Capital Investment and Financial Decisions

Second Edition

HAIM LEVY & MARSHALL SARNAT

Hebrew University of Jerusalem

Prentice/Hall PHI International

Englewood Cliffs, New Jersey   London   New Delhi
Singapore   Sydney   Tokyo   Toronto   Wellington

Library of Congress Cataloging in Publication Data

Levy, Haim.
    Capital investment and financial decisions.

    Includes bibliographies and index.
    1. Capital investments.   2. Business enterprises
--Finance.   I. Sarnat, Marshall.   II. Title.
HG4028.C4L48   1982   658.1'5   81-15340
ISBN 0-13-113589-9   AACR2

British Library Cataloging in Publication Data

Levy, Haim
    Capital investment and financial decisions — 2nd ed.
    1. Capital investment—Decision making
    I. Title   II. Sarnat, Marshall
    658.1'52   HG4028.C4

    ISBN 0-13-113589-9

PRENTICE-HALL INTERNATIONAL, INC., *London*
PRENTICE-HALL OF AUSTRALIA PTY., LTD., *Sydney*
PRENTICE-HALL CANADA, INC., *Toronto*
PRENTICE-HALL OF INDIA PRIVATE LIMITED, *New Delhi*
PRENTICE-HALL OF JAPAN, INC., *Tokyo*
PRENTICE-HALL OF SOUTHEAST ASIA PTE., LTD., *Singapore*
PRENTICE-HALL, INC., *Englewood Cliffs, New Jersey*
WHITEHALL BOOKS LIMITED, *Wellington, New Zealand*

Printed in the United States of America

10 9 8 7 6 5 4 3 2 1

Table of Contents

Part II — Risk and Uncertainty, 195

Part III — Long-term Financial Decisions, 329

Introduction, 330

Preface

"Some questions can be decided even if not answered"
MR JUSTICE BRANDEIS

This book is about financial policy with special emphasis on the allocation of a firm's long-term capital resources. Investment and financing decisions, which for better or for worse, fix the future course of the firm, have a great deal in common: they refer to a highly uncertain future, they must be made on the basis of incomplete information, and only a few of the relevant variables are controllable. But perhaps the salient characteristic of such decisions is that they cannot be avoided. "No decision" is itself a "decision".

Under these circumstances, Mr. Justice Brandeis' famous dictum regarding cases before the Court, provides an appropriate motto for the financial manager, whose objective is not to answer the unanswerable, but rather to spell out an operational framework for reaching the *best attainable* financial decisions. The book is a product of our underlying conviction that the theory of finance can provide such guidelines for practical financial management. To paraphrase John Maynard Keynes (the leading economic theorist of his generation, and a highly successful investor as well), the theory of finance ... "is a method rather than a doctrine ... a technique of thinking which helps its possessor to draw correct conclusions". Accordingly, we have emphasized the practical application of financial theory in uncertain environments.

The resurgence in recent years of double-digit inflation has had a profound effect on the theory and practice of finance, and, as a result, on the second edition of this book. Clearly, the problems posed by inflation are not new; but much of the theory of finance was developed in the more tranquil atmosphere of the 1950s and 1960s in which price level changes typically were ignored or at best swept aside after a minimum of lip service. Using the nominal theory as a guide

viii

to corporate decisions in the turbulent decade of the 1980s is a little like looking in a dark room for a black cat ... which is probably not there!

In this revised edition, we focus attention on the impact of inflation on corporate investment, the *effective* corporate tax rate and reported earnings. Special emphasis is given to corporate financial decisions and the crucial importance of the uncertainty generated by *unanticipated* changes in the level of prices. Wherever necessary, nominal values are clearly differentiated from their *real* counterparts and the significance of inflation for financial decision-making has been spelled out. Two separate chapters, (seven and twenty-two) are devoted solely to the analysis of inflation. In addition the remaining chapters have been rewritten to reflect the financial atmosphere, and economic conditions of the 1980s. The sections dealing wth capital budgeting, taxation, and leverage have been expanded; the chapter on dividend policy has been completely rewritten to reflect recent theoretical advances, and a new chapter on the important lease or buy decision has been added. Since we feel that valuation remains the key to understanding corporate financial decisions, the sections dealing with the portfolio analysis of decisions under uncertainty and the application of the capital asset pricing model have been expanded and rewritten to reflect the actual problems currently facing the business firm.

As was true for the first edition, the emphasis throughout the book is on the practical application of the modern theory of finance to realistic corporate decisions. To facilitate this goal numerous problems and mini-cases have been appended at the end of each chapter. Although instructors and students differ widely in their tastes, probably everyone will want to spend some time discussing the end-of-chapter questions and problems. We have tested the problems in our own classes, but room for improvement surely remains; and we would appreciate hearing of your experience with the problems and the suggested solutions which appear in the Teachers' Manual.

The book is suitable as a core text for courses in Corporate Financial Theory and Policy. The approach reflects our belief that the "technique of thinking" called financial management can be learnt best by considering the long-term problems of capital investment, financial structure, cost of capital and dividend policy. However, in recognition of the large variance in teaching methods and programs, the book has been designed to provide a highly flexible teaching instrument. It can be used for courses in capital budgeting, engineering economy and applied micro-economics, as well as for financial management.

Finally, a word to the student who has carelessly wandered into this preface: a finance course can be a challenging experience, as well as a lot of fun, just as writing this book has been for us. Unnecessary complexities and mathematical formulations have been ruthlessly weeded out. If you have an eye for a graph and don't have an aversion for numerical examples, you are well prepared to understand the text and perhaps, to improve it as well.

There remains the pleasant task of acknowledging the generous help of colleagues and friends. Our appreciation goes to Michael Adler, Fred Arditti, Moshe Ben-Horino, S. Benninga, M. Brenner, Mary Broske, David Cohen, R. Dunbar, S. Ekern, D. Galai, David Goldenberg, M. Gordon, P. Geleff,

G. Grundy, G.S. Hatjoullis, R. Holtgrieve, R. Mesznik, B. Rapp, R. Rundfelt, W. Sharpe, R. Stapleton, R. Westerfield, and R. Wubbels for critical comments and suggestions on various chapters. We also wish to thank Moshe Smith, Zvi Lerman, George Szpiro, Rogelio Saenz, Jim Craig and Mates Beja, Ronnie Zukerman, who provided research assistance, suggested questions and problems and prepared the solutions for the Teachers' Manual; and Marcia Don, who very ably saw the manuscript through all of the stages from typescript to page proof. Once again, we wish to thank Ronald Decent and Henry Hirschberg of Prentice-Hall, who by now have become experts in financial management, or at least in handling the authors of textbooks on that august subject with good humor and great skill.

H.L.
M.S.

Part I
Capital Budgeting

Introduction

Part I is devoted to the basic elements of the firm's capital budgeting process: project evaluation, the importance of the time element, and the principles underlying the composition of the cash flow. Alternative goals of the firm are discussed in Chapter 1 which also presents the arguments on behalf of our choice of wealth maximization. Chapter 2 gives an overview of the investment decision-making process; while Chapter 3 focuses attention on the crucial role played by the timing of future cash flows. Chapter 4 sets out the theoretical arguments on behalf of the Net Present Value method of appraising alternative investment proposals. Chapter 5 is devoted to a discussion of the principles underlying the firm's estimate of the relevant pre-tax cash flows of an investment project; the impact of corporate taxes and inflation on these flows is discussed in Chapter 6. Chapter 7 recasts traditional capital budgeting techniques in order to take "double-digit" inflation into account. Chapter 8 concludes this section of the book with a critical appraisal of the relationship of the popular rules of thumb which are often used to evaluate capital expenditures with the time-discounted measures of investment worth which were presented in the earlier chapters of this section.

The Goal of the Firm

A business firm is confronted daily by many decisions — some important and others less so; some with long-run implications and some which are more amenable than others to quantification. This book is devoted to a particular group of business decisions: those which determine a firm's capital expenditures and their financing. This class of decision problems has much to recommend it. Perhaps more than any single factor, the investment strategy adopted by the firm determines its future growth and profitability. Strategic capital investment decisions, such as the decision to "go international", diversify into new product lines or pursue an important innovation, can materially change the character of even the largest of firms in a single decade. Consider, for example, the phenomenal rise of the multinational and conglomerate corporations and the (perhaps ill-fated) British—French joint venture into the development of a supersonic commercial airliner. Future success, however, depends not only on finding an appropriate investment strategy but also on the way in which that strategy is implemented. Tactical decisions, such as the decision to buy rather than to produce component parts or to lease rather than to buy warehouse space, are often no less important than even the most elaborately planned long-term strategy.

ALTERNATIVE GOALS FOR THE FIRM

By its very nature financial decision-making involves purposeful behavior, which implies the existence of a goal, or what is much more likely, some combination of goals. In the absence of any objective, the firm would have no criterion for choosing among alternative investment strategies and projects. Surely there is no need to tell the firm that two million dollars is better than one. Yet even this decision is not always that simple; for example, an investment strategy which promises two million dollars accompanied by the risk of possible bankruptcy should the venture go sour may not be preferable to a conservative strategy which offers a payoff of only one million dollars but permits the directors of the firm to sleep soundly.

Once the complexity of the financial decision-making process is recognized it is fairly easy to conjure up a large number of possible candidates for "the goal of the firm". A very partial listing of some of those which have been mentioned at one time or another would include:

(1)   maximization of profits
(2)   maximization of sales
(3)   survival of the firm
(4)   achieving a "satisfactory" level of profits
(5)   achieving a target market share
(6)   some minimum level of employee turnover
(7)   "internal peace" or no ulcers for management as this objective is often called
(8)   maximization of managerial salaries.

The listing of possible objectives for the firm is a near endless game, more likely to leave its players exhausted than enlightened. However, we think the essential point has been made; no single "goal" can express *all* of the complexities of the decision process. But despite this, we shall see in what follows that a "goal" for corporate decision making can be found which serves well as a foundation for the firm's critically important investment, financing and dividend decisions.

Since the first four goals listed are most frequently encountered, let us now subject them to closer scrutiny. Following this, we shall spell out an appropriate goal which will enable us to feel somewhat more comfortable in discussing the numerous other candidates for the title, "goal of the firm".

MAXIMIZING PROFITS

Almost every introductory textbook in economics and especially those in price theory assume (apparently as self-evident) the goal of maximization of profits.[1] Though appealing to many economists, upon reflection it is clear that this highly simplified model of corporate behavior rests squarely on the assumption that future profits are known with *certainty*. Taking the maximization of profits as the corporation's objective implies that when the firm chooses among alternative strategies, it can forecast with certainty all of the relevant future

---

1 The simplest model of this type states that the firm should seek the output q which maximizes the function:

$$\pi = qp - C(q)$$

where: π denotes net profit; q the number of units that the firm produces; $C(q)$ the total production cost, which changes with the level of output; and p equals the price of each unit sold.

Applying the "maximum profit" goal, the firm should seek to produce that quantity q which maximizes its total profits, π.

revenues and costs, and hence profit, associated with each policy. However, reality is not so accommodating. Yet even if we are willing to accept the "certainty" assumption, the goal profit maximization is at best ambiguous. Consider, for example, the following problems.

What profit should the firm maximize? Short-run profits (say next year) or long-run profits over the next decade? To illustrate the problem, let us assume that the firm is confronted with two alternative investment strategies. If it adopts strategy "A", the firm will earn a net profit of $10,000 a year for ten years:

Strategy A					
year	1	2	3	. . .	9	10
net profit	10,000	10,000	10,000	. . .	10,000	10,000

On the other hand, adopting the alternative investment strategy, "B", will yield the following stream of profits:

Strategy B									
year	1	2	3	4	5	6	7	8	9	10
net profit	0	0	0	20,000	30,000	40,000	50,000	50,000	50,000	50,000

Which strategy should the firm choose in order to maximize its profits? Since the firm is an "on-going" organization, it is almost intuitively obvious that profits in the long run (i.e. over the entire ten-year period) and not just the profits in the first year, or over some arbitrary number of years, are relevant.

The maximization of long-run profits, however, implies the need to reduce the stream of future receipts and outlays to some common denominator so that meaningful comparisons can be made. And while this is no mean feat, the technique of discounting future cash flows, which will be developed in Chapters 3 and 4, provides a neat solution to this problem. In the jargon of this approach, the firm should choose that strategy which maximizes the discounted *present value* of the stream of long-run profits (see Chapter 3). However, the simplicity and elegance of the present value solution should not obscure the fact that the goal of maximizing long-run profits is neither simple nor obvious once we relax the assumption of certainty and assume a more realistic setting in which uncertainty regarding future cash flows prevails. Given the highly uncertain environment in which most firms operate, a number of alternative objective functions have been proposed — the maximization of sales or market share being perhaps the best known.

Many firms tend to state their objective solely in terms of total sales or market share.[2] The possible explanation for this tendency is straightforward:

---

2 The best known theoretical proponent of this approach is William J. Baumol: see his *Business Behavior, Value, and Growth*, New York, Macmillan, 1959.

market share is often a very good "proxy" for profits, since market share and profits often move together. In a study of fifty-seven companies, Buzzell, Gale and Sultan[3] found a positive correlation between a firm's market share and its profitability (see Fig. 1.1). On the average, an increase of 10% in market share was accompanied by an increase of about 5% in the pre-tax return on investment. Although one can find many possible explanations for this relationship, one thing is clear; the goals "maximum profit" and "maximum sales", or "maximum market share", are closely related.

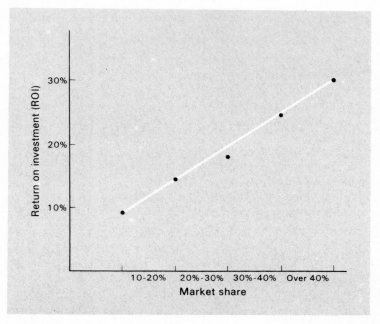

Fig. 1.1

The Relationship Between Pre-tax Return on Investment and Market Share
Source: Robert D. Buzzell, Bradley T. Gale and Ralph G.M. Sultan, "Market Share — a Key to Profitability", *Harvard Business Review*, Jan – Feb 1975, p.98. Copyright © 1974 by the President and Fellows of Harvard College; all rights reserved

SURVIVAL

"Survival" is another alternative which is often mentioned as the goal of the firm. Clearly, this objective cannot stand alone! If the firm's goal is purely to survive, why not invest all of its resources in short-term Government securities which guarantee a perfectly certain fixed income and therefore also guarantee survival. However, when a businessman speaks of "survival" as a motivating policy goal, he is probably referring to the avoidance of "very great" risks.

3 See Robert D. Buzzell, Bradley T. Gale and Ralph G. M. Sultan, "Market Share — a key to profitability", *Harvard Business Review*, January – February 1975.

Thus it is true that many firms will prefer to avoid a chance of earning even exceptionally high profits if the particular project endangers the financial stability of the firm. In this context the objective of business survival can be recast in terms of a goal of "safety first". Such an approach would identify some minimum level which the firm must meet at all costs. For example, assume that $100,000 is required to service the firm's annual debt payments. A "safety-first" rule would be to *minimize* the probability of earnings falling below $100,000.

SATISFACTORY PROFITS

Explorations along the boundaries of economics and psychology have led to the development of an organizational or behavioral approach. The firm is viewed as a complex pattern of personal relationships. Perhaps the best-known advocate of such an approach is Herbert Simon, who in a variety of publications developed what has proved to be a very influential concept of the firm and its goals.[4]

Although Simon agrees that the concept of a goal is indispensable to organization theory, he emphasizes that the object of corporate action is seldom single-valued. In his view, the decision-making mechanism is imperfect; the firm is confronted by the necessity to choose among alternatives without knowing exactly the outcomes of each choice. Not knowing the *best* alternative, the decision-maker does not seek a maximum profit, but is content with some satisfactory level of profit. Or as Simon has put it, the businessmen (organization) cannot maximize profits; they can only hope to *satisfice*. Thus in Simon's view, it is "satisficing" rather than maximizing behavior which characterizes the business firm.

Treating the firm as a complex organization has much to recommend it. There are many situations in which it is more fruitful to view decision-making as the search for courses of action which satisfy a number of constraints rather than as the pursuit of a single-valued goal such as profit maximization. This is especially true in the realistic setting of uncertainty. But its strength is also its weakness; the major drawback of the approach is its complexity, that is the large number of variables which must be considered. Thus greater organizational realism is acquired, but only at a price — in this instance the ease with which these types of models can be used to explain and predict corporate action.

SOME EMPIRICAL EVIDENCE

In a well-known article, Robert F. Lanzillotti examined the objectives upon

---

4 See, for example, Herbert A. Simon, *Administrative Behavior*, 2nd edn., New York, Macmillan, 1957, and his "On the Concept of Organizational Goal", *Administrative Science Quarterly*, June 1964. Somewhat similar views have been expounded by R. M. Cyert and J. G. March, *A Behavioral Theory of the Firm*, Englewood Cliffs N.J., Prentice-Hall, 1963.

Table 1.1
Pricing Goals of Twenty Large Industrial Corporations

Company	Principal Pricing Model	Collateral Pricing Goals
Alcoa	20% on investment (before taxes); higher on new products (about 10% effective rate after taxes)	(a) "Promotive" policy on new products (b) Price stabilization
American Can	Maintenance of market share	(a) "Meeting competition (using cost of substitute products to determine price) (b) Price stabilization
A & P	Increasing market share	"General promotive" (low-margin policy)
du Pont	Target return on investment — no specific figure given	(a) Charging what traffic will bear over long run (b) Maximum return for new products — "life cycle" pricing
Esso (Standard Oil of NJ)	"Fair-return" target — no specific figure given	(a) Maintaining market share (b) Price stabilization
General Electric	20% on investment (after taxes); 7% on sales (after taxes)	(a) Promotive policy on new products (b) Price stabilization on nationally advertised products
General Foods	$33\frac{1}{3}$% gross margin: ("one-third to make, one-third to sell, and one-third for profit") expectation of realizing target only on new products	(a) Full line of food products and novelties (b) Maintaining market share
General Motors	20% on investment (after taxes)	Maintaining market share
Goodyear	"Meeting competitors"	(a) Maintain "position" (b) Price stabilization
Gulf	Follow price of most important marketer in each area	(a) Maintain market share (b) Price stabilization
International Harvester	10% on investment (after taxes)	Market share: ceiling of "less than a dominant share of any market"
Johns-Manville	Return on investment greater than last fifteen-year average (about 15% after taxes); higher target for new products	(a) Market share not greater than 20% (b) Stabilization of prices
Kennecott	Stabilization of prices	
Kroger	Maintaining market share	Target return of 20% on investment before taxes
National Steel	Matching the market-price follower	Increase market share
Sears Roebuck	Increasing market share (8% – 10% regarded as satisfactory share)	(a) Realization of traditional return on investment of 10% – 15% (after taxes) (b) General promotive (low margin) policy
Standard Oil (Indiana)	Maintain market share	(a) Stabilize prices (b) Target return on investment (none specified)
Swift	Maintenance of market share in livestock buying and meat packing	
Union Carbide	Target return on investment	Promotive policy on new products; "life cycle" pricing on chemicals generally
US Steel	8% on investment (after taxes)	(a) Target market share of 30% (b) Stable price (c) Stable margin

Source: Robert Lanzillotti, "Pricing Objectives in Large Companies", *American Economic Review*, XLVIII, December 1958, pp. 924 – 6.

which business firms base their pricing decisions.[5] By intensive interviewing of the officials of twenty very large US companies, he was able to identify their principal, as well as their secondary goals. Table 1.1 presents a summary of his findings.

As can be seen from the data, a very wide variety of goals are mentioned, but four recurring objectives can be identified:

(1)   target returns on investment
(2)   stabilization of prices and margins
(3)   target market share
(4)   "meeting" or preventing competition.

Although every firm did not mention all the above four points, a majority included these four basic targets, either as principal or secondary objectives. Most of the firms also indicated that they have a *minimum* target profit which serves as a basis for the acceptance or rejection decision.

Summarizing his study, Lanzillotti concluded that "no single theory of the firm — and certainly no single motivational hypothesis such as profit maximization — is likely to impose an unambiguous course of action for the firm for any given situation".[6] Profits, stability, market share, etc. all appear to influence decision-making, and many firms aim at some combination of these goals, although no firm could articulate the precise formula with which it combines or assigns weights to the various goals.

WEALTH MAXIMIZATION

Although business motivation is admittedly very complex, the Lanzillotti evidence helps us to focus attention on what appear to be the two primary concerns of management:

(a)   long-run profitability
(b)   stability.

Although these goals appear to be inconsistent — attempts to increase profits often involve greater risks, i.e. less stability — a way must be found to combine them if our definition of the goal of the firm is to reflect accurately the objectives of business management. One way out of this dilemma is to assume that management takes as its goal the maximization of the market value of shareholders' wealth, or what comes to the same thing, the maximization of the market value of its existing common stock.[7] Although anyone who has ever attended a board meeting is not likely to underestimate the ability of management to act in their own self-interest, maximizing the financial well-being of the

---

5 See Robert F. Lanzillotti, "Pricing Objectives in Large Companies", *American Economic Review*, December 1958, pp. 921 – 40.

6 Ibid., pp. 938 – 9.

7 The formal equivalence between wealth maximization and the maximization of the market value of a firm's common stock is shown in Appendix 14A below.

shareholders is not necessarily incompatible with management's interests. On the contrary, it may well be an optimal strategy for maximizing management's welfare as well.

Taking shareholders' wealth as the firm's goal has the important advantage of permitting us to combine the profitability and riskiness of alternative courses of action into one quantitative measure. Consider a case of two firms, A and B, with identical expected profits (say $1 per share of common stock). Now assume that firm B expects to earn its profit by a very risky undertaking, e.g. financing a textbook on corporate investment. In such a case, the price (market value) of the common stock of firm A will be higher than that of firm B, since both offer investors the same expected future earnings, but one of them has a much higher risk. The situation is more complex if we assume the more realistic case in which the risky venture also offers *higher* expected earnings. For example, suppose that the firm can earn $1 per share with certainty, or alternatively, $2 per share with a 90% probability, but that there also exists a 10% chance that the firm will go bankrupt. The decision in this case is not easy. Is the additional $1 of profit sufficient to offset the 10% chance of going bankrupt? The answer depends upon the market's evaluation of the risk-return tradeoff implicit in this venture. If the greater expectation of return outweighs the increase in risk, we expect the price of the stock to rise if the project is undertaken. Conversely, for the case in which the riskiness outweighs the increase in expected returns, we would expect

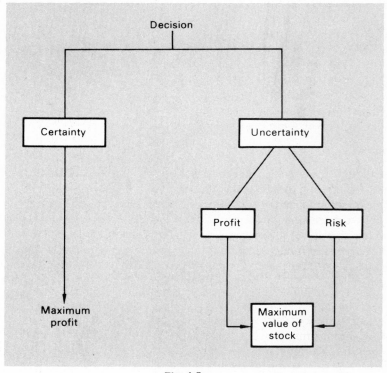

Fig. 1.2

the share price to fall. Thus defining the goal of the firm in terms of market value of the stock implies an effort on the part of management to seek an optimum balance between risk and profitability, which is consistent with much of the theory and empirical evidence on the motivation of corporate action.

Figure 1.2 summarizes the general decision problem faced by the firm. In the unrealistic case in which the results of all decisions are known in advance with certainty, the goal of the firm should be the maximization of the firm's long-run profit. However, when uncertainty prevails, as it always does in the real world, the firm must consider risk as well as profits, and therefore chooses that combination of risk and profit which maximizes the market value of its stock. Those firms who place greater emphasis on the goal of "survival" can be viewed as giving a very large weight to risk, but this is not necessarily inconsistent with the goal of maximizing the market value of the firm's common stock.

SUMMARY

The appropriateness of a decision rule can only be evaluated when one knows the firm's objective or goal. Empirical evidence indicates that some firms state their objectives in terms of their sales or market share, while others emphasize profits. "Safety" and "survival" are also widely mentioned as goals of the firm. However, a careful examination of the empirical evidence shows that most firms appear to have multidimensional goals. The two most important factors appear to be profitability (or market share, which is highly correlated with profits) and risk (i.e. "safety" or "survival"). The selection of the combination of expected profit and risk which is appropriate for a firm's stockholders is not an easy task, but by taking stockholders' interests as the goal of the firm, an operational method can be found for incorporating *both* risk and profitability into the firm's goal function. The rest of this book is devoted to spelling out the financial decision rules which are implied by the assumed goal of wealth maximization.

QUESTIONS AND PROBLEMS

1.1 Inquire at a number of corporations in your city as to whether or not they have determined a set of stated objectives. Evaluate their answers. Does the absence of a fixed goal (or goals) necessarily indicate that the firm's actions are random?

1.2 In a recent study of 500 corporations Professor Jack Skeptic found that not one firm mentioned maximizing shareholders' wealth as an objective of the firm. On the contrary, most of the firms stressed profitability and risk as the key variables affecting their decision regarding the assumption of the maximization of shareholders' wealth as the goal of the firm. Discuss the implications of these findings.

1.3 In what sense does Lanzillotti's empirical evidence support Herbert

Simon's organizational approach to the firm? In what sense do his findings lend support to the decision to define the firm's objective in terms of shareholders' interests?

1.4 "We have no goals for the firm, we are too busy making money." Why might this be a perfectly acceptable motto for a corporate president?

Why might this same motto be unacceptable for the authors of a textbook on capital budgeting?

1.5 The table below gives the price and the fixed and variable production cost as a function of the quantity produced (Q).

Quantity	Price ($)	Fixed Cost ($)	Total Variable Cost ($)
0	—	100	0
10	5.50	100	20
20	5.25	100	30
30	5.00	100	50
40	4.75	100	80
50	4.30	100	110
60	3.50	100	160

(a) Calculate: marginal cost per unit; total revenue; marginal revenue per unit; and profit per unit for each quantity level.
(b) How many units should the firm produce? What is its profit at that level of production?

1.6 Assume, Cost $= 4.5Q + 25Q^2$
Price $= 8 - \frac{1}{2}Q$ where Q is the quantity produced.

(a) Compute the optimal output and maximum profit.
(b) Graph the cost, marginal cost and marginal revenue functions.

1.7 The table below provides recent financial data of firms belonging to the Food and Lodging industry.

(a) Examine the hypothesis that there is a positive correlation between the two goals: return on common equity and profit margins (use the 2nd QTR 1978 data for profit margins).
(b) Examine the hypothesis that return on common equity and market share of sales are positively correlated (use the sales figures for 6 months of 1978). First calculate the market share of each firm as a percentage of the total sales in the industry.

Food & Lodging

	Sales 6 mo. 1978 ($ mil.)	Profit margins 2nd quarter (%)	Return com. eqy. 12 months ending 6-30
ARA Services	874.2	2.7	12.5
Church's Fried Chicken	123.1	9.3	36.8
Gino's	146.0	3.0	10.9
Hilton Hotels	219.4	16.3	22.7
Holiday Inns	551.3	7.3	12.6
Host International	147.5	4.6	21.1
Howard Johnson	262.4	6.7	13.2
Hyatt	208.3	4.4	26.5
Marriot	582.1	4.3	12.1
McDonald's	793.7	10.5	25.4
Ramada Inns	154.2	2.7	6.7
Webb (Del E.)	244.8	3.4	18.4
Industry composite	4307.0	6.4	17.1

Source: *Business Week*, August 21, 1978.

1.8 The table below reports sales, assets and net income of the eight largest oil companies in the US for the years 1977 – 78.

Firm	Sales ($000)		Assets ($000)		Net Income	
	1977	1978	1977	1978	1977	1978
Exxon	54,126,219	60,334,527	38,453,336	41,530,804	2,422,964	2,763,000
Mobil	32,125,828	34,736,045	20,575,967	22,611,489	1,004,670	1,125,638
Texaco	27,920,499	28,607,521	18,926,026	20,249,143	930,789	852,461
Std.Oil (Cal)	20,917,331	23,232,413	14,882,347	16,861,021	1,016,360	1,105,881
Gulf Oil	17,840,000	18,069,000	14,225,000	15,036,000	752,000	791,000
Std.Oil (Ind)	13,019,939	14,961,489	12,884,286	14,109,264	1,011,575	1,076,412
Atlantic Richfield	10,969,091	12,298,403	11,119,012	12,060,210	701,515	804,355
Shell Oil	10,112,062	11,062,883	8,876,754	10,453,358	735,094	803,623

Source: Fortune 500

For each firm
(1) Calculate the average net income as a percentage of average assets for the two years.
(2) Draw a scatter diagram with net income (as a percentage of assets) on the vertical axis and market share (as a percentage of total market) on the horizontal axis.
(3) Calculate the regression line and the correlation coefficient between the variables (net income and market share in percent). Is market share a good proxy for profit in the oil industry?

SELECTED REFERENCES

Branch, Ben, "Corporate Objectives and Market Performance", *Financial Management*, Summer 1973.

Bkara, S. and Wilson, R., "On the Theory of the Firm in an Economy with Incomplete Markets", *Bell Journal of Economics*, 5 (1974) 171 – 80.

Fama, Eugene F., "Agency Problems and the Theory of the Firm", *Journal of Political Economy*, 1980.

Findlay, M. Chapman, III and Whitmore, G.A., "Beyond Shareholder Wealth Maximization", *Financial Management*, Winter 1974.

Jennergren, I. Peter, "On the Design of Incentives in Business Firms — A Survey of Some Research", *Management Science*, February 1980.

Jensen, M.C. and Meckling, W.H., "Theory of the Firm: Managerial Behavior, Agency Costs and Ownership Structure", *Journal of Financial Economics*, October 1976.

Jensen, M.C. and Meckling, W.H., "Can the Corporation Survive?" *Financial Analysts Journal*, January – February 1978.

Lee, Sang M. and Lerro, A.J., "Capital Budgeting for Multiple Objectives", *Financial Management*, Spring 1974.

Osteryoung, J.S., "A Survey into the Goals Used by Fortune's 500 Companies in Capital Budgeting Decisions", *Arkon Business and Economic Review*, Fall 1973.

Simon, H.A., *Administrative Behavior*, New York: Macmillan, 1957.

Weston, J.F., *The Scope and Methodology of Finance*, Englewood Cliffs, N.J.: Prentice-Hall, 1966.

Yarrow, G.K., "On the Predictions of Managerial Theories of the Firm", *Journal of Industrial Economics*, June 1976.

2

Capital Budgeting:
An Overview

The investment decisions of business enterprises involve very large sums of money and have a significant impact on the investing firms and on the economy as a whole. In 1980 total business expenditures in the United States for new plant and equipment exceeded $195 billion.[1] As the accompanying chart shows, this figure represents almost a tenfold increase over the $20 billion invested by business in 1950. Taken in the aggregate, these capital expenditures constitute the economy's link with the future; the current investment decisions made by individual firms are a major determining factor of tomorrow's output. To the firm these decisions, which shape both the pattern and growth of future output, constitute one of the most demanding challenges confronting management since in large measure the future benefits are determined irrevocably by today's capital budgeting decisions. In this chapter we shall sketch in broad outline some of the considerations underlying these capital expenditure decisions.

DEFINING CAPITAL EXPENDITURES

What is a capital expenditure? In the typical capital investment decision management makes a commitment of current resources in order to secure a stream of benefits in future years. However, there is no sharp conceptual difference between so-called capital and current expenditures; it is fair to say that *all* of the firm's expenditures are made in expectation of realizing future benefits. The firm is continuously confronted by the problem of deciding if a proposed use of resources is worthwhile in terms of the prospective benefits. However, when the time horizon of the problem is relatively short, say less than one year (for example an increase in inventories or trade credit) *both* the costs and the

---

1 *Economic Report of the President, January 1980*, Washington, D.C., United States Government Printing Office, 1980.

benefits of a given proposal can be set out in *current* dollars; but when a significant period of time elapses between the outlay and the benefits the problem of evaluating and comparing costs and benefits becomes more difficult. As a result, many firms apply formal capital budgeting procedures only to projects in which more than one year elapses between the initial investment outlay and the receipt

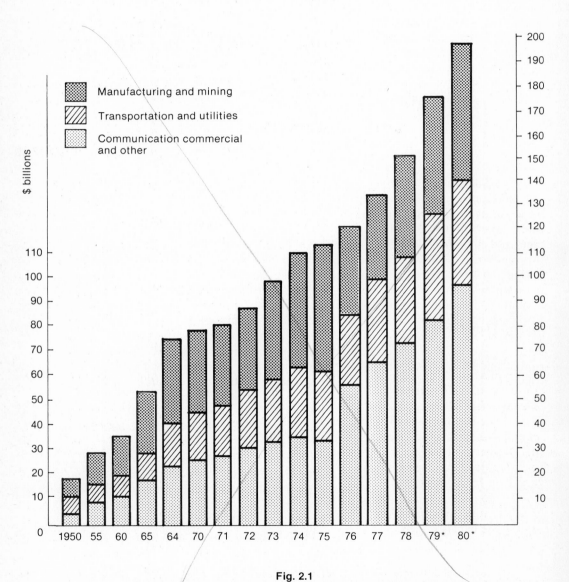

Fig. 2.1
Business Expenditures for New Plant and Equipment: 1950 – 1980.
*estimate
Source: Economic Report of the President, 1980.

of the project's final benefits. This distinction is completely arbitrary and reflects the underlying assumption that the timing of receipts can be ignored for time periods of less than one year.[2]

Many firms also limit their formal capital budgeting procedures to relatively large expenditures. This constraint is necessary if management time (a resource in short supply in most firms) is to be economized. The board of directors or capital appropriations committee are usually unwilling to discuss the merits of a proposed switch to electric pencil sharpeners despite the fact that the benefits from such an expenditure are expected to accrue over a number of years. Of course, the concept of a *relatively large* expenditure has no precise meaning outside the context of the particular problem at hand, and clearly this is one instance in which a decision that is good for General Motors may *not* be appropriate for the local ice cream company.

THE CAPITAL BUDGETING PROCESS

Capital budgeting is a many-sided activity which includes: the formulation and articulation of long-term goals; searching for new and profitable uses for investment funds; the preparing of engineering, marketing and financial forecasts and estimates; the preparation of appropriation and control budgets and the integration of these budgets in the firm's information system; the economic evaluation of alternative projects; and the post-audit of the performance of past projects.

Long-Term Goals

A systematic approach to capital investment decisions requires the formulation of a set of long-term goals which can serve as a guide for managerial decisions. As already noted in Chapter 1, we shall assume throughout the book that management is concerned with maximizing the value of the firm's common stock. For the purposes of capital budgeting this means that other things being equal, management will strive to secure the highest net dollar return on its capital investments which is compatible with the risks incurred. Of course many investment projects cannot be described completely in terms of monetary costs and benefits; for example a new cafeteria for the workers or an executive dining room. However, even in these cases a systematic calculation of the profitability of alternative investments can provide a benchmark for evaluating the otherwise intangible benefits.

---

2 Of course, the difference between a time lag of say six months and six years is not a difference of kind but only one of degree. However, in this context, it may be worthwhile to recall Norbert Wiener's remark that the difference between *fatal* and *medicinal* doses of strychnine is also only a matter of degree.

Generating Investment Proposals

Another prerequisite for systematic capital management is so obvious that it is often neglected. A good investment proposal is not just born — someone has to suggest it! In the absence of a creative search for new investment opportunities even the most sophisticated of evaluation techniques is worthless. In addition, someone within the firm must be willing to "listen" to such proposals; in other words a method must also be found for transferring proposals to the decision level. Clearly, the optimal method for identifying and generating investment proposals differs from industry to industry and even from firm to firm. A large chemical plant or electrical manufacturer is likely to have a well-equipped research and development division charged with the task of finding economically feasible and attractive uses for sophisticated new products or processes. In a small machine shop the search for investment possibilities may be less formal or structured. It often takes the form of an employees' "suggestion box" or discussion during a coffee break.

Depending on the size and organization of the firm, formal requests for investment funds are made by heads of operating divisions or departments often in conjunction with research and planning units. These requests are usually based explicitly on an expanding volume of sales of existing products, market research, technical engineering and methods studies, employee suggestions, significant changes in the competitive environment, and so on.

From the viewpoint of capital budgeting a broad interpretation of the term investment is desirable. Thus the search for investment opportunities should encompass the acquisition of *existing* production and marketing facilities by means of a merger with another company as well as the expansion of the company's own facilities or the creation of an entirely new division. The problems created by business mergers are sufficiently different and important to warrant separate treatment. In many large companies a staff of trained specialists concentrate on discovering and analyzing the benefits of potential acquisitions of existing firms by the parent corporation. The need for specially trained staff reflects the complex legal, tax, financing and accounting considerations attendant with external acquisitions.

Estimating Cash Flows and Classifying Projects

From the very inception of the proposal, the expected costs and revenues generated by the project must be estimated. Often the rough preliminary estimates which are prepared when the project is first defined have to be revised and refined when the proposal is incorporated in the firm's formal budget. Finally, on the eve of the actual budgeting decision, these revised estimates must be further refined and presented in the form of an appropriation request.

The relevant engineering, marketing and financial data must be compiled and collated from numerous departments and divisions throughout the firm. In the final stage, many of the cost estimates will be replaced by the actual offers made by supplying companies which include firm prices. However, the timing and magnitude of future cash flows of course usually retain their uncertainty throughout the budgeting process, and for that matter over the course of the project's lifetime as well.

The estimation of cash flows is sufficiently important to warrant separate treatment and Chapter 5 is devoted to a detailed examination of the principles underlying such forecasts. It may be well worth our while, however, to consider some alternative classifications of investment projects which can help the firm to develop standardized estimation and administration procedures for handling particular classes of proposals. Classification is especially helpful in the following cases:

(1)   When the accuracy of cost-revenue estimates varies widely. This depends on the type of investment proposal being considered: for some types no quantitative forecast is possible; for others costs can be estimated within relatively narrow bounds.

(2)   When the definition and methods of estimating future cash flows differ significantly. This can be especially important in a conglomerate firm which pursues very different lines of activity.

(3)   When a project has an impact beyond its direct monetary contribution. The firm may desire to give such projects priority or special consideration when examining their desirability.

In general, the grouping of projects into different categories simplifies the decision process, but it should be emphasized from the outset that no magic formula exists; each company has to adopt the classification best suited to its own needs.[3]

Let us consider briefly a few of the many possible ways of classifying investment projects.

BY PROJECT SIZE

The amount of cash resources required to implement the project provides a useful way of differentiating three classes of investments: major projects, regular capital expenditures, and small proposals. For example, one firm affords separate treatment to "major projects", defined as initial expenditures of over $250,000. Another applies formal capital budgeting procedures to expenditures in excess of $5,000; while smaller projects are exempted from formal approval. Similarly projects can be classified by the type of scarce resources used: land, key management personnel, floor space, and so on.

3 Of course, the "best" classification scheme for some firms may be not to classify projects at all beyond their estimated profitability and probability of success. This is the practice in many smaller companies in which the executives are familiar with almost all aspects of the projects being considered. See National Association of Accountants, *Financial Analysis to Guide Capital Expenditure Decisions*, Research Report 43, July 1967, Chapter 3.

BY TYPE OF BENEFIT

Benefits can arise either from cost reductions, expansion of sales of existing products, expansion into new lines of activities, risk reduction or social overhead investments designed to improve general working conditions. Hot showers for workers, improved antipollution facilities, and perhaps even a contribution to the community welfare fund are examples of the latter type of investment.

BY DEGREE OF DEPENDENCE

Interdependence between two investment projects can arise for several reasons:

(a) It may be technically impossible to undertake both investment *A* and investment *B*. Such investments will be referred to as being *mutually exclusive*, since the acceptance of one effectively precludes the acceptance of the other. The early identification of mutually exclusive alternatives is crucial for a logical screening of investments; much effort, even more patience and often money are wasted when two divisions independently investigate, develop and initiate projects which are recognized later as mutually exclusive. Numerous examples of such investments leap to mind: a basketball court and a swimming pool cannot be constructed on the same vacant lot; when a manufacturing plant is located near the sources of raw materials this may often mean that it cannot be close to the market; a power generating plant can be nuclear or coal fired — not both.

(b) If the decision to execute the first investment increases the expected benefits from the second project, the proposals are said to be *complements*. For example the construction of a water recycling facility may have a positive impact on the profitability of a number of other projects.

(c) If the acceptance of one project decreases the profitability of a second project they are said to be *substitutes*. Thus when a large razor blade manufacturer such as Gillette contemplated the introduction of stainless steel blades, the forecasted revenue from the sale of new blades was offset, in part, by a decline in the expected sales of its conventional blades. No such consideration hampered Wilkinson Ltd, the English firm which first introduced stainless steel blades. Presumably they assumed that the proceeds from razor blade sales were *economically independent* of the revenue from their other line of ceremonial swords. (They ignored the possibility that naval officers who previously shaved with their Wilkinson sabers would now switch to Wilkinson blades, thereby decreasing the replacement demand for the former.)

(d) Economic independence or dependence must be distinguished from another type of interrelationship, namely *statistical independence* (*dependence*). Two projects are said to be statistically dependent when increases (decreases) in the benefits from the one are accompanied over time by an increase (decrease) in the benefits of the second. Thus, the revenue from two lines of luxury goods (for example caviar and Cadillacs) are likely to fluctuate over time together.[4]

BY TYPE OF CASH FLOW

Another type of classification is technical in nature but can prove useful when analyzing alternative measures of profitability. Here projects' forecasted cash flows are examined and classified either as "conventional" or "non-conventional". A conventional investment project is defined as one in which the initial outlay is followed by a stream of net receipts of the form: $- + + + \ldots$; or if the outlay takes place over a number of years, the cash flow has the form: $- - + + \ldots$. Some numerical examples will help to clarify the point. Consider the following investment projects whose cash flows are all of the "conventional" type.

	Year					
	0	*1*	*2*	*3*	*4*	*5*
Project A	− 100	+ 110	—	—	—	—
Project B	− 100	—	—	—	+ 150	—
Project C	− 100	+ 40	+ 40	+ 40	+ 40	+ 40
Project D	− 100	− 100	+ 80	+ 100	+ 50	+ 75

As can be seen from these examples a conventional investment project is one whose cash flow has only one *change* in sign from a negative number to a positive number:[5] $- / + + +$ or $- - / + + +$ or $- / +$. Hence projects with net terminal costs which have cash flows of the form $- / + + + / -$ are "non-conventional" since such projects have *two* changes in sign: the first following the initial investment outlay and the second preceding the terminal year. An example of a non-conventional project is provided by the case of a strip mining or quarrying project in which the company is required to restore the physical appearance of the concession after the supply of ore (stone) has been exhausted. Similarly, projects with initial positive receipts of the form $+ / - / + + +$ also have non-conventional cash flows. Writing a textbook on capital budgeting provides an example of such a project; the initial receipt reflects the publisher's advance payment which precedes both the author's investment outlay and (hopefully) the later stream of royalties.

Clearly many other classifications are possible. Some firms assign a priority rating to alternative proposals; classifying projects as "urgent", "required", "desirable", and so on. Others classify investment alternatives by the location

---

4 The statistical relationship among investment returns is an important factor when analyzing decisions under uncertainty, and is discussed in greater detail in Chapter 10 below.

5 A conventional loan also has a cash flow with only one change in sign but in reverse order, that is from the receipt to the negative repayments: $+ / - -$, or $+ + / - - -$, and so on.

of the projects within the firm or within a division. The various classification schemes are *not* mutually exclusive; a firm can, and many do, use all of the above-mentioned classifications at one stage or another of their budgeting process.

THE ADMINISTRATIVE FRAMEWORK

A systematic approach to capital budgeting requires an administrative framework which facilitates the gathering and transfer of relevant information on alternative courses of action both for purposes of decision-making as well as for the control of expenditures, once these decisions have been reached. This requires a uniform set of procedures and forms which can be used to check project estimates for accuracy and against budget limits as well as to transfer the proposals to the decision level.

Figure 2.2 sets out a highly simplified flow chart for a typical investment

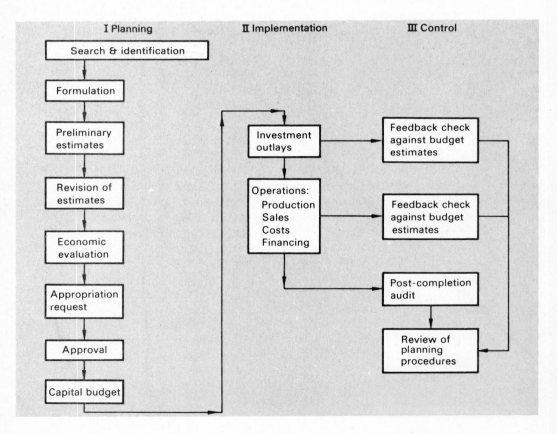

Fig. 2.2
Project Planning

proposal. The emphasis is on the importance of feedback from operating results both for control and for the future planning of new projects. The flow chart assumes that the firm employs a formal capital budget based on intensive financial planning. Practice, however, is far from uniform even among the medium-sized and large firms which typically budget their capital expenditures. Length of budget period, definition of projects, evaluation techniques and administrative procedures vary greatly from firm to firm. Many firms divide their efforts between a long-term planning budget which rarely exceeds five years and a short-term one-year capital budget. The former is usually general in nature and often indicates *areas* of future interest rather than specific investment proposals. For example, the rough order of magnitudes of planned investment in fixed assets such as land, buildings and machines is projected by divisions, by product line or by manufacturing process. The short-term budget is more specific and includes the final estimates for the proposed project. It is this budget which provides the cornerstone of the firm's control of its capital expenditures, and in fact, except in firms of very moderate size some sort of short-term budget appears to be a necessity if management is to control its capital expenditures.

The post-completion audit of capital investment projects is one stage of the decision-making process which is often overlooked. Strictly speaking the post-audit is not part of the current decision-making process since it refers to implemented projects. However, a systematic program of evaluating past decisions can contribute to the improvement of current decision-making by analyzing the patterns of past estimation errors by department, by personnel, or by type of expenditure. The accumulated information can be extremely valuable in revising current forecasting and evaluation methods.

The post-audit is a necessary management tool because unlike the movies of the 1930s, even the best laid plans of management may not have a happy ending. Although past mistakes cannot be undone, a careful analysis of the deviations of actual from planned performance may help to prevent history from repeating itself. If investment outlays are consistently underestimated by 5 – 10% a rule of thumb correction of that order of magnitude may be called for. In general, the post-audit can be a sobering and rewarding experience for most decision-makers.

SUMMARY

This chapter has sketched out a broad overview of the capital budgeting process. A capital investment project can be distinguished from current expenditures by two features:

   such projects are relatively large;
   a significant period of time (more than one year) elapses between the
      investment outlay and the receipt of the benefits.

As a result, most medium-sized and large firms have developed special procedures and methods for dealing with these decisions. A systematic approach to
capital budgeting implies:

> the formulation of long-term goals;
> the creative search for and identification of new investment opportunities;
> classification of projects and recognition of economically and/or statisti-
> cally dependent proposals;
> the estimation and forecasting of current and future cash flows;
> a suitable administrative framework capable of transferring the required
> information to the decision level;
> the controlling of expenditures and careful monitoring of crucial aspects
> of project execution.

Finally, a set of decision rules which can differentiate acceptable from unacceptable alternatives is required. And it is to this key problem that we turn
our attention in the next chapter.

QUESTIONS AND PROBLEMS

2.1   Why is it necessary to assume a goal for the firm when applying capital
budgeting methods?

2.2   Give two examples for each one of the following types of investment
projects:

(a)   mutually exclusive projects
(b)   complementary projects
(c)   substitute projects
(d)   independent projects

2.3   Define "conventional" and "non-conventional" projects.

2.4   Set out the cash flow generated by the following activities:

(a)   Developing a new product requires an investment of $800,000. This
product will generate annual receipts of $250,000 for the next six
years.
(b)   A firm invests $3 million in a new project and expects annual receipts
of $600,000 for the first three years and $900,000 during the last five
years.
(c)   Mr. Smith borrows $5,000 from the bank. The loan is repayable in
seven equal annual instalments of $950 each.
(d)   An investment of $75,000 in new equipment is expected to generate
annual net receipts of $45,000 for four years starting at the third year.
(e)   A firm takes a three-year loan of $100,000 which is to be repaid at
the end of the third year in a lump sum payment of $130,000.

2.5 The Western Company is considering introducing a new product line. The required investment outlay is $650,000 this year and $550,000 the following year. The expected net receipts are $750,000 two years from now, $500,000 in the third year and $250,000 in the fourth year. At the beginning of the fourth year the firm will have to invest an additional $600,000 to improve the product in order to generate net receipts of $400,000 in the fifth year and sixth year, and $500,000 in the seventh year. Set out the cash flow of this project.

2.6 "Improving capital investment decisions in practice is relatively simple; after all it all boils down to finding the correct decision rule." Evaluate this statement.

SELECTED REFERENCES

Ang, J.S., "A Graphical Presentation of an Integrated Capital Budgeting Model", *Engineering Economist*, Winter 1978.

Bierman, Harold Jr. and Smidt, Seymour, *The Capital Budgeting Decision*, Fourth Edition, New York: Macmillan, 1975.

Dean, Joel, *Capital Budgeting*, New York: Columbia University Press, 1951.

Jean, William H., *Capital Budgeting*, Scranton: International Textbook Co., 1969.

Johnson, Robert W., *Capital Budgeting*, Belmont, Calif.: Wadsworth Publishing Co., 1970.

Lutz, Friederich and Lutz, Vera, *The Theory of Investment of the Firm*, Princeton, N.J.: Princeton University Press, 1951.

Mao, J.C.T., "Survey of Capital Budgeting: Theory and Practice", *Journal of Finance*, May 1970.

Merrett, A.J. and Sykes, Allen, *Capital Budgeting and Company Finance*, London: Longmans, Green & Co. Ltd., 1966.

Petty, J.W., Scott, Jr., D.F. and Bird, M.M., "The Capital Expenditure Decision-Making Process of Large Corporations", *The Engineering Economist*, Spring 1975.

Robichek, Alexander, and Myers, Stewart C., *Optimal Financing Decisions*, Englewood Cliffs, N.J.: Prentice-Hall, 1965.

Sihler, William W., "Presenting Capital Expenditure Requests to Management", *Financial Executive*, April 1973.

Solomon, Ezra, *The Theory of Financial Management*, New York: Columbia University Press, 1963.

Shashua L., and Goldschmidt, Y., "An Index for Evaluating Financial Performance", *Journal of Finance*, June 1974.

Wellington, Roger, "Capital Budgeting", *Journal of Accountancy*, May 1963.

Williams, R.B., "Industry Practice in Allocating Capital Resources", *Managerial Planning*, May – June 1970.

3

*The Economic Evaluation
of Investment Proposals*

We now turn our attention to a problem which lies at the very heart of the capital budgeting process — the economic evaluation of a project's desirability. This requires the stipulation of a decision rule for accepting or rejecting investment projects. But before this can be done we must first consider the time element which is, as we have already noted, a distinguishing feature of capital investment decisions.

THE TIME VALUE OF MONEY

The expression "time is money" is considered by many to be almost as American as apple pie. However, from the standpoint of investment analysis, its significance stems not from its national origin but from the fact that a dollar received "tomorrow" is not equivalent to a dollar in hand "today". And as the typical capital investment decision invariably involves the comparison of present outlays and future benefits, problems relating to the timing of receipts and outlays lie at the very heart of the capital budgeting process.

In order to focus attention on the implications of the time value of money for decision-making let us initially assume that the costs and benefits of alternative investment projects are known with *certainty*. But even if the magnitudes of the relevant cash flows are known, attention must still be paid to their timing when weighing the desirability of an investment proposal. This will become clear if we consider the following example of a project which requires an immediate investment outlay of $1,000, and which returns $1,100 with certainty exactly one year later. Does it pay to make such an investment, i.e. does it pay to give up $1,000 today in order to receive $1,100 one year hence? Clearly the answer depends on the alternative use which we have for the $1,000. If, for example, we assume that we can earn 12% interest by depositing the $1,000 in a bank, the value of the deposit at the end of the year will be $1,120. And since $1,120 exceeds $1,100, the proposed investment is *not* desirable. On the other hand, if the bank pays only 8% interest, the value of the account at the end of the year will be $1,080. Since $1,080 is less than $1,100, the original proposal is worthwhile and, other things being equal, is to be preferred over the bank account.

Clearly, an intelligent investment decision requires the comparison of alternatives; and it is the fact that money always can earn a positive return that lends importance to the time dimension of the typical capital investment project. A dollar given up today is not the equivalent of a dollar received in the future as long as there exists the alternative of earning a positive return on the dollar during the interim.

Let us denote the relevant alternative rate of return which can be earned in the market, independent of the decision under consideration, by the letter k, which should be read as $k\%$. Now what is the value to the firm of a dollar which will be received one year from now? To answer this question let us first check the *future value* (*FV*) of 1 dollar, i.e. the principal plus accumulated interest at the end of the year. Given the alternative return of k, the future value of a dollar is given by

$$FV_1 = 1 \cdot (1 + k)$$

where FV_1 denotes the future value of 1 dollar at the end of year 1. If $k = 10\%$ we have

$$FV_1 = 1 \cdot (1 + 0.10) = 1 + 0.10 = \$1.10$$

What is the future value of 1 dollar at the end of two years?[1] As we have already noted its terminal value at the end of the first year will be $1.10, so that in the second year an additional 10% will be earned on the $1.10:

$$FV_2 = 1.10 + 0.11 = \$1.21$$

where FV_2 denotes the value at end of two years, or in symbols:

$$FV_2 = 1 \cdot (1 + k)(1 + k) = 1 \cdot (1 + k)^2$$

In general, the future value of 1 dollar at the end of n years will be

$$FV_n = 1 \cdot (1 + k)^n$$

Now let us take a concrete example and find the future value of $1,000 after five years assuming that k is again equal to 10%. The relevant calculations are set out in Table 3.1. The future value at the end of two years is the same as that which we found using the formula for 1 dollar, multiplied of course by 1,000

---

1 Throughout the discussion we assume annual compounding; for the effects of alternative assumptions regarding the frequency of compounding see Appendix 3A at the end of the chapter.

$(1.21 \times 1,000 = \$1,210)$. Similarly the future value after three years is given by:

$$FV_3 = FV_2 (1 + 0.10) = 1,210 (1 + 0.10) = \$1,331$$

But as $FV_2 = FV_1 (1 + k)$ and $FV_1 = V_0 (1 + k)$ where V_0 denotes the amount invested at the beginning of the first year, we can set the same result as follows:

$$FV_3 = V_0 (1 + k)^3$$

Table 3.1
Future Value Calculations

Year	(1) Amount at Beginning of Year ($)	(2) Interest Factor (k = 10%)	(3) = (1) × (2) Future Value ($)
1	1,000	1.10	1,100
2	1,100	1.10	1,210
3	1,210	1.10	1,331
4	1,331	1.10	1,464
5	1,464	1.10	1,611

Applying this formula to the above example we obtain

$$FV_5 = V_0 \cdot (1 + k)^5$$
$$= 1,000 (1 + 0.10)^5 = \$1,611$$

Again V_0 denotes the amount invested at the beginning of the first year, which in this example is equal to $1,000. Of course, this equation is a special version of the general formula for compound interest over time and can be applied to any amount of money using any interest rate. Thus if we want to know the future value to which V_0 dollars will accumulate in n years when it is compounded annually at some rate of interest i, we can write

$$V_n = V_0 (1 + i)^n$$

where i denotes the appropriate compounding rate.

In a world of electronic computers, the calculation of compound future values has been reduced to the mechanical reading of numbers from a table. Using the above compound interest formula we can easily generate the figures of Table 3.2 which gives the value of $(1 + i)^t$ for alternative values of i and t. The future value of any initial amount can be found by multiplying that amount by the relevant interest factor from Table 3.2. In our previous example we assumed a 10% compound rate and a five-year time horizon. The corresponding interest factor, 1.611, is found in line 5, column 10 of Table 3.2, and the future value of $1,000 at the end of five years is $1,611 as before:

$$1,000 \times 1.611 = \$1,611$$

It requires only a minor extension of the compound interest formula to

Table 3.2
Compounded Future Value of $1

Years Hence	1%	2%	3%	4%	5%	6%	7%	8%	9%	10%
1	1.010	1.020	1.030	1.040	1.050	1.060	1.070	1.080	1.090	1.100
2	1.020	1.040	1.061	1.082	1.102	1.124	1.145	1.166	1.188	1.210
3	1.030	1.061	1.093	1.125	1.158	1.191	1.225	1.260	1.295	1.331
4	1.041	1.082	1.126	1.170	1.216	1.262	1.311	1.360	1.412	1.464
5	1.051	1.104	1.159	1.217	1.276	1.338	1.403	1.469	1.539	**1.611**
6	1.062	1.126	1.194	1.265	1.340	1.419	1.501	1.587	1.677	1.772
7	1.072	1.149	1.230	1.316	1.407	1.504	1.605	1.714	1.828	1.949
8	1.083	1.172	1.267	1.369	1.477	1.594	1.718	1.851	1.993	2.144
9	1.094	1.195	1.305	1.423	1.551	1.689	1.838	1.999	2.172	2.358
10	1.105	1.219	1.344	1.480	1.629	1.791	1.967	2.159	2.367	2.594

derive the formula for *present value (PV)*, rather than future value. Denoting V_0 by PV and dividing both sides of the formula $FV_n = PV(1+i)^n$ by $(1+i)^n$ we derive:

$$PV = \frac{FV_n}{(1+i)^n}$$

which can be read as the present value (PV) of V_n dollars received at the end of n years. This is perhaps the less familiar formula for *discounting* future sums to their present values, and is, as we have seen, the obverse side of the compound interest formula. If we again assume that the firm's alternative rate of return is given by ($k = 10\%$) we can write the present value formula as follows:

$$PV = \frac{FV}{(1 + k)^n}$$

Applying this formula to our previous one-year example we get

$$PV = \frac{FV_1}{1 + k} = \frac{1.10}{1 + 0.10} = \$1$$

that is the present value of $1.10 to be received at the end of one year is 1 dollar. Similarly, the present value of $1.21 to be received at the end of two years is equal to 1 dollar:

$$\frac{FV_2}{(1 + k)^2} = \frac{1.21}{(1 + 0.10)^2} = \$1$$

The line of reasoning behind the formula is very simple: given the alternative of earning 10% on his money, an individual (or firm) should never offer (invest) more than $1,000 to obtain $1,100 with certainty at the end of the year. If he pays more, say $1,010, he could have reached a higher future value by investing the $1,010 at 10%:

$$\$1,010 \, (1 + 0.10) = \$1,111 > 1,100$$

Alternatively we can apply the present value formula directly by noting that

$$PV = \frac{1,100}{1+0.10} = 1,000 < 1,010$$

The present value of $1,100 received one year hence is only $1,000, which is less than the proposed investment outlay of $1,010 and therefore the proposed investment is not worthwhile. Modern time-discounted methods for evaluating investment projects are straightforward generalizations of this future value-present value relationship.

NET PRESENT VALUE (*NPV*)

The Net Present Value (*NPV*) method of evaluating the desirability of investments can be defined as follows:

$$NPV = \frac{S_1}{1+k} + \frac{S_2}{(1+k)^2} + \frac{S_3}{(1+k)^3} + \ldots + \frac{S_n}{(1+k)^n} - I_0$$

$$NPV = \sum_{t=1}^{n} \frac{S_t}{(1+k)^t} - I_0$$

where:
S_t = the net cash receipt at the end of year t
I_0 = the initial investment outlay[2]
k = the discount rate, i.e. the required minimum rate of return on new investment
n = the project's duration in years

Table 3.3
Present Value of $1

Years Hence	1%	2%	4%	5%	6%	8%	10%
1	.990	.980	.962	.952	.943	.926	.909
2	.980	.961	.925	.907	.890	.857	.826
3	.971	.942	.889	.864	.840	.794	.751
4	.961	.924	.855	.823	.792	.735	.683
5	.951	.906	.822	.784	.747	.681	.621
6	.942	.888	.790	.746	.705	.630	.564
7	.933	.871	.760	.711	.665	.583	.513
8	.923	.853	.731	.677	.627	.540	.467
9	.914	.837	.703	.645	.592	.500	.424
10	.905	.820	.676	.614	.558	.463	.386

An investment proposal's *NPV* is derived by discounting the net cash receipts at a rate which reflects the value of the alternative use of the funds, summing them

2 Since the investment outlay may stretch over an extended period, a more general formulation would be to define I_0 as the present value of the investment outlays.

over the life of the proposal and deducting the initial outlay. The actual calculation can be reduced to a very simple procedure by using Table 3.3. The 10%
discount factors of Table 3.3 which are used to reduce the receipts to their present
values are defined as follows:

$$q_{(1,10\%)} = \frac{1}{(1+0.10)} = 0.909$$

$$q_{(2,10\%)} = \frac{1}{(1+0.10)^2} = 0.826$$

$$q_{(3,10\%)} = \frac{1}{(1+0.10)^3} = 0.751$$

where the two subscripts of each q denote the year in which the dollar was
received and the 10% discount rate respectively. They also indicate the relevant
line (year) and column (discount rate) of Table 3.3. Thus $q_{(6,8\%)}$ is found by
taking the factor appearing in line 6 and the 8% column of Table 3.3, that is
0.630.

If we denote years by the letter t and discount (interest) rates by i, a general
formula for calculating the discount factor can be written

$$q_{(t,i)} = \frac{1}{(1+i)^t}$$

The solution of the above equation, for selected values of t and i, generates
Table 3.3. To find the present value of any given sum S received in any year t,
we multiply S by the appropriate discount factor. In the case of a business firm
the discount rate used, k, is the minimum required rate of return on new investment, or "cost of capital" as it is often called.

$$S \cdot q_{(t,k)} = S \cdot \frac{1}{(1+k)^t} = \frac{S}{(1+k)^t}$$

The actual calculation of the present value of the receipts, using Table 3.3,
can be illustrated by the following example of a three-year project:

Year (t)	Net Receipt (S)	Discount Factor $q_{(t,10)}$	Present Value of Cash Flow
1	400	.909	363.60
2	600	.826	495.60
3	500	.751	375.50
		Total	1,234.70
	Less Initial Outlay (I_0)		− 1,000.00
		NPV	**+ 234.70**

3 A more complete table of present value factors is given in the Appendix Tables at the end of
the book.

In the case of an annuity (uniform annual receipts) the calculation can be facilitated further by using Table 3.4 which is merely a summation of the relevant annual discount factors of Table 3.3. Thus, to find the present value of a five-year one-dollar annuity at 10% discount, we multiply 1 dollar by the factor appearing in line 5 of the 10% column of Table 3.4, that is 3.791 which is a summation of the first five factors in the 10% column of Table 3.3.

Table 3.4
Present Value of an Annuity of $1

Year	1%	2%	4%	5%	6%	8%	10%
1	0.990	0.980	0.962	0.952	0.943	0.926	0.909
2	1.970	1.942	1.886	1.859	1.833	1.783	1.736
3	2.941	2.884	2.775	2.723	2.673	2.577	**2.487**
4	3.902	3.808	3.630	3.546	3.465	3.312	3.170
5	4.853	4.713	4.452	4.329	4.212	3.993	3.791
6	5.795	5.601	5.242	5.076	4.917	4.623	4.355
7	6.728	6.472	6.002	5.786	5.582	5.206	4.868
8	7.652	7.325	6.733	6.463	6.210	5.747	5.335
9	8.566	8.162	7.435	7.108	6.802	6.247	5.759
10	9.471	8.983	8.111	7.722	7.360	6.710	6.145

The calculation of the NPV of an annuity can be illustrated by considering the example of an investment which for an initial outlay of $1,000 offers a net receipt of $400 per year for three years. First we find the relevant discount factor for a three-year annuity and a 10% discount rate, that is the discount factor appearing in line 3 of the 10% column of Table 3.4, 2.487. The present value of the receipts is given by:

$$400 \cdot 2.487 = 994.8$$

and therefore the NPV of the project is negative, -5.2, since the initial investment outlay exceeds the present value of the receipts,

$$994.8 - 1,000 = -5.2$$

Before we can apply the NPV method of investment appraisal a decision rule must be defined, but this requires the stipulation of a goal for the firm. Assuming that management desires *more* rather than *less* "bang for its buck" the following decision rules should be adopted:

If NPV is positive, accept the project
If NPV is negative, reject the project

where the present values are calculated using a discount rate which reflects the alternative return which the firm can earn on the capital in the market. Thus the firm should execute projects with a positive NPV and reject those proposals whose NPVs are negative. These decision rules follow directly from the assumption that firms operate so as to maximize the market value of their

---

4 We ignore projects with zero NPV since by definition the firm is indifferent to such proposals.

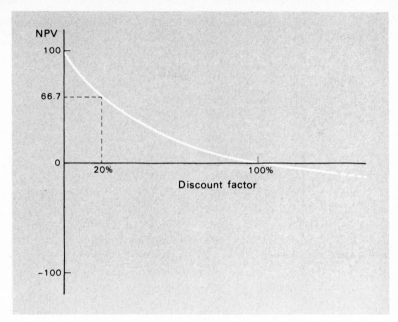

Fig. 3.1

common stock, since under the assumed conditions of certainty the prices of all assets, including common stocks, are determined by their discounted present values. These decision rules result in an *optimal* choice of projects, because under the assumed conditions no other group of projects can be found which will increase the value of the firm.

A Graphical Representation of *NPV*

The size of a project's *NPV* depends, among other things, on the discount rate. This dependence can be "visualized" by using a simple graphical device. Consider the following numerical example of a $100 investment which generates a $200 receipt at the end of one year:

$$NPV = \frac{S_1}{1+k} - I_0 = \frac{200}{1+k} - 100$$

Fig. 3.1 graphs the *NPV* of this project as a function of the discount rate. When the discount rate is zero (at the intercept on the vertical axis) the *NPV* is given by:

$$NPV = \frac{200}{1+0} - 100 = 100$$

5 A formal proof of this proposition was given by P.A. Samuelson, "Some Aspects of the Pure Theory of Capital", *Quarterly Journal of Economics*, May 1937, pp. 469 – 96.

Conversely, if we let the discount rate become indefinitely large, and approach infinity (∞), we get

$$NPV = \frac{200}{1+\infty} - 100 = -100$$

If we set the discount rate equal to 100%, the *NPV* is exactly zero which determines the intercept with the horizontal axis:

$$NPV = \frac{200}{1+1} - 100 = 0$$

These calculations determine three points on the *NPV* profile of the project which is drawn in Fig. 3.1; the remaining points of the profile have been sketched in by permitting the discount rate to vary between zero and infinity. From the diagram it is clear that the project's *NPV* is positive for all discount rates below 100%, and therefore should be accepted if the minimum required rate of return is less than 100%. For example, if $k = 20\%$, the project has a positive *NPV* of $66.70:

$$NPV = \frac{200}{1+0.2} - 100 = 166.70 - 100 = \$66.70$$

The meaning of the *NPV* decision rule is clear. Assuming a 20% required rate of return, it pays the firm to invest $100 today in a one-year project if the return received at the end of the year exceeds $120. Since the project in question promises a return of $200, that is $80 in excess of the minimum required receipt ($120), the project should be accepted. The reader can also verify that the present value of the $80 profit is $80/1.2 = \$66.70$, which is the project's *NPV*.

Figure 3.2 generalizes the analysis for conventional multiperiod projects, that is investment proposals having cash inflows in more than one year:

$$NPV = \sum_{t=1}^{n} \frac{S_t}{(1+k)^t} - I_0$$

When the discount rate $= 0$ (at the intercept with the vertical axis) the *NPV* equals the algebraic sum of the stream of undiscounted net receipts minus the initial investment outlay:

$$\sum_{t=1}^{n} S_t - I_0$$

As the discount rate approaches infinity the *NPV* reduces to $-I_0$. Since we have assumed a conventional form of cash flow ($- + + + \ldots$) the function slopes downwards as the discount rate increases. For every increase in the discount

---

6 We confine ourselves to positive values since the discount rate cannot be negative as long as money can earn a positive rate of interest in an alternative use.

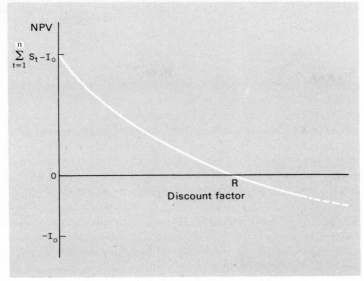

$$\sum_{t=1}^{n} S_t - I_0$$

NPV

0

R
Discount factor

$-I_0$

Fig. 3.2

rate the present value of the positive cash flow is decreased while the initial investment outlay remains unchanged, so that the project's *NPV* declines. Figure 3.2 shows that the project's *NPV* is positive, and therefore the proposal should be accepted for all discount rates (costs of capital) which are less than *R*.

THE INTERNAL RATE OF RETURN

The *internal rate of return* (*IRR*) is another time-discounted measure of investment worth. The internal rate of return is defined as that rate of discount which equates the present value of the stream of net receipts with the initial investment outlay:

$$I_0 = \frac{S_1}{(1+R)} + \frac{S_2}{(1+R)^2} + \frac{S_3}{(1+R)^3} + \dots + \frac{S_n}{(1+R)^n}$$

$$= \sum_{t=1}^{n} \frac{S_t}{(1+R)^t}$$

where *R* denotes the internal rate of return. An alternative and equivalent definition of the *IRR* is "that rate of discount which equates the *NPV* of the cash flow to zero":

7 Applied to the investment in real assets, this method is known under a variety of names including "marginal efficiency of capital", "discounted cash flow", "investor's method", and so on. This is also the method which is used to compute the yield to maturity on a bond. The term "internal rate of return" was first introduced by K. Boulding, "The Theory of a Single Investment", *Quarterly Journal of Economics*, May 1935, pp. 475 – 94.

$$\sum_{t=1}^{n} \frac{S_t}{(1+R)^t} - I_0 = 0$$

The latter formula is somewhat more helpful in calculating the *IRR*, which for investments whose cash flow is received over a period of years, requires an iterative or "trial and error" solution. The computational procedure is as follows: given the cash flow and investment outlay, choose a discount rate at random, and calculate the project's *NPV*. If the *NPV* is positive, choose a *higher* discount rate and repeat the procedure; if the *NPV* is negative, choose a *lower* discount rate and repeat the procedure. That discount rate which makes the *NPV* = 0 is the *IRR*, and the procedure is completed. Table 3.5 gives an example of such a calculation. Using an 8% discount factor the *NPV* is positive (+ 67.8) and therefore a higher rate, 15%, is chosen. This discount rate, however, results in a negative *NPV* (− 45.9) so that a discount rate which is lower than 15% but higher than 8% is required. A 12% discount rate reduces the project's *NPV* to zero so that by definition the project's *IRR* is 12%.

In cases of annuities, that is projects with equal annual receipts, Table 3.4 enables us to make a convenient short cut.

Consider the following:

$$\sum_{t=1}^{n} \frac{S}{(1+R)^t} = I_0$$

where: S = a constant, that is, $S_1 = S_2 = \ldots = S_n$. If we let $Q_{(t, k)}$ denote the discount factor in line (t) of Table 3.4, we can rewrite the *IRR* formula for an annuity as follows:

$$S \sum_{t=1}^{n} \frac{1}{(1+R)^t} = I_0 \text{ or } SQ_{(n,R)} = I_0$$

Since the investment outlay (I_0) and the uniform annual receipt (S) are known, the discount factor Q can be determined by dividing S into I_0:

$$Q_{(n,R)} = \frac{I_0}{S}$$

The project's *IRR* is determined by looking along line n of Table 3.4 to find the column which includes this particular discount factor. Now let us apply the simplified annuity formula to a concrete example:

$$\text{Let } S = \$20 \text{ per year}$$
$$n = 7 \text{ years}$$
$$I_0 = \$120$$

8 For most projects, the *IRR* can be calculated by hand in a few minutes, but where necessary, standard computer programs are available to facilitate the calculations.

Table 3.5
Calculation of IRR for a Hypothetical Project

Year	Net Cash Flow	Discount Factor	Present Value of Cash Flow
	First Iteration: 8% Discount Rate		
1	452	0.926	418.6
2	500	0.857	428.5
3	278	0.794	220.7
	PV of Receipts		1,067.8
	Less: Initial Outlay		− 1,000.0
	NPV		+ 67.8
	Second Iteration: 15% Discount Rate		
1	452	0.870	393.2
2	500	0.756	378.0
3	278	0.658	182.9
	PV of Receipts		954.1
	Less: Initial Outlay		− 1,000.0
	NPV		− 45.9
	Final Iteration: 12% Discount Rate		
1	452	0.893	403.6
2	500	0.797	398.5
3	278	0.712	197.9
	PV of Receipts		1,000.0
	Less: Initial Outlay		− 1,000.0
	NPV		0

First we find the discount factor,

$$Q_{(7,R)} = \frac{I_0}{S} = \frac{120}{20} = 6$$

A glance at line 7 of Table 3.4 shows that $Q_{(7,R)} = 6.002$, which is approximately equal to 6, appears in the 4% column; hence the *IRR* of the annuity is approximately 4%.

Looking back at Fig. 3.2, which graphs a project's *NPV* as a function of the discount rate, the *IRR* is located at the intercept with the horizontal axis, that is at point R, since this is the rate of discount which reduces the *NPV* to zero. The reader can verify from this graph that for all $k < R$ the *NPV* is positive; conversely for all $k > R$ the *NPV* is negative. Unlike the *NPV* which can be either positive or negative depending on the discount rate chosen, a project's *IRR* is fixed once-and-for-all independent of the discount rate. Thus the *IRR* decision rules must take the minimum required rate of return, k, explicitly into account:

> If R is greater than k, accept the project.
> If R is less than k, reject the project.

We again ignore the possibility of $R = k$ in which case the firm would be indifferent to the project.

AN ECONOMIC RATIONALE FOR THE *IRR* RULE

Although the *IRR* is easily calculated, its economic significance may not be intuitively obvious. What is the exact meaning of a 10% or 15% internal rate of return? Why must the *IRR* be higher than the opportunity cost of capital if the project is to be accepted? The answers to these questions can best be given within the context of a numerical example. Consider the cash flow of the following hypothetical two-year investment proposal:

	Year		
	0	*1*	*2*
Cash Flow	-173.60	$+100$	$+100$

Dividing the uniform annual cash receipt (100) into the investment outlay (173.60) we find that the discount factor $Q(_2, R) = 1.736$. A glance at line 2 of Table 3.4 shows that this corresponds to an *IRR* of 10%. According to the *IRR* decision rule that proposal should be accepted as long as the discount rate is less than 10%.

Common sense suggests that if the project earns 10% and we borrow the money needed to finance it at *less* than 10%, a profit will be made. That is we should be able to repay the principal and interest out of the proceeds from the project and still have some money left. Should the bank demand more than 10%, the project's cash flow will be insufficient and a loss will be incurred; and if the interest rate exactly equals the project's *IRR* the project will neither earn a profit nor suffer a loss, but will just break even. If these relationships do not hold we may be in very serious trouble because it would no longer be clear (to us at least) just why a project whose *IRR* is greater than k should be accepted.

To check the meaning of the *IRR* let us assume that the firm borrows from a bank the $173.60 necessary to implement the project, and that the bank charges 10% interest, that is an interest rate which just equals the project's *IRR*. If the *IRR* rule is to be meaningful such a situation should result in a zero profit to the firm. Table 3.6 sets out the relevant transactions between the bank and the firm. At the end of the first year the firm pays the bank 10% interest on its loan of $173.60, that is $17.30 out of the cash proceeds from the project. But as the firm earned $100 from the project it is now able to repay part of the principal of the loan ($82.70) as well. At the end of the second year the interest payment to the bank is only $9.10 since the outstanding loan in the second year is only $90.90 (10% × 90.90 ≅ 9.10). After paying the interest, $90.90 remains, which is just sufficient to repay the outstanding balance of the loan, so that the firm neither gains nor loses from the project. We leave it to the reader to verify that had the bank charged 15% interest the proceeds from the project would not have sufficed to pay the interest and principal on the loan. If we now generalize the arguments and substitute the minimum required rate of return (i.e. cost of capital[9]) for the interest rate on the bank loan, we can readily see the economic rationale for demanding $R > k$ as the necessary condition for accepting a project.

Table 3.6

	First Year	Second Year
Cash Inflow	+ 100.00	+ 100.00
Interest Payment	− 17.30	− 9.10
Payment of Principal	− 82.70	− 90.90
Loan Outstanding beginning of year	173.60	90.90
Loan Outstanding end of year*	90.90	—

*173.60 − 82.70 = 90.90.

MEASURING THE RETURN ON MONEY UNDER INFLATIONARY CONDITIONS

Although inflation is not a new phenomenon, until recently investors often ignored price level changes when measuring the return on money. However, the appearance of double digit inflation in the US and other highly industrialized countries during the 1970s has forced knowledgeable investors to consider explicitly the impact of inflation on the profitability of investments.

For simplicity, let us assume an inflation of $h\%$ a year, and an annual nominal interest rate paid on savings accounts of $R_n\%$. Thus, for each $100 deposited, such accounts grow to $100 \cdot (1 + R_n)$ at the end of the year. However, as we have assumed an inflation rate of $h\%$ during the year, the value of one's savings in *real terms* (i.e. in terms of their purchasing power) is only $100 (1 + R_n) \div (1 + h)$ at the end of the year. Clearly, if both the interest rate and the inflation rate are equal, say 5%, the account grows to $105 in nominal terms, but remains constant, $105/1.05 = $100, in terms of real purchasing power.

In general, the nominal future value of the savings (FV_n) at the end of the year is,

$$FV_n = \$100 (1 + R_n)$$

and its *future* value in real terms, FV_{real}, is given by,

$$FV_{real} = FV_n \div (1 + h) = \$100 (1 + R_n) \div (1 + h)$$

9 For further discussion of the cost of capital and its measurement, see Chapters 17 and 18 below.

Since we are dealing with a one-year investment, the internal rate of return (IRR) in real terms, which we denote by R_{real}, is given by the following formula:

$$\$100 = \frac{FV_{real}}{1 + R_{real}}$$

and

$$R_{real} = \frac{1 + R_n}{1 + h} - 1$$

Now let us apply this formula to some actual cases. During most of the 1950s and early 1960s one-year saving accounts (or an investment in Treasury bills) earned only 3% interest. But as the inflation rate averaged only about 1% (for example, the annual inflation rate in the US was 1% in 1961 and 1962 and only 0.9% in 1964), the IRR in *real* terms on such an investment was positive:

$$R_{real} = \frac{1 + 0.03}{1 + 0.01} - 1 \cong 0.0198, \text{ i.e., approximately } 2\%.$$

In March 1980, on the other hand, investors in the US could earn as much as 16% per year on an investment in Treasury bills and other short-term low-risk investments. However, since the inflation rate was expected to be about 15%, we find, using the formula for a one-year investment, that the *real IRR* on such investments was actually lower in March 1980 than during the early 1960s:

$$\frac{1 + 0.16}{1 + 0.15} - 1 = 1.0086 - 1 \simeq 0.9\%, \text{ i.e. less than } 1\%!$$

Thus, the accelerated rate of inflation reduced the real rate of return on investments in Government Treasury bills despite the sharp rise in the nominal interest paid on them.

Taxes and Inflation

This decline is even more serious once we consider the impact of personal taxes.

Unfortunately, Uncle Sam does not readily agree to forgo his share in interest income and as a result most of us have to pay income tax on our interest earnings. Suppose that the relevant marginal personal income tax rate is $T_p = 0.30$, i.e. 30% of interest income goes to the tax collector. In this case, the nominal future value (after one year) of $100 deposited at the beginning of the year grows, on an after-tax basis, to

$$FV_n = 100[1 + R_n(1 - T_p)]$$

because only $R_n(1 - T_p)$ is left after making the income tax payment. For example if R_n is 5%, $FV_n = 100[1 + 0.05(1 - 0.3)] = 103.5$. And given an inflation rate of $h\%$, the future value after taxes is, in real terms,

$$FV_{real} = 100[1 + R_n(1 + T_p)] \div (1 + h)$$

In this instance the after-tax real *IRR* can be derived from the following equation:

$$\frac{FV_{real}}{1 + R_{real}} = \frac{\$100 \; [1 + R_n \, (1 - T_p) \div (1 + h)]}{1 + R_{real}} = \$100$$

Hence,

$$R_{real} = \frac{[1 + R_n \, (1 + T_p)]}{1 + h} - 1$$

Let us apply this formula to the previous two cases, on the assumption that the personal tax rate T_p is 30%. Given the relative low interest and inflation rates which prevailed during most of the 1950s and early 1960s, we have $R_n = 3\%$, $h = 1\%$, and the real after tax rate of return was

$$R_{real} = \frac{1 + 0.03 \cdot (1 - 0.30)}{1.01} - 1 = \frac{1.021}{1.01} - 1 = 0.01089 \simeq 1.09\%$$

Thus the after-tax real *IRR* was not much different from its pre-tax counterpart. Now consider the after-tax *IRR* on savings in the high inflation period. Assuming a 16% interest rate and 15% inflation, but retaining the same tax rate,

$$R_{real} = \frac{1 + 0.16 \, (1 - 0.30)}{1.15} - 1 = \frac{1.112}{1.115} - 1 = - 0.033 \simeq - 3.3\%$$

Clearly, the need to pay taxes reduces the real return on savings; hence for the earlier period in question the after-tax real rate of return is only 1.09% as compared with a pre-tax return of 1.98%. The striking feature of the exercise, however, is the much more drastic fall in the after-tax rate of return for the hypothetical high inflation case, even though we have assumed the same tax rate. In this instance, the real rate of return falls from 0.9% to *minus* 3.3% when personal taxes are considered. The reason for this negative *IRR* is that savers must pay taxes on "inflationary" profits. Although 16% interest was earned on the investment the 15% inflation reduces the *real* profit to slightly less than 1%. However, under existing tax law *all* the 16% interest income is subject to tax and hence savers are taxed on "paper profits," that is "inflationary" profits which represent no increase in their purchasing power. The higher the inflation rate, the higher is the tax on inflationary profits, and the greater is the negative impact on after-tax real rates of return.[10]

Before we end this section a word of caution seems appropriate. These results, which often characterize an inflationary economy do not mean that all investors (after reading this section) should run out and withdraw all their savings or sell their holdings of Treasury bills, but it does mean that taxes and inflation are important factors to be considered when making an investment decision.[11]

10 Of course the nominal interest rate might rise sufficiently in an inflationary economy to compensate investors for this "tax loss", but this does not always seem to have been the case in the United States and western Europe.

11 For a detailed discussion of the impact of taxes and inflation on the evaluation of investments, see Chapters 6 and 7 below.

SUMMARY

In this chapter, problems raised by the time lag between a project's initial investment outlay and the receipt of the benefits have been examined. When evaluating the desirability of an investment proposal, consideration must be given to both the timing of the net receipts and their magnitude, since a dollar invested "today" is not the equivalent of a dollar received "tomorrow", so long as there exists an alternative possibility of earning a positive return during the interim.

Two time-discounted methods of evaluating capital investment expenditures are defined: *Net Present Value* (*NPV*) which is derived by discounting a project's cash receipts using the minimum required rate of return on new investment (cost of capital), summing them over the lifetime of the proposal and deducting the initial investment outlay; the *Internal Rate of Return* (*IRR*) which is defined as that rate of discount which equates the present value of the stream of net receipts with the inital outlay. All of the necessary calculations can be reduced to very simple procedures by using tables of present value which have been constructed for this purpose.

Assuming that the firm wishes to maximize the wealth of its shareholders, the following decision rules can be derived for the *NPV* method:

When *NPV* is positive, accept the project.
When *NPV* is negative, reject the project.

The following decision rules are associated with the *IRR* method:

If *IRR* exceeds the discount rate, accept the project.
If *IRR* is less than the discount rate, reject the project.

Since these two methods are closely related, we devote the next chapter to a comparison of their relative effectiveness in screening capital investment proposals.

The chapter ends with a brief discussion of the impact of inflation on the rate of return earned on savings. Nominal and *real* calculations of the rate of return are distinguished and the problem of the taxation of inflationary profits is raised. We shall return to these important issues in Chapters 6 and 7.

QUESTIONS AND PROBLEMS

3.1   Define the following terms:

(a) time value of money
(b) present value
(c) future value
(d) internal rate of return (*IRR*)
(e) net present value (*NPV*)

3.2 You are given the choice between $1,000 now or some amount of money one year from now.

    (a) How large would the amount one year from now have to be for you to be indifferent between the two choices?

    (b) What does the answer to this question imply about the rate of interest during this time period?

3.3 How long does it take for $100 to be double compounded at 8%? How much would you get at the end of this period of time, if the $100 were an annuity?

3.4 If you decide to buy a house for which you have to pay $4,000 per year for eight years, and the interest rate is 10%, what is the equivalent price of the house if paid in a lump sum today?

3.5 Given the following cash flow:

			Year		
0	*1*	*2*	*3*	*4*	*5*
− 3,352	1,000	1,000	1,000	1,000	1,000

    (a) Calculate the net present value of the project using the following discount rates: 6, 10, 14, 15, 16, 20 and 24%.

    (b) Graph the *NPV* of the project as a function of the discount rate.

    (c) Find the internal rate of return, mathematically and graphically.

3.6 For each of the following investment projects, calculate:

    (a) The net present value using a 15% discount rate.

    (b) The internal rate of return.

				Cash Flow				
Year	*0*	*1*	*2*	*3*	*4*	*5*	*6*	*7*
Project A	− 4,564	1,000	1,000	1,000	1,000	1,000	1,000	1,000
Project B	− 2,000	524.7	524.7	524.7	524.7	524.7	524.7	524.7
Project C	− 21,000	3,000	3,000	3,000	3,000	3,000	3,000	3,000

3.7 For each of the following projects calculate:

    (a) The net present value using a 20% discount rate.

    (b) The internal rate of return.

Cash Flow

Year	0	1	2	3	4	5
Project A	− 370	—	—	—	—	1,000
Project B	− 240	60	60	60	60	—
Project C	− 263.5	100	100	100	100	100
Project D	− 200	56.8	56.8	56.8	56.8	56.8

3.8 For each of the following three projects, calculate:

(a) The net present value using a 16% discount rate.

(b) The internal rate of return.

(c) Graph the *NPV* of each project as a function of a discount rate (Hint: calculate three points and draw the remaining segments of the curve in freehand), and check your graphical answer with question (b).

Cash Flow

Year	0	1	2	3	4
Project A	− 800	350	350	350	100
Project B	− 70	40	25	25	25
Project C	− 20,000	2,000	8,000	14,000	4,466

3.9 A firm examines the following cash flow:

Year	0	1	2	3
Cash Flow	− 10,000	2,000	2,000	12,000

Assume a 12% cost of capital. Should the firm accept the project? Also present the solution graphically.

3.10 Your business is expanding rapidly and as a result you are in need of additional capital. The bank offers you a loan under the following conditions: a loan of $100,000 repayable in five equal annual payments of $28,000 (the first payment at the end of the first year). Plot the *NPV* of the loan as a function of the discount rate by calculating the intercepts on the horizontal and vertical axis, and a third point of your own choice.

3.11 For each of the following cash flows:

(a) Calculate the net present value using a 10% discount rate.

(b) Calculate the Internal Rate of Return.

Year	0	1	2	3	4	5
Flow						
A	− 50	17	17	17	17	17
B	50	− 17	− 17	− 17	− 17	− 17
C	− 100	—	—	—	100	—
D	0	5	5	5	5	5

3.12 The XYZ corporation is evaluating the following two *mutually exclusive* projects:

Project A: Investment of $1,000, which generates an annual cash flow of $90 during the next 100 years.

Project B: Investment of $400, which generates an annual cash flow of $50 during the next 100 years.

Assume that the relevant discount rate (cost of capital) is 10%. Which of the projects should be preferred? *Answer without the use of the present value tables.*

3.13 Early in 1980, the interest rate on US Treasury bills was quite high but by June it had dropped to only 8%. Assume that the expected rate of inflation in June 1980 was about 15% on an annual basis, and suppose that an investor invested $10,000 in Treasury bills. Calculate the *real* after-tax *IRR* for each of the following assumptions:

(a) The investor is exempt from the payment of personal income taxes.
(b) He pays 30% tax on the interest earned.
(c) He pays 50% tax on the interest earned.

3.14 Consider the following investments A through E all of which have a five-year duration. These are the only investments available to the firm, and the cost of capital, k, is 10%.

Investment	0	1	2	3	4	5
			Year			
A	− 3,000	1,000	1,000	1,000	1,000	1,000
B	− 4,000	1,500	1,200	900	600	300
C	− 2,200	650	650	600	600	200
D	− 400	300	300	300	300	300
E	− 2,000	300	600	900	1,200	1,500

Assume that the cash flow of each of the above investments will be realized only if the investment is undertaken alone. For example, if investment A is chosen and B through E are rejected, then A's cash flow is as indicated above. However, if more than one investment are executed the following results will be realized:

(a) If A *and* B are both executed each cash flow will increase 10% while the initial investment will not be affected.

(b) If B *and* C are executed each cash flow will decrease 15% while the initial investment will not be affected.

(c) If A *and* C are executed the cash flow of each will increase by 30%; the initial investment outlay will not be affected.

(d) If A, B *and* C are executed, the initial investment outlay will not be affected but the cash flow of all three projects will increase by 7%.

(e) Executing A, B, C or any combination of these projects, excludes the possibility of choosing D or E.

(f) If D *and* E are executed the cash flow of D will increase by 50%, the cash flow of E will decrease by 20% and the total initial investment of both projects (combined) will decrease by 10%.

Using the definition given in Chapter 2 above,

(i) Classify the investment combinations of A, B, C, D and E as mutually exclusive, substitutes, complements or independent.

(ii) Which investments should be undertaken and which should be rejected.

APPENDIX 3A CONTINUOUS COMPOUNDING AND DISCOUNTING

The fledgling, and perhaps also the not so fledgling, student of finance is often puzzled by the bewildering variety of interest rates which banks and savings and loan associations offer on deposits. In addition to an array of toasters, casseroles and alarm clocks, many thrift institutions offer interest which is compounded "semi-annually", "quarterly" or even "daily". To this point we have assumed annual discounting, but to make sense out of the various offers we must adjust the interest formulas developed in the text to cover alternative assumptions regarding the frequency of compounding.

Obviously, for a given interest rate, the greater the frequency with which interest is compounded the higher the future value of the deposit, so that the investor is better off. Consider the following example: an individual deposits $100 in a bank for one year at an annual interest rate of 6%. The value of his account at the end of the year will be $100(1 + 0.06) = \$106$. Now, suppose the interest is compounded twice a year. In this case the value of the deposit at the end of the year is given by:

$$100 \left(1 + \frac{0.06}{2} \right) \left(1 + \frac{0.06}{2} \right) = 100 \left(1 + \frac{0.06}{2} \right)^2 = \$106.10$$

The only difference between this calculation and the previous one is that in this instance the bank credits the account with $3 interest after six months have elapsed, so that for the next six months the investor earns 3% on $103 (and not on $100) or $3.10. The economic meaning of compounding within a given period is that the bank pays interest on the principal and the accumulated interest up to the compounding date. It follows that in the case of quarterly compounding the terminal value of the deposit is $100\left(1 + \dfrac{0.06}{4}\right)^4$ and where interest is compounded daily the terminal value is $100\left(1 + \dfrac{0.06}{365}\right)^{365}$. The maximum end-of-year value is achieved should the bank compound continously; in this extreme case, the terminal value of the deposit equals $100 \cdot e^{0.06}$ (where e denotes the base of the natural logarithms).

These results can be generalized for deposits of any duration. The terminal value of the $100 deposit at the end of n years is given by the following formulas:

Annual compounding $100(1 + 0.06)^n$

Semi-annual compounding $100\left(1 + \dfrac{0.06}{2}\right)^{2n}$

Quarterly compounding $100\left(1 + \dfrac{0.06}{4}\right)^{4n}$

Monthly compounding $100\left(1 + \dfrac{0.06}{12}\right)^{12n}$

Daily compounding $100\left(1 + \dfrac{0.06}{365}\right)^{365n}$

Continuous compounding $100\, e^{0.06n}$

Figure 3A.1 graphs the value of the deposit as a function of the frequency of compounding and of deposit duration. In this particular example, we have assumed an interest rate of 12%. However, it is worth noting that for short durations and for low interest rates the differences induced by the various compounding methods are negligible. In general, the higher the interest rate and the longer the duration, the greater is the impact of the compounding method. Thus when a bank declares that the annual interest of, say 6%, is compounded several times a year, this is tantamount to raising the simple interest rate.

Discounting more than once in a given period is the obverse side of the frequency with which interest is compounded. What is the value of $100 received one year from now? If the discount rate is 10%, the present value is equal to $\dfrac{100}{(1 + 0.1)}$, but if the cash flow is discounted twice a year, the present value is smaller, and equals $\dfrac{100}{\left(1 + \dfrac{0.1}{2}\right)^2}$. In general, the value of $100 received n years

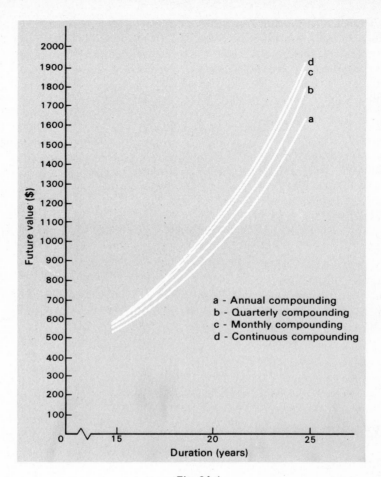

Fig. 3A.1
Future Value of $100 Received in the *n*th Year Compounded at 12%

from now, and discounted m times a year is $\dfrac{100}{\left(1 + \dfrac{0.1}{m}\right)^{mn}}$. In the extreme case

of continuous discounting, the present value is $100e^{-0.1n}$. In Table 3A.1 the present value of $100 received n years from now is calculated for several alternative assumptions regarding the frequency of compounding. These figures show that an increase in the frequency of compounding decreases the present value.

Formulas for Future and Present Value: The Continuous Case

The value of 1 dollar received n years from now and compounded m times

Table 3A.1
Present Value of $100 Received in the *n*th Year Discounted at 12%

	Year			
	1	5	10	20
Compounded Annually	89.3	56.7	38.2	10.4
Compounded Quarterly	88.8	55.4	30.6	9.4
Compounded Monthly	88.7	55.0	30.2	9.2
Compounded Continuously	88.7	54.9	30.1	9.1

each year is $1\left(1 + \dfrac{r}{m}\right)^{mn}$, where r denotes the interest rate. As m approaches

infinity, the future value of 1 dollar is given by:[1]

$$\lim_{m \to \infty} 1\left(1 + \frac{r}{m}\right)^{mn} = e^{rn}$$

Similarly, if we invest S dollars instead of 1 dollar, the future value compounded continuously is $S \cdot e^{rn}$. Thus where we deposit S_t dollars continuously in the bank in period t, the future value of all these deposits compounded continuously is given by:

$$\int_0^n S_t e^{rt} dt$$

By the same token, the present value of $1 received n years from now and

discounted at $k\%$, and compounded m times each year is $\dfrac{1}{\left(1 + \dfrac{k}{m}\right)^{mn}}$. As m

approaches infinite, we get

$$PV = \lim_{m \to \infty} \frac{1}{\left(1 + \dfrac{k}{m}\right)^{mn}} = \frac{1}{e^{kn}} = e^{-kn}$$

Similarly, the present value of S dollars is given by $S\,e^{-kn}$. And where the cash flows are received continuously (S_t dollars in period t), the present value is given by the following formula:

$$PV = \int_0^n S_t e^{-kt} dt$$

It is worth noting that for many firms, the assumption that cash flows are received continuously is more realistic than the assumption that they are received at the end of the year, since the company incurs outlays and receipts more or less continuously throughout the year.

QUESTIONS AND PROBLEMS

3A.1 What is the future (terminal) value of $500 invested at 12% for five years if interest is:

(a) compounded annually
(b) compounded semi-annually
(c) compounded quarterly
(d) compounded monthly
(e) compounded continuously?

3A.2 If you want to establish a fund of $6,000 for a trip around the world which you plan to take in three years, what would be the investment required now if money earns 8% compounded quarterly?

3A.3 You now have $2,500 in a savings account which earns 12% compounded semi-annually. How long will it take to accumulate:

(a) $5,000
(b) $10,000
(c) $12,500
(d) $25,000?

3A.4 How much money will you have at the end of four years if you deposit $200 per month in a savings account at 12% interest compounded monthly?

3A.5 If you decide to buy a speedboat for which you will have to pay $90 per month for two years, how much can you afford to pay today for the speedboat if the interest rate is 12%?

3A.6 If you borrow $2,500 to be repaid over two-and-a-half years at 12% interest, what will be the monthly payment?

3A.7 What would be the annual rate of interest that an investor would earn if he were to pay $9,457 for a six-year program of quarterly receipts of $500?

3A.8 How long will it take to repay an 8% loan of $29,130 with semi-annual payments of $2,500?

3A.9 You are asked to examine the savings plans of three banks. The first bank offers interest of 8.2% compounded annually, the second bank offers 8% compounded quarterly while the third one pays 7.8% compounded daily.

(a) On the assumption that you intend to save $1,000 for five years, which plan do you prefer? Explain.
(b) Does your answer change if the period of saving is ten years?

SELECTED REFERENCES

Ang, J.S. and Chua, J.H. "Composite Measures for the Evaluation of Investment Performance", *Journal of Financial and Quantitative Analysis*, June 1979.

Bauman, W. Scott, "Investment Returns and Present Values", *Financial Analysts Journal*, November – December 1969.

Dean, Joel, "Measuring the Productivity of Capital", *Harvard Business Review*, January – February 1954.

de la Mare, R.F., "An Investigation into the Discounting Formulae Used in Capital Budgeting Models", *Journal of Business Finance & Accounting*, Summer 1975.

Franklin, Peter J., "The Normal Cost Theory of Price and the Internal Rate of Return Method of Investment Appraisal: An Integration", *Journal of Business Finance & Accounting*, Spring 1977.

Grinyer, J.R., "Relevant Criterion Rates in Capital Budgeting", *Journal of Business Finance & Accounting*, Autumn 1974.

Haynes, W. Warren and Solomon, Martin B. Jr., "A Misplaced Emphasis in Capital Budgeting", *Quarterly Review of Economics and Business*, February 1962.

Jarrett, Jeffrey E., "A Note on Investment Criteria and the Estimation Problem in Financial Accounting", *Journal of Business Finance & Accounting*, Summer 1980.

King, Paul, "Is the Emphasis of Capital Budgeting Theory Misplaced?" *Journal of Business Finance & Accounting*, Winter 1975.

Merville, L.J. and Tavis, L.A., "A Total Real Asset Planning System", *Journal of Financial and Quantitative Analysis*, January 1974.

Norstrum, C., "A Note on 'Mathematical Analysis' of Rates of Return under Certainty", *Management Science*, January 1967.

Porterfield, J.T.S., *Investment Decisions and Capital Costs*, Englewood Cliffs, N.J.: Prentice-Hall, 1965.

Quirin, G. David, *The Capital Expenditure Decision*, Homewood, Ill.: Irwin, 1967.

Soldofsky, Robert M., "The History of Bond Tables and Stock Valuation Models", *Journal of Finance*, March 1966.

Teichroew, Daniel, Robichek, Alexander A. and Montalbano, Michael, "An Analysis of Criteria for Investment and Financing Decisions under Uncertainty", *Management Science*, November 1965.

4

Net Present Value Versus
Internal Rate of Return

It is already clear from the previous chapter that the Net Present Value (*NPV*) and Internal Rate of Return (*IRR*) methods of selecting capital investment proposals are closely related. Both are "time-adjusted" measures of profitability, that is they take the crucial element of timing into consideration. Even their mathematical formulas appear, at least on the surface, to be almost identical in form. However, unless the two investment criteria *invariably* lead to identical decisions, one cannot avoid the necessity of choosing between the two methods of measuring the desirability of capital investment proposals. With this in mind we now turn to the analysis and comparison of the *NPV* and *IRR* rules in order to determine which of the two is the *optimal* (best possible) investment criterion for a wealth-maximizing firm. In order to focus attention on the crucial properties of the two decision criteria we continue to abstract from risk, and therefore assume throughout this chapter that the magnitude and timing of investment outlays and receipts are known with perfect certainty.[1] This also permits us to postpone the discussion of the "cost of capital" (see Part III below). Under the assumption of certainty, the cost of capital (discount rate) is simply the riskless rate of interest.

NPV vs *IRR*: INDEPENDENT PROJECTS

If we limit the discussion to conventional projects (those having only one change in sign, for example $-/++\ldots$) which are economically independent of one

---

1 The assumption that all investments yield perfectly certain cash flows is unnecessarily restrictive. For the purposes of the comparison of *NPV* to *IRR*, it is sufficient to assume that all investments are homogeneous with respect to risk. Thus the acceptance of a particular project will not cause the market to reassess the riskiness of the firm.

another (that is the selection of a particular project does not preclude the choice of the other) no problem arises. In this case both the *NPV* and *IRR* rules lead to identical accept or reject decisions. But rather than simply stating this result as an axiomatic truth, it might be more convincing, especially to our more skeptical readers, if some evidence were offered in support of the claim that the two criteria lead to the same acceptance (rejection) decisions. Of course, a number of specific examples could be examined which might remove some, but certainly not all, doubt. But conjuring up numerical examples, or "proof by exhaustion" as it might be called, is a never-ending task. Fortunately for both authors and readers, the equivalence of the *NPV* and *IRR* rules with respect to conventional independent projects can readily be proved.

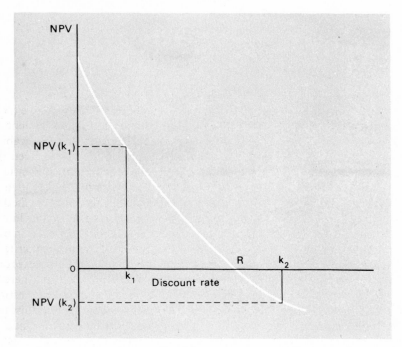

Fig. 4.1

The equivalence can be seen in Fig. 4.1 which again graphs the *NPV* of a conventional investment project as a function of the discount rate. Recall that the intercept with the horizontal axis, point *R*, denotes the internal rate of return. (By definition *R* is the discount rate which reduces the project's *NPV* to zero.) The graph shows that where the *NPV* is positive, for example using a discount rate (cost of capital) of k_1, *R* exceeds k_1. The *NPV*, which is measured by the height of the line connecting k_1 with the *NPV* function, is clearly positive and *R* lies to the right of k_1 along the horizontal axis. Conversely, where the *NPV* is negative, for example using the discount rate k_2, *R* is less than k_2. In sum, both methods result in identical accept-reject decisions; if the *NPV* criterion is fulfilled, the *IRR* criterion must also be satisfied, and vice versa.

Thus a firm which is faced with the problem of screening acceptable from unacceptable investment proposals will be indifferent as to which method is employed.

The mathematical proof of this equivalence is also straightforward. Let us assume that the project under consideration has a positive *NPV* and therefore should be accepted by the firm, that is

$$\sum_{t=1}^{n} \frac{S_t}{(1+k)^t} - I_0 > 0 \quad \text{or} \quad \sum_{t=1}^{n} \frac{S_t}{(1+k)^t} > I_0 \tag{1}$$

The *IRR* of the *same* project is the value *R* which solves the following equation,

$$\sum_{t=1}^{n} \frac{S_t}{(1+R)^t} = I_0 \tag{2}$$

It follows that the left-hand side of equation (2), which equals I_0, must be smaller than the left-hand side of inequality (1) which is greater than I_0, and since by definition the numerators (S_t) are identical (and positive) in both instances this also implies that *R* must be greater than *k*, and conversely for the assumption of a negative *NPV*. Note that if the *NPV* is assumed to be zero, $R = k$, so that by both methods the firm will be indifferent to such a project. Hence for any conventional project, independent of the project's size or duration, the *IRR* and *NPV* rules invariably lead to the same acceptance (rejection) signal.

NPV vs *IRR*: DEPENDENT PROJECTS

A direct confrontation between the two time-adjusted methods of profitability analysis cannot be avoided once we drop the assumption of independence. As we noted in the previous chapter, mutually exclusive alternatives often crop up in a modern business enterprise; numerous examples of projects whose acceptance precludes the execution of another proposal come to mind. Both a five-storey apartment building and a ten-storey office building cannot be built on the same plot of land; similarly, the purchase of an IBM computer precludes the alternative of leasing the same computer.

The problems raised by such extreme dependency can be illustrated by considering the following numerical example of two one-year projects:

	Initial Investment Outlay	Net Inflow at the End of the Year
Project A	— 10,000	12,000
Project B	— 15,000	17,700

Since both projects have one-year durations their *IRR*s can be calculated directly, without recourse to present value tables:

$$\frac{12,000}{1 + R_A} = 10,000, \text{ hence } IRR_A = 20\%$$

$$\frac{17,700}{1 + R_B} = 15,000, \text{ hence } IRR_B = 18\%$$

Assuming a cost capital $k = 10\%$ (discount factor $= 0.909$), the *NPV*s of the two projects are given by:

	Net Inflow		Discount Factor	Less Initial Outlay		NPV
Project A	12,000	×	0.909	$-10,000$	=	908
Project B	17,700	×	0.909	$-15,000$	=	1,089

Thus despite the fact that project A has the higher internal rate of return, project B has the larger net present value:

	IRR	NPV
Project A	**20**%	908
Project B	18%	**1,089**

Now if the proposals are independent, both A and B are accepted, using either the *NPV* or the *IRR* rules, which is as it should be. But which of the two projects is the "better buy"? If the firm is forced to choose between them, for example, if they are *mutually exclusive* alternatives, *which* of the two projects should be accepted? In such a case the method of analysis becomes crucial: if the firm uses the *NPV* criterion, project B will be chosen since it has the higher *NPV* (1,089 > 908); however, if the firm uses the *IRR* criterion, project A, which has the higher *IRR* (20% > 18%), will be preferred.

   This paradoxical result reflects the fact that the two decision criteria do not necessarily *rank* projects the same. In the case of independent proposals ranking is not important; essentially the firm is indifferent as to the "order" in which projects are accepted, because the acceptance of one does not prevent the acceptance of the other. However, in the case of mutually exclusive investments, ranking becomes crucial. Only one of a group of mutually exclusive alternatives (presumably that with the highest rank) can be executed, and since the ranking depends on the investment criterion used, one can no longer be indifferent between the *NPV* and *IRR* methods.

   To clarify the difference in ranking we have drawn the *NPV* curves for each of the above projects in Fig. 4.2. The ranking of the projects by their internal rates of return is constant: 20% always exceeds 18%! On the other hand, the ranking of the projects by their net present values is not fixed.

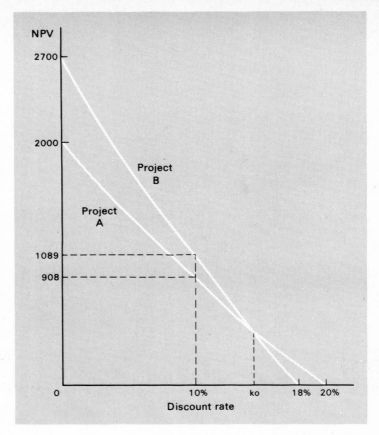

Fig. 4.2

Figure 4.2 clearly shows that the *NPV* ranking depends on the discount rate assumed. For costs of capital greater than k_0 no contradiction arises; both the *IRR* and *NPV* methods rank project A first. However, for discount rates which are smaller than k_0 the two methods result in different rankings; project B has the higher *NPV* while project A has the higher *IRR*. In general, if the two functions intersect in the positive quadrant of the diagram, and such is the case in Fig. 4.2, the dominance of one project over another by the *NPV* rule will not be absolute, and as a result, there exists a range of values of the discount rate in which contradictory rankings can arise. In the following sections we shall attempt to provide an intuitively appealing argument for preferring the *NPV* ranking.

DIFFERENCES IN THE SCALE OF INVESTMENT

Differences in the ranking of projects by the two methods may arise for a variety of reasons. Consider, for example, the cash flows of the following two projects:

	Years			
	0	*1*	*2*	*3*
Project A	− 1,000	505	505	505
Project B	− 11,000	5,000	5,000	5,000

If we assume a 10% discount rate, that is if we assume that the firm can acquire funds or find alternative uses for funds at 10%, both projects are acceptable by either the *IRR* or *NPV* methods since the *IRR*s of both exceed the cost of capital and therefore both projects also have positive net present values:

	IRR	*NPV*
Project A	**24%**	256
Project B	17%	**1,435**

Now let us assume that these two projects are *mutually exclusive*. If we invoke the *IRR* rule, project A with a 24% rate of return is preferable to project B which has only a 17% rate of return. However, by the *NPV* rule, project B should be preferred over project A since the former's *NPV* is larger. What is the reason for this disparity in the rankings of the projects? Figure 4.3 graphs the

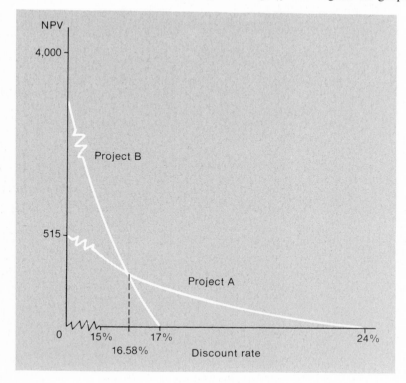

Fig. 4.3

*NPV*s of the two projects as functions of the discount rate. As can be seen from the diagram, the functions intersect at a discount rate of 16.58%. The interpretation of the diagram is straightforward; given the necessity of making a choice between the two projects, the larger project will be preferred to the smaller one if the cost of capital is below 16.58%, the opposite holds if the cost of capital is above 16.58%. In fact, for discount rates above 17%, only the smaller project is feasible; the *NPV* of project B becomes negative after that point.

The arithmetic of capital budgeting aside, how can we account for the fact that for discount rates below 16.58% the *NPV* method gives priority to project B despite its relatively low rate of return? The source of this preference can be clarified by considering the *incremental* cash flow which such a choice represents. This is done in Table 4.1 and in Fig. 4.4.

Table 4.1

	0	1	2	3
Project B	− 11,000	5,000	5,000	5,000
Project A	− 1,000	505	505	505
"B minus A"	− 10,000	4,495	4,495	4,495

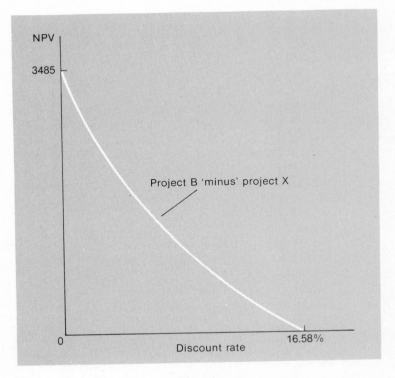

Fig. 4.4

Initially, let us assume that the firm uses the *IRR* rule exclusively and therefore plans to execute project A. Now, would it be worthwhile to add the additional investment labelled "B minus A"? If the answer is affirmative the total investment will be A + (B − A) = B, that is to say the firm would shift from project A to project B. Choosing project B rather than project A is tantamount to choosing a hypothetical project "B minus A" which represents the *incremental* cash flow resulting from such a decision. Thus, the choice of the larger project (B) is equivalent to choosing the smaller project (A) plus an additional investment outlay of $10,000 on which $4,495 will be realized each year, for three years. The internal rate of return on this incremental cash flow is 16.58%, and given a 10% cost of capital, this represents a profitable opportunity, and should be accepted.

Using the *IRR* criterion, the firm chooses project A, but as we have just seen would also like to accept the hypothetical cash flow "B minus A". This results in a total cash flow to the firm of A + (B − A) = B. Thus, the *IRR* rule when used properly (i.e. on an incremental basis) leads the firm to prefer project B, but this is precisely the project which has the higher *NPV*! In this example the superiority of the *NPV* rule has been established even though we used the *IRR* rule, that is the *IRR* analysis has been contradicted using the *IRR* rule itself![2]

To complete the analysis, it is worth noting that if the cost of capital is greater than 16.58%, it does not pay to make the additional commitment of resources and the hypothetical project "B − A" should be rejected. And this is precisely what the *NPV* method prescribes: looking back at Fig. 4.3 we note that the intersection of the two functions takes place at a discount rate of 16.58% which is the same as the internal rate of return on the incremental cash flow (see Fig. 4.4). This follows from the fact that the point of intersection represents a discount rate which *equates* the net present values of the two projects, and this is equivalent to the discount rate which equates their difference to zero. The latter, by definition, is the internal rate of return on the *incremental* cash flow. To sum up, if the cost of capital is greater than 16.58% the firm should stick to project A (B − A should be rejected). But this is precisely the case in which the *NPV* of project A is greater than the *NPV* of project B (see Fig. 4.3) so that again the *IRR* rule can be used to justify the use of the *NPV* criterion.

By *automatically* examining and comparing the incremental cash flows against the cost of capital, the *NPV* method ensures that the firm will reach the optimal *scale* of investment. The *IRR* criterion — which is expressed in terms of percent rather than in terms of absolute dollar returns — ignores this important facet of an investment decision. Put in the crudest of terms, the *IRR* method always prefers a 500% return on 1 dollar to a 20% return on 100 dollars. To most of us (assuming a cost of capital below 20%) the optimal solution is to

---

2 Of course the above example could also be used to support the conclusion that a *modified IRR* method which systematically examines the incremental flows between all pairs of projects could be substituted for the *NPV* method. However, when non-conventional projects are introduced even the modified version of the *IRR* fails to yield consistently correct results; see page 80 below.

take advantage of *both* opportunities, but where a choice *between* the two must be made, few indeed would argue in favor of the *IRR* solution. Most individuals, as is true of most firms, have goal functions which are set out in terms of *absolute* returns, and not in percentage terms. And since the *NPV* reflects absolute returns, this ensures optimality when mutually exclusive choice situations arise.

The Profitability Index

Before going on to the other reasons for the difference in rankings, this might be a good place to pause to see if we can use the results of the previous section to analyze a very popular variant of the *NPV* criterion, the so-called Profitability Index.[3]

The Profitability Index is defined as the present value of the project divided by its initial outlay, that is

$$\text{Profitability Index} = \frac{\text{Present value of cash flow}}{\text{Initial Investment}} = \frac{PV}{I_0}$$

The following decision rule is associated with the Profitability Index:

accept the project if the index is greater than 1;
reject the project is the index is less than 1.

Clearly in the case of independent projects, the Profitability Index and the *NPV* criterion yield the same acceptance – rejection decision. If $NPV > 0$, we necessarily have $NPV = PV - I_0 > 0$, and therefore, $PV > I_0$. Dividing both sides by I_0 we get $\frac{PV}{I_0} > 1$, that is, the Profitability Index is also greater than 1. Hence, if a project is acceptable by the *NPV* criterion it must also be acceptable by the Profitability Index.

For many people the Profitability Index is more intuitively appealing than the *NPV* criterion. The statement that a particular investment has a *NPV* of say $20 is not sufficiently clear to many people who prefer a relative measure of profitability. By adding the information that the project's initial outlay (I_0) is $100, the Profitability Index $(120/100 = 1.2)$ provides a meaningful measure of the project's relative profitability in more readily understandable terms. It is then only a small step to convert the index of 1.2 to 20%.

However once again problems can arise when mutually exclusive alternatives are considered. As we have seen in the previous section, one advantage of the *NPV* criterion over the *IRR* criterion in mutually exclusive choice situations stems from the fact that the *NPV* criterion reflects the *absolute* magnitudes of the investment proposals. The *IRR*, being a pure number, does not. But by converting the *NPV* criterion to a *relative* measure, the Profitability Index, which is itself a pure number, no longer reflects differences in investment scale and as a

3 For a critical analysis of the properties of the Profitability Index, see H.M. Weingartner, "The Excess Present Value Index — A Theoretical Basis and Critique", *Journal of Accounting Research*, Autumn 1963, pp. 213 – 24.

result recreates the very paradox that the *NPV* criterion is designed to avoid. Consider, for example, the following two *mutually exclusive* proposals:

	Present Value of Cash Flow	Initial Investment Outlay	Profitability Index
Project A	100	50	2
Project B	1,500	1,000	1.5

According to the Profitability Index project A, which has an index of 2, should be preferred. But it is equally clear that a firm which desires to maximize its absolute present value rather than percentage return would prefer project B, because the *NPV* of project B ($500) is greater than the *NPV* of project A ($50). Thus, while the Profitability Index may be useful for exposition it should not be used as a measure of investment worth for projects of differing size when mutually exclusive choices have to be made.

THE TIMING OF THE CASH FLOW

The fact that the *NPV* rule takes differences in the scale of investments into account while the *IRR* rule does not might lead to the erroneous conclusion that if the initial investment outlays of two projects are the same, the *IRR* and *NPV* will rank the proposals in the same manner. The following example shows that even in the case of identical initial outlays the rankings by the *IRR* and by the *NPV* can differ.

	Initial Outlay	Cash Flow	
		First Year	Second Year
Project A	− 100	20	120
Project B	− 100	100	31.25
"A minus B"	0	− 80	88.75

Assuming a cost of capital of 10% let us calculate the *NPV* and the *IRR* for these two projects.[4]

	NPV	IRR
Project A	**17.3**	20%
Project B	16.7	**25%**
"A minus B"	0.6	10.9%

4 The *NPV* is calculated by using Table 3.3; the *IRR* is calculated by "trial and error" using the same table. However, for the incremental cash flow (A − B) the *IRR* can be calculated directly as follows:

$80/(1 + R) = 88.75/(1 + R)^2$ which reduces to $80 = 88.75/(1 + R)$

Hence $R = 88.75/80 - 1 = 10.9\%$.

Again a contradiction in the ranking arises. The *NPV* ranks project A first, while the *IRR* gives first priority to project B even though both projects have identical initial outlays. Thus in this instance we cannot use the scale of investment argument to justify the choice of A; however, we can still use the same incremental technique.

Let us again assume that a firm uses the *IRR* criterion. If A and B are mutually exclusive, project B will be accepted and project A will be rejected. Before executing project B it is legitimate to ask whether or not it is worthwhile to add the incremental (hypothetical) investment "A minus B". Since the *IRR* of the incremental investment is 10.9% and therefore exceeds the cost of capital (10%), the hypothetical project should be accepted. But as B + (A − B) = A, this is tantamount to accepting project A, that is the alternative with the higher *NPV*.

This result is illustrated graphically in Fig. 4.5. For discount rates below 10.9% the incremental investment "A minus B" is acceptable, which coincides with the range over which project A has the higher *NPV*. Thus even when initial

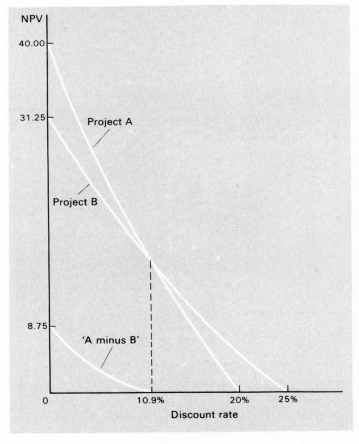

Fig. 4.5

investment outlays are the same, the two methods can still give contradictory rankings, that is the *NPV* curves may still intersect (see Fig. 4.5). In general, it is the failure of the *IRR* method to evaluate properly the alternative use of funds (it ranks projects *independent* of the cost of capital) which leads to differences in ranking. And this can occur even if the projects have the same initial outlays and even the same durations, so long as they do not have identical annual cash flows. (If they did, of course the projects themselves would be identical.) Any difference in the magnitude or timing of the cash flow can potentially cause a difference in the rankings of projects by the two methods.

REINVESTMENT RATES

How can one account for this superiority of the *NPV* rule even when differences in the scale of investment do not exist? The answer can be found by considering the element of time which is so crucial to investment analysis. Although both the *NPV* and the *IRR* take the time element into account, the time-adjustment made in the *IRR* method is incorrect. This can be seen more clearly by examining the *implicit* assumptions made by the two methods regarding the "reinvestment" of interim cash flows. The *IRR* tacitly assumes that a project's annual cash flows can be reinvested at the project's internal rate of return; the *NPV* method assumes that the cash flows can be reinvested at the firm's opportunity cost of capital.

Since these assumptions are implicit, a more formal demonstration can help to clarify the meaning and significance of the reinvestment rates. Consider any project with a given initial outlay I_0, a duration of n years, and a stream of cash receipts $S_1, S_2, \ldots, S_n$. The internal rate of return (R) of this project is given by

$$I_0 = \frac{S_1}{1 + R} + \frac{S_2}{(1 + R)^2} + \cdots + \frac{S_{n-1}}{(1 + R)^{n-1}} + \frac{S_n}{(1 + R)^n}$$

which can also be written as

$$I_0 = \sum_{t=1}^{n-1} \frac{S_t}{(1 + R)^t} + \frac{S_n}{(1 + R)^n} \tag{1}$$

For simplicity let us further assume that the same project has a positive *NPV*. Assuming a cost of capital equal to k, the *NPV* formula for the same project can be written as

$$I_0 < \frac{S_1}{1 + k} + \frac{S_2}{(1 + k)^2} + \cdots + \frac{S_{n-1}}{(1 + k)^{n-1}} + \frac{S_n}{(1 + k)^n}$$

or $\tag{2}$

$$I_0 < \sum_{t=1}^{n-1} \frac{S_t}{(1 + k)^t} + \frac{S_n}{(1 + k)^n}$$

In order to make the reinvestment rates explicit, let us rewrite (1) and (2) in their future value forms. This is done by multiplying both sides of (1) by $(1 + R)^n$:

$$I_0(1 + R)^n = \sum_{t=1}^{n-1} S_t(1 + R)^{n-t} + S_n \qquad (3)$$

Similarly, we multiply both sides of (2) by $(1 + k)^n$:

$$I_0(1 + k)^n < \sum_{t=1}^{n-1} S_t(1 + k)^{n-t} + S_n \qquad (4)$$

Thus even if the initial investment outlays and the durations of the projects are the same, it is clear from these equations that the interim receipts are compounded forward (the other side of discounting) at different rates — R in the *IRR* formula and k in the *NPV* formula.[5] Nor can this problem be avoided, since it arises out of the very need to discount the cash flows of different time periods to some common denominator.

The economic counterpart of these compounding rates is a "reinvestment" rate, i.e. the time-discounting process which underlies both methods implicitly makes an assumption regarding the "value" to the firm of the interim receipts. In the *NPV* method it is assumed, as it should be, that all receipts can be reinvested at the cost of capital k. If this does *not* hold true, the cost of capital has been incorrectly estimated. This makes sense, since by definition k should reflect the alternative use of funds, and in calculating the profitability of a project we want to evaluate it against that alternative use. This, of course, is the very essence of the *NPV* calculation.

The *IRR* method, on the other hand, assumes reinvestment at the project's own internal rate of return, R. This has no economic basis; clearly the alternative cost of capital to the firm cannot be R and k at one and the same time. If R does not equal k, and this is the only case where differences in ranking are of interest, assuming the future reinvestment of the interim proceeds at the rate R might be unrealistic, to the extent that such high-return projects (in cases where $R > k$) simply may not be available in the future. But even if we could be certain of their physical availability, the *IRR*'s reinvestment assumption is still in error. Such high-return projects, if available, will always be executed if the cost of capital is equal to k, *independent* of the decision on the current project under consideration. It is an error, therefore, to "credit" the current project with any benefits accruing from the reinvestment of the interim proceeds at rates of return above k. The *NPV* method isolates and evaluates the profitability of the current project alone, since the net present value of the proceeds reinvested at a rate of return *equal* to the cost of capital is zero.

The crucial importance of the reinvestment rate assumption can be made even more explicit if we assume that for any one of a variety of reasons, the firm expects the cost of capital to differ in future years. For simplicity, let us consider

---

5 Except for one-year projects, in which case there is no need for compounding. In such cases the *NPV* and *IRR* rank conventional projects consistently as long as the initial outlays are the same.

a case where the discount rate is expected to rise over time, so that $k_1 < k_2 < k_3 < \ldots < k_n$. Clearly, no change occurs in the internal rate of return calculation, and equation (3) still holds, that is the interim proceeds are still assumed to be reinvested at the average rate of return, R. But it is no longer clear that the *IRR* decision rule which relates the rate of return to the cost of capital can be used. Comparison of a single-valued rate of return with a series of discount rates k_1, k_2, ..., k_n will not, in general, yield meaningful results. It is sufficient to consider an example of a three-year project with a rate of return equal to 15%, and the following costs of capital:

$$k_1 = 10\%, \ k_2 = 15\% \text{ and } k_3 = 20\%.$$

A similar problem does *not* arise with respect to the net present value method. Given the series of discount rates, the *NPV* of a three-year project can be formulated as follows:

$$I_0 \gtreqless \frac{S_1}{(1 + k_1)} + \frac{S_2}{(1 + k_1)(1 + k_2)} + \frac{S_3}{(1 + k_1)(1 + k_2)(1 + k_3)}$$

Multiplying both sides of this equation by the expression

$$(1 + k_1)(1 + k_2)(1 + k_3)$$

we obtain:

$$I_0(1 + k_1)(1 + k_2)(1 + k_3) \gtreqless S_1(1 + k_2)(1 + k_3) + S_2(1 + k_3) + S_3$$

Thus the *NPV* calculation remains meaningful even if we assume non-uniform short-term discount rates. The interim receipts are compounded forward (reinvested) in this case at the appropriate opportunity cost for each relevant period. The first-year receipts are reinvested during the second year at that year's cost of capital, k_2, and during the third year at k_3, and so on.

To sum up, the *NPV* method provides an optimal solution to the capital budgeting problem given the assumptions that future cash flows and the cost of capital (discount rate) are known. Both the *NPV* and *IRR* are weighted averages: the former using the appropriate short-term weights, k_1, k_2, ..., k_n, while the latter method uses the inappropriate long-term rate of return, R.

THE HORIZON PROBLEM

The reinvestment argument in favor of the *NPV* method which was set out in the text is completely general and holds even for cases where projects differ in their durations. However, the reinvestment problem, or horizon problem as it is often called, which arises when alternative investment projects have different durations is of special interest and has been the subject of much dispute in the finance literature.[6]

---

6 The horizon problem in general, as well as the specific numerical example of the text are due to Ezra Solomon, "The Arithmetic of Capital Budgeting Decisions", *Journal of Business*, April 1956.

Consider the following example of two mutually exclusive projects:

	Initial Outlay	First Year	Cash Inflow Second Year	Third Year	Fourth Year
Project A	− 100	120	—	—	—
Project B	− 100	—	—	—	174

Assuming a 10% cost of capital, the *NPV* and *IRR* of the above two projects are:

	NPV	*IRR*
Project A	9	20%
Project B	19	15%

Once again the *IRR* and *NPV* rankings are contradictory. As has already been shown, project B should be preferred because it has the higher *NPV*. What then is the horizon problem? Since project A earns its return of 120 at the end of the first year while in project B the cash inflow of 174 is not received until the end of the fourth year, it has been argued that the appropriate comparison is with the cash flow of the earlier project *repeated* three more times. Denoting the "repetitive" project by A*, we rewrite the cash flows as follows:

	Initial Outlay	First Year	Cash Inflow Second Year	Third Year	Fourth Year
		120	120	120	
		− 100	− 100	− 100	
Project A*	− 100	20	20	20	120
Project B	− 100	—	—	—	174

Out of the cash flow of $120 received at the end of the first year, $100 are reinvested, so that the *net* cash flow is only $20. However, the reinvestment produces another cash inflow of $120 at the end of the second year, and so on. By repeating investment A we generate a new compound project A* whose time horizon is identical to that of project B, i.e. four years.

The *NPV* and *IRR* of projects A* and B are:

	NPV	*IRR*
Project A*	31.7	20%
Project B	19.0	15%

Thus, the paradoxical difference in ranking is resolved, and project A* dominates project B by both the *IRR* and the *NPV* rules.

But is it proper to repeat project A until a common duration is reached? The argument in favor of such a procedure rests on the fact that the cash flows of project A are realized earlier than those of project B so that the firm has "extra" time to reinvest the money. *In general, this argument is not valid*! A firm whose cost of capital is 10%, can by definition always raise money at this rate, and therefore can take advantage of an investment opportunity at the end of the first year, independent of the particular project (A or B) which it executes in the first year. However, three special cases are of interest.

(a) What if the later investments are closely related to project A? For example, let's assume that the investment in the first year is only the initial stage of a larger project (such as the road for a factory which will be built in the following year). In such a case the cash flows of all of the components of the compound project should be combined since in essence they constitute a single project. And in fact, isolating the first year cash flow of such a project would be a conceptual error.

(b) Another noteworthy possibility is the case in which proposals A and B utilize the same physical resource. For example, suppose that project A and B are two alternative crops to be grown on the same acre of land. For simplicity, we assume that the amount of land is limited, and for some reason the firm cannot sell this land. Project A is a one-year crop, for example cucumbers destined to be pickles, while Project B is a four-year crop, such as a fruit orchard. Once again a straightforward comparison of projects A and B is conceptually incorrect. Only after equating the two time horizons will the comparison be meaningful. In this special case, we must consider the alternative uses of the land in the interim years, before comparing it with the four-year alternative.

(c) Similarly, where replication is obvious, for example in technical cost minimization problems, such as equipment replacement, equalization of time horizons is necessary. Replacement chains are discussed in detail in Chapter 5.

A THEORETICAL JUSTIFICATION FOR NET PRESENT VALUE

In this section, we shall present a theoretically rigorous analysis of the advantages of *NPV* vs *IRR*.[7] For simplicity the discussion will be confined to two-period investments.[8] To further simplify the analysis we initially examine the case of an investor, with given available resources W_0, who has to decide how much of his present wealth (W_0) to consume this year, and how much to invest in order to provide for consumption in the next year. But before we go on to the analysis proper we can greatly facilitate matters by introducing the concept of an investment schedule.

---

[7] The discussion is based on the classic article by Jack Hirshleifer, "On the Theory of Optimal Investment Decision", *Journal of Political Economy*, August 1958.

[8] The reader who wishes to generalize the analysis to the case of multiperiod investments should consult M.J. Bailey, "Formal Criteria for Investment Decisions", *Journal of Political Economy*, October 1959.

Table 4.2

Project	Required Investment Outlay	Net Cash Receipt at end of year	Internal Rate of Return
A	100	200	100%
B	100	150	50%
C	500	600	20%
D	300	315	5%

The Investment Schedule

Consider an investor with an initial endowment equal to W_0, who must decide how to divide his wealth between current consumption and investment in productive resources. As a first step let us assume that he arrays all of his potential productive opportunities in descending order of profitability, that is by their internal rates of return (see Table 4.2).

In a one-year investment in which the investment outlay takes place at the beginning of the year and the net cash receipt is received at the end of the year, a project's *IRR* is readily calculated by dividing the net receipt by the initial

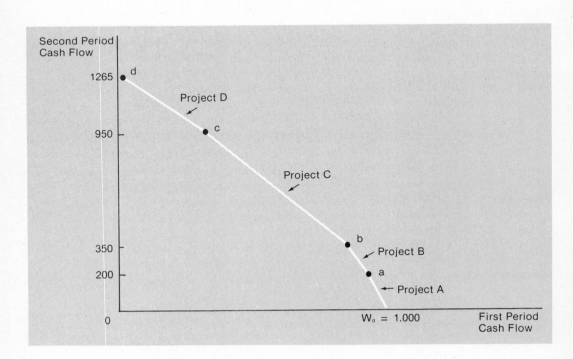

Fig. 4.6

outlay, and then reducing the quotient by one. Assuming an initial endowment of $1,000 such a productivity schedule (which is also called the transformation curve) is illustrated graphically in Fig. 4.6.

Points W_0, *a, b, c* and *d* represent the attainable combinations of current and future consumption, given the investor's initial endowment of $1,000 and the four investment opportunities A, B, C and D. For example he can consume W_0 this year and nothing next year, but even though this alternative is physically available it cannot be recommended to an individual who desires to survive next year. On the other hand, if investment A is executed he can reach point *a* which denotes current consumption of $900 ($W_0$ less the required investment outlay of project A) and consumption of $200 next year which is the cash flow that project A produces in the second period. Similarly by executing the other investment alternatives the individual can reach points *b, c* and *d*.

To simplify the presentation the attainable points of Fig. 4.6 are connected to form the investment productivity curve W_0d. This is tantamount to assuming that the projects are infinitely divisible, that is they can be broken down into very small components so that the investment alternatives can be represented by a continuous curve instead of by a series of discontinuous points. The reader should also note that when moving from W_0 to *d*, the slope of the productivity curve declines which reflects the fact that the projects have been arrayed in descending order of profitability from point W_0 to point *d*. Now which projects should be accepted, or in other words which point on the investment productivity curve is optimal? But before we can answer this question a way must be found to represent investors' tastes. This can be done by introducing another important tool of analysis, the *indifference curve*.

The Meaning of Indifference Curves

Consider a rational[9] individual who is faced with the problem of choosing that combination of current and future consumption (c_0, c_1) which will maximize his satisfaction, where c_0 and c_1 denote cash flows (consumption) in the first and second periods respectively. One possible combination is represented by point *M* in Fig. 4.7. Whenever a combination such as *M* is replaced by an alternative located in the direction of the arrow marked *a* the satisfaction derived from the cash flow combination is increased; every movement along the line *Ma* increases current consumption without altering future consumption. Conversely, any movement in the direction of arrow *b* is undesirable, because consumption in the second period is reduced without any compensating increase in first period consumption, which is clearly to the individual's disadvantage. Since any movement in the direction of arrow *b* reduces the investor's satisfaction while any movement in the direction of arrow *a* increases it, a point can be found between *a* and *b* (for example *N*) at which the individual's satisfaction is

9 By "rational" we simply mean that other things being equal such an individual prefers *more* to *less* consumption.

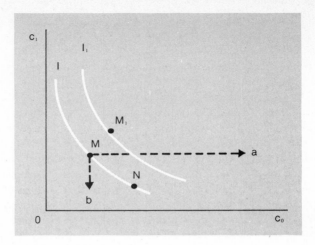

Fig. 4.7

neither increased nor decreased. If we substitute combination N for combination M, the first period cashflow increases and the second period cashflow decreases, but as we have assumed that the individual's satisfaction remains unchanged, the impact of the increase in c_0 on the individual's satisfaction is exactly offset by the decrease in c_1. Hence the investor is indifferent to the choice between the two consumption combinations represented by points M and N.[10] Other combinations of (c_0, c_1) can also be found which leave the individual indifferent, that is, with the same level of satisfaction which he derived from combination M. In principle all such combinations can be plotted along an "indifference curve" such as I of Fig. 4.7. If we start with a point such as M_1, we can repeat the process and generate yet another indifference curve such as I_1, and so on until an entire indifference map is constructed which represents an investor's tastes with respect to current and future cashflows (consumption).

The indifference curves of Fig. 4.7 decline from left to right which indicates that the rational investor must be compensated by an increase in future consumption when his current consumption is reduced. The curves also have been drawn convex to the origin on the assumption that each additional decrease in current consumption requires increasingly larger increments of future consumption if the individual is to remain indifferent to the change.

Another important property of the indifference map is that the indifference curves of a single individual *cannot* intersect. This can be proved by examining Fig. 4.8 in which two indifference curves I and I_1 of the *same* individual intersect at point R. Since R and R_1 are located on the same indifference curve (I), the

10 To facilitate the graphical representation the indifference curves of Fig. 4.7 have been drawn as continuous curves, that is independent of the actual available alternatives. Clearly, no potential investment option may exist which permits an individual to achieve the consumption pattern represented by a point such as M or N. However, from the fact that both these points lie on the same indifference curve we can conclude that had such alternatives been available, the individual would have been indifferent between them.

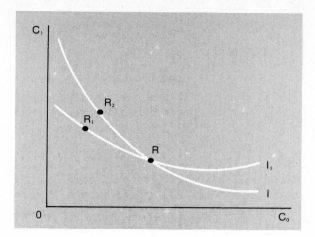

Fig. 4.8

individual, by definition, must be indifferent between them. R_2 and R also lie on a single indifference curve (I_1) so that the individual is also indifferent between these two alternatives. It follows that the individual must also be indifferent between R_1 and R_2, but this contradicts the assumption that the investor is rational, because R_2 represents a larger cashflow in both periods.

An investor's final choice out of all available cashflow combinations depends on his tastes. He will choose that combination which allows him to reach the highest indifference curve, for the higher the curve, the greater his satisfaction or what is called in the economist's jargon "utility". Fig. 4.9 superimposes an individual's indifference map on an opportunity set of alternative cashflow combinations denoted by points *a, b, d, e* and *f*.

The individual would prefer a combination which would allow him to reach indifference curve I_5, but such a combination is not attainable (indifference curve I_5 does not intersect or touch any of the attainable points). The best that he can do, given the opportunity set, is to choose combination *a*, the option which lies on indifference curve I_3. As no other choice will permit him to reach a higher level of satisfaction (utility), the cashflow pattern represented by point *a* constitutes his *optimal* choice. Should he choose another alternative out of the available set, say point *f*, his satisfaction will fall since this option only permits him to reach indifference curve I_2, which represents a lower level of utility.

Can we infer from this analysis that no individual will ever prefer option *f*; or alternatively, does option *a* represent the optimal choice for all individuals? Because the shape of the indifference curves varies from one individual to another it is conceivable that a second individual may have an indifference map, representing his individual preferences, in which the highest indifference curve touches point *f* rather than point *a*. In fact depending on the shape of the curves some other alternative may constitute the optimal choice for a particular in-

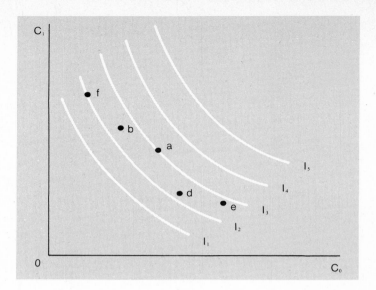

Fig. 4.9

dividual. This is illustrated in Fig. 4.10 which sets out the indifference curves of two *different* individuals.[11] From the shape of their indifference curves we can see that the individual whose tastes are represented by curve I_A would choose point *a* while the other would prefer point *f*.

The reader should note that the indifference curve I_A is steeper than curve I_B. This means that when his current consumption (c_0) is decreased by one unit individual A requires a greater compensatory increase in future consumption (c_1). For individual B, on the other hand, a lower current consumption represents a lesser drawback and therefore this individual requires a smaller compensating increase in future consumption in order to leave his level of satisfaction unchanged.

Optimal Investment Decisions

Now we are in a position to combine the concepts of an investment productivity curve and an indifference map in order to determine optimal investment policy for the individual or firm. Figure 4.11 superimposes the indifference curves of a hypothetical individual confronted by the investment opportunities which are summarized in the investment productivity curve $W_0 d$. Note that his initial endowment equals W_0. From Fig. 4.11 it is clear that the cashflow pattern

---

11 The reader should note that the intersection of the indifference curves of two *different* individuals does not contradict our previous proof that the indifference curves of the *same* individual cannot intersect.

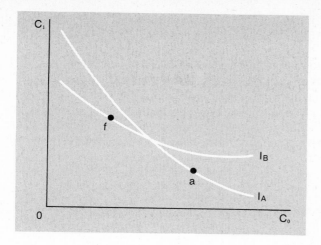

Fig. 4.10

(c_0^*, c_1^*) denoted by c^* permits the individual to reach his highest indifference curve (I_2). This occurs at the point of tangency between the productivity curve and an indifference curve. The *optimal* consumption combination also dictates the optimal investment policy: point c^* can be attained by consuming c_0^* in the

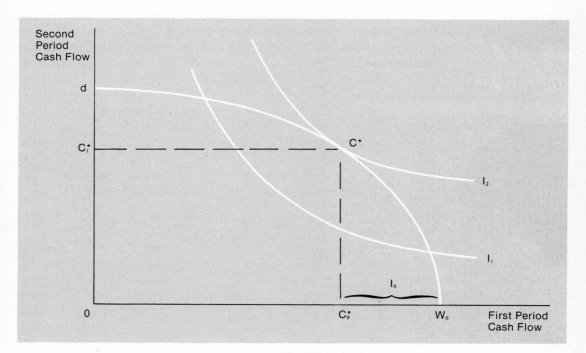

Fig. 4.11

current period and investing the amount $W_0 - c_0^* = I_0$ in order to provide a cashflow in the second period which is just sufficient to support a consumption of c_1^*.

Let us now apply the basic properties of this analysis to reevaluate somewhat more rigorously the relationship of *NPV* to *IRR*. We shall start by assuming that all of the alternative projects are independent of one another, and have conventional cashflows, i.e., the initial investment outlay in the first period is followed by a positive cashflow in the second period. Although the analysis is confined to two periods, the period which elapses between the investment outlay and the receipt of the cashflow can be as long or as short as is required. For convenience we assume throughout that the investment horizon is one year.

The Money Market Line

Consider an individual confronted by the net cashflows c_0 in period one and c_1 in the second period. Recalling the discussion in the text of the time element, the net present value of these cashflows clearly is not $c_0 + c_1$ but rather the discounted sum:

$$NPV = c_0 + \frac{c_1}{1+k}$$

where k denotes the individual's opportunity cost of capital which in a perfect market under conditions of certainty is also equal to the riskless interest rate in both borrowing and lending. For any given value of *NPV* (for example $NPV_1 = 1$) an infinite number of combinations of c_0 and c_1 can be found which yield this value. Hence we can write the following *linear* (hence the name market line) relationship between c_1 and c_0:

$$c_1 = NPV_1 (1+k) - c_0 (1+k)$$

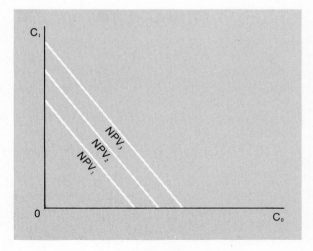

Fig. 4.12

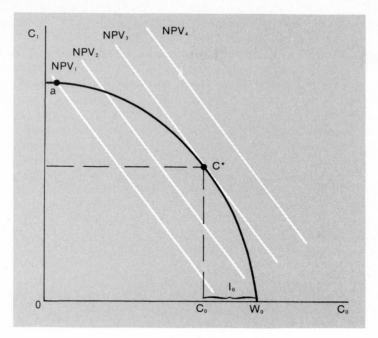

Fig. 4.13

Since k is a constant, the intercept of this line with the vertical axis is the constant $NPV_1 (1 + k)$ and the slope of the line is given by $-(1 + k)$. All the combinations of cashflows (c_0, c_1) which lie on this line yield the same net present value, which in this particular case is equal to NPV_1. Now, suppose that we wish to find all the combinations (c_0, c_1) which yield a higher NPV, say NPV_2. In this case we substitute NPV_2 for NPV_1 in the above equation, thereby generating another line *with the same* slope, but with a higher intercept on the vertical axis. By considering alternative values of NPV we derive a family of parallel straight lines each with the property that all combinations on a given line represent the same NPV; hence, the name iso-NPV or equal NPV lines.

Let us examine the set of typical iso-NPV lines drawn in Fig. 4.12. Which NPV line will the investor desire to reach? Obviously, he would prefer the highest line NPV_3 since this line includes the combinations of c_0 and c_1 with the highest NPV. But not all of these lines represent attainable cashflow combinations; the feasibility of an iso-NPV line depends on the individual's initial endowment, W_0, as well as the available investment opportunities (the investment productivity curve).

Figure 4.13 superimposes the investment productivity curve on a family of iso-NPV lines. The initial endowment is denoted by point W_0 on the horizontal axis. The individual would prefer to reach line NPV_4; however, none of the combinations (c_1, c_2) which lie on this line are attainable because this line lies to the right of the investment curve. Point "a" is attainable as he can invest part of his initial endowment and "move" along the investment curve to this point. But will he choose this point? The answer is unequivocally negative, because point c^* which is also attainable (by investing I_0) represents a higher level of *NPV* ($NPV_3 > NPV_1$). Given the productive investment opportunities and his initial endowment, the combination of net cashflows (c_0^*, c_1^*) denoted by point c^*, and the current investment outlay I_0 required to achieve this combination, are the best possible alternatives in the sense that they maximize the net present value of the cashflows.

Will an individual whose cost of capital is equal to k necessarily choose the cashflow (consumption) combination denoted by point c^*? To answer this question the individual's tastes (indifference map) must be taken into account and, moreover, the analysis must incorporate the fact that the individual is confronted by financial as well as productive investment opportunities. This is done in Fig. 4.14 which superimposes the individual's indifference curves on the investment productivity curve and iso-*NPV* line of Fig. 4.13.

As before, the individual invests the amount I_0 thereby reaching point c^* the point of tangency between the highest attainable iso-*NPV* line and the productivity curve. But the indifference curve which passes through point c^* (I_1) lies below I_2, which is also attainable if financial alternatives are taken into account. Given his tastes (the shape of his indifference curves) the individual

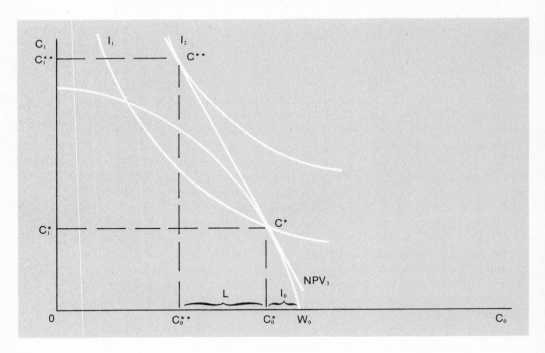

Fig. 4.14

can reach a higher level of satisfaction by lending the amount L at the opportunity cost of capital k. This is indicated by a movement along the iso-*NPV* line to c^{**} at which point the iso-*NPV* line is tangent to indifference curve I_2. The individual prefers lending to investing beyond point c^* because he will receive in period 2 $L(1+k)$ in return for the loan; the effective rate of interest on the financial transaction k, therefore, is greater than the rate of return on productive investment beyond this point as a comparison of the slopes of the investment curve and *NPV* line clearly shows.

Should the point of tangency with the indifference curve lie to the right of point c^*, the individual would again invest up to point c^* as before, but would borrow the amount B in order to increase his current consumption, see Fig. 4.15.

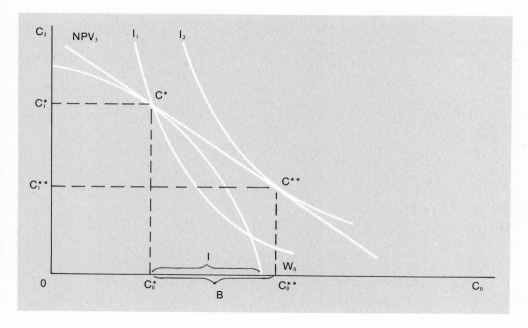

Fig. 4.15

Note that the indifference curves of Fig. 4.15 have been drawn much steeper which indicates that this individual gives high priority to current relative to future cashflows (consumption). However, despite this strong preference for current consumption, the individual in this case first takes advantage of his productive opportunities and invests I_0, that is up to the point c^*; the preferred consumption pattern is achieved by a financial transaction, in this instance borrowing. Finally if an indifference curve is tangent to the investment productivity curve at point c^* itself, the individual neither borrows nor lends, and point c^* represents the optimum combination of cashflows (consumption).

Separation of Investment and Financing Decisions

The striking feature of the analysis is that the optimal investment decision denoted by point c^* does *not* depend on the shape of the indifference curves. Whether the individual desires to redistribute his consumption over time by either borrowing or lending, the investment decision, as we have just seen, remains the same. The projects represented by the segment W_0c^* of the investment curve are accepted; this is the subset of projects having a positive *NPV* at the cost of capital, k, which permits the individual to reach the highest attainable *NPV* line. Thus, as long as the individual chooses investments so as to maximize *NPV*, that is to reach the highest attainable iso-*NPV* line, he also ensures that he will be able to maximize his satisfaction (utility) by redistributing (if necessary) his consumption over time by means of borrowing or lending. In this sense the *NPV* rule is *optimal*; making investment decisions by the *NPV* rule is tantamount to the maximization of investors' utility as well.

The independence of investment and financing (i.e. borrowing or lending) decisions is called "separation" and lies at the very heart of the modern theory of finance. It is the existence of an efficient capital market which permits the individual (firm) to reach its productive investment decisions without *explicitly* considering its financing decisions, as long as the opportunity cost of using its capital resources is fully reflected in the evaluation of its economic investment opportunities. And as we have already noted, the cost of capital, k, is an integral feature of the decision rule in the *NPV* method.

NPV vs *IRR*: Independent Projects

Now under the assumed condition of independence, does the internal rate of return rule also lead to the investment decision which maximizes investors' utility? The *IRR* criterion asserts that all projects with an *IRR* greater than k should be accepted. Then it also takes the opportunity cost of using the firm's capital resources into account. Looking back at Fig. 4.6, it is clear that by construction, the *IRR* of each project is given by the slope of the investment productivity curve at the appropriate point.[12] Looking at Fig. 4.15 the slope of the investment curve at point c^* equals $-(1 + k)$ which is the slope of the iso-*NPV* line tangent to the curve at that point. Along the segment W_0c^* the slope of the investment curve is greater than the slope of the *NPV* lines; hence the *IRR*s of all the projects on this segment are higher than the cost of capital k, and therefore all these projects should be accepted by the *IRR* rule. By the same token all projects which lie to the left of point c^* have *IRR*s which are less than the cost of capital and accordingly they should be rejected by the *IRR* rule. But

---

12 For the first project, an outlay of \$100 returns \$200 in the second period, the *IRR* is given by $100 = 200/(1 + R)$ or $1 + R = 200/100$, and $R = 100\%$. Since the slope of the investment curve in this segment is negative, we have $-(1 + R) = -200/100$; hence $R = 100\%$. In the continuous case the *IRR* of each additional dollar invested is measured by the slope of the investment function at that point.

this is precisely the investment decision which maximizes investors' utility. Thus, in sum, both the *NPV* and *IRR* rules lead to an optimal investment decision, in the sense that both lead to the acceptance – rejection decision which maximizes investors' utility, that is to the investment decision which permits investors to reach their highest possible indifference curves.

NPV vs *IRR*: Mutually Exclusive Projects

When mutually exclusive proposals exist the investment decision can no longer be analyzed in terms of a single investment productivity function. If two projects, A and B, are mutually exclusive two investment curves must be constructed: one which includes all of the independent projects, *plus project A*; and a second which includes the independent projects *plus project B*. If more than two projects are mutually exclusive the number of possible investment curves increases accordingly so that the optimal investment curve, as well as the optimal point on it, must be chosen.

Unlike the previous case of independence, when mutually exclusive projects exist the *NPV* and *IRR* solutions no longer coincide; the *NPV* remains an optimal rule but the *IRR* may fail to yield the optimal investment decision. To prove this contention let us consider the two investment curves A and B of Fig. 4.16.

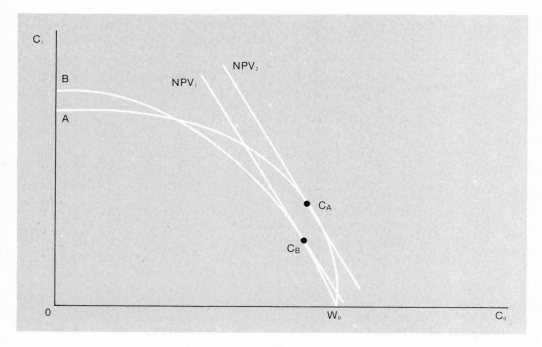

Fig. 4.16

Curve A represents all the independent projects, plus project A, and curve B represents all the independent projects plus project B. This is tantamount to assuming that A and B are the only two mutually exclusive proposals. We continue to assume initial endowment of W_0. The *IRR* criterion cannot distinguish between alternatives A and B. In this example, if alternative A is chosen, all projects up to point c_A should be accepted; if alternative B is chosen all projects up to c_B should be accepted. But which alternative enables investors to reach higher indifference (utility) curves? The *IRR* rule has no clear answer to this crucial problem and hence cannot guarantee optimal results. The *NPV* rule, on the other hand, provides a clear cut answer to the question. The *NPV* of alternative A is greater than that of B and, therefore, permits a tangency with a higher indifference curve. Thus A is the optimal choice between the mutually exclusive alternatives A and B, and c_A is the optimal cutoff point for new investment.

NONCONVENTIONAL CASH FLOWS

Theoretically appropriate decision rules are often complicated, difficult to calculate and impractical to apply, the famous marginal revenue = marginal cost dictum of economic theory being a case in point. The *NPV* decision criterion, however, is an exception to this rule. In all respects it is less complicated and easier to calculate and apply than the alternative *IRR* method. This is especially true once we drop the assumption of conventional cash flows. When nonconventional projects are considered, a proposal's *IRR* may not exist, or if it does, it may not be unique.

Absence of a Real Solution

Consider the following nonconventional cash flow:

0	1	2
+ 100	− 200	+ 150

What is the *IRR* of this project? Should it be accepted by a firm if the cost of capital is 10%?

Anyone who attempts to solve the *IRR* by trial and error will exhaust most of his patience, as well as all of his computer budget, but will still not succeed. The reason for this statement is simple; no "real" *IRR* for this project exists! This can readily be seen by solving the following equation:

$$100 - \frac{200}{1 + R} + \frac{150}{(1 + R)^2} = 0$$

Dividing through by 100 (for simplicity only) and denoting $\frac{1}{1 + R}$ by x, we derive the following quadratic equation:

$$1.5x^2 - 2x + 1 = 0$$

The values of x which solve this equation are called the *roots* of the equation; if at least one real root exists, we can safely assert that there are values of x (and hence values of R) which equate the *NPV* to zero. But if we cannot find real values of x which equate the formula to zero this is tantamount to asserting that the *IRR* does not exist. Using the conventional formula for solving a quadratic equation[13] we get,

$$x_1 = \frac{2 + \sqrt{[4 - 4(1.5)]}}{3} = \frac{2 + \sqrt{-2}}{3}$$

$$x_2 = \frac{2 - \sqrt{[4 - 4(1.5)]}}{3} = \frac{2 - \sqrt{-2}}{3}$$

Since the square root of -2 is an *imaginary* rather than a real number, the *IRR* is also imaginary in this case, that is no real *IRR* exists. This is clear from Fig. 4.17 which graphs the *NPV* of this nonconventional project as a function of the discount rate. At a zero discount rate, the *NPV* is simply the algebraic sum of the cash flow: $100 - 200 + 150 = 50$. As the discount rate approaches infinity the *NPV* approaches 100. Between these values, the curve is U-shaped but always positive, that is there is no positive discount rate at which the *NPV* becomes zero.[14] As Fig. 4.17 shows, the project in question is acceptable by the *NPV* criterion, at any cost of capital; but despite this the *IRR* rule cannot be applied because the *IRR* for such a project does not exist! Nor is this merely an intellectual curiosity; as we noted in Chapter 2, such nonconventional cash flows may be generated whenever a proposal which calls for an advance payment or terminal costs is being evaluated.

Multiple Solutions

In general, the *IRR* formula relates to n years and, therefore, has n roots.

---

13 In general a quadratic equation $ax^2 + bx + c = 0$ has two roots which we denote by x_1 and x_2, that is to say if we substitute either x_1 or x_2 in the above equation the value of the equation is equal to zero. x_1 and x_2 can be found by applying the standard formula:

$$x_1 = \frac{-b - \sqrt{(b^2 - 4ac)}}{2a} \text{ and } x_2 = \frac{-b + \sqrt{(b^2 - 4ac)}}{2a}$$

In cases where $b^2 - 4ac < 0$, no real roots exist, and the function $ax^2 + bx + c$ can never intersect the horizontal axis of a diagram such as Fig. 4.17.

14 The mathematically inclined reader (if such an animal really exists) can readily verify that the function reaches a minimum at a discount rate of 50% by setting the first derivative equal to zero:

$$\frac{\partial NPV}{\partial x} = 3x - 2 = 0$$

Hence $x = \frac{2}{3}$ and since by definition $x = \frac{1}{1 + R}$, $R = 50\%$.

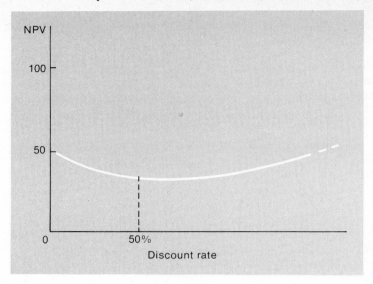

Fig. 4.17

Thus there are always *n* values of *R* which solve the *IRR* equation. However, if the cash flow is conventional only one of these values of *R* is a real number; the other *n* − 1 roots are imaginary numbers which are of importance in higher mathematics but have no economic meaning. In this sense we can say that a conventional project has a *unique* rate of return. The *NPV* function of such a proposal crosses the horizontal axis of a diagram such as Fig. 4.17 *once, and only once.*

If the project is nonconventional, that is we are confronted by a cash flow which has more than one change in sign, the number of real solutions for the *IRR* can vary from zero to *n*.[15] In our previous example we examined a case of a nonconventional, but economically meaningful, project which has no real *IRR*; we now turn to an example of a nonconventional project which has *more than one* real *IRR*.

Consider the following problem: a firm has an old machine which will produce a net return of $300 at the end of the first year, and $1,400 at the end of the second year. The current market value of this machine is zero. The firm is considering the alternative of replacing the old machine with a new one which costs $100, but which will produce a net return of $1,000 at the end of the first year, and only $200 at the end of the second year. The replacement problem requires the evaluation of the *incremental* cash flow stemming from the decision. The necessary data are summarized in the following table:

15 The *maximum* number of real solutions is equal to the number of sign changes in the cash flow. See, for example, D. Teichrow, A.A. Robichek and M. Montalbano, "An Analysis of Criteria for Investment and Financing Decisions under Certainty", *Management Science*, January 1965. A valid economic interpretation of the multiple roots problem can be given by carefully differentiating the project's net inflows and outflows over time. Proponents of this approach would introduce explicitly the reinvestment rate for positive cash balance during the life of the project in order to estimate the maximum rate of interest that could be paid to finance the project without loss.

	Cash flow	
	1st year	*2nd year*
New Machine	-100 1,000	200
Old Machine	300	1,400
Incremental Flow*	-100 $+700$	$-1,200$

*Cash flow of new machine minus cash flow of old machine.

Should the firm replace the old machine? Using the *IRR* rule, we first must solve the following equation for R:

$$-100 + \frac{700}{1 + R} - \frac{1200}{(1 + R)^2} = 0$$

Dividing through by 100 and denoting $\frac{1}{1 + R}$ by x, the following must hold:

$$-12x^2 + 7x - 1 = 0$$

Solving this equation by the standard formula yields *two* real roots:

$$x_1 = \frac{-7 + \sqrt{(49 - 48)}}{-24} = \tfrac{1}{4} \text{ and since } x = \frac{1}{1 + R}, R_1 = 300\%$$

Similarly,

$$x_2 = \frac{-7 - \sqrt{(49 - 48)}}{-24} = \tfrac{1}{3}, \text{ so that } R_2 = 200\%$$

Now, for sake of argument, assume that the cost of capital is 250%. Should the old machine be replaced? The *IRR* rule breaks down in such a case since contradictory answers are indicated depending on which rate of return is chosen:

$R_1 = 200\% < 250$; don't replace
$R_2 = 300\% > 250$; replace

And, moreover, we have no way of discriminating between the two solutions.

The dilemma can be resolved by examining Fig. 4.18 which plots the *NPV* profiles of the cash flows of the new machine and the old machine as well as the incremental cash flow of the replacement decision. The dual rate of return reflects the fact that the *NPV* functions of the old and new machines intersect *twice* — at discount rates of 200% and 300%. These rates are also, by definition, the internal rates of return of the incremental cash flow as they equate the *NPV* of the two alternatives. Applying the *NPV* rule to the diagram we note that for discount rates *between* 200% and 300%, the *NPV* of the new machine is greater than the *NPV* of the old machine and as a result the *NPV* of the incremental cash flow is positive over this range as well. Thus for these discount rates, the replacement is worthwhile. However, if the discount rate is below 200% or over 300% the old machine should not be replaced.

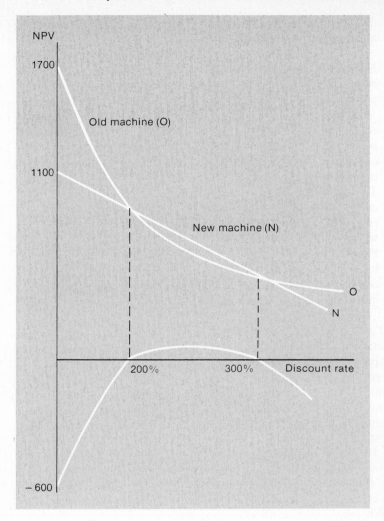

Fig. 4.18

SUMMARY

This chapter has analyzed and compared two time-adjusted measures of invest-ment worth: Net Present Value (*NPV*) and the Internal Rate of Return (*IRR*). Although both criteria give equivalent results with regard to independent con-ventional projects, they do not *rank* projects the same. This difference in ranking becomes crucial in mutually exclusive choice situations, that is when the firm must choose the best (presumably highest ranking) proposal out of two or more alternatives. *NPV* provides the more attractive criterion for the following reasons:

(a)   *NPV* reflects the *absolute* magnitude of the projects while the *IRR* does not. This is a point in the *NPV*'s favor, because the firm is concerned with absolute profits and not merely with the rate of profit. Similarly, this provides the reason for rejecting the "Profitability Index" as a measure of investment worth.

(b) *NPV* implicitly assumes reinvestment of the interim proceeds at the cost of capital; the *IRR* assumes reinvestment at the project's own rate of return. Once again this is a point in favor of the *NPV* since projects which earn more than their opportunity cost would be accepted anyway, *independent* of the current investment decision, Hence, the investment worth of a current project should not be credited with returns on interim receipts in excess of the cost of capital.

(c) The reinvestment assumption is of critical importance if we assume a changing cost of capital in future years. Under such circumstances the *IRR* rule breaks down because the comparison of a single-valued rate of return with a series of different short-term discount rates is not meaningful.

(d) Finally, the *NPV* is not only theoretically superior to the *IRR* but also has important technical advantages. When nonconventional cash flows are considered, a real solution for the project's *IRR* may not exist; or in other instances more than one *IRR* may be found for a single project.

To sum up, the *NPV* provides an optimal solution to the firm's capital budgeting problems on the assumption that the future cash flows and the appropriate cost of capital (discount rate) are known. The popularity of the *IRR* is in part psychological; a measure of investment worth which is set out in percentage terms is appealing to many executives. The rate of return can readily be compared with the cost of funds to yield a "margin of profit". This is a valid consideration and much can be said in favor of *presenting* the results of a feasibility study in a form which is preferred by management, that is in terms of the *IRR*. However, the intuitive appeal of the *IRR* should not be permitted to obscure the fundamental fact that when mutually exclusive decisions have to be made, they should be dictated by differences between the alternative proposals' net present values and not by their internal rates of return.

With this technical material under our belts we now turn, in Chapter 5, to the "real world" problem of applying our evaluation methods and decision rules to actual cash flows within the complex framework of a modern corporate organization.

QUESTIONS AND PROBLEMS

4.1 (a) The *NPV* and *IRR* criteria always lead to the same decisions, when the projects are independent. Prove this statement.

(b) The *NPV* and *IRR* may lead to different decisions when the projects are mutually exclusive. Explain.

4.2 Assume that you are confronted by the following three projects:

Year	Cash Flow					
	0	*1*	*2*	*3*	*4*	*5*
Project A	−1,000	100	100	100	100	1,100
Project B	−1,000	264	264	264	264	264
Project C	−1,000	—	—	—	—	1,611

(a) Calculate the net present value of each of the above projects, assuming a 10% discount rate, and rank the projects.

(b) Calculate the internal rate of return for each of the above projects and rank the projects.

(c) Calculate the net present value of each of the projects using a 6% discount rate and rank the projects.

(d) Calculate the net present value of the projects assuming a 15% discount rate and rank the projects.

(e) Compare and explain the rankings which you obtained in parts (a) – (d) above using a diagram which graphs the *NPV* as a function of the discount rate.

4.3 Consider the following two *mutually exclusive* investment opportunities:

Year	*0*	*1*	*2*	*3*	*4*	*5*
Project A	−48,700	17,000	17,000	17,000	17,000	17,000
Project B	−31,600	12,000	12,000	12,000	12,000	12,000

(a) Calculate each project's net present value and internal rate of return. (Assume that the cost of capital is 8%.)

(b) Which of the two projects would be chosen according to the *IRR* criterion? Which according to the *NPV* criterion?

(c) How can you explain the differences in rankings given by the *NPV* and *IRR* methods in this case?

4.4 A company is confronted with the following two *mutually exclusive* investment opportunities:

Year	*0*	*1*	*2*	*3*	*4*
Project C	−80,000	28,000	28,000	28,000	28,000
Project D	−24,000	9,800	9,800	9,800	9,800

(a) Calculate the net present value of each of the above projects assuming a 10% discount rate.

(b) Calculate the internal rate of return of each project.

(c) Which of the two projects would be chosen according to the *NPV* criterion? Which according to the *IRR*?

(d) Describe the hypothetical cash flow "C minus D" and calculate its *NPV* and *IRR*. Use this result to "defend" the *NPV* decision.

(e) Graph the *NPV* of each project (including the project "C – D") as a function of the discount rate.

4.5 Consider the following two *mutually exclusive* projects:

Year	0	1	2
Project A	– 10,000	6,700	5,700
Project B	– 2,000	1,900	900

(a) For each project, calculate the net present value, internal rate of return and the "profitability index", assuming an 8% discount rate.

(b) Which of the two projects is preferred according to each of the three methods?

(c) How can you explain the differences in rankings given by the *NPV* criterion and the profitability index?

(d) Which of the two methods is the correct one?

(e) Calculate the internal rate of return of the project "A – B". Does it confirm your answer to part (d)? Explain.

4.6 Having proven yourself to be a superior student (your choice of this course being a case in point) your university offers you a choice between an outright *gift* of $1,000 or a $7,000 *interest-free loan* to be paid back in seven equal annual installments of $1,000 each.

(a) Which alternative would represent the optimal choice for you? Explain your decision.

(b) Under what circumstances would you reverse your choice. Be specific.

(Use a graph to illustrate your answer.)

4.7 The NAYOT corporation is examining the following two *mutually exclusive* investment proposals:

Proposal A: Initial outlay of $100,000 and receipts of $25,000 in the first year and $125,000 in the second year.

Proposal B: Initial outlay of $100,000 and receipts of $95,000 in the first year and $45,500 in the second year.

(a) Calculate each project's net present value and internal rate of return, assuming a cost of capital of 10%.

(b) Which of the two projects would be chosen according to the *NPV* criterion? Which according to the *IRR* criterion?

(c) How can you explain the differences in rankings given by the *NPV* and *IRR* methods *in this case*? Use the incremental cash flow "A – B" in your explanation.

(d) How would your answers to parts (a) – (c) be changed if you assume that the cost of capital is 16%? Be specific.

4.8 One of the main differences between the net present value and the internal rate of return methods lies in the implicit assumptions concerning the reinvestment of interim cash flows.

(a) Identify the implicit assumption in each of these methods.
(b) In the light of your answer to part (a), which method should be preferred? Explain your choice.

4.9 Under what assumptions will the *IRR* and *NPV* methods rank all projects in the same order of priority? Prove your answer. (Hint: Use a graph.)

4.10 Critically comment on the following quotations:

(a) "The problem of reinvestment rates can be avoided by considering only projects of the same duration."
(b) "The problem of reinvestment does not exist when the two projects have the same duration and require the same investment outlay."
(c) "The *IRR* method does not assume that interim receipts are reinvested."

4.11 The following cash flow represents an investment in an energy saving machine for a firm faced with a cost of capital of 12%.

	0	1	2	3
Cashflow	− 1000	400	500	600

(a) Calculate the project's *NPV* and *IRR*.
(b) Show numerically that if the firm borrows $1,000 at an interest rate which is equal to the project's *IRR*, it will end up with a zero cash balance at the end of the project.
(c) Show numerically that if the firm pays interest on the loan at the rate of $k\%$ per year ($k = 12\%$) and any cash which remains is used to pay the principal, then what is left at the end of the project will be exactly equal to the future value of the project's net present value.

4.12 Consider the following cash flows:

Year	0	1	2
Project A	500	− 700	300
Project B	− 60	120	− 100

(a) Calculate the internal rate of return and the net present value (at a discount rate of 12%) for each project.
(b) Plot the *NPV* profile for each project as a function of the discount rate. Explain your results.

4.13 Consider the following cash flows:

Year	0	1	2
Project A	− 40	130	− 100
Project B	25	− 140	160
Project C	− 100	500	− 600

(a) Calculate each project's *NPV* and *IRR* (assume a discount rate of 10%).

(b) Plot each project's *NPV* profile as a function of the discount rate. Indicate the intercepts on both axes.

(c) What is the economic meaning of the *IRR* when a project has two rates of return?

4.14 The examination of a project revealed that it has two internal rates of return: 10% and 30%. Assume that the cost of capital is 15%. Should the firm accept this investment project? Explain your answer.

4.15 (1) The Olive Oil company is examining the following two mutually exclusive investment projects:

	Initial Outlay	Cash Flow First Year	Second Year
Project A	−1,000	1,180	—
Project B	−1,000	—	1,300

(a) Calculate the net present value and the internal rate of return of each project; assume an 8% cost of capital.

(b) Rank the projects according to each of the two methods.

(2) The Super Deluxe company was confronted by the following two *mutually exclusive* investment opportunities:

	0	1	Year 2	3	4
Project C	−500	—	—	—	1037
Project D	−500	625	—	—	—

(a) Calculate each project's net present value and internal rate of return. (Assume that the cost of capital is 8%).

(b) Which of the two projects would be chosen according to the *NPV* criterion? According to *IRR* criterion?

(c) How can you explain the difference in rankings in this case?

(d) Build a "repetitive" project to show that the paradoxical difference in ranking can be resolved.

(3) (a) In view of your answers to parts (1) and (2) above, which of the two methods, in your opinion, provides the *optimal* decision in each of the cases? Explain and defend your choice.

(b) How would you qualify your answer in the absence of mutual exclusiveness, that is, if the projects were economically *independent*?

4.16 The Eastern Metals company is confronted with the following two-period independent projects:

Project	Required Investment Outlay ($)	Net Cash Receipts at the End of the Year ($)
A	750,000	900,000
B	400,000	420,000
C	200,000	260,000
D	300,000	330,000
E	250,000	400,000
F	100,000	140,000

The firm has initial available resources of 2 million dollars.

(a) Plot the productivity schedule of the firm.
(b) Calculate, and show on the graph, how much the firm can "consume" next year if it "consumes":
(1) $350,000 this year?
(2) $1,300,000 this year?

Which projects would it execute in each case?

4.17 Define the following terms:

(a) Rational individual
(b) Indifference curve
(c) Optimal choice.

4.18 An individual is indifferent between the following consumption combinations:

This year ($)	Next year ($)
4,000	3,200
3,700	3,500
3,200	4,000
2,900	4,400

(a) Plot the indifference curve that represents the individual's tastes with respect to current and future consumption.
(b) What is the meaning of a *convex* indifference curve? Is the curve which you plotted in part (a) convex? Prove your answer.

4.19 (1) "I am indifferent between the consumption combinations ($2,200 this year; $2,500 next year) and ($2,600 this year; $2,000 next year)".
(2) "Consumption of $2,800 this year and $2,100 next year gives me the same satisfaction as consumption of $2,200 this year and $2,500 next year".

Regarding the above two quotations:
(a) Is it possible that both statements were made by the same individual?

(b) Is it possible that each statement was made by two different individuals? Prove your answers.

4.20 Illustrate graphically the two-period consumption – investment model for the case of independent projects.

(a) What are the equilibrium conditions when the only possibilities are investment and consumption?
(b) What are the equilibrium conditions when it is also possible to lend or borrow?

4.21 An investor with an initial endowment of $2500 is confronted with the following two-period independent investment options:

Project	Required Investment ($)	First-year Receipts ($)
A	200	260
B	300	450
C	100	175
D	500	525
E	200	310
F	100	110
G	200	250
H	300	300
I	400	460
J	200	360

Assume that the investor's indifference curve is defined in the following manner: he requires compensation of 1.35 units of future consumption when his current consumption is decreased by one unit. Answer the following questions, assuming that there is no possibility to borrow or lend money.

(a) Plot the investor's productivity schedule.
(b) How much will the investor invest in production?
(c) What is the optimal consumption combination?
(d) Is it possible that the investor will choose to consume $1300 this year? Explain.

4.22 Assume that the investor is allowed to lend and borrow at an interest rate of 20%.
Answer the following questions with regard to the data in question 4.21.

(a) How much will the investor invest in production?
(b) What is the net present value of the investment chosen by the investor?
(c) What is the present value of the investor's total consumption in both periods?

(d) What is the future value of the investor's total consumption in both periods?

4.23 An investor with initial endowment of $2,000 is confronted with the same ten investment options that appeared in question 4.21. Assume that projects A, C and G exclude projects H and J, that is if the investor decides to execute A, C or G, he cannot execute H or J, and likewise, if he chooses H or J he cannot choose A, C or G. Assume also that the interest rate is 20%, and answer the following questions:

(a) Illustrate graphically the two mutually exclusive investment (productivity) curves.

(b) Show and prove that the *NPV* rule gives the optimal investment decision in this case.

(c) How much will the investor invest in production? Which projects will he carry out?

(d) What is the present value of the total consumption in both periods?

4.24 "The two-period investment – consumption model gives a unique solution for the investment problem even when all the projects confronting the firm have the same *IRR*".
Appraise, for both the case of independent projects and the case of mutually exclusive projects.

4.25 "One who is not concerned about future consumption need not bother investing in production".
Appraise and prove your answer.

4.26 An investor with an initial endowment of $16,000 is confronted with the following productivity curve:

$$c_1 = 240 \, (16{,}000 - c_0)^{\frac{1}{2}}$$

where c_0 indicates consumption at present and c_1-consumption in the future. Assume that the interest rate (for borrowing and lending) is equal to 20%. The investor's utility function, from which it is possible to derive his indifference curves, is defined as: $u(c_0, c_1) = c_0 \cdot c_1$.
Answer the following questions, using the two-period investment consumption model:

(a) How much will the investor invest in production?

(b) What is the *NPV* of the investment chosen by the investor?

(c) What is the net present value of his total consumption?

(d) Does the investor borrow or lend in the capital market? Give a numerical answer.

(e) What is the optimal allocation of consumption for the two periods?

Illustrate your answers graphically.

4.27 Another investor with an initial endowment of $32,000 is confronted with the productivity curve defined as follows:

$$c_1 = 36(32{,}000 - c_0)^{\frac{1}{2}}$$

where c_0 indicates consumption at present and c_1 = consumption in the future. Assume that the interest rate (for borrowing and lending) is equal to 20%. The investor's utility function, from which it is possible to derive his indifference curves, is defined as:

$$u(c_0, c_1) = 12c_0^2 + 100\ c_0 c_1.$$

Answer the following questions, using the two-period model of investment-consumption:

(a) How much will the investor invest in production?

(b) What is the *NPV* of the investment chosen by the investor?

(c) What is the net present value of his total consumption in both periods?

(d) Does the investor borrow or lend in the capital market? Give a numerical answer.

(e) What is the optimal allocation of consumption for the two periods? Illustrate your answer graphically.

4.28 Consider an investment in physical capital when the initial wealth W_0 is $100. The investment transformation curve between current consumption (c_0) and future consumption (c_1) is such that the marginal return on successive investments of $10 is as follows:

Marginal Investment	Total Return ($)	Marginal Net Return ($)
10	67.0	57.0
10	83.0	6.0
10	98.0	5.0
10	112.0	4.0
10	125.0	3.0
10	137.0	2.0
10	148.5	1.5
10	159.5	1.0
10	170.0	0.5
10	180.0	0.0

Assume that the borrowing and lending rate is 35% (i.e., $r = 0.35$).

(a) What is the optimal investment at time t_0? Show your solution on a diagram.

(b) Assume now that an individual has the following indifference curves between current and future consumption:

$$c_1 = a + \frac{1}{20} \cdot (c_0 - 100)^2 \qquad 0 \leqslant c_0 \leqslant 100$$

where a is a constant along any indifference curve. Determine the optimal amount to be borrowed or lent by the individual at time t_0 as well as his total consumption at t_0 and at t_1.

(c) Work out parts (a) and (b) once again, this time assuming the following indifference curve:

$$c_1 = a + \frac{1}{20} \cdot (c_0 - 60)^2 \qquad 0 \leqslant c_0 \leqslant 60$$

Is there any change in the investment decision compared to parts (a) and (b)? Why?

4.29 (1) Consider a two-period investment productivity curve defined by the equation

$$c_1 = 300(12{,}000 - c_0)^{\frac{1}{2}}$$

where c_0 is the current period consumption and c_1 is the next period consumption. The investor's initial endowment is $W_0 = \$12{,}000$.

(a) Draw the investment productivity curve in the (c_0, c_1) plane by calculating several points of the curve.

(b) What is the maximum attainable current consumption? What is the corresponding future consumption?

(c) What is the maximum investment that can be made in the current period? What are the corresponding consumption levels c_0 and c_1? What is the average return on investment?

(d) Suppose the investor with total endowment $W_0 = \$12{,}000$ decides to invest \$4,900 in production. What are his consumption levels in the two periods, c_0 and c_1? Show the resulting two-period consumption strategy on your graph and indicate the production projects in which the individual invested his capital. What is his *average* return on investment? What is the marginal rate of return on investment?

(2) Now consider three investors whose indifference maps are described by the following two-period utility functions:

Investor A: $u(c_0, c_1) = c_0 + c_1$
Investor B: $u(c_0, c_1) = 3c_0 + c_1$
Investor C: $u(c_0, c_1) = c_0 \cdot c_1$

(Each indifference curve corresponds to some constant value of the utility function, $u(c_0, c_1) = $ constant.)

(a) Show graphically the optimum consumption combination that each investor will choose.

(b) Find the corresponding optimum consumption combination analytically.

(c) How much will each individual invest in production?

(d) What is the marginal rate of return on investment at the optimum point for each investor? What is the average rate of return of total investment?

(3) Now suppose that in addition to the investment productivity curve there is a perfect capital market in which all investors can borrow and lend at a constant rate of $r = 50\%$. Hence, 50% is in this case the cost of capital for all investors.

(a) Find analytically the optimum *production* policies of the three investors. Show your results graphically.

(b) What is the total amount invested by each investor in production?

(c) What is the marginal rate of return on production investments for each investor?

(d) What is the net present value of the optimum production strategy of each investor? What is the future value? What is the equation of the money market line through the optimum production point?

(e) Find analytically the optimum consumption combination of investor C. Indicate whether investor C acts as a borrower or a lender in the money market. What is the amount of borrowing or lending?

(f) Is investor C better off with or without the money market?

4.30 In the Bible we find the following quotation:

> The Lord shall open unto thee his good treasure, the heaven to give the rain unto thy land in his season, and to bless all the work of thine hand: and thou shalt lend unto many nations, and thou shalt not borrow. (Deuteronomy 28: 12.)

Suppose that God opens his treasures to an investor and his initial wealth grows from W_0 to say $5W_0$. There is no change in the projects available and in the market interest rate. Show graphically a case where the investor changes, as a result of the increase in his wealth, from a borrower to a lender.

APPENDIX 4A CALCULATING THE OPTIMAL INVESTMENT – CONSUMPTION COMBINATION IN A TWO-PERIOD MODEL

Denoting by f the production function, we can find the optimal production strategy at the tangency point between f and the NPV line by equating the slope of f to the slope of the NPV line, i.e.,

$$\left(\frac{dc_1}{dc_0}\right)_f = -(1 + k)$$

To find the optimal borrowing, we equate the slope of the NPV line to the slope of the indifference curve, thus

$$\left(\frac{dc_1}{dc_0}\right)_u = -(1 + k)$$

where u denotes differentiation along a particular indifference curve corresponding to the value u of the utility function.

Example: Suppose that the productivity curve is defined as $c_1 = 250(18,000 - c_0)^{\frac{1}{2}}$ and the interest rate, k, is equal to 25%, so that

$$\left(\frac{dc_1}{dc_0}\right)_f = -125(18,000 - c_0)^{-\frac{1}{2}} \text{ and } -(1 + k) = -1.25$$

$$\frac{-125}{(18,000 - c_0)^{\frac{1}{2}}} = -1.25$$

$$(18,000 - c_0)^{\frac{1}{2}} = 100$$

$$18,000 - c_0 = 10,000$$

$$\text{or } c_0^* = 18,000 - 10,000 = \textbf{\$8000}.$$

If the initial endowment is $18,000 then the investment in production is $I_0 = 18,000 - 8000 = \textbf{\$10,000}$ and $c_1^* = 250(18,000 - c_0^*)^{\frac{1}{2}} = 250(10,000)^{\frac{1}{2}} = 250\cdot100 = \textbf{\$25,000}$.

The *NPV* of the investment is equal to $\dfrac{c_1}{1 + k} - I_0$ and the *NPV* of the total consumption is equal to

$$\frac{c_1}{1 + k} + c_0^* = \frac{25,000}{1.25} + 8,000 = \textbf{\$28,000}$$

The optimal consumption point is the point where the iso-*NPV* line is tangent to the indifference curve, so that to find this point we have to equate the derivative of the indifference curve $\left(\dfrac{dc_1}{dc_0}\right)_u$ to the slope of the iso-*NPV* line.

Suppose that $u(c_0, c_1) = 2c_0 \cdot c_1$

$$\left(\frac{dc_1}{dc_0}\right)_u = \frac{-\partial u(c_0, c_1)}{\partial c_0} \left/ \frac{\partial u(c_0, c_1)}{\partial c_1} \right. = \frac{-2c_1}{2c_0} = -\frac{c_1}{c_0}$$

so that $\dfrac{dc_1}{dc_0} = -(1 + k) \Leftrightarrow -\dfrac{c_1}{c_0} = -1.25$

$$\text{or } c_1^{**} = \textbf{1.25}c_0^{**}.$$

Since this point lies on the same iso-*NPV* lines as (c_0^*, c_1^*)

$$\frac{c_1^{**}}{1 + k} + c_0^{**} = \frac{c_1^*}{1 + k} + c_0^* = 28,000$$

$$\text{or } \frac{1.25c_0^{**}}{1.25} + c_0 = c_0^{**} + c_0^{**} = 2c_0^{**} = 28,000$$

$$\text{therefore } c_0^{**} = \textbf{\$14,000}$$

$$\text{and } c_1^{**} = 1.25c_0^{**} = 1.25 \cdot 14,000 = \textbf{\$17,500}$$

SELECTED REFERENCES

Alchian, A.A., "The Rate of Interest, Fisher's Rate of Return over Cost, and Keynes' Internal Rate of Return", *American Economic Review*, December 1955.

Bailey, M.J., "Formal Criteria for Investment Decisions", *Journal of Political Economy*, October 1959.

Ben Shahar, Haim and Sarnat, M., "Reinvestment and the Rate of Return on Common Stocks", *Journal of Finance*, December 1965.

Beranek, W., "Some New Capital Budgeting Theorems", *Journal of Financial and Quantitative Analysis*, December 1977.

Beranek, W., "The AB Procedure and Capital Budgeting", *Journal of Financial and Quantitative Analysis*, June 1980.

Bernardo, J.J. and Lanser, H.P. "A Capital Budgeting Decision Model with Subjective Criteria", *Journal of Financial and Quantitative Analysis*, June 1977.

Bernhard, R.H., "Discount Methods for Expenditure Evaluation — A Clarification of Their Assumptions", *Journal of Industrial Engineering*, January – February 1962.

Bernhard, R.H. and Norstrom, Carl, J., "A Further Note on Unrecovered Investment, Uniqueness of the Internal Rate, and the Question of Project Acceptability", *Journal of Financial and Quantitative Analysis*, June 1980.

Brick, J.R. and Thompson, H.E., "The Economic Life of an Investment and the Appropriate Discount Rate", *Journal of Financial and Quantitative Analysis*, December 1978.

Capettini, R., Grimlund, R.A. and Toole, H.R., "Comment: The Unique, Real Internal Rate of Return", *Journal of Financial and Quantitative Analysis*, December 1979.

Carlson, C. Robert, Lawrence, Michael and Wort, Donald H., "Clarification of the Reinvestment Assumption in Capital Analysis", *Journal of Business Research*, April 1974.

Chateau, Jean-Pierre, D., "The Capital Budgeting Problem Under Conflicting Financial Policies", *Journal of Business Finance & Accounting*, Winter 1975.

Greer, Willis R. Jr., "Capital Budgeting Analysis with the Timing of Events Uncertain", *Accounting Review*, January 1970.

Haskins, C.G., "Benefit Cost Ratios vs. Net Present Value: Revisited", *Journal of Business Finance & Accounting*, Summer 1974.

Herbst, A., "The Unique, Real Internal Rate of Return: *Caveat Emptor!*", *Journal of Financial and Quantitative Analysis*, June 1978.

Hirshleifer, J.H., "On the Theory of Optimal Investment Decision", *Journal of Political Economy*, August 1958.

Hoskins, Colin G., "Benefit – Cost Ratio Ranking for Size Disparity Problems", *Journal of Business Finance & Accounting*, 4,2 (1977).

Jeynes, Paul H., "The Significance of Reinvestment Rate", *Engineering Economist*, XI (Fall 1965), 1 – 9.

Lere, John C., "Deterministic Net Present Value as an Approximation of Expected Net Present Value", *Journal of Business Finance & Accounting*, Summer 1980.

Lerner, Eugene M. and Rappaport, Alfred, "Limit DCF in Capital Budgeting", *Harvard Business Review*, September – October 1968.

Lin, S.A.Y., "The Modified Internal Rate of Return and Investment Criterion", *Engineering Economist*, Summer 1976.

Litzenberger, R.H. and Joy, O.M., "Decentralized Capital Budgeting Decisions and Shareholder Wealth Maximization", *Journal of Finance*, September 1975.

Longbottom, D.A. and Wiper, L., "Capital Appraisal and the Case for Average Rate of Return", *Journal of Business Finance and Accounting*, Vol. 4, No. 4, 1977.

Longbottom, David and Wiper, Linda, "Necessary Conditions for the Existence of Multiple Rates in the Use of Internal Rate of Return", *Journal of Business Finance & Accounting*, Winter 1978.

Lopez Leautaud, J.I. and Swalm, R., "On the Internal Rate of Return Criterion: A Note on the Notes and Replies", *Engineering Economist*, Summer 1976.

Mao, James C.T., "The Internal Rate of Return as a Ranking Criterion", *Engineering Economist*, Winter 1966.

Meyer, R.L., "A Note on Capital Budgeting Techniques and the Reinvestment Rate", *Journal of Finance*, December 1979.

Oakford, R.V., Bhimjee, S.A. and Jucker, J.V., "The Internal Rate of Return, the Pseudo Internal Rate of Return, and the *NPV* and their Use in Financial Decision Making", *Engineering Economist*, Spring 1977.

Peasnell, K.V., "Capital Budgeting and Discounted Cash Equivalents: Some Clarifying Comments", *Abacus*, December 1979.

Rapp, Birger, "The Internal Rate of Return Method — A Critical Study", *Engineering Costs and Production Economics*, Vol. 5, 1980.

Robichek, Alexander A. and Van Horne, James C., "Abandonment Value and Capital Budgeting", *Journal of Finance*, December 1967.

Robinson, R., "The Rate of Interest, Fisher's Rate of Return over Costs and Keynes' Internal Rate of Return: Comment", *American Economic Review*, December 1956.

Ross, Stephen A., Spatt, Chester S. and Dybvig, Philip H., "Present Values and Internal Rates of Return", *Journal of Economic Theory*, August 1980.

Schwab, Bernhard and Lusztig, Peter, "A Comparative Analysis of the Net Present Value and the Benefit – Cost Ratios as Measures of the Economic Desirability of Investments", *Journal of Finance*, June 1969.

Scott, David F. Jr., Gray, Otha L. and Bird, Monroe M., "Investing and Financing Behavior of Small Manufacturing Firms", *MSU Business Topics*, Summer 1972, Vol. 20, No. 3, pp. 29 – 38.

Stapleton, R.C., "The Acquisition Decision as a Capital Budgeting Problem", *Journal of Business Finance & Accounting*, Summer 1975.

Sundem, G.L., "Evaluating Capital Budgeting Models in Simulated Environments", *Journal of Finance*, September 1975.

5

Using Cash Flows
to Evaluate Investments

In the two preceding chapters alternative investment decision criteria were analyzed on the assumption that the annual cash flows are known. No attempt was made to determine how the receipts and outlays should be defined or measured. We cannot overemphasize the importance of accuracy of both projected capital costs and estimated revenues as well as the extreme difficulty in arriving at both in an actual business situation. Modern corporations are often very large and complex organizations which for a variety of reasons (including extreme uncertainty) often use a number of alternative capital budgeting methods. Moreover, for internal political reasons management on occasion will be prepared to rearrange project priorities.

In a sense the capital budgeting decision represents a resolution of conflict (hopefully not too unfriendly) among colleagues in the same organization. In reality, the management of each division or subsidiary is constantly trying to outmaneuver its internal competition within the firm in order to win a bigger slice of the available funds. In such a situation political and prestige factors may sometimes overrule rational decision-making, but in the longer run the race is not always to the swift, and the ability to present cogent arguments based on careful and accurate forecasts of the relevant cashflow is crucial. The purpose of this chapter is to prepare the groundwork for the practical application of capital budgeting techniques. To this end we shall first examine the principles underlying the measurement of a project's cash flows; following this, the capital budgeting model will be applied to a recurring problem of great importance to most firms: the analysis of equipment replacement decisions.[1]

---

1 The important question of the impact of corporate income taxes on the cash flows will be dealt with in the next chapter. For the purpose of this chapter the reader should assume that the cash flows are *net* of the relevant tax deductions.

INCREMENTAL CASH FLOWS

Underlying modern feasibility analysis is the principle of *incremental cash flows*, which states that a project should be evaluated by considering all of the cash inflows and outflows induced by the investment decision in question. It follows that attention must be given to the magnitude and timing of the cash flows, rather than to the accounting concepts of income and expenses. To help clarify the cash flow principle let us consider an extreme hypothetical example. Assume that Avirone Aircraft Corporation signs a contract to supply five jet aeroplanes to Pan World Airlines in 1980. The contract is signed in 1978, and Pan World pays an advance of $20 million to help Avirone finance the project. To Avirone's accountant, no profit from this contract will have an impact on the corporation's reported profits either in 1978 or 1979. Only in 1980, when the jets are delivered to Pan World, will the profit (or loss) generated by this transaction be reflected in Avirone's accounts, that is to say the $20 million which were received in 1978 do not affect the accounting revenues of the project. Thus from the viewpoint of reported accounting earnings, Avirone Aircraft Corporation's decision to undertake such a project would not be influenced by the receipt of the advance payment.

Clearly, this does not make economic sense and in practice a firm will always prefer, other things being equal, to receive as large a cash advance as possible, thereby reducing the cost of financing the project. In order to reflect this important dimension of the decision process, modern time-adjusted investment criteria are based on cash, rather than accounting, inflows and outlays. Hence the exact timing of each component of the cash flow must be accurately determined if a proposal's full economic impact is to be gauged correctly.

The difference between the cash flow and accounting concepts can also be illustrated by considering the case of trade credit. Let us assume that the annual sales in 1978 of the ABC company were $100,000, and that the company's policy was to offer two-year payment terms to its customers. The accounting department of the ABC company will report gross revenues of $100,000 for the year. Now suppose that the total cost of producing and selling the product in question is $80,000, and that this outlay also occurred in 1978. The company's balance sheet for 1978 will include an entry *accounts receivable* of $100,000, and its income statement will report a profit of $20,000. However, from the viewpoint of capital budgeting, the impact on *NPV* is considerably smaller. Since the outlay of $80,000 occurs in 1978 no adjustment is required (for simplicity we assume that the costs were incurred on the first day of the year); but this is not true of the revenues from sales as they will only be realized in 1980, that is two years later. The calculation of the "cash flow" profit, therefore, is as follows:

1978	1979	1980
− 80,000	—	+ 100,000

Obviously, the accounting and the cash flow profits are the same only for the trivial and unrealistic case of a zero cost of capital (discount rate). At all positive discount rates the cash flow profit will be smaller. For example, if we assume a 10% discount rate, the calculation of the discounted value of the profit is:

$$\frac{100,000}{(1.1)^2} - 80,000 = \$2,600$$

Thus the contribution to *NPV* is $2,600, and not $20,000. And as we have already noted, the *NPV* of cash flows is the relevant concept for the maximization of the value of the owners' equity.

Invoking the cash flow principle is not in itself sufficient to resolve all of the conceptual difficulties which plague the measurement of the costs and benefits of a typical investment project. Some of these problems can best be examined by considering yet another example. Suppose that the Atlantic Electric Company is considering an investment in a new power unit, and that the gross cash inflows from this unit are expected to be $100,000 per year, while the annual cash outflows for fuel, labor, etc., are expected to be $75,000. In addition the cost accounting department estimates that overhead costs of $20,000 per year should be charged to the new power unit. These costs include the new project's share in managerial salaries, general administrative expenses, etc. For simplicity we shall assume that those overhead costs include $10,000 of *fixed costs*, that is costs which will be incurred even if the project is not implemented. An example of such a cost would be the fraction of the company president's salary which is allocated to the new power unit. The remaining $10,000 is assumed to be variable, that is these costs will be incurred only if the project is accepted. In addition, it has been estimated that the company's net receipts from its other power units will *decrease* by $5,000 per year should the new power unit be installed.

Table 5.1 summarizes the above information on the receipts and outlays of the proposed project. Clearly the annual cash inflow of $100,000 is part of the project's cash flow, but it is not equally clear that all of the four types of outlays listed in Table 5.1 should be deducted from the inflow when calculating the project's net annual cash flow. In general, the fixed overhead expenses should *not* be deducted from the project's receipts as they do not represent an incremental cash outflow induced by the decision to invest in the new power unit. By definition, these fixed costs (president's salary, etc.) will remain the same *independent* of the investment decision in question, and therefore they should not be "charged" against the project. Variable overhead costs and the direct costs (fuel, labor, etc.) should be deducted since they do not represent incremental outlays induced by the decision to invest in the new unit.

Table 5.1
Annual Receipts and Outlays of New Power Unit
($)

Annual Inflow	100,000
Annual Outflow:	
Fuel, labor, etc.	75,000
Fixed overhead	10,000
Variable overhead	10,000
Decrease in net receipts from other power units	5,000

The last item of Table 5.1, the decrease in net receipts elsewhere in the firm, should also be deducted; by the incremental cash flow principle, this is a (negative) cash flow which occurs as a direct result of the decision to invest in the new unit. The fact that the change in the cash flow takes place with respect to other power units, or in another department, is relevant; we seek to measure the net change in the firm's *total* cash flow which will be induced by the decision to invest. Thus any impact of the new project on the cash flows of existing units is germane to the investment decision, and therefore should be reflected in the estimated cash flows of the new unit. Hence, when developing a new model car, Ford and General Motors try to introduce the type of car which will not compete with their existing models. A very "successful" new car which drastically reduces revenues from the sales of existing models might prove a disaster, and therefore must be evaluated on an incremental cash flow basis if its true impact is to be reflected in the profitability calculation.

Initial Investment Outlay and Depreciation

Having examined the underlying principle of incremental cash flows, let us now turn to some additional problems which can arise when defining project cash flows. Suppose, for example, that the ABC company acquires a machine which costs $10,000, has an expected economic life of ten years and is expected to produce a net annual cash inflow of S dollars. The cash flow for such a machine can be written as follows:

Years

0	1	2	3 ... 10
(− 10,000)	S	S	S ... S

Now, let us consider the problem confronting the company's accountant, who must allocate the project's revenues and cost to particular years in order to estimate the annual net profit in his report to the shareholders. To do this he must first calculate that part of the machine's original purchase price which erodes each year. The most popular solution to this problem is to divide the original cost of the machine by its expected economic life, thereby deriving the *depreciation* figure which must be deducted from the annual receipts when calculating the accounting profit for the year. In our example the annual depreciation expense is $1,000 (10,000 ÷ 10 = 1,000) and the net annual profit is S minus $1,000.

Obviously, the deduction of a depreciation allowance is a compromise between reality and the legal requirement to calculate an annual profit figure; however, when evaluating the profitability of a proposed capital investment one can (and should) ignore interim profits and consider the project's entire life as one decision unit. Thus, in capital budgeting the allocation of costs to particular years can be ignored and attention can be focused on the cash flows at the precise time that they occur.

Since the machine in question is to be purchased and paid for at the outset of the project, an outlay of $10,000 at the beginning of the first year is taken into account, rather than deducting an allowance for depreciation of $1,000 in each of the next ten years. Clearly, the two alternative ways of handling the initial investment outlay are equivalent only for the special case in which the discount rate is equal to zero. In general the two methods differ, and in choosing a method of incorporating capital costs we prefer to deduct the initial investment outlay when it is incurred because it is an actual cash flow. Since the capital cost is fully taken into account by deducting the initial investment outlay from the project's cash flow when calculating *NPV*, accounting depreciation should *not* be deducted from the net receipts (*S*); deducting an annual depreciation allowance would *double count* investment costs!

Working Capital

In addition to depreciable assets (buildings, machinery, etc.) the investment in a new project often requires an investment in working capital (cash, inventories, etc.). The treatment of working capital requires special attention. Consider the following hypothetical example:

Let:
I = initial investment outlay
W = investment in working capital
S = annual net receipts
I_n = terminal (salvage) value of the depreciable assets
n = economic duration of the project
The cash flow of such a project can be written as follows:

Year

0	1	2	3 ...	n
$-(I + W)$	S	S	S	$S + I_n + W$

The reader should note that in the last year of the project's expected lifetime, the salvage (market) value of the investment in fixed assets and the total amount of working capital are added back to the cash flow of that year. This reflects the fact that the fixed assets may still have some value at the end of the project and that termination of the project releases the *entire* amount of funds which were previously tied up in working capital.[2]

---

2 An alternative, and fully equivalent, way of handling the investment in working capital would be to exclude working capital from the initial outlay and to charge each year's cash flow with *imputed interest* (kW) using the cost of capital, k. The two methods are equivalent, since the present value of the stream of imputed interest is exactly equal to the difference between W and $W/(1 + k)^n$.

The present value of a stream of annual outlays of kW for n years is given by:

$$-\left[\frac{kW}{1 + k} + \frac{kW}{(1 + k)^2} + \cdots + \frac{kW}{(1 + k)^n}\right] =$$

$$-\left[\frac{kW}{1 + k}\left(1 - \left(\frac{1}{1 + k}\right)^n\right)\middle/ 1 - \frac{1}{1 + k}\right] = -\frac{kW}{k}\left[1 - \frac{1}{(1 + k)^n}\right] = \frac{W}{(1 + k)^n} - W$$

Interest

Unlike accounting depreciation, interest often represents an actual cash outflow. Despite this, interest should *not* be deducted from the annual cash flow, because the discounting process already takes the interest outlay into account. Should interest payments be deducted from the discounted cash flow, the interest charges would be double counted (once in the numerator of the *NPV* equation and again in the denominator) and the project's net present value would be understated.

Opportunity Costs

When estimating the cash flow of a proposed capital investment project, the "opportunity" or "alternative" costs and not just the direct outlay costs, must be taken into consideration. Consider, for example, the case of a firm which is evaluating a project which among other things requires 10,000 cubic feet of cold storage area. Let us further assume that the firm has 20,000 cubic feet of suitable storage space available, only half of which is currently being used for the firm's other products. Under the circumstances, what should be the storage cost (if any) which is assigned to the proposed project? The answer to this question is neither simple nor straightforward. If one adopts the incremental cash flow principle, it would appear, on the surface at least, that storage costs should *not* be charged. Clearly the firm already has the storage space available and therefore no additional cash outflow is incurred. But, suppose the firm can rent this space, say at a net annual rental of $20 per cubic foot. By executing the new project the firm suffers a loss of alternative income of $200,000 per year. In such a case the *opportunity cost* of using the storage space, that is $200,000, should be subtracted from the annual cash inflow of the new project. The problem is even more complicated if we assume, for some reason, that the firm cannot rent the unused storage space to outsiders. Here it would seem that in the absence of an alternative use (recall that only 10,000 cubic feet are currently being used) excess capacity exists whose opportunity cost is zero, and therefore no storage cost should be charged to the new project. However, if we are concerned with a project whose economic life is say ten years, we must, in fact, examine the possible alternative uses for the storage space over the entire ten-year period. If, for example, we expect the "excess capacity" to disappear after the second year due to the expansion of the firm's other activities, the cost of acquiring additional storage space in the third and later years must be charged to the project under consideration. In such a case the storage cost is zero for two years, and positive from the third year onwards.

Similarly, the opportunity cost of using the limited services of key personnel may have to be estimated, especially if their involvement in the new project creates a need to hire additional people elsewhere in the firm. Despite the difficulties involved, a careful analysis of the opportunity costs of transferring existing assets (both human and physical) to the new project must be made in order to ensure that the overall return to the firm as a whole is reflected in our calculations.

EQUIPMENT REPLACEMENT DECISIONS

To this point the cash flow analysis has been applied to conventional type capital budgeting decisions. In this section we extend the discussion to the closely related problem of optimal replacement. Consider a machine which costs $10,000, has a five-year duration, and generates a net cash inflow of $5,000 a year. The firm is faced with the alternative of using the machine for five years, or selling it before the five years are up and replacing it with a new machine. Let us further assume that the market value of the old machine at the end of year t is as follows:

Year	Market Value of Old Machine (I_t)
1	$8,000
2	7,000
3	6,000
4	2,000
5	0

On the basis of the above information the firm seeks to determine the optimal replacement period: but this requires the prior construction of the appropriate cash flow for each alternative course of action. Assuming a discount rate of 10% and that the machine is sold at the end of the first year, the net present value of this alternative (NPV_1) is given by:

$$NPV_1 = (-10,000) + \frac{5,000}{1.1} + \frac{8,000}{1.1} = \$1,817$$

Similarly, if the machine is sold after t years ($t = 2, 3, 4, 5$) the following NPV calculations are generated:

$$NPV_2 = (-10,000) + \frac{5,000}{1.1} + \frac{5,000}{(1.1)^2} + \frac{7,000}{(1.1)^2} = \$4,462$$

$$NPV_3 = (-10,000) + \frac{5,000}{1.1} + \frac{5,000}{(1.1)^2} + \frac{5,000}{(1.1)^3} + \frac{6,000}{(1.1)^3} = \$6,941$$

$$NPV_4 = (-10,000) + \frac{5,000}{1.1} + \frac{5,000}{(1.1)^2} + \frac{5,000}{(1.1)^3} + \frac{5,000}{(1.1)^4} + \frac{2,000}{(1.1)^4} = \$7,216$$

$$NPV_5 = (-10,000) + \frac{5,000}{1.1} + \frac{5,000}{(1.1)^2} + \frac{5,000}{(1.1)^3} + \frac{5,000}{(1.1)^4} + \frac{5,000}{(1.1)^5} = \$8,955$$

The above figures can be misleading. While using the machine for five years yields the highest net present value ($NPV_5 = \$8,955$), this does *not* necessarily mean that the optimal decision is to replace after five years. Since we are seeking the optimal replacement policy, one must compare different policies for *equal economic horizons*. For example, if we want to compare the policy of replacement every two years with the policy of replacement every four years, we must repeat the shorter cash flows for another two-year period if the comparison is to make economic sense. Repeating the two-year replacement option yields the following cash flow:

$$NPV = (-10,000) + \frac{5,000}{1 + k} + \frac{5,000}{(1 + k)^2} + \frac{7,000}{(1 + k)^2} +$$

$$\left[-\frac{10,000}{(1 + k)^2} + \frac{5,000}{(1 + k)^3} + \frac{5,000}{(1 + k)^4} + \frac{7,000}{(1 + k)^4} \right]$$

At a 10% discount rate, the *NPV* of the two-year replacement chain is equal to $8,148:

$$4462 + \frac{4462}{(1.1)^2} = \$8,148$$

which, for example, is preferable to a policy of replacing the machine at the end of four years (*NPV* = $7,216). The crucial point in the above illustration is that in replacement problems one must consider the cash flows of alternative policies over *equal* time periods. Otherwise, the calculation discriminates against short replacement policies. In the above example, one might compare all five alternative replacement policies up to a common horizon of say, sixty years. Thus the policy to replace every year would be repeated sixty times, the policy to replace every two years would be repeated thirty times, and so on.[3]

We also note that the policy of annual replacement, extended to infinity, yields the following cash flow:

$$NPV_1 + \frac{NPV_1}{1 + k} + \frac{NPV_1}{(1 + k)^2} + \ldots = NPV_1 \sum_{t=0}^{\infty} \frac{1}{(1 + k)^t} =$$

$$\frac{NPV_1(1 + k)}{k} = \frac{1,998.7}{0.1} = \$19,987$$

Similarly, the two-year replacement policy extended to infinity yields:[4]

3 Changing the common horizon, say to 120 years, will not affect the ranking of alternatives as long as all alternatives are brought to the new *common* horizon.

4 If one repeats the same investment two years from now, we obtain the same NPV_2 but two years later, and consequently the net present value of the cash flow resulting from the second replacement is only $NPV_2/(1 + k)^2$. Similarly, the net present value of the third replacement (four years from now) is $NPV_2/(1 + k)^4$.

In general if one replaces the machine every *m* years, we get:

$$NPV = NPV_m + \frac{NPV_m}{(1 + k)^m} + \frac{NPV_m}{(1 + k)^{2m}} \ldots = NPV_m \sum_{t=0}^{\infty} \frac{1}{(1 + k)^{tm}}$$

Applying the formula for the summation of a geometric progression:

$$NPV = NPV_m \left| 1 - \frac{1}{(1 + k)^m} \right.$$

$$NPV_2 + \frac{NPV_2}{(1 + k)^2} + \frac{NPV_2}{(1 + k)^4} + \ldots = NPV_2 \sum_{t=0}^{\infty} \frac{1}{(1 + k)^{2t}} =$$

$$NPV_2 / 1 - \frac{1}{(1 + k)^2} = 4,462 \left/ 1 - \frac{1}{(1.1)^2} \right. = \$25,644$$

Applying the same approach, we can readily calculate the net present value for three-, four- and five-year replacement policies as well:

$$NPV_3 = \$27,876$$
$$NPV_4 = \$22,763$$
$$NPV_5 = \$23,628$$

Thus, in our particular example, the optimal policy would be to replace the machine every three years.

PROJECTS WITH UNEQUAL LIVES: THE UNIFORM ANNUITY SERIES (*UAS*)[5]

To this point, optimal replacement policy of equipment has been discussed using a specific case of mutually exclusive projects of unequal duration. For example, replacement of the machinery every two or four years may be considered as two mutually exclusive projects with unequal lives. The correct approach when choosing between such alternatives is simply to repeat the project with the shortest duration until the two alternatives have equal duration, or to repeat both projects to infinity.

Another way to deal with mutually exclusive projects of unequal duration is to find the uniform annual series (*UAS*) of each alternative and then choose the project with the highest *UAS*. The *UAS* is defined as the *annuity* whose present value equals the *NPV* of the investment project in question:

$$NPV = \sum_{t=1}^{n} \frac{UAS}{(1 + k)^t}$$

$$\text{hence, } UAS = NPV \left/ \sum_{t=1}^{n} \frac{1}{(1 + k)^t} \right.$$

Suppose that project A has a net present value of \$200.00 and a duration of 10 years, then assuming a 9% discount rate its *UAS* is \$31.16:

---

5 The reader should be cautioned, once again, that the equalization of time horizons, and the equivalent alternative method of finding the uniform annuity series, are appropriate methods *if, and only if*, the relevant projects can be repeated indefinitely. Clearly, such an assumption may be appropriate for technical problems such as finding the optimal replacement period. However, it is equally clear that it would be a very unrealistic assumption for evaluating the construction of a plant designed to produce a new chemical product, where economic life, due to obsolescence, competition, etc., may be less than a decade.

$$\text{Project A:} \quad \$31.16 = 200 \Bigg/ \sum_{t=1}^{10} \frac{1}{(1.09)^t}$$

$$200 = \sum_{t=1}^{10} \frac{31.16}{(1.09)^t}$$

Similarly, if project B's net present value is assumed to be $100 and its duration is two years, its *UAS* will be $56.85 since:

$$\text{Project B:} \quad 100 = \sum_{t=1}^{2} \frac{56.85}{(1.09)^t}$$

Suppose that the above two projects are mutually exclusive. The two alternatives could be compared, if we assume that replication is an appropriate *assumption* in this instance, by repeating the two-year project five times or by repeating each into infinity. However, there really is no need to compare such replications; the *UAS* approach immediately shows that the shorter alternative is preferable. It yields a cash flow which is equivalent to an annuity of $56.85 and since we are assuming a case in which the projects can be repeated, $56.85 will be received in each year that the project is repeated. The ten-year project has a *UAS* of only $31.16 and hence it is inferior.

The *NPV* of the two-year project is $100 and its *UAS* for two years is a cash flow of $56.85. Since the *same* project can be repeated every two years, each replication creates a *NPV* which is identical to the original, i.e., present value of $100 and a cash flow of $56.85 each year. Hence we obtain an annuity of $56.85. The other project earns a *NPV* of $200 every ten years, but it only has an equivalent equal annual cash flow of $31.16. Thus the project with the shorter duration has a higher *NPV* on a comparable basis, namely for equal durations or when each project is repeated until infinity.

In the preceding section we solved the equipment replacement problem by extending each policy to infinity and calculating the appropriate *NPV* for each replacement policy. In the example in question the optimal policy is three-year replacement. Let us solve the same problem using the *UAS* approach. We have already found that,

$$NPV_1 = \$1,817 \text{ for one-year replacement}$$
$$NPV_2 = \$4,462 \text{ for two-year replacement}$$
$$NPV_3 = \$6,941 \text{ for three-year replacement}$$
$$NPV_4 = \$7,216 \text{ for four-year replacement}$$
$$NPV_5 = \$8,955 \text{ for five-year replacement}$$

Since the assumed cost of capital is 10%, one can readily calculate the *UAS* for each replacement policy and then choose the strategy with the highest *UAS*. Applying the formula for the uniform annuity series:

$$UAS = NPV \bigg/ \sum_{t=1}^{n} \frac{1}{(1 + k)^t}$$

and plugging in the 10% discount rate ($k = 10\%$), we find:

$UAS_1 = 1817 \div 0.909 = 1998.90$ for a one-year replacement policy
$UAS_2 = 4462 \div 1.736 = 2570.28$ for a two-year replacement policy
$UAS_3 = 6941 \div 2.487 = \mathbf{2790.91}$ for a three-year replacement policy
$UAS_4 = 7216 \div 3.170 = 2276.34$ for a four-year replacement policy
$UAS_5 = 8955 \div 3.791 = 2362.17$ for a five-year replacement policy

Here too, the *UAS* approach identifies the optimal policy, i.e. replacement every three years.

Technically, the two equivalent methods (infinite replication or *UAS*) involve the same number of calculations, but the *UAS* approach is for many people the more intuitively appealing of the two. Repeating a project to infinity appears unrealistic; but despite their outward differences it should be recalled that both methods imply the same replication assumption.

SUMMARY

This chapter has examined the incremental principle underlying the definition of the major components of a project's cash flow. Special attention must be paid to the timing of receipts and outlays; and the handling of fixed and variable costs, accounting depreciation, working capital, interest expense and opportunity costs. In general, a project's cash flow should reflect all of the cash flows generated by the investment decision, independent of whether they occur directly in the department in question, or elsewhere in the firm. The chapter concludes with a description of the relevant cash flow for an important class of investment decision – equipment replacement.

QUESTIONS AND PROBLEMS

5.1 The Melany Boat Company builds fishing boats to order. In 1977, the firm examined a proposal for building ten fishing boats for a large client. The receipts and outlays during the project's first year were expected to be $500,000 and $300,000 respectively. The terms of the contract permit the client to pay only 40% of the total receipts in the first year, 30% in the following year and the remainder in the next year. Assume that the cost of capital is 12% and answer the following questions:

(a) Calculate the accounting profit of the project.
(b) Calculate the cash flow profit of the project.

5.2 The Norton Loading Company is considering opening a new loading dock.

In order to do so the company must purchase $280,000 of new equipment. The gross annual receipts are expected to be $250,000, and the annual costs of the new unit are estimated as follows:

Direct labor cost	$65,000
Fuel	50,000
Electricity	17,000
Direct administrative costs	23,000
Fixed overhead expense	26,000
General administrative cost (pro rata share of office expenses)	29,000

In addition, it has been estimated that the company's *net* receipts from its other loading docks will decrease by $25,000 per year when the new loading unit is installed.

(a) Construct the net annual cash flow for the investment in the new loading dock. Explain your calculations.

(b) Assume that the new equipment's economic life is eight years, and a cost of capital of 16%. Is it worthwhile for the firm to open the new loading dock?

5.3 Mr. Jones is offered the opportunity to invest $5,000 with a promise of a return of $5,700 at the end of one year.

"I refused to make this investment", Mr. Jones said. "I had only $1,000 of my own, and for a $4,000 loan which I would have had to take, the bank wanted 10% interest so that my net return would have been only $5,300. Would you be satisfied with a 6% return in these days?" Appraise Mr. Jones's statement.

5.4 When Mr. Milford, the manager of the new computer unit, made his feasibility report on the proposed unit, he didn't charge his own salary. "I am not a new worker in the company", Mr. Milford said. "I used to be the manager of the laboratory, and my deputy there took over my place." Critically appraise Mr. Milford's logic.

5.5 In 1970 the Western Metals Company (WMC) was forced to discontinue operations of its Export Division owing to the closing of the foreign market for its particular product. While it would have been possible to sell limited amounts of the product on the local market, a careful feasibility study showed that such limited production could be carried on only at a loss, even if fixed costs were ignored. As a result of this study, production of the item was completely discontinued.

In 1977 it not only became possible to export the item in question again, but in much larger amounts. In order to permit the expanded scale of production, WMC would have to acquire two additional machines. The cost of the two machines was $400,000 and $300,000, and the machines had expected economic lives of four and five years respectively.

The company's production manager also pointed out that the division's old equipment had been transferred to the Maintenance Department and it would now be necessary to return it to the Export Division. While the book value of the old equipment was zero, the production manager estimated its market value at $150,000. He also stated that when the old equipment is transferred, WMC will have to acquire additional used equipment to replace it in the Maintenance Department. He estimated the cost of this equipment at $200,000. The production manager estimated that the old equipment still had a useful economic life of four years.

The expected receipts of the Export Department from the expanded scale of production were estimated at $600,000 per year.

Annual expenses were estimated as follows:

Raw materials	$40,000
Salaries	60,000
Other expenses	20,000
Fixed expenses of the company (120% of the salaries)	72,000
Straight-line depreciation	160,000
Total	$352,000

Renewed production would also require an additional $500,000 for working capital — principally inventories of raw materials and finished goods.

Assume that the cost of capital (i.e. minimum required rate of return) is 15% and that the company does *not* pay taxes.

Write a report to the President of WMC on the economic feasibility of reopening the Export Division.

5.6 Assume that the duration of a project is ten years (most of the equipment will serve ten years), but that a few machines will last for five years, while the buildings are expected to last for approximately twenty years. How is the cash flow affected by these facts?

5.7 The Pelem Lock Company is using a new lathe which costs $120,000, has six years' duration and generates a net annual cash inflow of $42,000. The firm is faced with the alternative of using the lathe for the next six years or selling it before the six years are up and replacing it with a new lathe.

The finance manager asks you to determine the optimal replacement period for the lathe. You have the following information regarding the market value of the lathe:

End of Year	Market Value of Old Lathe
1	$100,000
2	85,000
3	75,000
4	60,000
5	32,000
6	6,000

Assume a 12% cost of capital and answer the following questions (ignoring corporate taxes):

(a) What is the optimal replacement policy for the firm?

(b) How would your answer to part (a) change if the lathe generated a net annual cash inflow of $60,000?

(c) What would your advice be to the finance manager if the lathe generated a net annual cash inflow of $24,000?

5.8 The United Carpenters Company is using a machine with a life expectancy of five years. The company is considering its replacement, and for this purpose, has gathered the following data:

The purchase price of a new machine (P_0) is $97,000.

The market price of the machine at time t (P_t) and the operating expenses at time t (C_t) are estimated as follows:

Year (t)	Market Value at End of Year (P_t)	Operating Expenses at t (C_t)
1	$70,000	$16,000
2	60,000	20,000
3	50,000	27,000
4	35,000	36,000
5	5,000	42,000

Note: The price for the last year is the salvage value. The operating expenses are calculated gross of depreciation and interest.

Assume that technological changes are not expected and therefore operating expenses and equipment prices will remain constant over time.

Assume also that the cost of capital is 15%, and that there are no taxes.

(a) On the assumption that the company only considers the possibility of purchasing new equipment, what is the optimal replacement policy?

(b) On the assumption that the company also considers the possibility of buying used equipment (machine), what is the optimal replacement policy? (Assume that there are no commissions on buying and selling, and therefore the selling price is equal to the buying price.)

(c) What would be your answer to part (a) if there were no possibility of selling used equipment?

5.9 Answer once again question 5.8 section (b) with the additional assumption that there is a $5,000 cost each time it incurs a transaction. Thus if the machine is sold and another is purchased the firm incurs transaction costs of $10,000. Compare your results with those of 5.8(b). How do you explain the difference? What would be the direction of change in optimal replacement policy if the transaction cost exceeds $5,000?

SELECTED REFERENCES

Becker, S.W., Ronen, J. and Sorter, G.H., "Opportunity Costs — An Experimental Approach", *Journal of Accounting Research*, Autumn 1974.

Chant, P.D., "On the Predictability of Corporate Earnings per Share Behavior", *Journal of Finance*, March 1980.

Dopuch, N. and Sunder, S., "FASB's Statements on Objectives and Elements of Financial Accounting: A Review", *Accounting Review*, January 1980.

Drury, D.H., "Effects of Accounting Practice Divergence: Canada and the United States", *Journal of International Business Studies*, Fall 1979.

Ijiri, Yuji, "An Introduction to Corporate Accounting Standards: A Review", *Accounting Review*, October 1980.

Livnat, J., Ronen, J. and Swirski, M., "Disaggregation of Deviations in Cost Analysis", *OMEGA, The International Journal of Management*, Vol. 9, No. 1. 1981.

Winsen, J. and Ng, D., "Investor Behavior and Changes in Accounting Methods", *Journal of Financial and Quantitative Analysis*, December 1976.

6

Impact of Corporate Income Taxes on Projects' Cash Flows

In the previous chapter we argued that investment decisions should be based on the cash flows emanating from the proposal. Accounting conventions, for example those affecting the allocation of depreciation expense over time, were ignored. However, the accounting treatment of individual cost items does influence the measurement and timing of net income and therefore the amount and timing of corporate income tax payments as well. In that hypothetical and incidentally very happy world in which no taxes are levied, the investment decision would not be influenced by the method of accounting used to evaluate revenue and expenses. But as neither death nor taxes can be avoided — at least not for long — the accounting treatment used for computing the tax burden must be considered if the cash flow is to be accurately estimated. This is especially necessary, since, as we shall see below, corporate income taxes do *not* affect all investments in the same manner and therefore the cash flows must be expressed on an after-tax basis if meaningful comparisons are to be made.

FORMAL TREATMENT OF TAXES

Corporate taxes are a real outflow and must be taken into account when evaluating a project's desirability. Suppose, for simplicity, that the tax rate is $T\%$; the annual cash flow before deducting interest and depreciation is S, and the annual depreciation allowance is D. As we mentioned earlier, depreciation is not an actual outflow and should not be subtracted from the annual cash flow. However, the fact that depreciation is tax-deductible does decrease the tax burden and therefore must be considered when calculating the after-tax annual cash flow. Hence, in order to estimate the corporate tax we first calculate the net income by subtracting D from S, and then the amount of tax, $T(S-D)$, is deducted from the pre-tax cash flow. However, as we subtract D solely in order

114

to calculate the corporate tax burden we add it back, thereby deriving the *after-tax cash flow*:[1]

$$(1 - T)(S - D) + D$$

It is often convenient to use an alternative version of the post-tax cash flow:

$$(1 - T)(S - D) + D = (1 - T)S + TD$$

Note that the annual pre-tax cash flows, as well as the annual depreciation allowances, are not necessarily constant. In general, the pre-tax and post-tax net present values are calculated using the following two formulas:

$$NPV_{BT} = \sum_{t=1}^{n} \frac{S_t}{(1 + k)^t} - I$$

$$NPV_{AT} = \sum_{t=1}^{n} \frac{(1 - T)S_t}{(1 + k^*)^t} + \sum_{t=1}^{n} \frac{TD_t}{(1 + r)^t} - I$$

where:

k	= the before-tax discount rate
k^*	= the after-tax discount rate
r	= the pre-tax riskless interest rate
D_t	= the depreciation allowance in year t
I	= the initial outlay
n	= the proposal's duration
NPV_{BT}	= the proposal's net present value, before taxes
NPV_{AT}	= the proposal's net present value, after taxes

The only peculiarity of the after-tax formula is the fact that the *tax shelter, TD*, is discounted at the pre-tax riskless interest rate, r, rather than the after-tax cost of capital k^*. The tax benefit of deducting depreciation is essentially *certain*, and can be used to reduce the corporate tax burden even in a year in which no taxable profits are earned.[2]

The use of the pre-tax interest rate reflects the fact that the relevant alternative facing the investor in the case of riskless income streams would be the *direct* purchase of riskless bonds, thereby avoiding the corporate tax rate. Clearly

---

1 Interest, like depreciation, is also tax-deductible. However, instead of adjusting the cash flow, we prefer to adopt an alternative procedure and adjust the discount rate. For example, suppose that the interest rate is $r\%$. The after-tax interest rate is only $(1 - T)r$ since T is the government's participation in the interest bill, due to its willingness to recognize interest as a tax deduction. This in turn lowers the post-tax discount rate (see Part III below). Thus the tax-deductibility of interest is reflected in the denominator of the NPV formula via the discount rate rather than in the cash flow of the numerator.

2 In such a case the tax benefits can still be realized through the provision of the US internal revenue code which permits losses to be offset against past or future income. For further details regarding the definition and measurement of the cost of capital see Chapters 17 and 18 below.

this argument does not hold for risky returns; in such a case the relevant alternative is to invest indirectly via shares in a business enterprise, thereby incurring the corporate tax.

As we have just seen, the firm should separate the risky cash flow S_t from the depreciation tax shelter (TD_t) which for all practical purposes can be considered an almost certain cashflow; each component, in turn, should be discounted at the appropriate post-tax or pre-tax discount rate. However, in practice many firms apply a single discount rate to the entire cashflow. Of course most executives are aware that the greater a project's depreciation tax shelter, the lower should be the discount rate, but they are deterred by the apparent complexity of the theoretically correct approach which requires the application of different discount rates to the various components of the cashflow.

In principle, the use of a single-valued discount rate does *not* preclude the firm from reaching the theoretically correct investment decision. Thus before you fire the firm's financial manager you may wish to ponder the following example. Consider a project with the characteristics:

$S_t = 400$, $T = 0.50$, $I = 1000$
$n = 10$
$k^* = 10\%$ and $r = 5\%$
$D_t = 100$, using (straight-line) depreciation

Applying the theoretically correct formula, the project's *NPV* is **615.10**:

$$NPV = \sum_{t=1}^{10} \frac{(1-T)S_t}{(1+k^*)^t} + \sum_{t=1}^{10} \frac{TD_t}{(1+r)^t} - I$$

$$= \sum_{t=1}^{10} \frac{200}{(1.1)^t} + \sum_{t=1}^{10} \frac{50}{(1.05)^t} - 1,000$$

$$= 200\,(6.145) + 50\,(7.722) - 1,000$$
$$= 1229 + 386.1 - 1,000 = \mathbf{615.10}$$

Note, however, that the firm could have obtained the same *NPV* by applying a single rate to the entire annual cashflow $(1-T)S_t + TD_t$. In our specific example the annual cashflow is 250:

$$(1-T)\,S_t + TD_t = 0.5\,(400) + 0.5\,(100) = 250$$

and the single-valued discount rate which equates the *NPV*s is approximately 8.85%:

$$\sum_{t=1}^{10} \frac{250}{(1+k)^t} - 1,000 = 615.10$$

From the present value tables in the appendix we find that the critical value of k lies between 8% and 9%.[3]

THE MAKE OR BUY DECISION

Now let's consider a concrete example in which the use of multiple discount rates to reflect the depreciation tax shelter can be very helpful to the decision-maker.

Almost every firm at one time or another has been confronted by the problem of choosing between the production or purchase of the component parts of its final product. Of course some companies produce all of their components themselves, but many, and perhaps most, do purchase part of their components from outside suppliers.

The decision to *make* or *buy* a given component depends on many factors. For example, should the firm decide to purchase the parts from an outside supplier, it must weigh the risk of delay in their delivery. If the market for the particular component is competitive, and there are many suppliers, this risk may be negligible. However, if there is only a limited number of suppliers, the risk of non-delivery or delay, and the subsequent financial loss to the firm, may be substantial. Similarly, considerations of quality control or even secrecy may preclude the firm from utilizing the services of an outside supplier even when the profitability calculation indicates that this is the preferred alternative. On the other hand, patents, lack of know-how or other technological and legal barriers may preclude a firm from producing the component.

In this section attention is focused on the quantitative analysis of the very large and important subset of decisions in which *both* the make and buy alternatives are technically feasible. Under these circumstances make or buy decisions, like any investment, should be based on the present values of the cash flows generated by the two alternatives.

In the absence of taxes, the solution to this problem is straightforward; the introduction of taxes, however, complicates the analysis and great care must be taken if the present values are to be expressed correctly on an after-tax basis.

As a first step in the present value analysis we define the annual after-tax cash flow generated by the decision to produce rather than purchase a particular component.

Let:
T = the corporate tax rate
P = the per unit purchase price from an outside supplier
C = the production cost per unit in the firm (excluding interest and depreciation)
Q = the number of units that the firm requires per year
I = investment outlay for production equipment
D = the annual depreciation allowance

3 The exact value of k is 8.85%, but needless to add, in practice one would expect a *rule-of-thumb* downward adjustment of the discount rate to account for the impact of the tax shelter.

Clearly, the annual cash flow involves the comparison of the per unit purchase price (P) with the per unit production cost (C) multiplied by the estimated number of units required (Q). And to be relevant, the comparison must be effected on an *after-tax* basis. In the production alternative, moreover, the depreciation of equipment is also tax-deductible; hence it must be deducted when calculating the tax burden. For simplicity, we shall assume straight-line, i.e. equal annual, depreciation; however, as we subtract depreciation solely in order to calculate the corporate tax bill we subsequently add it back, thereby deriving the after-tax cash flow for the make rather than buy alternative:

$$(1 - T)[(P - C)Q - D] + D = (1 - T)(P - C)Q + TD$$

In order to decide which alternative course of action is preferable, we next calculate the present value of the annual cash flow saving and then subtract the initial investment outlay (I) required for the production equipment. The magnitude of the post-tax saving is uncertain because the quantities needed (Q) are uncertain and therefore should be discounted using the appropriate[4] after-tax discount rate, k. However, as we have already noted, the tax shield (TD) is essentially certain, independent of the firm's income; hence the tax shield should be discounted at the pre-tax *riskless* interest rate (r), i.e. at a rate below k.

It follows that a firm should make rather than buy a component if the net present value of the cost saving is positive:

$$NPV(m) = \sum_{t=1}^{n} \frac{(1 - T)(P - C)Q}{(1 + k^*)^t} + \sum_{t=1}^{n} \frac{TD}{(1 + r)^t} - I$$

where:
$NPV(m)$ = the net present value of the decision to make rather than buy and
          P, C, Q, T, D and I are defined as before
n = the economic life of the equipment which for simplicity we assume
          to be equal to its accounting life
k^* = the firm's after-tax discount rate
r = the riskless interest rate

If the net present value of making the component is positive ($NPV(m) > 0$), the firm should produce the part in question; however, if the net present value of producing the component is negative ($NPV(m) < 0$), the part should be purchased from the outside supplier.[5]

The *NPV* formula shows that the make or buy decision depends on a number of factors: the spread between the per unit purchase price and manufacturing cost ($P - C$), the quantity required (Q), the discount rates (r and k^*) and the initial investment outlay (I). The degree of dependence of the make or

---

4 Risk-adjusted discount rates are discussed in detail in Part II below. The concept of a weighted-average cost of capital is introduced in Chapters 17 and 18 below.
5 The reader should note that this formula assumes that the components must be acquired in one way or another. Hence we are only checking to find the least expensive manner in which they can be obtained.

buy decision on these factors can be made more transparent by considering a specific numerical example.

Let:

I	$=$	$200,000
P	$=$	$9
C	$=$	$5
n	$=$	10 years
D	$=$	$I/n = $20,000
k^*	$=$	10%
r	$=$	5%
T	$=$	50%

Plugging these values into the $NPV(m)$ formula we find that the investment outlay *less* the present value of the tax shield is $122,780:

$$I - \sum_{t=1}^{n} \frac{TD}{(1 + r)^t} = 200,000 - 10,000 \sum_{t=1}^{10} \frac{1}{(1 + .05)^t} = 122,780$$

But before deciding whether to buy or make the component the firm must first identify another factor, i.e. the estimated quantity required (Q) each year. The crucial role in the decision played by this factor can be seen by examining Table 6.1 which sets out the net present value of manufacturing the component for various assumptions regarding the quantity of parts required. For example, if the firm requires 5,000 units per year the annual pre-tax saving will be $20,000 (5,000 units times $4, the spread between the purchase price and the per unit manufacturing cost). On an after-tax basis, the annual saving is half this amount, that is $10,000. Over a ten-year period, the present value of the post-tax saving equals $61,450. However, the saving can only be obtained at a net cost of $122,780 (the initial outlay on the equipment *less* the tax shield). The present

Table 6.1
Net Present Value of Producing the Component

Annual Quantity Required (Q)	Annual Pre-tax Saving (P − C) Q	Annual Post-tax Saving (1 − T)(P − C) Q	Present Value of Post-tax Saving*	Net Present Value of Post-tax Saving†
5,000	20,000	10,000	61,450	− 61,330
7,500	30,000	15,000	92,175	− 30,605
9,990	**39,960**	**19,980**	**122,777**	**~0**
10,000	40,000	20,000	122,900	+ 120
12,500	50,000	25,000	153,625	+ 30,845
15,000	60,000	30,000	184,350	+ 61,570

*Cost of capital = 10%.
†After deducting the initial investment outlay *less* the PV of the tax shield, that is $122,780.

value of producing the parts is negative $(61,450 - 122,780 = -61,330)$ when 5,000 units are required, and the components should be purchased from the outside supplier. An examination of Table 6.1 shows that up to an annual requirement of 9,990 units, the purchase option is preferable; beyond that quantity it pays to acquire the equipment and produce the components.

Now let us examine a situation in which the firm is considering buying more expensive production equipment. This equipment involves a more substantial investment, say $300,000, but it is also more efficient. The components can be produced at a per unit cost of only $3 which means a saving of $6 per unit relative to the purchase price of $9. The relevant present value calculations[6] for this case are given in Table 6.2.

Table 6.2
Net Present Value of Producing the Component, Using Expensive Equipment

Annual Quantity Required (Q)	Annual Pre-tax Saving $(P - C) Q$	Annual Post-tax Saving $(1 - T) (P - C) Q$	Present Value of Post-tax Saving*	Net Present Value of Post-tax Saving†
5,000	30,000	15,000	92,175	− 91,995
7,500	45,000	22,500	138,263	− 45,907
9,990	**59,940**	**29,970**	**184,165**	**~0**
10,000	60,000	30,000	184,350	+ 180
12,500	75,000	37,500	230,438	+ 46,268
15,000	90,000	45,000	276,525	+ 92,355

*Cost of capital = 10%.
†After deducting the initial investment outlay *less* the PV of the tax shield, that is $184,170.

The example given in Table 6.2 has been constructed in a manner which preserves the 9,990 unit break-even point. Now which equipment should the firm acquire? In a hypothetical world of perfect certainty the answer to this question is straightforward. For example, if we can be *absolutely certain* that the firm will require 12,500 units per year during the next ten years, the net present value using the less expensive production equipment is only $30,845 (see Table 6.1) while the *NPV* using the more expensive equipment is $46,268 (see Table 6.2). Clearly, in such a case the more expensive machinery should be acquired. In the real world, however, the firm cannot be absolutely certain regarding its future needs. Suppose that its best estimate of the annual requirement is 9,990 units, but that substantial deviations from this figure are possible. In this instance which equipment should be acquired? Taking into account the basic uncertainty regarding the future need for the component, it is apparent

6 In this instance the annual depreciation allowance is $15,000 and the present value of the tax shield at a 5% discount rate equals $115,830 ($15,000 \times 7.722 = $115,830$). The present value of the investment outlay *less* the present value of the tax shield equals $184,170 ($300,000 − 115,830 = $184,170$).

that the more expensive equipment constitutes the more risky choice. Although it is true that such equipment will provide a larger profit if the firm should need relatively large quantities of the component in the future, it also induces a greater loss should the firm's future requirements prove to be more modest.

This contention is illustrated in Fig. 6.1 which graphs the *NPV* as a function of the annual quantities required for each of the two alternatives. The line denoted as A represents the less expensive machinery. As can be seen, line B is considerably steeper which means that any given change in the quantity required (*Q*), induces a relatively large shift in net present value.

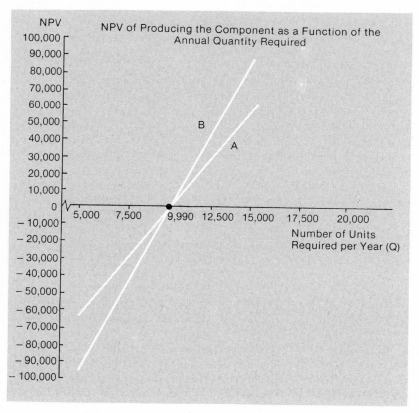

Fig. 6.1

Now let's examine the sensitivity of the make or buy decision to a change in the cost of capital. Tables 6.3 and 6.4 repeat the calculations of the net present value of producing the component with one change: in the two latter tables we assume that the cost of capital is 20% instead of 10% as had been assumed previously. The reader should note that this does *not* change the value of the investment outlay less the present value of the tax shield, since the tax shelter is still discounted at the 5% interest rate.

As might have been expected, the increase in the cost of capital has a negative

Table 6.3

Net Present Value of Producing the Component Using Less Expensive Equipment

Annual Quantity (Q)	Annual Pre-tax Saving (P − C) Q	Post-tax Saving (1 − T) (P − C) Q	Present Value of Post-tax Saving*	Net Present Value of Post-tax Saving†
7,500	30,000	15,000	62,880	− 59,900
10,000	40,000	20,000	83,840	− 38,940
14,645	**58,580**	**29,290**	**122,784**	**~0**
15,000	60,000	30,000	125,760	+ 2,980
17,500	70,000	35,000	146,720	+ 23,940
20,000	80,000	40,000	167,680	+ 44,900

*Cost of capital = 20%
†After deducting the initial investment outlay *less* the PV of the tax shield, that is, $122,780.

Table 6.4

Net Present Value of Producing the Component Using More Expensive Equipment

Annual Quantity (Q)	Annual Pre-tax Saving (P − C) Q	Annual Post-tax Saving (1 − T) (P − C) Q	Present Value of Post-tax Saving*	Net Present Value of Post-tax Saving†
7,500	45,000	22,500	94,320	− 89,850
10,000	60,000	30,000	125,760	− 58,410
14,645	**87,870**	**43,935**	**184,176**	**~0**
15,000	90,000	45,000	188,640	+ 4,470
17,500	105,000	52,500	220,080	+ 35,910
20,000	120,000	60,000	251,520	+ 67,350

*Cost of capital = 20%
†After deducting the initial outlay *less* the PV of the tax shield, that is, $184,170.

impact on the production alternative — the break-even quantity rises from 9,990 units to 14,645 units. For annual requirements below 14,645 it now pays the firm to purchase rather than produce the components. On the other hand, the acquisition of the more expensive equipment (Table 6.4) remains the riskier of the two options; any given fluctuation in the quantity required induces a larger change in *NPV* if the more expensive equipment is used.

TAXES AND THE OPTIMAL METHOD OF DEPRECIATION

The annual depreciation allowance depends on the depreciation method employed as well as on the proposal's duration. The Internal Revenue Service establishes for various classes of assets the minimum number of years to be used in calculating depreciation for tax purposes. Firms are permitted to use one of several depreciation methods and we shall discuss below the relative merits of using each of these methods.

Clearly, a firm should, for tax purposes, try to depreciate its assets in the shortest possible period, since by so doing it will enjoy the tax benefits at an earlier date. To avoid any misunderstanding the reader should note that the particular depreciation method chosen does *not* affect the actual economic depreciation of the assets, that is it neither lengthens or shortens the asset's useful economic duration.

Several alternative depreciation methods are available:

Straight Line Method (SL)

Assume that a proposal's duration is n years, and that the original cost of the asset is I. The annual depreciation allowance using the *straight line* method is given by the formula $D = I/n$.

Double Declining Balance Method (DDB)

DDB is one of many ways of accelerating the depreciation allowance. By this method, the firm is permitted to depreciate more than I/n in the first years of an asset's lifetime, but less than I/n in later years. For the years $t = 1, 2, \ldots n-1$, the *DDB* depreciation allowance is calculated using the following formula:

$$D_t = \frac{2}{n}\left(I - \sum_{i=1}^{t} D_{i-1}\right)$$

Clearly, $D_O = 0$ by definition.

The depreciation allowance in the *nth* year is given by the formula:

$$D_n = I - \sum_{t=1}^{n-1} D_t$$

A numerical example can help to clarify the logic of this method. Assume that $n = 4$ and $I = \$10,000$. Using the *DDB* formula the annual depreciation allowance in the first year is given by

$$D_1 = \frac{2}{4}(10,000 - D_0) = \frac{2}{4}(10,000 - 0) = \$5,000$$

Similarly, for years 2, 3 and 4 the annual depreciation allowances are:

$$D_2 = \frac{2}{4}(10,000 - 5,000) = \frac{2}{4}\,5,000 = \$2,500$$

$$D_3 = \frac{2}{4}\left[10,000 - (5,000 + 2,500)\right] = \frac{2}{4}\,2,500 = \$1,250$$

$$D_4 = I_0 - \sum_{t=1}^{3} D_t = 10,000 - 8,750 = \$1,250$$

Thus the depreciation allowance in the first year is double the *straight line* depreciation $\left(D_1 = \frac{2}{n} I\right)$, and in succeeding years (apart from the last year) the allowance is $\frac{2}{n}$ times the undepreciated balance. The depreciation allowance in the last year is of course the residual value which has not been depreciated in the previous $n-1$ years.

Sum of the Year's Digits Method (*SYD*)

Another method of accelerated depreciation is the *Sum of the Year's Digits* (*SYD*). Using this approach we derive the following schedule of annual depreciation allowances:

$$D_1 = \frac{n}{(SYD)}\,I$$

$$D_2 = \frac{n-1}{(SYD)}\,I$$

$$D_3 = \frac{n-2}{(SYD)}\,I$$

$$\begin{array}{cc} \cdot & \cdot \\ \cdot & \cdot \\ \cdot & \cdot \end{array}$$

$$D_n = \frac{1}{(SYD)}\,I$$

where n denotes the asset's duration and SYD is the sum of all the year's digits corresponding to that duration:

$$SYD = n+(n-1)+(n-2) \ldots +1 = \frac{n(n+1)}{2}$$

Again, a specific numerical example can help clarify this method. Consider the previously mentioned project in which $n = 4$ years and $I = \$10,000$.

The sum of the year's digits is given by:

$$SYD = 4+3+2+1 = \frac{4 \cdot 5}{2} = 10$$

The depreciation allowance in the first year equals $\frac{4}{10} \cdot 10{,}000 = \$4{,}000$

For years 2, 3 and 4 the annual depreciation allowances are:

$$D_2 = \frac{3}{10} \cdot 10{,}000 = \$3{,}000$$

$$D_3 = \frac{2}{10} \cdot 10{,}000 = \$2{,}000$$

$$D_4 = \frac{1}{10} \cdot 10{,}000 = \$1{,}000$$

CHOOSING THE OPTIMAL DEPRECIATION METHOD

Now let us rewrite the after-tax *NPV* of a project as follows:

$$NPV_{AT} = \sum_{t=1}^{n} \frac{(1 - T)S_t}{(1 + k^*)^t} + \sum_{t=1}^{n} \frac{TD_t}{(1 + r)^t}$$

$$= \sum_{t=1}^{n} \frac{(1 - T)S_t}{(1 + k^*)^t} + T \sum_{t=1}^{n} \frac{D_t}{(1 + r)^t}$$

The first term is not affected by the depreciation method used; consequently, the firm should choose that method of depreciation which maximizes the second term,

$$T \sum_{t=1}^{n} \frac{D_t}{(1 + r)^t}$$

Hence, for a given corporate tax rate T, the optimal depreciation method depends on a proposal's duration, n, and the riskless interest rate.

For example, let us consider a project with the following characteristics:

$$S = \$500$$
$$I = \$1{,}000$$
$$n = 4 \text{ years}$$
$$T = 50\%$$

In order to find the optimal depreciation method we have calculated in Table 6.5 the depreciation schedule for the above project using three alternative depreciation methods. Note that no matter which method is employed, the *total* depreciation allowance remains $1,000. Thus by switching from one depreciation method to another one can only change the time-pattern, but not the total amount, of the depreciation allowance.

Table 6.5
Annual Depreciation Allowances Using Three Alternative Methods

Year	Straight Line SL	Double Declining Balance DDB	Sum of Year's Digits SYD
1	250	500	400
2	250	250	300
3	250	125	200
4	250	125	100
Total Depreciation	1,000	1,000	1,000

Assuming a 50% corporate tax rate, the *NPV* of the tax benefits stemming from the tax deductibility of the depreciation allowance can readily be calculated using the formula

$$T \sum_{t=1}^{n} \frac{D_t}{(1 + r)^t}$$

In our numerical example, we find that the Double Declining Balance method (*DDB*) is the optimal method of depreciation for this special case; for all relevant discount rates it yields the highest present value. This result is summarized in Fig. 6.2. Note that at zero or infinite discount rates the three methods

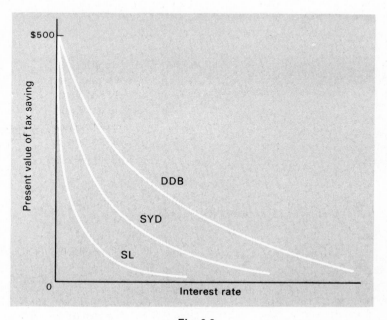

Fig. 6.2

yield the same present values; however, for all other positive discount rates the depreciation methods can be ranked in the following order: *DDB*, *SYD*, and lastly *SL*.

One should not argue from this one specific example that the *DDB* method is always preferable. For example, a situation such as that described in Fig. 6.3 may arise, that is to say for interest rates below r_0, the *DDB* is the optimal method, while for discount rates greater than r_0 the *SYD* method is preferable.[7]

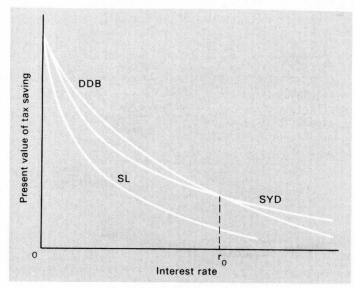

Fig. 6.3

A slight complication arises when salvage values are considered. Assume that a machine whose initial cost is $10,000 is to be depreciated over a ten-year period, but that the machine has an expected salvage value of $1,000 at the end of the tenth year. In this case the total depreciable value is $9,000 rather than $10,000. Assuming straight-line depreciation, the annual depreciation charge is $900 and not $1,000. However, in the tenth year one has to add the estimated salvage value ($1,000) to the cash flow. A similar adjustment can easily be made in the accelerated depreciation formulas as well.

The firm does not have to use complicated formulas to calculate the present value of the depreciation charges for each specific project. Tables which give the present value of depreciation charges for $1 of assets are available for all relevant depreciation periods and discount rates. By using the relevant tables for *DDB* and *SYD* the firm can easily choose the method of depreciation which is optimal for its projects. (See Appendix Tables at the end of the book.)

---

7 For such a situation to arise, project durations must be greater than (or equal to) six years. For the impact of inflation on the choice of optimal depreciation method, see Appendix 6B at the end of this chapter.

INVESTMENT TAX CREDIT

Another complication which must be considered when evaluating the tax impact on a project's desirability stems from the governmental policy designed to encourage capital investment. Recently, the government has allowed many corporations to deduct (for tax purposes) 10% of the initial cost of qualified investments.[8]

In order to measure the impact of the 10% tax credit on a project's profitability, let us first write the project's internal rate of return after taxes but before the tax credit:

$$I = \sum_{t=1}^{n} \frac{(1 - T)S + TD}{(1 + R^*)^t} = \sum_{t=1}^{n} \frac{(1 - T)S + T \cdot I/n}{(1 + R^*)^t}$$

where $D = I/n$, i.e. we assume straight-line depreciation. The project's internal rate of return, taking the tax credit into account, is given by R_1^*, which by definition, is higher than R^*,

$$0.90I = \sum_{t=1}^{n} \frac{(1 - T)S + T \cdot 0.90I/n}{(1 + R_1^*)^t}$$

The reader should note that the Internal Revenue Service permits the firm to calculate depreciation only on 90% of the initial investment, I, since this is its *net* investment once the tax credit is taken into account.

From time to time the tax credit has been changed. Thus for example in 1964 the tax regulations were amended to allow firms to deduct the full amount of I for depreciation purposes, which of course effectively increased the firm's tax benefit. In such a case the project's "post-tax credit" internal rate of return is given by R_2^*,

$$0.90I = \sum_{t=1}^{n} \frac{(1 - T)S + TI/n}{(1 + R_2^*)^t}$$

Clearly, $R_2 > R_1 > R$. Similarly the percentage tax credit allowed has fluctuated over time and, depending on economic conditions, has been cancelled altogether

---

8 The tax credit granted depends on the project's duration. For example, if we assume a tax credit of 10%, an initial investment outlay of $1000, and the proposal's duration, n, is greater or equal to seven years, the full 10% credit of $100 is allowed. Hence, in such cases the firm's *net* investment outlay, is only $900. However, for project durations of five or six years ($5 \leqslant n < 7$), only two-thirds of the 10% credit is allowed. In this instance the tax credit is only $66.60. Only one-third of the tax credit is taken into account if the project duration is 3 or 4 years; and no tax credit at all is granted for projects with a duration of less than three years.

in some periods. For example, in 1971 the tax credit was raised temporarily from 7% to 10%.

The actual impact of the tax credit on the profitability of capital investment projects is quantified in Table 6.6 which shows the *post*-tax credit rates of return for projects with varying *pre*-tax credit rates of return and durations. (The calculations assume a 10% tax credit and that the entire gross investment can be depreciated.) As the Table shows, we assume that no tax credit is granted to projects of less than three years' duration, so that the before and after tax-credit rates of return are the same. The figures also show that the impact of the tax credit is proportionately greater for projects of relatively low pre-incentives profitability and for medium rather than long-term proposals.

Table 6.6
Post-Tax Credit Rates of Return for Alternative Pre-Tax Credit Rates of Return and Project Durations*
(%)

Project Duration (in years)	Pre-tax Credit IRR			
	6.00	8.00	10.00	20.00
2	6.00	8.00	10.00	20.00
3	7.85	9.90	11.95	22.19
5	8.59	10.67	12.76	23.21
7	9.05	11.17	13.30	23.98
15	7.66	9.78	11.91	22.65
25	7.14	9.28	11.42	22.31

*Assuming a 10% investment tax credit and that the entire gross investment can be depreciated for tax purposes.

Let's illustrate now exactly how the numbers of Table 6.6 are calculated. Consider, for example, a project with a duration of three years ($n = 3$) and an *IRR*, before any tax credit, of six percent ($R = 6\%$). For convenience, and with no loss of generality we assume an initial investment outlay of one hundred dollars ($I = 100$). Let's denote the annual cash receipt by S and assume straight-line depreciation, $TI/3$ is the depreciation tax shelter for this case. Hence, by definition, the following equality must hold:

$$I = 100 = \sum_{t=1}^{3} \frac{(1 - T)S + (TI/3)}{(1 + .06)^t}$$

or equivalently

$$100 = \left[(1 - T)S + \frac{TI}{3} \right] \cdot \sum_{t=1}^{3} \frac{1}{(1 + .06)^t}$$

From Appendix Table B, we find the value of $\sum\limits_{t=1}^{3} \dfrac{1}{(1 + .06)^t}$ is 2.673. Using this value we can solve for the annual cash flow:

$$(1 - T)S + \frac{TI}{3} = \frac{100}{2.673} = 37.41.$$

Since the project's duration is three years only one-third of the $10 tax credit is received (see footnote 8). Hence, the initial investment outlay after deducting the tax credit is $96.67 (i.e., $100 - \frac{1}{3} \cdot 10$). The post-tax credit *IRR* which appears in line two column two of Table 6.6 is the rate of discount, *R*, which equates:

$$96.67 = \frac{37.41}{(1 + R)} + \frac{37.41}{(1 + R)^2} + \frac{37.41}{(1 + R)^3}$$

By trial and error, and with the aid of a pocket calculator, we find *R* to be 7.85%. Using this method all of the rates of return of Table 6.6 were generated; care being taken to reflect in the calculations only the relevant portion of the tax credit for short-lived projects.

INFLATION AND THE DEPRECIATION TAX SHELTER[9]

As we have already noted a project's after-tax cashflow in any year t is given by: $(1 - T)S_t + TD_t$, where TD_t is the depreciation tax shelter. A project's net present value is given by:

$$NPV = \sum_{t=1}^{n} \frac{(1 - T)S_t}{(1 + k^*)^t} + \sum_{t=1}^{n} \frac{TD_t}{(1 - r)^t} - I$$

Since the first term on the right-hand side and the investment outlay, *I*, do not vary with a change in the method of calculating depreciation, the firm should select that method which minimizes the second term, that is the present value of the depreciation tax shield.

In the absence of inflation the present value of the tax shelter from depreciation is given by

$$PV(TD) = \sum_{t=1}^{n} \frac{TD_t}{(1 + r)^t}$$

Since depreciation allowances are based on historical cost, the present value of

9 For further details see Yoram Landskroner and Haim Levy, "Inflation, Depreciation and Optimal Production", *European Economic Review* (October, 1979); and Moshe Ben-Horim and Haim Levy, "Financial Management in an Inflationary Environment", *Financial Handbook*, 5th Edition, New York: Wiley, forthcoming.

the tax shield, $PV(TD)$, does not vary with inflation. However, the present value of the tax shield in *real* terms (i.e. in dollars of constant purchasing power) will fall in an inflationary environment. To be more specific, given an inflation rate of $h\%$ per year, the present value of the depreciation tax shelter in *constant* dollars, reduces to:[10]

$$PV(TD,h) = \sum_{t=1}^{n} \frac{TD_t/(1 + h)^t}{(1 + r)^t} \Bigg| = \sum_{t=1}^{n} \frac{TD_t}{(1 + r)^t(1 + h)^t}$$

Note that the *nominal* depreciation tax shield in year t remains TD_t, but as we now assume that prices are rising at an annual rate of $h\%$, the undiscounted value of the depreciation tax shield in real terms (constant dollars) becomes $TD_t/(1 + h)^t$, and its present value, after discounting at the *real* riskless interest rate[11] r, is $\dfrac{TD_t}{(1 + h)^t (1 + r)^t}$. Since this relationship holds for all years ($t = 1, 2, \ldots, n$) we can easily show that for $h > 0$, $PV(TD,h) < PV(TD)$, that is, inflation, other things being equal, reduces the real present value of the depreciation tax shield.

Thus in the absence of inflation if a project's economic duration is n years and the firm uses straight-line depreciation, the present value of the depreciation tax shield, in *real* terms, is given by

$$PV_{SL}(TD) = \sum_{t=1}^{n} \frac{TD}{(1 + r)^t}$$

where SL denotes straight-line depreciation. If we now assume an inflation rate of $h\%$ per year, the real present value of the tax shelter, as above, is given by:

$$PV_{SL}(TD,h) = \sum_{t=1}^{n} \frac{TD}{(1 + h)^t (1 + r)^t}$$

The accelerated depreciation methods discussed earlier in the chapter (SYD and DDB) were introduced in the United States (and other countries) for the purpose of stimulating growth. However, as we have seen, the impact of inflation, *per se*, decreases projects' net present values, thereby discouraging new investment. Thus during periods of high inflation more tax stimuli are required to induce a given increase in investment. In the case of accelerated depreciation that part of the negative impact of inflation on investment which stems from the legal convention that depreciation for tax purposes can only be based on

---

10 For the economic logic underlying the calculation in *real* terms, see Chapter 22 below.

11 We previously used r to denote the rate of interest, in the absence of inflation. This is equivalent to the *real* rate since in that case the real and nominal rates are identical.

historical rather than replacement cost, will be fully offset only if the following inequality holds:

$$PV_{AM}(TD,h) = \sum_{t=1}^{n} \frac{TD_t}{(1 + r)^t (1 + h)^t} \geq PV_{SL}(TD) = \sum_{t=1}^{n} \frac{TD_t}{(1 + r)^t}$$

where *AM* denotes an accelerated depreciation method. In other words we require that the present value of the depreciation tax shelter in real terms must be no smaller than the present value of the straight-line depreciation tax shield in the absence of inflation. If the real present value of the tax shield with accelerated amortization is less than its value with straight-line depreciation and *no* inflation, the firm is undercompensated. Alternatively, these relationships can be summarized as follows:

$PV_{AM}(TD_t,h) \div PV_{SL}(TD_t) > 1$ implies overcompensation for inflation.

$PV_{AM}(TD_t,h) \div PV_{SL}(TD_t) < 1$ implies undercompensation for inflation.

$PV_{AM}(TD_t,h) \div PV_{SL}(TD_t) = 1$ implies exact compensation for inflation.

The British Experience

The British economy has suffered a much higher rate of inflation than the US. Hence, the depreciation tax shield in the United Kingdom has diminished dramatically in real terms, and industrial firms have reduced their investment expenditures. In order to encourage investment, the Heath government introduced in 1972 a 100% first-year depreciation allowance on investment in new plant and equipment. Thus, for an initial investment outlay of *I*, the present values of the depreciation tax shield, in the absence of inflation, and before the special provision, was given by

$$PV_{SL}(TD) = \sum_{t=1}^{n} \frac{TD_t}{(1 + r)^t}$$

Under the Heath government's provision, and assuming an inflation rate of $h\%$, the real present value of the tax shield becomes:

$$PV_{UK}(TD,h) = \frac{TI}{(1 + r)(1 + h)} = \frac{TnD}{(1 + r)(1 + h)}$$

where UK denotes the special case of the United Kingdom. Note that the firm depreciates all of the investment in the first year, and as the straight-line method, $D = I/n$, is used in the UK, we simply deduct $I = nD$ from the taxable income at the end of the first year. This implies a tax shield, in real terms, of $TnD/(1 + h) \cdot (1 + r)$. If the investment is made at the end of the year, and depreciation is deducted in that same year, the present value of the tax shield is even larger.

Once again, if $PV_{UK}(TD,h) > PV_{SL}(TD)$ the accelerated depreciation allowance overcompensates British firms for inflation; the opposite holds if the

Table 6.7

Ratio* of Real Present Value of the Special British Tax Shelter to the Straight-Line Zero Inflation Benchmark for Selected Project Durations and Inflation Rates

Project Duration (Years)	Inflation Rate (%)							
	5	10	15	20	25	30	35	40
1	0.95	0.91	0.87	0.83	0.80	0.77	0.74	0.71
2	0.98	0.93	0.90	0.85	0.82	0.79	0.76	0.73
3	1.00	0.95	0.91	0.87	0.84	0.81	0.78	0.75
4	1.02	0.98	0.93	0.90	0.86	0.83	0.80	0.77
5	1.06	1.01	0.96	0.92	0.89	0.85	0.82	0.79
6	1.07	1.02	0.98	0.94	0.90	0.88	0.83	0.80
7	1.10	1.05	1.00	0.96	0.92	0.89	0.85	0.82
8	1.12	1.07	1.02	0.98	0.94	0.91	0.87	0.84
9	1.15	1.10	1.05	1.01	0.96	0.93	0.89	0.86
10	1.18	1.12	1.07	1.03	0.99	0.95	0.91	0.88
15	1.31	1.25	1.20	1.15	1.10	1.06	1.02	0.98
20	1.46	1.39	1.33	1.27	1.22	1.17	1.13	1.09

$$\text{*Ratio:} \quad \frac{TnD}{(1+r)(1+h)} \Bigg/ \sum_{t=1}^{n} \frac{TD}{(1+r)^t(1+h)^t}$$

$$= \frac{n}{(1+r)(1+h)} \Bigg/ \sum_{t=1}^{n} \frac{1}{(1+r)^t(1+h)^t}$$

The present value calculations assume a 5% real interest rate ($r = 5\%$)

inequality is reversed. Table 6.7 presents the ratio of the real present value of the tax shield, as allowed by the Heath government, to the present value of the depreciation tax shield under the straight-line method in an economy without inflation.[12] In the calculation we have assumed a real riskless discount rate of 5%. Whenever the ratio is greater than one, there is overcompensation by the British government for inflation. For example, for an inflation rate of 15% and project duration of seven years, the ratio is exactly one which implies an exact offset. As one would expect, the British accelerated depreciation provision overcompensates firms for projects with long durations and undercompensates those with a short duration. For example, for annual inflation rates of 15%–25%, projects with durations of less than seven years are undercompensated.

The American Experience

Unlike the United Kingdom, the US government permits firms to depreciate

---

12 Note that this ratio is independent of the corporate tax rate (T) since the T's cancel out.

Table 6.8

Ratio of the Real Present Value* of the *DDB* and *SYD* Depreciation Tax Shelters to the Straight-Line, Zero Inflation Benchmark, for Selected Project Durations and Inflation Rates

Inflation Rate (%)		Project Duration (Years)									
		3	4	5	6	7	8	12	16	18	20
0	DDB	1.03	1.03	1.03	1.04	1.04	1.05	1.06	1.08	1.09	1.09
	SYD	1.02	1.02	1.03	1.04	1.05	1.06	1.09	1.12	1.14	1.15
1	DDB	1.01	1.01	1.01	1.01	1.01	1.01	1.01	1.02	1.02	1.02
	SYD	1.00	1.00	1.01	1.01	1.02	1.02	1.04	1.06	1.07	1.08
2	DDB	1.00	0.99	0.99	0.99	0.98	0.98	0.97	0.96	0.96	0.96
	SYD	0.98	0.99	0.99	0.99	0.99	0.99	1.00	1.01	1.02	1.02
3	DDB	0.99	0.98	0.97	0.96	0.96	0.95	0.93	0.91	0.91	0.90
	SYD	0.97	0.97	0.97	0.97	0.96	0.96	0.96	0.96	0.96	0.96
5	DDB	0.96	0.94	0.93	0.92	0.91	0.89	0.86	0.83	0.82	0.81
	SYD	0.94	0.93	0.93	0.92	0.92	0.91	0.89	0.88	0.87	0.87
10	DDB	0.90	0.87	0.84	0.82	0.80	0.78	0.71	0.67	0.64	0.69
	SYD	0.87	0.85	0.84	0.82	0.81	0.80	0.75	0.71	0.70	0.69
15	DDB	0.85	0.81	0.77	0.74	0.71	0.69	0.61	0.56	0.54	0.52
	SYD	0.81	0.79	0.76	0.74	0.72	0.70	0.64	0.60	0.58	0.56
20	DDB	0.80	0.75	0.71	0.68	0.64	0.62	0.53	0.48	0.46	0.45
	SYD	0.76	0.73	0.70	0.67	0.65	0.63	0.56	0.51	0.49	0.48
40	DDB	0.65	0.59	0.54	0.50	0.46	0.43	0.36	0.31	0.29	0.28
	SYD	0.60	0.56	0.52	0.49	0.46	0.44	0.37	0.32	0.30	0.29

$$\text{*} PV = \sum_{t=1}^{n} \frac{D_t}{(1 + r)^t (1 + h)^t}$$

where: $r = 5\%$ and D_t is determined by the various depreciation methods. The tax shield is obtained by multiplying the relevant D_t by the tax rate T.

their assets by *SYD* or *DDB* and not just by the straight-line method. In order to gauge the extent with which the accelerated methods compensate firms for inflation, the following ratios have been calculated in Table 6.8.

$$PV_{SYD}(TD_t, h) \div PV_{SL}(TD_t)$$
$$\text{and} \quad PV_{DDB}(TD_t, h) \div PV_{SL}(TD_t)$$

These calculations represent the ratio of the present value of the depreciation tax shield in real terms under the two accelerated methods to the percent value of the straight-line tax shield in the absence of inflation. Once again a riskless real interest rate has been assumed.

A number greater than unity means that the accelerated method over-compensates for inflation, a figure smaller than unity indicates undercompensation, and unity indicates exact compensation. For example, assuming a project duration of eight years and an annual inflation rate of 1%, both accelerated methods overcompensate for inflation. That is, the present value of the depreciation tax shield in real terms is increased by 1% using the *DDB* method and by 2% using the *SYD* method, compared to the benchmark value using the *SL* method in the absence of inflation. On the other hand, if we take the same project, but assume an inflation rate of 5%, both accelerated methods *undercompensate* the firm for inflation. The real present value of depreciation tax shelter is reduced by 11% using the *DDB* method and by 9% using the *SYD* method. The main finding of Table 6.6 is that the accelerated methods provide full protection only at very low inflation rates, i.e., up to 2%. The *DDB* method fully compensates only up to 1% inflation and the *SYD* method up to 2%. This occurs independently of the asset's service life. It is interesting to note that within the range of relatively low inflation rates, the overcompensation increases with the duration of the asset. The rate of increase, however, is greater for the *SYD*. Thus, the use of accelerated depreciation during periods of low inflation provides a greater incentive to projects of long duration. The opposite occurs during periods of more pronounced inflation (over 2%). Here the accelerated methods do not fully compensate for inflation; and the degree of undercompensation *increases* with the asset's life. Thus, the accelerated methods provide a greater incentive for the investment in short-lived assets.

It is of some interest to compare these findings with the American experience with inflation during the last quarter of a century. Using the Consumer Price Index (CPI) to calculate inflation rates, the period 1950−79 can be divided into the following subperiods. 1950−65 was a period of relatively little inflation: the arithmetic mean of the annual rates of inflation during the period was only 1.8%. In the second subperiod, 1966−76, inflation rates were generally higher and they greatly accelerated during the decade of the seventies, a phenomenon common to practically all the Western world. The arithmetic mean for this period was 6.1%. In the period 1977−79 the average annual inflation rate was 9%, and in 1979 the rate of inflation exceeded 13%. Clearly, the accelerated depreciation methods which were sufficient to protect firms against inflation in the earlier years were completely inadequate for this purpose in the decade of the seventies.

SUMMARY

This chapter has been devoted to a discussion of the way in which corporate taxation affects a project's cash flow. Taxes are of especial importance because they do *not* affect all investments in the same manner; hence cash flows must be expressed on a post-tax basis if meaningful comparisons are to be made.

In general the after-tax cash flow in any year can be written as

$$(1 - T)S + TD$$

where:

S = the net pre-tax receipt
T = the corporate tax rate
D = the annual depreciation allowance

When calculating the net present value of a stream of net receipts, the after-tax receipts are discounted using the post-tax cost of capital, but the *tax shelter* (TD) is discounted using the riskless interest rate. This reflects the fact that the value of the tax shield to the firm is absolutely certain, since the deduction can be used to reduce the corporate tax burden even in years of no profit. This follows from the provision in the tax code which permits the tax shield to be applied against the income of past or future years. The importance of carefully spelling out the relevant *after-tax* cash flows was illustrated using the "make or buy" decision which often confronts many business firms.

Given the tax deductibility of depreciation expense for tax purposes, three popular methods of calculating depreciation — "Straight-line", "Double Declining Balance" and "Sum of the Digits" — were examined in order to determine the "best" method from the viewpoint of the firm. This was followed by a discussion of the impact of tax incentives on the profitability of investment projects. The chapter concludes with an analysis of the impact of inflation on the real value of the depreciation tax shelter and its implications for investment incentives using for this purpose the underlying tax structures of the United States and Great Britain.

QUESTIONS AND PROBLEMS

6.1 "In the calculation of *NPV*, depreciation is not deducted from the net cash flow despite the fact that depreciation is a real economic cost, and is also recognized by the tax authorities." Critically appraise this statement.

6.2 The Yellow Box Company is considering buying for $200,000 special equipment whose economic life span is expected to be eight years. The annual cash flow (before deducting interest and taxes) generated by the equipment is expected to be $40,000. Assume that the corporate tax rate is 40%, the after-tax cost of capital is 8%, and that the riskless interest rate is 5% and answer the following questions:

(a) Set out the post-tax annual cash flow of the "project", assuming straight-line depreciation.
(b) Should the firm buy the equipment? Support your answer.
(c) Assume now a riskless interest rate of 7%. Should the firm buy the machine in this case?

6.3 "Taxes can't be all bad. Any increase in the corporate tax rate T will improve the profitability of the project, since the tax shield TD will also increase."
Appraise the above quotation.

6.4 (a) What are the most common methods of calculating depreciation?

(b) For a corporation that does *not* pay taxes, which method of depreciation is optimal for capital budgeting purposes?

(c) Assume that the firm pays corporate taxes, and that this rate will be the same in the future. Which depreciation method is preferable?

6.5 International Forest Products is planning to build a new plant in a developing country. There are two possibilities: to establish the plant in Woodland, where straight-line depreciation is permitted, or in Forestania, where the Double Declining Balance method is used.

   The required investment is $25 million, and the duration of the project is five years. Annual net receipts are expected to be the same in both countries, except for transportation costs which will be $200,000 more per year if the plant is built in Forestania.

   Assume a corporate tax of 50% and riskless interest rate of 6% in both countries.

(a) Set out the after-tax cash flow for each alternative.

(b) Which country will the company prefer, if the after-tax cost of capital is 8%?

(c) Would your answer to part (b) be changed if the company is given a government grant of 50% of the investment and is allowed to charge depreciation on its own net investment only (i.e. 50% of the total investment)?

6.6 The government of a developing country is very interested in encouraging the execution of an investment project in textiles. The required investment outlay is $14 million and the economic life of the project is expected to be seven years.

The investor is offered the choice between two alternatives:

(i) A government grant which is given when the investment is carried out (for depreciation purposes, the investment equals $14 million, and the method of depreciation must be straight line).

(ii) The possibility to charge depreciation using the Sum of the Year's Digits method.
   (Assume a tax rate of 50% and 7% riskless rate of interest.)

   (a) How large a grant is required to make the investor indifferent between the two alternatives?

(b) Assume now that the government grant is equal to $500,000. What is the minimum net annual cash receipt (before deducting depreciation and taxes) the investor would require in order to carry out the project assuming that after-tax cost of capital is 9%?

6.7 Assume an investment outlay of $200,000 which generates a net annual pre-tax cash flow of $56,000 for ten years.

(a) Calculate the pre-tax internal rate of return of this investment.

(b) Calculate the post-tax internal rate of return, assuming a 50% tax rate.

(c) Assume now that the investment is $72,000 and that its annual net cash flow is $50,000 for two years. Calculate the investment's pre-tax and post-tax internal rate of return.

(d) Compare your results in part (c) to the results you got in parts (a) and (b). In which case does the rule of thumb method for calculating the post-tax internal rate of return yield better results?

6.8 (a) In order to encourage investment, the Heath government in the UK introduced a 100% depreciation allowance in the first year of the asset's life. For what inflation rate ($h\%$) does the 100% depreciation allowance exactly offset the attrition of inflation? Assume firms use straight-line depreciation; that the risk-free interest rate (in real terms) is 5% ($r = 0.05$), and that the project duration is five years ($n = 5$).

(b) Answer the same question assuming a project duration of ten years ($n = 10$).

6.9 In order to encourage investment in Puerto Rico the government offers investors the incentives described on the following table taken from the Wall Street Journal on February 6, 1980.

Income Tax Calculation	$
Sales	10,000,000
Production Worker Payroll	1,700,000
Profit Before Tax	1,000,000
Eligible Incentives:	
A. 5% Production Worker Payroll Deduction	85,000
B. Income Tax and Property Tax Exemption at Partial Rates	
Pre-Tax Income	1,000,000
Production Worker Payroll Deduction	85,000
Adjusted Taxable Income	915,000

Annual Income Tax Calculation by Period*

Years	1 – 5	6 – 10	11 – 15	16 – 20
% Tax Exempt	90%	75%	65%	55%
% Taxable Income	10%	25%	35%	45%
Taxable Income	$91,500	228,750	320,250	411,750
Calculated Tax	$26,115	82,613	122,863	164,038
Effective Tax Rate	2.61%	8.26%	12.29%	16.40%

*Duration of tax exemption depends upon geographical zone in which the firm has been established.

Assume that you are considering the alternative of locating a plant either in Ohio or in Puerto Rico and the *pre-tax* financial characteristics of your project are as those described in the table.

Find the *post-tax* internal rate of return of your project when your plant is located in Puerto Rico assuming an economic duration of your project of $n = 5$, $n = 10$, $n = 15$ and $n = 20$ years, under the following two alternative assumptions:

(a) You estimate that the post-tax internal rate of return of your project when the plant is located in Ohio will be 10%.

(b) You estimate that the post-tax internal rate of return of your project when the plant is located in Ohio will be zero.

Assume straight-line depreciation, and a 50% corporate tax rate ($T = 0.5$) if the plant is located in Ohio. In your answer consider only the corporate tax advantage and the worker payroll deduction but ignore any other benefits which might be provided (e.g. property tax exemption, etc.)

6.10 The following article on a new depreciation proposal was published in the Wall Street Journal on July 24, 1980.

A Look at '10-5-3' Depreciation Proposal, Focus of Attention in Tax-Cut Climate

By CHRISTOPHER CONTE
Staff Reporter of THE WALL STREET JOURNAL

WASHINGTON — The Senate Finance Committee opened hearings yesterday on tax reduction, amid a strong consensus here that says the next tax cut should include provisions designed to stimulate business investment.

The proposal that has drawn the most attention so far is known as "10-5-3."

Sen. Russell Long (D., La.), chairman of the committee, reported strong congressional support for a tax reduction in 1981. Regardless of the timing, most observers expect some form of liberalized depreciation to be a major feature of any tax legislation that emerges from Congress.

The following questions and answers explore the 10-5-3 plan and its implications:

Q. What, broadly speaking, is 10-5-3?

A. It is a plan for legislation to liberalize tax write-offs for depreciating business investments.

Q. What do the numbers stand for?

A. They represent the number of years in which business could write off various kinds of investments for tax purposes. Buildings could be depreciated in 10 years, equipment in five years and cars and light trucks in three years.

Q. How would that differ from present depreciation rules?

A. It would allow business to write off investments more quickly. For buildings, the depreciation period would be about one-third the average time allowed by Treasury rules. For equipment, the write-off period would be shortened by about five years, on average. For cars and trucks, the reduction would be about half a year.

Q. Is that all the 10-5-3 plan would do?

A. No. In addition, the existing investment tax credit, which lets a business claim a 10% tax credit on most equipment, would be enlarged. (A

---

credit is subtracted directly from taxes owed.) For example, a business could take the full amount of the credit for equipment that the Treasury figures will last just five or six years; under present rules, only two thirds of the credit can be taken for such equipment.

Q. How would that benefit business?

A. By shortening the period in which businesses could write off investments, companies could deduct larger amounts each year for tax purposes. This would lower their tax bill and presumably be an incentive to invest.

Q. Is any other change included?

A. Yes. Beyond the time changes, the method of calculating depreciation would be liberalized so that even more of a business investment's cost could be written off in the early years.

Q. Who is pushing the 10-5-3 plan, and why?

A. Business groups, on the ground that the country's capital investment has been lagging dangerously and that present tax rules discourage needed investment.

Q. What effect would the proposal have on businesses' tax burden?

A. It would provide substantial relief, according to the Treasury. It estimates that corporate income taxes would be cut in half by the time the proposal took full effect. That would mean a $50 billion cut in 1984.

Q. Is that reduction really needed?

A. Businessmen generally say it is, and most economists agree that inflation has seriously eroded the value of depreciation deductions. That's because depreciation is based on the actual cost of an asset. During periods of inflation, depreciation allowances lose their value each year. In the meantime, the cost of replacing equipment rises, with the result that the amount of money saved through depreciation falls farther behind replacement cost.

Q. Who opposes 10-5-3?

A. The Carter administration. So do some high-technology industries that invest mostly in research and development rather than machinery and buildings.

Q. Why does the administration object?

A. Officials think 10-5-3 would be too costly. Also the administration argues that it would divide the tax relief very unevenly. Those industries that use short-lived equipment wouldn't benefit nearly as much as those with longer-lived equipment. For the construction industry, for instance, tax savings would amount to only 5% of investment, while utilities would save 20%.

Q. Will the administration favor some other form of liberalized depreciation?

A. Probably. Officials generally agree that inflation has diminished the tax advantages of depreciation. The Commerce Department estimates that inadequate inventory and depreciation deductions had the effect of overstating last year's $237 billion in pretax corporate profits by $58.5 billion. Federal and state income taxes on those swollen profits totalled $92.7 billion, so an effective corporate income tax rate of 39.1% became an inflation-adjusted rate of 51.9%.

Q. Has that tax burden really deterred investment?

A. It's hard to tell, but many businessmen and economists think it has. There is a growing consensus that investment has been lagging in the US in recent years. That's difficult to prove, however. Last year, businesses' fixed investment amounted to 10.6% of gross national product (the total output of goods and services), at the high end of the 8.5%-to-11% range that has prevailed since World War II. On the other hand, investment hasn't grown as rapidly as the labor force. That may explain why productivity, or output per worker, has been declining.

Q. Are there alternatives to 10-5-3?

A. Yes. One is a plan suggested by Rep. Al Ullman (D., Ore.), chairman of the House Ways and Means Committee. It would reduce the standard depreciation life of business equipment by about 35%. Instead of a single five-year depreciation period for equipment, it would create four classes of three, six, nine and 12 years. Rep. Ullman believes his plan would cost much less than 10-5-3, and would cause less economic distortion because the four new classes would be more closely related to the actual useful lives of equipment.

Q. Does the Carter administration support that proposal?

A. A spokesman says only that it's a step in the right direction. The White House hasn't proposed a plan of its own, partly because it hasn't decided exactly what it would like to do. It appears that the administration will favor a plan that tries to preserve the idea that depreciation deductions be taken over the actual useful life of an asset. Its plan will probably include more classes of equipment than the Ullman proposal.

Q. Aren't there less complex ways to increase funds businesses have for investment?

A. Lots of them. You could simply increase the investment tax credit, or cut corporate tax rates. But many people prefer accelerated depreciation because it's focused directly at promoting investment. A general tax-rate cut would benefit companies no matter how they spend their money, but liberalized depreciation would go only to businesses that invest in new buildings or equipment. That makes it more acceptable to liberals who agree that investment should be encouraged but object to no-strings-attached corporate tax breaks. Moreover, corporate tax rates were cut as recently as 1978, and the investment tax was increased in 1975. Depreciation rules haven't been touched since 1971.

Wall Street Journal, 24 July 1980

Assume three alternative investments of $100 each, yielding constant annual before-tax cash flows of $40 (excluding interest and depreciation) for $n = 5, 10, 20$ years, respectively. The firm uses sum of the year's digits (*SYD*) depreciation and the applicable tax rate $T = 0.50$ (ignore tax credits).

(a) Calculate the original post-tax *IRR* of the three investments and the *IRR* that would obtain if the investments qualify for the five-year depreciation plan.

(b) Why does "high-technology" industry object to this proposal? Why do industries using short-lived equipment object? Explain.

(c) What would be the impact of the new proposal on investment in research and development? On investment in the heavy industry or in utilities?

(d) Rep. Al Ullman suggests reducing the standard depreciation time of business equipment by 35%. Determine the *IRR* of the three investments under this plan and compare the results to (a). How does this proposal affect your answer to parts (b) and (c)? (Note: in determining the project's life we round the number of years to the closest integer number.)

(e) Now assume that there is a 10% annual inflation every year for the entire duration of the project. The operating cash flows fully adjust to inflation, while the depreciation is calculated in nominal dollars.

Calculate the *IRR* of constant-dollar cash flows before and after the proposed five-year depreciation plan. Discuss your results comparing them to those in part (a).

APPENDIX 6A RULE OF THUMB CALCULATIONS OF POST-TAX RETURNS

Clearly, project evaluation should only be carried out on a post-tax basis. This follows both from the fact that tax payments are a real cash outlay induced by the investment decision, and even more important, because the goal of the firm (maximizing the market value of the owners' equity) depends on the firm's *after-tax* profitability. However, some firms persist in using a short-cut rule of thumb type of calculation to reflect the tax impact on a project's desirability. To be more specific, let us assume that the firm uses the internal rate of return as a measure of a project's profitability; we further assume straight-line depreciation, and an annual pre-tax cash flow of S. The pre-tax internal rate of return is given by the discount rate R which solves the following equation:

$$I = \frac{S}{1 + R} + \frac{S}{(1 + R)^2} + \cdots + \frac{S}{(1 + R)^n}$$

The post-tax internal rate of return for the same project is the discount rate, R^*, which solves the following equation:

$$I = \frac{(1 - T)S + TD}{1 + R^*} + \frac{(1 - T)S + TD}{(1 + R^*)^2} + \cdots + \frac{(1 - T)S + TD}{(1 + R^*)^n}$$

Clearly R^* is the conceptually correct measure of the project's post-tax rate of return since it is calculated on the basis of the actual after-tax cash flow. But for simplicity some firms use the pre-tax equation to calculate the pre-tax internal rate of return R, and then use the following rule of thumb, to estimate the project's post-tax rate of return:

$$R_e^* = (1 - T)R$$

where R_e^* is the rule of thumb estimate of the true post-tax rate of return, R^*.

The relationship of R_e^* to R^* is set out in Fig. 6A.1 which plots the rule of thumb estimate as a function of proposal duration. The rule of thumb provides a completely accurate approximation of the true post-tax rate of return only for proposals of one-year or infinite durations. For all other durations between one and infinity the estimated post-tax rate of return R_e^* is less than the true post-tax rate of return, R^*. Thus, the rule of thumb yields a *conservative* under-estimate of R^*. In the relevant range of project durations ($n < 20$) which includes almost all of a firm's projects, the larger the duration n is, the greater is the discrepancy between R^* and R_e^*. In other words, the longer a project's duration, the more conservative is the estimate, which perhaps should be regarded as a built-in adjustment for the greater risks involved in projects of long duration.[1]

---

[1] For further discussion of the formal relationship between R_e^* and R^*, see H. Levy, "The Connection between Pre-Tax and Post-Tax Rates of Return", *Journal of Business*, October, 1968.

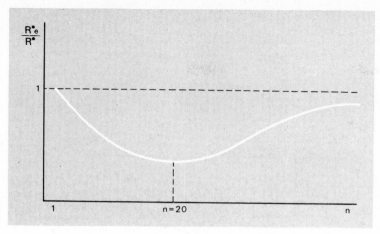

Fig. 6A.1

QUESTIONS AND PROBLEMS

6A.1 Consider a project which requires $50,000 as an initial investment and generates an annual pre-tax cash flow of $10,000 for ten years. Answer the following questions assuming straight-line depreciation and a 48% corporate tax rate:

   (a) Calculate the project's pre-tax internal rate of return.
   (b) Calculate the post-tax internal rate of return.
   (c) What is the rule of thumb estimate of the post-tax rate of return?

6A.2 (a) Calculate the post-tax internal rate of return (R^*) and the rule of thumb estimate of the post-tax rate of return (R_e^*) of a project which requires $100,000 as an initial investment, and which generates an annual cash flow of $25,000 before taxes, for each of the following project durations (n);

     (Assume a 50% corporate tax rate and straight-line depreciation.)
     (1) 5 years;
     (2) 10 years;
     (3) 20 years;
     (4) 50 years;
     (5) 100 years.

   (b) Use the results of part (a) to plot the ratio (R_e^*/R^*) as a function of the project's duration. Which duration gives you the biggest deviation between R_e^* and R^*? Explain your results.

APPENDIX 6B INFLATION AND THE OPTIMAL DEPRECIATION METHOD

Table 6B.1 presents the present value of depreciation per dollar of investment using alternative depreciation methods and for various rates of inflation and asset duration. The calculations assume a real discount rate of 5%.

Table 6B.1

Present Value of Depreciation per Dollar of Investment Using the Straight-Line (*SL*) and Accelerated Methods (*DDB* and *SYD*) of Depreciation*

Inflation Rate %		Asset Duration								
		3	4	5	6	7	8	12	16	20
0	SL	.908	.886	.866	.846	.827	.808	.739	.677	.623
	DDB	.923	.914	.896	.878	.861	.845	.784	.730	.682
	SYD	.923	.908	.894	.880	.867	.854	.804	.759	.718
2	SL	.873	.845	.818	.792	.767	.744	.658	.587	.526
	DDB	.907	.882	.858	.835	.813	.792	.716	.652	.598
	SYD	.893	.874	.855	.837	.820	.803	.740	.685	.636
5	SL	.825	.788	.753	.721	.690	.661	.561	.482	.419
	DDB	.870	.837	.806	.776	.749	.723	.632	.561	.503
	SYD	.852	.827	.802	.779	.757	.735	.659	.595	.540
10	SL	.755	.707	.663	.622	.586	.552	.442	.363	.305
	DDB	.816	.772	.731	.694	.661	.629	.528	.453	.396
	SYD	.791	.757	.726	.696	.668	.643	.544	.483	.427
15	SL	.694	.638	.588	.544	.505	.469	.360	.286	.235
	DDB	.768	.715	.669	.627	.590	.556	.452	.380	.327
	SYD	.737	.698	.661	.628	.597	.569	.475	.405	.351
20	SL	.641	.580	.527	.481	.440	.405	.300	.234	.190
	DDB	.725	.666	.616	.571	.533	.498	.395	.327	.279
	SYD	.690	.646	.606	.571	.538	.508	.414	.346	.297
40	SL	.486	.418	.381	.319	.283	.254	.176	.133	.106
	DDB	.591	.522	.466	.420	.382	.350	.263	.210	.175
	SYD	.547	.495	.451	.414	.381	.353	.270	.217	.181

*The table presents the present value of depreciation per dollar of investment; that is

$$DV(D,h) = \sum_{t=1}^{n} \frac{1/n}{(1 + r)^t (1 + h)^t}$$

The present value of the tax shield can be obtained by multiplying the above by the tax rate, *T*.

A number of conclusions can be drawn from the table. Firstly, as the inflation rate increases, the advantage of both accelerated methods over the straight-line method increases. This occurs because higher inflation rates imply a higher nominal discount rate $(1 + r)(1 + h)$, which in turn increases the relative weight of the depreciation charges in the early years. Secondly, in comparing the *DDB* and the *SYD* methods, it can be observed that short-lived assets and high inflation rates, individually or taken together, favor the *DDB* method of calculating

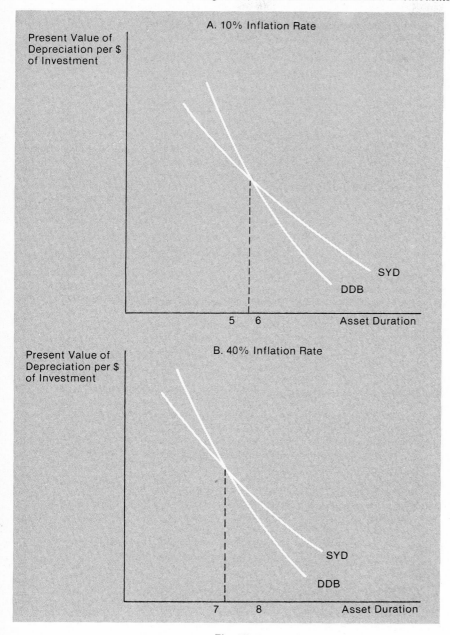

Fig. 6B.1

the depreciation allowance. High inflation rates favor the *DDB* method because of the large first-year charge, the weight of which increases in proportion to the rise in inflation rates and nominal discount rates. But this superiority of the *DDB* over the *SYD* holds only for short durations. For example, assuming a real discount rate of 5%, the superiority of *DDB* holds for assets of less than 5—6 years duration, for all inflation rates up to 20%.

From the point of view of financial management, the most significant finding is that the choice of the optimal depreciation method is invariant to inflation in the relevant range of inflation in the US. For annual rates of inflation up to 20%, there is an unambiguous choice of the optimal depreciation method which depends solely on asset duration. Specifically, if $n \leqslant 5$, *DDB* is optimal, and if $n > 5$, *SYD* is optimal, *independent* of the rate of inflation so long as the latter does not exceed 20%. This is illustrated in Figure 6B.1 which graphs the present value of depreciation per dollar of investment as a function of asset duration for two alternative inflation rates, 10% and 40%.

SELECTED REFERENCES

Arditti, F.D., "Discounting the Components of an Income Stream: Reply", *Journal of Finance*, March 1977.

Baran, A., Lakonishok, J. and Ofer, A.R., "The Information Content of General Price Level Adjusted Earnings: Some Empirical Evidence", *Accounting Review*, January 1980.

Bierman, H. Jr. and Dukes, R.E., "Limitations of Replacement Cost", *Quarterly Review of Economics and Business*, Spring 1979.

Brennan, M.J., "An Approach to the Valuation of Uncertain Income Streams", *Journal of Finance*, June 1973.

Coen, Robert M., "Investment Behavior, The Measurement of Depreciation and Tax Policy", *The American Economic Review*, March 1975.

Fabozzi, F.J. and Shiffrin, L.M., "Replacement Cost Accounting: Application to the Pharmaceutical Industry", *Quarterly Review of Economics and Business*, Spring 1979.

Gee, K.P. and Peasnell, K.V., "A Comment on Replacement Cost as the Upper Limit of Value to the Owner", *Accounting and Business Research*, Autumn 1977.

Gheyara, Kelly and Boatsman, James, "Market Reaction to the 1976 Replacement Cost Disclosures", *Journal of Accounting and Economics*, August 1980.

Kistler, L.H. and Carter, C.P., "Replacement Cost Measures: Their Impact on Income, Dividends, and Investment Return", *Quarterly Review of Economics and Business*, Spring 1979.

Lembke, V.C. and Toole, H.R., "Differences in Depreciation Methods and the Analysis of Supplemental Current-Cost and Replacement Cost Data", *Journal of Accounting Auditing and Finance*, Winter 1981.

Osteryoung, J.S., McCarty, D.E. and Fortin, K., "A Note on the Optimal Tax Lives for Assets Qualifying for the Investment Tax Credit", *Accounting Review*, April 1980.

Popoff, Boris, "Replacement Cost as the Upper Limit of Value to the Owner", *Accounting and Business Research*, Autumn 1977.

Ro, Byung, T., "The Adjustment of Security Returns to the Disclosure of Replacement Cost Accounting Information", *Journal of Accounting and Economics*, August 1980.

Samuelson, R.A., "Should Replacement-Cost Changes be Included in Income?" *Accounting Review*, April 1980.

Scheiner, J.H. and Morese, W.J., "The Impact of SEC Replacement Cost Reporting Requirements: An Analysis", *Quarterly Review of Economics and Business*, Spring 1979.

Stark, M.E., "A Survey of LIFO Inventory Application Techniques", *Accounting Review*, January 1978.

Sunder, S., "A Note on Estimating the Economic Impact of the LIFO Method of Inventory Valuation", *Accounting Review*, April 1976.

Turnbull, S.M., "Discounting the Components of an Income Stream: Comment", *Journal of Finance*, March 1977.

Watts, Ross, L. and Zimmerman, Jerold L., "On the Irrelevance of Replacement Cost Disclosures for Security Prices", *Journal of Accounting and Economics*, August 1980.

Winston, Joseph K., "Capital Market Behaviour and Accounting Policy Decisions", *Accounting and Business Research*, Spring 1977.

Zimmer, Robert K. and Gray, Jack, "The Economic Advantage of the Optimum Depreciation Procedure", *Decision Sciences*, January and April 1970.

7

Capital Budgeting and Inflation

The double-digit inflation which erupted in many countries during the 1970s has refocused attention on the financial and economic implications of monetary instability. This chapter spells out some of the implications of the decline in purchasing power for the underlying logic of corporate financial decision-making. Such a reassessment is necessary since much of the theory of finance emerged in a more tranquil (and perhaps happier) atmosphere in which the then minor fluctuations of the price level could be safely ignored.

Given the current magnitude of world-wide inflation, imperfectly anticipated rises in the price level can generate massive, and often socially undesirable, shifts in the allocation of wealth between the buyers and sellers of some goods and services and between debtors and creditors. And although these gains and losses cancel in the aggregate, this provides little solace to the corporation and its shareholders who find themselves unwilling "victims" of the inflationary process. Rational decision-making, therefore, must take the impact of inflation explicitly into account; and to this end some of the familiar concepts of financial theory must be recast.

ACCOUNTING vs ECONOMIC EARNINGS

Let's begin with a brief review of the salient differences between the accountants' and economists' concepts of profitability which exist even in a world of no inflation, but are aggravated by the presence of price instability.

As we have already noted in Chapter 5, reported (accounting) profits often differ from the actual cash flows which the firm receives. As a result a firm which shows a low accounting profit may still be very profitable in economic terms. Of course, the opposite situation may also prevail, that is an economically weak firm may report a rather large accounting profit. Among the factors which contribute to the discrepancy between accounting and economic profitability we find:

(a) *Accounts Receivable*: Standard accounting practice includes credit sales in the current income statement despite the fact that the firm may actually obtain the proceeds from cash sales much later. Hence, measured on a cashflow basis, profits may be much lower. (Remember, time is money!)

(b) *Accounts Payable*: Now assume that the firm has purchased raw materials for $1,000,000. This amount would appear (after appropriate inventory corrections) in the accounting income statement as an expense. But should the firm pay the $1,000,000 a year later, this would imply a higher profit on a cashflow basis. (Recall that the firm may earn interest on the $1,000,000 during the interim.)

(c) *Depreciation*: Suppose that in 1975 the firm bought machinery that cost $10,000,000 and depreciates it over ten years using the straight-line method. In the 1981 income statement, for example, we would find a depreciation allowance of $1,000,000 listed as an expense. The firm's overall *economic* profit is really smaller since the $1,000,000 will already have been taken into account in the year in which the total investment outlay originally occurred.

(d) *Inventory Valuation*: If a firm adopts the "first-in first-out" (FIFO) method of inventory valuation, its reported net profit will be higher if prices are rising since it considers the older inventory items, which were cheaper to produce or acquire, as expenses. It might seem optimal, there-fore, to use this technique because reported accounting earnings will be higher. But as we shall see below, using the FIFO method may be an inferior strategy during inflationary times since taxes must be paid on such profits.

As a result of these (and other) factors, accounting and economic measures of earnings will, in general, diverge. However, in periods of relatively stable prices, the differences between the two are often slight and sufficiently systematic to permit the use of reported accounting profits as a proxy for true economic earnings when analyzing trends within the firm, or when comparing the profitability of firms in various industries.

The situation is radically different under conditions of inflation. As infla-tion accelerates, the gap between reported and economic earnings also increases. This is especially true for firms with little or no debt. For such firms, reported earnings *systematically* distort the true economic picture during periods of rapid inflation. However, for firms who borrow, there is another offsetting factor which may reduce the gap between reported earnings and economic profits; inflation also reduces the *real* value of interest and debt repayment.

The increase in inflationary pressures in the US and western Europe during the decade of the 1970s led to the modification of long accepted accounting standards. In October 1979 the Financial Accounting Standards Board (FASB) ruled that all publicly held US firms, with over one billion dollars in assets or over 125 million dollars invested in property, plant and equipment, must include inflation-adjusted data (with explanations) in their annual reports. Thus, the financial community has recognized the extent of the impact of inflation on reported profits. We shall see below that inflation also significantly affects individual project evaluation, but first we shall turn to the impact of inflation on reported earnings, the crucial factor which led to the FASB ruling.

IMPACT OF INFLATION ON REPORTED EARNINGS

In the absence of inflation, as we have already noted, reported earnings provide a reasonably correct picture of the trends in economic earnings. The relationship of reported to economic profits however, is seriously distorted during periods of monetary instability. In our discussion three principal factors will be singled out for attention: inventory valuation, depreciation allowances and the treatment of debt financing.

Inventory Valuation and Inflation

Alternative accounting treatments of inventory valuation can affect a firm's reported earnings, tax bill, and cash position. For example this can occur should a firm switch from a first-in first-out (FIFO) to a last-in first-out (LIFO) formula for evaluating its inventories. Consider a firm which has $200 million in revenues from sales and suppose, for the sake of simplicity, that it incurs no expenses other than the cost of the goods sold. Some additional relevant information concerning our hypothetical firm is given below:

	Units (millions)	*Cost per Unit* ($)
Inventory at the beginning of the year	100	1.0
Materials bought during the year	100	1.5
Sales during the year	100	. . .
Inventory at the end of the year	100	. . .

Note that the cost per unit of inventory at the beginning of the year was $1, but due to inflation, the cost of acquiring additional materials during the year rose to $1.50 per unit. Since the cost of goods sold is calculated by the following formula:

Cost of goods sold = inventory at the beginning of the year
plus (+) new purchases during the year
minus (−) inventory at the end of the year,

it is clear that the method chosen to evaluate the end-of-year inventory affects the calculation of cost of goods sold. For example, either the 100 million units which were actually sold during the year can be assumed to have been taken out of the beginning inventory (FIFO) or out of the purchases made during the year (LIFO). Using FIFO, sales during the year cost $100 million. Using LIFO they cost $150 million. Hence reported profits, and therefore the corporate tax bill, will be affected as follows:

	Using FIFO	Using LIFO
	(millions of dollars)	
Revenue from sales	200	200
Cost of goods sold	− 100	− 150
Net profit before tax	100	50
Corporate taxes (50%)	− 50	− 25
Net profit after tax	50	25

Under FIFO, the units sold during the year are assumed to be the ones that the firm acquired at a cost of $1 per unit. Thus, the remaining end-of-year inventory is valued at $150 million (100 million units times $1.50). Under LIFO, the units sold are assumed to be those bought during the year at a cost of $1.50 per unit; and the end-of-year inventory is only $100 million (100 million units valued at $1.00 per unit). It is clear, in this instance, that the LIFO method measures economic profitability more accurately since it is based on prices which are closer to the true replacement cost (market value) of the inventory than are the historical costs on which the FIFO method is based. And the higher the inflation rate, the greater is the discrepancy between the measures.

The LIFO method, however, leaves much to be desired. In essence, the company's accounts (balance sheet and profit and loss account) are a mixture of "apples and oranges," that is dollars of different purchasing power. For example, the closing inventory at the end of the year should also be valued in dollars of constant purchasing power if an accurate picture of a firm's financial position is to be had.

In many countries, including the US, firms are permitted to switch from FIFO to LIFO. What are the financial implications of such a switch during inflation? As we have seen, use of FIFO may permit the firm to show higher *reported* profit than does the LIFO method ($50 million versus $25 million in our example). Thus, switching from FIFO to LIFO *decreases* reported earnings. Nonetheless, the switch from FIFO to LIFO may still be advantageous to the firm. Recalling that the cash outlay for the materials purchased during the year was $150 million, the total cash flow under the two alternative methods can be set out as follows:

	Cash Flow	
	(in millions of dollars)	
	FIFO	LIFO
Revenue from sales	+ 200	+ 200
New purchases	− 150	− 150
Taxes	− 50	− 25
Net cash flow	0	+ 25

Clearly, from a purely economic standpoint the LIFO method is the better of the two alternatives. Switching from FIFO to LIFO reduces the tax burden, thereby increasing the net cash flow of the firm by $25 million. Since the *replacement cost* of the inventory units is $150 million, the firm's true economic profit is $50 million, independent of the particular accounting convention used to value the inventory. Employing LIFO results in a tax bill of $25 million, that is a 50% tax rate, but employing FIFO results in a tax bill of $50 million, which represents an effective tax rate of 100% on economic profits! Thus, in this instance, LIFO measures the firm's earnings more accurately and also reduces the corporate tax burden.[1]

In most cases[2] LIFO provides a more accurate picture of a firm's earnings under inflation and, as we have just seen, has economic advantages since it results in a lower effective corporate tax rate. It is surprising therefore that despite this two-fold advantage, only about one-third of US firms use the LIFO method. This is probably the consequence of the IRS rule which does not permit firms to value their inventories by two different methods — one for tax purposes and the other for financial reporting. Hence, along with the lower tax rate, a switch from FIFO to LIFO means that reported profits will be lower. Since many financial managers feel that their own performance, as well as that of the firm, is evaluated and judged in the market largely on the basis of reported earnings, they are willing to forego the tax advantages of LIFO in order to report a higher (albeit illusory) level of net accounting earnings. This reluctance of firms to switch from FIFO to LIFO may also reflect the fear that they will appear less profitable than other firms in the same industry who use FIFO.[3]

Depreciation

The federal income tax code recognizes depreciation allowances only on an historical (rather than replacement) cost basis. Consider a firm which invested $100 million in depreciable assets having a ten-year lifetime, so that the annual straight-line depreciation allowance is $10 million. Now, if we assume a 20% rise in prices, the second year's depreciation allowance, on a replacement cost basis, is $12 million. The tax code, however, does *not* permit replacement cost depreciation, nor does it permit the indexation of the depreciation expense.[4] Although the depreciation expense in current dollars is $12 million, the Tax Code only recognizes $10 million. As a result the depreciation allowance may be insufficient to keep the capital investment intact during a prolonged period of inflation.

---

1 This assumes a neutral inflation. In the case of a non-neutral inflation neither LIFO nor FIFO measures economic profits correctly, and some combination of the two methods would have to be employed in order to measure the true economic profit.

2 The qualification is necessary to provide for cases in which the firm reduces its inventory levels during the year.

3 It is reasonable to assume that the willingness to change accounting methods will increase as more firms in an industry make the switch.

4 For a discussion of the relative merits of indexing vs. accelerated depreciation, see Martin Feldstein, "Adjusting Depreciation in an Inflationary Economy: Indexing Versus Acceleration", Working Paper No. 395, National Bureau of Economic Research (October 1979).

Corporate executives are well aware that under existing legislation part of the funds required to replace worn-out physical assets is being taxed as income. This has led some firms to seek immediate relief by trying to shorten the period over which it depreciates its assets, thereby increasing current allowances. For example, US Steel Corporation depreciates its equipment over 18 years, but when reacting to inflation, Bracy D. Smith, the company's comptroller, asserted recently that 12 years would be a more "realistic" period over which the equipment should be depreciated.[5]

Inventories and depreciation allowances are calculated, in general, at their historical, rather than replacement, cost. As a result reported earnings during inflation systematically *overstate* true economic profits; and the higher the inflation rate the greater is the overstatement. For example, in 1978 US firms earned a total of $202 billion before tax, and $118 billion after tax. This is 16% more than the net earnings in 1977 and 68% more than in 1975. However, about a third of the reported earnings in 1978 were illusionary since the accounting rules for inventory and depreciation *understated* true economic costs.[6] Thus, the effective tax rates levied on US corporations were much higher than they might have been. In 1974, for example, the average effective tax rate paid by US corporations was 63%! This could have been significantly decreased if more corporations had switched to the LIFO method, or alternatively, if the federal law recognized depreciation on a replacement cost basis for tax purposes.

Corporate Debt

Many firms finance operations partially by debt. Since the debt payments are not indexed to the cost of living, inflation increases the real wealth of debtors because the debt repayment is made with dollars of less purchasing power. This gain is *not* reported in the firm's balance sheets or income statements. Adjusting a firm's accounts for this factor tends to increase its profit. Consider a firm which is borrowing $100 million (say by issuing bonds) on which it pays 10% interest. In the absence of inflation the income statements would look like this:

	$m
Profit before interest and taxes	300
Interest payments	10
Profit before tax	290
Tax (50%)	145
Net profit	145

Now suppose that there is a 10% *fully anticipated* inflation. In this case the creditors (bondholders) require a 21% return if they are to earn a *real* return of 10%.[7] Assuming that all prices increase by 10%, then reported earnings will

5 See *Business Week*, March 19, 1979, p. 112.
6 Ibid.
7 Without inflation, bondholders lend $100 to get back $110 at the end of the year (principal plus interest). With 10% inflation they must get back 121 in order to obtain a purchasing power of 110 ($121 ÷ 1.1 = $110).

also grow by 10% in nominal terms. Hence, the income statement becomes: (remember that the firm is issuing new debt, it is *not* already outstanding)

	$m
Profit before interest and taxes	330
Interest (21% on $100 million)	21
Profit before tax	309
Tax (50%)	154.5
Net profit	154.5

The $154.5 million of net profit cannot be compared to the previous profit of $145 million, in the absence of inflation, since the $154.5 million represents *less* purchasing power. The firm's *real* profit, given a 10% rate of inflation, is only $140.45 million:

$$\frac{154.5}{1 + \text{inflation rate}} = \frac{154.5}{1.1} = \mathbf{140.45}$$

However, the $100 million of debt which the firm repays at the end of the year has a purchasing power of only $90.9 million (100 ÷ 1.1 = 90.9). Thus, the firm gains $9.1 million in real terms due to the erosion of the purchasing power of the money borrowed. Since such monetary gains are not reported in corporate income statements true economic profits are understated; clearly this factor is important for firms with relatively large debts.[8]

The net impact of inflation on reported profit depends on all three of the above-mentioned factors. For firms with no debt the first two factors (inventory and depreciation) cause reported earnings to be higher than the true economic profit. For firms with debt, the last factor may partially (or even completely) offset the first two.

In a world of double-digit inflation, unadjusted reported earnings are misleading if not meaningless. Despite the great need to adjust reported income statements for inflation confusion still persists regarding the proper method of adjustment. The FASB did not specify exactly where the adjusted data should appear in the annual statement or even what format should be used. Some companies put the figures in a separate section accompanied by lengthy explanations; others simply bury the figures in a footnote.

Much of the confusion which has plagued the introduction of the new disclosure regulations stems from the fact that the FASB requires two different versions of inflation adjustment. The first, known as "constant dollar" accounting, adjusts for changes in the consumer price index (CPI); the other method values individual items at their *current* (replacement) cost rather than *historical* (original) cost. Thus a firm which uses silver or gold as a raw material may show an enormous loss, rather than profit, should a sharp increase in the price of the

---

8 The failure of the financial community to recognize the increase in true corporate profits due to the erosion of the real value of debt has been emphasized by Franco Modigliani and Richard A. Cohn, "Inflation, Rational Valuation and the Market", *Financial Analysts Journal* (March–April, 1979).

Table 7.1

IBM 1979 Statement of Earnings Adjusted for General Inflation (Constant Dollar)

	As Reported in Financial Statements	Adjusted for General Inflation
	(Dollars in millions except per share amounts)	
Gross income from sales, rentals and services	$22,863	$22,863
Cost of sales, rentals and services	$8,413	$9,083
Expenses and other income	8,897	8,991
Provision for US Federal and non-US income taxes	2,542	2,542
	19,852	20,616
Net earnings	$3,011	$2,247
Earnings per share†	$5.16	$3.85
Net assets	$14,961	$16.624
Loss from decline in purchasing power of net monetary assets		$455

†Adjusted for 1979 stock split.
Source: IBM *1979 Annual Report*

metals occur at the end of the year. Since inflation rarely affects all prices equally, using the CPI to adjust income statements typically yields very different results than does the "current replacement" approach. In this context it should be emphasized that the constant dollar method is to be preferred on theoretical grounds. Deflating by a general index of prices (e.g. the CPI) eliminates the effects of the upward drift of the absolute price level without disturbing *relative* prices. And this is as it should be! Changes in the relationship between individual prices reflect changes in productivity, efficiency, or in the underlying supply and demand conditions rather than the effects of inflation *per se*, and therefore should *not* be eliminated.

Whatever the method employed, the impact of inflation-adjustments on reported earnings can be crucial for a proper evaluation of corporate profitability.[9] To illustrate the magnitude of this impact Table 7.1 presents International Business Machines' 1979 Income Statement, adjusted for inflation using the *constant dollar* method. IBM prepared the adjusted information by converting reported inventory, plant, rental machines and other property, cost

---

9 A very strong case for price-level adjustments not only as a supplementary statement, but as a guide for business decisions as well has been made by Avraham Beja and Yair Aharoni, "Some Aspects of Conventional Accounting Profits in an Inflationary Environment", *Journal of Accounting Research*, Autumn 1977.

of sales, rentals and services, and depreciation expense, into dollars with pur-chasing power equivalent to average 1979 dollars. This was done by applying to the original cost of the applicable assets, the increase in the CPI for the elapsed period from acquisition to 1979. The related depreciation expenses were similarly adjusted and charged against earnings, using the company's established depre-ciation policies. Gross income and expenses other than depreciation are con-sidered proportionately over the year, and therefore they are restated in terms of end-of-1979 dollars.

Depreciation charged to restated costs and expenses amounted to $2,343 million, as compared with reported depreciation of $1,970 million. The loss from decline in purchasing power results from holding net monetary assets during periods of inflation. Net monetary assets include cash and claims to cash, and amounts owed, which are fixed in terms of number of dollars to be received or paid.

The impact of inflation on earnings, as presented in the constant dollar adjustments, is *not* deductible for corporate income tax purposes. As a result, after giving effect to these adjustments, corporate income taxes consume 53.1% of earnings as compared to 45.8% reported in the financial statements. Although IBM has reservations regarding the degree to which the constant dollar method properly reflects the impact of inflation,[10] the adjusted figures do give an indi-cation of the significant hidden impacts of corporate taxation in periods of high inflation and the adverse effects on a firm's ability to retain earnings to meet the escalating cost of replacing and expanding productive capacity. Clearly part of this problem is caused by legal (and other institutional) constraints based on accounting methods which were devised for a non-inflationary environment.

As we have already noted, inflation rarely affects all prices, and as a result all firms, equally. The *differential* impact of inflation on profitability makes the inflation-adjustment imperative if meaningful comparisons of earnings are to be made between individual companies and industries. To illustrate this point, consider the 1979 earnings per share (net profit ÷ by number of shares outstanding) of IBM and General Motors:

	Reported EPS	*Inflation-adjusted EPS*
IBM	$5.16	$3.85
GM	$10.00	$5.00

Note that the *adjusted* earnings per share of IBM comprises 75% of the reported nominal figure. For General Motors the results are more serious; the adjust-ment reduces its EPS by 50%, from $10 to $5. Since GM's dividend is $5.30, it did not earn enough (in *real* economic terms) to cover the dividend.[11]

---

10 See IBM, *Annual Report 1979*.

11 The analysis of the dividend employs the second adjustment method, i.e. the current (replacement) cost method. The reader should also note that both IBM and GM had relatively low levels of debt in 1979 so the offsetting real gain from nominal debt is only marginal in this instance. For a further discussion of the impact of inflation on dividend policy, see Chapter 19 below.

PROJECT EVALUATION UNDER INFLATION

Not only does inflation distort reported profits, but it also can have a significant impact on corporate investment decisions. It is quite possible that a project that would be accepted in the absence of inflation may be rejected in an inflationary environment. Moreover, inflation may change the *ranking* of mutually exclusive projects, thereby altering the firm's investment priorities.

As we have noted in Chapter 4 above, the net present value (*NPV*) of an investment project is the most widely accepted theoretical measure of invest-ment profitability. Like other measures of profitability, special care must be exercised when applying the *NPV* criterion to a cash flow under conditions of inflation. For simplicity only, let's start with the case of a "neutral" inflation, in which gross income, labor costs, raw materials, prices, etc., all increase at the same rate, say $h\%$ a year. Also assume that the cost of capital in real terms, k_R, is 10%, so that an investment of $100 will only be attractive if the cash flow at the end of the year is $110 in *real* terms. The real net present value of such a project is, by definition, zero:

$$NPV = \frac{110}{1.1} - 100 = 0$$

If the cash flow in real terms is greater than $110, the project's *NPV* is positive and it would be accepted.

Now suppose that all prices (costs) are rising by 20% per year. What is the *minimum* required cash flow which will induce the firm to execute the project? Since the zero *NPV* cash flow, in the absence of inflation, is 110, the critical minimum required nominal cash flow, given an annual inflation rate of 20%, must be $(110) \cdot (1.20) = 132$. In other words, the cash flow must increase by 20% in order to preserve the project's previous *NPV*. Thus, for a 20% inflation, the minimum required nominal cash flow is 132; the real value of which remains 110 ($132/1.20 = 110$). Any net receipt in excess of 132 will generate a positive *NPV*.

Measuring a project's *NPV* in an inflationary environment can be done in one of two ways:

(a) Reduce the nominal cash flow to *real* terms and then discount at the *real* cost of capital. In our example the *NPV* of the project is:

$$NPV = \frac{132/1.20}{1.1} - 100 = \frac{110}{1.1} - 100 = 0$$

(b) The same result can be obtained by using the nominal cost of capital to discount the nominal cash flow. In this particular example, the nominal cost of capital is 32%, and the *NPV* of the project is given by,

$$NPV = \frac{132}{(1.2)(1.1)} - 100 = \frac{\$132}{1.32} - 100 = 0$$

As we have just seen cash flow can be discounted either in nominal or in real (constant purchasing) terms. Correctly done, shifting from one method to the other will *not* affect a firm's investment decisions. To illustrate this point, consider a firm which invests I dollars in order to obtain a future cash flow of S_1, S_2, ... S_n, and for the moment, also assume the absence of depreciable assets and taxes. As before, all prices rise by $h\%$ per year and the real and nominal discount rates are k_R and k_N, respectively. Since S_t is the nominal cash flow in year t, it increases every subsequent year as a result of inflation. In order to calculate a project's *NPV* in real terms (i.e., in constant dollars) the nominal cash flows must first be deflated using the annual inflation rate. The real present value of the first year cash flow is $S_1/(1 + h)$, and the real present value of the second year cash flow is given by $S_2/(1 + h)^2$. The raising of the inflation term $(1 + h)$ to the second power reflects the underlying economic fact that prices rise at *compounded* rates. Hence, in general, the present value, *in constant dollars*, of a nominal receipt S_t is given by the formula $S_t/(1 + h)^t$; and the real *NPV* of a project, that is its *NPV* in dollars of *constant* purchasing power, is given by the following formula:

$$NPV_R = \sum_{t=1}^{n} \frac{S_t/(1 + h)^t}{(1 + k_R)^t} - I$$

where NPV_R denotes the *NPV* in real terms.

Since real cash flows are in the numerator, the appropriate discount rate is k_R, the *real* rate. However, the shift to nominal discounting is straightforward. The above equation can be rewritten as follows:

$$NPV_N = \sum_{t=1}^{n} \frac{S_t}{(1 + k_R)^t(1 + h)^t} - I = \sum_{t=1}^{n} \frac{S_t}{[(1 + k_R)(1 + h)]^t} - I$$

$$= \sum_{t=1}^{n} \frac{S_t}{(1 + k_N)^t} - I$$

where: NPV_N denotes nominal net present value and k_N denotes the nominal discount rate.

Thus project analysis can be carried out either in terms of current (nominal) or real (constant) dollars. However, the projects' *NPV* will be the same under both methods if, and only if, the real discount rate is applied to the constant dollar cashflows and the appropriate nominal rate is used to discount the cash flows in terms of current dollars. More specifically

$$NPV_R = NPV_N \text{ if and only if } (1 + k_N) = (1 + k_R)(1 + h)$$

From this condition we can readily see that the nominal cost of capital equals the real cost of capital plus an adjustment for inflation:[12]

$$k_N = k_R + h + k_R h$$

For example, suppose that one puts \$100 in the bank and obtains (in the absence of inflation) $k_R = 10\%$ in interest. With a 10% inflation one would now require a nominal interest rate of k_N in order to retain the same real income:

$$k_N = 0.10 + 0.10 + 0.10 \cdot 0.10 = 0.21 = 21\%$$

Since the investor earns 10% in the absence of inflation, he now requires 21%: 10% to compensate him for the loss of purchasing power of the principal; plus an additional 11%, which in real terms equals 10% ($0.11/1.1 = 0.10$). This is exactly the same rate of interest that he earned before the inflation. Hence, an interest rate of 21% fully compensates the investor for the 10% inflation.

One is tempted to use a simple rule of thumb to estimate the nominal rate by simply adding the inflation rate to the real rate ($k_N = k_R + h$), but this ignores the additional correction factor, $k_R \cdot h$. In our example, such a procedure would imply the use of 20% rather than 21% as the nominal discount rate, a procedure which introduces an upward bias to our estimate of a project's profitability (*NPV*).

Unfortunately the rule of thumb cannot be recommended for project analysis in a world of double-digit inflation. Moreover the magnitude of the error engendered by the use of the rule of thumb increases with project duration, due to the compounded nature of the inflationary process.

In the extreme case of a project with an infinite life the error may even be as large as the present value of the project times the inflation rate ($PV \cdot h$). For example, assume a constant cash flow S which increases every year at the inflation rate, h. Its *NPV* in constant dollars is given by,

$$NPV_R = \sum_{t=1}^{\infty} \frac{S}{(1 + k_R)^t} - I = \frac{S}{k_R} - I$$

Alternatively, we may discount the nominal cashflow using the nominal discount rate k_N:

$$NPV_N = \sum_{t=1}^{\infty} \frac{S(1 + h)^t}{(1 + k_N)^t} - I = \frac{S(1 + h)}{1 + k_N} \Big/ 1 - \frac{1 + h}{0 + k_N} - I$$

After rearrangement of terms this becomes:

$$NPV_N = \frac{S(1 + h)}{k_N - h} - I$$

If we now substitute the precise value of k_N, that is $k_N = k_R + h + k_R \cdot h$,

---

12 The derivation of this formula is given in Chapter 22 below.

the nominal net present value, NPV_N, can be rewritten as follows:

$$NPV_N = \frac{S(1 + h)}{k_R + h + k_R h - h} - I = \frac{S(1 + h)}{k_R (1 + h)} - I = \frac{S}{k_R} - I$$

which is exactly the *same NPV* as was obtained above using the constant dollar cash flow and real discount rate.

Thus, when the correct formula for k_N is applied, we find $NPV_R = NPV_N$ which implies that either formula can be used to evaluate projects without changing the firm's investment decision.

However, if we apply the rule of thumb approximation $k_N = k_R + h$ we get,

$$NPV_N = \frac{S(1 + h)}{k_R + h - h} - I = \frac{S(1 + h)}{k_R} - I = \left(\frac{S}{k_R} - I\right) + \frac{Sh}{k_R}$$

or

$$NPV_N = NPV_R + \frac{Sh}{k_R}$$

Since NPV_R is the correct measure of the project's value, use of the approximation induces an error of the size $(S/k_R) \cdot h$ which is the present value of the project multiplied by the inflation rate.[13] An error of this magnitude may well reverse an investment decision.

A Numerical Example

This can best be illustrated by means of a simple numerical example. Assume a neutral 10% inflation ($h = 0.10$) and consider an investment project of infinite duration whose real present value and initial investment outlay are $PV = 10,000$ and $I = 10,500$, respectively. Clearly this project should be rejected since its NPV is negative (-500).

However, if we use the rule of thumb approximation for the nominal rate we obtain:

$$NPV_N = \left(\frac{S}{k_R} - I\right) + \frac{Sh}{k_R} = NPV_R + PV \cdot h$$

Plugging in the values from our example we get $-500 + 10,000 \cdot (0.10) = -500 + 1000 = 500$. Thus, using the rule of thumb, the project's real NPV is *positive* ($+500$) and therefore should be accepted which *reverses* the previous investment decision.

Our numerical example represents an extreme case in which the error is compounded an *infinite* number of times and hence yields the maximum possible error. In general, the longer a project's duration (n), the larger is the possible error caused by the rule of thumb approximation ($k_N = k_R + h$). Table 7.2 illus-

---

13 Note that the error is a function of the present value and not of the net present value, since $S/k_R = PV$.

Table 7.2

The Error from Using the Rule of Thumb Approximation of the True Nominal Discount Rates for Alternative Project Durations, assuming a 10% Real Discount Rate and 15% Inflation

Duration	Initial Outlay	Value of $100 Annuity*		Value of Annuity of $100 $(1 + h)^t$ Using Rule of Thumb Approximation**		Error
(n)	(I)	(PV)	(NPV)	PV_A	NPV_A	
1	$40.9	$90.9	$50	$92.00	$51.10	$1.10
2	123.6	173.6	50	176.64	53.04	3.04
3	198.7	248.7	50	254.51	55.81	5.81
4	267.0	317.0	50	326.22	59.22	9.22
5	329.1	379.1	50	392.18	63.08	13.08
6	385.5	435.5	50	452.78	67.28	17.28
7	436.8	486.8	50	508.64	71.84	21.84
8	483.0	533.5	50	560.03	77.03	27.03
9	525.9	575.9	50	607.16	81.25	31.26
10	564.0	614.5	50	650.45	86.45	36.45
15	710.6	760.6	50	820.17	109.57	59.57
20	801.1	851.1	50	932.01	130.94	80.94
∞	950	1,000	50	1,150	200	150

* Calculated using real discount rate $k_R = 10\%$.
** Calculated using the rule of thumb approximation, $k_A = k_R + h = 0.10 + 0.15 = 25\%$.

trates the magnitude of the error for alternative project durations. We assume a real discount rate of 10%, an inflation rate of 15%, and a real cashflow of 100 in constant dollars, or $100 (1 + h)^t$ in nominal dollars. Once the present value is calculated, various values of I are assumed such that for all durations the real net present value (NPV_R) is 50.

The right-hand side of Table 7.2 sets out the present value of the nominal cashflow using the rule of thumb approximation:

$$PV_A = \frac{S(1 + h)^t}{(1 + 0.25)^t}$$

where the subscript A denotes that the approximation is being used ($k_N = k_R + h = 0.10 + 0.15 = 25\%$). Then the initial investment outlay, I, is subtracted in order to obtain NPV_A. The difference between NPV_A and the true NPV is the error involved in using the rule of thumb approximation. It is very small for short durations but increases systematically as project duration increases. The maximum error is 150 ($PV \cdot h = 1,000 \cdot 0.15$) for $n = \infty$. It is worth noting that for reasonable durations the error is *not* negligible. For $n = 10$, the error is 36.45 compared to NPV of 50, i.e. an error of 73%.[14]

[14] Obviously, the magnitude of this error is a function of the selected numerical example.

To sum up, a project's net present value can be calculated either in constant dollars using the real discount rate k_R or in current dollars discounted at the nominal cost of capital $k_N = k_R + h + k_R \cdot h$. Used correctly, the two methods yield the *same NPV*. However, if one applies the rule of thumb approximation, $k_N = k_R + h$, the project's *NPV* will be overstated with the magnitude of the error increasing monotonically as project duration increases.

INFLATION, TAXES AND THE RANKING OF PROJECTS

As we have just seen, a *neutral* inflation in which all prices (costs) rise in equal proportion, should not affect a project's estimated *NPV*, independent of whether the analysis is carried out in real or nominal terms. This reflects the fact that in such a case both the cash flows and the appropriate discount rate increase at the same rate as the inflation. But even in the extreme case of neutrality, not all cash flows will be affected equally by inflation.

An outstanding example of the differential impact of inflation on project cash flow is the depreciation tax shelter which is calculated on the basis of historical costs. The failure of the fiscal authorities to permit an upward adjustment of depreciation allowances, *for tax purposes*, produces the well-known negative impact of inflation on capital investment, even when the underlying inflationary process is neutral.

In the absence of inflation a project's after-tax cash flow in any year t is given by:

$$(1 - T)(S_t - D_t) + D_t = (1 - T)S_t + TD_t$$

and its *NPV with no inflation* (denoted as NPV_{NI}) is,

$$NPV_{NI} = \sum_{t=1}^{n} \frac{(1 - T)S_t}{(1 + k_R)^t} + \sum_{t=1}^{n} \frac{TD_t}{(1 + r)^t} - I$$

In the absence of inflation, k_R is the firm's *real* cost of capital and r is the *real* riskless interest rate. Note that the firm considers the tax-shelter, TD_t, to be a virtually riskless cash flow and therefore discounts it at the risk-free rate, r. If we now assume a neutral inflation of $h\%$ per year, the cash flow S_t increases each year by $h\%$ and the nominal cost of capital, k_N, becomes $(1 + k_R)(1 + h)$. Note however that the depreciation tax shelter, TD_t, does *not* increase with inflation since it is calculated on the basis of historical value. Hence the project's *NPV with inflation*, denoted as NPV_I, becomes:

$$NPV_I = \sum_{t=1}^{n} \frac{(1 - T)S_t (1 + h)^t}{[(1 + k_R)(1 + h)]^t} + \sum_{t=1}^{n} \frac{TD_t}{[(1 + r)(1 + h)]^t} - I$$

which can be rewritten as

$$NPV_I = \sum_{t=1}^{n} \frac{(1 - T)S_t}{(1 + k_R)^t} + \sum_{t=1}^{n} \frac{TD_t/(1 + h)^t}{(1 + r)^t} - I$$

Thus, given a *fully anticipated neutral* inflation in which all prices, including the nominal interest rate, rise at the rate of inflation, the discount rate becomes (in nominal terms) $(1 + r)(1 + h)$ where r denotes the risk-free rate in the absence of inflation. As before, one may first calculate the depreciation tax shield in constant dollars, $TD_t/(1 + h)^t$, and then discount it at the real rate, i.e., by r; or alternatively, one may calculate all the cash flows in current dollars, and then apply the appropriate nominal discount rates: $(1 + k_R)(1 + h)$ and $(1 + r)(1 + h)$.

Since NPV_I, which is the correct measure of profitability with inflation, is less than NPV_{NI}, the correct measure in the absence of inflation, it is clear that even a neutral inflation reduces a project's profitability via its negative impact on the depreciation tax shield.[15] And the greater the inflation rate, the greater is the gap between NPV_{NI} and NPV_I. Moreover, it is quite possible that $NPV_{NI} > 0$ while $NPV_I < 0$ so that a project which would have been accepted in the absence of inflation might be rejected under inflationary conditions. This reduction in NPV is also a function of the relative importance of labor and capital inputs. In general, the more capital intensive the project, the larger will be the tax shelter. Since the real value of the latter is reduced by inflation, we expect capital-intensive projects to suffer more from inflation than otherwise comparable labor-intensive projects.

For example, suppose that a firm is considering three projects. Project A does not involve any initial investment (all machines and buildings are rented so there are annual rent payments but no initial outlay). Project B has an initial outlay (I_B) as does project C (I_C). All projects have a ten-year duration and the firm uses straight-line depreciation. The cost of capital is 20%, the risk-free interest rate is 5% and the corporate tax rate is 50%.

Table 7.3 sets out the calculation of the projects' net present values using the familiar formula:

$$NPV = \sum_{t=1}^{n} \frac{(1 - T)S}{(1 + k)^t} + \sum_{t=1}^{n} \frac{TD}{(1 + r)^t} - I$$

In the absence of inflation, all three projects have the same NPV, in this case $1000, so the firm is indifferent between them. Let us now assume a neutral inflation of $h\%$. As a result, S will increase annually by $h\%$ and the appropriate discount rate will also adjust to the inflation. As we have shown before, a neutral inflation will *not* change the real value of the first term on the right-hand

15 The reader should note that firms having fixed obligations (such as lease contracts) may gain from inflation since the real value of their fixed commitments decreases with inflation, see Chapter 22 below.

Table 7.3

Net Present Values of Three Hypothetical Projects in the Absence of Inflation

			Projects	
		A	B	C
(1)	Initial Investment Outlay I	0	1,000	10,000
(2)	Project Duration	10	10	10
(3)	Depreciation $(D = I/n)$	0	100	1,000
(4)	Annual Cashflow (S)	477.1	770	3,406
(5)	$\sum\limits_{t=1}^{10} \dfrac{(1 - T)S}{(1 + k)^t}$	1,000	1,613.9	7,139
(6)	$\sum\limits_{t=1}^{10} \dfrac{TD}{(1 + r)^t}$	0	386.1	3,861
(7)	$NPV = (5) + (6) - (1)$	1,000	1,000	1,000

side of the *NPV* equation, but it does reduce the present value of the tax shield:

$$\sum_{t=1}^{10} \frac{TD}{[(1 + r)(1 + h)]^t}$$

Clearly, the *NPV* of project A is not affected by inflation since $TD = 0$. However, we expect projects B and C to be adversely affected by inflation. The effect is particularly great in the case of project C since it involves a larger capital expenditure. To show this we first calculate the appropriate nominal riskless discount rates for alternative inflation rates, assuming that the real rate is 5%:

Annual Inflation Rate (h)	$(1.05)(1 + h)$
4.76%	1.10
9.52%	1.15
14.29%	1.20
23.81%	1.30

Note that the discount factor for the tax shelter becomes $(1.05)(1 + h)$. The net present values of the three projects for each of the alternative inflation rates are given in Table 7.4. Although the *NPV* of project A is unaffected by inflation, the *NPV* of project B is decreased and that of project C even becomes negative. The differential impact of inflation (even of the neutral variety) on projects' net present values is of crucial importance. A glance at Table 7.4 suffices to show

Table 7.4

Net Present Value of Three Hypothetical Projects with Alternative Inflation Rates (h)

			Projects	
		A	B	C
(1)	Investment Outlay I	0	1,000	10,000
(2)	Present Value of Risky Cashflow	1,000	1,613.9	7,139
(3)	Depreciation	0	100	1,000
(4)	Present value of Tax Shelter			
	$h = 4.76$	0	307.3	3,073
	$h = 9.52$	0	250.9	2,509
	$h = 14.29$	0	209.6	2,096
	$h = 23.81$	0	154.6	1,546
(5)	Net Present Value			
	$[(2)+(4)-(1)]$ $h = 4.76$	1,000	921.2	212
	$h = 9.52$	1,000	864.8	-352
	$h = 14.29$	1,000	823.5	-765
	$h = 23.81$	1,000	768.5	$-1,315$

that inflation can change a project's *NPV* from positive to negative depending on its degree of capital intensity and the rate of inflation. Thus for a moderate level of inflation (4.76%) all three projects are acceptable (i.e., have positive *NPV*s); but for higher rates of inflation (for example 9.5%) project C has a negative *NPV*. Consider, for example, two hypothetical projects D and L. The first is assumed to be capital-intensive; the second project, L, is labor-intensive and has no investment in fixed assets. Let's further assume that in the absence of inflation project D is preferred to project L, which is tantamount to assuming that project D has a higher *NPV*. If we introduce a neutral inflation, other things equal, the *NPV* of project D decreases in *real* terms because the real value of its depreciation tax shield shrinks. The *NPV* of project L, however, does not change with inflation; it has no tax shield and, therefore, its entire cash flow rises proportionately at the inflation rate.

This situation is illustrated in Fig. 7.1 which plots the *NPV*s of the two projects in relation to the inflation rate. For zero inflation and for all rates of inflation below h_0, project D has the higher *NPV*. But for the rates of inflation beyond h% the negative impact on the real value of the depreciation tax shelter becomes dominant, and beyond this point the labor-intensive project L has the higher *NPV*. Clearly, the ranking of the two projects depends upon the rate of inflation. And should the two projects happen to be mutually exclusive, an estimate of the rate of inflation must be made before the firm can choose between them.[16]

16 Inflation also affects project risk and the cost of capital; for a discussion of those two important problems see Chapter 22 below.

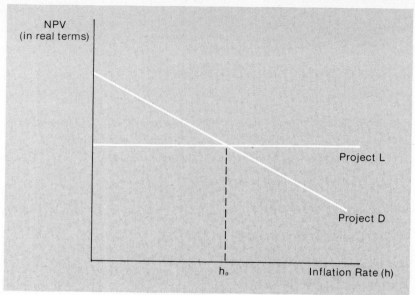

Fig. 7.1

SUMMARY

This chapter has been devoted to the analysis of the impact of inflation on corporate profitability and project selection. Inflation seriously undermines the economic significance of reported corporate profits. The source of much of this distortion can be traced to three elements:

(a)   use of historical costs to value inventories;
(b)   estimation of the depreciation of fixed assets on the basis of their historical cost rather than their cost in current dollars;
(c)   failure to recognize the implicit gain in an inflationary environment to those firms who are net debtors.

The financial implications for corporate profits stemming from the use of two alternative methods of inventory evaluation (FIFO and LIFO) are examined. The chapter goes on to examine some of the implications of the 1979 ruling of the Financial Accounting Standards Board which requires firms to include inflation-adjusted data in their annual reports.

Inflation can also be a significant factor in the evaluation of capital investments, and care should be exercised when defining cash flows and the appropriate discount rates. In general inflation has a differential impact on capital-intensive investments via the reduction in the real value of the depreciation tax shelter, and therefore it can affect a firm's investment priorities. The higher the inflation the greater is the tendency to prefer labor-intensive rather than capital-intensive projects.

QUESTIONS AND PROBLEMS

7.1 How does inflation influence the reported income, the effective tax rate and cashflow of the firm?

7.2 Which of the two methods, LIFO or FIFO, is preferable under the following conditions?

(a) in the absence of inflation
(b) when a neutral inflation exists

Regarding your answer to part (b) how do you explain the fact that a great many firms in the US use FIFO?

7.3 Superfine is a firm engaged in retail trade. Its sales and inventory for 1981 were as follows:

Opening inventory on December 31, 1980	500,000 units
Purchases during 1981	200,000 units
Sales during 1981	300,000 units
Closing inventory on December 31, 1981	400,000 units

For the sake of simplicity assume the company sells only one product whose cost on December 31, 1980 was $1.00 and that the company's profit margin is 10% on sales. The company pays 50% corporate income tax and the consumer price index rose 10% in the period December 31, 1980– December 31, 1981. Compute the company's net profit after taxes using FIFO and LIFO.

7.4 The Temopil company imports Japanese cars. Assume for simplicity that the company imports one model only. The importer's cost per car in 1980 was $5,000. On 1 January, 1981 the manufacturer announced a price increase of 20%. The importer's profit margin on the sale of the cars is 10%. The following data relate to its inventory, sales and purchases during 1981:

	No. of units	Cost per unit
Inventory on 31 December, 1980	3,000	$5,000
Purchases during 1981	5,000	$6,000
Sales during 1981	4,000	$6,600
Closing inventory on 31 December, 1981	4,000	

The Temopil company finances the purchase of its cars by means of a six-month line of credit from the bank at an annual interest rate of 18%. The company pays 50% income tax. Compute the company's net profit after taxes, first using FIFO and then LIFO.

7.5 "Neutral inflation doesn't change the firm's cost of capital or the real present value of its projects."
Critically evaluate this statement.

7.6 Explain the use of the constant dollar method in contrast to the replacement cost method on financial statements under inflationary conditions. Under what conditions would you prefer to use each one of the methods?

7.7 A textile firm is considering switching from hand looms to automatic machines. The new machines will allow the firm to reduce its labor and production costs by 50%. Without the change, annual sales and expenses for the next ten years are expected to be as follows:

Proceeds from sales	$30,000,000
Expenses (excluding depreciation)	$20,000,000
Depreciation (straight-line)	$ 2,000,000

The firm is considering acquiring machines which cost $40,000,000 and have an expected economic life of ten years. The introduction of the machines will decrease expenses (excluding depreciation) to $10,000,000 annually while sales will remain at the same level. The real cost of capital is 12%, and the real riskless interest rate is 8%. The firm pays 50% income tax. The predicted annual inflation rate for the next 10 years is 10% annually.

(a) Is it worthwhile for the firm to purchase the machines? (Assume that the acquisition of the machines is out of the firm's own capital.)
(b) How would your answer to (a) change if the riskless interest rate was 10%?

7.8 A firm is considering an investment of $50,000,000 to set up a new production line. The economic life span of the machinery is ten years. The expected annual receipts from the investment are $20,000,000 and the annual expense (including straight-line depreciation) is $10,000,000. The real cost of capital is 15% and riskless interest rate is 10%. The firm's financial analysts predict an annual inflation rate of 10% for the next decade.

(a) Is it worthwhile for the firm to make the investment?
(b) How might your answer to (a) change if the tax authorities agree to accept depreciation expenses calculated on the basis of replacement costs rather than historical costs?

7.9 A petrochemicals firm is considering a $20,000,000 investment in a new product. Sales and expenses are expected to be as follows:

s = annual sales of $13,000,000
c = annual expenses $6,000,000
k = real cost of capital of 15%
r = real riskless interest rate of 8%
T = corporate income tax rate of 50%
h = predicted annual inflation rate for the next ten years = 8%
n = economic duration of the equipment 10 years.

The firm has been offered the opportunity to sign a 10 year sales contract for its product, at a price *linked* to the increase in the consumer price index. Assume, therefore, that revenues and expenses will increase at the same rate over the ten-year period.

(a) Is it worthwhile for the firm to make the investment under the above assumptions?

The firm's advisors on the price of oil are divided in their opinion. One group says that because of the surplus of oil its price is not expected to increase any higher than the world inflation rate. Others estimate that due to an increase in demand, and a decrease in production, oil prices will increase at double the inflation rate.

(b) If you assume that oil prices grow at double the average inflation rate, how does this affect the feasibility of the project?

7.10 One factor which causes the deviation of reported accounting from economic earnings in an inflationary economy is depreciation. The table below presents selected items from the income statement of the Bethlehem Steel Corporation and the inflation rate for the years 1971–78.

(a) Calculate Bethlehem's net income when depreciation is calculated at replacement cost. The latter is determined by increasing the original depreciation allowance at the annual inflation rate.
(b) Use the inflation-adjusted figures obtained in (a) to calculate the firm's inflation-adjusted earnings per share (EPS).

In your calculations make the assumption that the depreciation given in each year for any particular asset continues at least until 1974, so that the increase in depreciation for each year is due to *new* capital expenditures which have been made at the beginning of the appropriate year. (Recall that the IRS does *not* allow firms to deduct indexed depreciation for tax purposes!)

Bethlehem Steel Corporation

Selected data 1971–78

Year	Depreciation	Net Income	Number of Shares	Earning per Share	Inflation Rate (%)
1971	159.3	139.2	44,483	3.13	4.30
1972	180.8	134.6	44,469	3.03	3.30
1973	196.1	206.6	43,467	4.75	6.23
1974	210.9	342.0	43,666	7.85	10.97
1975	234.2	242.0	43,665	5.54	9.14
1976	275.6	168.0	43,666	3.85	5.77
1977	300.1	− 448.2	43,665	− 10.26	6.48
1978	321.9	225.1	43,665	5.16	9.33

Source: Bethlehem Steel Annual Reports

7.11 The following case study of the Artex Corporation focuses on aspects of capital budgeting under inflation. Read the case and answer the questions below. In your answer, assume that the decision to lease rather than buy the machine is the correct one, i.e., do not analyze the lease vs. buy decision.

1. Assuming that all facts are correct, do you accept the cashflow as presented by Artex? Would you make any changes? Explain.
2. How does Artex deal with inflation and the adjustment to its cost of capital? Do you accept Artex's method? If yes, defend it. If no, carry out the calculations by the method that you think is more accurate.
3. How does Artex handle risk? What is the "true" risk premium that Artex required on the machine?

ARTEX CORPORATION

Equipment Replacement Decision Under Conditions of Inflation

In the recent years there has been a rapid growth in the activities of Artex Corporation in printing and finishing textiles. The British company specializes in high-quality printing of knits, curtains, bedclothes and fine fabrics.

In 1975 two of Artex's major customers notified the company that they were about to begin manufacturing sheets 2.00 meters wide to meet the market demand for wide bedclothes.

Artex had a printing machine for fabrics 1.60 meters wide. It was clear to Artex that without advanced printing equipment, it would lose some of its customers. This apprehension was compounded when the company forecast the possibility of an indirect loss much larger than the direct loss in printing jobs of bedclothes 2.00 meters wide. It was feared that some of the customers would transfer most of their orders to other companies in the textile printing business which have a wide-printing capability, and Artex's market share would slip. It was clear to Artex that a customer who prints 2-meter-wide sheets with one company would try and concentrate all the printing orders with that company.

A superficial survey showed that there was a considerable market potential for wide bedclothes (in addition to curtains wider than 1.60 meters). It was believed that several textile companies with printing requirements of millions of meters might be persuaded to use Artex's facilities.

Investment Alternatives

Artex examined four investment alternatives for printing fabrics wider than 2.00 m.:

(a) Adding a wide rotary printing machine
(b) Replacing the existing rotary machine by a wide rotary printing machine
(c) Adding a flat screen wide-printing machine
(d) Trading-in the existing flat printing machine for a wide flat printing machine

It was estimated that the initial printing demand would not exceed 1,500,000 meters per month.

The company examined the four alternatives and found that the first and third ones did not seem profitable since currently only half the existing rotary machine's capacity was used, and it did not seem possible to utilize the additional capacity in the near future. The fourth alternative was rejected because a rotary machine is technically preferable to a flat one, while the cost difference between the two machines is negligible.

After discussing the problem, Artex's Managing Director decided to recommend the second alternative, that is, replacing the existing rotary printing machine by a wide rotary machine.

The company found it could trade in the fully depreciated old machine for £625,000. Originally it cost £1.6 million.

Increase in Capacity

The rotary machine will print any fabric up to 220–290 cm. wide. This machine will expand the company's printing capacity by 10 printing hours per day and add 2,000,000 meters of wide sheets to the monthly output.

Artex estimated the additional revenue from printing an additional 1,000,000 meters per month in the first six months at £500,000 per month. The monthly printing output would increase by an additional 500,000 meters after the first six months.

In checking the feasibility of the project, Artex completely ignored the possible additional orders from a sister company owned by the same conglomerate. It was not clear whether the sister company would be willing to pay the market price and whether the parent corporation would show any special interest in the arrangement. According to Artex's controller:

> If the sister company pays the market price, the profitability calculations will not change markedly. If, however, we are forced to allow preferential terms and turn away other paying customers, the results will not be too good.

Lease Financing

Artex could acquire the new machine under a five-year lease financing contract. The company would pay about 2.85% of the purchase price per month (about £60,000 per month) for 60 months. The company would deposit 10% of the machine's value (£207,000). At the termination of the leasing period the ownership of the printing machine will pass to the company.

An investment of £4,600,000 in infrastructure and building for the new machine was to be financed from internal funds. Building the infrastructure and running in the machine takes about a year. Though the infrastructure has an economic life of ten years at least for tax purposes the firm is allowed to depreciate it over seven years.

Table 1   Projected Profit-and-Loss (£'000)

	1976 (6 months)	1977	1978	1979	1980
Sales	3,000	10,350	11,902	13,687	15,740
Cost of Sales					
Variable cost:					
Dyes and Chemicals	879	3,033			
Electricity	76	262			
Fuel	246	849			
Water	13	45			
Maintenance	111	383			
Labor	120	414			
Total Variable Cost	1,445	4,986	5,734	6,594	7,583
Machine Rental	350	700	700	700	700
Depreciation*	330	660	660	660	660
Total Cost of Sales	2,125	6,346	7,094	7,954	8,943
Gross Income	875	4,004	4,808	5,733	6,797
Financing Expense**	280	560	560	560	560
Selling Expenses	50	115	132	152	175
Pretax Income	545	3,329	4,116	5,021	6,062
Income Tax (61%)	332	2,031	2,511	3,063	3,698
Net Income	213	1,298	1,605	1,958	2,364

*   Straight-line depreciation of the building (£4,600,000) over seven years (rounded).
**   Financing expense on working capital — the financing expenses are paid to the government which allocates to the firm a subsidized loan for working capital. The subsidy represents a new policy of the British Government to encourage investment.

Table 2   Projected Cash Flow (£'000)

	1976	1977	1978	1979	1980
Receipts					
Collection of Sales	1,700	8,545	11,437	13,153	15,125
Reduction of Working Capital					4,722
Total Receipts	1,700	8,545	11,437	13,153	19,847
Payments					
Building	4,600				
Deposit on Machine	207				
Running-in Costs	100				
Cost of Production (without Depreciation)	1,795	5,686	6,434	7,294	8,283
Selling Expenses	50	115	132	152	175
Income Tax	332	2,031	2,511	3,063	3,698
Total Payments	7,084	7,832	9,077	10,509	12,156
Annual Surplus (Deficit)	(5,384)	713	2,360	2,644	7,691
PV Coefficients (25%)	0.800	0.640	0.512	0.410	0.328
NPV (25%)	(4,307)	456	1,208	1,084	2,522
Cumulative *NPV* (25%)					963
PV Coefficients (30%)	0.769	0.592	0.455	0.350	0.269
NPV (30%)	(4,140)	422	1,074	925	2,069
Cumulative *NPV* (30%)					350

The Profitability of the Investment

When analyzing the profitability of the investment, the company assumed the machine's life to be five years, although the machine wears out technologically in a longer period of at least ten years. According to the company's economist:

> The uncertainty beyond five years is so great that our policy is to disregard the income (and expenses) that are expected after five years.

Inflation rates are expected to range around 15% annually. It was estimated that the income from the machine and variable costs will rise at this rate. Since the real cost of capital is 10% (which is appropriate to the risk that is characteristic of the cashflows of this project), "the profitability of the machine must be examined with a nominal cost of capital of 25%, which is the rate of expected inflation added to the real cost of capital." The project was also examined with a cost capital of 30%, that is an expected rate of inflation of 15% added to a real cost of capital of 15%.

The incremental profit and loss statement attributed to the additional output from the new machine is presented in Table 1. The cash flow analysis done by the company and profitability forecasts with cost of capital of 25% and 30% are presented in Table 2. In the cash flow analysis it was assumed that the company collects 70% of sales in the current year, and 30% in the following year.* Thus the reduction of working capital in 1980 represents the balance of receivables for the sales in the last year of the machine's operation.

On the basis of these calculations it was decided to lease the machine.

---

* Except for the sales of the first six months of 1976 where only 57% would be collected in that year, and the rest in 1977.

SELECTED REFERENCES

Agrawall, S.P., "Accounting for the Impact of Inflation on a Business Enterprise", *Accounting Review*, October 1977.

Beja, Avraham and Aharoni, Yair, "Some Aspects of Conventional Accounting Profits in an Inflationary Environment", *Journal of Accounting Research*, Autumn 1977.

Brooks, L.D. and Buckmaster, D., "Price-Change Accounting Models and Disaggregated Monetary Gains and Losses", *Quarterly Review of Economics and Business*, Spring 1979.

Call, W.L., "General versus Specific Price-Level Adjustment: A Graphic Analysis", *Accounting Review*, January 1977.

Cross, Stephen, M., "A Note on Inflation, Taxation and Investment Returns", *Journal of Finance*, March 1980.

Ijiri, Y., "The Price-Level Restatement and its Dual Interpretation", *Accounting Review*, April 1976.

Kaplan, R.S., "Purchasing Power Gains on Debt: The Effect of Expected and Unexpected Inflation", *Accounting Review*, April 1977.

Kim, M.K., "Inflationary Effects in the Capital Investment Process: An Empirical Examination", *Journal of Finance*, September 1979.

Leech, S.A., Pratt, D.J. and Magill, W.G.W., "Company Assets Revaluations and Inflation in Australia, 1950 to 1975", *Journal of Business Finance & Accounting*, Winter 1978.

Nelson, C.R., "Inflation and Capital Budgeting", *Journal of Finance*, June 1976.

Perrin, J., "Inflation Accounting: Survey of Academic Opinion", *Journal of Business Financing & Accounting*, Spring 1976.

Piper, A.G., "Reporting the Effects of Inflation in Company Accounts in the United Kingdom", *Quarterly Review of Economics and Business*, Spring 1979.

Poengsen, Otto H. and Straub, Hubert, "Inflation and the Corporate Investment Decision", *Management International Review*, Vol. 16, No. 4, 1976.

Schoenfeld, H.-M.W., "Inflation Accounting — Development of Theory and Practice in Continental Europe", *Quarterly Review of Economics and Business*, Spring 1979.

Shashua, L. and Goldschmidt, Y. "A Tool for Inflation Adjustment of Financial Statements", *Journal of Business Finance and Accounting*, Spring 1976.

Singh, S.P., "Inflation and the Profitability of Firms in Canada", *Journal of Business Finance & Accounting*, Winter 1975.

Tysseland, M.S. and Gandhi, D.K., "Depreciation, Inflation and Capital Formation in Public Utilities: One Possible Approach towards a Solution", *Quarterly Review of Economics and Business*, Spring 1979.

Van Horne, J.C., "A Note on Biases in Capital Budgeting Introduced by Inflation", *Journal of Financial and Quantitative Analysis*, January 1971.

Vasarhelyi, M.A. and Pearson, E.F., "Studies in Inflation Accounting: A Taxonomization Approach", *Quarterly Review of Economics and Business*, Spring 1979.

8

Traditional Measures of Investment Worth

The preceding chapters of the book have spelled out in great detail normative guidelines for reaching capital expenditure decisions; the main thrust of the argument resting on the need to discount the cash flows generated by alternative projects. However, many businessmen still use non-discounted rules of thumb such as a simple payback formula or accounting rate of return when estimating the profitability of alternative investments. In this chapter, therefore, we change our perspective and focus attention on the perplexing question of why many business firms have persisted in using short-cut rules of thumb, rather than (or as a supplement to) one of the more sophisticated time-discounted decision rules. Here the analysis will be essentially *positive*, rather than normative; that is we shall be using the tools at our disposal not to improve the decision-making process, but rather to account for, and hopefully to understand, the observed behavior of many corporate executives.

RULES OF THUMB FOR PROJECT EVALUATION

One of the more pervasive facts of economic life has been the continued wide-spread use of a variety of short-cut rules of thumb to evaluate capital investment projects. Actual business practice suggests that the only effective limit on the number of different methods employed has been the ingenuity of management in devising additional variants of existing profitability measures. But despite differences in detail, almost all of the popular rules of thumb fall into one of two broad classes: payback measures or undiscounted accounting rates of return.

Payback

Many firms still use a simple payback formula, that is the number of years

175

required to recover the initial investment outlay out of the project's future cash flow, as their index of an investment's desirability. For example, if a proposal requires an initial outlay of $1 million and is expected to give rise to a net cash flow of $250,000 per year, for say ten years, the project has a *four-year* payback. Had the expected annual cash flow been $500,000 per year, the payback period would be two years, and so on for any combination of investment outlay and cash receipts.

If we assume that all projects have equal annual receipts (as in the above-mentioned examples) the payback can be calculated from the following formula:

$$\text{Payback Period} = \frac{\text{Initial Investment Outlay}}{\text{Annual Cash Receipt}}$$

Even if the receipts are expected to fluctuate over time the payback period is still easily calculated by summing the receipts until the initial investment outlay is covered. For example, Table 8.1 sets out the cash flows of two hypothetical projects, A and B. The former has a payback period of three years; summing the annual receipts of project B gives a somewhat larger payback of five years for that proposal.

Table 8.1

Investment Outlay	Project A (1,000,000)	Project B (1,000,000)
Net Cash Flow:		
First year	500,000	400,000
Second year	400,000	300,000
Third year	100,000	100,000
Fourth year	0	100,000
Fifth year	0	100,000
.	.	.
.	.	.
.	.	.
Tenth year	0	100,000

The payback formula has some rather obvious defects. The formula does not discount for the future returns, and perhaps even more important it concentrates attention solely on the receipts *within* the payback period; receipts in later years are ignored. Thus Project A of Table 8.1 has a shorter payback, and therefore is presumably more desirable than Project B, despite the fact that the internal rate of return of Project A is zero while that of B is positive!

Accounting Rate of Return

Another widely used measure of investment profitability is the accounting rate of return. This rate of return is calculated by dividing a proposal's annual net profit (after deducting depreciation) by either the *total* or the *average* initial investment outlay:

$$\frac{\text{Accounting Rate of Return}}{\text{on Total Investment}} = \frac{\text{Net Annual Profit}}{\text{Investment Outlay}}$$

$$\frac{\text{Accounting Rate of Return}}{\text{on Average Investment}} = \frac{\text{Net Annual Profit}}{\text{Investment Outlay} \div 2}$$

Taking our previous example of a project with initial investment outlay of $1 million and annual net receipts of $250,000 for ten years, and assuming straight-line depreciation of $100,000 per year, the accounting rates of return on total and average investment are given by:

$$\frac{\text{ARR on Total}}{\text{Investment}} = \frac{250,000 - 100,000}{1,000,000} = 15\%$$

$$\frac{\text{ARR on Average}}{\text{Investment}} = \frac{250,000 - 100,000}{500,000} = 30\%$$

Once again we can note some very obvious defects of both versions of the accounting rate of return. As was true of payback, the accounting rate also neglects the timing of receipts, that is no provision is made for discounting the future cash flows. Moreover, the accounting rate of return implicitly assumes *stable* cash receipts over time. Needless to add, this measure is particularly inappropriate where cash flows are expected to change over the life of the project.

THE HISTORICAL RECORD

Man's knowledge of the principles of compound interest can be traced back to the Old Babylonian period (circa 1800-1600 B.C.) in Mesopotamia, and present value tables not unlike the ones used in this book can be found in the mathematical and early accounting literature of medieval Europe.[1] Despite this, time-discounted methods of project evaluation were not applied to *nonfinancial* investments until the nineteenth century when an American civil engineer, A.M. Wellington, anticipated many of the concepts of modern capital investment analysis in his work on the location of railways,[2] but as late as 1950, a study of 25 large electric utilities reported that none of the firms surveyed used time-discounted methods, *all* of the firms preferring the simple accounting rate of return on total assets as their measure of profitability.[3] Similarly, a 1950 field

1 For an informative and highly entertaining survey of the historical development of discounting, see R.H. Parker, "Discounted Cash Flow in Historical Perspective", *Journal of Accounting Research*, Spring 1968.

2 Ibid., p. 62. Wellington's book, *The Economic Theory of the Location of Railways*, New York, Wiley 1887, is discussed by M.B. Scorgie, "Rate of Return", *Abacus*, September 1965, and by R.J. Stephens, "A Note on an Early Reference to Cost-Volume Relationships", *Abacus*, September 1965.

3 Michael Gort, "The Planning of Investment: A Study of Capital Budgeting in the Electric Power Industry", *Journal of Business*, April 1951 and July 1951.

study[4] of corporate investment decisions in manufacturing firms found a marked preference for the use of undiscounted payback periods; no firm surveyed reported the use of time-discounting when evaluating their capital expenditure programs.

It was not until the second half of the 1950s that US business firms seriously began to consider the use of time-discounting for project evaluation. Since that time a virtual army of academic researchers has descended periodically upon the largest of US corporations in an effort to monitor the procedures and techniques which they use to evaluate capital investment proposals.[5] A sample of the findings of these surveys is given in Table 8.2. Clearly a preference for the use of rule of thumb evaluation methods continued well into the 1960s and the reliance on simple rules of thumb remains significant to this day.

Thus despite the theoretical arguments presented in Chapters 3 and 4, 38% of the firms surveyed in 1970 relied on simple rule of thumb estimates of profitability for evaluating capital investments. Moreover, as both the surveys reported in Table 8.2 relate to very large US corporations the data probably *understate* the reliance on rules of thumb. Size and (observable) sophistication have a strong tendency to be positively correlated in the business world! It appears reasonable to conclude that many (if not most) business executives still use short-cut rules of thumb such as a payback formula or accounting rate of return when analyzing capital budgeting decisions.

On the other hand it is equally clear from Table 8.2 that the use of time-discounting (principally the *IRR*) has been increasing over time. This shift to more sophisticated methods of project evaluation is not surprising. After an

---

4 See Walter W. Heller, "The Anatomy of Investment Decisions", *Harvard Business Review*, March 1951.

5 A far from exhaustive listing of such studies includes: Eugene F. Brigham, "Hurdle Rates for Screening Capital Expenditure Proposals", *Financial Management*, Autumn 1975; G.A. Christy, *Capital Budgeting: Current Practices and Their Efficiency*, Eugene, Oregon: Bureau of Business and Economic Research, University of Oregon, 1966; James M. Fremgen, "Capital Budgeting Practices: A Survey", *Management Accounting*, May 1973; Lawrence J. Gitman and J.R. Forrester, Jr., "A Survey of Capital Budgeting Techniques Used by Major US Firms", *Financial Management*, Fall 1977; Donald Istvan, *Capital Expenditure Decisions: How They are Made in Large Corporations*, Bloomington, Indiana: Bureau of Business Research, Indiana University, 1961; Thomas Klammer, "Empirical Evidence of the Adoption of Sophisticated Capital Budgeting Techniques", *Journal of Business*, July 1972; James C.T. Mao, "Survey of Capital Budgeting: Theory and Practice", *Journal of Finance*, May 1970; James H. Miller, "A Glimpse at Practice in Calculating and Using Return on Investment", *N.A.A. Bulletin*, June 1960; J. William Petty, David F. Scott, Jr. and Monroe M. Bird, "The Capital Expenditure Decision-Making Process of Large Corporations", *The Engineering Economist*, Spring 1975; J. William Petty and David F. Scott, Jr., "Capital Budgeting Practices in Large American Firms: A Retrospective Analysis and Update", forthcoming; Lawrence D. Schall, Gary L. Sundem and William R. Geijsbeek, Jr., "Sulvey and Analysis of Capital Budgeting Methods", *Journal of Finance*, March 1978; and Jerry Viscione and John Neuhauser, "Capital Expenditure Decisions in Moderately Sized Firms", *Financial Review*, 1974.

For a methodological critique of these studies, see Raj Agarwal, "Corporate Use of Sophisticated Budgeting Techniques: A Strategic Perspective and a Critique of Survey Results", *Interfaces*, April 1980; Allen Rappaport, "A Critique of Capital Budgeting Questionnaires", *Interfaces*, May 1979; and Meir J. Rosenblatt and James V. Jucker, "Capital Expenditure Decision-Making: Some Tools and Trends", *Interfaces*, February 1979.

Table 8.2

Project Evaluation Techniques

	Percentages used in			
	1976*	*1970***	*1964***	*1959***
Discounting (*IRR, NPV* or Profitability Index)	66	57	38	19
Accounting Rate of Return	25	26	30	34
Payback or Payback Reciprocal	9	12	24	34
Qualitative Methods		5	8	13
	100	100	100	100

*Based on *primary* evaluation technique used.
**Only *most* sophisticated method reported was counted.

Sources: For the years 1970, 1964 and 1959: Thomas Klammer, "Empirical Evidence of the Adoption of Sophisticated Capital Budgeting Techniques", *Journal of Business*, July 1972. For 1976: Lawrence J. Gitman and John R. Forrester Jr., "A Survey of Capital Budgeting Techniques Used by Major US Firms", *Financial Management*, Fall 1977.

understandable lag, capital budgeting theory, developed in the 1950s, became the practice of business firms in the 1970s. But, despite this trend, three nagging questions are raised by the empirical evidence:

(1) How can we account for the persistence with which many knowledgeable businessmen continue to use simple rule of thumb calculations?
(2) What changes in the economic and business environment account for the observed shift to time-discounted methods?
(3) How can we explain managements' preferences for the internal rate of return over other time-discounted methods such as *NPV*?

The remainder of the chapter will be devoted to an attempt to answer each of these questions, but to do this we must first analyze the precise relationship between traditional rules of thumb and modern time-discounted methods of project evaluation.

THE RELATIONSHIP BETWEEN TRADITIONAL AND MODERN INVESTMENT ANALYSIS

As we have already noted, many businessmen still use short-cut measures of investment worth when evaluating capital expenditures. Although it can readily be shown that the popular rules of thumb may distort investment decisions, they provide close approximations of the discounted rate of return in a number of important situations.

In Chapter 3 an investment proposal's internal rate of return was defined as that rate of discount which equates the present value of the net cash receipts generated by the proposal with the initial investment outlay.

$$I = \frac{S_1}{(1 + R)} + \frac{S_2}{(1 + R)^2} + \cdots + \frac{S_n}{(1 + R)^n}$$

where:

R = the internal rate of return

I = the present value of the investment outlay

S_t = the net pre-tax cash receipt in period t, before deducting depreciation expenses.

Assuming equal annual net receipts and zero terminal values, this formula can be rewritten as

$$I = \frac{S}{1 + R} \cdot \left[1 + \frac{1}{(1 + R)} + \frac{1}{(1 + R)^2} + \cdots + \frac{1}{(1 + R)^{n-1}} \right]$$

Summing the geometric progression within the square brackets and rearranging terms yields

$$R = \frac{S}{I} - \frac{S}{I} \left(\frac{1}{1 + R} \right)^n$$

Under these same two assumptions the reciprocal of an investment proposal's payback period, R_p, can be defined as

$$R_p = \frac{S}{I}$$

Comparing the definition of the payback reciprocal with the *IRR* formula clearly shows that the internal rate of return always lies below the payback reciprocal for all investment projects of finite duration, the margin of error being given by the expression $S/I[1/(1 + R)^n]$. The margin of error depends not only on an investment proposal's duration, but also on its internal rate of return. This can be seen by substituting the payback reciprocal into the *IRR* equation and rearranging terms:

$$R = R_p - R_p \left(\frac{1}{1 + R} \right)^n$$

$$R_p = R \bigg/ \left[1 - \left(\frac{1}{1 + R} \right)^n \right]$$

The above relationship provides a convenient equation for carrying out a numerical analysis of the general relationship between the payback reciprocal

Table 8.3

Percentage Point Deviations of the Payback Reciprocal R_p from the Internal Rate of Return for Selected Values of R and n

Internal Rate of Return R in Percent	Project Duration in n Years								
	2	5	8	10	15	20	40	60	100
5	+ 48.8	+ 18.1	+ 10.5	+ 8.0	+ 4.6	+ 3.0	+ 0.8	+ 0.3	—
10	+ 47.6	+ 16.4	+ 8.7	+ 6.3	+ 3.2	+ 1.8	+ 0.2	—	—
15	+ 46.5	+ 14.8	+ 7.3	+ 4.9	+ 2.1	+ 1.0	+ 0.1	—	—
20	+ 45.4	+ 13.4	+ 6.1	+ 3.9	+ 1.4	+ 0.5	—	—	—
30	+ 43.5	+ 11.1	+ 4.2	+ 2.4	+ 0.6	+ 0.2	—	—	—
40	+ 41.7	+ 9.1	+ 2.9	+ 1.4	+ 0.3	—	—	—	—
50	+ 40.0	+ 7.6	+ 2.0	+ 0.9	+ 0.1	—	—	—	—
60	+ 38.5	+ 6.3	+ 1.4	+ 0.6	—	—	—	—	—

The symbol "—" represents deviations of less than 0.1 percentage points.

and the internal rate of return.[6] The results of the numerical calculations are given in Table 8.3. An examination of the data confirms that the sign of the deviation is always positive (i.e. the payback reciprocal always exceeds the internal rate of return) and that for any given rate of return, the deviation decreases as an investment proposal's economic life increases.[7] However Table 8.3 also clearly shows that for any *given* proposal duration, the deviation of the payback reciprocal from the internal rate also decreases as the internal rate increases. For investment proposals with internal rates of return greater than 30% and with economic lives exceeding ten years (the relevant region for much of US industry) the deviation is negligible and the payback reciprocal provides a very good estimate of the discounted rate of return. On the other hand, for proposals with relatively low internal rates of return ($R < 8\%$), which is the relevant domain for regulated industries such as the electric power industry, the deviations remain substantial for all economic lives of less than twenty years, which helps to explain why the payback period has never been popular in such industries. Similarly, proposals of short duration (less than five years) exhibit substantial deviations even for large values of the *IRR*. Thus despite the fact that the payback period is often considered as a conservative rule of thumb which emphasizes liquidity considerations, its use may impart a significant *upward* bias to profitability estimates.

6 For the purposes of this comparison, otherwise important differences between the internal rate of return and net present value investment criteria can be safely ignored. Strictly speaking, the use of the internal rate of return as a benchmark in the analysis is equivalent to assuming (a) that no mutually exclusive investment alternatives exist and (b) that the relevant discount rate does not change over time, cf. Ch. 4 above.

7 The percentage point deviations given in Table 8.3 were calculated by deducting R from R_p for each combination of R and n. For example, when $R = 10\%$ and $n = 10$ years, $R_p = 16.3\%$; the percentage point deviation, therefore, is given by $16.3 - 10 = +6.3$.

Table 8.4

Percentage Point Deviations of the Accounting Rate of Return on Total Investment R_t from the Internal Rate of Return R for Selected Values of R and n

Internal Rate of Return R in Percent	Project Duration in n Years								
	1	2	5	10	15	20	40	60	100
5	0	− 1.2	− 1.9	− 2.0	− 2.0	− 2.0	− 1.7	− 1.4	− 1.0
10	0	− 2.4	− 3.6	− 3.7	− 3.5	− 3.2	− 2.3	− 1.6	− 1.0
15	0	− 3.5	− 5.2	− 5.1	− 4.6	− 4.0	− 2.4	− 1.7	− 1.0
20	0	− 4.6	− 6.6	− 6.2	− 5.3	− 4.5	− 2.6	− 1.7	− 1.0
30	0	− 6.5	− 8.9	− 7.6	− 6.1	− 4.8	− 2.5	− 1.7	− 1.0
40	0	− 8.3	− 10.9	− 8.6	− 6.4	− 5.0	− 2.5	− 1.7	− 1.0
50	0	− 10.0	− 12.4	− 9.1	− 6.6	− 5.0	− 2.5	− 1.7	− 1.0
60	0	− 11.5	− 13.7	− 9.4	− 6.6	− 5.0	− 2.5	− 1.7	− 1.0

In a similar manner, the relationship between the accounting rate of return and the *IRR* can be specified.[8] The essential properties of the accounting rate of return on total investment (R_t) are analyzed in Table 8.4 which gives the percentage point deviations of the accounting rate of return on total investment, R_t from the internal rate of return, *R*, for a wide range of values of *R* and *n*.

In sharp contrast to the payback reciprocal, the sign of the deviation of the accounting rate on total investment from the internal rate is uniformly *negative* for all finite proposal durations greater than one year. The deviations, moreover, *increase* initially as proposal duration is increased, but after a point, R_t also asymptotically approaches the *IRR* as longer proposal durations are considered. However, in the case of the accounting rate the approach is not nearly as rapid as was true for the payback reciprocal, and over most of the economically relevant range the deviations remain significantly large.

---

8 We shall consider the following popular variants of the accounting rate of return:

$$R_t = \frac{S - D}{I} = \frac{S}{I} - \frac{I/n}{I} = R_p - \frac{1}{n}$$

$$R_a = \frac{S - D}{I/2} = \frac{2S}{I} - \frac{2}{n} = 2\left(R_p - \frac{1}{n}\right)$$

where:
D = annual "straight-line" depreciation, i.e. I/n
R_t = the accounting rate of return on total investment
R_a = the accounting rate of return on average investment
Substituting the formula for the payback reciprocal which was derived above into these two formulas yields:

$$R_t = \frac{R}{1 - \left(\frac{1}{1 + R}\right)^n} - \frac{1}{n}$$

$$R_a = 2\left[\frac{R}{1 - \left(\frac{1}{1 + R}\right)^n} - \frac{1}{n}\right]$$

Since the accounting rate of return on average investment, R_a is a constant multiple of R_t, the relationship of the former to the internal rate of return is simply a constant vertical displacement of the latter's relationship. For proposal durations of one year, $R_a = 2R$; and as proposal duration increases, R_a first decreases but beyond some critical value of n it increases; as n approaches infinity R_a approaches $2R$. For all other values of n the sign of the deviation of R_a from R remains *positive*. Thus the accounting rate of return on average investment *overstates*, while the accounting rate of return on total investment *understates* investment proposals' internal rates of return.[9]

RECONCILING THEORY WITH PRACTICE

Having determined the formal relationship between the rules of thumb and the *IRR*, let us return to the questions regarding the persistence with which many businessmen continue to use simple short-cut measures of profitability and the observed trend towards the use of time-discounted methods in the 1960s and 1970s. But before we do this, a preliminary warning may be in order. Despite the systematic nature of the relationship of short-cut methods to the time adjusted internal rate of return, these results have *no* significance for the normative theory of the investment of the firm.[10] Even minor deviations of the rules of thumb from the internal rate may lead to decision errors. However, the systematic nature of the relationships between rules of thumb and the internal rate, and the range over which the deviations remain relatively small, are very relevant for the positive theory of investment. They can help to account for the fact that most successful business firms used short-cut rules of thumb in the past and explain why many still persist in their use today, even in the face of the overwhelming theoretical arguments in favor of time discounting.

Use of Rules of Thumb

Considerable evidence exists that most of the industrial firms who employed the payback rule operated in the range of project durations and profitability in which the rule of thumb provided a very close approximation of the project's true *IRR*. Almost all of the researchers who reported on the use of the payback rule comment on the fact that firms demanded relatively short payback periods while applying the rule to projects of rather long duration.[11]

9 For simplicity the analysis has been carried out in terms of pre-tax cash flows. In Appendix 8A at the end of this chapter it is shown that these general relationships between the rules of thumb and the *IRR* hold for the after-tax case as well.

10 This section employs Milton Friedman's familiar distinction between normative and positive theories. The term normative refers to propositions concerning what should or ought to be; positive refers to propositions designed to explain or predict reality as it actually exists. See Milton Friedman, *Essays in Positive Economics*, Chicago, University of Chicago Press, 1953, pp. 3–43.

11 See, for example, Donald F. Istvan, "The Economic Evaluation of Capital Expenditures", *Journal of Business*, January 1961.

But these are precisely the conditions (high profitability and long economic life) which ensure a very close approximation of the rule of thumb estimate to the project's true profitability. Thus, the use of the crude measure of profitability need not lead, in such instances, to a *decision error*, that is to a reversal of the decision which would have been reached using the *IRR*.

Similarly, the results of the analysis can be used to explain the observed use of the accounting rate of return on total investment (R_t) rather than on average investment (R_a). On the surface, the latter would seem to have the greater appeal — especially for accountants, who might be expected to argue that the investment (denominator of the ratio) should be progressively reduced as the initial outlay is recouped through depreciation allowances.

In this case, the popularity of R_t can be traced to the systematic *downward* bias which it imparts to the profitability estimate. (The reader should recall that the sign of the deviation is always negative). The use of R_t can only lead to .a decision error in which a project which would have been accepted had its *IRR* been calculated, is rejected. Conversely, the use of the conservative R_t formula can never lead to the acceptance of a project which should be rejected. The opposite holds true for R_a and since most financial executives tend to prefer an "opportunity loss" to an actual money loss, the preference for R_t is not surprising. The conservative downward bias which results from the use of total, rather than average, investment in the formula for the accounting rate of return can also be rationalized as a crude adjustment for risk and/or timing, both of which are ignored in the numerator of the rule of thumb calculation.

Shift to Time Discounting

Now let us turn to the even more perplexing question of why many of these same firms began to make the transition to more sophisticated time-discounted measures of investment worth in the 1960s and 1970s. First credit must be given to the generation of specialists in corporate finance, managerial economics and engineering economy who refined and strengthened the theoretical foundations of modern investment analysis. Secondly, the transition to modern evaluation techniques coincides with a "revolution" in corporate forecasting capability. The corporations of the post-World War II period had an arsenal of newly created tools at their disposal to help forecast the uncertain future; and soon econometricians and systems analysts began to make their appearance on corporate planning teams and even in the boardroom. Perhaps the best known example of the post-war transition is provided by the Ford Motor Company which appointed a former Harvard University professor of accounting (McNamara) as its president and a former University of Chicago professor of econometrics (Yntema) as its financial vice-president.

In this context the reader should recall that our analysis of the popular rules of thumb rests on the assumption of *equal annual* receipts. As long as business firms were unable to refine their forecasts beyond a ball park estimate of the average annual cash flow and the economic life of the project — e.g. "a million dollars for ten years", the rules of thumb worked well. An in fact, considering the trauma which often afflicts executives when radically new techniques are introduced, there was little economic justification for making the transition to *IRR* or *NPV* until better forecasts became available. However, once a firm is able to estimate both the magnitude and timing of the cash flow, the transition to evaluation methods which reflect the impact of the differential timing of receipts and outlays is almost inevitable. Under these circumstances rules of thumb become as obsolete as the fabled gray mare and readers of books like this begin the long trek to positions of corporate responsibility.

Preference for *IRR* over *NPV*

A detailed examination of more recent empirical surveys shows that management has a very strong preference for the *IRR* over its other time-discounted counterparts such as *NPV*. Moreover, most large corporations, which still use a rule of thumb such as payback, do so in combination with the internal rate of return.[12] Thus despite the theoretical difficulties which academics have with the *IRR* it is very popular with practitioners. And by the principle of revealed preference, it is clear that, by and large, management is unconcerned with the theoretical and technical shortcomings of the *IRR* which we have spelled out in great detail in Chapter 4 above.

In this context we should recall that the *theoretical shortcomings* of the *IRR* method relate only to mutually exclusive choice situations. Thus with respect to many (and perhaps most) capital expenditure decisions, the *IRR* is not inferior to net present value. But, even though it gives good results in most cases why should management prefer the *IRR* when an even better method (i.e., *NPV*) is available.

Unlike the case of payback, one cannot rationalize the use of *IRR* on grounds of simplicity. On the contrary, the *IRR* is actually somewhat more difficult to calculate than the *NPV*; and, moreover, it is plagued on occasion by the technical problem of multiple roots. Nor can we gain much insight from that old textbook dictum about *NPV* requiring an estimate of the cost of capital, for as we have already seen, such an estimate is also required if the *IRR* is to be used as a decision rule. It appears, not unlikely, that the preference for *IRR* reflects a very strong but perhaps subconscious, preference for measures of profitability which are stated in terms of percent. "Everyone knows what 10% means; what in the devil is a positive net present value?" How can the fledgling executive reconcile this with his theoretical conscience? There are two alternatives.

(1) Give your boss a crash course in capital budgeting; this may temporarily inflate your ego but will probably shorten the duration of your stay with the firm!

(2) A more political alternative is to plug for, and use, *IRR* but always make

---

12 See Petty and Scott, op. cit.

room for an Appendix on *NPV* in your feasibility reports in mutually exclusive choice situations!

SUMMARY

This chapter has been devoted to the analysis of nondiscounted methods of evaluating capital investment proposals. Two popular rules of thumb are analyzed in detail; the payback (and its reciprocal) and the undiscounted accounting rate of return on total investment. (The accounting rate of return on *average* investments is simply twice the latter.)

Assuming equal annual receipts the payback and accounting rate of return are defined as follows:

$$\text{Payback Period} = \frac{\text{Initial Investment Outlay}}{\text{Annual Cash Receipt}}$$

$$\begin{array}{l}\text{Accounting Rate of} \\ \text{Return on Total} \\ \text{Investment}\end{array} = \frac{\text{Net Annual Profit}}{\text{Initial Investment Outlay}}$$

Despite some very obvious defects, a majority of all business firms probably still employ such methods, although in more recent years more and more larger firms have been making the transition to time-discounted measures of investment worth.

An analysis of the formal relationship between the rules of thumb and the time-discounted *IRR* shows that as long as the firm assumes equal annual receipts, the simple rules of thumb often provide a very close approximation to a project's true *IRR* in the domain of project duration and profitability which is relevant for the firm in practice. It is only when more sophisticated techniques are used to forecast the components and timing of the cash flow that the use of time-discounted methods becomes an imperative for rational decision-making. Finally, we should mention that although the comparison between the internal rate of return and the rules of thumb ignored corporate taxes, the same basic relationship holds for the post-tax cash flows as well.

QUESTIONS AND PROBLEMS

8.1   Define the following terms:

(a) Payback period
(b) Accounting rate of return.

8.2   For each of the following cash flows, calculate the payback period:

Year	0	1	2	3	4	5	6	7	8
A	−2,000	400	400	400	400	400	400	400	400
B	−9,000	3,000	2,500	2,000	1,500	1,000	500	—	—
C	−12,000	10,000	2,000	—	—	—	—	—	—
D	−12,000	2,400	2,400	2,400	2,400	2,400	14,400	—	—
E	−12,000	2,000	2,000	2,000	2,000	2,400	2,000	2,000	2,000

8.3 What is the payback period of a project which requires $1,000 initial investment, and has receipts of $500 for five years? What will be its payback if the receipts are $500 for two years? What is the economic significance of your answer?

8.4 For each of the following cash flows, calculate the accounting rate of return (on total investment), assuming straight-line depreciations:

Year	0	1	2	3	4	5	6	7	Duration
F	−1,400	300	300	300	300	300	300	300	7 years
G	−25,000	12,500	12,500	12,500	12,500	12,500	—	—	5 years
I	−10,000	4,000	4,000	4,000	4,000	—	—	—	4 years
J	−2,000	1,500	1,500	—	—	—	—	—	2 years

8.5 Calculate the payback period and its reciprocal for each of the cash flows appearing in Question 8.4. Compare and explain your answer using the two rules of thumb.

8.6 Set out the formal relationships between the following rules of thumb for project evaluation and the internal rate of return.

(a) Payback period (reciprocal)
(b) Accounting rate of return on total investment
(c) Accounting rate of return on average investment

8.7 What is the significance of the formal relationship between rules of thumb and the *IRR* for investment decision-making?

8.8 "It is surprising that large US firms often use short payback periods to appraise long-lived projects." Critically comment on this statement.

8.9 For each of the following projects, calculate the payback reciprocal, the accounting rate of return on total investment and the internal rate of return. Assume straight-line depreciation:

Project A. Initial investment of $10,000 and, annual gross receipts (before deducting depreciation) of $2,000, for ten years.

Project B. Initial investment of $10,000 and annual gross receipts of $2,000 for twenty years.

Project C. Initial investment of $10,000 and annual gross receipts of $2,000 for forty years.

Compare and explain your results.

8.10 For each of the following projects, calculate the payback reciprocal and the accounting rates of return on total and average investment, and the internal rate of return. (Assume straight-line depreciation.)

Project D. Initial investment of $20,000 and annual gross receipts of $3,000 for ten years.

Project E. Initial investment of $20,000 and annual gross receipts of $6,000 for ten years.

Project F. Initial investment of $20,000 and annual gross receipts of $9,000 for ten years.

Compare and explain your results.

8.11 The Gordon Investment Company was established in 1963. The company's policy was to concentrate its investments in industrial firms in an effort to gain control. The parent company created a decentralized management system which gave the managers of the subsidiaries a considerable freedom, and as a result different methods of project evaluation are employed by the subsidiaries.

Alpha Company uses the "payback" criterion, where the cash flow is taken on a "before interest and depreciation" basis. According to Alpha's criterion, a project is acceptable if the payback period does not exceed four years. Another subsidiary, Beta, uses the "accounting method" which is defined as follows: compute the rate of return by dividing the net receipt (before interest but after depreciation) by the total investment. If this accounting rate of return exceeds 20%, the project is acceptable.

In February 1975, the management of the Gordon Investment Company asked Mr. Smith, a management consultant, for his professional judgment of the methods used by Alpha and Beta. As a first step, Smith chose a sample of investment projects being evaluated by the two subsidiaries.

Projects considered by Alpha

Project 1. An investment of $10,000. The net receipts (after deducting depreciation and interest) are $1,600 per annum. The yearly interest charge is $700 and the annual depreciation is $500.

Project 2. An investment of $60,000. The net receipts (after deducting depreciation and interest) are $3,000 per annum. The yearly interest and depreciation charges are $4,200 and $10,000 respectively.

Project 3. An investment of $150,000. The net annual receipts, after deducting depreciation and interest, are $10,000 during the first five years and $40,000 per annum in the next ten years. The yearly depreciation charge is $10,000 and the yearly interest charge is $15,000.

Projects considered by Beta

Project 1. An investment of $600,000; net receipts, before interest but after depreciation, are $100,000. The yearly depreciation is $200,000.

Project 2. An investment of $1 million. Net receipts, before interest but after depreciation, are $240,000. The yearly depreciation is $25,000.

Mr. Smith also made the following assumptions:

(1) The investment projects are *not* mutually exclusive.
(2) The salvage value of all projects at the end of their economic life is zero.
(3) Straight-line depreciation is used.
(4) Due to differences in risk, the appropriate cost of capital for Alpha is 25% and the appropriate rate for Beta is 20%.
(5) Corporate taxes are not payable by the companies and therefore can be ignored.
(6) The sample of projects is *representative* of the type of projects evaluated by the firms.

Assume that you are Mr. Smith and recommend an optimal decision rule for evaluating investments.

(a) What rule do you recommend? Why?
(b) In defending your answer compare the decisions reached by the subsidiaries using their methods with the decisions which you reach using the proposed optimal method. Carefully explain your results.

8.12 Consider a project with a pre-tax internal rate of return of 10%, and a duration of five years. The project's initial investment is $100 (I). Assuming a constant annual cash flow S, solve for the pre-tax and post-tax accounting rates of return (R_a and R_t) and for the payback reciprocal (R_p). Assume straight-line depreciation and a corporate tax of 50% ($T = 0.5$).

8.13 Distinguish between "opportunity loss" and "financial loss". Which rule of thumb leads to each type of loss? Explain your answer.

APPENDIX 8A THE POST-TAX RELATIONSHIPS BETWEEN RULES OF THUMB AND THE INTERNAL RATE OF RETURN

In this appendix the effects of introducing corporate taxes into the analysis are examined. The post-tax relationships between the rules of thumb and the internal rate of return are of crucial importance since it may be presumed that profit-oriented firms are concerned solely with errors in post-tax profitability estimates.[1] Fortunately for our purposes, it can be shown that the relationships among the alternative measures of return depicted in Tables 8.3 and 8.4 of the text remain

---

1 Of course this "concern" need not (and presumably often does not) exist at a conscious level.

invariant for any level of taxation. The general proof of this proposition follows the notation and method of analysis used in the pre-tax case.[2]

Retaining the assumptions of equal annual pre-tax cash receipts and straight-line depreciation, and letting T equal the tax rate, the net post-tax receipt before depreciation is defined as $(S - D)(1 - T) + D$. Hence

$$I = \frac{(S - D)(1 - T) + D}{(1 + R^*)} + \frac{(S - D)(1 - T) + D}{(1 + R^*)^2}$$

$$+ \ldots + \frac{(S - D)(1 - T) + D}{(1 + R^*)^n}$$

$$= \frac{(S - D)(1 - T) + D}{(1 + R^*)} \cdot \left[1 - \left(\frac{1}{1 + R^*} \right)^n \middle/ 1 - \left(\frac{1}{1 + R^*} \right) \right]$$

where:
R^* = the post-tax internal rate of return
T = the income tax rate.

Simplifying and rearranging terms yields

$$R^* = \frac{(S - D)(1 - T) + D}{I} \cdot \left[1 - \left(\frac{1}{1 + R^*} \right)^n \right]$$

Under the same assumptions the post-tax payback reciprocal (R_p^*) is defined as

$$R_p^* = \frac{(S - D)(1 - T) + D}{I}$$

Substituting this definition into the preceding equation and rearranging terms yields

$$R_p^* = \frac{R^*}{1 - \left(\dfrac{1}{1 + R^*} \right)^n}$$

Comparing the relevant pre-tax and post-tax formulae clearly shows that the relationship of the post-tax payback reciprocal to the post-tax internal rate of return is *identical* to the pre-tax relationship and, therefore, has the same general properties. It follows that the deviations given in Table 8.3 of the text hold equally for both the before-tax and after-tax cases.

A similar result can readily be proven for the accounting rates of return as well. Let us define the post-tax accounting rate of return on total investment R_i^* as follows:

$$R_i^* = \frac{(1 - T)(S - D)}{I}$$

Recalling that under the assumption of straight-line depreciation $D = I/n$, we

---

2 After-tax variables are distinguished from their pre-tax counterparts by an asterisk.

can rewrite the post-tax *IRR* as

$$R^* = \frac{(S - D)(1 - T)}{I} \cdot \left[1 - \left(\frac{1}{1 + R^*} \right)^n \right] + \frac{1}{n} \cdot \left[1 - \left(\frac{1}{1 + R^*} \right)^n \right]$$

Substituting the definition of R_i^* into this equation and rearranging terms gives

$$R_i^* = \frac{R^*}{1 - \left(\dfrac{1}{1 + R^*} \right)^n} - \frac{1}{n},$$

which also has the identical form of the pre-tax relationship.[3] Here again it follows that the deviations presented in Table 8.4 of the text hold for both the before- and after-tax cases. Thus all of the general properties of the pre-tax relationships hold with equal force for the after-tax case as well, *independent* of the tax rate assumed.[4]

QUESTIONS AND PROBLEMS

8A.1 For each of the following cashflows, calculate the post-tax payback reciprocal (R_p^*), the post-tax accounting rate of return (R^*) and the post-tax *IRR*; assuming a 50% corporate income tax rate and straight-line depreciation:

Cashflow	The PV of the Investment Outlay ($)	The Annual Pre-tax Cash Receipts ($)	Duration Life (in years)
A	20,000	9,000	5
B	12,000	4,000	6
C	50,000	11,000	10
D	100,000	30,000	20

8A.2 The "Bazak" Company deals with projects with constant annual cashflows whose duration is more than 30 years. The firm uses the payback method and accepts every project with a payback period of five years or less. "Bazak" pays no corporate taxes.

(a) "The above method is an unreasonable investment rule, particularly in the case of projects with a long duration." Do you agree with the above quotation? Prove your answer.

---

3 Since the post-tax accounting rate of return on average investment is a constant multiple of the post-tax rate of return on total investment, this result holds for that relationship as well.

4 The analysis can readily be extended to other than straight-line depreciation methods, for example, "sum-of-the-year's-digits" and "twice-the-straight-line-declining-balance", both of which are permitted by the income tax authorities. However, it should be noted that in the latter two cases the annual post-tax cash receipts will vary even when the pre-tax cash flow is constant. As a result, the post-tax relationship of the rules of thumb to the internal rate of return will no longer be independent of the assumed tax rate.

(b) Assume now that the above firm has to pay 50% corporate tax. After the tax has been levied on the firm, an economic consultant recommends to use the "accounting method" instead of the payback method. He claims that when the tax is taken into account the "accounting method" yields the best approximation to the internal rate of return. Do you agree with the above recommendation? Explain carefully.

SELECTED REFERENCES

Aggarwal, Raj, "Corporate Use of Sophisticated Capital Budgeting Techniques: A Strategic Perspective and a Critique of Survey Results", *Interfaces*, April 1980.

Baker, James C. and Beardsley, Lawrence, "Multinational Companies Use of Risk Evaluation and Profit Measurement for Capital Budgeting Decisions", *Journal of Business Finance*, Spring 1973.

Brigham, Eugene F., "Hurdle Rates for Screening Capital Expenditure Proposals", *Financial Management*, Autumn 1975.

Brigham, Eugene F. and Pettway, Richard H., "Capital Budgeting by Utilities", *Financial Management*, Autumn 1973.

Eisner, Robert, "Determinants of Capital Expenditures: An Interview Study", *Studies in Business Expectations and Planning*, Urbana: University of Illinois, 1956.

Fremgen, James, "Capital Budgeting Practices: A Survey", *Management Accounting*, May 1973.

Gitman, Lawrence J. and Forrester, John R., Jr., "A Survey of Capital Budgeting Techniques Used by Major US Firms", *Financial Management*, Fall 1977.

Gordon, Lawrence A., "Accounting Rate of Return vs. Economic Rate of Return", *Journal of Business Finance & Accounting*, Autumn 1974.

Gordon, Lawrence A., "Further Thoughts on the Accounting Rate of Return vs. The Economic Rate of Return", *Journal of Business Finance & Accounting*, Spring 1977.

Gordon, Myron J., "The Payoff Period and the Rate of Profit", *Journal of Business*, October 1955.

Gort, Michael, "The Planning of Investment: A Study of Capital Budgeting in the Electric Power Industry", *Journal of Business*, April 1951 and July 1951.

Hoskins, C.G. and Mumey, G.A., "Payback: A Maligned Method of Asset Ranking?" *Engineering Economist*, Fall 1979.

Istvan, Donald F., *Capital-Expenditure Decisions: How They Are Made in Large Corporations*, Bloomington, Indiana: Bureau of Business Research, Indiana University, 1961.

Istvan, Donald F., "The Economic Evaluation of Capital Expenditures", *Journal of Business*, January 1961.

Kim, Suk H., "Capital Budgeting Practices in Large Corporations and Their Impact on Overall Profitability", *Baylor Business Studies*, November–December 1978, January 1979.

Klammer, T., "Empirical Evidence of the Adoption of Sophisticated Capital Budgeting Techniques", *Journal of Business*, July 1972.

Levy, Haim, "A Note on the Payback Method", *Journal of Financial and Quantitative Analysis*, 3 December 1968.

Longbottom, D.A. and Wiper, L., "Capital Appraisal and the Case for Average Rate of Return", *Journal of Business Finance & Accounting*, 4,4 (1977).

Maher, P. Michael and Rubenstein, Albert A., "Factors Affecting Adoption of a Quantitative Method for R&D Project Selection", *Management Science Application*, October 1974.

Miller, James H., "A Glimpse at Practice in Calculating and Using Return on Investment", *N.A.A. Bulletin*, June 1960.

Neuhauser, John J. and Viscione, Jerry A., "How Managers Feel About Advanced Capital Budgeting Methods", *Management Review*, November 1973.

Oblak, David J. and Helm, Roy J. Jr., "Survey and Analysis of Capital Budgeting Methods Used by Multinationals", *Financial Management*, Winter 1980.

Petry, Glenn H., "Effective Use of Capital Budgeting Tools", *Business Horizons*, October 1975.

Pullara, S.J. and Walker, L.R., "The Evaluation of Capital Expenditure Proposals; A Survey of Firms in the Chemical Industry", *Journal of Business*, October 1965.

Rosenblatt, Meir J., "A Survey and Analysis of Capital Budgeting Decision Processes in Multi-Division Firms", *The Engineering Economist*, Summer 1980.

Sarnat, Marshall and Levy, Haim, "The Relationship of Rules of Thumb to the Internal Rates of Return: A Restatement and Generalization", *Journal of Finance*, June 1969.

Schall, L.D.; Sundem, G.L. and Geijsbeek, W.R., Jr., "Survey and Analysis of Capital Budgeting Methods", *Journal of Finance*, March 1978.

Stephen, Frank H., "On Deriving the Internal Rate of Return from the Accountant's Rate of Return", *Journal of Business Finance & Accounting*, Summer 1976.

Stonehill, Arthur I. and Nathanson, Leonard, "Capital Budgeting and the Multinational Corporation", *California Management Review*, Summer 1968.

Weingartner, H. Martin, "Some New Views on the Payback Period and Capital Budgeting Decisions", *Management Science*, August 1969.

Williams, Ronald B. Jr., "Industry Practice in Allocating Capital Resources", *Managerial Planning*, May–June 1970.

PART 1: SUGGESTIONS FOR FURTHER READING

The reader with an historical bent can turn to the pioneering articles by Boulding and Samuelson:

K. Boulding, "The Theory of a Single Investment", *Quarterly Journal of Economics*, May 1935.

P.A. Samuelson, "Some Aspects of the Pure Theory of Capital", *Quarterly Journal of Economics*, May 1937.

The capital budgeting problem was rediscovered in the beginning of the 1950s by:

J. Dean, *Capital Budgeting*, New York, Columbia University Press, 1951.

F. Lutz and V. Lutz, *The Theory of Investment of the Firm*, Princeton, N.J., Princeton University Press, 1951.

The theoretical foundation for capital budgeting under certainty can be found in:

J.H. Hirshleifer, "On The Theory of Optimal Investment Decision", *Journal of Political Economy*, August 1958.

M.J. Bailey, "Formal Criteria for Investment Decisions", *Journal of Political Economy*, October 1959.

E. Solomon, *The Management of Corporate Capital*, New York, The Free Press, 1959.

The tax aspects of capital budgeting are examined in detail by:

S. Davidson and D.F. Drake, "Capital Budgeting and the 'Best' Tax Depreciation Method", *Journal of Business*, October 1961.

N. Dopuch and S. Sunder, "FASB's Statements on Objectives and Elements of Financial Accounting: A Review", *Accounting Review*, January 1980.

V.C. Lembke and H.R. Toole, "Differences in Depreciation Methods and the Analysis of Supplemental Current-Cost and Replacement Cost Data", *Journal of Accounting Auditing and Finance*, Winter 1981.

The impact of inflation on capital investment decisions is discussed in

C.R. Nelson, "Inflation and Capital Budgeting", *Journal of Finance*, June 1976.

M.K. Kim, "Inflationary Effects in the Capital Investment Process: An Empirical Examination", *Journal of Finance*, September 1979.

J.C. Van Horne, "A Note on Biases in Capital Budgeting Introduced by Inflation", *Journal of Financial and Quantitative Analysis*. January 1971. Finally the reader who is skeptical of "optimal" decision methods might do well to study the literature on the relationship of popular rules of thumb to their theoretical superior counterparts.

M.J. Gordon, "The Payoff Period and the Rate of Profit", *Journal of Business*, October 1955.

H. Levy, "A Note on the Payback Method", *Journal of Financial and Quantitative Analysis,* December, 1968.

M. Sarnat and H. Levy, "The Relationship of Rules of Thumb to the Internal Rate of Return", *Journal of Finance,* June 1969.

Part II

Risk and Uncertainty

Introduction

Risk and uncertainty lie at the very heart of the capital investment decision. The formal treatment of risk, however, is often quite complicated; hence we preferred to expose the reader first to the basic methods of project evaluation, to the importance of the timing of the cash flow and to the analysis of the factors which determine the components of the cash flow. Forearmed with this knowledge we believe the reader will be better prepared to grapple with the problems created by the existence of uncertainty.

In the following five chapters we shall examine several alternative ways of explicity incorporating risk into the analysis of the firm's investment decisions. Our main purpose is to prove beyond any shadow of doubt the importance of not ignoring uncertainty, rather than suggesting that all firms adopt some of the more sophisticated tools which we shall be using. Technical and administrative difficulties often preclude the use of such methods in actual decision making, but even if for many firms formal risk analysis is not as yet feasible, they must still devise rough, but practical rules of thumb for taking uncertainty into account. Hopefully, the methods of risk evaluation presented in this section will at least provide a benchmark for determining actual decision strategies in practice.

Chapter 9 briefly sets out the utility foundations of modern risk analysis; the popular mean variance decision rule is derived in Chapter 10. Chapter 11 discusses some practical applications of risk analysis. Chapter 12 presents the basic elements of modern portfolio analysis, while the capital asset pricing model, which is derived from the mean variance portfolio analysis, is described in Chapter 13.

9

Foundations of Risk Analysis

As we noted in Part I, the firm's capital investment decisions depend on its estimates of the cash flows of alternative investment opportunities. Forecasting the future is at best a risky business, and in this chapter we shall attempt to lay a firm conceptual foundation for reaching budgeting decisions under conditions of risk or uncertainty.

THE ESSENCE OF RISK

A firm's expectations of the possible future gains from investment must be based in part on more or less certain historical data of past performance, and in part on forecasts of future events, which can usually be made only on a highly tentative basis. As a result, management rarely has very precise expectations regarding the future profit to be derived from a particular venture. In fact, the best that the firm can reasonably be expected to do is to make some estimate of the range of possible future costs and benefits and the relative chances of earning a high or low profit on the investment.

Formally, we shall distinguish between two states of expectation: certainty and risk (uncertainty).

Certainty

Strictly speaking, perfect certainty refers to cases in which expectations are single-valued; that is the firm views prospective profits in terms of a particular outcome, and not in terms of a range of alternative possible returns. We shall also use the term certainty to describe those situations in which investors' expectations regarding future profit are bounded within a very narrow range. But do

197

such investments actually exist outside of the realm of textbooks? At first glance it may appear that no investment yields a perfectly certain income stream, but on reflection several illustrations can be found. For example, suppose that the firm decides to invest in three-month Treasury bills. Short-term Treasury bills permit the firm to calculate the exact return which will be received upon redemption, i.e. at the end of three months, with what amounts to absolute certainty; we simply ignore the insignificant probability of a revolution or of a war which might destroy the existing monetary system. For the time being we also ignore the important question of inflation and its impact on the *real* return from investment, that is on the return in terms of purchasing power.[1] Similarly if we are willing to ignore the remote possibility of bankruptcy or financial default in such giants as General Motors and AT&T, the short-term notes of these companies can also be considered, for all practical purposes, as investments yielding safe returns.

Investment companies and mutual funds may invest relatively large proportions of their assets in such riskless assets, but most firms invest in productive assets rather than in financial assets, i.e. most firms are typically confronted by risky investment alternatives. Although the opportunity to invest in Treasury bills exists for all investors, this opportunity is irrelevant for most firms, since the stockholder can readily acquire the riskless assets directly. As a result, there would be no incentive for an individual to invest in the shares of a company, which in turn invested a significant proportion of its equity in riskless assets.

Risk

The term *risk* or equivalently *uncertainty* will be used to describe an option whose profit is not known in advance with absolute certainty, but for which an array of alternative outcomes and their probabilities are known.[2] In other words, a risky investment is one for which the *distribution* of profits is known. The distribution may have been estimated on the basis of either objective or purely subjective probabilities.

An example of such a frequency distribution is given in Table 9.1 which sets out the historical record of the profit from a hypothetical investment over the past forty years. The data of Table 9.1 were then used to prepare the histogram, drawn in Fig. 9.1. Historical data of this sort are often available for financial investments, and can be used to facilitate current investment decisions. But even where a long record of past profitability is available, the decision to invest remains complex. There often may be no reason why the future distribution of profits should resemble their distribution in the past, and before arriving

---

1 The impact of inflation on the decision-making process is discussed in Chapters 7 and 22.
2 Frank Knight distinguished between "risk" as defined in the text and "uncertainty" which he defined as an option for which only the array of possible outcomes, but *not* their probabilities, is known. See his *Risk, Uncertainty and Profit*, Boston and New York: Houghton Mifflin Company, 1921, Chapter 7. The reader should note that the introduction of subjective probability has greatly diminished the significance of the distinction between risk and uncertainty. By assigning *subjective* probabilities to decision problems, an inherently *uncertain* situation can be transformed into a *risky* choice.

Table 9.1
An Example of a Frequency Distribution of Profits

Profit*	Frequency (number of years)
− 30.00 to − 20.01	2
− 20.00 to − 10.01	3
− 10.00 to − 0.01	5
0.00 to 9.99	10
10.00 to 19.99	9
20.00 to 29.99	6
30.00 to 39.99	3
40.00 to 49.99	2
TOTAL	40

*To facilitate comparison, the returns are expressed as percentages.

at a decision all of the factors that might indicate future changes in the distribution must be carefully weighed. Moreover, even if the distribution can be expected to remain unchanged, realizing a high profit (the right-hand side of the histogram) or a loss (the left-hand side of the histogram) in any particular year is largely a matter of chance.

Firms with a lot of experience or those who are confronted with repetitive investments which are renewed every few years are confronted with situations similar to the one portrayed in Fig. 9.1. However, more often the firm has little or no past experience to draw upon, particularly when investments in new products or processes are being considered, and therefore relevant historical data cannot be found which can serve as a guide for current decisions. In such cases

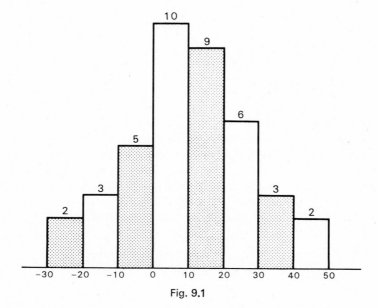

Fig. 9.1

the firm must base its decision solely on subjective probabilities, i.e. on personal judgment regarding the chances of gain or loss.

ALTERNATIVE INVESTMENT CRITERIA

Having defined risk let us now turn to the crucial question of devising a relevant decision rule for evaluating investments with risky, i.e. uncertain, returns.

The Maximum *NPV* Criterion

Let us initially assume a uniform investment period, for example one year, and let us further assume that the decision-maker can choose only a single investment alternative.[3] What decision rule should the investor apply in order to choose the best possible alternative? To define the problem more precisely consider a firm that is confronted by the five alternatives given in Table 9.2. Two of the proposals (A and B) represent perfectly certain investments, while the other three alternatives (C, D and E) entail varying degrees of risk. Such a situation is quite realistic: the entrepreneur can typically buy riskless short-term government bonds or deposit his money in a savings bank; alternatively, he can acquire productive facilities, the income and profit from whcih must be considered as highly uncertain.

Table 9.2

Distribution of Possible Outcomes of Five Alternative Investments*

A NPV	A Probability	B NPV	B Probability	C NPV	C Probability	D NPV	D Probability	E NPV	E Probability
8	1	10	1	−8	1/4	−4	1/4	−20	1/10
				16	1/2	8	1/2	0	6/10
				24	1/4	12	1/4	50	3/10

*Using the riskless interest rate to discount the cash flows.

Only in the unrealistic case in which the firm restricts itself to "safe" investments, that is to proposals A and B, is the choice simple. In this instance the company should choose the alternative that offers the highest net present value (see Chapter 3), and the riskless interest rate should be used as the discount rate. In our example, investment B which affords a *NPV* of 10 as compared with the *NPV* of 8 offered by alternative A, would be chosen.

Such simple choice situations are hardly representative of the alternatives

---

3 Discussion of combinations of investments, i.e. the very important portfolio problem is deferred to Chapter 11, while analysis of the no less important multiperiod capital budgeting problem is postponed to Chapter 13.

faced by modern corporations; reality is much more complicated and for that matter much more interesting as well. Firms do not confine themselves solely to safe proposals. A more realistic problem, therefore, is how to select the "best" investment out of the five alternative choices, A, B, C, D and E.

Can we still apply the maximum *NPV* criterion? Clearly we cannot do so without major qualifications. Whereas in the previous example, profits were known with certainty (8 and 10 respectively), this does not hold for the other three proposals. Suppose we try to compare proposals B and C: the *NPV* of B is 10 but what *NPV* can we attribute to C? If we assume a negative *NPV* of -8, project B is clearly preferable; however, if we assume the *NPV* of C will be 16 or 24, then it is equally clear that investment C represents the better alternative. Since there is no *a priori* reason to single out any one of three possible outcomes of project C, the maximum *NPV* criterion breaks down. Thus once uncertainty is introduced, finding an appropriate investment criterion is unavoidable; the maximum *NPV* criterion which is appropriate in a world of perfect certainty is no longer applicable in a realistic setting in which risk prevails.

The Maximum Expected *NPV* Criterion

To compare the desirability of alternative investments under conditions of uncertainty, we must first devise a measure which can reflect the entire distribution of returns. One possible solution to this problem stipulates that decisions should be reached on the basis of an investment's *expected* profit, where expected profit is defined as the mean of the *NPV* distribution weighted by the probabilities of occurrence. For example, if we consider project C of Table 9.2 the *expected NPV* can be calculated as follows:

$$\tfrac{1}{4} \times (-8) + \tfrac{1}{2} \times 16 + \tfrac{1}{4} \times 24 = 12$$

Similarly, we can readily calculate the expected *NPVs* for the other alternatives:

Projects	Expected NPV
A	8
B	10
C	12
D	6
E	13

Having calculated the expectations for each of the five alternative projects, we can now choose that project with the highest *expected NPV*; in our example this is project E with an expected *NPV* of 13.

The *expected NPV* criterion can be applied to uncertain investments since each investment can be characterized by a single measure of profitability, and therefore all investment proposals can be ranked according to this criterion. However, the fact that the maximum expected *NPV* criterion *can* be applied by no means indicates that it *should* be used. On the contrary, in most cases this

Table 9.3

Calculation of Expected *NPV*

	Project A	Project B
	($)	($)
Present Value of Net Receipts:		
Economic Recession with Probability of 0.2	100	1,100
Economic Prosperity		
(with Probability of 0.8)	2,000	1,750
Expected *PV* of Net Receipts*	1,620	1,620
Less Initial Outlay	− 1,000	− 1,000
Expected *NPV*	620	620

*The expected net income of project A is 0.2 × 100 + 0.8 × 2,000 = $1,620; the expected net income of project B is 0.2 × 1,100 + 0.8 × 1,750 = $1,620.

criterion is inappropriate because it does not take risk explicitly into account. The following example illustrates the drawbacks of using this criterion for evaluating risky investments.

Suppose that the firm has to choose between proposals such as A and B of Table 9.3. Both projects require an initial outlay of $1,000; however, the demand for the products produced under A (say luxury products) is very vulnerable to general economic conditions, that is to say in prosperity demand increases rapidly but in recession the demand falls off drastically. On the other hand, the demand for the products of project B (say a basic food item) is less affected by general economic conditions; hence the monetary returns from investment A are less stable than those of proposal B.

The two proposals yield the same expected profit, i.e. an *NPV* of $620; but clearly they are not equivalent. The outcome of proposal A is more uncertain than B; and the fact that their expected profits are identical confirms the contention that the expected *NPV* criterion does *not* take risk into account. As a result the expected *NPV* criterion, *by itself*, does not provide an appropriate decision criterion to use when uncertainty prevails.

The fact that project A is riskier than project B can be seen even more clearly if the distributions of expected profit are drawn. Figure 9.2 shows that the possible outcomes under proposal B are much closer to one another than is true for proposal A. Moreover, the greater risk inherent in project A is also illustrated by the fact that this project has a 20% chance of a $900 loss; the probability of loss is zero should project B be accepted. Hence, while the calculation of expected *NPV* can serve as a measure of profitability, it can not in itself serve as a measure of risk.

In the following chapters, we shall examine several possible measures of risk which can be used along with the expected *NPV* when reaching investment decisions under conditions of uncertainty. But first, we shall turn to the theory of expected utility in order to gain additional insight into the nature of investment risk.

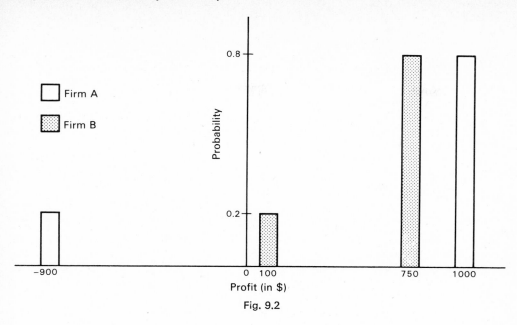

Fig. 9.2

RISK AND UTILITY

The numerical examples of the preceding section suffice to show the inadequacies of a decision criterion based solely on expected profit. In their classic book on the theory of games,[4] John von Neumann and Oskar Morgenstern showed that an appropriate criterion can be found if the expected *utility* derived from the monetary income is substituted for the money profits themselves. Such a criterion has the advantage of taking both the profitability and the risk inherent in an uncertain investment project into account simultaneously.

In order to introduce the concept of utility, consider the case of an individual who must choose between the two alternatives given in Table 9.4. (To simplify the discussion we shall assume that the receipts and outlays occur instantaneously so there is no need to discount the cash flow.) Note that the two projects under consideration have the same expected profit, i.e. $2,000. A glance at the two options suffices to show that the risk of project B is greater than that of project A. We shall show below that despite the equal expected profits, project A is indeed preferable to project B. The intuitive explanation for the preference of investment A over investment B can be clarified if we examine the difference in the monetary outcomes of the two proposals. Suppose that the investor who tentatively chooses project A considers shifting from

4 J. von Neumann and O. Morgenstern, *Theory of Games and Economic Behavior*, 2nd ed., Princeton, N.J., Princeton University Press, 1953. A more popular version is given in R.D. Luce and H. Raiffa, *Games and Decisions*, New York, Wiley, 1966.

Table 9.4

| | Investment A | | Investment B | |
	Net Profit	Probability	Net Profit	Probability
	($)		($)	
	1,000	1/2	0	1/2
	3,000	1/2	4,000	1/2
Expected				
Profit	2,000		2,000	

project A to project B. What changes are induced by such a shift? Clearly, the differences between the two projects can be summarized as follows: in a poor year he will realize $1,000 less on investment B relative to project A, while in a good year investment B yields $1,000 more. Thus, if the investor changes his decision and shifts from investment A to investment B, he has a 50% chance of gaining $1,000, but he also has a 50% chance of losing $1,000. Is it worthwhile to shift from investment A to investment B?

In general, most investors will not switch from A to B since the subjective satisfaction (or utility) that they derive from the additional $1,000 is less than the utility that they must give up if they lose $1,000. To help clarify this argument consider an individual who invests his money for one period and then uses the monetary return to buy consumer goods. For most individuals the additional satisfaction (utility) from consumption diminishes as consumption increases. That is to say, the consumer initially satisfies his more essential needs and hence the utility that he derives from spending say the first $1,000 is relatively large. Once he satisfies his more basic needs we expect that the additional utility which he derives from spending the second $1,000 will be lower, and so on for additional increments of income.

The concept of *diminishing marginal utility* is illustrated in Table 9.5. As we can see, total utility increases as income rises, that is to say the higher the income, the larger is the satisfaction derived from the income. However, the marginal utility is diminishing; the utility of the first $1,000 is 1, for the second $1,000 it is 0.8, for the third $1,000 it is 7 and so the fourth $1,000 it is only 0.5. Combining the relevant figures from Tables 9.4 and 9.5, Table 9.6 presents investment A and investment B in terms of the utility which is derived from these two proposals. The data of Table 9.6 indicate that while proposals A and B are characterized by the same expected profit, they differ with respect to their expected utility. The expected utility derived from investment A is 1.75 as compared with investment B's expected utility of only 1.5. Thus despite the fact that the expected profit criterion cannot discriminate between proposals A and B, the expected utility criterion indicates a clear preference for proposal A, which as we have already noted is considerably less risky. Moreover the ranking of investment A over B holds for all utility functions, so long as the utility function has the property of diminishing marginal utility. This statement can be proved by examining individuals' attitudes towards risk.

Table 9.5

Income	Utility	Marginal Utility
($)		
0	0	
1,000	1	1
2,000	1.8	0.8
3,000	2.5	0.7
4,000	3.0	0.5

Table 9.6

| | Investment A | | | Investment B | | |
	Probability	Profit	Utility	Probability	Profit	Utility
		($)			($)	
	1/2	1,000	1	1/2	0	0
	1/2	3,000	2.5	1/2	4,000	3.0
Expected Net Profit		2,000			2,000	
Expected Utility*		1.75			1.5	

*The expected utility of investments A and B is given by 1/2 × 1 + 1/2 × 2.5 = 1.75 and 1/2 × 0 + 1/2 × 3 = 1.5 respectively.

ALTERNATIVE ATTITUDES TOWARD RISK

It is convenient for the purposes of the analysis to distinguish between two classes of investors: those who dislike risk whom we shall call "risk averters", and those who prefer risky prospects, whom we shall call "risk lovers". As the bulk of the theoretical and empirical evidence supports the view that the typical investor is risk averse we shall concentrate on that broad class of individuals.

Consider the following hypothetical example. Suppose an individual is offered the opportunity of purchasing for $10 the following investment option:

End-of-period Value	Probability
9	1/2
11	1/2

The expected end-of-period value of such an investment is 1/2 × 9 + 1/2 × 11 = 10; that is the expected value equals the initial purchase price. In other words, the expected monetary profit from this investment is zero. (We continue to ignore the discount factor, which is tantamount to assuming a very short investment period.) Can an individual be expected to purchase such an option? Since we have rejected the principle of expected profit and tentatively replaced it with the principle of expected utility, our answer depends on the individual's attitude toward risk, that is on the degree to which he "likes" or "dislikes" to trade a safe prospect for an uncertain one.

Definition: An individual whose utility function is concave will be called a risk averter.

A concave utility function has the property that the marginal utility of money declines over the entire relevant range. Thus investors whose preferences are characterized by diminishing marginal utility will be called risk averters. It follows that every risk averter prefers a perfectly certain investment to an investment with an equal but uncertain expected return. Taking our example, a risk-averse individual will *not* purchase the above option because in terms of utility, the possible loss of 1 dollar more than offsets the equal possible gain of 1 dollar.

This conclusion can be confirmed by using a graphical device. Fig. 9.3 sets out the same investment problem: the purchase for $10 of an option whose end-of-period value has an equal probability of being $9 or $11. The possible end-of-period values are measured along the horizontal axis and utility is measured along the vertical axis. The individual's utility function is drawn in Fig. 9.3 as a *concave* curve rising from the origin; this is tantamount to assuming that he is risk-averse. The expected utility is represented graphically by point C of Fig. 9.3, the point at which a perpendicular rising from the point marked 10 on the horizontal axis intersects the chord connecting points A and B. The expected utility, given by point C, is equal to $1/2\ U(9) + 1/2\ U(11)$ (where U stands for utility). A glance at the diagram shows that the utility of the purchase price, $U(10)$, which corresponds to point D on the utility curve, is greater than the expected utility of the investment option, which corresponds to point C. Thus a risk-averse individual will not purchase an uncertain option whose expected value is equal

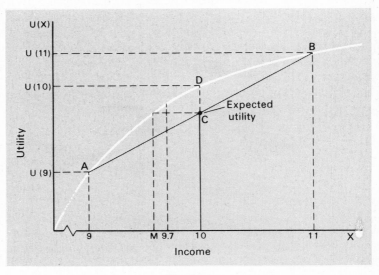

Fig. 9.3

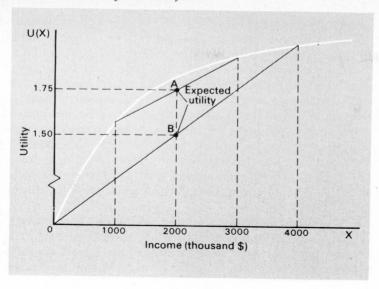

Fig. 9.4

to its purchase price, since the concavity of his utility function translates the *zero monetary gain* into a *utility loss*.

Now let us assume that the same individual is offered the same option, but at a lower price, say $9.70. The expected end-of-period value remains $10 so that the option has a positive expected return ($10 − 9.70 = $0.30). Will the risk-averse individual purchase the option? Despite the lower price, Fig. 9.3 clearly shows that he will not be willing to purchase the option because the utility of a perfectly certain sum of $9.70 still exceeds the expected utility of the risky option (point C). How far must the price fall before our risk-averse investor will be willing to acquire it? Again the answer can be readily inferred from Fig. 9.3. The maximum price that he will be willing to pay is represented by point M on the horizontal axis. At this price, $U(M)$ is just equal to the expected utility from the risky investment option. The distance between 10 and M measures the *risk premium* required to induce the risk-averse individual to purchase the option.[5] At prices lower than M (points to the left of M on the horizontal axis) the invest-ment option is attractive since it represents a gain in utility; conversely, at prices above M, as we have already seen, the risky investment represents a loss of utility for the risk-averse investor. The value M represents the *certainty equivalent* value of the risky option and we will make further use of this concept in Chapter 11.

Having got the basic properties of risk aversion under our belts, let us put the graphical analysis through its paces by returning to the original example given in Table 9.6 above. Recall that we have asserted, but as yet not proved,

5 This is the first of the many risk premia that characterize modern risk analysis. As a tribute to the inventors of the graphical measurement presented in Fig. 9.3, we shall call it the "Friedman–Savage risk premium". See Milton Friedman and Leonard J. Savage, "The Utility Analysis of Choices Involving Risk", *Journal of Political Economy*, August 1948.

that *all* risk averters (i.e. individuals characterized by diminishing marginal utility of money) will prefer proposal A to proposal B, due to the greater dispersion of the latter for an equal expected profit. Fig. 9.4 graphs the data of Table 9.6. Since we are assuming risk aversion, the utility function is drawn as a concave curve rising from the origin. The expected utility of project A is simply 1/2 *U*(1000) + 1/2 *U*(3000) = 1/2 (1) + 1/2 (2.5) = 1.75 (where *U* stands for utility). This value corresponds to point A of Fig. 9.4; i.e. the intersection of the vertical line rising from point 2,000 on the horizontal axis (which is the expected monetary return) with the appropriate chord on the utility function. Similarly, point B indicates the expected utility from investment B. Since point A lies above point B (and this relationship holds for *all* concave utility functions), it follows that every risk averter will prefer investment A over investment B, independent of the degree of his risk aversion.

The reason for this result can also be inferred from Fig. 9.4. Other things being equal, risk averters do not like a wide dispersion of outcomes. From the graph, it is clear that both projects have the same expected profit but the range of outcomes of proposal B is much greater than the range of outcomes of proposal A. Hence all risk averters will prefer proposal A over proposal B.

Two additional classes of possible investors can be identified. First we have those optimistic fellows who have a preference, rather than an aversion, for risk. In terms of our analysis such an individual is characterized by a *convex* utility function, which means that the marginal utility of each additional dollar increases, which upon reflection is not a very realistic assumption.

Second, we have those investors who are "risk neutral", i.e. are neither risk averters nor risk lovers. Such an individual has a linear utility function, and displays constant marginal utility of money. Risk neutrality constitutes a borderline case between risk lovers and risk averters. A risk-neutral individual chooses his investments solely according to their expected profit, and completely ignores the dispersion of the returns.[6]

The expected utility criterion provides an elegant and theoretically impeccable solution to the problem of investment under certainty. However, an individual (or corporation) seeking investment advice will not be grateful for the suggestion that he should maximize his expected utility. The expected utility rule is not operational; in general we do not know the precise shape of the utility function, and hence cannot calculate expected utilities. Moreover, corporations typically have many stockholders, each with a presumably different utility function. Consequently we must look elsewhere for additional investment criteria which are capable of application to actual decision problems; however in formulating these rules we shall be using the insights which we have derived from the examination of the expected utility criterion.

SUMMARY

The purpose of this chapter has been to set out the utility foundation of the theory of investment choice under conditions of risk and uncertainty. A risky

6 We leave the graphical proof of this statement to the reader.

(or uncertain) investment is defined as an option whose monetary return is not known with perfect certainty, but for which an array of alternative returns and their (objective or subjective) probabilities are known. After a demonstration that the maximum *NPV* (profits) and maximum *expected NPV* (profits) criteria do not provide a straightforward solution to our problem, attention was directed to the theory of expected utility. Three broad classes of risk attitudes, corresponding to three types of investors, were distinguished:

(a)   risk averters — individuals with concave utility functions;
(b)   risk lovers — individuals with convex utility functions; and
(c)   risk-neutral individuals — those with linear utility functions.

The introduction of utility into the analysis provides an elegant solution to the investment decision problem under uncertainty by permitting us to assign *unequal* weights to different monetary outcomes. However, the chapter closes with a warning regarding the inability to apply the utility principle directly to decision problems, and therefore we shall turn in the following chapters to an examination of operational decision rules which while they reflect the insight gained from the utility analysis, are *not* set out explicitly in terms of immeasurable utilities.

QUESTIONS AND PROBLEMS

9.1   The following table sets out the annual percentage changes in the Standard & Poor's 500 Stock Index during the period 1952–79.

Year	Annual Change	Year	Annual Change
1952	11.8	1966	− 13.1
1953	− 6.6	1967	20.1
1954	45.0	1968	7.7
1955	26.4	1969	− 11.4
1956	2.6	1970	0.1
1957	− 14.3	1971	10.8
1958	38.1	1972	15.7
1959	8.5	1973	− 17.4
1960	− 3.0	1974	− 29.7
1961	23.1	1975	31.5
1962	− 11.8	1976	19.2
1963	18.9	1977	− 11.5
1964	13.0	1978	9.88
1965	9.1	1979	12.05

(a)   Calculate the frequency distribution of the annual changes in a table; starting at " − 20.0 to − 10.1" and finishing at "40.0 to 49.9".
(b)   Use the data of part (a) to draw a histogram of the historical record.

9.2   Assume that an individual is confronted with the problem of choosing one
of the following investment options:

Option A		Option B		Option C		Option D		Option E	
NPV	Probability	NPV	Probability	NPV	Probability	NPV	Probability	NPV	Probability
7	1	6	1/2	−12	1/4	−30	2/10	−16	1/8
		16	1/2	12	1/2	12	4/10	−4	2/8
				24	1/4	24	3/10	8	2/8
						60	1/10	24	3/8

(a) Which option will be chosen according to the maximum expected
    NPV criterion?

(b) What is the major shortcoming of this rule for decision-making under
    uncertainty?

9.3   Assume than an individual must choose between the following two investment alternatives:

Investment A		Investment B	
NPV ($)	Probability	NPV ($)	Probability
100	3/10	300	3/10
400	4/10	400	4/10
700	3/10	500	3/10

(a) Which alternative will be chosen according to the maximum expected
    NPV criterion?

(b) Which alternative will the individual choose according to the maximum
    expected utility criterion; if his utility function is given by the following
    table:

Income ($)	Utility
0	0
100	20
200	39
300	57
400	73
500	87
600	98
700	105

    (c) Calculate the marginal utility of money implied by the utility function given in the table above.

9.4 "A risk averter never enters a fair game of chance." Prove this statement graphically. In your answer indicate the "risk premium" necessary to induce him to agree to play.

9.5 An investor whose utility function is given by $U(X) = \sqrt{X}$, where X denotes money profits, is offered a chance to choose one of the following investment options:

Option A		Option B	
Probability	Profit	Probability	Profit
1/2	16	1/2	81
1/2	196	1/2	121

    (a) Which option will be chosen?
    (b) Prove your answer graphically.
    (c) What is the maximum price that such an investor will be willing to pay for each option? Compare the price you get for each option to its expected profit.
    (d) Graph your answer to (c) using the graph you drew in part (b).

9.6 An individual with the utility function

$$U(X) = \left(\frac{X}{10}\right)^2$$

is known to be indifferent between two lotteries A and B, which offer the following prizes:

Lottery A		Lottery B	
Probability	Prize	Probability	Prize
1/2	110	p	90
1/2	130	$1 - p$	150

Find the value of p.

9.7 "A risk-neutral investor, that is one who has a linear utility function, makes his investment decisions in accordance with the principle of maximum expected *NPV*, rather than with that of maximum expected utility." Is this statement correct? Prove your answer using a graph of the utility function.

9.8   Assume an investor with the following utility function:

PV ($)	Utility
-2,000	-600
-1,000	-150
0	0
1,000	80
2,000	150
3,000	210
4,000	250
5,000	280
10,000	340

(a) Graph the investor's utility function.

(b) Will this investor be willing to execute an investment project that requires an outlay of $2,000 and has an equal chance to be a complete loss or to generate a cash flow with *PV* of $5,000?

(c) What is the maximum amount the investor would agree to invest in a project with a cash flow with an equal probability, a *PV* of $1,000 or a *PV* of $10,000?

(d) Answer parts (b) and (c) graphically.

9.9   Answer question 9.8, assuming that the investor is risk-neutral.

SELECTED REFERENCES

Amihud, Yakov, "A Note on Risk Aversion and Indifference Curves", *Journal of Financial and Quantitative Analysis*, September 1977.

Amihud, Yakov, "General Risk Aversion and an Attitude towards Risk", *The Journal of Finance*, June 1980.

Arrow, K.J., "Alternative Approaches to the Theory of Choice in Risk Taking Situations", *Econometrica*, October 1951.

Baker, H.K., Hargrove, M.B. and Haslem, J.A., "An Empirical Analysis of the Risk-Return Preferences of Individual Investors", *Journal of Financial and Quantitative Analysis*, September 1977.

Baron, D.P., "On the Utility Theoretic Foundations of Mean-Variance Analysis", *Journal of Finance*, December 1977.

Bernoulli, D., "Exposition of a New Theory on the Measurement of Risk", *Econometrica*, January 1954.

Borch, K., *The Economics of Uncertainty*, Princeton, N.J.: Princeton University Press, 1968.

Friedman, M. and Savage, L.J., "The Expected Utility Hypothesis and the Measurability of Utility", *Journal of Political Economy*, December 1952.

Graves, P.E., "Relative Risk Aversion: Increasing or Decreasing?" *Journal of Financial and Quantitative Analysis*, June 1979.

Hakansson, Nils, H., "Friedman-Savage Utility Functions Consistent with Risk Aversion", *Quarterly Journal of Economics*, August 1970.

Hanoch, G. and Levy, H., "The Efficiency Analysis of Choices Involving Risk", *Review of Economic Studies*, July 1969.

Hirshleifer, J., "Investment Decision Under Uncertainty: Choice-Theoretic Approaches", *Quarterly Journal of Economics*, November 1965.

Jean, William H., "The Geometric Mean and Stochastic Dominance", *The Journal of Finance*, March 1980.

Kihlstrom, R.E. and Laffont, J.-J., "A General Equilibrium Entrepreneurial Theory of Firm Formation Based on Risk Aversion", *Journal of Political Economy*, August 1979.

Knight, F.H., *Risk, Uncertainty and Profit*, Boston and New York: Houghton Mifflin, 1921.

Levy, Haim and Sarnat, M., *Investment and Portfolio Analysis*, New York: Wiley, 1972.

Meyer, J., "Mean-Variance Efficient Sets and Expected Utility", *Journal of Finance*, December 1979.

Miller, Stephen M., "Measures of Risk Aversion: Some Clarifying Comments", *Journal of Financial and Quantitative Analysis*, June 1975.

Moore, P.G. and Thomas H., "Measuring Uncertainty", *Omega*, December 1975.

Pratt, J.W., "Risk Aversion in the Small and in the Large", *Econometrica*, January–April 1964.

Quirk, J.P. and Saposnik, R., "Admissibility and Measurable Utility Functions", *Review of Economic Studies*, February 1962.

Von Neumann, J. and Morgenstern, O., *Theory of Games and Economic Behavior*, Princeton, N.J.: Princeton University Press, 1953.

10

Measuring Risk

If the analysis of risk is to be meaningful for the firm, a method must be found to translate the utility analysis of the preceding chapter into operational decision rules which do not depend on the measurement of that elusive will o' the wisp, "utility". Clearly there are many ways to incorporate risk into decision problems. Common to almost all of the approaches, however, is the need to develop an index which will *directly* reflect the risk inherent in an investment proposal.[1] For simplicity, and in order to focus our attention on the role of uncertainty, we shall initially ignore the element of time and the need to discount future returns by assuming a very short investment period. In the later sections of the chapter this restriction is relaxed and the analysis is carried out in terms of net present values and their associated risk.

MEASURING RISK BY THE VARIABILITY OF RETURNS

Although in modern parlance the term risk has come to mean "hazard" or "danger of loss", the Latin word *risicum* retained some positive connotations at least up to the Middle Ages. In this earlier form, risk refers to chance or luck — *both* good and bad. Modern investment analysis has returned to the original meaning of risk, identifying the latter with the dispersion of returns, i.e. with possible deviations (both positive and negative) from the expected return.[2] The most widely used method of risk analysis utilizes the expected (mean) profit as an indicator of an investment's anticipated profitability and the variance (or standard deviation) as an indicator of its risk.

---

1 The implications of combining projects into portfolios are spelled out in Chapters 12 and 13.
2 The case for associating the derivation of the Latin *risicum* from the Arabic *rizq*, is argued by Benjamin Z. Kedar, "Again: Arabic *Rizq* Medieval Latin *Risicum*", *Studi Medievali*, Centro Italiano Di Studi Sull' Alto Medioevo, Spoleto, 1970.

Expected Profit

The expected value of a project's profitability is given by

$$E(x) = \sum_{i=1}^{n} P_i x_i$$

where:
$E(x)$ = the expected value
x_i = the ith possible outcome (profit)
P_i = the probability of obtaining the ith outcome x_i
n = the number of possible outcomes

Consider, for example, an investment which offers a 50% chance of earning a net profit of $1,000, a 25% chance of breaking even and a 25% chance of a $400 loss. The *expected value* of the investment is simply the weighted average of the possible outcomes:

$$1/2 \cdot 1,000 + 1/4 \cdot 0 + 1/4 \cdot (-400) = \mathbf{400}$$

Variance as a Measure of Risk

The variance, or the standard deviation, measures the dispersion of profits around the mean (expected) value. It provides information on the extent of the possible deviations of the actual return from the expected return.

The variance of the distribution (σ^2) is given by the formula:

$$\sigma^2(x) = \sum_{i=1}^{n} P_i(x_i - Ex)^2 = E(x - Ex)^2$$

To determine the variance we first calculate the deviation of each possible outcome from the expected value i.e. $(x_i - Ex)$, then raise it to the second power and multiply this term by the probability of getting x_i, that is by P_i. The summation of all these products serves as a measure of the distribution's variability, and is called the variance. The reader should note that since the distribution of future profit x_i is measured in dollars, the dimension of σ^2 is dollars squared, which of course is economically meaningless. Hence we take the square root of the variance, thereby obtaining the standard deviation, σ, which also measures the variability of the distribution but has the further advantage of being set out in terms of dollars. However despite this difference in dimensions the reader should note that if investment A is more risky than investment B, in terms of the variance, i.e. $\sigma_A^2 > \sigma_B^2$, its standard deviation must also be greater, i.e. $\sigma_A > \sigma_B$.

Thus for ranking investment proposals according to their risk one can use the variance or standard deviation interchangeably.[3]

In practice the actual calculation of the variance is somewhat easier if the following formula is used:

$$\sigma^2(x) = \sum_{i=1}^{n} P_i x_i^2 - \left(\sum_{i=1}^{n} P_i x_i \right)^2$$

AN EXAMPLE

Let us calculate the expected value and the variance of the following distribution:

Profits *(in dollars)*	*Probability of Occurrence*
(x)	$P(x)$
80	1/2
100	1/4
200	1/4

The expected profit is given by

$$E(x) = P_1 x_1 + P_2 x_2 + P_3 x_3 = 1/2 \cdot 80 + 1/4 \cdot 100 + 1/4 \cdot 200 = \$115$$

and the variance is

$$\sigma^2(x) = \sum_{i=1}^{3} P_i x_i^2 - \left(\sum_{i=1}^{3} P_i x_i \right)^2 = 1/2 \cdot 80^2 + 1/4 \cdot 100^2 + 1/4 \cdot 200^2 - 115^2$$

$$= 15,700 - 13,225 = 2,475$$

This method of calculation is very simple even for relatively large problems; however, the reader can verify that calculating the variance from its basic definition gives the same results, but the calculations are somewhat more tedious:

$$\sigma^2(x) = \sum_{i=1}^{3} P_i (x_i - Ex)^2 = 1/2(80 - 115)^2 + 1/4(100 - 115)^2 + 1/4(200 - 115)^2$$

$$= 1/2 \cdot 1,225 + 1/4 \cdot 225 + 1/4 \cdot 7,225 = 2,475$$

3 One might legitimately ask: if we desire a risk index in terms of dollars rather than in terms of dollars squared, why raise all terms to the second power in the first place? Why not directly calculate the term $\sum_{i=1}^{n} P_i(x_i - Ex)$ which has the dimension of dollars? However, the reader should note that this term is *always* equal to zero, which explains the need to "square" the deviations.

The standard deviation, which is simply the square root of the variance, is given by:

$$\sigma = \sqrt{2,475} = 49.75$$

COVARIANCE AND THE CORRELATION COEFFICIENT

Consider an individual who invests part of his money in the construction industry. Since profits in this industry fluctuate strongly, he may be interested in investing part of his money in another industry to stabilize his income. This stabilization can be facilitated by investing part of his money in an industry whose profits fluctuate either independently or negatively with those of the construction industry. By so doing, the investor can achieve a fairly stable average return; when the return on one type of stock is relatively low, the return from the other stocks will be relatively high, and vice versa. The degree to which diversification stabilizes the return is a function of the relation between the two random variables. The two closely related concepts which serve as quantitative measures of the relation between the fluctuations of two random variables are the *covariance* and the *correlation coefficient*.

The Covariance

We define the covariance of two random variables x and y as

$$Cov(x,y) = E(x - Ex)(y - Ey)$$

In the discrete case we get[4]

$$Cov(x,y) = \sum_{i=1}^{n} (x_i - Ex)(y_i - Ey)P_{ii}$$

where P_{ii} stands for the probability of getting x_i and y_i simultaneously. The above definition of $Cov(x, y)$ can be found to be

$$Cov(x,y) = E[(x - Ex)(y - Ey)] = E[xy - yEx - xEy + ExEy]$$

$$= E(xy) - 2ExEy + ExEy = E(xy) - ExEy$$

or

$$Cov(x,y) = E(xy) - ExEy$$

where $E(xy)$ is the expected value of the random variable xy.

---

4 In the continuous case we have

$$Cov(x,y) = \iint (x - Ex)(y - Ey)f(x,y)\, dx\, dy$$

or

$$Cov(x,y) = \iint xy\, f(x,y)dxdy - (\int xf(x)\, dx \int yf(y)dy)$$

where $f(x,y)$ denotes the joint density function of x and y.

We can explain the intuitive meaning of the covariance as follows:

Look at the expression $(x - Ex)(y - Ey)$.

Suppose $x - Ex > 0$ (x exceeds Ex) and $y - Ey > 0$ (y exceeds Ey)

Then $(x - Ex)(y - Ey) > 0$

We will get a positive value also when both the returns x and y are below their average. However, if

$$(x - Ex) > 0 \text{ and } (y - Ey) < 0$$

or

$$(x - Ex) < 0 \text{ and } (y - Ey) > 0$$

which means that the return on one asset is above its average and the other is below the average, then

$$(x - Ex)(y - Ey) < 0$$

Consequently if we get $Cov(x,y) = E(x - Ex)(y - Ey) > 0$, we have to conclude that x and y simultaneously tend either to exceed their respective average or to be below it. However, if $Cov(x,y) < 0$, we can say that they tend to disperse from their average in opposite directions. That is why our hypothetical investor will try to choose an industry whose returns have a *negative* covariance with the returns in the construction industry.[5]

Correlation Coefficient

The covariance has been shown to be an indicator of the direction of the dependence between two variables. This indicator, however, changes with any change in the unit of measurement (cents, dimes or dollars) of the random variables. We need, therefore, an indicator which will be independent of the units used in measuring the outcomes. Furthermore, we desire information concerning *both* the direction and the power of the relationship between the variables. The index which has the required characteristics is called the correlation coefficient and is given by

$$R(x,y) = \frac{Cov\,(x,y)}{\sigma(x)\sigma(y)}$$

This coefficient always satisfies

$$-1 \leqslant R(x,y) \leqslant 1$$

and is independent of the units of measurement.

5 It is worthwhile to mention that the relationship between x and y can be written as

$$y_t = a + bx_t + e_t$$

where a,b are constants, t stands for year t, and e_t is the deviation of y_t from the straight line. The line which minimizes the Σe_t^2 is called the regression line of y on x. By using this "best" line we find that the slope of the line is:

$$b = \frac{Cov\,(x,y)}{\sigma^2(x)}$$

When R lies between zero and one, the relation between the returns on the two assets is of a positive nature; and the closer we approach to 1, the stronger is the relationship. When $R = 1$ there is a *perfect positive* correlation. In other words, the relation is linear, which means there are b and a such that $y = a + bx$ where $b > 0$. When $0 \geqslant R \geqslant -1$ the relation is negative and the smaller R, the stronger is the negative relation. In the extreme case where $R = -1$ we have

$$y = a + bx \text{ with } b < 0.$$

The impact of the degree of correlation on portfolio choice will be deferred until Chapter 12. We shall use the concept in this chapter to examine the relationship between the correlation of a project's cashflows and the variance of the *NPV*.

THE MEAN VARIANCE RULE

A very popular decision rule has been developed by Harry Markowitz for evaluating investments on the basis of their expected return and variance (standard deviation).[6] The "expected return-variance" or "mean-variance" rule (also referred to in the literature as the $E - V$ rule) can be defined as follows: project A will be preferred to project B if one of the following two combinations holds:

(1) Expected return of A exceeds (or is equal to) the expected return of B *and* the variance of A is less than the variance of B
or
(2) Expected return of A exceeds that of B *and* the variance of A is less than (or equal to) that of B.[7]

Thus the expected return is taken as an indicator of a project's profitability and the variance serves as the index of its risk.

To illustrate the application of the $E - V$ rule, consider the example of the two projects whose distributions of profits are given in Table 10.1. (These are

Table 10.1

	Investment A		Investment B	
Net Profit ($)		Probability	Net Profit ($)	Probability
1,000		1/2	0	1/2
3,000		1/2	4,000	1/2
Expected profit	**2,000**		**2,000**	
Standard deviation	**1,000**		**2,000**	

6 See his pioneering article "Portfolio Selection", *Journal of Finance,* March 1952.
7 Equivalently in symbols, the $E - V$ preference rule implies preference for A if either

$$E(A) \geqslant E(B) \text{ and } Var (A) < Var (B)$$

or

$$E(A) > E(B) \text{ and } Var (A) \leqslant Var (B)$$

the same two projects which were analyzed using the expected utility rule in Table 9.6 of the previous chapter.) Both projects A and B have the same expected profit:

$$E(A) = 1/2 \cdot 1,000 + 1/2 \cdot 3,000 = \mathbf{2,000}$$
$$E(B) = 1/2 \cdot 0 \quad\quad + 1/2 \cdot 4,000 = \mathbf{2,000}$$

The variance of project A is 1,000,000:

$$\sigma^2(A) = 1/2(1,000 - 2,000)^2 + 1/2(3,000 - 2,000)^2 = 1,000,000$$

Hence the standard deviation of project A which is the square root of the variance is 1,000.

$$\sigma(A) = \sqrt{1,000,000} = 1,000$$

Similarly the variance and standard deviation of project B are 4,000,000 and 2,000 respectively:

$$\sigma^2(B) = 1/2(0 - 2,000)^2 + 1/2(4,000 - 2,000)^2 = 4,000,000$$

and

$$\sigma(B) = \sqrt{4,000,000} = 2,000$$

Thus if we adopt the Markowitz expected return-variance rule, we can confirm that project A is preferred to project B. Both have the same expected profit (2,000) but project B is the more risky in terms of the variance, a result which is consistent with the expected utility solution to the same problem.

The importance of the $E - V$ criterion stems from the fact that it can be derived from the expected utility rule. If we assume that returns are normally distributed so that the mean and the variance provide us with all of the relevant information about their distributions, all risk averters will reach their investment decisions according to the $E - V$ rule.[8] Thus in many important cases the $E - V$ rule can be substituted for the theoretically correct, but non-operational, expected utility analysis.

THE VARIANCE OF *NPV* AS A MEASURE OF RISK

To this point we have analyzed the problem of risky investment on the assumption that the element of time could be ignored. However, since capital budgeting typically deals with multiperiod investments, some of which constitute mutually exclusive alternatives, expected net present value must be substituted for expected profit as our measure of a project's profitability, and by analogy the variance of net present value is used as the risk indicator. However, employing the variance as a measure of risk when dealing with

---

8 The same result obtains if we assume a quadratic utility function. For further details of the utility foundations of mean-variance analysis, see Harry Markowitz, *Portfolio Selection*, New York, Wiley, 1959; and Haim Levy and Marshall Sarnat, *Investment and Portfolio Analysis*, New York, Wiley, 1972. See also Appendix 10A.

multiperiod capital investments raises some thought-provoking questions:

(a) How should the variance within years be handled? Should the measure of risk reflect the sum of the annual variances or an average annual figure?

(b) How should we account, in the case of multiperiod investments, for the fact that risks are incurred in different years?

(c) What should be done about the variability between projects which arises from differences in the levels of each year's average return: that is how should the variance between years be handled?

Independent Cashflows

To simplify the analysis we shall assume investment projects involving an immediate cash outlay followed by positive net cash flows in each of two subsequent years. Given this assumption, the expected *NPV* of an investment proposal is defined as the sum of the present values of the expected net cash flows in the first and second years, less the initial investment outlay:

$$E(NPV) = \alpha EX_1 + \alpha^2 EX_2 - I$$

where:

EX_1 = the expected value of the net cash flow in the first year
EX_2 = the expected value of the net cash flow in the second year
I = the initial investment outlay
α = $1/(1 + r)$ = a coefficient for capitalizing cash flows over time, where r denotes the riskless interest rate.
$E(NPV)$ = the expected net present value.

Given the assumption that the net cash flow of the second year is statistically independent of the first year's outcome we can define the variance of net present value as follows:

$$\sigma^2 = \sum_i \sum_j P_i P_j [\alpha X_{1i} + \alpha^2 X_{2j} - I - (\alpha EX_1 + \alpha^2 EX_2 - I)]^2$$

where:

X_{1i} denotes the net cash flow in year 1, with a probability of occurrence = P_i
X_{2j} denotes the net cash flow in year 2, with a probability of occurrence = P_j

This equation shows that the variance of net present value depends on all possible combinations of cash flows in years 1 and 2 multiplied by their probability of occurrence, which equals the product $P_i P_j$ in the case of independence. This formula can be rewritten as

$$\sigma^2 = \alpha^2 \sigma_1^2 + \alpha^4 \sigma_2^2$$

$$= \frac{\sigma_1^2}{(1 + r)^2} + \frac{\sigma_2^2}{(1 + r)^4}$$

where:

σ_1^2 = the variance of the cash flow distribution in year 1
σ_2^2 = the variance of the cash flow distribution in year 2

Given the assumption of statistical independence, the total variance of *NPV* is equal to the discounted sum of the annual variances. Thus the overall measure of risk depends on the *time-adjusted* risks incurred in each year, with the discounting of all annual risks to their present values serving to make the expected risks of more distant years comparable to those of earlier years. This can be illustrated by considering the following case of a firm confronted by two investment proposals, A and B, each having the same expected *NPV* but different time patterns of *undiscounted* annual variances:

	σ_1^2	σ_2^2	σ^2
Project A	1	3	4
Project B	3	1	4

In the absence of discounting (i.e. if we assume that $\alpha = 0$) the firm would be indifferent to these two "equal risk" projects despite the fact that project A defers the larger risk to the second year. The discounting of annual variances (inherent in the variance of *NPV* calculation) ensures that the time pattern of risk will be taken into account. In this particular example, project A would be preferred since its total discounted variance is smaller than that of project B, at all positive discount rates.

The only peculiarity in this formulation of the "riskiness" of multiperiod investment projects stems from the exponents applied to the discount rate. Thus, in apparent contradiction to the usual capital budgeting analysis the discount factor of the first year is equal to $1/(1 + r)^2$ rather than $1/(1 + r)$, while the discount factor for year 2 is raised to the fourth power rather than to the second power. This anomaly arises because we have used the variance, rather than the standard deviation, as the measure of dispersion. An alternative would be to set out the measure of risk directly in terms of the discounted standard deviation rather than the variance, thereby obtaining the measures of risk, $\sigma_1/1 + r)$ and $\sigma_2/(1 + r)^2$, in the first and second year respectively. But since the variance provides a mathematically (and statistically) more convenient variable, these expressions are raised to their second power.

As can readily be seen from the formula, the total variance of *NPV* depends on the variability of possible outcomes within each year, but is completely independent of the variance between years. Thus the variance which arises from shifts in the expected cash flow over time is *not* a factor influencing this measure of risk. This can be illustrated by examining the numerical example given in Table 10.2. In this example the variance of both projects, in both years, is equal to 1. Assuming a capitalization rate of *r* the total variance of *NPV* for both projects is equal to $1/(1 + r)^2 + 1/(1 + r)^4$. Since the intra-year variances are the same (equal to 1 in each year) for both projects, the total risk incurred in each project is also considered to be equal, despite the additional upward shift of project B's distribution in the second year.

At first glance the failure to reflect the variance *between* years, along with the variance *within* each year, would appear to be a serious shortcoming of the

Table 10.2

	I	First Year		Second Year	
		X_i	P_i	X_j	P_j
Project A	− 1	1	1/2	1	1/2
		3	1/2	3	1/2
Project B	− 1	1	1/2	9	1/2
		3	1/2	11	1/2

variance of *NPV* as an indicator of risk. On further reflection, however, it is clear that while upward or downward shifts of the cash flow distribution in any particular year must affect a project's expected value, they do not necessarily affect its risk. Again this can be illustrated by the numerical example given in Table 10.2. Ignoring the common capitalization factor, project A has in the second year a maximum net cash flow of 3 and a minimum of 1; the relevant figures for project B are 11 and 9 respectively. As can be seen from these calculations one can increase expected profitability (net present value) by shifting from project A to project B, but such a shift does not involve any change in risk (that is any change in the dispersion of outcomes). Since risk is measured by the variance around the expected *NPV*, each of these projects carries the same risk index, independent of the upward shift of project B's expected receipts in the second year. Far from being a shortcoming, the neglect of such shifts is conceptually correct; such shifts properly affect a project's profitability but not its risk index.

As we have already noted, the variance of *NPV* reflects the discounted sum of the annual variances, and not the average annual variance. With the aid of the numerical example given in Table 10.3, it can be shown that the measure of dispersion based on the sum of the annual variances, rather than the annual average, provides the more appropriate risk indicator. Let us assume a set of initial investment outlays for the two projects which equate their net present values. (This, of course, implies $I > I^*$.) Which project involves the most risk? If we measure risk by the variance of *NPV*, that is by the discounted sum of the annual variances, project B is less risky because its variance is smaller than that of project A. The variances of projects A and B are given by:

Table 10.3

	Initial Investment Outlay	First year		Second year	
		X_i	P_i	X_j	P_j
Project A	I	10	1/2	10	1/2
		30	1/2	30	1/2
Project B	I*	10	1/2	—	—
		30	1/2	—	—

$$Var\,(B) = \frac{\sigma_1^2}{(1\,+\,r)^2} = \frac{100}{(1\,+\,r)^2}$$

$$Var\,(A) = \frac{\sigma_1^2}{(1\,+\,r)^2} + \frac{\sigma_2^2}{(1\,+\,r)^4} = \frac{100}{(1\,+\,r)^2} + \frac{100}{(1\,+\,r)^4} > \frac{100}{(1\,+\,r)^2}$$

Clearly, the variance of project A, which reflects the sum of two equal annual variances, is greater than that of B which reflects the same annual variance, but for only one year. However the result is reversed, and project A becomes less risky than project B, when the *average* annual variance is used as a risk indicator:

$$\frac{1}{2}\left[\frac{100}{(1\,+\,r)^2} + \frac{100}{(1\,+\,r)^4}\right] < \frac{100}{(1\,+\,r)^2}$$

Clearly, the sum of the variances provides the more appropriate measure of risk; project A affords the same expected *NPV* as project B, but requires the firm to sustain a given degree of risk for two years. Thus the sum of the variances gives the intuitively appealing result that, *other things being equal*, the longer the duration of the project, the greater is the risk incurred.

To sum up the discussion: given the assumption of statistical independence between the cash flows of the various projects over time, the total variance of the *NPV* is equal to the discounted sum of the annual variances, and has the following properties:

(a)   This measure of risk depends on the variance of all possible outcomes within each year, but is completely independent of the variance between years.

(b)   The annual variances are discounted to their present values, thereby making the risks of more distant years comparable to those of earlier years.

Dependent Cashflows

In the above section we assumed for simplicity that the project's cashflows in the two years are statistically independent. In reality this is not often the case. For example, when a firm invests in the development of a new product success in the first year is more likely to be followed by success in the second year. Similarly, a failure in the first year is often the harbinger of bad news in the second year. Thus, in general, we expect the cashflows of a project across years to be *positively correlated*.

Let us apply the covariance and correlation concepts, defined above, to the calculation of the variance of a project's *NPV* for the case of statistically dependent cashflows.

Using the same notation as before, $E(NPV)$ is given by

$$E(NPV) = \alpha EX_1 + \alpha^2\,EX_2 - I$$

which is the same as in the case of independent annual cashflows. However, the variance of *NPV* is affected by the dependence association. The previous formula for calculating the variance no longer holds and one has to substitute P_{ij} for P_i and P_j where P_{ij} is the *joint* probability to obtain cashflow X_i in the first year and cashflow X_j in the second year. Thus, in general,

$$\sigma^2 = \sum_i \sum_j P_{ij} \left[\alpha X_{1i} + \alpha^2 X_{2j} - I - (\alpha EX_1 + \alpha^2 EX_2 - I) \right].$$

After cancelling out the investment *I*, and rearrangement of terms, this variance can be rewritten in the following general form,

$$\sigma^2 = E[\alpha(X_1 - EX_1) + \alpha^2(X_2 - EX_2)]^2$$

when X_1 and X_2 are the cashflows (random variables) in the first and second year, respectively.

Hence,

$$\sigma^2 = E[\alpha^2(X_1 - EX_1)^2 + \alpha^4(X_2 - EX_2)^2 + 2\alpha^3(X_1 - EX_1)(X_2 - EX_2)]$$

Since α is not a random variable, the variance can be rewritten as,

$$\sigma^2 = \alpha^2 \sigma_1^2 + \alpha^4 \sigma_2^2 + 2 \alpha^3 \, Cov \, (X_1, X_2)$$

where by definition $E(X_1 - EX_1)(X_2 - EX_2) = Cov(X_1, X_2)$. Employing the relationship between correlation coefficient and covariance, the variance of the *NPV* can also be rewritten as,

$$\sigma^2 = \alpha^2 \sigma_1^2 + \alpha^4 \sigma_2^2 + 2\alpha^3 R(X_1, X_2) \sigma_1 \sigma_2$$

where R is the correlation coefficient between X_1 and X_2.

Thus we have obtained the same formula as in the case of independence, but with an additional term for the covariance between the first and the second year cashflows. This formula has the following characteristics:

(a) If the cashflows are independent, then by definition, $cov(X_1, X_2) = 0$ and the formula reduces to the previous one.[9]

(b) If there is a positive association between the cashflows X_1 and X_2, the variance of the *NPV* increases relative to the case of independence. The opposite holds regarding negative association between X_1 and X_2.

(c) It is interesting to note that the covariance is due to the continuation of the first-year cashflows, which are discounted by α^2, and second-year cashflows, which are discounted by α^4, and hence it is discounted by the intermediate value α^3.

A NUMERICAL EXAMPLE

Suppose that the firm considers two projects, A and B, both with an economic duration of two years and with an initial investment outlay of $40 million. Table 10.4 gives the cashflows of these projects. In project A the pro-

---

9 If X_1 and X_2 are independent we have
$$2\alpha^3 E(X_1 - EX_1)(X_2 - EX_2) = 2\alpha^3 E(X_1 - EX_1)E(X_2 - EX_2) = 0$$
since $E(X_1 - EX_1) = E(X_2 - EX_2) = 0$

Table 10.4

First-year Cashflow	Project A Second-year Cashflow	Joint Probability
20	10	1/3
30	20	1/3
40	30	1/3

First-year Cashflow	Project B Second-year Cashflow	Joint Probability
20	30	1/3
30	20	1/3
40	10	1/3

bability of earning $20 million in the first year and $10 million in the second year is 1/3; similarly the probability of getting $30 million in the first year and $20 million in the second year is also 1/3, as is the probability of earning $40 million in the first year and $30 million in the second year.

For simplicity only assume that the discount factor $\alpha = 1$. Which project is preferred by the Mean-Variance Rule? In order to answer this question a few calculations are called for. First let us calculate the expected *NPV* of each project:

$$E(NPV_A) = \tfrac{1}{3}(20 + 10) + \tfrac{1}{3}(30 + 20) + \tfrac{1}{3}(40 + 30) - 40 = \$10 \text{ million}$$

(recall that we are assuming that $\alpha = 1$ and an investment outlay of $40 million).

$$E(NPV_B) = \tfrac{1}{3}(20 + 30) + \tfrac{1}{3}(30 + 20) + \tfrac{1}{3}(40 + 10) - 40 = \$10 \text{ million}$$

Thus the two projects provide the same mean net present value. Now let's determine their risk, i.e. the variance of the *NPV, Var (NPV)*. With $\alpha = 1$ we have the following formula:

$$Var(NPV) = \sigma_1^2 + \sigma_2^2 + 2Cov(X_1, X_2)$$

and for project A this yields:[10]

$$EX_1(A) = \tfrac{1}{3}20 + \tfrac{1}{3}30 + \tfrac{1}{3}40 = \$30 \text{ million}$$
$$EX_2(A) = \tfrac{1}{3}10 + \tfrac{1}{3}20 + \tfrac{1}{3}30 = \$20 \text{ million}$$

Hence

$$\sigma_1^2(A) = \tfrac{1}{3}(20 - 30)^2 + \tfrac{1}{3}(30 - 30)^2 + \tfrac{1}{3}(40 - 30)^2 = \frac{200}{3}$$

$$\sigma_2^2(A) = \tfrac{1}{3}(10 - 20)^2 + \tfrac{1}{3}(20 - 20)^2 + \tfrac{1}{3}(30 - 20)^2 = \frac{200}{3}$$

10 Since in this example there is only one possibility of receiving $20 million in the first year year, the joint probability of getting $20 million in the first year and $10 million in the second year is also the marginal probability of earning $20 million in the first year.

Applying the covariance formula we have,

$$Cov_A(X_1, X_2) = \sum_{i=1}^{3} P_{ii}(X_{1i} - EX_1)(X_{2i} - EX_2)$$

where $P_{ii} = \frac{1}{3}$ which is the joint probability to get the ith pair of cashflows in the first and second year as given in Table 10.4. Thus

$$Cov_A(X_1, X_2) = \frac{1}{3}(20-30)(10-20) + \frac{1}{3}(30-30)(20-20) + \frac{1}{3}(40-30)(30-20)$$

$$= \frac{1}{3}(-10)\cdot(-10) + \frac{1}{3} 10 \times 10 = \frac{200}{3}$$

Collecting all these results we have

$$Var(NPV_A) = \sigma_1^2 + \sigma_2^2 + 2Cov(X_1, X_2)$$

$$= \frac{200}{3} + \frac{200}{3} + 2\frac{200}{3} = \frac{800}{3}$$

Now let's calculate the components of the variance of NPV for project B. First,

$$EX_1(B) = \frac{1}{3} 20 + \frac{1}{3} 30 + \frac{1}{3} 40 = \$30 \text{ million}$$

$$EX_2(B) = \frac{1}{3} 30 + \frac{1}{3} 20 + \frac{1}{3} 10 = \$20 \text{ million}$$

Hence

$$\sigma_1^2(B) = \frac{1}{3}(20-30)^2 + \frac{1}{3}(30-30)^2 + \frac{1}{3}(40-30)^2 = \frac{200}{3}$$

$$\sigma_2^2(B) = \frac{1}{3}(30-20)^2 + \frac{1}{3}(20-20)^2 + \frac{1}{3}(10-20)^2 = \frac{200}{3}$$

and

$$Cov_B(X_1, X_2) = \frac{1}{3}(20-30)(30-20) + \frac{1}{3}(30-30)(20-20) + \frac{1}{3}(40-30)(10-20)$$

$$= \frac{1}{3}(-10)(10) + \frac{1}{3}(10)(-10) = -\frac{200}{3}$$

Hence

$$Var(NPV_B) = \sigma_1^2 + \sigma_2^2 + 2Cov(X_1, X_2)$$

$$= \frac{200}{3} + \frac{200}{3} + 2 - \frac{200}{3} = 0$$

To summarize, the two projects A and B are identical in all respects apart from the covariance between their annual cashflows. Specifically the expected values of their cashflows are the same in each year:

$$EX_1(A) = EX_1(B); \ EX_2(A) = EX_2(B)$$

and so are the variances of each year's cash flow:

$$\sigma_1^2(A) = \sigma_1^2(B); \ \sigma_2^2(A) = \sigma_2^2(B)$$

Hence ignoring the covariance effect the firm would be indifferent between the two projects. However, once we recognize the effect of the covariance, project B is clearly superior. Its expected NPV is the same as project A but project B has zero variance. The economic advantage of project B is quite clear: should its first-year cashflow be below average its second-year cashflow will be above average, which stabilizes the total cashflow of this project. Thus, it is the negative correlation between the annual cashflow of project B, which creates the preference for that project.

Since we have assumed, for simplicity, that $\alpha = 1$, one can easily check the formulas and also gain additional insight into the covariance effect by simply summing up the two years' cashflows, which in the case of $\alpha = 1$ is equal to the *PV*.

	Project A				*Project B*		
PV	*Investment*	*NPV*	*Probability*	*PV*	*Investment*	*NPV*	*Probability*
$(20 + 10) = 30$	40	-10	1/3	$(20 + 30) = 50$	40	10	1/3
$(30 + 20) = 50$	40	10	1/3	$(30 + 20) = 50$	40	10	1/3
$(40 + 30) = 70$	40	30	1/3	$(40 + 10) = 50$	40	10	1/3

It is obvious that $Var(NPV_B) = 0$ since we always have an *NPV* of \$10 million. If we note that $E(NPV_A) = \$10$ million, the variance of the *NPV* of project A is given by,

$$Var(NPV_A) = \tfrac{1}{3}(-10 - 10)^2 + \tfrac{1}{3}(10 - 10)^2 + \tfrac{1}{3}(30 - 10)^2$$

$$= \frac{400}{3} + \frac{400}{3} = \frac{800}{3}$$

exactly as we obtained before by applying the formula which incorporates explicitly the covariance between the annual cashflows.

We illustrated the crucial role of the covariance by considering two extreme cases; one with a perfect positive correlation (project A) and one with a perfect negative correlation, project B.[11] In real life most projects are characterized by positive association of cashflows across years, but normally this association yields a correlation between any pair of years of considerably less than + 1.

MEASURING RISK BY THE COEFFICIENT OF VARIATION

Occasionally using the variance (or standard deviation) as an indicator of risk can be misleading. Clearly, the larger is the variance of earnings the larger is the

---

11 The correlation coefficient for project A is

$$R(X_1, X_2) = \frac{Cov\ (X_1, X_2)}{\sigma_1 \sigma_2} = \frac{200/3}{\sqrt{200/3}\ \sqrt{200/3}} = +1$$

and for project B

$$R(X_1, X_1) = \frac{Cov(X_1, X_2)}{\sigma_1 \sigma_2} = \frac{-200/3}{\sqrt{200/3}\ \sqrt{200/3}} = -1$$

Table 10.5

	Expected Profit	Standard Deviation	Coefficient of Variation (σ/E)
Investment A	100	10	0.10
Investment B	500	25	0.05

chance that the actual return will deviate significantly from the average or expected return. However, in some cases the expected profit of the proposal under consideration may be so large that the proposal should be considered relatively safe even if it has a large variance.

The expected profit and the standard deviation of two hypothetical investments are given in Table 10.5. As can be seen the expected profit of project B is $500, i.e. significantly larger than the expected profit of investment A which is only $100. Can we, as a result, say with assurance that project B should be preferred to project A? If we examine the standard deviations of the two proposals, we note that although proposal B is the more profitable of the two on the average, it is also the more risky (its standard deviation is 25 as compared with a deviation of only 10 in project A). Thus, the mean-variance (or the mean-standard deviation) rule cannot discriminate between the two proposals, and therefore we cannot determine which proposal is preferable.

This simple example illustrates one of the major drawbacks of using the standard deviation (or variance) as a risk index. Intuitively we can say that most, if not all, investors will prefer proposals B even though the $E - V$ rule does not indicate a clear-cut preference over A. And, as we shall see, this is one instance in which our intuition, rather than our arithmetic, should be relied upon. The reason is straightforward: project B's profitability is so high that it more than compensates for its greater risk (variability). For example, should the earnings of proposal B deviate by four standard deviations[12] to the left-hand side of its distribution (i.e. a very pessimistic result) and the profit of proposal A by four standard deviations to the right side (i.e. a very optimistic outcome), an individual would be better off with investment B. Even if the very unlikely above-mentioned combination of deviations should occur, the return on B would be still $400 (500 − 4 × 25) as compared with A's profit of only $140 (100 + 4 × 10).[13]

This simple numerical example is sufficient to show that in some cases the standard deviation (or variance) does not provide an appropriate measure of

---

12 The reader should note that the probability of such a large deviation is extremely small; for example, if the distribution is normal the probability of such a deviation is only 0.003%.

13 A similar line of reasoning has been used by William J. Baumol in an attempt to develop an efficiency criterion which can replace the $E - V$ rule. See his "Expected Gain-Confidence Limit Criterion for Portfolio Selection", *Management Science,* October 1963. A detailed critique of the Baumol analysis is given in H. Levy and M. Sarnat, *Investment and Portfolio Analysis,* New York, Wiley, 1972. See also Paul Halpern and Yehuda Kahane, "A Pedagogical Note on Baumol's Gain-Confidence Limit Criterion for Portfolio Selection and the Probability of Ruin", *Journal of Banking and Finance,* June 1980.

risk. In order to overcome these shortcomings some writers have advocated that the *coefficient of variation*:

$$c = \sigma/E$$

be used instead of the standard deviation as the measure of an investment's risk.[14] (The reader should note that the coefficient of variation is defined simply as the standard deviation divided (normalized) by the expected profit.) And indeed, if we replace the standard deviation by the coefficient of variation in our numerical example, intuition is vindicated, and proposal B is clearly preferable to proposal A. Looking back at Table 10.5 we note that project B has both a *higher* expected profit and a *lower* coefficient of variation. Thus if we employ the expected return-coefficient of variation rule, it follows that an investor will be better off if he chooses proposal B rather than proposal A.

Does the replacement of the standard deviation by the coefficient of variation overcome all the difficulties encountered in measuring risk? The answer is clearly negative. Although the coefficient of variation can serve as a better measure of risk in some cases,[15] it by no means resolves *all* the problems relating to the meaning of risk. This contention is illustrated in Table 10.6 which sets out the relevant data for two hypothetical alternative investments.

Table 10.6

	Investment A		Investment B	
	Profit	Probability	Profit	Probability
	2	1	5	1/2
			15	1/2
Expected Profit (E)	2		10	
Variance (σ^2)	0		25	
Standard Deviation (σ)	0		5	
Coefficient of Variation (σ/E)	0		1/2	

The expected values of proposals A and B are given by $1 \times 2 = \$2$, and $1/2 \times \$5 + 1/2 \times \$15 = \$10$ respectively. Similarly, the variance of the two proposals is given by:

$$1(2-2)^2 = 0 \text{ for A}$$

and

$$1/2(5-10)^2 + 1/2(15-10)^2 = 25 \text{ for B}$$

Again the $E - V$ rule cannot distinguish between the two proposals; investment B is the more profitable but is also the more risky of the two. Nor does the expected profit-coefficient of variation rule help resolve the issue; the coefficient of variation of project B is also larger than that of A (1/2 as compared with zero). Thus neither the expected profit-standard deviation criterion nor the expected profit-coefficient of variation criterion can choose between the two

---

14 See for example, J. Fred Weston and Eugene F. Brigham, *Managerial Finance,* 4th edn., New York, Holt, Rinehart & Winston, 1972.

15 For example, the coefficient of variation is the theoretically correct measure of risk if we assume a lognormal distribution of returns and risk-averse investors; see Haim Levy, "Stochastic Dominance among Log Normal Prospects", *International Economic Review,* October 1973.

proposals, even though upon reflection common sense alone is sufficient to indicate that investment B is preferable to investment A. Every rational individual would choose project B rather than project A, because even the *worst* possible outcome of investment B ($5) is higher than the profit offered by alternative A ($2). Clearly the decision maker must exercise considerable caution when using either of these two popular measures of investment risk, if paradoxical choices are to be avoided.[16]

SENSITIVITY ANALYSIS

Having clarified somewhat the underlying concepts of risk, we turn in this section to a practical pragmatic way of handling project risk. Probably the most common method of evaluating a project's risk in practice is *sensitivity analysis* in which the firm makes its best estimate of the revenues and costs involved in a project, calculates the project's *NPV* (or the *IRR* for that matter), and then checks the sensitivity of the *NPV* to possible estimation errors of the gross revenue and the various cost items.

For example, what will be the *NPV* should the estimate of the annual revenues be too high by 5% or by 10%? If a small error proves critical, in the sense that the *NPV* becomes negative, the project is considered very risky, since small estimation errors are very likely to occur. On the other hand, suppose that for errors in the range of 1% – 15% the *NPV* remains positive. In this instance the *NPV* is relatively insensitive to errors in the estimate of future cashflows and therefore the project will be considered to have low risk. Even if one overestimates the revenue by as much as 14% the project's *NPV* is still positive.[17]

A NUMERICAL EXAMPLE

Let's illustrate the way a sensitive analysis is carried out with a numerical example. Consider a project with zero initial outlay (e.g., renting or leasing a machine) and the annual gross revenue and costs set out in Table 10.7.

Let's further assume that the proposal's economic duration is ten years ($n = 10$) and the cost of capital is ten percent ($k = 0.1$). Hence, the firm's best estimate of the project's *NPV* is

$$NPV_0 = \sum_{t=1}^{10} \frac{\$10}{(1 + 0.1)^t} = 10 \cdot 6.145 \cong \$61.5 \text{ million}$$

(recall that in this specific case $I = 0$; hence $NPV_0 = PV_0$)

---

16 A way out of this dilemma can be found if information on the entire distribution of returns is available; see Appendix 10A.

17 The reader should note that by changing the annual *cashflow* of each year by $X\%$, the firm is implicitly assuming in such analysis the extreme case of perfect positive correlation between the cashflows of each pair of years, an assumption which probably is not unduly unrealistic for most projects.

Table 10.7

Best Estimate of Future Annual Cashflows

		(million $)
Gross revenue	R	100
Costs:		
Labor	C_1	10
Energy	C_2	60
Materials	C_3	5
Other	C_4	5
Total annual costs	ΣC_i	80
Annual Income (before tax)		20
Tax (at 50%)		10
Net annual income		10

The *NPV* can be written in general form as follows

$$NPV_0 = \sum_{t=1}^{n} \frac{(1-T)R}{(1+k)^t} - \sum_{t=1}^{n} \frac{(1-T)C_1}{(1+k)^t} - \sum_{t=1}^{n} \frac{(1-T)C_2}{(1+k)^t} - \sum_{t=1}^{n} \frac{(1-T)C_3}{(1+k)^t} - \sum_{t=1}^{n} \frac{(1-T)C_4}{(1+k)^t}$$

The advantage of this decomposition is that the firm can examine the sensitivity of the *NPV* to changes in revenue or in each of the cost components. For example, suppose that there is an error of $\alpha\%$ in the estimate of the revenue (R) but there is no change in any of the other components. We obtain a new estimate of the project's net present value, NPV_α, which is given by:

$$NPV_\alpha = NPV_0 + (1-T) \sum_{t=1}^{n} \frac{\alpha R}{(1+k)^t}$$

If $\alpha > 0$, $NPV_\alpha > NPV_0$ and if $\alpha < 0$, $NPV_\alpha < NPV_0$. In a similar manner the sensitivity of the project's profitability to errors in the estimates of each of the cost components can be examined.

Table 10.8 presents the results of the sensitivity analysis. The table gives the new *NPV*, i.e. *NPV* after a change of $\alpha\%$ has been made in one of the various components. For example, if the revenue is reduced by 10% ($\alpha = -10\%$) then the *NPV* drops from $61.5 million to $30.7 million. However, an increase in energy costs, component C_2, by 10% decreases the *NPV* from 61.5 to 43.0.

An examination of the sensitivity matrix permits the firm to reach a number of conclusions relating to the project's riskiness:

(a)   Even if the gross revenue is overestimated by as much as 20% the NPV_α is still positive.

(b)   The price of energy may go up in the future, but as long as the price rise is 33%, or less, the project remains profitable.

(c)   The project's desirability is not seriously affected by the other cost components.

Table 10.8

Sensitivity Analysis of Hypothetical Project* (in millions of $)

Estimation Error	Revenue	Labor Cost	Energy Cost	Material Cost	Other Costs
α	R	C_1	C_2	C_3	C_4
-50%	-92.2	76.8	153.6	69.2	69.1
-40%	-61.4	73.7	135.1	67.6	67.6
-30%	-30.7	70.7	116.8	66.1	66.1
-20%	0.0	67.6	98.3	64.5	64.5
-10%	30.7	64.5	79.9	63.0	63.0
0	61.5	61.5	61.5	61.5	61.5
$+10\%$	92.9	58.4	43.0	59.9	59.9
$+20\%$	122.9	55.3	24.6	58.4	58.4
$+30\%$	153.6	52.2	6.2	56.8	56.8
$+40\%$	184.4	49.2	-12.3	55.3	55.3
$+50\%$	215.1	46.1	-30.7	53.8	53.8

$$*NPV_0 = \sum_{t=1}^{10} \frac{10}{(1 + 0.1)^t} = \$61.5 \text{ million}$$

Since NPV_α is a linear function of α, one can write for example,

$$NPV_\alpha = NPV_0 + \alpha(1 - T) \sum_{t=1}^{n} \frac{R}{(1 + k)^t}$$

and as the after-tax present value of revenue is a constant (for any given initial R) we can simply write

$$NPV_\alpha = NPV_0 + b\alpha$$

where

$$b \equiv (1 + T) \sum_{t=1}^{n} \frac{R}{(1 + k)^t}$$

In the same way each of the cost components can be set out as linear equations. This allows us to present the sensitivity analysis in a simple diagram.

Figure 10.1 summarizes the sensitivity of the project to changes in revenue (R) as well as to each of the cost components. It is clear from the diagram that changes in each of the cost components of C_1, C_3 and C_4 have only a minor impact on the project's NPV. (The straight lines corresponding to these cost items are relatively flat.) On the other hand, lines for R and C_2 are relatively steep and here the firm would be well advised to take greater pains when predicting these two items. An error here could mean serious losses.

The linear property of the sensitivity relationship has two principal advantages: (a) by extending the lines, the firm can consider all levels of α up to any α which it considers to be relevant without additional calculation; (b) errors in

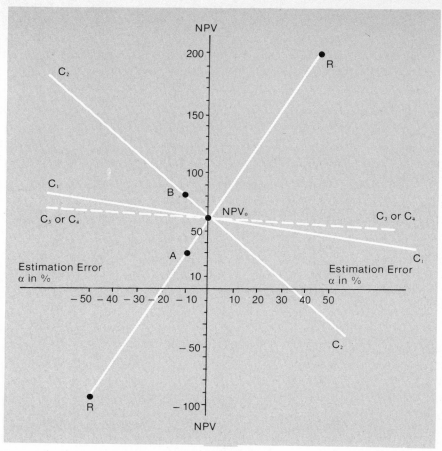

Fig. 10.1

various components can be combined. For example, suppose that the sales are over estimated by 10%, but if the firm sells less, it also consumes about 10% less energy. Thus, a reduction of 10% in R decreases the NPV from $61.5 million to about $30 million (Point A) but the parallel reduction in energy costs (C_1) decreases the NPV from $61.5 million to about $80 million (Point B). The net effect of the reduction in revenue, therefore, would be a decrease in the NPV of about $10 million, and so the project would remain profitable, i.e., its NPV is still positive.

SUMMARY

This chapter has examined the popular mean-variance ($E - V$) rule for reaching investment decisions. When returns can be assumed to be normally distributed the mean-variance analysis provides a decision rule which is compatible with the maximization of expected utility. Moreover, the $E - V$ rule can be generalized to cover multiperiod capital budgeting problems by taking the expected value and variance of the NPV as indicators of a project's profitability and risk.

Despite its widespread use, the variance does not always provide a meaningful definition of risk; as a result, decision-makers must still exercise considerable caution when using this popular measure of investment risk, if decision errors are to be avoided. In cases where returns are not normally distributed, decisions can be improved by considering the entire cumulative probability distribution. Two decision criteria, based on the total distribution, are spelled out in Appendix 10A.

Despite these limitations, the variance of returns is still by far the most popular and convenient measure of investment risk. Although in some situations more appropriate risk indexes than the variability of returns can be found, there is no other *operational* risk indicator which in general is better than the variance of the returns. In many important cases the variance is the best possible measure of risk, while in other cases it can usefully serve as a proxy for the risk inherent in an investment. In both instances, the risk-averse entrepreneur will seek an investment strategy which will stabilize his returns, i.e. which will minimize the variance of returns, for a given expected profit. However, in practice, a great many firms try to resolve some of the riskiness of projects by applying sensitivity analysis to the major components of the cashflow.

QUESTIONS AND PROBLEMS

10.1 Consider the following two investments:

	Investment A		Investment B	
	Return	*Probability*	*Return*	*Probability*
	$ 500	1/8	$ 800	1/8
	1,000	3/4	1,000	3/4
	1,500	1/8	1,200	1/8

(a) Calculate the expected return of each investment.
(b) Calculate the variance and the standard deviation of each.
(c) Which investment would you prefer using the mean-variance rule?

10.2 Examine the following two investment proposals, each with an initial investment of $5,000. The net cash flow of the proposals is as follows:

	Project A				Project B			
	Year 1		*Year 2*		*Year 1*		*Year 2*	
Prob.	*Cash flow($)*	*Prob.*	*Cash flow($)*	*Prob.*	*Cash flow($)*	*Prob.*	*Cash flow($)*
1/10	2,000	1/3	2,000	1/3	2,000	1/10	2,000
8/10	3,000	1/3	3,000	1/3	3,000	8/10	3,000
1/10	4,000	1/3	4,000	1/3	4,000	1/10	4,000

Assume that in each project the net cash flow in the second year is statistically independent of the first year's outcome.

(a) Calculate each project's expected net present value and variance of *NPV*, assuming a discount rate of 8%.

(b) Which project do you prefer? Explain.

10.3 The Nelson Company is considering the possibility of selling one of its machines. The selling price of the machine is dependent on the results of a public tender, the possible outcomes of which after taxes are:

$14,700 with a probability of 0.1
$ 8,000 with a probability of 0.8
$ 4,300 with a probability of 0.1

The alternative is to use the machine in the company. The cash flows generated by the machine are not known with certainty, and are listed below on an after-tax basis:

Year 1		Year 2	
Cashflow ($)	Probability	Cashflow ($)	Probability
3,500	0.4	3,000	0.5
6,000	0.6	5,000	0.25
		9,000	0.25

(Note that if the company sells the machine, it receives the money at once. Note also that once the company submits a formal offer to sell, it cannot change its mind.)

Assume an after-tax discount rate of 6% and answer the following questions:

(a) Calculate each alternative's expected net present value and variance of *NPV*.

(b) Which alternative is preferable according to the mean-variance criterion?

(c) Assume now that the after-tax cost of capital rises to 8%. Will the firm choose to sell the machine? Briefly explain your results.

10.4 "Risk deferment always pays." Evaluate this statement.

10.5 Express the expected value, the variance and the standard deviation of a variable *y*, in terms of *x* on the assumption that $y = a + bx$.

10.6 The Multiplier Investment Company can invest in one of two mutually exclusive projects. The two proposals have the following probability distributions of net present value:

Project C		Project D	
Probability	*NPV ($)*	*Probability*	*NPV ($)*
8/25	3,000	2/25	800
9/25	5,000	21/25	4,800
8/25	7,000	2/25	8,800

(a) Which project will be chosen according to the mean-variance rule?

(b) Which project will be preferred according to the expected return-coefficient of variation rule?

10.7 Consider the following investments:

Investment A		Investment B	
NPV	*Probability*	*NPV*	*Probability*
$ 700	2/9	$1,700	1/2
1,000	5/9	2,300	1/2
1,300	2/9		

(a) Which alternative will be preferred according to the mean-variance criterion?

(b) Which alternative will be preferred according to the expected return coefficient of variation rule?

(c) According to your intuition, which alternative would be preferred by most investors? Explain.

APPENDIX 10A CUMULATIVE DISTRIBUTIONS AND RISK

As we noted in the text, if investment returns are normally distributed one can safely use the $E - V$ rule as the decision criterion. Given this assumption, the expected NPV and the variance of NPV provide us with all the required information regarding the distribution of outcomes. The $E - V$ rule can also be used without imposing any restrictions on the distributions of returns if we assume a quadratic utility function. In this case we have,

$$U(X) = X + \beta X^2 \text{ with } U' = 1 + 2\beta X > 0 \text{ and } U'' = 2\beta < 0$$

Assuming such a utility function, we have for two investments X and Y:

$$EU(X) = EX + \beta EX^2 = EX + \beta(EX)^2 + \beta\sigma_X^2$$

and

$$EU(Y) = EY + \beta(EY)^2 + \beta\sigma_Y^2$$

If X is better than Y by the $E - V$ rule we have

$$EX > EY$$

$$\sigma_X < \sigma_Y$$

It follows that in this case $EU(X) > EU(Y)$ for *all* quadratic utility functions. To see this we employ the fact that for a quadratic function $\Delta EU/\Delta E > 0$ (based on the property that $U' > 0$) and $\Delta EU/\Delta \sigma^2 < 0$ (using the property $U'' < 0$). However, this utility function has its drawbacks. First, for all values of $X > -1/(2\beta)$ it declines and second it is characterized by an increasing risk premium as wealth increases which is quite contrary to observed investor behavior. But these inadequacies of quadratic utility functions return us to the assumption that returns are distributed normally. However, in cases where the returns are not distributed normally, the mean-variance rule often can be misleading.

Recognition of such a possibility led Frederick Hillier and David Hertz to the conclusion that investment decision making might be improved by examining the *entire* cumulative distribution of possible outcomes.[1] With the tools at their disposal, Hillier and Hertz succeeded in analyzing investment problems in which the cumulative distributions of alternative proposals do *not* intersect, but experienced considerable difficulty in interpreting their results when such intersections did occur. The purpose of this Appendix is to extend their work by applying some relatively new techniques which permit us (in a number of important instances) to make an unambiguous choice between investment alternatives even if their cumulative distributions intersect. But first let us digress for a moment and refresh our memories regarding some of the basic properties of probability distributions.

The Probability Distribution and the Cumulative Distribution Function

The probability distribution provides information regarding the probability that a random variable will get some value x. We can use this information, in turn, to define the *cumulative distribution function*, or in short the *distribution function,* which sets out the probability that the random variable will attain a value smaller or equal to some x, that is $P(X \leq x)$. A common notation for the cumulative distribution is $F(x) = P(X \leq x)$. In this section we shall familiarize ourselves with the chief characteristics of this type of probability distribution which will then be used to study problems of investment choice.

AN EXAMPLE

Assume the following probability distribution of net present value for a

---

1 See F.S. Hillier, "The Derivation of Probabilistic Information for the Evaluation of Risky Investments", *Management Science,* April 1963, and David B. Hertz, "Risk Analysis in Capital Investment", *Harvard Business Review,* January – February 1964.

hypothetical investment proposal:

NPV (in dollars) x	Probability P(x)
80	0.2
90	0.2
110	0.4
120	0.2

If we want to know the probability that the project's *NPV* will be "smaller or equal" to any particular value, the answer can be derived from the following *cumulative* probability function:

$$F(x) = P(X \leqslant x) = \begin{cases} 0 & x < 80 \\ 0.2 & 80 \leqslant x < 90 \\ 0.4 & 90 \leqslant x < 110 \\ 0.8 & 110 \leqslant x < 120 \\ 1 & x \geqslant 120 \end{cases}$$

For example, if one wants to know the probability that the *NPV* will be smaller than (or equal to) $112.5 the appropriate interval ($110 \leqslant x < 120$) can be examined and a probability of 80% is the answer. Graphical representations of the probability distribution, and the cumulative probability distribution, are given in Fig. 10A.1. The reader should note that this particular cumulative distribution is a "step-function" which reflects the fact that we used an example of a *discrete* random variable. With respect to a continuous random variable, such as the normal distribution, the cumulative distribution rises continuously in a smooth (rather than stepwise) fashion.

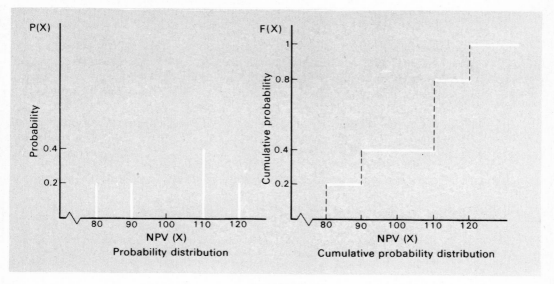

Probability distribution   Cumulative probability distribution

Fig. 10A.1

Distribution Free Investment Analysis

Now let us use the concept of a cumulative distribution to analyze investment choice. Consider again the simple example given at the end of Chapter 10 in which investment A yields a profit of $2 with a probability of 1, while alternative B yields a profit of $5 with a probability of 1/2 or $15 with a probability of 1/2. As we have already pointed out, neither the $E - V$ nor the mean-coefficient of variation rules can distinguish between these two alternative investments, despite the fact that investment B is obviously preferable to A, since *all* possible outcomes of B exceed the outcome of A.

The superiority of investment B is easily demonstrated by examining the cumulative distributions of the two investments. In Fig. 10A.2 the cumulative

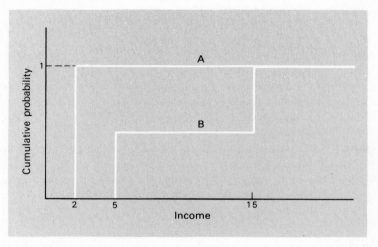

Fig. 10A.2

probability distribution of B lies to the right of that of investment A. In the simple case considered, in which the cumulative distributions do not intersect, a decision which is consistent with the expected utility rule can always be identified, without recourse to the shapes of individuals' utility functions, by applying the following general rule of *First Degree Stochastic Dominance* (*FSD*) which is set out in terms of monetary outcomes and their probabilities and not in terms of utilities:[2]

> *Any investment B is preferable to investment A if $F_B(x) \leqslant F_A(x)$, for all values of x, i.e. if the cumulative probability distribution of B lies to the right of that A.*

2 For the derivation of this technique see J.P. Quirk and R. Saposnik, "Admissibility and Measurable Utility Functions", *Review of Economic Studies,* February 1962; J. Hadar and W.R. Russell, "Rules for Ordering Uncertain Prospects", *American Economic Review,* March 1969, and G. Hanoch and H. Levy, "The Efficiency Analysis of Choices Involving Risk", *Review of Economic Studies,* July 1969. A detailed discussion of the implications of stochastic dominance for financial analysis is given in H. Levy and M. Sarnat, *Investment and Portfolio Analysis,* New York, Wiley, 1972, chs. 8 and 9.

This is tantamount to the requirement that the two cumulative probability distributions do not intersect. This condition also means that the probability of receiving a return greater than or equal to some level *k* must always be *higher* in alternative B than in investment A. Since the chance of earning higher returns is always greater, investment B will be preferred by all investors.

Some Numerical Examples

In order to demonstrate the simplicity of the stochastic dominance technique, let us examine a specific numerical example.

EXAMPLE NO. 1

Consider first the two alternative investments, denoted as A and B, in Table 10A.1. A comparison of investments A and B clearly shows that investment A is preferable to investment B since investment A offers an equal probability of double the income. This is equivalent to confronting an individual

Table 10A.1

| | Investment A | | | Investment B | |
Probability (P)	Cumulative Probability F_A	Net present Value (x)	Probability (P)	Cumulative Probability F_B	Net present Value (x)
1/3	1/3	10	1/3	1/3	5
1/3	2/3	20	1/3	2/3	10
1/3	1	30	1/3	1	15

with the choice of betting on either of two unbiased roulette wheels, one of which pays the winner double the amount of the other for the same wager. Clearly all rational persons would choose to play on the roulette wheel having the equal probability of the larger payoffs (represented by alternative A), since common sense alone suffices to tell us that this option is preferable. Despite this, the $E - V$ rule cannot discriminate between the two options: investment A has both a higher expected *NPV* and a greater risk (variance).

Now let us check to see if the use of cumulative distributions can help to eliminate this anomaly. The cumulative probability distributions of both options are given in Table 10A.1, and these figures were used to construct Table 10A.2 which sets out the relevant data for *comparing* the cumulative probability functions of the two investments. The left-hand column includes all attainable returns from investments A and B, as well as several values of returns which are not attainable in either of the options.[3]

3 The reader can verify that the cumulative probability distributions are not affected by considering the unattainable levels of return. In other words, the cumulative probability distribution of a discrete random variable is a step function, remaining constant for those values of *x* which have a zero probability and rising in jump fashion at those values of *x* for which probability is positive.

Table 10A.2

Income	Cumulative Probability of Investment B F_B	Cumulative Probability of Investment A F_A	F_B Minus F_A
−5	0	0	0
0	0	0	0
5	1/3	0	1/3
7	1/3	0	1/3
10	2/3	1/3	1/3
12	2/3	1/3	1/3
15	1	1/3	2/3
17	1	1/3	2/3
20	1	2/3	1/3
22	1	2/3	1/3
25	1	2/3	1/3
28	1	2/3	1/3
30	1	1	0
35	1	1	0

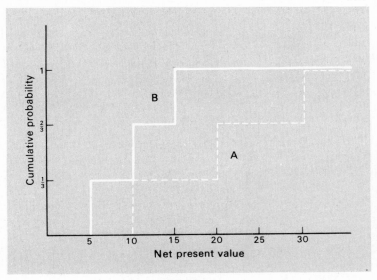

Fig. 10A.3

From the right-hand column of Table 10A.2 we can see the $F_B(x) - F_A(x) > 0$ for all levels of x; or alternatively we can write $F_A(x) \leqslant F_B(x)$. This result is shown in Fig. 10A.3 which plots the cumulative probability functions for the two investments. The "roulette wheel" with the smaller payoffs is denoted by B and the other alternative by A. Since the cumulative distribution of A lies to the right of B the First Degree Stochastic Dominance Criterion is fulfilled, and investment A (the roulette wheel with the larger payoff) is preferable to, i.e.

dominates, investment B, independent of the shape of the utility function, which is as it should be.

Unfortunately the firm is not always confronted with simple choice situations which are characterized by non-intersecting cumulative distributions. In general, as Hillier and Hertz found, the distributions often intersect once or even a number of times. In such situations the decision is somewhat more complicated, but if we make the usual assumption of risk aversion, we can discriminate between projects in a number of important cases, even though their distributions do intersect, by applying the following risk-aversion criterion, or Second Degree Stochastic Dominance (*SSD*) as it is often called:

> *Investment B is preferable to investment A for all risk averters if the cumulative difference between F_A and F_B is non-negative over the entire domain of x.*[4]

If the risk-aversion criterion is fulfilled, the expected utility of project B is higher than the expected utility of project A (for all risk averters). Thus we can choose between the two alternatives in a manner which is consistent with expected utility theory, but *without* the need to know the detailed shape of the utility function beyond the realistic assumption of risk aversion. Hence such a rule is doubly blessed: it is consistent with the utility theory which underlies most of modern risk analysis while at the same time it provides a practical tool for actual decision analysis.

The meaning of this criterion can readily be visualized by considering the two investments A and B whose (continuous) cumulative probability distributions have been drawn in Fig. 10A.4. According to the risk-aversion criterion, the cumulative probability distributions may intersect, but the cumulative difference between F_A and F_B must remain non-negative over the entire domain of x. In Fig. 10A.4 the differences between the two distributions are marked with a plus sign where $F_A > F_B$ and with a minus sign where $F_B > F_A$. A glance at the diagram suffices to show that over the entire range of returns the cumulative area between the two distributions always remains positive. Hence the risk-aversion criterion is fulfilled and investment B *dominates* investment A for all risk averters. This is true since up to x_0 the distribution of A lies above that of B and therefore the area under A exceeds the area under B. And while it is true that between x_0 and x_1 distribution B lies above A, the preceding shaded area

---

4 That is if the following condition holds:

$$\int_{-\infty}^{x} [F_A(t) - F_B(t)]\, dt > 0 \text{ for all values of } x.$$

See Hadar and Russell, *op. cit.,* Hanoch and Levy, *op. cit.,* and Levy and Sarnat, *loc. cit.* If, in addition to risk aversion, we assume a decreasing absolute risk premium the third derivation will be non-negative. For this case Whitmore has derived a stochastic dominance rule which asserts that A is preferred over B if $E_A(X) \geq E_B(X)$ and in addition

$$\int_{-\infty}^{x} \left(\int_{-\infty}^{v} [F_A(t) - F_B(t)]\, dt \right) dv \geq 0 \text{ for all values } x.$$

See G.A. Whitmore, "Third Degree Stochastic Dominance", *American Economic Review,* Vol. 60, 1970, pp. 457 – 59.

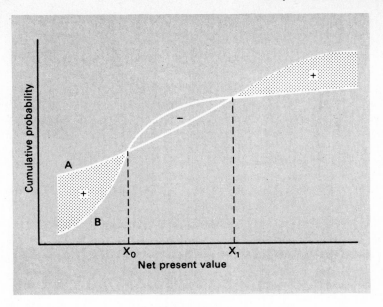

Fig. 10A.4

marked with a plus sign is larger than the area marked with a minus sign. Since beyond x_1, A again exceeds B, the *cumulative* shaded areas always exceed the areas marked with a minus sign over the entire range of x.

In order to clarify this investment rule we shall apply it to the specific numerical examples given in Table 10A.3. From the data of this Table we have computed the cumulative probability distributions for the two alternatives; these distributions are plotted in Fig. 10A.5. Since the two distributions intersect, options A and B do *not* dominate each other by the first degree stochastic dominance criterion. But if we invoke the risk-aversion criterion, investment B is clearly preferable to investment A; it is clear by inspection that the cumulative shaded area under A is always greater than the cumulative area under B.

Of course it may not always be an easy matter to verify the dominance of one investment over another by inspection, especially in cases where the probability distributions intersect a number of times. In such instances the area under

Table 10A.3

	Investment B			Investment A	
Net Present Value	*Probability*	*Cumulative Probability*	*Net Present Value*	*Probability*	*Cumulative Probability*
1	1/4	1/4	1/2	3/16	3/16
2	1/4	1/2	3/2	3/16	6/16
			5/2	4/16	10/16
9	1/4	3/4	7/2	3/16	13/16
10	1/4	1	9/2	3/16	1

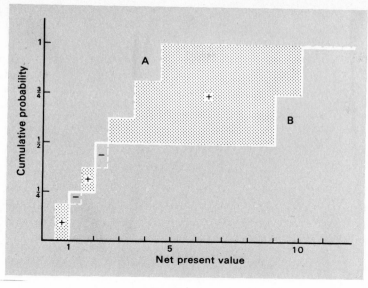

Fig. 10A.5

the cumulative probability distributions can be calculated by hand, or a simple computer program can be utilized for screening the projects by this choice criterion.

QUESTIONS AND PROBLEMS

10A.1 A publisher tries to estimate the sales of a new book in the current month relying on the sales figures during the preceding month. He expects that the sales will have the following distribution:

Probability $P(X_2)$	Number of Copies which will be Sold in the Current Month X_2
1/10	$X_1 - 1,000$
2/10	$X_1 - 500$
4/10	X_1
2/10	$X_1 + 500$
1/10	$X_1 + 1,000$

where X_1 denotes the quantity of copies of the book sold during the preceding month.

(a) Calculate the expected number of copies, $E(X_2)$, which will be sold in the current month.

(b) Calculate the variance of X_2.

(c) Calculate the cumulative probability function of X_2, assuming that $X_1 = 1,500$. (Graph your results.)

(d) Use the cumulative probability function you calculated in (c) to find the probability that X_2 will be smaller than (or equal to) 1,600.

10A.2 (a) Define the *First Degree Stochastic Dominance* criterion (*FSD*).

(b) Consider the following two investment options:

A		B	
Probability (P)	NPV (X)	Probability (P)	NPV (X)
2/5	10	1/5	5
1/5	15	2/5	10
2/5	30	1/5	15
		1/5	30

Which option is preferable by the First Degree Stochastic Dominance criterion? Prove your answer graphically.

10A.3 Consider the following two investment options:

C		D	
Probability (P)	NPV (X)	Probability (P)	NPV (X)
1/8	10	1/8	5
2/8	15	1/8	8
1/8	20	1/8	15
3/8	30	2/8	22
1/8	35	3/8	25

Which option is preferable by the *FSD* criterion? Prove your answer graphically.

10A.4 Consider the following two investment options:

A		B	
Probability (P)	NPV (X)	Probability (P)	NPV (X)
2/10	4	3/10	8
3/10	12	4/10	18
5/10	26	3/10	30

Which option is preferable by the risk-aversion criterion? Prove your answer graphically.

10A.5 "If investment A is preferable to investment B by the *FSD* rule then necessarily A is preferable to B by the risk-aversion criterion." Appraise this quotation.

10A.6 Consider the following two investment options:

C		D	
Probability (P)	NPV (X)	Probability (P)	NPV (X)
1/2	10	1	15
1/2	20		

(a) Which option is preferable by the *FSD* criterion?

(b) Which option is preferable by the risk-aversion criterion? Prove your answer graphically.

(c) Is your approach to part (b) consistent with the expected utility approach?

SELECTED REFERENCES

Aharony, Joseph and Loeb, Martin, "Mean-Variance vs Stochastic Dominance: Some Empirical Findings on Efficient Sets", *Journal of Banking and Finance*, June 1977.

Ali, M.M., "Stochastic Dominance and Portfolio Analysis", *Journal of Financial Economics*, June 1975.

Arditti, Fred D., "Risk and the Required Return on Equity", *Journal of Finance*, March 1967.

Arzac, Enrique R., "Structural Planning Under Controllable Business Risk", *Journal of Finance*, December 1975.

Bawa, V.S., "Safety-First, Stochastic Dominance, and Optimal Portfolio Choice, *Journal of Financial and Quantitative Analysis*, June 1978.

Bawa, V.S., "Optimal Rules for Ordering Uncertain Prospects", *Journal of Financial Economics*, March 1975.

Ben-Horim, M. and Levy, H., *Statistics: Decisions and Applications in Business and Economics*, New York, Random House, 1981.

Cooley, P.L., Roenfeldt, R.L. and Modani, N.K., "Interdependence of Market Risk Measures", *Journal of Business*, July 1977.

Cox, J.C., Ingersoll, J.E. Jr., and Ross, S.A., "Duration and the Measurement of Basic Risk", *Journal of Business*, January 1979.

Cramer, R.H. and Seifert, J.A., "Measuring the Impact of Maturity on Expected Return and Risk", *Journal of Bank Research*, Autumn 1976.

Fishburn, P.C., "Mean-Risk Analysis with Risk Associated with Below-Target Returns", *American Economic Review*, March 1977.

Dimson, Elroy, "Risk Measurement when Shares are Subject to Infrequent Trading", *Journal of Financial Economics*, 1979.

Falk, H. and Heintz, J.A., "Assessing Industry Risk by Ratio Analysis", *Accounting Review*, October 1975.

Friend, I. and Blume, M.E., "The Demand for Risky Assets", *American Economic Review*, December 1975.

Gehr, A.K. Jr., "Risk and Return", *Journal of Finance*, September 1979.

Hadar, J. and Russell, W.R., "Rules for Ordering Uncertain Prospects", *American Economic Review*, March 1969.

Hogan, William W. and Warren, James M., "Toward the Development of an Equilibrium Capital-Market Model Based on Semivariance", *Journal of Financial and Quantitative Analysis*, January 1974.

Huang, C.C., Vertinsky, I. and Ziemba, W.T., "On Multiperiod Stochastic Dominance", *Journal of Financial and Quantitative Analysis*, March 1978.

Jean, W.H., "The Geometric Mean and Stochastic Dominance", *Journal of Finance*, March 1980.

Johnson, K.H. and Burgess, R.C., "The Effects of Sample Sizes on the Accuracy of EV and SSD Efficiency Criteria", *Journal of Financial and Quantitative Analysis*, December 1975.

Kearns, R.B. and Burgess, R.C., "An Effective Algorithm for Estimating Stochastic Dominance Efficient Sets", *Journal of Financial and Quantitative Analysis*, September 1979.

Latane, H.A. and Tuttle, Donald L., "Decision Theory and Financial Management", *Journal of Finance*, May 1966.

Levy, H. and Kroll, Y., "Ordering Uncertain Options with Borrowing and Lending", *Journal of Finance*, May 1978.

Levy, H. and Paroush, Jacob, "Multi-Period Stochastic Dominance", *Management Science Application*, December 1974.

Mao, James C.T. and Helliwell, John F., "Investment Decisions under Uncertainty: Theory and Practice", *Journal of Finance*, May 1969.

McEnally, R.W. and Upton, D.E., "A Re-examination of the Ex Post Risk-Return Tradeoff on Common Stocks", *Journal of Financial and Quantitative Analysis*, June 1979.

Murphy, Joseph E. Jr and Osborne, M.F.M., "Games of Chance and the Probability of Corporate Profit or Loss", *Financial Management*, Summer 1979.

Meyer, J. "Further Applications of Stochastic Dominance to Mutual Fund Performance", *Journal of Financial and Quantitative Analysis*, June 1977.

Modigliani, Franco and Pogue, Gerald A., "An Introduction to Risk and Return", *Financial Analysts Journal*, March/April 1974. Part II, May/June 1974.

Perrakis, S. and Zerbinis, J., "Identifying the SSD Portion of the EV Frontier: A Note", *Journal of Financial and Quantitative Analysis*, March 1978.

Philippatos, George C. and Gressis, Nicolas, "Conditions of Equivalence Among E-V, SSD, and E-H Portfolio Selection Criteria — The Case for Uniform Normal and Lognormal Distributions", *Management Science Application*, February 1957.

Porter, R.B., Bey, R.P. and Lewis D.C., "The Development of a Mean-Semivariance Approach to Capital Budgeting", *Journal of Financial and Quantitative Analysis*, November 1975.

Porter, R.B. and Bey, R.P., "An Evaluation of the Empirical Significance of Optimal Seeking Algorithms in Portfolio Selection", *Journal of Finance*, December 1974.

Pratt, J.W. and Hammond, J.S. III, "Evaluating and Comparing Projects: Simple Detection of False Alarms", *Journal of Finance*, December 1979.

Robison, L.J. and Barry, P.J., "Risk Efficiency Using Stochastic Dominance and Expected Gain-Confidence Limits", *Journal of Finance*, September 1978.

Roy, A.D., "Safety First and the Holding of Assets", *Econometrica*, July 1952.

Saunders, Anthony, Ward, Charles and Woodward, Richard, "Stochastic Dominance and the Performance of UK Unit Trusts", *Journal of Financial and Quantitative Analysis*, June 1980.

Schlarbaum, Gary G. and Racette, George A., "Measuring Risk: Some Theoretical and Empirical Issues", *Journal of Business Research*, July 1974.

Schwendiman, Carl J. and Pinches, George E., "An Analysis of Alternative Measures of Investment Risk", *Journal of Finance*, March 1975.

Scott, Robert C. and Horvath, Philip A., "On the Direction of Preference for Moments of Higher Order than the Variance", *Journal of Finance*, September 1980.

Tehranian, H., "Empirical Studies in Portfolio Performance Using Higher Degrees of Stochastic Dominance", *Journal of Finance*, March 1980.

Vickson, R.G., "Stochastic Dominance for Decreasing Absolute Risk Aversion", *Journal of Financial and Quantitative Analysis*, December 1975.

Vickson, R.G. and Altmann, M., "On the Relative Effectiveness of Stochastic Dominance Rules: Extension to Decreasingly Risk-Averse Utility Functions", *Journal of Financial and Quantitative Analysis*, March 1977.

Wachowicz, John M. Jr. and Shrieves, Ronald E., "An Argument for 'Generalized' Mean-Coefficient or Variation Analysis", *Financial Management*, Winter 1980.

Whitmore, G.A., "The Theory of Skewness Preference", *Journal of Business Administration*, Spring 1975.

11

Applications of
Risk Analysis

To this point we have focused attention on the *principles* of risk measurement in an attempt to determine the fundamental properties of some of the better-known risk indices and decision rules. With this theoretical background to build upon, let us turn now to the no less important problems concerning the use of risk analysis in actual practice.

This chapter is devoted to the practical application of risk analysis. Two *indirect* methods for adjusting the *NPV* calculation for risk are discussed:

(a)   The Certainty Equivalent Method.
(b)   The Adjusted Discount Method, which is a popular rule of thumb used by firms who do *not* estimate the riskiness of individual projects.

After showing that the rule of thumb method is equivalent to the more sophisticated techniques based on the discounting of certainty-equivalent cash flows, the remainder of the chapter is devoted to two practical applications of *direct* adjustments for risk for those firms which are able to estimate the probability distributions of individual projects:

(a)   Simulation Analysis
(b)   Decision Trees.

APPLYING RISK ANALYSIS: THE EMPIRICAL EVIDENCE

As was noted in Chapter 8 above, the actual practice of firms has tended to lag behind academic research with respect to the use of relatively sophisticated capital budgeting methods. Many firms still rely on simpler rules of thumb to adjust for the timing of the cash flow, although these rules of thumb are often applied in a sophisticated manner. It is not too surprising, therefore, to learn

Table 11.1

Percentage of Firms Using Risk Analysis Techniques, in Selected Years

	1970	*1964*	*1959*
Raising Required Return	21	16	12
Shortening Payback Period	10	9	9
Determining Probability Distribution	13	7	7
Measuring Covariance of Projects	3	2	1
Other	7	2	1
At least One of Above	39	24	19

Source: Thomas Klammer, "Empirical Evidence of the Adoption of Sophisticated Capital Budgeting Techniques", *Journal of Business,* vol. 45, 1972, p. 391.

that a recent survey[1] of large U.S. manufacturing corporations reported that only 39% of the respondents make formal adjustments for risk in their capital budgeting procedures. (See Table 11.1.)

A noteworthy feature of Table 11.1 is the steadily rising percentage of firms which use one or more techniques of risk analysis. Only 19% of the firms surveyed applied formal risk analysis in 1959; the relevant figure for 1970 is 39%. And the trend has continued throughout the 1970s. Table 11.2 combines data drawn from several surveys on the percentage of firms which explicitly consider risk when evaluating capital expenditures. Although the data are not strictly comparable, the increasing tendency for firms to explicitly recognize project risk as an important facet of capital budgeting is clearly discernible. And by the end of the 1970s it would appear reasonable to conclude that at least two-thirds of the largest US firms apply some sort of risk adjustment (formal or informal) when assessing the feasibility of a capital investment proposal. Thus, once again, the theory which was developed in the 1950s and early 1960s (in this instance risk analysis) has increasingly been reflected in the actual practice of large corporations during the 1970s.

Another noteworthy feature of the empirical evidence is that the majority of firms which do apply risk analysis tend to use a short-cut rule of thumb adjustment for risk,[2] for example raising the discount rate (or equivalently shortening the payback period). Such firms make an "indirect" adjustment for risk, rather than explicitly expressing the risk of each proposal (or portfolio of proposals) in terms of the dispersion of returns. Hence in what follows we shall focus attention initially on the properties of the "indirect" rule of thumb adjustment of the discount rate, and then go on to some practical applications of the "direct" adjustment for risk for those firms which estimate the probability distributions of individual investment projects.

1 See Thomas Klammer, "Empirical Evidence of the Adoption of Sophisticated Capital Budgeting Techniques", *Journal of Business,* July 1972, p. 391.
2 See Table 11.1. This finding has been corroborated by a large number of more recent studies, see for example Petty and Scott, *op. cit.*

Table 11.2
Explicit Consideration of Project Risk

Year in which Survey was Published	Percent of Firms Considering Risk
1972	39*
1973	67
1975	71
1977	71
1978	96**

*This percentage reflects only those firms that use a specific formal method for assessing risk; see Table 11.1.

**In this study, 36% of the respondents indicated use of a quantitative technique for assessing risk. The other 60% represents subjective adjustments.

Source: J. William Petty II and David F. Scott Jr., "Capital Budgeting Practices in Large American Firms: A Retrospective Analysis and Update", forthcoming.

INDIRECT ADJUSTMENT FOR RISK

In the preceding chapter it was assumed implicitly that each investment project could be characterized by two indices, one which measures the investment's profitability and a second which reflects its risk. This type of approach is a *direct method* of incorporating risk into the decision-making process since we directly attempt to measure the risk of each investment proposal or combination of proposals. One example of such an approach is the $E - V$ (expected *NPV*-Variance of *NPV*) rule.

An alternative, and as we have just seen the most popular, way to incorporate risk into the decision-making procedure is to include it *indirectly* in the discount rate for calculating the *NPV*. In this type of approach we characterize each project by a *single* indicator of investment worth, i.e. its "risk-adjusted" net present value. Thus the measure of attractiveness, in this instance the project's *NPV*, contains an indirect or implicit factor which reflects the project's risk, and no attempt is made to explicitly express the risk of each proposal or portfolio of proposals.

In order to isolate the theoretical properties of the rule of thumb adjustment of the discount rate, we shall first set out an alternative theoretical method for adjusting a project's cash flow for risk, based on the expected utility principle. This "certainty-equivalent" method will then be used as a benchmark for evaluating the popular rule of thumb.

Certainty Equivalent Method

Suppose that an investor is offered the following future net receipt: $5 with a probability of 1/2 and $15 with a probability of 1/2. What is the present value of his return? One way to answer this question is to find the *certainty equivalent*

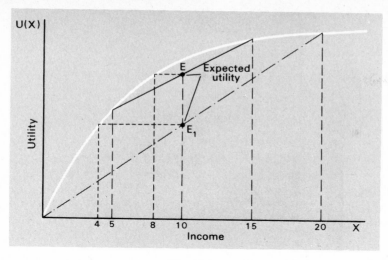

Fig. 11.1

of this probability distribution. In principle, the certainty equivalent depends on the investor's preferences, i.e. on his utility function. Let us assume that point E of Fig. 11.1 represents the distribution's expected utility to our hypothetical investor. Note that point E is simply the weighted average of the two outcomes $(1/2\ U(5) + 1/2\ U(15))$ and, as before, is given by the intersection of the vertical line rising from \$10 (which is the expected monetary return) with the chord connecting the two alternative outcomes on the utility function.

Now, suppose that we offer the investor a *perfectly certain* sum of money instead of the uncertain distribution. What is the amount of money which must be offered to ensure that the investor will be indifferent between the risky and perfectly certain alternatives? As was explained in Chapter 9, the answer is that sum which provides the *same level of utility*, i.e. \$8 in the example given in Fig. 11.1. Hence, \$8 is the *certainty equivalent* of a risky distribution which offers an equal probability of receiving \$5 or \$15.

Now, what is the present value of this risky prospect? Since, as we have just seen, the certainty equivalent of the distribution is \$8, its present value will be $8/(1 + r)$, where r denotes the *riskless* interest rate. We discount the cash flow using the riskless interest rate, because we first reduced the cash flow (i.e. the numerator of the equation) to its certainty equivalent.

AN EXAMPLE

Another example may help clarify this line of reasoning. Suppose that the initial outlay of a given investment proposal is \$50 and that its net annual cash flow for the next twenty years is \$5 with probability of 1/2 and \$15 with a probability of 1/2. Hence, the certainty equivalent of the annual cash receipt again is \$8. Assuming a riskless interest rate of 5%, the proposal's net present value is

$$\$8 \times 12.462 - \$50 = \$99.70 - \$50 = \$49.70$$

where 12.462 is the appropriate coefficient in the present value table used in Chapter 3.

Note that the *expected* annual cash flow is

$$1/2 \times 5 + 1/2 \times 15 = \$10$$

Thus, the proposal's *expected* net present value is given by

$$10 \times 12.462 - 50 = \$74.62$$

which is higher than the *risk-adjusted* net present value ($49.70). The difference can be interpreted as follows: the *NPV* of $74.62 is *not* adjusted for risk and therefore only measures the proposal's expected profitability; the previous calculation of $49.70 measures the net present value *adjusted for risk*. It follows that the *difference* between $74.62 and $49.70 measures the "value" of the risk inherent in the investment project in question; and at least in principle, the investor (or firm) would be willing to pay this amount (i.e. $24.92) to induce an insurance company to underwrite this risk.

The higher is the variability of future outcomes, the greater is the risk, and therefore we would expect the risk-adjusted *NPV* to decline even further. For example, suppose we replace the previous distribution by an equal probability of earning $20 or nothing. The average annual cash flow remains $10 as before, but the variability (variance) of the possible outcomes is increased considerably. This new proposal is represented by the dashed line of Fig. 11.1. As can be seen from the diagram, the expected utility of the more risky cash flow, denoted by E_1, has a certainty equivalent of only $4. The project's risk-adjusted net present value (again using a horizon of twenty years and a 5% riskless discount rate) is given by

$$\$4 \times 12.462 - \$50 = \$49.8 - \$50 = -\$0.20$$

Thus for a given *expected* net present value, the larger the dispersion (variance) the lower will be the certainty-equivalent cash flow and hence the lower will be the risk-adjusted *NPV*. This result of the certainty-equivalent approach is consistent with both the expected utility and mean-variance methods which were discussed in earlier chapters, although clearly it utilizes a very different technique for carrying out the risk-adjustment.

Adjusting the Discount Rate

As we have just seen the risk-adjusted *NPV* can be calculated using the riskless rate of interest as the discount rate, if the future cash flow is first reduced to its certainty-equivalent value. Alternatively, this adjustment can be effected by raising the discount rate, i.e. by adjusting the denominator rather than the numerator of the *NPV* equation. Clearly, the greater the risk, the higher will be the adjusted discount rate and therefore the lower will be the project's risk-adjusted *NPV*. In this case, the difference between the risk-adjusted discount rate and the riskless interest rate measures the required *risk premium*.

AN EXAMPLE

Consider an investment proposal which requires an initial outlay of $100 and provides an equal probability of earning a net annual cash flow of $50 or $150 for ten years, i.e. an expected (mean) annual cash receipt of $100:

$$1/2 \times \$50 + 1/2 \times \$150 = \$100$$

If we again assume a 5% riskless rate of interest, the *unadjusted NPV* of this proposal is $672.20:

$$\$100 \times 7.722 - \$100 = \$772.20 - \$100 = \$672.20$$

where 7.722 is the appropriate present value coefficient assuming a 5% discount rate and a ten-year cash flow. However, since the future cash flow is *not* known with certainty, let us assume that the firm requires an additional 5% as a premium to compensate for the risk incurred and therefore calculates the *NPV* of the project using a 10% discount rate. In this case, the *risk-adjusted NPV* is only $514.50:

$$\$100 \times 6.145 - \$100 = \$614.50 - \$100 = \$514.50$$

Thus even though the project's expected *NPV* is $672.20, due to its risk, the firm values the proposal at only $514.50.

Now suppose that we hold the average receipt constant at $100, but increase its variability. For example, suppose that for the same initial outlay we have another project which provides an equal probability of receiving an annual cash flow of either $200 or nothing for ten years. Note that the expected (mean) annual cash flow remains $100. Since the variance increases, we can assume that the required risk premium will also be larger, say 15%, and as a result the adjusted discount rate will be 20% (5% riskless interest rate plus 15% risk premium). In this case the risk-adjusted *NPV* is only $319.20.

$$\$100 \times 4.192 - \$100 = \$419.20 - \$100 = \$319.20$$

where 4.192 is the appropriate present value coefficient for a 20% discount rate and ten-year cash flow. Thus the higher the variance, the greater will be the discount rate, and hence the lower will be the risk-adjusted *NPV*. Once again this result is consistent with the expected utility and mean-variance principles.

Certainty Equivalent vs Discount Rate Adjustments

The certainty equivalent method adjusts the project's cash flow while in the second rule of thumb method the discount rate is adjusted. Although it may not be intuitively obvious, the two methods are equivalent, in the sense that they provide the *same NPV* if the respective risk adjustments are carried out in an appropriate manner. To show this, consider a case in which the expected net cash receipt one year hence is $\overline{C}$ dollars. Now assume that the certainty equivalent of this sum is C^*, which, of course, must be smaller than $\overline{C}$. Thus, one can always write

$$C^* = q\overline{C} \text{ (where } 0 < q < 1)$$

The risk-adjusted present value of the cash receipt, using the certainty equivalent approach, is

$$\frac{C^*}{1 + r}$$

where r denotes the riskless interest rate. But as $C^* = q\overline{C}$, the present value can be rewritten as follows:

$$\frac{q\overline{C}}{1 + r} = \frac{\overline{C}}{(1 + r)/q} = \frac{\overline{C}}{1 + k}$$

where $1 + k = (1 + r)/q$.

By definition, k must be greater than r, so the expression $\overline{C}/(1 + k)$ can be interpreted as the risk-adjusted present value when the adjustment is effected by raising the discount rate. Thus, if the adjusted discount rate is determined by the relationship $(1 + r)/q = 1 + k$, the two methods will yield the same adjusted present values. For example if $r = 5\%$ and $q = 0.9$, the adjusted discount rate can be calculated as follows:

$$k = (1.05 \div 0.9) - 1 = \textbf{16.7\%}$$

If on the other hand the risk is larger and hence q is smaller, say $q = 0.8$, the adjusted discount rate is approximately 31%:

$$(1.05 \div 0.8) - 1 = \textbf{31.2\%}$$

In sum, the larger the risk, the smaller is the certainty equivalent C^* in comparison to the mean cash flow $\overline{C}$ and, therefore, the factor q must also be smaller. This, in turn, implies a higher adjusted discount rate.[3]

Thus the popular rule of thumb adjustment of the discount rate is conceptually equivalent to the more sophisticated techniques, based on the discounting of certainty-equivalent cash flows, which are advocated in the theoretical literature.[4]

APPLYING PROBABILITY MEASURES IN PRACTICE

Now let us turn our attention to that subset of firms who are able to apply the more sophisticated techniques of direct risk analysis discussed. It is noteworthy that the various measures of risk and return which have been proposed share an important characteristic; all the indices and decision rules require the prior assignment of a probability to each of the possible outcomes of the risky invest-

---

3 Although the algebra is somewhat more complicated, this equivalence holds for multiperiod projects as well.

4 This is of considerable importance, not only for interpreting the actual practices of firms, but for the theory of finance as well; see Part III below.

ment option. As we have seen, one straightforward way to handle this problem is to assign probabilities to different outcomes in terms of the proposal's net present value. These probabilities may be objective, or subjective, or what is probably more often the case, some mixture of objective information regarding the possible outcomes with a large measure of subjective judgment.

Simulation Analysis

In order to improve the process by which the probabilities are assigned one should recall that a project's *NPV* is a sort of summary outcome of the proposal's prospects which is based on forecasts of sales, market prices, costs, etc. Once we explicitly recognize the economic roots which determine the *NPV*, the analysis becomes considerably more complex because a probability distribution must be assigned to each of the relevant economic factors. The probability distribution of the *NPV*, in turn, is derived from the distributions of the underlying real economic factors. Of course, the larger the number of economic factors considered the more difficult it becomes to derive the *NPV* distribution. However, it must be emphasized that such an analysis of the basic factors which determine the project's *NPV* is necessary for improving our estimate of the project's chances of success or failure.

In order to help overcome the technical difficulties of handling and evaluating so many economic factors, David Hertz has proposed the use of a simulation technique to evaluate the profitability of investment projects when their probability distributions are derived from the probability distributions of underlying economic factors.[5] Hertz distinguishes between market analysis, investment analysis and cost analysis (see Fig. 11.2). Each of these categories is subdivided; for example under the heading market analysis we find the following subdivisions: market size, selling price, market growth rate, and market share. To each of these factors one has to assign some probability distribution. For example, suppose that the firm assigns the following probabilities to the selling price of the product under consideration:

Selling Price ($)	*Probability*
5	0.05
6	0.10
7	0.10
8	0.50
9	0.10
10	0.10
11	0.05

5 David B. Hertz, "Risk Analysis in Capital Investment", *Harvard Business Review,* January – February 1964, pp. 95 – 106; and "Investment Policies that Pay Off", *Harvard Business Review,* January – February 1968, pp. 96 – 108.

and that the following probabilities are assigned to the firm's market share:

Market Share (in units)	Probability
100,000	0.25
150,000	0.50
200,000	0.25

Now suppose that we spin two roulette wheels. The first is a proxy for the selling prices and has 100 numbers; numbers 1 to 5 stand for a price of $5, numbers 6 to 15 for a market price of $6, and so on. The other roulette wheel also has 100 numbers, with numbers 1 to 25 standing for sales of 100,000 units, numbers 26 to 75 representing 150,000 units of sales, and numbers 76 to 100 sales of 200,000 units.

Now assume that after spinning both wheels, the first stops on number 9,

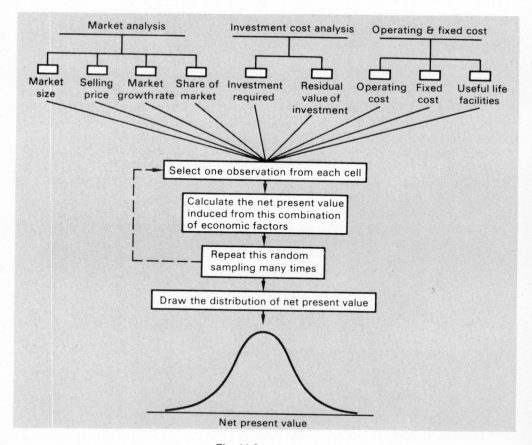

Fig. 11.2

which means that we are in the $6 price zone, and the other wheel stops at number 23, which means that sales will be 100,000 units. As a result, gross revenue will be $6 × 100,000 = $600,000. Of course, we should have many other "roulette wheels", one for each of the factors which determine the net profit. Spinning all the wheels simultaneously, we can calculate the profit or the net present value. Now we repeat this procedure many times and obtain the frequency distribution, i.e. the statistical distribution of outcomes of *NPV* resulting from various combinations of the underlying economic factors. Obviously, once we have more than two economic factors to consider, it helps to use a computer to carry out the simulation.

Finally, two warnings are in order. First, the economic factors set out in Fig. 11.2 are, in general, statistically dependent. For example, market size, and especially the firm's market share, is related to its operating costs, which often decline significantly as output increases. This can, and should, be handled by allowing for interdependencies between the statistical distributions of the relevant factors. Secondly, one should remember that the simulation approach facilitates, and hopefully improves, the estimate of the statistical distribution of *NPV*; however it does not absolve the firm from evaluating this distribution in terms of its profitability and risk. For example suppose that the firm desires to evaluate two mutally exclusive investments, A and B. Running the simulations for the two projects results in the two distributions drawn in Fig. 11.3. Both the expected *NPV* and risk (variance) of project B are larger than their counterparts in investment A. Thus, the firm must weigh the implied tradeoff between the higher expected profit and greater risk when choosing between these two investment alternatives. The simulation provides us with better estimates of the distributions but cannot by itself reach a decision. The computer simulation facilitates the process of decision-making but does *not* replace the decision-maker which perhaps explains why you are reading this book.

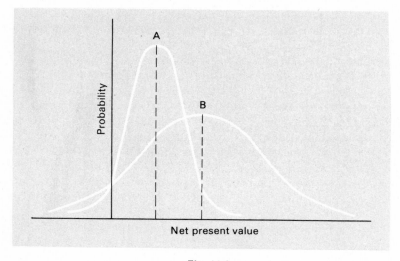

Fig. 11.3

DECISION TREE

The decision flow diagram, or "decision tree" as it is often called, is another technique which can facilitate investment decision-making when uncertainty prevails, especially when the problem involves a sequence of decisions.[6] In a sequential decision problem, in which the actions taken at one stage depend on actions previously taken in earlier stages, the evaluation of investment alternatives can become very complicated. In such cases, the "decision tree" technique facilitates project evaluation by enabling the firm to write down all the possible future decisions, as well as their monetary outcomes, in a systematic manner. As is true of simulation analysis, the use of decision trees does not obviate the need to reach decisions regarding projects having different expected profit-risk profiles. However, the use of the decision tree does make the implications of alternative possible courses of action more transparent, especially when the firm is confronted by a complex sequence of decisions.

Perhaps the best way to explain the decision tree is to demonstrate its use by a specific example. Suppose that an oil company owns drilling rights in a given area and that the company initially faces a decision whether or not to make a seismic test which would indicate the chances of finding oil in this area. Hence, making the test (which of course costs money) or avoiding it, is the *first decision* in our sequence of decisions (see Fig. 11.4). In stage 2, the firm again faces two alternatives: either to sell its drilling rights to another company, or to drill with the hope of finding oil. However, as one can see from Fig. 11.4, these two simple alternatives yield radically different monetary rewards, depending on the action taken in stage one, i.e. whether or not the seismic test is made, and on its sucess or failure in the event that the firm decides to make the test. Hence, the first stage is characterized in Fig. 11.4 by two branches of possible action denoted by A_1 and A_2. If the firm decides to make the seismic test (i.e. to follow branch A_2) it will, in the second stage, again be confronted by two branches of possible decisions (branches B_1 and B_2). Thus each successive decision in the sequence has its own branches to represent further decisions; hence the name decision "tree".

Now let us turn to the specific numerical example of the oil company given in Fig. 11.4. If the firm decides not to carry out the seismic test it can sell the drilling rights for $9 million (see branch G_9); alternatively the company can drill for oil without making the seismic test. In the latter event, the monetary outcome depends solely on whether or not oil is actually found. Suppose that the oil company estimates the probability of finding oil at 0.6, and the probability of a dry hole at 0.4. If we assume that the drilling cost is $12,500,000, there is a probability of 0.4 of losing this sum (see branch G_8). On the other hand, there is a probability of 0.6 of striking oil, in which case the firm will earn an *NPV* (after deducting the drilling and other costs) of $25 million (see branch G_7). The

6 The reader who wishes to pursue this subject further can consult John F. Magee, "Decision Trees for Decision Making", *Harvard Business Review,* July – August 1964; and "How to Use Decision Trees in Capital Investment", *Harvard Business Review,* September – October 1964; or Howard Raiffa, *Decision Analysis: Introductory Lectures on Choices Under Uncertainty,* Reading, Mass., Addison – Wesley, 1968.

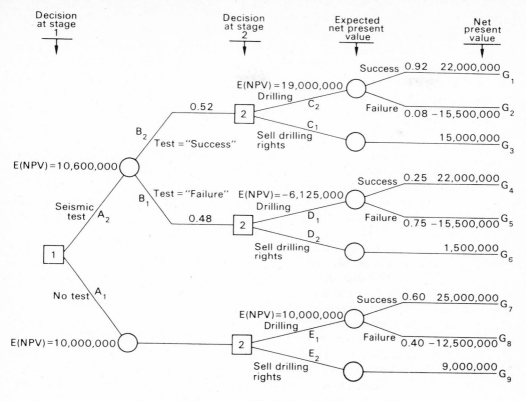

Decision at stage 1	Decision at stage 2	Expected net present value	Net present value

Fig. 11.4

expected NPV, should the firm decide to drill, *without* a seismic test, is $10 million:

$$E(NPV) = 0.6 \times \$25,000,000 + 0.4 \times (-\$12,500,000) = \mathbf{\$10,000,000}$$

Let us turn now to the monetary consequences of following branch A_2, i.e. we now shall assume that the firm decides to make the seismic test in the first stage. We further assume that this seismic test costs $3 million and that there exists a probability of 0.52 that the test will yield good results (denoted as "success" in Fig. 11.4), and a probability of 0.48 that it will fail. The decision in stage 2 obviously will depend on the test results. Should the company decide to sell the drilling rights after the seismic test fails, it will realize a lower price than it could have obtained without the seismic test. Clearly the poor results of the test (which we assume are public knowledge) decrease the market value of the drilling rights. Let us assume that if the test fails the firm can sell its concession for $4,500,000, which will net the firm only $1,500,000 because we have assumed that the seismic test costs $3 million (see branch G_6). On the other hand, the firm might still decide to drill despite the failure of the seismic test. However, as a result of the failure of the test, the company revises its estimates of the probability of finding oil. The probability of hitting oil is now estimated to be only 0.25 (as compared with 0.6 without the additional information provided by the seismic test). Should the firm fail to find oil, the loss will be $15,500,000 — the assumed drilling cost of $12,500,000 plus the $3 million cost of the seismic test (see branch G_5). Should the firm strike oil the net present value will be $22 million, which reflects a present value of $25 million from the net oil revenues minus the cost of the seismic test (see branch G_4). The *expected NPV*, should the firm decide to drill even if the seismic test fails, is $-$ \$6,125,000:

$$E(NPV) = 0.25 \times \$22,000,000 + 0.75 \times (-\$15,500,000) = -\mathbf{\$6,125,000}$$

The second possibility, i.e. the case of a successful seismic test, is described by branch B_2. Clearly a successful test will increase the value of the drilling rights, say to $18 million, and since the company spent $3 million on the seismic test, its net income from selling the rights would be $15 million (see branch G_3). Obviously, a successful seismic test also increases the probability of finding oil so we assume that the firm now estimates this probability at 0.92 (branch G_1). Thus the expected *NPV*, should the firm decide to drill following a successful seismic test, is $19 million:

$$E(NPV) = 0.92 \times \$22,000,000 + 0.08 \times (-\$15,500,000) = \mathbf{\$19,000,000}$$

Having obtained the monetary outcomes from all possible branches of Fig. 11.4, which decision sequence is optimal? Clearly, the decision depends on the utility that the firm attributes to each possible outcome. However, in order to demonstrate the use of the decision-tree technique, let us first assume, for simplicity, that the firm reaches its decisions according to the maximum expected *NPV* criterion. Following this rule, we calculate the expected *NPV* for each branch of Fig. 11.4 and that course of action represented by the branch with the highest expected *NPV* will be chosen. However, this is not as simple as it might seem. First we must examine the *NPV*s of stage 2 in order to choose the optimal course of action (branch) for stage 2; only then can we "fold back" the tree and choose the optimal decision for stage 1.

To illustrate the type of calculation required, let us examine the specific problem given in Fig. 11.4. Our first step is to compare the expected *NPV*s of the branches in stage 2. Assuming that the firm makes the seismic test the expected *NPV* of branch C_2 ($19 million) is higher than the *NPV* from selling the contract, branch C_1; hence the course of action denoted by branch C_1 can be discarded and should be ignored in our further calculations. Similarly, branch D_2 results in a higher expected *NPV* than does branch D_1, and therefore D_1 can also be discarded. If on the other hand, the firm decides not to make the seismic test, branch E_1 has a higher expected *NPV* than E_2 and therefore the latter can be discarded. Having first made these eliminations in the second stage decisions, we can then evaluate the first-stage decision as follows: the expected *NPV* of the seismic test becomes $10,600,000:

$$0.52 \times \$19,000,000 + 0.48 \times \$1,500,000 = \mathbf{\$10,600,000}$$

Note that this calculation of stage 1 exploits the previous screening of the alternatives of stage 2. If the test is successful, branch C_2 is chosen, so the expected *NPV* of that alternative is $19 million with a probability of 0.52. If the test is unsuccessful, the best path to follow is branch D_2, which results in a *NPV* of $1,500,000 with a probability of 0.48. Similarly, if we "fold back" the other branches, the maximum expected *NPV*, if the seismic test is *not* made, is the $10 million which rebults from the option of drilling without the test.

Examining our results, we find that the optimal decision in the first stage, using the maximum expected *NPV* criterion, is to make the seismic test. If successful, the firm will go ahead in stage 2 with the decision to drill for oil; should the test prove unsuccessful, the optimal second stage decision will be to sell the drilling rights. In terms of Fig. 11.4, the optimal path follows branches A_2, B_2 and C_2 if the test is a success; and branches A_2, B_1 and D_2 should it fail. Note that in both cases we start with branch A_2, i.e. with the decision to make the seismic test; the next decision in the sequence being taken only after the results of the test have been obtained. In summary, the decision-tree technique permits us to transport ourselves in "conceptual time" to the extremities of the tree where expectations are calculated in terms of the alternative outcomes and their probabilities of occurrence. Then we worked our way back by folding back, so to speak, the branches of the tree, choosing only those paths which yield the *maximum NPV* at each decision junction.

Decision Trees and Risk

In order to simplify the above example, we made the very unrealistic assumption that the firm seeks to maximize its expected *NPV*, i.e. that it completely ignores the risk incurred in each of the possible courses of action. Conceptually, risk can be incorporated into the analysis very easily, simply by assigning a utility to each monetary outcome and then choosing that branch which maximizes the *expected utility*. Such a procedure provides an acceptable theoretical solution to the problem but, as we have already noted, is not capable of practical application. Alternatively, the firm can examine the risk-return profile of each possible course of action in stage 2, in order to eliminate some branches on the basis of their expected profit and risk. Then the firm can "fold back" the decision tree to find the best *sequence of decisions*, taking both risk and expected *NPV* into account.

The expected *NPV*s and standard deviations of the alternative actions open to the firm in stage 2 are set out in Table 11.3. Taking risk into account, it is no longer clear that the firm will eliminate branch E_2 (i.e. the sale of the drilling rights without the test). Although the expected value of branch E_1 (i.e. drilling without the test) is greater than the expected *NPV* of branch E_2, the risk incurred is also greater. Thus, the firm must try to eliminate either E_1 or E_2 on the basis of the implicit tradeoff between *NPV* and risk. This decision depends, to a great extent, on the firm's subjective valuation of the cost of the risk incurred if branch E_1 is followed. Similarly, the firm must choose between branches C_1 and C_2. However, the choice between branches D_1 and D_2 is very simple, since D_2 yields both the *higher* expected *NPV* and the *lower* risk. Hence D_1 can be eliminated without recourse to a further subjective evaluation of its risk.

Thus, each of the actions C_2 or C_1, D_2 and E_1 or E_2 are potential choices in

Table 11.3

	Probability	Net Present Value	Probability	Net Present Value
		E_1		E_2
	0.6	25	1	9
	0.4	− 12.5		
Expected Value		10		9
Standard Deviation		18.37		0
		D_1		D_2
	0.25	22	1	1.5
	0.75	− 15.5		
Expected Value		− 6.125		1.5
Standard Deviation		20.34		0
		C_1		C_2
	1	15	0.92	22
			0.08	− 15.5
Expected Value		15		19
Standard Deviation		0		10.17

the second-stage decision. However, by "rolling back" the decision tree in terms of expected profit and risk we can further refine the decision set by eliminating action E_1. To show how we can eliminate a course of action by rolling back the branches of the decision tree, consider the following strategy:

i.e. make the test and if successful drill; or if the test is not successful, sell the drilling rights. The expected value of such a strategy is:

$$0.52 \times 0.92 \times 22,000,000$$
$$+ \ 0.52 \times 0.08 \times (- \ 15,500,000)$$
$$+ \ 0.48 \times 1,500,000 = \$10,600,000$$

Similarly, the variance of this overall strategy is

$$\sigma^2 = 0.52 \times 0.92 \ [22,000,000 - 10,600,000]^2$$
$$+ \ 0.52 \times 0.08 \ [- \ 15,500,000 - 10,600,000]^2$$
$$+ \ 0.48 \ [1,500,000 - 10,600,000]^2$$

Hence the standard deviation of this strategy, that is the square root of the above term, is equal to \$11,410,000.

In a similar manner, we can calculate the expected values and standard deviations of each of the remaining alternative strategies:

$$A_2 \nearrow B_2C_1 \searrow B_1D_2 \quad, \ A_1E_1 \text{ and } A_1E_2$$

The expected values and standard deviations of each of the alternative strategies are given in Table 11.4. A glance at this table confirms that when we

Table 11.4

Expected Values and Standard Deviation of Alternative Strategies

	$A_2 \nearrow B_2C_2 \searrow B_1D_2$	$A_2 \nearrow B_2C_1 \searrow B_1D_2$	A_1E_2	A_1E_1
(Million \$)				
Expected Value	10.60	8.52	9.00	10.00
Standard Deviation	11.41	6.74	0	18.37

consider the entire branch, strategy A_2E_1 can be eliminated from further consideration:

$$\text{strategy } A_2 \nearrow B_2C_2 \searrow B_1D_2 \quad \text{dominates strategy } A_1E_1$$

since the former has a greater expected profit and a smaller risk. Similarly:

$$\text{strategy } A_1E_2 \text{ dominates } A_2 \nearrow B_2C_1 \searrow B_1D_2 \quad \text{and therefore the latter can be eliminated.}$$

As a result, we are left with only two strategies to choose from:

$$A_1E_2 \text{ and } A_2 \nearrow B_2C_2 \searrow B_1D_2$$

Thus even though we were initially unable to distinguish between alternatives E_1 and E_2, an examination (i.e. rolling back) of the entire decision tree permits us to eliminate E_1.

To sum up, using the decision-tree technique becomes almost a necessity when the firm is confronted by a complex sequence of decisions. If the firm is willing to ignore risk, it can easily determine that course of action which will maximize expected *NPV*. However, when risk is recognized, the firm's risk-return tradeoff must be incorporated into the decision-tree framework if a final decision which reflects both these elements is to be reached.

SUMMARY

This chapter has been devoted to the practical application of risk analysis. As is true of capital budgeting techniques in general, the adoption of sophisticated risk analysis by business firms has lagged behind the theoretical literature. However, it should be noted that the percentage of firms using risk evaluation techniques is steadily rising, although the majority of such firms still prefer an *indirect* "rule of thumb" adjustment of the discount rate to the more sophisticated method of directly estimating the probability distributions of individual projects.

Two *indirect* methods of adjusting *NPV* calculations for risk are discussed:

(a)   the Certainty Equivalent Method
(b)   the Adjusted Discount Method.

The former adjusts the projects' cash flow and discounts the stream using the riskless rate of interest; in the latter method the discount rate, rather than the cash flow, is adjusted. Although it is not intuitively obvious, the two methods are equivalent, in the sense that they provide the *same NPV* if the respective adjustments are carried out appropriately. Thus, the popular rule of thumb adjustment of the discount rate is conceptually equivalent to the more sophisticated techniques based on the discounting of certainty-equivalent cash flows.

The remainder of the chapter is devoted to two practical applications of the "direct" adjustment for risk for those firms which estimate the probability distributions of their investment projects:

Simulation Analysis: A method for deriving the probability distribution of the projects' cash flows from the probability distribution of underlying economic factors.

Decision Tree: A decision flow diagram which can facilitate investment decision-making when uncertainty prevails, especially when the problem involves a sequence of decisions.

Neither of these two techniques eliminates the need to reach decisions regarding the tradeoff between the higher expected *NPV* and greater risk which characterizes so many investment alternatives, but they can provide us with better estimates of the distributions, thereby clarifying the implications of alternative courses of action. However, no matter how sophisticated the analytical technique, it *cannot* replace the decision-maker.

QUESTIONS AND PROBLEMS

11.1   Define and explain the "Certainty Equivalent Method".

11.2   Assume an investor with the following utility function:

Dollars	Utility
− 1,000	− 30
0	0
1,000	20
2,000	38
3,000	54
4,000	68
5,000	70
10,000	105

The investor is faced with a project which requires an initial outlay of $15,000 and yields a net annual cash flow of $2,000 with a probability of 1/2 and $5,000 with a probability of 1/2, for the following eight years. Assume a 6% riskless interest rate.

(a) Calculate the annual risk-adjusted net cash flow, using the *certainty equivalent method*.

(b) Calculate the risk-adjusted net present value of the project. Should the investor accept this project?

(c) Find the "value" of the risk inherent in the project.

11.3   The ABC Food Company is confronted with the following two investment proposals A and B:

Proposal A requires an initial outlay of $100,000 and provides an equal probability of earning a net annual cash flow of $12,000 or $28,000 for fifteen years.

Proposal B requires the same initial outlay and provides an equal probability of earning a net annual cash flow of $5,000 or $45,000 for fifteen years.

Assume that the riskless interest rate is 6% and that the firm requires a risk premium of 1.5% for every 10% of coefficient of variation (σ/E).

(a) Calculate the unadjusted net present value of each proposal.

(b) Which investment proposal will be preferred if the firm uses the adjusted *discount rate* method?

11.4   The Melkor Tool Corporation is examining the following project: the initial outlay is $400,000 and the net annual cash flow for the next ten years is $60,000 with a probability of 2/3 and $150,000 with a probability of 1/3.

Assume a 7% riskless interest rate and answer the following questions:

(a) What is the *risk premium* (in terms of the discount rate) required by the firm, if you know that the project has a risk-adjusted *NPV* of $35,000?

(b) What is the *maximum* risk premium the firm could demand and still accept the project?

11.5 Assume a project which requires $30,000 as an initial outlay and its *expected* net cash receipt is $36,000 for one year. Assume also that the certainty equivalent of this sum is $33,300, and that the riskless interest rate is 7%. Answer the following questions:

(a) Calculate the risk-adjusted net present value of the project (using the certainty equivalent method).

(b) Find the adjusted discount rate that will yield the same adjusted *NPV*.

(c) What would be the appropriate discount rate under the assumption that the risk of the project is larger and hence the certainty equivalent of its expected receipt is only $30,600?

11.6 You are asked to examine the following proposal: an investment outlay of $3,500 and one year's net receipts of $1,600 or $6,400 with equal probability. Suppose that your utility function is determined by $U(x) = \sqrt{x}$. Answer the following questions, assuming 6% riskless interest rate:

(a) Would you accept this proposal?

(b) Find the adjusted discount rate that will yield the same adjusted *NPV* as the certainty-equivalent method.

11.7 Define and explain the use of the following two techniques in decision making:

(a) Simulation analysis.

(b) The decision tree.

11.8 The Nefton Oil Company owns drilling rights in a given area for ten years and has two possibilities: either to drill with the hope of finding oil, or to sell its drilling rights to another company.

Suppose that the company estimates the probability of finding oil ("success") 0.55 and the probability of a dry hole ("failure") 0.45. Assume that the drilling cost is $14 million so that in the case of failure, the company loses this sum, and on the other hand, in the case of striking oil, the company will earn a net present value (after deducting the drilling and other costs) of $36 million.

The oil company initially is faced with a decision whether or not to make a seismic test, which would add more information on the chances of finding oil in the given area. Assume that this test costs $4 million and there is an equal probability that the test will succeed or fail.

The probability of a successful test *and* striking oil is 45%.

The probability of a successful test *and* striking a dry hole is 5%.

The probability of an unsuccessful test and striking oil is 10% and the probability of an unsuccessful test and not finding oil is 40%.

Denoting a successful test as "*Ts*", an unsuccessful test as "*Tf*", striking oil as "*S*", and not striking oil as "*F*", the probability of striking oil given that the test succeeds, i.e. $P(S \mid Ts)$, is 90%. The probability of not finding oil even though the test succeeds $P(F \mid Ts)$, is 10%. The probability of a success in finding oil although the test fails, $P(S \mid Tf)$, is 20% and the probability of not finding oil when the test fails, $P(F \mid Tf)$, is 80%.

The company can sell the drilling rights, but the price realized depends on its timing:

If the firm decides not to carry out the seismic test, it can sell the drilling rights for $12 million.

If the firm proposes to sell the drilling rights after it carries out the test and the results are a success, the firm can realize $24 million. But if the test fails, the poor results of the test decrease the market value of the rights and the firm can sell its concessions for only $6 million.

(Note that if the firm carries out the seismic test, any price must be decreased by the cost of the test, which is $4 million.) Answer the following questions:

(a) Draw a decision tree which describes the sequence of decisions which follows from the initial decision whether to make a seismic test or not.

(b) What is the optimal decision using the maximum expected *NPV* criterion?

(c) Which alternative will be chosen if the firm uses the $E - V$ criterion?

11.9 The Starlight Electronic Corporation (SEC) is confronted with the problem of building a large or small plant for producing a newly-developed product which has an expected economic life of ten years. The decision depends, among other things, on the size of the market for the new product. The demand may be high in the first three years, but if many of the potential users find that the product does not fulfil their wishes, the demand may then fall to a lower level. On the other hand, an initial high demand may point to the possibility of a permanent market.

The marketing manager developed the following market forecast:

(1) The probability of high demand in the first three years (marked as H_3) and high demand for the last seven years (H_7) is 45%.

(2) The probability of a high demand in the first three years (H_3) followed by low demand in the last seven years (L_7) is 15%.

(3) The probability of low demand in the first three years (L_3) and low demand in the last seven years (L_7) is 30%.

(4) The probability of L_3 and H_7 is 10%.

If the firm sets up a big plant now, it has to continue running it for the next ten years, regardless of the demand, but if the firm builds a smaller plant, it will have the option to expand it after the first three years.

The financial vice-president provided the following financial appraisal:

(1) With a high demand, a big plant will realize a net annual cash flow of $1,600,000.

(2) The net annual cash flow of a big plant with low demand will be only $200,000, because of the high overhead costs and inefficiency.

(3) In case of low demand a small plant will be the more efficient one, and will yield a net annual cash flow of $500,000.

(4) The net annual cash flow of a small plant in a high demand market will be $700,000. (This reflects the possibility of raising prices.)

(5) If the small plant is expanded after three years and if the market demand is high during the last seven years, the net annual cash flow will be $1,500,000 (in these years). We assume that the plant will be slightly less efficient than a large plant which is built today.

(6) If the small plant is expanded after three years, but the demand is low through the remaining seven years, the net annual cash flow will be only $100,000 in each of these years.

According to the engineering estimates, the cost of building a big plant will be $3 million; a small plant will cost only $1,500,000, but if expanded after three years it will cost an additional $2 million.

Mr. McNeal, the chief executive officer of SEC, has to prepare a recommendation to the board of directors.

(a) Draw the decision tree which describes the sequence of decisions, implied by the initial decision whether to build a big or a small plant.

(b) What will be the chief executive officer's optimal decision if he uses a 10% discount rate and the maximum expected *NPV* criterion? (Ignore taxes.)

(c) Which alternative will be chosen according to the mean-variance criterion? For this question, assume that the annual cash flows are statistically independent.

(Hint: Note that the probability of a high demand in the last seven years given a low demand in the first three years is

$$P(H_7 \mid L_3) = \frac{0.10}{0.40} = 25\%. \text{ Similarly, } P(H_7 \mid H_3) = \frac{0.45}{0.60} = 75\%$$

$$P(L_7 \mid L_3) = \frac{0.30}{0.40} = 75\% \text{ and } P(L_7 \mid H_3) = \frac{0.15}{0.60} = 25\%$$

where *P* denotes probability and " | " means conditional.)

SELECTED REFERENCES

Adler, F. Michael, "On Risk-Adjusted Capitalization Rates and Valuation by Individuals", *Journal of Finance*, September 1970.

Bar-Yosef, S. and Mesznik, R. "On Some Definitional Problems with the Method of Certainty Equivalents", *Journal of Finance*, December 1977.

Baum, S., Carlson, R.C. and Jucker, J.V., "Some Problems in Applying the Continuous Portfolio Selection Model to the Discrete Capital Budgeting Problem", *Journal of Financial and Quantitative Analysis*, June 1978.

Ben-Shahar, H. and Werner, F.M., "Multiperiod Capital Budgeting under Uncertainty: A Suggested Application", *Journal of Financial and Quantitative Analysis*, December 1977.

Berg, Claus C., "Individual Decisions Concerning the Allocation of Resources for Projects with Uncertain Consequences", *Management Science Theory*, September 1974.

Bierman, Harold Jr. and Hass, Jerome E., "Capital Budgeting Under Uncertanty: A Reformulation", *Journal of Finance*, March 1973.

Blatt, John M., "Investment Evaluation Under Uncertainty", *Financial Management*, Summer 1979.

Bogue, Marcus, C. and Roll, Richard, "Capital Budgeting of Risky Projects with 'Imperfect' Markets for Physical Capital", *Journal of Finance*, May 1974.

Brumelle, Shelby L. and Schwab, Bernhard, "Capital Budgeting with Uncertain Future Opportunities: A Markovian Approach", *Journal of Financial and Quantitative Analysis*, January 1973.

Bussey, Lynn E. and Stevens, G.T. Jr., "Formulating Correlated Cash Flow Streams", *The Engineering Economist*, Fall 1972.

Castagna, A.D. and Matolcsy, Z.P., "The Relationship between Accounting Variables and Systematic Risk and the Prediction of Systematic Risk", *Australian Journal of Management*, October 1978.

Celec, S.E. and Pettway, R.H., "Some Observations on Risk-Adjusted Discount Rates: A Comment", *Journal of Finance*, September 1979.

Copeland, T.E., "A Probability Model of Asset Trading", *Journal of Financial and Quantitative Analysis*, November 1977.

Constantinides, G.M., "Market Risk Adjustment in Project Valuation", *Journal of Finance*, May 1978.

Cozzolino, John M., "Controlling Risk in Capital Budgeting: A Practical Use of Utility Theory for Measurement and Control of Petroleum Exploration Risk", *The Engineering Economist*, Spring 1980.

Ekern, Steinar, "On the Inadequacy of a Probabilistic Internal Rate of Return", *Journal of Business Finance and Accounting*, 6, 2, 1979.

Falk, Haim and Heintz, James A., "The Predictability of Relative Risk Over Time", *Journal of Business Finance and Accounting*, Spring 1977.

Frankfurter, G.M. and Frecker, T.J., "Efficient Portfolios and Superfluous Diversification", *Journal of Financial and Quantitative Analysis*, December 1979.

Fuller, Russel J. and Lang-Hoon, Kim, "Inter-Temporal Correlation of Cash Flows and the Risk of Multi-Period Investment Projects", *Journal of Financial and Quantitative Analysis*, December 1980.

Gitman L.J., "Capturing Risk Exposure in the Evaluation of Capital Budgeting Projects", *The Engineering Economist*, Summer 1977.

Grayson, F. Jackson Jr., *Decisions Under Uncertainty: Drilling Decisions by Oil and Gas Operators*, Boston: Division of Research, Harvard Business School, 1960.

Gregory D.D., "Multiplicative Risk Premiums", *Journal of Financial and Quantitative Analysis*, December 1978.

Hertz, David B., "Risk Analysis in Capital Investment", *Harvard Business Review*, January-February 1964.

Hespos, Richard F. and Strassman, Paula A., "Stochastic Decision Trees for the Analysis of Investment Decisions", *Management Science*, August 1965.

Hillier, Frederick S., "The Derivation of Probabilistic Information for the Evaluation of Risky Investments", *Management Science*, April 1963.

Hoskins, C.G., "Capital Budgeting Decision Rules for Risky Projects Derived from a Capital Market Model Based on Semivariance", *The Engineering Economist*, Summer 1978.

Hsiao, F.S.T. and Smith, W.J., "An Analytic Approach to Sensitivity Analysis of the Internal Rate of Return Model", *Journal of Finance*, May 1978.

Huefner, Ronald L., "Sensitivity Analysis and Risk Evaluation", *Decision Sciences*, July 1972.

Keeley, Robert H. and Westerfield, Randolph, "A Problem in Probability Distribution Techniques for Capital Budgeting", *The Journal of Finance*, June 1972.

Kudla, Ronald J., "Some Pitfalls in Using Certainty-Equivalents: A Note", *Journal of Business Finance and Accounting*, Summer 1980.

Lessard, Donald R. and Bower, Richard S., "An Operational Approach to Risk Screening", *Journal of Finance*, June 1972.

Lewellen, W.G., "Some Observations on Risk Adjusted Discount Rates", *Journal of Finance*, September 1977.

Lockett, A. Geoffrey and Gear, Anthony E., "Multistage Capital Budgeting under Uncertainty", *Journal of Financial and Quantitative Analysis*, March 1975.

Lucken, J.A. and Stuhr, D.P., "Decision Trees and Risky Projects", *The Engineering Economist*, Winter 1978.

Magee, John F., "Decision Trees for Decision Making", *Harvard Business Review*, July-August 1964.

Miller, Edward M., "Uncertainty Induced Bias in Capital Budgeting", *Financial Management*, Autumn 1978.

Myers, Stewart C., "Procedures for Capital Budgeting under Uncertainty", *Industrial Management Review*, Spring 1968.

Obel, Borge and van der Weide, James, "On the Decentralized Capital Budgeting Problem under Uncertainty", *Management Science*, September 1979.

Parkinson, M. "The Extreme Value Method for Estimating the Variance of the Rate of Return", *Journal of Business*, January 1980.

Perrakis, Stylianos, "Certainty Equivalents and Timing Uncertainty", *Journal of Financial and Quantitative Analysis*, March 1975.

Petty, William J. and Bowlin, Oswald D., "The Financial Manager and Quantitative Decision Models", *Financial Management*, Winter 1976.

Raiffa, H., *Decision Analysis*, Reading Mass: Addison-Wesley, 1968.

Ross, S.A., "A Simple Approach to the Valuation of Risky Streams", *Journal of Business*, July 1978.

Salazar, Rudolfo C. and Sen, Subrata K., "A Simulation Model of Capital Budgeting under Uncertainty", *Management Science*, December 1968.

Schwab, Bernhard, "Conceptual Problems in the Use of Risk-Adjusted Discount Rates with Disaggregated Cash Flows", *Journal of Business Finance and Accounting*, Winter 1978.

Whisler, W.D., "Sensitivity Analysis of Return", *Journal of Finance*, March 1976.

Zinn, C.D., Lesso, W.G. and Motazed, B., "A Probabilistic Approach to Risk Analysis in Capital Investment Projects", *The Engineering Economist*, Summer 1977.

12

Decreasing Risk by Diversification: The Portfolio Approach

To this point we have ignored the old maxim, "Don't put all of your eggs into one basket." In the preceding three chapters alternative investments were treated as independent individual projects; any interaction between them was not taken into account. In this chapter we focus attention on the possibility of such inter-action. Here we shall emphasize the possibility that risk diversification can be facilitated by combining investments into a *portfolio*.

The theory of portfolio selection was originally developed for the analysis and management of financial assets, such as securities.[1] In this chapter we shall set out the basic elements of the theory explicitly in terms of the expected returns and variance (standard deviation) of the returns from securities. The portfolio approach will then be applied to the analysis of capital market equilibrium and problems of capital budgeting at the level of the firm in Chapter 13.

MEASURING THE RETURN ON FINANCIAL INVESTMENTS

In Part I of the book the Net Present Value method was used to determine the feasibility capital expenditures. But the investment in financial securities, by its

---

1 The theory was first set out in the pioneering work of Harry Markowitz, "Portfolio Selec-tion", *Journal of Finance,* March 1952. Important extensions have been made by Markowitz, *Portfolio Selection,* New York, Wiley 1959; James Tobin, "Liquidity Preference as Behaviour Towards Risk", *Review of Economic Studies,* February 1958; William F. Sharpe, "Capital Asset Prices: A Theory of Market Equilibrium Under Condi-tions of Risk", *Journal of Finance*, September 1964; John Lintner, "The Valuation of Risk Assets and the Selection of Risky Investments in Stock Portfolios and Capital Budgets", *Review of Economics and Statistics,* February 1965; Jan Mossin, "Equilibrium in a Capital Assets Market", *Econometrica,* October 1966; J.L. Treynor, "Toward a Theory of Market Value of Risky Assets", unpublished manuscript, 1961; and Eugene F. Fama, "Risk, Return and Equilibrium", *Journal of Political Economy,* January/February 1971.

very nature, tends to differ from the investment in physical assets: financial assets tend to be highly divisible — you cannot build two-thirds of a bridge but you can buy one-millionth of a share in the ownership of AT&T. Thus for all practical purposes, scale problems can usually be ignored when analyzing the return on securities.

The investment in capital goods usually involves a long-term commitment of resources over a fixed number of years (that is, disinvestment is costly and often uneconomic); most securities, independent of their date of maturity (if any),[2] can be held for as short or as long a period as is desired; in other words, investments in securities are highly reversible. Finally, while the firm is often faced with mutually exclusive alternatives, the decision to purchase a share of AT&T does not generally preclude the purchase of GM stock.

Thus, when analyzing investments in securities, differences in scale and duration among alternative investments can safely be ignored. This property of financial investments is of considerable importance since we seek a measure which can rank investments by return without determining their individual discount rates. (The vast number of investors in a financial market precludes any attempt at making meaningful *NPV* calculations of stocks and bonds.) What is required is an index which provides an objective measure of financial investments' profitability for all investors. The measure of return which has this property[3] is the *holding period rate of return* (*HPR*). The underlying idea is to specify the holding-period (e.g. one year) and then assume that all benefits received during the period are *reinvested*.

Consider, for example, the one-year *HPR* on a share of common stock:

$$1 + HPR = \frac{\text{value at end of holding period}}{\text{value at beginning of holding period}} = \frac{V_t}{V_{t-1}}$$

The value at the beginning of the year (ignoring transaction costs) is simply the market price of the share. Its value at the end of the year is found by multiplying the end of year price by the *number* of shares held. Recall that cash dividends, stock dividends etc. have been assumed to be reinvested. A numerical example can help clarify this type of calculation.

Consider a stock which sold for $35 at the beginning of the year, paid a cash dividend of $1.50 per share on the last day of the year, split 2 for 1 in the July of that year and sold for only $17.75 on the last day of the year. What is the *HPR* of that stock? The initial value is clearly $35; but the end of period value is certainly *not* $17.75. Due to the 2:1 split of the stock in July, our hypothetical investor holds *two* shares at the end of the year, and moreover he receives a dividend of $1.50 on *each* of the two shares held. Hence the end of period value is $38.50 (2 · $17.75 + 2 · $1.50 = $38.50) and the *HPR* is 10%:

2 Common stock or preferred stock as well as perpetual bonds have no formal redemption dates.

3 For a proof of the equivalence between *NPV* and *HPR* rankings, see Haim Ben-Shahar and Marshall Sarnat, "Reinvestment and the Rate of Return on Common Stocks", *Journal of Finance*, December 1966.

$$HPR = \frac{38.50}{35.00} - 1 = 0.10.$$

For multiperiod investments the *HPR* can readily be converted to an equivalent return *per period* by calculating the *compounded* average rate of return ($\overline{HPR}$). This is accomplished by taking the geometric mean of the single period returns:

$$\overline{HPR} = \sqrt[N]{[(1 + HPR_1)(1 + HPR_2) \ldots (1 + HPR_N)]} - 1$$

where $\overline{HPR}$ = the compounded per period rate of return
$1 + HPR_i$ = the holding period return in period i
N = the number of periods.

These holding-period returns are the basic building blocks of the portfolio model, and will be used below to calculate the expected returns, variances and covariances which are the inputs of the portfolio selection model.

IMPROVING THE RISK-RETURN RELATIONSHIP BY DIVERSIFICATION

Underlying the portfolio approach to decision making is the contention that by combining a number of securities into a "portfolio", some degree of income stabilization can be achieved, without impairing the expected profit. This proposition can be illustrated by considering the example of two securities given in Table 12.1. For simplicity, let us assume that the individual can either invest all of his resources in one of the two securities, A or B; or alternatively, he can diversify his investment by putting half of his resources in A and the other half in B. For emphasis, the distribution of the returns on security A is assumed to be *identical* to the distribution of returns on security B. (The distributions given in Table 12.1 reflect an investment of 100% of the investor's resources, say $100, either in A or in B.) Now consider an investor with $100 at his disposal who must decide whether to put all his resources in one of the securities or to diversify his investment between the two alternatives. If he invests the entire amount in a single security (either A or B) he has a 50% chance of losing $20 and a 50% chance of earning $30. In both A and B, the expected return is $5 with a variance of 625 (i.e. a standard deviation of $25).

Now what are the relevant expected earnings and risk should our hypothetical investor decide to diversify his holdings, say by investing $50 in A and $50 in B? The answer depends on the *statistical relationship* between the two distributions. Let us initially assume that the income streams of the two projects are statistically independent of each other; in other words, that the correlation between the returns from the two securities is zero. In such a case the probability of getting any pair of returns from the two projects is equal to the product of their individual probabilities. For example, the *joint probability* that the return on both investments will be $-$20 is $1/2 \times 1/2 = 1/4$, so that by

Table 12.1

	Security A		Security B	
	− 10	1/2	− 20	1/2
	30	1/2	30	1/2
Expected Return	5		5	
Variance of Returns	625		625	
Standard Deviation of Returns	25		25	

diversifying his resources equally between A and B our entrepreneur has only a 25% chance of losing $20.[4]

Using this approach we can calculate the probability distribution of the returns on a *mixed portfolio* comprised of equal proportions in securities A and B (see Table 12.2). The expected return of such a portfolio is $5, that is the same as for each of the individual securities; however, the variance is considerably reduced. In addition to the extreme results (+ 30 and − 20) which are attainable from each of the single investments, the portfolio provides an intermediate result (+ 5) as well. Thus, the diversified portfolio reduces the dispersion of outcomes, and the chances of suffering a major loss (− $20) are lowered from a probability of 1/2 for each single investment to a probability of only 1/4 for the mixed portfolio. Moreover this risk reduction property of portfolio diversifications exists even though we assumed that the two projects had *identical* earnings and risk characteristics.

The above example demonstrates how an investor can improve his risk-return position by diversifying when the income streams in question are assumed to be statistically independent. In practice, however, the analysis is somewhat more complicated: the income streams of individual securities (or projects) are

Table 12.2
A Mixed Portfolio: 50% Invested in A and 50% Invested in B

	Return	Probability
	− 20	1/4
	+ 5	1/2*
	+ 30	1/4
Expected Return	+ 5	
Variance of Return†	312.5	

*Since the two alternatives are independent events the probability of earning $5 results from a 1/4 chance that A will lose $20 while B earns $30, and from a 1/4 probability that A will earn $30 while B loses $20.
†The variance is given by $1/4(-20-5)^2 + 1/2(5-5)^2 + 1/4(30-5)^2 = 312.5$.

4 Note that there is a 25% chance that the outcome of investment A will be − $20 and a similar chance that the outcome of investment B will be − $20. But since the investor "buys" only half of each security, he will lose $10 in A and $10 in B, so that his total loss will be $20 with a probability of 25%.

not necessarily statistically independent, but as long as they are not *perfectly* (positively) correlated, diversification can reduce risk. The degree of risk reduction depends on the degree of the statistical interdependence between the income streams of the different investments and on the number of securities over which the investor can spread his risk. The lower the interdependence, and the greater the number of investments, the greater will be the potential gain from risk diversification. Let us turn now to the more general analysis of the portfolio selection problem.

THE CONCEPT OF AN EFFICIENT PORTFOLIO

To analyze the portfolio effects of combining the returns of different investments, let us assume that an individual is confronted by two securities A and B, the expected returns and standard deviations of which are (μ_1 and σ_1) and (μ_2 and σ_2) respectively. These two securities are plotted as points A and B in Fig. 12.1. Should the individual decide to diversify his investment by purchasing a portfolio in the proportions p_1 of A and $p_2(p_2 = 1 - p_1)$ of B, the expected return on such a portfolio is given by

$$\mu = p_1\mu_1 + (1 - p_1)\mu_2$$

with a variance of

$$Var(x) = p_1^2\sigma_1^2 + (1 - p_1)^2\sigma_2^2 + 2p_1(1 - p_1)\ Cov(x_1,x_2)$$

where the random variables x_1 and x_2 denote the returns on securities A and B respectively, and $Cov(x_1,x_2)$ denotes the covariance between x_1 and x_2. The equation for the variance can also be written as follows:[5]

$$Var(x) = p_1^2\sigma_1^2 + (1 - p_1)^2\sigma_2^2 + 2p_1(1 - p_1)\ R\sigma_1\sigma_2$$

where R denotes the coefficient of correlation between the returns of the two securities.

Let us now examine the effects of combining the two securities in a portfolio, under varying assumptions regarding the coefficient of correlation R. When $R = 0$ the transformation curve, which represents the pairs of expected return and variance which result from combining the two securities in all possible proportions, takes the form of the locus ACB of Fig. 12.1. This curve has its minimum variance (standard deviation) at point C. All the portfolios (points) on curve ACB correspond to the different proportions in which the amount invested is divided between the two securities.

Only the solid portion of the curve represents *efficient* portfolios of securities A and B, an efficient portfolio being defined as a combination of securities which maximizes the expected return for a given variance (standard deviation). The dashed segment AC is irrelevant, since these portfolios are by

---

5 Since the coefficient of correlation $R = \dfrac{Cov(x_1,x_2)}{\sigma_1\sigma_2}$ the two equations are equivalent.

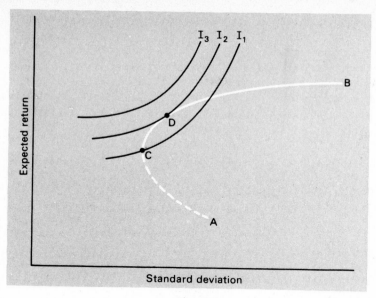

Fig. 12.1

definition inefficient because alternatives exist which offer higher expected
returns for the same levels of risk. The statement can readily be proved by
examining Fig. 12.2. For every point on section AC a corresponding point
which is preferable can be found on section BC. For example, Point G′
dominates G since it has a higher mean and an equal variance. Therefore, section AC represents inefficient portfolios which will never be chosen by a rational
investor.

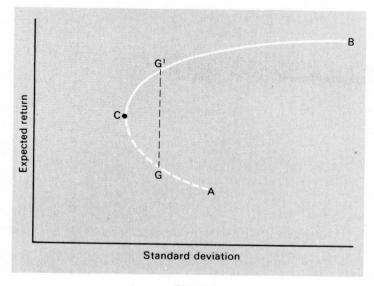

Fig. 12.2

To complete the graphical representation of investment choice, the indifference curves of a hypothetical risk-averse investor have been superimposed on the transformation curve of Fig. 12.1. The indifference curves rise from left to right which indicates that the investor must be compensated with a higher expected return as the variance increases. The curves are drawn convex downwards on the assumption that additional increments of variance (risk) require increasingly larger increments of expected return to compensate the individual. The investor's *final* choice out of the efficient set depends on his tastes. And in accordance with the expected utility maxim, he will choose that portfolio which permits him to reach the highest indifference curve, because the higher is the indifference curve, the greater is his utility. The *optimal* portfolio for the hypothetical investor of Fig. 12.1 is denoted by point D which lies on indifference curve I_2.

THE GAINS FROM DIVERSIFICATION

As we noted earlier, the degree to which a two-security portfolio reduces the variance of returns depends on the degree of correlation between the returns of the securities. To quantify this relationship let us assume the following expected returns and variances for two hypothetical securities A and B:

$$
\begin{array}{ll}
\qquad\qquad A & \qquad\qquad B \\
\mu_1 = 10 & \mu_2 = 20 \\
\sigma_1^2 = 100 & \sigma_2^2 = 900
\end{array}
$$

The expected returns and variances for portfolios of varying proportions and for four alternative assumptions regarding the degree of correlation between returns are given in Table 12.3. The data clearly show that diversification can reduce the variance of returns, and moreover, the lower is the coefficient of correlation, the greater is the reduction in the variance. For example, if we choose the proportions p_1 and p_2 which minimize the variance, in this case $p_1 = 3/4$ and $p_2 = 1/4$, and assume $R = -1$, the portfolio variance can be reduced to zero:

$$\sigma^2 = p_1^2\sigma_1^2 + p_2^2\sigma_2^2 - 2p_1p_2\sigma_1\sigma_2$$

$$= 9/16 \times 100 + 1/16 \times 900 - 2 \times 3/4 \times 1/4 \times 10 \times 30$$

$$= \frac{900 + 900 - 1800}{16} = 0$$

In general diversification will reduce the minimum attainable variance if the correlation coefficient is less than the ratio of the smaller standard deviation to the larger one.

The inverse relationship between the degree of correlation and the degree of variance reduction can be seen even more clearly in Fig. 12.3, which presents a family of transformation curves for varying assumptions regarding the degree

Table 12.3

Proportion of Portfolio Invested in Security A	Expected Return on Portfolio*	Variance of Returns for Alternative Coefficients of Correlation†				
		R = + 1	R = + 1/2	R = 0	R = − 1/2	R = − 1
0	20	900	900	900	900	900
1/5	18	676	628	580	532	484
2/5	16	484	412	340	268	196
3/5	14	324	252	180	108	36
4/5	12	196	148	100	52	4
1	10	100	100	100	100	100

* The mean is independent of R, and is obtained from the formula

$\mu = p_1\mu_1 + p_2\mu_2$

† The formula for the variance is

$Var(x) = p_1^2\sigma_1^2 + p_2^2\sigma_2^2 + 2p_1p_2R\sigma_1\sigma_2$

of correlation. Diversification in this diagram reduces variance except in the extreme case where the returns are perfectly correlated ($R = + 1$). On such an assumption the transformation curve reduces to a straight line joining points A and B.[6] As the correlation coefficient is reduced from + 1 to + 1/2, 0, and − 1/2, the transformation curve bulges out farther and farther to the left, and if we were to superimpose a set of indifference curves on the same plane, we could readily see that the risk-averse investor reaches higher levels of utility (i.e. a higher indifference curve), the smaller is the coefficient of correlation. It should also be noted that in the case of perfect negative correlation between the returns of the two securities, the transformation curve will at one point touch the vertical axis, which means that there exists a portfolio which can completely eliminate the variance. Of course, the final decision to choose the minimum variance portfolio or some other point on the curve depends on individuals' tastes (that is on the slope of the indifference curves).

In reality, the returns on investment are not perfectly correlated, either positively or negatively. In most cases, some positive correlation, reflecting general economic conditions, exists, and at best the cash flows may have zero, or slightly negative correlation. As a result, portfolio diversification can help to stabilize the returns, but cannot entirely eliminate the fluctuations (variance) of investment returns. In general, diversification reduces, but does not completely eliminate, risk; however, this does not mean that the individual should seek diversification at any cost. The mere fact that two particular securities have a low degree of correlation is not in itself sufficient to indicate that both should be included in the portfolio.

6 In the particular case where $R = + 1$ the variance of the portfolio is given by $\sigma^2 = p_1^2\sigma_1^2 + p_2^2\sigma_2^2 + 2p_1p_2\sigma_1\sigma_2 = (p_1\sigma_1 + p_2\sigma_2)^2$, and hence $\sigma = p_1\sigma_1 + p_2\sigma_2$. The last equation describes a straight line connecting points A and B.

In the other extreme case of perfect negative correlation in which $R = − 1$, the portfolio variance is given by $\sigma^2 = p_1^2\sigma_1^2 + p_2^2\sigma_2^2 − 2p_1p_2\sigma_1\sigma_2 = (p_1\sigma_1 − p_2\sigma_2)^2$. The investment proportions which minimize the variance are given by $p_1/p_2 = \sigma_2/\sigma_1$. In this case the variance of the portfolio is equal to zero; hence AB touches the vertical axis.

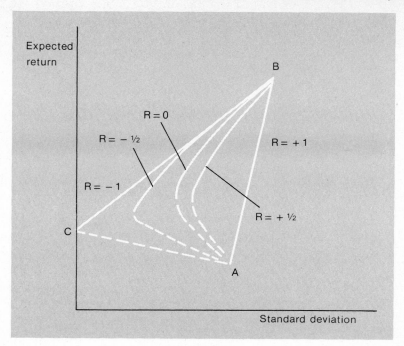

Fig. 12.3

THE NUMBER OF SECURITIES AND THE GAINS
FROM DIVERSIFICATION

In order to examine the relationship between the number of projects included in the portfolio and the gain from diversification, let us assume that we now are confronted by three securities, A, B, and C, the price of each of which is $100. The expected return and variance of each of these securities are given in Table 12.4. For the sake of convenience we shall assume zero coefficients of correlation between the returns of each pair of securities. We also assume that the investments are completely divisible, that is the investor can combine the securities in any proportion.

The three-security case is illustrated in Fig. 12.4. The investor is confronted with three mutually exclusive alternatives: (a) invest in a portfolio which includes all three securities; (b) confine himself to a two-security port-

Table 12.4

		Securities	
	A	*B*	*C*
Expected Return	10	20	30
Variance of Returns	100	900	2,500

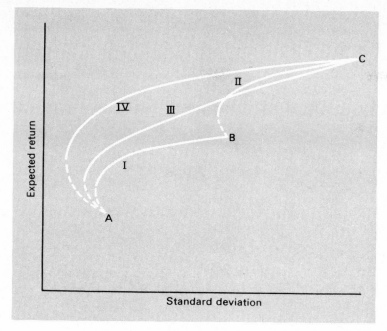

Fig. 12.4

folio; (c) put all of his money into a single security. Curve I of Fig. 12.4 represents the transformation curve of portfolios comprised of differing proportions of securities A and B; curve II and curve III are the relevant transformation curves for portfolios which include B and C, and A and C, respectively. Curve IV represents the transformation curve for portfolios which include all possible three-security combinations. In the latter case the investor is offered an additional degree of freedom, and is in a better position to reduce the variance for any given expected return, that is curve IV lies to the left of the other three curves. This *additional* possibility for diversifying his investment can only increase, and not decrease, an investor's utility since he still remains free to put his money into only two of the three securities. And this relationship holds for portfolios which include four, five or more securities.

It would seem to follow that investors who select their portfolios according to the mean-variance rule and who desire to benefit from diversification should tend to build large portfolios. In practice, however, the degree of diversification is often limited, for one or more of the following reasons:[7]

7 Empirical studies, based on the capital asset pricing model (see Chapter 13 below) have shown that randomly chosen portfolios with as few as 10 to 15 securities capture almost all of the potential reduction of risk through diversification. See J. Evans and S.H. Archer, "Diversification and the Reduction of Dispersion: An Empirical Analysis", *Journal of Finance,* December 1968; and K.H. Johnson and D.S. Shannon, "A Note on Diversification and the Reduction of Dispersion", *Journal of Financial Economics,* December 1974. Compare also Bruno Solnik, "Why not Diversify Internationally Rather than Domestically?" *Financial Analysts Journal*, July/August 1974.

(a)   Sometimes an investor has only a relatively small amount of money at his disposal so that diversifying over a large number of securities would mean investing very small amounts in each security.

(b)   An individual investor may find it difficult and expensive to keep track of a large number of securities; even a cursory check of the past performance and future outlook of a large number of securities is likely to prove a difficult and tedious task for most investors. Thus outside of the realm of textbooks, investors usually restrict themselves to a relatively small number of securities; however, the individual investor can, and often does, hold a large number of securities in his portfolio *indirectly* by investing in the shares of mutual funds or investment companies.

THE EFFICIENCY FRONTIER WITH BORROWING AND LENDING

A further significant increase in utility can be achieved if investors are permitted to borrow or lend money at some *riskless* interest rate r. To illustrate this line of argument suppose that some risky security A exists with an expected return and standard deviation of $E(A)$ and $\sigma(A)$ (see Fig. 12.5). Clearly an investor might confine himself to the risky asset; however, given the opportunity to borrow or lend at $r\%$, he can also combine A with riskless bonds (or with debt). Denoting by y the return generated by a portfolio which blends the risky asset A with riskless bonds (or debt) we can write the return on such a portfolio as follows:

$$y = pr + (1 - p)A$$

where p denotes the proportion invested in bonds (or in debt if p is negative), $(1 - p)$ denotes the proportion invested in security A, and y is a random variable which denotes the return of the new portfolio. The expected return and standard deviation of the new portfolio are given by

$$E(y) = pr + (1 - p)\, E(A)$$

$$\sigma(y) = (1 - p)\sigma(A)$$

and hence $(1 - p) = \dfrac{\sigma(y)}{\sigma(A)}$ and $p = 1 - \dfrac{\sigma(y)}{\sigma(A)}$

Substituting these expressions for p and $1 - p$ in the formula for the expected portfolio return yields:

$$E(y) = r + \frac{E(A) - r}{\sigma(A)} \, \sigma(y)$$

All the combinations of $E(y)$ and $\sigma(y)$ lie on a straight line and represent the set of efficient portfolios (see Fig. 12.5). If the investor chooses to be at point A he neither borrows nor lends, and the optimal investment proportion in bonds is $p = 0$. If he chooses a point on the line to the right of point A, this signifies a levered portfolio, i.e. he borrows money at r, and invests his own resources plus

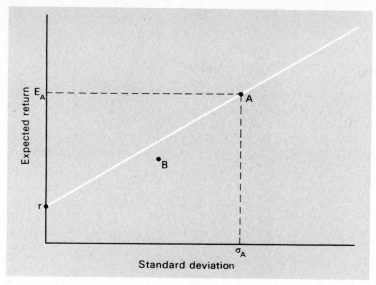

Fig. 12.5

the borrowed money in A (i.e. $p < 0$). If on the other hand his optimal choice is a point located to the left of point A, this means that the investor prefers to diversify his investment between the risky asset A and the riskless bonds (i.e. $p > 0$). Finally, should he choose to be at point r, this would represent a case of extreme risk aversion in which all of his resources are invested in the riskless asset.

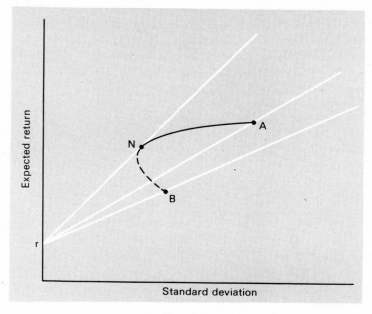

Fig. 12.6

Obviously, if given the opportunity to invest in another asset, say *B*, the investor could construct another straight line of attainable mixed or levered portfolios by blending this new risky asset with riskless bonds (or with debt). However, in general investors will prefer to diversify their holdings over both risk assets as well as riskless bonds (debt). This is illustrated in Fig. 12.6 which sets out the risk-return characteristics of each of the two securities, *A* and *B*, as well as the curve of portfolios of varying combinations of *A* and *B*. It is clear that the efficiency frontier which connects point *r* with point *N* represents the best possible alternative for all risk-averse investors. For every point on line *rA* or *rB* one can find a point on line *rN* which promises a higher expected return for the same risk. If we recall that point *N* itself represents a mixed portfolio of risk securities *A* and *B*, we can summarize Fig. 12.6 as follows: if an individual chooses to be at point *N* he places all of his resources in the portfolio of risky assets and neither buys bonds (lends) nor borrows. If he chooses a point to the left of *N*, this signifies the blending of the risky portfolio *N* with riskless bonds; points to the right of *N* represent levered portfolios in which money is borrowed and invested in the risky portfolio represented by *N*.

SUMMARY

This chapter has presented a graphical analysis of the portfolio selection process. In general, risk can be reduced by combining individual securities in a portfolio; the degree of risk reduction depending on the degree of correlation among returns and the number of securities included in the portfolio. The lower the correlation and the greater the number of securities, the greater are the gains from diversification. Investors' utility can also be increased by permitting them the additional option of borrowing and/or lending at a riskless interest rate. In this case, the efficiency frontier is linear, a property which will be used in the following chapter which extends the $E - V$ analysis to the market as a whole.

QUESTIONS AND PROBLEMS

12.1   Assume that an individual can either invest all of his resources in one of the two securities *A* or *B*; or alternatively, he can diversify his investment between the two.
The distributions of the returns are as follows:

	Security A			Security B	
Return		*Probability*	*Return*		*Probability*
−10		$\frac{1}{2}$	−20		$\frac{1}{2}$
50		$\frac{1}{2}$	60		$\frac{1}{2}$

Assume that the correlation between the returns from the two securities is zero, and answer the following questions:

(a) Calculate each security's expected return, variance and standard deviation.

(b) Calculate the probability distribution of the returns on a *mixed portfolio* comprised of equal proportions of securities A and B. Also calculate the expected return, variance and standard deviation.

(c) Calculate the expected return and the variance of a mixed portfolio comprised of 75% of security A and 25% of security B.

12.2 The securities of companies Z and Y have the following expected returns and standard deviations:

	Company Z	*Company Y*
Expected Return (%)	15	35
Standard Deviation (%)	20	40

Assume that the correlation between the returns of the two securities is 0.25.

(a) Calculate the expected return and standard deviation for the following portfolios:

(1) $100\% Z$
(2) $75\% Z + 25\% Y$
(3) $50\% Z + 50\% Y$
(4) $25\% Z + 75\% Y$
(5) $100\% Y$

(b) Graph your results.

(c) Which of the portfolios in part (a) is optimal? Explain.

12.3 Distinguish between an *efficient portfolio* and an *optimal portfolio*.

12.4 Given the following two securities A and B:

	A	*B*
Expected Return (%)	12	24
Standard Deviation (%)	6	36

(a) Will an individual ever concentrate all of his investment in security A?

(b) Will he ever concentrate all of his investment in security B?

12.5 Given the following securities C and D:

	Security C	*Security D*
Expected Return (%)	8	20
Standard Deviation (%)	18	24

(a) Calculate the expected return and the variance for the following portfolios, assuming that the returns are perfectly correlated ($R = +1$):

(1) $100\%C$	(4) $25\%C + 75\%D$
(2) $75\%C + 25\%D$	(5) $100\%D$
(3) $50\%C + 50\%D$	

Use these points to graph the transformation curve between C and D.

(b) Answer part (a), assuming that $R = +0.5$.

(c) Answer part (a) for the case of zero correlation between the two securities ($R = 0$).

(d) Graph the transformation curve for the following cases:

$$R = -0.5, R = -1$$

(e) Can you find the proportions of C and D in the mixed portfolio that reduce the portfolio's variance to zero? (Assume $R = -1$)

12.6 What is the general relationship between the gains from diversification and the correlation among security returns?

12.7 "In the case of perfect positive correlation between two securities ($R = +1$), an investor will never diversify his investment between the two." Do you agree? In your answer analyze several alternative situations and use diagrammatic proofs.

12.8 What is the relationship between the number of available securities and the gains from diversification? Does this have any implications for the small investor?

12.9 Given the following three securities:

	A_1	A_2	A_3
Expected Return (%)	10	15	20
Standard Deviation (%)	20	30	40

(a) Calculate the expected return and the variance (assuming that the correlation for each pair of securities (R_{ij}) is equal to zero) for each of the following two-security portfolios:

(1) $p_1 = 2/5$	(2) $p_1 = 2/5$	(3) $p_1 = 0$
$\quad p_2 = 3/5$	$\quad p_2 = 0$	$\quad p_2 = 3/5$
$\quad p_3 = 0$	$\quad p_3 = 3/5$	$\quad p_3 = 2/5$

where p_i denotes the proportion of security i in the portfolio.

(b) Find, for each of the above portfolios, the three-security portfolio that gives the same expected return as the two-security portfolio.

(c) Calculate the variance of returns for each one of the three-security portfolios and compare your results to the results you got in part (a).

12.10 Assume that an investor wishes to invest $1,000 in a portfolio which includes only one common stock. The rate of interest on riskless bonds (r) is 7% and the expected return and standard deviation of the single stock are 17% and 25% respectively.

(a) Graph the frontier of efficient portfolios for this case.

(b) Suppose that the investor selects a portfolio composed of 60% stock and 40% bonds; what is the expected return and standard deviation of this portfolio?

(c) Suppose now that the investor found it optimal to invest in a portfolio with a 20% standard deviation. How much (in dollars) must he invest in stock and how much in bonds to achieve this risk level? What is the expected return of this portfolio?

SELECTED REFERENCES

Alexander, G.J., "A Re-evaluation of Alternative Portfolio Selection Models Applied to Common Stocks", *Journal of Financial and Quantitative Analysis*, March 1978.

Baron, D.P., "Investment Policy, Optimality, and the Mean-Variance Model: Review Article", *Journal of Finance*, March 1979

Barry, C.B. and Winkler, R.L., "Nonstationarity and Portfolio Choice", *Journal of Financial and Quantitative Analysis*, June 1976.

Bawa, V.S., Elton, E.J. and Gruber, M.J., "Simple Rules for Optimal Portfolio Selection in Stable Paretian Markets", *Journal of Finance*, September 1979.

Bawa, V.S., "Admissible Portfolios for All Individuals", *Journal of Finance*, September 1976.

Blume, Marshall E., "Portfolio Theory. A Step Towards its Practical Application", *Journal of Business*, April 1970.

Brealey, R.A. and Hodges, S.D., "Playing with Portfolios", *Journal of Finance*, March 1975.

Brennan, M.J., "The Optimal Number of Securities in a Risky Asset Portfolio Where There are Fixed Costs of Transacting: Theory and Some Empirical Results", *Journal of Financial and Quantitative Analysis*, September 1975.

Brito, N.O., "Portfolio Selection in an Economy with Marketability and Short Sales Restrictions", *Journal of Finance*, May 1978.

Chen, A.H., "Portfolio Selection with Stochastic Cash Demand", *Journal of Financial and Quantitative Analysis*, June 1977.

Chen, Andrew H.Y., Jen, Frank C. and Zionts, Stanley, "The Joint Determination of Portfolio and Transaction Demands for Money", *Journal of Finance*, March 1974.

Dhingra, Harbans L., "Effects of Estimation Risk on Efficient Portfolios: A Monte Carlo Simulation Study", *Journal of Finance and Accounting*, Summer 1980.

Dickinson, J.P., "The Reliability of Estimation Procedures in Portfolio Analysis", *Journal of Financial and Quantitative Analysis*, June 1974.

Elton, E.J. and Gruber, Martin J., "On the Optimality of Some Multi-period Portfolio Selection Criteria", *The Journal of Business*, April 1974.

Elton, E.J., Gruber, M.J. and Padberg, M.W., "Simple Criteria for Optimal Portfolio Selection", *Journal of Finance*, December 1976.

Elton, E.J., Gruber, M.J. and Padberg, M.W., "Simple Criteria for Optimal Portfolio Selection: Tracing out the Efficient Frontier", *Journal of Finance*, March 1978.

Fielitz, Bruce D., "Indirect versus Direct Diversification", *Financial Management*, Winter 1974.

Frankfurter, George M. and Phillips, Herbert E., "Portfolio Selection: An Analytic Approach for Selecting Securities from a large Universe", *Journal of Financial and Quantitative Analysis*, June 1980.

Goldsmith, D., "Transactions Costs and the Theory of Portfolio Selection", *Journal of Finance*, September 1976.

Gonzalez, N., Litzenberger, R. and Rolfo, J., "On Mean Variance Models of Capital Structure and the Absurdity of Their Predictions", *Journal of Financial and Quantitative Analysis*, June 1977.

Gressis, N., Philippatos, G.C. and Hayya, J., "Multiperiod Portfolio Analysis and the Inefficiency of the Market Portfolio", *Journal of Finance*, September 1976.

Hamada, Robert S., "Portfolio Analysis, Market Equilibrium and Corporation Finance", *Journal of Finance*, March 1969.

Jacob, Nancy L., "A Limited Diversification Portfolio Selection Model for the Small Investor", *Journal of Finance*, June 1974.

Jaffe, Jeffrey P. and Merville, Larry J., "Stock Price Dependencies and the Valuation of Risky Assets with Discontinuous Temporal Returns", *Journal of Finance*, December 1974.

James, J.A., "Portfolio Selection with an Imperfectly Competitive Asset Market", *Journal of Financial and Quantitative Analysis*, December 1976.

Klein, R.W. and Bawa, V.S., "The Effect of Estimation Risk on Optimal Portfolio Choice", *Journal of Financial Economics*, June 1976.

Klemkosky, R.C. and Maness, T.S., "The Predictability of Real Portfolio Risk Levels", *Journal of Finance*, May 1978.

Klemkosky, R.C. and Martin, John D., "The Effect of Market Risk on Portfolio Diversification", *Journal of Finance*, March 1975.

Levy, H. and Sarnat, M., "The Portfolio Analysis of Multiperiod Capital Investment Under Conditions of Risk", *Engineering Economist*, Fall 1970.

Levy, H and Sarnat, M., "The World Oil Crisis: A Portfolio Interpretation", *Economic Inquiry*, September 1975.

Markowitz, Harry M., "Portfolio Selection", *Journal of Finance*, March 1952

Markowitz, Harry M., *Portfolio Selection*, New York: Wiley 1959.

Martin, J.D. and Keown, A.J., "Interest Rate Sensitivity and Portfolio Risk", *Journal of Financial and Quantitative Analysis*, June 1977.

Mossin, Jan, "Equilibrium in a Capital Assets Market", *Econometrica*, October 1966.

Rubinstein, Mark E., "A Mean-Variance Synthesis of Corporate Financial Theory", *Journal of Finance*, March 1973.

Saniga, E., Gressis, N. and Hayya, J., "The Effects of Sample Size and Correlation on the Accuracy of the EV Efficiency Criterion", *Journal of Financial and Quantitative Analysis*, September 1979.

Schneller, M.I., "Mean-Variance Portfolio Composition When Investors' Revision Horizon is Very Long", *Journal of Finance*, December 1975.

Schwartz, R.A. and Whitcomb, D.K., "The Time-Variance Relationship: Evidence on Autocorrelation in Common Stock Returns", *Journal of Finance*, March 1977.

Senbet, L.W. and Thompson, H.E., "The Equivalence of Alternative Mean-Variance Capital Budgeting Models", *Journal of Finance*, May 1978.

Sharpe, William F., "A Simplified Model for Portfolio Analysis", *Management Science*, January 1963.

Simkowitz, M.A. and Beedles, W.L., "Diversification in a Three-Moment World", *Journal of Financial and Quantitative Analysis*, December 1978.

Tobin, James, "Liquidity Preference as Behavior Towards Risk", *Review of Economic Studies*, February 1958.

Van Horne, James C., "Capital Budgeting Decisions Involving Combinations of Risky Investments", *Management Science*, October 1966.

Winkler, Robert L. and Barry, Christopher B., "A Bayesian Model for Portfolio Selection and Revision", *Journal of Finance*, March 1975.

Wallingford B.A., "A Survey and Comparison of Portfolio Selection Models", *Journal of Financial and Quantitative Analysis*, June 1967.

Williams, J.T., "A Note on Indifference Curves in the Mean-Varaince Model", *Journal of Financial and Quantitative Analysis*, March 1977.

Ziemba, W.T., Parkan, C. and Brooks-Hill, R., "Calculation of Investment Portfolios with Risk Free Borrowing and Lending", *Management Science Application*, October 1974.

13

The Capital Asset Pricing Model

Throughout the book we have taken the maximization of the market value of the shareholders' equity as the goal of the firm. A direct implication of this assumption is that the firm should choose its investment program and financing policy so as to maximize the price (value) of its common stock. This in turn requires some sort of model of the forces which influence and determine stock prices. This chapter will be devoted to a model of the securities market based explicitly on the portfolio analysis of the preceding chapter. In this chapter we examine the equilibrium relationship between expected return and risk; this relationship will be derived from a formal model, known in the literature as the capital asset pricing model (*CAPM*). In Part III below, this model will be used to help determine the discount rate (cost of capital) to be used in firms' financial decisions.

An important advantage of this model lies in the fact that it takes uncertainty directly into account and, therefore, allows us to study the dual impact of profitability and risk upon the value of a firm's shares. A shortcoming of the model is the fact that it rests on very restrictive assumptions; however, the capital asset pricing model does provide significant insights into the problem of capital budgeting under uncertainty. Moreover, the logic which underlies the model can help the firm devise operational rules of thumb for reaching investment and financing decisions in practice.

THE MODEL[1]

A modern securities market is a complex mechanism incorporating thousands

---

1 The capital asset pricing model was developed by: William F. Sharpe, "Capital Asset Prices: A Theory of Market Equilibrium Under Conditions of Risk", *Journal of Finance*, September 1964; John Lintner, "Security Prices Risk and Maximal Gains from Diversification", *Journal of Finance*, December 1965; Jan Mossin, "Equilibrium in a Capital Asset Market", *Econometrica*, October 1966; and E.F. Fama, "Risk, Return and Equilibrium: Some Clarifying Comments", *Journal of Finance*, March 1968.

of decision variables, and therefore any attempt to gain insight into the workings of such a market requires a high degree of abstraction. Thus the fascinating world of brokers, speculators and market tips will be ruthlessly shunted aside in order to focus our attention on the all-important relationship between risk and return. For this purpose we shall assume that securities are traded in a hypothetical "perfect" capital market in which:

(a)   there are no transaction costs or taxes;
(b)   all relevant information regarding securities is freely available to all investors;
(c)   all investors can borrow or lend any amount in the relevant range without affecting the interest rate, and there is no risk of bankruptcy;
(d)   there is a given uniform investment period for all investors;
(e)   investors are risk averse and reach their decisions using the mean variance rule.

For simplicity, let us initially assume that the market is comprised of only five securities, A, B, C, D and E. Fig. 13.1 sets out the risk-return characteristics of each of these securities; the shaded area represents the various combinations of two or more of the risky securities in portfolios of differing proportions. Now let us consider an investor who for some reason restricts himself to a portfolio which includes only securities A and E: the curve I, connecting points A

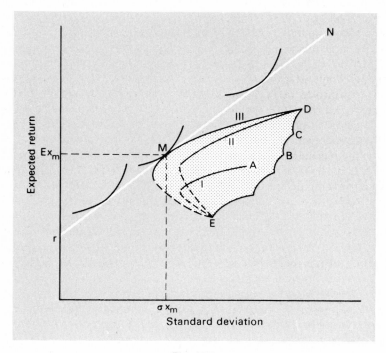

Fig. 13.1

and E, represents all the attainable risk-return combinations from this two-security portfolio, with each point on the curve representing a different set of investment proportions. (Note that only the solid part of the curve represents efficient portfolios; the dashed part of the curve represents inefficient combinations.) Similarly, transformation curve II is the appropriate curve for portfolios which include various proportions of D and E. Clearly, similar curves could also be generated for other two-security combinations or for portfolios which include three, four or more securities.

If we permit the investor to build his portfolio as he wishes, choosing any proportion of all the five securities assumed to comprise the market, the envelope curve of the five-security portfolios will lie to the left of the transformation curves of the constrained portfolios which include four or fewer securities. The envelope curve for the five-security case is denoted as III in Fig. 13.1. This curve sets out all of the combinations of expected return and standard deviation which can be obtained by freely building a portfolio of risk assets using all of the securities available in the market. The shaded area to the right of curve III represents portfolios which are *inefficient* relative to the portfolios on the solid part of curve III. Here again the lower, dashed part of the curve is also inefficient since these portfolios are dominated by the upper segment of curve III.

THE CAPITAL MARKET LINE

Now let us assume that the investor can borrow or lend (buy bonds) at the riskless rate *r*. This option, which is represented in Fig. 13.1 by the *capital market line* (*CML*) denoted as *r*N which rises from the interest rate *r* on the vertical axis and which is tangent to transformation curve III at point M, sets out all the alternative combinations of the risk portfolio M with riskless borrowing and lending. The segment from point *r* to point M includes the mixed portfolios of risky securities and bonds. Levered portfolios (combinations of M with riskless loans) are represented by points along the line beyond point M. Point M represents the risk-return characteristics of the *market portfolio* which has optimal proportions of the five risky securities. This portfolio is optimal since given the option of riskless borrowing or lending at rate *r*, portfolio M permits the investor to reach the highest market line, thereby permitting him to reach the highest possible indifference curve. Note that the optimal risk portfolio, represented by point M, has the property of maximizing the angle formed when a straight line is drawn from point *r* to any point on the transformation curve. Thus the line *r*N has the highest possible slope of any market line drawn to any point on the transformation curve.

If an investor's indifference curve is tangent to point M, this individual will invest all of his resources in risky securities. Of course, the indifference curves of most investors presumably will *not* be tangent to point M. Tangency solutions which lie on the segment *r*M represent mixed portfolios which combine risky securities and riskless bonds. Those which occur on the segment MN represent levered portfolios, that is the risky portfolio M financed partly by loans. However, it must be emphasized that in our idealized market all investors must have one important characteristic in common. Whether he chooses a pure risk, mixed, or levered portfolio, an investor who chooses to invest in risky assets invariably builds a risk portfolio which has the optimal proportions represented by point M. Hence the proportions of each security in the risky portion of the portfolios of all investors are the same, independent of their individual tastes. Despite the differences in tastes, all individuals will diversify the risky portion of their portfolios in the same proportions among the individual securities. Differences in individual tastes are operative only in determining the proportion of bonds (loans) which the investor buys (takes). The indifference curves enter the analysis only after the optimal proportions of the risk portfolio (represented by point M) have been established, and serve to determine the tangency point with the market line rN, but do not alter the tangency of the market line with point M itself.

The capital market line indicates that the expected return and risk (standard deviation) of all *efficient portfolios* lie on a straight line rN (see Fig. 13.1). To show this relationship, we denote by E_p and σ_p the expected return and the standard deviation of *efficient* portfolios. Since the efficient portfolio is a simple mix of the riskless asset and the portfolio M, we have

$$E_p = pr + (1 - p)Ex_m$$

$$\sigma_p = (1 - p)\,\sigma_m$$

where p denotes the proportion invested in the riskless asset. And substituting $(1 - p) = \sigma_p/\sigma_m$ from the second equation into the first one we derive the capital market line *CML*,

$$E_p = r + \frac{Ex_m - r}{\sigma_m}\sigma_p$$

All efficient portfolios lie on this straight line. Obviously, in the specific case of the market portfolio (which is also efficient) we have $\sigma_p = \sigma_m$ and hence $E_p = Ex_m$. The other extreme case is that of the riskless asset. By definition the riskless asset is also efficient with $\sigma_p = 0$ and hence, $E_p = r$.

THE OPTIMAL INVESTMENT PROPORTIONS

As we have just seen, in an idealized perfect capital market in which riskless lending and borrowing opportunities are available without transaction costs, all investors will desire to hold the same proportions of risky securities in their portfolios. This raises two questions: which securities are held, and in what proportions? The answer to the first question is straightforward. In a perfect market, in which all lenders and borrowers face the same (riskless) interest rate, the risk portfolios of all investors will include the same securities independent of their tastes. Thus if a particular security is not included in portfolio M, no investor holds it. But if no investor desires to hold a security, its price must fall, thereby raising its return, until it becomes sufficiently attractive to be included in portfolio M. It follows that in equilibrium, *all* available securities will be included in the risk portfolios of all investors. The answer to the second question regarding the proportions in which the securities are held is somewhat more difficult, and requires additional analysis.

In order to find the optimal proportion of securities that are included in M, we must first analyze the process by which the optimal point M is derived. Let Ex_0 and σ_0 denote the expected return per dollar investment and standard deviation of any risky portfolio; the formula for these two measures of portfolio return and risk are given by:

$$Ex_0 = \sum_{i=1}^{n} p_i Ex_i$$

and

$$\sigma_0^2 = \sum_{i=1}^{n} p_i^2 \sigma_i^2 + 2 \sum_{\substack{i=1 \\ j>i}}^{n} p_i p_j \, Cov(x_g, x_j)$$

where:

p_i = the proportion of an investor's wealth invested in the ith security
n = the number of different securities available in the market
σ_i^2 = the variance of returns (per dollar invested) in the ith security
Ex_i = the expected return (per dollar invested) in the ith security
$Cov(x_i, x_j)$ = the covariance between securities i and j

The expression $Cov(x_i, x_j)$ in the formula for the portfolio variance represents the covariance between all pairs of securities; thus it reflects the correlation between the fluctuations in the returns of the two securities from period to period. Note that since the above formula holds for any portfolio, the investment proportions p_i need *not* be optimal.

In general, $\sum_{i=1}^{n} p_i \neq 1$, that is the investment proportions will not add up to $1 because the investor may also buy riskless bonds or borrow. When the latter two possibilities are taken into account the investment proportions (including riskless bonds or loans) must add to 1: $\sum_{i=1}^{n} p_i + p_r = 1$, where p_r denotes the proportion invested in riskless bonds (or loans). If the investor borrows, $p_r < 0$ and $\sum_{i=1}^{n} p_i > 1$; if the investor buys bonds, $p_r > 0$ and $\sum_{i=1}^{n} p_i < 1$; and if the investor neither borrows nor lends, $p_r = 0$ and $\sum_{i=1}^{n} p_i = 1$. The latter possibility represents the special case where the indifference curve is tangent to the market line at point M itself.

Recalling our discussion of Fig. 13.1 the problem confronting the investor is how to choose a point (Ex_0, σ_0) on the envelope curve so that the capital market line (CML) connecting it to the point r on the vertical axis forms a maximum angle α thereby permitting him to reach the highest possible indifference curve. In analytical terms, the investor must find the investment proportions p_i which maximize the following expression:

$$tg\ \alpha\ =\ \frac{Ex_0\ -\ r}{\sigma_0}\ =\ \frac{\sum\limits_{i=1}^{n} p_i Ex_i\ -\ r}{\left[\ \sum\limits_{i=1}^{n} p_i^2 \sigma_i^2\ +\ 2\ \sum\limits_{\substack{i=1 \\ j>i}}^{n} p_i p_j Cov(x_i,x_j)\right]^{1/2}}$$

Portfolio M in the example given in Fig. 13.1 maximizes this expression, and therefore represents the optimum unlevered risky portfolio. The investment proportions of this portfolio are optimal for all investors. Note that we are discussing the first stage of the decision process in which the optimal risk portfolio is determined, that is we are locating the optimal point on the efficiency curve, and *not* the tangency of the curve to an indifference curve.

THE SECURITY MARKET LINE (*SML*)

The preceding formula can now be used to derive the following equilibrium condition between the risk and return of a security:[2]

$$Ex_i\ =\ r\ +\ \frac{Ex_m\ -\ r}{\sigma_m^2} Cov(x_i,\ x_m)$$

where x_m and Ex_m denote, respectively, the return and expected return of the optimal portfolio of risky securities, the proportions of which are fixed for all investors; this portfolio, which we shall call the *Market Portfolio*, corresponds to point M of Fig. 13.1. The equilibrium relationship between expected return and risk must hold for *every* security i in the market. Thus the expected return of each security reflects the pure riskless interest rate plus a *risk premium* which is related to that security's contribution to the overall risk of the market portfolio. From the formula it is also clear that the *higher* the association between the return on the individual security and the return of the market portfolio, the greater is the required risk premium.

The relationship between the expected return of each risky asset and its risk is called the *security market line (SML)*, which constitutes a linear relationship between expected return and risk. Denoting the market price of risk (as measured by the variance) by

$$\frac{Ex_m\ -\ r}{\sigma_m^2}\ \equiv\ \lambda,$$

2 The formal derivation is given in Appendix 13A at the end of this chapter.

the last equation can be rewritten as

$$Ex_i = r + \lambda\, Cov(x_i, x_m)$$

Thus, Ex_i, the expected rate of return on the ith security, is equal to the risk-free rate plus the market price of risk λ multiplied by the contribution of the ith security to the portfolio risk i.e. by $Cov(x_i, x_m)$. Since λ is a constant factor for all securities one can put Ex_i on the vertical axis and $Cov(x_i, x_m)$ on the horizontal axis and derive a linear relationship between Ex_i and $Cov(x_i, x_m)$.

However, the most common way to present the linear relationship between Ex_i and risk is as follows: First recall that if one runs the following time regression

$$x_{it} = r + \beta_i\, x_{mt} + e_t$$

then by definition of the regression slope we have

$$\beta_i = \frac{Cov(x_i, x_m)}{\sigma_m^2}$$

Substituting β_i for $Cov(x_i, x_m)/\sigma_m^2$ in the risk return equation, we get the following Security Market Line

$$Ex_i = r + (Ex_m - r)\beta_i$$

Fig. 13.2 illustrates this linear relationship.

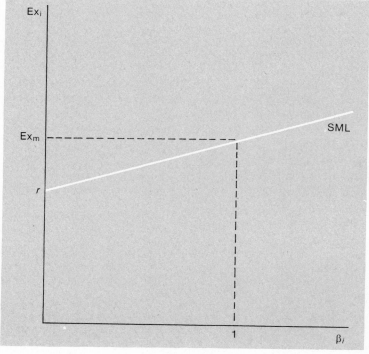

Fig. 13.2

Note that if $\beta_i = 1$ the security has the same risk as the market portfolio and hence

$$Ex_i = r + (Ex_m - r) \cdot 1 = Ex_m$$

If $\beta_i = 0$, the ith security makes a zero contribution to the portfolio's risk and hence the expected return on the security is equal to the riskless rate r. In general, Ex_i increases linearly with increases in β_i.

SYSTEMATIC AND NON-SYSTEMATIC RISK

The risk of each security (or of a portfolio) can be decomposed into two parts. The first component is that part of a security's risk which can be eliminated by combining it in a diversified portfolio. This *diversifiable* component of risk is often called the *non-systematic risk*, since no systematic relationship exists between this portion of the security's risk and the market. The *non-diversifiable* component of a security's risk, i.e. the part of the risk of its returns which *cannot* be eliminated by including the security in a diversified portfolio, is usually called the *systematic risk*. The latter stems from the general market fluctuations, or more specifically from that component of a security's risk which reflects the relationship of its fluctuations to those of the market portfolio. It is this non-diversifiable portion of the risk which gives rise to the risk premium; the non-systematic risk requires no such premium since it can be eliminated through diversification. The higher a security's Beta (other things being constant), the higher is its non-diversifiable risk, and therefore the higher is the expected return on this security.

In order to identify the two risk components and their impact on a security's risk premium, let us write the two linear equations of the *CML* and of the *SML*:

By the *CML* we have,

$$E_p = r + \frac{Ex_m - r}{\sigma_m} \sigma_p$$

where p denotes an efficient portfolio.

By the *SML*, however, we have the following equation

$$Ex_i = r + (Ex_m - r)\beta_i$$

which holds for all individual securities and portfolios, whether efficient or not.

Dividing and multiplying the *SML* by σ_m we rewrite it as

$$Ex_i = r + \frac{(Ex_m - r)}{\sigma_m} (\beta_i \cdot \sigma_m)$$

which is the same as the *CML* with the exception that $\beta_i \sigma_m$ is written instead of σ_p and hence it is this factor that determines the individual security's risk premium. Thus, the risk component of the individual security which determines the risk premium is the factor $\beta_i \sigma_m$. Each individual stock's standard deviation

σ_i can be decomposed into two components; the systematic risk $\beta_i \sigma_m$ and the non-systematic risk σ_i^{NS}:[3]

$$\sigma_i^{NS} = \sigma_i - \beta_i \sigma_m$$

To sum up, define the following notations for security i:

Diversifiable risk $= \sigma_i^D$, Non-Diversifiable risk $= \sigma_i^{ND}$
Non-Systematic risk $= \sigma_i^{NS}$, Systematic risk $= \sigma_i^S$

and we have

$$\sigma_i^{ND} \equiv \sigma_i^S = \beta_i \sigma_m$$

and

$$\sigma_i^D \equiv \sigma_i^{NS} = \sigma_i - \beta_i \sigma_m$$

The graphical decomposition of a security's standard deviation into the systematic and non-systematic risk is illustrated in Fig. 13.3 which depicts the Capital Market Line, the market portfolio M, an efficient portfolio P and two securities i and j.

Portfolio P and security i, both have the same expected rate of return, thus $E_p = Ex_i$. Since for efficient portfolios we have $E_p = \dfrac{Ex_m - r}{\sigma_m} . \sigma_p$ and for the ith security we have $Ex_i = r + \dfrac{Ex_m - r}{\sigma_m} (\beta_i \sigma_m)$, for the case when $Ex_i = E_p$ we also must have $\beta_i \sigma_m = \sigma_p$, and then $\beta_i \sigma_m = \sigma_i^{ND} = \sigma_i^S$

Thus the non-diversifiable risk of a security is measured by the horizontal distance of the vertical axis from the *CML*, at the security's level of expected rate of return. In order to measure the security's risk component which determines the risk premium $Ex_i - r$, we draw a line from point i (representing the security's mean and standard deviation) to the *CML*, parallel to the horizontal axis; at the point of intersection with the *CML* we reach σ_p, which is identical to the ith security's systematic risk. The non-systematic risk is simply the total risk σ_i minus the systematic risk, or

$$\sigma^{NS} = \sigma_i - \beta_i \sigma_m$$

Figure 13.3 shows that the non-diversifiable risk of a security may be negative

---

3 It is more common in the financial literature to decompose the variance rather than the standard deviation:

$$\sigma_i^{2 NS} = \sigma_i^2 - \beta_i^2 \sigma_m^2$$

However, as can be seen from the equilibrium equation, $\beta_i \sigma_m$ and not $\beta_i^2 \sigma_m^2$ determines the risk-premium and hence $\beta_i^2 \sigma_m^2$ cannot serve as the systematic risk index. Moreover, suppose that you have two securities with $\beta_i = +\frac{1}{2}$ and $\beta_j = -\frac{1}{2}$, respectively. The decomposition of its standard deviation can distinguish between the systematic risk of these two stocks, but $\beta_i^2 \sigma_m^2 = \beta_j^2 \sigma_m^2$ and hence the decomposition of σ^2 is inappropriate since it indicates that the two stocks have the *same* systematic risk. See M. Ben Horim and H. Levy, "Total Risk, Diversifiable Risk and Nondiversifiable Risk: A Pedagogic Note", *JFQA*, June 1980.

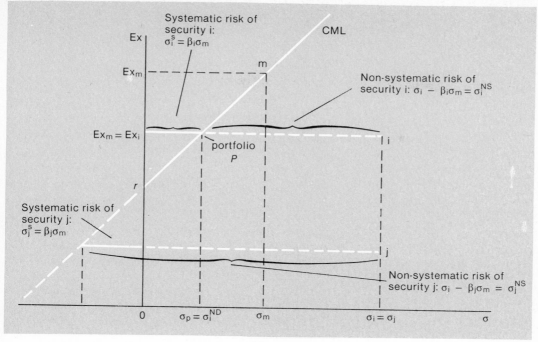

Fig. 13.3

(see for example, security *j*) so that its diversifiable risk is greater than the total risk, σ_j. Adding security *j* to an efficient portfolio, not only does not add to the portfolio's risk, but lends stability to the portfolio. This analysis shows that for all cases where $\beta \geqslant 0$, the terms "diversifiable risk" and "non-diversifiable risk" best convey their own meaning. Some readers, however, may find the terms "non-systematic risk" and "systematic risk" more appropriate, especially for the cases where $\beta < 0$. A negative systematic risk is best understood, perhaps, as negative systematic co-movement of the rate of return of the security under consideration with that of the market portfolio.

Equilibrium Value of Risky Assets

A security's rate of return is given by

$$x_i = \frac{R_i}{P_{i0}} - 1$$

where R_i denotes the (uncertain) end-of-period *return* (and *not* the rate of return) and P_{i0} is the equilibrium price of the *i*th stock at the beginning of the period. From the risk-return relationship of the SML we thus obtain

$$E\left(\frac{R_i}{P_{i0}} - 1\right) = r + \lambda \, Cov\left[\left(\frac{R_i}{P_{i0}} - 1\right), x_m\right]$$

since P_{i0} is a constant and $Cov(-1, x_m) = 0$, we get

$$\frac{E(R_i)}{P_{i0}} - 1 = r + \lambda\left(\frac{1}{P_{i0}}\right)Cov(R_i, x_m)$$

and finally after rearrangement of terms

$$P_{i0} = \frac{E(R_i) - \lambda\,Cov(R_i, x_m)}{1 + r}$$

Thus, the equilibrium price of a risky asset whose future (uncertain) return is R_i is the certainty equivalent, $E(R_i) - \lambda\,Cov(R_i, x_m)$ discounted at the risk-free interest rate r. Obviously, if R_i denotes the return from a risky asset, then P_{i0} is the equilibrium price (value) of this asset. Note that if we have risky bonds then B_{i0} would replace P_{i0} and if one can apply the same formula to derive the equilibrium price of bonds B_{i0}.

In order to obtain the *total* equilibrium value of a corporation's equity, S_{i0}, we should substitute the *total* return of equity; i.e., the end-of-period net earnings or income Y_i, for the return R_i in the above formulas.

CALCULATING BETA IN PRACTICE

In order to apply the capital asset pricing model, a method must be found for estimating each firm's *future* beta, i.e. the component of its risk which cannot be eliminated through diversification. Although beta might be estimated solely on the basis of subjective probability beliefs, it is the common practice to use past data to estimate future betas. However, where one expects the historical relationship between the rates of return on a given security and the rates of return on the market portfolio will be materially different in the future, the observed *ex-post* relationship should be modified to reflect such changes.

The method for estimating beta can be illustrated using the hypothetical data of Table 13.1 which sets out the rates of return for an individual security and for the market portfolio during the period 1971 – 80. If we further assume that the risk-free interest rate is equal to r percent per year, the systematic risk of the security can be estimated on the basis of the historical data using the following regression equation:

$$x_{i_t} = r + \beta_i x_{m_t} + e_t$$

where:

x_{i_t} = the rate of return on the ith security in year t
x_{m_t} = the rate of return on the market portfolio in year t
r = the riskless interest rate
e_t = the residual error about the regression line
β_i = ith security's systematic risk[4]

4 Although the systematic risk is given by $\beta_i\sigma_m$, σ_m is constant for all individual assets; hence, it is the common practice to identify the systematic risk with β_i alone.

Table 13.1

Years	Rate of Return on Security (1) x_i	Rate of Return on Market Portfolio (2) x_m	(2) × (2) x^2_m	(1) × (2) $x_i x_m$
1971	5.2	7.4	54.8	38.5
1972	7.3	8.2	67.2	59.9
1973	10.1	12.3	151.3	124.2
1974	15.4	16.9	285.6	260.3
1975	19.8	19.1	364.8	378.2
1976	24.9	22.5	506.3	560.3
1977	29.7	25.1	630.0	745.5
1978	35.2	26.4	697.0	929.3
1979	40.1	29.8	888.0	1195.0
1980	42.6	30.3	918.1	1290.8
Total	230.3	198.0	4563.1	5582.0
Annual average	23.0	19.8		

The estimate of the systematic risk, denoted by $\hat{\beta}_i$ is given by the standard formula:

$$\hat{\beta}_i = \frac{Cov(x_i, x_m)}{\sigma_m^2} = \frac{\sum\limits_{t=1}^{10}(x_i - \bar{x}_i)(x_{m_t} - \bar{x}_m)}{\sum\limits_{t=1}^{10}(x_{m_t} - \bar{x}_m)^2}$$

where $\bar{x}_i$ and $\bar{x}_m$ denote the arithmetic annual average rate of return of the ith security and market portfolio respectively and 10 represents the number of years in this specific example.

Employing some algebraic manipulation this equation can be rewritten as:

$$\hat{\beta}_i = \frac{\sum\limits_{t=1}^{10} x_{i_t} x_{m_t} - 10\,\bar{x}_i\,\bar{x}_m}{\sum\limits_{t=1}^{10} \bar{x}_{m_t}^2 - 10 x_{m_t}^2}$$

Plugging in the data from Table 13.1, we obtain an estimate of the security's future beta, $\hat{\beta}_i = 1.6$:

$$\hat{\beta}_i = \frac{5582.0 - 10 \times 23 \times 19.8}{4563.1 - 10 \times 392} = \frac{1028}{643.1} = 1.6$$

THE CHARACTERISTIC LINE

The regression line of x_i on x_m, or *characteristic line* as it is usually called, is plotted in Fig. 13.4. The reader should note that the characteristic line which is appropriate for the hypothetical example of Table 13.1 has a slope (beta) equal to 1.6. (The ten dots represent the ten annual plots of the relationship between the individual security's rate of return with that of the market portfolio.) The second characteristic line, denoted as beta = 1 has a slope of 45° and is appropriate for any security having the *same* risk as the market portfolio since the return in such security fluctuates, on the average, in the same way as the market as a whole.

The concept of a characteristic line also suggests the possibility of classifying companies by their systematic risk. Stocks having a beta greater than one ($\beta > 1$) are classified as *aggressive stocks* since they go up faster than the market in a "bull", i.e. rising market, but fall faster in a "bear", i.e. falling market. Stocks with betas less than one ($\beta < 1$) are *defensive*; their returns fluctuate less than the market as a whole. Finally, the limiting case of stocks with betas equal to unity are *neutral stocks* since they fluctuate, on the average, along with the market.

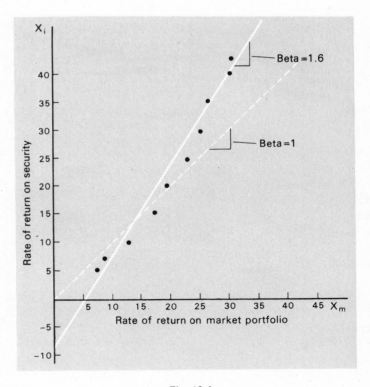

Fig. 13.4

Table 13.2

Defensive Stocks (β < 1)	
	Beta
Abbot Laboratory	0.42
General Telephone	0.60
Greyhound Corporation	0.62
R.H. Macy Corporation	0.65
Union Carbide Corporation	0.92
Aggressive Stocks (β > 1)	
	Beta
Bethlehem Steel	1.37
Hooper Chemical	1.43
Cerro Corporation	1.67
Medusa Portland	1.86
Conalco Inc.	3.44

The classification of stocks by their systematic risk is illustrated in Table 13.2. Using the regression technique described above and substituting the average return on all New York Stock Exchange stocks (the Fisher Index) for the market portfolio, betas were derived using the historical rates of return for a sample of firms over the period 1948 – 68. The betas of the defensive stocks ranged from 0.42 for Abbot Laboratory to 0.92 for Union Carbide. With respect to the aggressive securities, Bethlehem Steel had a beta of 1.37, while the highest beta was 3.44 for Conalco. Since the expected rate of return on common stock, in the context of the capital asset pricing model, is linked to systematic risk, we shall use the estimated betas of Table 13.2 as a basis for calculating the required return on equity in Chapter 18 below.[5]

CAPITAL ASSET PRICING MODEL AND CAPITAL BUDGETING

The implications of the capital asset pricing model for capital budgeting are straightforward. In a perfect capital market, combining investment projects whose cash flows have little, or even negative correlation, does not necessarily create opportunities for risk diversification over and beyond what was previously possible for individual (and institutional) investors.[6] In such a

---

5 Current estimates of beta for a wide variety of companies are available on a commercial basis. For example, Value Line and Merril Lynch, Pierce, Fenner and Smith provide current updates of estimated betas for the stocks of many corporations.

6 A number of authors have offered proofs of this proposition. See Jan Mossin, "Equilibrium in a Capital Asset Market", *Econometrica*, October 1966; Stewart C. Myers, "Procedures for Capital Budgeting Under Uncertainty", *Industrial Management Review*, Spring 1968; Haim Levy and Marshall Sarnat, "Diversification, Portfolio Analysis and the Uneasy Case for Conglomerate Mergers", *Journal of Finance*, September 1970.

market, portfolio diversification and corporate risk diversification are perfect substitutes, and as a result, the contribution of the project to the firm's variance can be ignored since the diversifiable unsystematic portion of the risk can be eliminated indirectly by the investors themselves when building their portfolios. Thus, given the assumption of a perfect capital market, each project should be evaluated solely in terms of its own expected return and undiversifiable systematic risk, i.e. the appropriate discount rate is equal to the risk free interest rate plus a risk premium which depends solely on the project's beta.

If we recall the equilibrium condition for individual securities, the required rate of return for each individual project is given by Ex_i.

$$Ex_i = r + (Ex_m - r)\beta_i$$

where β_i now denotes the undiversifiable risk of the i project. Recognizing that

$$\frac{Ex_m - r}{\sigma_m^2} = \lambda$$ represents the market price of risk, i.e. the market trade-off between return and risk, the required rate of return on the ith project can be rewritten as:

$$Ex_i = r + \lambda\ Cov(x_i, x_m)$$

Applying this concept we can explain some extreme cases which have plagued the capital budgeting literature. For example, should the firm consider the possibility of investing in riskless bonds, the required rate of return reduces to $Ex_i = r$, i.e. to the interest rate itself, because the covariance between the return on a riskless bond and the return on the market portfolio is zero. On the other hand, if $\beta_i = 1$, the required rate of return is

$$Ex_i = r + (Ex_m - r) \times 1 = Ex_m$$

Thus the required rate of return on a project whose returns fluctuate exactly like the market as a whole is the same as the expected return on the market portfolio. Moreover, in that happy world of negative betas, i.e. for projects whose returns fluctuate inversely with the market, the required rate of return may be *less* than the riskless interest rate, once their superior risk-reducing properties are recognized. In conclusion the higher a project's systematic risk (beta) the higher will be the required rate of return. The remainder of the projects' variance which emanates from random fluctuations which are not systematically associated with the market can be ignored.

APPLICATION TO CAPITAL BUDGETING: IMPERFECT MARKETS

Of course in the real world, capital markets are less than perfect, and investors' diversification is *not* a perfect costless substitute for corporate diversification. In reality, stabilizing the firms income stream is often an important (and valid) goal of corporate financial strategy.[7] The resulting reduction of lenders' risk may lead to significant cost savings when raising capital either by reducing the interest rate required on a given amount of capital, or by increasing the proportion of debt capital which can be raised at a given interest rate.[8] For example, in the extreme case in which investors hold only single-security portfolios, rather than the market portfolio, project risk is measured by the *variance* of the returns and the portfolio selection model of Chapter 12 can be applied directly to the capital budgeting problem using a project's *expected NPV* and the variance of *NPV* as the index of return and risk respectively.

As is true of the individual investor in securities, the firm is faced with the problem of choosing an optimal combination (portfolio) of projects out of the subset of efficient combinations (portfolios); and because of possible covariance between the cash flows of new investment proposals and those generated by existing projects, the combinations should include existing cash flows as well as newly proposed investments. These efficient investment combinations facing the firm can be illustrated by the envelope curve in Fig. 13.5. All of the remaining interior combinations should not be chosen since they represent *inefficient* options, in the sense that the firm can always improve its position (increase return with no increase in risk, or reduce risk without sacrifice of return) by choosing a different combination on the efficiency curve.[9]

If we recall that the distribution of the expected income stream accruing to shareholders reflects the past and present capital investment projects undertaken by the firm the slope of the opportunity line confronting the firm, Mb of Fig. 13.5, measures the market price of a unit of risk to the firm in an imperfect market. This measure of the trade-off between expected return and risk can be used to determine the firm's *optimal* capital budget; i.e. the point of tangency between the opportunity line and the curve of efficient combinations (point b) represents the *optimal* investment combination for our hypothetical firm.[10]

The explicit application of the mean-variance criterion to capital expenditure decisions can shed some further light on the paradoxical cases considered

---

7 The importance of recognizing the correlations among investment opportunities is almost intuitively obvious. Numerous examples of risk-reducing combinations of investments can be found: manufacturers of machine tools and other highly cyclical products often tend to diversify into consumer goods to help stabilize the income stream; risk reduction also provides one of the explanations for the recent spate of conglomerate mergers.

8 An analogous argument with respect to conglomerate mergers has been presented by Levy and Sarnat, *ibid.*, and by W.G. Lewellen, "A Pure Financial Rationale for the Conglomerate Merger", *Journal of Finance*, May 1971.

9 In the case of the firm the efficiency frontier may not be continuous owing to the indivisibility of investment projects. It should also be noted that a point on the efficiency curve cannot include more than one project out of a set of *mutually exclusive* alternatives.

10 The alternative of using the point of tangency between an indifference curve and the efficiency locus should not be applied to problems of capital budgeting since a firm's shareholders typically have different utility functions (indifference curves). Such a procedure also implicitly assumes that investors cannot lend or borrow.

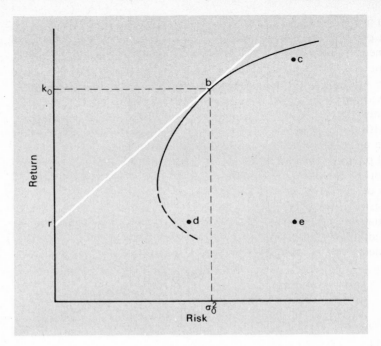

Fig. 13.5

earlier. If the firm is confronted with projects of varying risk, the mean-variance model suggests that the optimal portfolio (point b of Fig. 13.5) might have been achieved by combining two projects having the characteristics of points such as c and d; note that the first project has a higher expected return than k_0 and a higher variance than σ_0^2, the second project has an expected return lower than k_0, and also a variance lower than σ_0^2. Thus the explicit application of the mean-variance framework to the capital budgeting problem immediately suggests the possibility that situations may arise in which it pays the firm to accept a low-risk project even though its *NPV* is negative when discounted at the rate of k_0 that is the firm's average cost of capital (for example, a project of the type represented by point d in Fig. 13.5).

At first glance this result seems startling, but on further reflection it can readily be explained. Most firms holding low-risk assets such as bonds would find the net present value of such investments are negative when discounted at the firm's opportunity cost of capital, since the latter reflects the average risk of the firm, and is therefore higher (and usually substantially higher) than the interest rate on bonds.

The appropriateness of the simple *NPV* rule becomes even more dubious once we recognize the possibility of statistical interdependence between the cash flows of the various investment projects. In such circumstances it may pay to accept a project with a *negative NPV* even though its variance is higher than σ_0^2. (Such a project is represented by point e in Fig. 13.5.) Clearly, the negative covariance of such a project with the other proposals might conceivably be sufficient to combine with them into an "efficient" combination. Of course, if the firm was faced with the problem of choosing only one project, an alternative with the risk-return characteristics denoted by point e would be rejected by the mean-variance rule since it represents an inefficient alternative as compared with point d.

The application of a single-valued risk-adjusted discount rate to *all* individual projects represents a sort of rule-of-thumb solution (see Chapter 11). Such a procedure assumes that the individual characteristics of the alternative projects do not change the average risk level of the firm. However, where the firm must choose among investment opportunities with risk characteristics which materially change the average risk level of the firm, both the optimal investment mix and the appropriate discount rate must be simultaneously determined.

THE CAPITAL ASSET PRICING MODEL: THE EMPIRICAL EVIDENCE

The *CAPM* relates the expected return of a security, Ex_i to its systematic risk β_i in the following way

$$Ex_i = r + (Ex_m - r)\beta_i$$

The validity of the *CAPM* can be tested in two ways:

(a) By checking if the underlying assumptions of the model are logical and fit investors' behavior;

(b) By testing empirically the degree to which the *CAPM* explains, i.e. predicts, the behavior of security prices.

Many of the model's assumptions (e.g., no transaction costs, perfect divisibility of investments, homogeneous expectations regarding the future, uniform investment horizons, etc.) clearly do not hold in reality. However, one should not reject the *CAPM* on these grounds. Perhaps these deviations from reality are not crucial, so that the *CAPM* can still explain price behavior. As Milton Friedman[11] has emphasized, the "realism" of a theory's assumptions can be judged only by the degree to which the theory provides valid and meaningful explanations and predictions, and this requires an examination of the logical consequences of the theory against observed reality. In fact, to be meaningful and useful, the assumptions must be descriptively unrealistic in the sense that they must abstract from a complex reality. Few indeed would argue that

---

11 See Milton Friedman, "The Methodology of Positive Economics", in *Essays in Positive Economics*, Chicago and London: The University of Chicago Press, 1953.

the hair color of the president of the New York Stock Exchange is germane to the problem of explaining the determination of prices in that market. But how "unrealistic" can the assumptions be? We have no recourse but to test the model's predictions empirically.

In order to test the degree to which the *CAPM* explains stock price behavior, one normally uses ex-post data to estimate the ex-ante parameters of the model. Typically a time-series regression of the following form is used,

$$x_{it} = \alpha + \beta_i x_{mt} + e_t$$

where x_{it} and x_{mt} are the rates of return on the ith security and on the market portfolio in period t, and α and β_i are the regression coefficients. Now let us denote the estimate of the ith security's systematic risk by $\hat{\beta}_i$. Suppose that we include in our sample 100 securities, and for each one we have 26 observations of their annual rates of return. We then run 100 regression (time series regressions of each security against the market portfolio x_m) and the output of these 100 regressions are 100 matched pairs $(x_i, \hat{\beta})$ which are the average rate of return on the ith security and the estimate of its systematic risk. We then run a cross-section regression of the type

$$x_i = \gamma_0 + \gamma_1 \hat{\beta}_i$$

This regression is very similar to the theoretical relationship as presumed by the *CAPM*,

$$Ex_i = r + (Ex_m - r)\beta_i$$

with the following differences:

(a) In the regression analysis we use the ex-post average return $\bar{x}_i$ as an estimate of the expected rate of return Ex_i.

(b) We also use the ex-post estimate $\hat{\beta}_i$ instead of the ex-ante, and unknown, true systematic risk β_i.

If the *CAPM* provides a good approximation of stock price behavior, we would expect to find the following empirical results:

(1) γ_0 would not be significantly different from the risk-free interest rate r.

(2) γ_1 would not be significantly different from $(Ex_m - r)$. However, since Ex_m is not observable and therefore is not known, it is common to compare the estimate γ_i to the average *ex post* excess return $(\bar{x}_m - r)$.

(3) Obviously we also expect to find a reasonable value for the square of the correlation coefficient, R^2.

The number of papers which have tried to verify empirically the validity of the *CAPM* in this way (or by some other variation of the method explained above) is so large that we will not attempt to catalogue all of them.[12]

However, in general, the results tend to reject the *CAPM*. To be specific, the following findings characterize most of the empirical efforts:

(a) γ_0 is much larger than the risk-free interest rate which prevailed in the period covered by the relevant study;

(b) γ_1 is much smaller than $(\bar{x}_m - r)$; and

(c) The R^2 (using individual stocks rather than grouped data) is quite low, usually only around 20% if one uses annual rates of return; and is very close to zero when monthly rates of return are used.

Thus, the empirical findings do not support the *CAPM* in its pure form.[13] Indeed, if one recalls that the typical investor holds a small non-diversified portfolio consisting of less than four stocks on average[14] it is obvious that β which measures the covariability of the return of a given stock with a market portfolio (which no one holds!) can only play a very limited role in measuring a security's risk. Indeed, if one substitutes the ith security's variance for β and runs the naive regression

$$(\bar{x}_i = \gamma_{0i} + \gamma_i \sigma_i^2)$$

the coefficient of correlation actually increases from about 20% (when $\hat{\beta}_i$ is use) to about 40% when it is replaced by $\hat{\sigma}_i^2$. This is a result which makes sense only if investors hold extremely non-diversified portfolios.

---

12 See, for example, Irwin Friend and Marshall Blume, "Measurement of Portfolio Performance Under Certainty", *American Economic Review*, September 1970; Marshall Blume and Irwin Friend, "A New Look at the Capital Asset Pricing Model", *Journal of Finance*, March 1973; Irwin Friend and Randolph Westerfield, "Risk and Capital Asset Pricing", *Journal of Banking and Finance*, forthcoming; Fischer Black, Michael C. Jensen, and Myron Scholes, "The Capital Asset Pricing Model: Some Empirical Tests", in *Studies in the Theory of Capital Markets*, New York: Praeger, 1972; Merton H. Miller and Myron Scholes, "Rate of Return in Relation to Risk: a Reexamination of Some Recent Findings", in M.C. Jensen (ed.) *Studies in the Theory of Capital Markets*, New York: Praeger 1972; Haim Levy, "Equilibrium in an Imperfect Market: A Constraint on the Number of Securities in the Portfolio", *American Economic Review*, September 1978; and Eugene F. Fama and J. MacBeth, "Risk, Return and Equilibrium: Empirical Test", *Journal of Political Economy*, May/June 1973.

13 Clearly the use of predictions based on ex-post data is fraught with difficulties. See, for example, Robert C. Merton, "On Estimating the Expected Return on the Market: An Exploratory Investigation", Working Paper No. 444, National Bureau of Economic Research, February 1980; and Edwin H. Elton and Martin J. Gruber, "Estimating the Dependence Structure of Share Prices: Implications for Portfolio Selection", *Journal of Finance*, December 1973.

However the substitution of ex-ante data drawn directly from financial institutions does not change the conclusion that investors' assessments of a security's risk is not closely connected to its beta coefficient as implied by the *CAPM*; see Irwin Friend, Randolph Westerfield and Joao Ferreira, "The CAPM and Mean-Variance Efficient Portfolios: *Ex-Ante* and *Ex-Post* Data", Working Paper No. 10-80, Rodney L. White Center for Financial Research, University of Pennsylvania, October 1980.

14 See Marshall Blume, Jean Crockett and Irwin Friend, "Stock Ownership in the United States: Characteristics and Trends", *Survey of Current Business*, November 1974.

However, recall that $\hat{\sigma}_i^2$ by itself cannot serve as the risk index unless each investor holds only *one* stock in his portfolio. As mentioned above investors do diversify to some extent, which implies that the true measure of risk lies somewhere between σ_i^2 and β_i, but probably closer to σ_i^2 since investors' portfolios are closer to a pure non-diversified portfolio than to a fully diversified one comprised of all available risky assets.[15]

In a recent paper Richard Roll has made a serious methodological criticism of the empirical tests of the *CAPM*.[16] Roll questions the very testability of the *CAPM*. He shows that the absence of a perfect linear fit using empirical data merely implies that the selected market portfolio is mean-variance inefficient. Hence the failure of the empirical test may be simply a result of the researcher having chosen an inappropriate index for the market portfolio. Since, in theory, the market portfolio should include *all* risky assets[17] (e.g., stocks, bonds, land, gold, coins, human capital etc.) it is difficult, if not impossible, to test the *CAPM* empirically.

By now you may well be ready to ask, "If the *CAPM* is so bad ... why is it so popular in academic circles?" The answer can be found in a famous dictum of George Stigler, who in a completely different context, pointed out that "a theory can only be replaced by a better ... theory." Although the *CAPM* provides important insights, we shall be extremely cautious about applying it uncritically to corporations' capital investment decisions involving as they do millions, and often many millions, of shareholders' dollars. The need for caution is reflected in managements' observed reluctance to utilize techniques based on the *CAPM* when evaluating capital investments. In a recent survey of large U.S. corporations, 52% of the executives polled indicated that the concept of systematic risk seldom influences policy decisions, while another 40% stated flatly that the *CAPM* has no effect on corporation decisions.[18]

SUMMARY

This chapter has set out the basic principles of the capital asset pricing model. The model assumes a perfect capital market in which investors hold portfolios which are comprised of *all* securities available in the market. This very strong assumption permits us to define a number of important concepts:

   (a) The *capital market line* (*CML*) on which all efficient portfolios lie.
   (b) The *security market line* (*SML*) which sets out the linear relationship between expected return and risk.

15 For a theoretical equilibrium model of prices subject to the constraint that investors do *not* hold all risky assets, see Levy, *op cit.*, but this model has not yet been tested empirically.
16 See Richard Roll, "A Critique of Asset Pricing Theory's Tests", *Journal of Financial Economics*, March 1977.
17 See David Mayers, "Non-Marketable Assets and the Capital Market Equilibrium under Uncertainty", in *Studies in the Theory of Capital Markets*, New York: Praeger, 1972.
18 See J. William Petty II and David F. Scott, Jr., "Capital Budgeting Practices in Large American Firms: A Retrospective Analysis and Update", forthcoming.

(c) The analysis also permits the dichotomization of a security's risk into two components: the *diversifiable* component, or *non-systematic risk* as it is often called, which can be eliminated by combining it in a diversified portfolio; and the non-diversifiable component or *systematic risk* as it is called, which cannot be eliminated through portfolio diversification.

(d) The Beta coefficient which measures a security's systematic risk:

$$\beta_i = \frac{Cov(x_i, x_m)}{\sigma_m^2}$$

Although it was originally developed for the security market, the model also provides some important insights into the capital budgeting process. Applied to individual projects, the appropriate discount rate is given by the riskless interest rate plus a premium which is determined by the projects' non-diversifiable systematic risk. However, in an extremely imperfect market in which investors hold only single security portfolios, the firm's optimal capital budget can be found using the mean-variance rule. Clearly, the truth lies somewhere between these two extreme assumptions. And in fact empirical evidence drawn from the New York Stock Exchange suggests that a typical portfolio includes only a few individual common stocks.

Hopefully the reader has emerged from his baptism of fire in a world of risk and uncertainty with some additional insight and a degree of 'risk aversion' and skepticism for quick and easy formulas which are appropriate for a future corporate executive. With that in mind we turn in part III to the forces which determine the corporation's cutoff rate for investments, i.e., the cost of capital.

QUESTIONS AND PROBLEMS

13.1 In what sense does a perfect market separate the investment process into two stages?

13.2 What is the equilibrium relationship between return and risk which must hold for every risky asset in a perfect market?

13.3 Define "systematic" and "non-systematic risk".

13.4 The "betas" of four shares in a perfect market are as follows:

$$\beta_A = -1; \beta_B = 0; \beta_C = 1; \beta_D = 2$$

Assume that the market is in equilibrium; that the riskless interest rate is 6%; and that the expected return of the "market portfolio" is 14%. Calculate the expected return on shares *A, B, C* and *D*.

13.5 In what circumstances may a firm rationally decide to accept an investment which has a negative *NPV*?

13.6 Assume a perfect capital market in which investors are constrained to building single-stock risk portfolios; that borrowing or lending at a riskless interest rate is possible, and that in *equilibrium* the following relationship between two risky securities *i* and *j* holds:

	Share i	Share j
Expected Return (%)	26	18
Standard Deviation (%)	15	9

(a) What is the riskless rate of interest in this market? (Hint: in equilibrium under the above conditions both securities must lie on the same market lines, i.e. the following equation must hold:

$$\frac{Ex_i - r}{\sigma_i} = \frac{Ex_j - r}{\sigma_j}$$

(b) If the investor wishes to hold a portfolio with a standard deviation of only 6% what would be his investment strategy?

(c) What would his investment strategy be if he wanted to reach an expected return of 24%?

13.7   Assume the following rates of return on the market portfolio:

Year	Rate of Return	Year	Rate of Return
1968	10	1973	3
1969	32	1974	12
1970	20	1975	− 5
1971	18	1976	18
1972	17	1977	21

Set out the hypothetical rates of return for a defensive and an aggressive stock. Use your figures to calculate the betas of each stock. Draw the characteristic lines for each stock on the same graph.

13.8   The annual rate of return of the market portfolio x_m and the annual rate of return on a security j, x_j, for a period of eight years are given below:

Year	x_j	x_m
1	0.045	0.020
2	0.050	0.060
3	0.070	0.080
4	0.020	− 0.030
5	0.050	0.010
6	0.090	0.080
7	0.040	0.060
8	0.020	− 0.040

Estimate the Beta coefficient of security j, interpret it and classify the security as "aggressive" or "defensive".

13.9   Assume that the firm's current income Y_0 is equal to $10,000. The firm

is making investment $I_0 = \$2,000$, and the next-period income is uncertain. The expected next-period income is $\overline{Y}_1 = \$10,000$ and its covariance with the return on the market portfolio is $Cov(Y_1, x_m) = 250$; the expected return on the market portfolio is $\overline{x}_m = 0.10$ and the standard deviation of the market return $\sigma_m = 0.10$; the risk-free interest rate is $r = 0.04$. There are no taxes.
Calculate the value of the firm's equity.

13.10 A common stock (j) is expected to yield a (gross) return $R_j = \$40$. The following quantities are given: the expected rate of return on the market portfolio $\overline{x}_m = 0.10$; the standard deviation of the market return $\sigma_m = 0.08$; the covariance of the stock-j return with the market portfolio $Cov(R_j, x_m) = 0.50$; the risk-free rate $r = 0.04$.
What is the stock's equilibrium value?

13.11 Assume that the capital market is in equilibrium. The riskless rate is 6% and you buy a common stock (i) whose expected gross return is $\$120$. You pay $\$100$ for the stock. Is $Cov(R_i, x_m)$ positive or negative? Explain!

13.12 Assume that the capital market is in equilibrium. The risk-free interest rate is $r = 0.04$; the expected rate of return on the market portfolio is $\overline{x}_m = 0.10$; and the standard deviation of the market return is $\sigma_m = 0.09$.

(a) Write out and draw the capital market line (*CML*).
(b) Consider three securities whose returns (x_1, x_2 and x_3) have the following covariances with the return on the market portfolio:

$$Cov(x_1, x_m) = 0.0108$$

$$Cov(x_2, x_m) = 0.0027$$

$$Cov(x_3, x_m) = 0.0054$$

Write out and draw the security market line (*SML*), and determine the expected value of the above securities. Also, identify them on the *SML*.
(c) Determine the Beta coefficients of the three securities.
(d) If the standard deviations of the three securities are $\sigma_1 = 0.20$, $\sigma_2 = 0.05$, and $\sigma_3 = 0.16$, what is the *diversifiable* risk of each of these securities? (Decompose the standard deviation rather than the variance.)

13.13 Let S_0 be the value of a company's shares *just after current dividends are paid*. Assume no taxes, the expected next period's income is $\overline{Y}_1 = \$1000$ and $Cov(Y_1, x_m) = 40$. Also assume that the expected rate of return on the market portfolios is $\overline{x}_m = 0.10$, its standard deviation $\sigma_m = 0.10$, and the risk-free rate $r = 0.04$.

(a) Determine the value S_0 under the assumption that the firm is liquidated at the end of the period and all its assets are paid out as dividends D_1.
(b) Answer question (a) assuming that $Cov(Y_1, x_m) = 0$.

13.14   The annual rates of return (in percent) of two securities, *i* and *j*, and of the market portfolio for the four years 1977−80 were as follows:

Year	Security i	Security j	Market portfolio
1977	− 20	+ 30	+ 40
1978	0	+ 10	+ 20
1979	+ 20	− 10	0
1980	0	+ 10	+ 12

Assume riskless interest rate $r = 5\%$ and answer the following questions:

(a) Calculate the standard deviations of returns of securities *i* and *j* and the covariances between the returns of the two securities and between the returns of each security and the market.

(b) Calculate the systematic (non-diversifiable) risk of the two securities, σ_i^S and σ_j^S, and show graphically the location of the two securities and of the market portfolio in the average rate of return−systematic risk plane.

(c) Suppose that the market is in equilibrium. What would be the expected rate of return of the two securities? How can you account for the deviation of the above data from the calculated figures?

13.15   The table below provides the annual rates of return on General Motors, American Motors Corporation and the S & P Five Hundred Index, which is a proxy to the market portfolio. Assuming riskless interest rate of $r = 3\%$ answer the following questions.

Year	GM	AMC	Market Portfolio
1959	14.4	121.2	11.9
1960	− 22.2	− 33.9	.4
1961	47.5	3.7	26.9
1962	7.7	3.1	− 8.6
1963	42.8	17.2	22.8
1964	30.7	− 16.9	16.5
1965	11.4	− 32.8	12.5
1966	− 32.5	− 30.4	− 10.06
1967	30.5	114.0	23.9
1968	1.8	− 3.7	11.1
1969	− 6.2	− 33.0	− 8.5
1970	22.3	− 33.2	3.9
1971	4.3	21.6	14.3
1972	6.5	17.8	19.1
1973	− 37.8	7.5	− 14.7
1974	− 27.6	− 62.3	− 26.5
1975	97.1	65.4	37.3
1976	45.85	− 28.02	23.8
1977	− 11.25	− 6.33	− 7.15
1978	− 4.7	26.67	12.16

(a) Calculate the systematic risk $\beta_i \sigma_m$, the non-systematic risk ($\sigma_i - \beta_i \sigma_m$) and the total risk σ_i of the stocks of GM and AMC.

(b) For risk-free interest rate of $r = 3\%$ draw the *CML* and illustrate graphically the decomposition of the risk into the two components.

(c) Draw the *SML* and show the location of the two stocks on the line.

(d) Use the systematic risk σ^S to calculate the equilibrium risk-premium of GM and AMC. What was the actual estimate of the risk-premium during the years 1959–78? How do you explain the difference in the expected risk-premium?

13.16 Suppose that a firm operates for one period and at the end of the period stockholders get the liquidation value of the firm. Let Y be a random variable which denotes the total income for the stockholders at the end of the period. The joint probability to get income $Y = Y_i$ and that the rate of return on the market portfolio will be $x_m = x_{mj}$ is given by P_{ij} in the table:

		Total	Income Y_i	(in \$)	
		1,000	6,000	8,000	
	−20	0.05	0.00	0.00	
x_{mj} (%)	10	0.05	0.05	0.10	P_{ij}
	40	0.15	0.50	0.10	

(Note that the total probability $\underset{i \ j}{\Sigma\Sigma} P_{ij} = 1$)

The risk-free interest rate is 6%. In the absence of corporate tax answer the following questions:

(a) The firm intends to issue bonds with face value of \$2,000 and coupon interest rate of 10%. Is the bond riskless? Why? What is the total equilibrium market value of the bonds?

(b) Assume that the bonds as described in part (a) are the only debt the firm has. What is the value of the firm's stock in equilibrium?

(c) Suppose that the firm decides *not* to issue bonds, what is the market value of the stock? Is there any relationship between your answers to (a), (b) and (c)?

Hint: (1) If income is below \$2200, bondholders get whatever is available and the stockholders get nothing.

(2) The total investment in physical assets remains constant. Thus, issuing bonds implies that less shares are issued.

(3) $Cov(x_{mj}, Y_i) = \underset{i \ j}{\Sigma\Sigma} P_{ij} x_{mj} Y_i - Ex_m EY$

Where $P_{ij} = Pr(x_m = x_{mj}$ and $Y = Y_i)$

13.17 The future after-tax income of the firm one year from now is a random variable Y_1^T. The joint distribution of the firm's after tax future income Y_1^T [where $Y_1^T = (1 - T)$ (Revenue−Expenses−Depreciation)] and the return on the market portfolio x_m (also a random variable) is given by the following table:

		Y_1^T	
	$6,000	$10,000	$14,000
	Joint Probabilities		
	0.10%	0.10	0.15	0.05
x_m	0.10%	0.10	0.20	0.10
	0.30%	0.05	0.15	0.10

In addition assume a tax rate $T = 0.50$, *current* after-tax income $Y_0^T = \$6,000$, current investment $I_0 = \$5,000$, and the risk-free interest rate $r = 0.06$. The investment is fully depreciated in the one period and its residual value at $t = 1$ is zero.

(a) Determine the value of the firm (assume that current income has not been distributed yet). Assume zero debt at time $t = 0$. (Hint: recall that the depreciation tax shelter is certain!)

(b) Suppose the firm is increasing the current dividend out of the proceeds of a one-period bond issue, i.e., the new issue is not being used to finance an increase in the firm's activities. The bonds have $6,000 face value and a coupon rate of 7%. Are the bonds a risky asset? Find their market equilibrium value, B_0.

APPENDIX 13A THE DERIVATION OF THE CAPITAL ASSET PRICING MODEL

This appendix provides a formal demonstration of the derivation of the primary equilibrium condition of the Capital Asset Pricing Model (*CAPM*) — that is the proposition that in equilibrium the expected return on any risky asset (in a perfect capital market) will be given by:

$$Ex_i = r + (Ex_m - r)\,\beta_i$$

where:
Ex_i = the expected return on asset i
r = the risk-free interest rate
Ex_m = the expected return on the market portfolio (e.g. the Standard & Poors' index)
β_i = the ith asset's systematic risk

Optimal Investment Proportions

As noted in the text each individual investor in the market attempts to reach the highest feasible market line, for example, the line rN of Fig. 13.1 of the text which is reproduced here. The market line can be found by minimizing the standard deviation (σ_0) for any given portfolio's expected return (Ex_0):

$$Ex_0 = \sum_{i=1}^{n} p_i Ex_i + (1 - \sum_{i=1}^{n} p_i)r$$

$$\sigma_0 = \sqrt{\sum_{i=1}^{n} p_i^2 \sigma_i^2 + 2 \sum_{\substack{i=1 \\ j>i}}^{n} p_i p_j Cov(x_i,x_j)}$$

where p_i denotes the proportion of the portfolio invested in the ith asset.

Clearly the availability of riskless bonds (or loans) influences, and therefore appears, in the formula for the expected return. However, the inclusion of such bonds (loans) does *not* affect the standard deviation of the overall portfolio since the variance of a perfectly certain income (payments) stream r is zero. Hence the covariance of the bonds (loans) with the portfolio's risky assets (e.g. common stock) is also zero.

Now let us define the function C, as follows:

$$C = \sigma_0 + \lambda_1 [Ex - \sum_{i=1}^{n} p_i Ex_i - (1 - \sum_{i=1}^{n} p_i)r] \qquad (13A.1)$$

where λ_1 = a Lagrange multiplier.

The problem is to determine the vector of investment proportions which *minimizes* the overall portfolio standard deviation for all values of Ex_0. This is tantamount to finding the market line rN of Fig. 13.1 of the text, since by definition, that market line represents the feasible efficient set of alternatives facing the investor. Thus, each point on the line represents the overall portfolio (equities plus bonds or loans) which minimize the standard deviation, given the expected return. The market line can be generated analytically by differentiating Equation (13A.1) with respect to each p_i and with respect to the Lagrange multiplier λ_1, and setting the first derivatives equal to zero. This yields the following set of $n + 1$ equations:

$$\frac{\partial C}{\partial p_1} = \tfrac{1}{2}(\sigma_0^2)^{-\frac{1}{2}}[2p_1\sigma_1^2 + 2\sum_{j=2}^{n} p_j Cov(x_1,x_j)] - \lambda_1(Ex_1 - r) = 0$$

$$\frac{\partial C}{\partial p_2} = \tfrac{1}{2}(\sigma_0^2)^{-\frac{1}{2}}[2p_2\sigma_2^2 + 2\sum_{\substack{j=1 \\ j\neq 2}}^{n} p_j Cov(x_2,x_j)] - \lambda_1(Ex_2 - r) = 0$$

$$\vdots \qquad\qquad\qquad\qquad\qquad\qquad\qquad (13A.2)$$

$$\frac{\partial C}{\partial p_n} = \tfrac{1}{2}(\sigma_0^2)^{-\frac{1}{2}}[2p_n\sigma_n^2 + 2\sum_{j=1}^{n-1} p_j Cov(x_n,x_j)] - \lambda_1(Ex_n - r) = 0$$

$$\frac{\partial C}{\partial \lambda_1} = Ex_0 - \sum_{i=1}^{n} p_i Ex_i - (1 - \sum_{i=1}^{n} p_i)r = 0$$

Multiplying the first equation by p_1, the second equation by p_2, etc. and summing over all the equations yields,[1]

$$\sigma_0 = \lambda_1 \left(\sum_{i=1}^{n} p_i Ex_i - \sum_{i=1}^{n} p_i r \right)$$

$$= \lambda_1 \left[\sum_{i=1}^{n} p_i Ex_i + \left(1 - \sum_{i=1}^{n} p_i \right) r - r \right]$$

At the specific point where $\sum_{i=1}^{n} p_i = 1$ we obtain:[2]

$$\sigma_m = \lambda_1 (Ex_m - r) \text{ and hence } 1/\lambda_1 = \frac{(Ex_m - r)}{\sigma_m}$$

where m denotes the market portfolio, which is optimal for all investors (see Fig. 13A.1).

As we have already noted, the expression $(Ex_m - r)/\sigma_m$ defines the slope of the market line (rN of Fig. 13A.1). The reciprocal of the Langrange multiplier $(1/\lambda_1)$ measures the price of a unit of risk, that is the required increase in expected return when one unit of risk (in terms of the standard deviation) is added to the portfolio. Since the larger are the number of different shares which are available in the market, the greater are the opportunities to reduce risk, therefore the entire efficient set (market line) will shift to the left as the market grows. Thus for a given interest rate, the price of a unit of risk (slope of the market line) will be higher, other things being equal, in larger markets.

Let us now use the above results to determine the equilibrium relationship between an individual asset's expected return and its risk. Recall, in this context, that "risk" reflects not only the standard deviation of returns on the asset itself but also the covariance with the returns of all other risky assets in the market. In the previous section the relationship between a share's expected return and its contribution to the total risk of the optimal portfolio was stated in terms of the standard deviation. For mathematical convenience only we shall now use the portfolio variance to indicate risk, but this does *not* change the optimal solution.

Since this set of equations, from which we derive the equilibrium conditions for the individual investor must hold simultaneously for all investors, independent of their tastes, we can also use equations (13A.2) to derive the general relationship among the expected returns of all shares and their risk.

In general, the ith equation of (13.A.1), at the point $\sum_{i=1}^{n} p_i = 1$, can be rewritten as:

---

1 Note that the left side of this summation is simply σ_0.

2 Note that the slope of the market line is identical at all points. Thus, finding the highest slope by looking at the specific point where $\sum_{i=1}^{n} p = 1$ does not restrict the results, since the same slope holds for all other points.

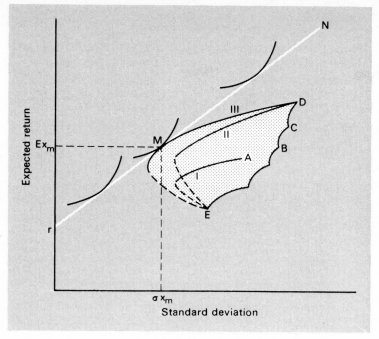

Fig. 13A.1

$$Ex_i = r + \frac{1}{\lambda_1 \sigma_m} \left[p_i \sigma_i^2 + \sum_{\substack{i=1 \\ j \neq i}}^{n} p_j Cov(x_i, x_j) \right]$$

Recalling the definition of λ_1, we obtain:

$$Ex_i = r + \frac{Ex_m - r}{\sigma_m^2} \left[p_i \sigma_i^2 + \sum_{\substack{i=1 \\ j \neq i}}^{n} p_j Cov(x_i, x_j) \right]$$

But since by definition, the return on the market portfolio is given by $x_m = \sum_{j=1}^{n} p_i x_i$

it can be shown[3] that the expected return on any risk asset can be written as:

$$Ex_i = r + \frac{Ex_m - r}{\sigma_m^2} Cov(x_i, x_m), \text{ or alternatively}$$

$$Ex_i = r + (Ex_m - r)\beta_i$$

where
$$\beta_i = \frac{Cov(x_i, x_m)}{\sigma_m^2}$$

which is precisely the equilibrium relationship which was presented in the text.

3 $Cov(x_i, x_m) = Cov \left[x_i, (p_1 x_1 + \ldots p_n x_n) \right] = p_i \sigma_i^2 + \sum_{\substack{j=1 \\ j \neq i}}^{n} p_j Cov(x_i, x_j).$

QUESTIONS AND PROBLEMS

13A.1   Assume that there are only three stocks in the market, and that the optimal investment proportion in each stock *A, B* and *C* is 1/3. Also assume:

$$\sigma_A^2 = 10, \ \sigma_B^2 = 8, \ \sigma_C^2 = 20, \text{ and}$$

$$Cov(A,B) = 8, \ Cov(B,C) = -10, \ Cov(A,C) = 4$$

Calculate:

(a) $Cov(A,M)$, $Cov(B,M)$, and $Cov(C,M)$ where M denotes the market portfolio.

(b) The systematic risk (beta) for each of the above three stocks.

13A.2   Assume that there are only two stocks (*A* and *B*) in the market, and that the risk-free interest rate is 5%. Also assume:

$$Ex_A = 10, \ \sigma_A^2 = 10 \text{ and}$$

$$Ex_B = 20, \ \sigma_B^2 = 20 \text{ and } Cov(A,B) = 0$$

(a) Find the optimal investment proportions in these two stocks on the assumption that the individual invests 100% of his resources in the two stocks.

(b) Find the optimal investment proportions for an individual who decides to invest 50% of his resources in these two stocks, and 50% in the riskless asset.

(c) What is the market price of risk? Show your calculation in detail.

SELECTED REFERENCES

Alexander, Gordon J. and Chervany, Norman L., "On the Estimation and Stability of Beta", *Journal of Financial and Quantitative Analysis*, March 1980.

Barry, C.B., "Effects of Uncertain and Non-Stationary Parameters upon Capital Market Equilibrium Conditions", *Journal of Financial and Quantitative Analysis*, September 1978.

Beja, Avraham and Goldman, Barry, "On the Dynamic Behavior of Prices in Disequilibrium", *The Journal of Finance*, May 1980.

Ben-Horim, Moshe and Levy, Haim, "Total Risk, Diversifiable Risk: A Pedagogic Note", *Journal of Financial and Quantitative Analysis*, June 1980.

Black, Fischer, "Capital Market Equilibrium with Restricted Borrowing", *Journal of Business*, 1972.

Blume, M.E., "Betas and Their Regression Tendencies: Some Further Evidence", *Journal of Finance*, March 1979.

Bolton, S.E. and Crockett, J.H., "The Influence of Liquidity Services on Beta", *Review of Business and Economic Research*, Spring 1978.

Bolton, S.E., Kretlow, S.J. and Oakes, J.H., "The Capital Asset Pricing Model under Certainty", *Review of Business and Economic Research*, Fall 1978.

Boyer, Marcel, Storoy, Sverre and Sten, Thore, "Equilibrium in Linear Capital Market Networks", *Journal of Finance*, December 1975.

Breeden, D.T., "An Intertemporal Asset Pricing Model with Stochastic Consumption and Investment Opportunities", *Journal of Financial Economics*, June 1979.

Brennan, Michael J., "Taxes, Market Valuation and Corporate Finance Policy", *National Tax Journal*, 23 (1970).

Brenner, Menachem and Smidt, Seymour, "Asset Characteristics and Systematic Risk", *Financial Management*, Winter 1978.

Brito, N.O., "Marketability Restrictions and the Valuation of Capital Assets under Uncertainty", *Journal of Finance*, September 1977.

Brown, S.L., "Autocorrelation, Market Imperfections, and the CAPM", *Journal of Financial and Quantitative Analysis*, December 1979.

Chen, A.H., Kim, E.H. and Kon, S.J., "Cash Demand, Liquidation Costs and Capital Market Equilibrium under Uncertainty", *Journal of Financial Economics*, September 1975.

Cheng, Pao L. and Grauer, Robert R., "An Alternative Test of the Capital Asset Pricing Model", *The American Economic Review*, September 1980.

Cornell, B. and Dietrich, J.K., "Mean-Absolute-Deviation Versus Least-Squares Regression Estimation of Beta Coefficients", *Journal of Financial and Quantitative Analysis*, March 1978.

Crockett, Jean and Friend, Irwin, "Capital Budgeting and Stock Valuation Comment", *American Economic Review*, March 1967.

Eddy, A.R., "Interest Rate Risk and Systematic Risk: An Interpretation", *Journal of Finance*, May 1978.

Elgers, P.T., Haltiner, J.R. and Hawthorne, W.H., "Beta Regression Tendencies: Statistical and Real Causes", *Journal of Finance*, March 1979.

Epstein, Larry G. and Turnbull, Stuart M., "Capital Asset Prices and the Temporal Resolution of Uncertainty", *The Journal of Finance*, June 1980.

Everett, James E. and Schwab, Bernhard, "On the Proper Adjustment for Risk Through Discount Rates in a Mean-Variance Framework", *Financial Management*, Summer 1979.

Fabozzi, F.J. and Francis, J.C., "Beta as a Random Coefficient", *Journal of Financial and Quantitative Analysis*, March 1978.

Fabry, Jaak and van Grembergen, Willy, "Further Evidence on the Stationarity of Betas and Errors in their Estimates", *Journal of Banking and Finance*, October 1978.

Fama, Eugene F., "Risk, Return, and Equilibrium: Some Clarifying Comments", *Journal of Finance*, March 1968.

Fama, Eugene; Fisher, Lawrence; Jensen, Michael and Roll, Richard, "The Adjustment of Stock Prices to New Information", *International Economic Review*, February 1969.

Foster, G., "Asset Pricing Models: Further Tests", *Journal of Financial and Quantitative Analysis*, March 1978.

Frankfurter, G.M., "The Effect of 'Market Indexes' on the Ex-Post Performance of the Sharpe Portfolio Selection Model", *Journal of Finance*, June 1976.

Friend, Irwin and Westerfield, Randolph, "Co-Skewedness and Capital Asset Pricing", *The Journal of Finance*, September 1980.

Friend, Irwin and Westerfield, Randolph, "Risk and Capital Asset Prices", *Journal of Banking and Finance*, forthcoming.

Friend, L., Westerfield, R. and Granito, M., "New Evidence on the Capital Asset Pricing Model", *Journal of Finance*, June 1978.

Gentry, James and Pike, John, "An Empirical Study of the Risk-Return Hypothesis Using Common Stock Portfolios of Life Insurance Companies", *Journal of Financial and Quantitative Analysis*, June 1970.

Goldberg, M.A. and Vora, A., "Bivariate Spectral Analysis of the Capital Asset Pricing Model", *Journal of Financial and Quantitative Analysis*, September 1978.

Grauer, R.R., "Generalized Two Parameter Asset Pricing Models: Some Empirical Evidence", *Journal of Financial Economics*, March 1978.

Harris, Richard G., "A General Equilibrium Analysis of the Capital Asset Pricing Model", *Journal of Financial and Quantitative Analysis*, March 1980.

Hess, A.C., "The Riskless Rate of Interest and the Market Price of Risk", *Quarterly Journal of Economics*, August 1975.

Hill, Ned C. and Stone, Bernell K., "Accounting Betas, Systematic Operating Risk, and Financial Leverage: A Risk-Composition Approach to the Determinants of Systematic Risk", *Journal of Financial and Quantitative Analysis*, September 1980.

Jahankhani, A., "E-V and E-S Capital Asset Pricing Models: Some Empirical Tests", *Journal of Financial and Quantitative Analysis*, September 1976.

Jarrow, Robert, "Heterogeneous Expectations, Restrictions on Short Sales, and Equilibrium Asset Prices", *Journal of Finance*, December 1980.

Jensen, Michael C. (Editor), *Studies in the Theory of Capital Markets*, New York: Praeger Publishers, 1972.

Jones-Lee, M.W. and Poskitt, D.S., "An Existence Proof for Equilibrium in a Capital Asset Market", *Journal of Business Finance & Accounting*, Autumn 1975.

Klemosky, R.C. and Martin, J.D. "The Adjustment of Beta Forecasts", *Journal of Finance*, September 1975.

Kon, S.L. and Ien, F.C., "Estimation of Time-Varying Systematic Risk and Performance for Mutual Fund Portfolios: An Application of Switching Regression", - *Journal of Finance*, May 1978.

Kraus, Alan and Litzenberger, Robert H., "Market Equilibrium in a Multiperiod State Preference Model with Logarithmic Utility", *Journal of Finance*, December 1975.

Kymn, K.O. and Page, W.P., "A Microeconomic and Geometric Interpretation of Beta in Models of Discrete Adaptive Expectations", *Review of Business and Economic Research*, Spring 1978.

Lakonishok, Josef, "Stock Market Returns Expectations: Some General Properties", *The Journal of Finance*, September 1980.

Landskroner, Y., "Intertemporal Determination of the Market Price of Risk", *Journal of Finance*, December 1977.

Lee, C.F. and Jen, F.C., "Effects of Measurement Errors on Systematic Risk and Performance Measure of a Portfolio", *Journal of Finance and Quantitative Analysis*, June 1978.

Lee, C.F., "On the Relationship between the Systematic Risk and the Investment Horizon", *Journal of Financial and Quantitative Analysis*, December 1976.

Lee, C.F., "Performance Measure, Systematic Risk, and Errors-in-Variables Estimation Method", *Journal of Economics and Business*, Winter 1977.

Leland, H., "Production Theory and the Stock Market", *Bell Journal of Economics*, 5, (1974) 125—144.

Levy, H., "The CAPM and Beta in an Imperfect Market", *Journal of Portfolio Management*, Winter 1980.

Lewellen, Wilbur G., Lease, Ronald C. and Schlarbaum, Gary G., "Portfolio Design and Portfolio Performance: the Individual Investor", *Journal of Economics and Business*, Spring/Summer 1980.

Lin, Winston T. and Jen, Frank C., "Consumption, Investment, Market Price of Risk, and the Risk-Free Rate", *Journal of Financial and Quantitative Analysis*, December 1980.

Lintner, John, "The Valuation of Risk Assets and the Selection of Risky Investments in Stock Portfolios and Capital Budgets", *Review of Economics and Statistics*, February 1965.

Lintner, John, "Security Prices, Risk and Maximal Gains from Diversification", *Journal of Finance*, December 1965.

Lintner, John, "The Aggregation of Investors' Diverse Judgments and Preferences in Purely Competitive Security Markets", *Journal of Financial and Quantitative Analysis*, December 1960.

Litzenberger, Robert H. and Budd, Alan P., "Corporate Investment Criteria and the Valuation of Risk Assets", *Journal of Financial and Quantitative Analysis*, December 1970.

Litzenberger, Robert H. and Joy, O.M., "Target Rates of Return and Corporate Asset and Liability Structure under Uncertainty", *Journal of Financial and Quantitative Analysis*, March 1971.

Merton, R.C., "Theory of Finance from the Perspective of Continuous Time", *Journal of Financial and Quantitative Analysis*, November 1975.

Milne, Frank and Smith, Clifford Jr., "Capital Asset Pricing with Proportional Transaction Costs", *Journal of Financial and Quantitative Analysis*, June 1980.

Myers, S.C. and Turnbull, S.M., "Capital Budgeting and the Capital Asset Pricing Model: Good News and Bad News", *Journal of Finance*, May 1977.

Nielson, N.C., "The Investment Decision of the Firm under Uncertainty and the Allocative Efficiency of Capital Markets", *Journal of Finance*, May 1976.

Officer, R.R., "Seasonality in Australian Capital Markets: Market Efficiency and Empirical Issues", *Journal of Financial Economics*, March 1975.

Owen, Joel and Rabinowitch, Ramon, "The Cost of Information and Equilibrium in the Capital Asset Market", *Journal of Financial and Quantitative Analysis*, September 1980.

Perrakis, Stylianos, "Capital Budgeting and Timing Uncertainty Within the Capital Asset Pricing Model", *Financial Management*, Autumn 1979.

Rabinovitch, R. and Owen, J., "Nonhomogeneous Expectations and Information in the Capital Asset Market", *Journal of Finance*, May 1979.

Rendleman, Richard J. Jr., "Ranking Errors in CAPM Capital Budgeting Applications", *Financial Management*, Winter 1978.

Robichek, Alexander A. and Cohn, Richard A., "The Economic Determinants of Systematic Risk", *Journal of Finance*, May 1974.

Roenfeldt, R.L., Griepentrof, G.L. and Pflaum, C.C., "Further Evidence on the Stationarity of Beta Coefficients", *Journal of Financial and Quantitative Analysis*, March 1978.

Roll, R., "Ambiguity when Performance is Measured by the Securities Market Line", *Journal of Finance*, September 1978.

Roll, R., "A Critique of the Asset Pricing Theory's Tests: Part I: On Past and Potential Testability of the Theory", *Journal of Financial Economics*, March 1977.

Roll, R. and Ross, S., "An Empirical Investigation of the Arbitrage Pricing Theory", *Journal of Finance*, December 1980.

Ross, S.A., "The Capital Asset Pricing Model (CAPM), Short-Sale Restrictions and Related Issues", *Journal of Finance*, March 1977.

Ross, S.A., "The Current Status of the Capital Asset Pricing Model (CAPM)", *Journal of Finance*, June 1978.

Scholes, M. and Williams, J., "Estimating Betas from Nonsynchronous Data", Journal of Financial Economics, December 1977.

Scott, E. and Brown, S., "Biased Estimators and Unstable Betas", *Journal of Finance*, March 1980.

Sharpe, William F., "Capital Asset Prices: A Theory of Market Equilibrium", *Journal of Finance*, September 1964.

Sharpe, William F., *Portfolio Theory and Capital Markets*, New York: McGraw-Hill, 1970.

Smith, K.V., "The Effect of Intervaling on Estimating Parameters of the Capital Asset Pricing Model", *Journal of Financial and Quantitative Analysis*, June 1978.

Stapleton, Richard C., "Portfolio Analysis, Stock Valuation and Capital Budgeting Decision Rules for Risky Projects", *Journal of Finance*, March 1971.

Stapleton, R.C. and Subrahmanyam, M.G., "Market Imperfections, Capital Market Equilibrium and Corporation Finance", *Journal of Finance*, May 1977.

Stapleton, R.C. and Subrahmanyam, M.G., "Marketability of Assets and the Price of Risk", *Journal of Financial and Quantitative Analysis*, March 1979.

Theobald, Michael, "An Analysis of the Market Model and Beta Factors Using U.K. Equity Share Data", *Journal of Business Finance and Accounting*, Spring 1980.

Trauring, M., "A Capital Asset Pricing Model with Investors' Taxes and Three Categories of Investment Income", *Journal of Financial and Quantitative Analysis*, September 1979.

Treynor, J.L., "Toward a Theory of Market Value of Risky Assets", *Unpublished manuscript*.

Turnbull, S.M., "Value and Systematic Risk", *Journal of Finance*, September 1977.

Umstead, D.A. and Bergstrom, G.L., "Dynamic Estimation of Portfolio Betas", *Journal of Financial and Quantitative Analysis*, September 1979.

Weston J. Fred, "Investment Decisions Using the Capital Asset Pricing Model", *Financial Management*, Spring 1973.

Williams, J.T., "Capital Asset Prices with Heterogeneous Beliefs", *Journal of Financial Economics*, Novemebr 1977.

PART II: SUGGESTIONS FOR FURTHER READING

The reader who has become interested in probability might still profit from the classic survey by Keynes:

J.M. Keynes, *A Treatise on Probability*, London, Macmillan, 1921.

The utility foundations of modern risk analysis can be found in:

J. von Neumann and O. Morgenstern, *Theory of Games and Economic Behavior*, 2nd edition, Princeton N.J., Princeton University Press, 1947.

K. Borch, *The Economics of Uncertainty*, Princeton N.J., Princeton University Press, 1968.

K.J. Arrow, *Essays in Risk Bearing*, Amsterdam, North Holland Press, 1970.

Useful collections of articles are to be found in:

K. Borch and J.E. Mossin (eds.), *Risk and Uncertainty*, London, Macmillan, 1968.

W. Edwards and A. Tversky, *Decision Making*, Harmondsworth, England, Penguin, 1967.

The mean-variance portfolio approach to decision-making was first set out in the classic works of Harry Markowitz and James Tobin.

H.M. Markowitz, "Portfolio Selection", *Journal of Finance*, March 1952.

H.M. Markowitz, *Portfolio Selection: Efficient Diversification of Investments*, New York, Wiley, 1959.

J. Tobin, "Liquidity Preference as Behavior Towards Risk", *Review of Economic Studies*, February 1958.

Building on this foundation the capital asset pricing model was developed in the mid 1960s:

W.F. Sharpe, "Capital Asset Prices: A Theory of Market Equilibrium", *Journal of Finance*, September 1964.

J. Lintner, "The Valuation of Risk Assets and the Selection of Risky Investments in Stock Portfolios and Capital Budgets", *Review of Economics and Statistics*, February 1965.

J. Mossin, "Equilibrium in a Capital Assets Market", *Econometrica*, October 1966.

E.F. Fama, "Risk Return and Equilibrium: Some Clarifying Comments", *Journal of Finance*, March 1968.

More recent extensions have been made by:

F. Black, "Capital Market Equilibrium With Restricted Borrowing", *Journal of Business*, July 1972.

R.C. Merton, "An Inter-temporal Capital Asset Pricing Model", *Econometrica*, 1973.

S.A. Ross, "The Arbitrage Theory of Capital Asset Pricing", *Econometrica*, Volume 13, 1976.

Less technically demanding introductions to portfolio theory and capital asset pricing can be found in:

R.A. Brealey, *An Introduction to Risk and Return from Common Stocks*, Cambridge, Mass., M.I.T. Press, 1969.

W.F. Sharpe, *Portfolio Theory and Capital Markets*, New York, McGraw-Hill, 1971.

E.J. Elton and M.J. Gruber, *Modern Portfolio Theory and Investment Analysis*, New York, Wiley, 1981.

The empirical evidence and problems regarding its interpretation are surveyed by:

I. Friend, "Recent Developments in Finance", *Journal of Banking and Finance*, Vol. 1 No. 2, 1977.

R. Roll, "A Critique of the Asset Pricing Theory's Tests; Part 1: On Past and Potential Testability of the Theory", *Journal of Financial Economics*, March 1977.

Specific applications of risk analysis and portfolio theory to capital budgeting can be found in:

C.J. Grayson Jr., *Decisions Under Uncertainty: Drilling Decisions by Oil and Gas Operators*, Boston, Mass., Division of Research, Harvard Business School, 1960.

S.C. Myers, "Procedures for Capital Budgeting Under Uncertainty", *Industrial Management Review*, Spring 1968.

R.H. Litzenberger and A.P. Budd, "Corporate Investment Criteria and the Valuation of Risk Assets", *Journal of Financial and Quantitative Analysis*, December 1970.

R.S. Hamada, "Investment Decisions with a General Equilibrium Approach", *Quarterly Journal of Economics*, November 1971.

R.C. Stapleton, "Portfolio Analysis, Stock Valuation and Capital Budgeting for Risky Projects", *Journal of Finance*, March 1971.

M.E. Rubenstein, "A Mean Variance Synthesis of Corporate Financial Theory", *Journal of Finance*, March 1973.

Part III
Long-term Financial Decisions

Introduction

To this point we have avoided a direct confrontation with financing decisions and the concept of the cost of capital. In the preceding chapters which were devoted to the analysis of investment decisions (under certainty and uncertainty) we explicitly assumed that the cost of capital problem was solved, thereby permitting the use of a given "riskless" or "risky" discount rate, as the analysis required. Questions relating to the economic determinants of the cost of capital and its measurement were carefully swept under a by now bulging carpet. However, postponement of the discussion until now, should *not* be construed as an indication that the cost of capital has only a secondary impact on financial decision-making. On the contrary, the cost of capital is of crucial importance since it serves as one of the direct determinants of the acceptability of capital investments within the individual firm, and therefore constitutes a key determinant of the economy's aggregate level of investment as well. Postponement of the analysis merely reflects the subject's complexity, and our hope is that the reader will be better prepared to handle this controversial subject, now that he has the fundamental tools of financial analysis under his belt.

Chapters 14 through 16 are devoted to the analysis of the impact of financial leverage on stockholders' earnings and risk; the relationship of financial structure to the value of the firm's securities; and the factors determining the firm's *optimal* financing mix, i.e. the financial structure which maximizes the market value of the firm to its shareholders. In Chapter 17 we define the cost of capital, which, of course, is a function of the firm's market value, and hence also depends directly on the choice of financial structure; and in Chapter 18 a method for measuring the cost of capital is spelled out, thereby providing a practical solution to the problem of determining a firm's cut-off rate on new investments. Chapter 19 discusses the recurring problem of dividend policy. Chapter 20 uses techniques of linear programming to analyze the importance of capital rationing on corporate investment decisions. Chapter 21 is devoted to the analysis of the lease or buy decision. The book's final chapter is devoted to perhaps the most important problem which has confronted corporate management in this decade — the impact of inflation on corporate planning and decision-making.

14

Financial Leverage

In the preceding chapters we assumed that the firm's risk-return profile could be changed only by altering its investment program. In this chapter we deal with an alternative means of influencing earnings and risk, by changing the firm's financial mix. Here we take the firm's investment program and its business risk as given, and seek to determine the influence of changes in capital structure on the rate of return, with a view to finding the particular capital structure which affords the best expected return-risk combination.

FINANCIAL LEVERAGE AND EARNINGS

What effect does financial leverage, i.e. the introduction of fixed-interest-bearing debt (or preferred stock), have on the return to the firm's shareholders and on the risk level of its common stock? To answer this question we start by considering a new company which faces a decision regarding its capital structure, that is, a decision with respect to the best debt-equity mix with which to finance its operations. For simplicity, let us initially assume that there are only two mutually exclusive alternatives: (A) financing the firm with 100% equity, and (B) financing the firm with equal amounts of stock and bonds; and that there are no taxes levied on either the firm's income or that of the shareholders.

Table 14.1 sets out the relevant data for these two alternatives. Since we are discussing two alternative financial plans for the same company, the operating income (earnings before interest) remains constant in both. Note also that the distribution of the operating income, and therefore the degree of business risk attached to these earnings, must be the same in both alternatives. The net income in alternative B declines from $1,000 to $750 since (by assumption) 5% interest must be paid on the $5,000 of capital raised via bonds. But as fewer shares are issued in alternative B, earnings per share (*EPS*), which is the relevant return to

331

Table 14.1

	Alternative A (100% equity) $	Alternative B (50% bonds, 50% equity) $
Net Operating Income (NOI)	1,000	1,000
Interest (5% on bonds)	—	250
Net Income (NI)	1,000	750
Capitalization:		
Stock	10,000	5,000
Bonds	—	5,000
Total Stocks and Bonds	10,000	10,000
Number of Shares	1,000	500
Earnings per Share (EPS)	**1.00**	**1.50**

the shareholders, rises in alternative B from \$1.00 to \$1.50. The change in *EPS* induced by the use of fixed payment securities to finance a company's operations is often referred to as *financial leverage:* the bonds in the example serving as a lever, so to speak, which raises *EPS* for a given net operating income (*NOI*). The reason for this is not hard to find: although the company pays out 5% interest on the bonds, it earns a return of 10% on the capital invested, thereby raising the return to the common shareholders. And since we are considering a case without taxes, substitution of a 5% preferred share for the bonds will result in the same leverage effect as the bonds.

If we introduce corporate taxes (say at the rate of 50%), net income will be reduced by one-half in both examples and *EPS* (after taxes) will be \$0.50 and \$0.75 in alternatives A and B respectively. The general line of reasoning remains the same; although the firms pays out 5% on the bonds, the effective cost in terms of after-tax income is only $(1 - T)r$, where T denotes the corporate tax rate and r the rate of interest. This reduction in the cost of debt follows directly from the tax deduction afforded interest payments. In our particular example the after-tax cost of the debt is $(1 - 0.50) \cdot 0.05 = 2\frac{1}{2}\%$. Since the firm earns a net *after-tax* return of 5% without leverage, the leverage effect again results from the difference between the effective (after-tax) rate of outlay on the bonds,[1] $2\frac{1}{2}\%$, and the (after-tax) rate of return earned by the company on the capital invested, 5%.

FINANCIAL LEVERAGE AND RISK

Financial leverage is a two-edged sword. In the previous example, we saw that the introduction of fixed-interest bearing securities in the capital structure can

---

1 Note, however, that in the after-tax example cited, substituting a 5% preferred stock no longer creates a leverage effect because the dividend paid on preferred stock is *not* tax deductible. The after-tax "cost" of the preferred dividend is 5%, that is just equal to the company's after-tax rate of return on invested capital, and the *EPS* remains constant or \$0.50.

Table 14.2

	Alternative A (100% equity) Probability		Alternative B (50% bonds, 50% equity) Probability	
	1/2	1/2	1/2	1/2
	$	$	$	$
Net Operating Income	1,000	250	1,000	250
Interest (5% on bonds)	—	—	250	250
Net Income	1,000	250	750	0
Capitalization:				
Stock	10,000	10,000	5,000	5,000
Bonds	—	—	5,000	5,000
Total Stocks and Bonds	10,000	10,000	10,000	10,000
Number of Shares	1,000	1,000	500	500
Earnings per Share (EPS)	1.00	0.25	1.50	0
Expected Value of EPS*	0.625		0.75	
Variance of EPS*	0.14		0.56	

* The expected value of EPS of firm A is given by $1/2 \times 1 + 1/2 \times 0.25 = \$0.625$ and its variance is calculated as follows: $1/2 \ (1 - 0.625)^2 + 1/2 \ (0.25 - 0.625)^2 = 0.14$ Similarly the expected value and variance of the EPS of firm B are given by $1/2 \times 1.50 + 1/2 \times 0 = \$0.75$ and $1/2 \ (1.50 - 0.75)^2 + 1/2 \ (0-0.75)^2 = 0.56$ respectively.

raise *EPS*, but upon reflection it might in certain circumstances also decrease *EPS*. This possibility of *negative* leverage creates a new type of financial risk, in addition to the business risk already inherent in the company's operations. How does negative leverage arise?

Surely, the firm does not *plan* to reduce *EPS*. The possible negative effects of leverage can be seen more clearly if we explicitly recognize that the firm's net operating income is not usually a constant. Consider again the example given in Table 14.1 above. (For simplicity only, we shall continue to use the example of a world without taxes.) Although the company expects an average annual income of $1,000, this expectation usually is not held with certainty. In general, earnings will fluctuate, so that in any given year the income from operations may be greater or less than $1,000. And of course there also might be some probability (presumably small) of incurring a loss in a particular year.

Let us assume that the firm's expectation regarding future net operating income can be characterized by the following distribution: $1,000 with a probability of 1/2 and $250 with a probability of 1/2. This assumption is incorporated explicitly in Table 14.2. Note that each alternative now has two outcomes (columns) corresponding to the two possible outcomes of future *NOI*. As can be seen from Table 14.2, introducing debt into the capital structure increases the *expected value* of the earnings per share from $0.625 to $0.75, but the leverage also has an impact on risk. If the net operating income turns out to be $1,000, leverage increases the *EPS* from $1.00 to $1.50; however, there is also a 50% likelihood of a less favorable result, i.e. of a net operating income of only $250. Should this occur, the use of debt will decrease the *EPS* from $0.25 to zero.

In general, we must take both the "bad" and the "good" into account if the financial decision is to properly reflect the underlying uncertainty of business life. Hence we calculate the variance (or standard deviation) of *EPS* as well as its expected value. Table 14.2 shows that the levered alternative is characterized by both a higher expected *EPS* and a higher variance, i.e. a greater variability of earnings. This result confronts financial management with the difficult problem of finding a way to weigh and compare the advantages and disadvantages of leverage. A first step in this direction is to evaluate the interaction between the firm's business and financial risks.

BUSINESS RISK vs FINANCIAL RISK

A firm's *business* or *economic risk* is related to the industry to which it belongs and to the general conditions of the economy. For example, the business risk of public utilities is usually significantly less than that of manufacturing firms. This reflects the tendency for the fluctuations in the demand for the services provided by utilities such as American Telephone and Telegraph to be small relative to industrial firms, the demand for whose products tends to be more unstable. This instability often reflects changes in fashion, or in the real income of consumers or shifts in the level of competition. Even if we assume that firms never issue debt, we would still expect to find a higher variability in the earnings per share of industrial firms than in the *EPS* of utilities. Thus we usually say that industrial firms have a greater *business risk* than public utilities. Moreover this risk is a function of general economic conditions and is *not* related to the firm's financial structure. Therefore, the variability of net operating income (or *NOI* per share), which is the firm's income *before* any interest payments, is an appropriate measure of such risk.

As we have previously noted, introducing financial leverage intensifies the variability of *EPS*, and we shall denote the *additional* variance of earnings induced by leverage as *financial risk*. The decision of a firm to enter a particular line of economic endeavour or undertake a particular investment program affects its economic risk; the decision to finance the investment (partially or completely) with debt determines the firm's financial risk. Clearly, the individual who holds the firm's stock is vulnerable to total risk, i.e. to the firm's business as well as its financial risk. In Table 14.2 above, the variance of alternative A, which represents a case of pure equity financing, is 0.14. This variance of the unlevered earnings measures the firm's business risk. Alternative B gives the results for the same firm, should it decide to introduce 50% debt. The variability of the *EPS* in the latter case is higher, i.e. 0.56, since this variance reflects *both* the economic as well as the financial risk.[2] However, only the 0.14 variance is due to business risk; the additional 0.42 is generated by the financial risk incurred from the use of debt.

---

2 For a discussion of leverage in the context of the Capital Asset Pricing Model, see Chapter 15 below.

GRAPHICAL SIMULATION

As we have seen, introducing financial leverage usually increases the average profitability of the firm as well as its risk. In good economic years the impact of financial leverage will most likely be positive, however the leverage effect may be negative in relatively bad years. One of the crucial tasks of management is to attempt to evaluate the risks of the leverage by forecasting the changes of "good" versus "bad" economic conditions. This task can be facilitated by using a special version of the well-known tool, Break-Even Analysis, in order to simulate the impact of financial leverage on *EPS* for varying levels of output and sales, or alternatively, for different levels of net operating income.[3]

Table 14.3

Alternative A: 100% Equity								
Net Operating Income	1,500	1,250	1,000	750	500	250	0	−500
Interest	—	—	—	—	—	—	—	—
Net Income	1,500	1,250	1,000	750	500	250	0	−500
Number of Shares	1,000	1,000	1,000	1,000	1,000	1,000	1,000	1,000
Earnings per Share	1.50	1.25	1.00	0.75	0.50	0.25	0	−0.50
Alternative B: 50% Shares, 50% Bonds								
Net Operating Income	1,500	1,250	1,000	750	500	250	0	−500
Interest	250	250	250	250	250	250	250	250
Net Income	1,250	1,000	750	500	250	0	−250	−750
Number of Shares	500	500	500	500	500	500	500	500
Earnings per Share	2.50	2.00	1.50	1.00	0.50	0	−0.50	−1.50

Table 14.3 sets out the earnings per share for the two alternative financing plans (A = 100% equity and B = 50% equity and 50% bonds) over a wide range of possible levels of future net operating incomes. A glance at the data of Table 14.3 shows that the financial leverage is positive (raises *EPS*) for *NOI* greater than $500, but is negative (decreases *EPS*) for cases in which the *NOI* is less than $500. The leverage is neutral (leaves *EPS* unchanged) for the cases in which *NOI* = $500. Hence, the "break-even" point in this example is $500. For levels of *NOI* above $500, the firm earns a rate of return on invested capital in excess of the 5% paid to the bondholders, thereby raising the *EPS* to its common shareholders; conversely, should net operating earnings fall below $500, the firm will earn less than 5% on its assets, so the bondholders can be compensated only at the "expense" of the shareholders, which reduces *EPS*.

The differential impact of financial leverage is illustrated in Fig. 14.1 which graphs *EPS* as a function of *NOI*. The dashed line ZZ which goes through the break-even point divides the chart into two sections; all points to the right of this line representing positive leverage (+), and all points to the left

---

3 A more general exposition of the derivation of the break-even point is given in the Appendix to this chapter.

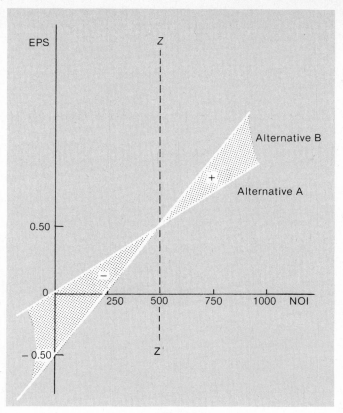

Fig. 14.1

representing negative leverage (−). Since risk is associated with the degree of fluctuation, the graph shows that the financial risk associated with the mixed capital structure (alternative B) is greater than that associated with the all equity structure (alternative A). The greater riskiness is reflected in the *steeper* slope of line B; for each per unit change in *NOI*, the induced change in *EPS* is greater in the case of the levered capital structure. Despite the identical economic risk (we are making alternative assumptions about the financing of the same company) the introduction of leverage magnifies the fluctuations of *EPS*, thereby increasing the risk associated with the investment in common stock. It follows that the riskiness of an investment in the shares of a company with a levered capital structure exceeds the risk associated with the same shares when the capital structure is unlevered.

　　This relationship can be seen even more clearly from Fig. 14.2 which plots the hypothetical fluctuations of *EPS* over time. The solid line, labeled A, represents the assumed fluctuations when the company is financed solely by common stock; the dotted line, marked B, represents the fluctuations in *EPS* for the same operating incomes when the firm is financed by equal proportions of bonds and stock. Note that the introduction of leverage magnifies the variability of the income stream to the shareholders in both directions. Once

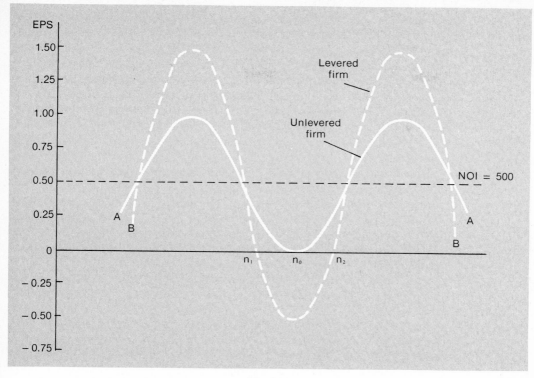

Fig. 14.2

again, the leverage break-down point is given by *NOI* = 500, which corresponds to the point *EPS* = 0.50 on the vertical axis of Fig. 14.2. (The guideline marked "*NOI* = 500" has been added to identify the critical points where the leverage changes from positive to negative.) Note also that while the firm never suffers an operating loss (we assume zero profits in only one year, point n_0 on the horizontal axis), when leverage is introduced, losses are incurred during the period between n_1 and n_2.

FACTORS DETERMINING THE CHOICE OF FINANCIAL STRUCTURE

In a fanciful world of no risk, in which the future volume of sales, prices, costs, and hence profits are known with absolute certainty, the use of financial leverage presents no particular difficulty. Given these unrealistic assumptions, management would know the exact point on the horizontal axis of Fig. 14.1 which denotes a future year's *NOI*. If the leverage is positive the firm would use a maximum of debt to finance its investments since in such a case, the greater the leverage the higher will be the *EPS*. On the other hand, if we knew *with certainty* that the *NOI* is located to the left of the break-even point, i.e., the leverage is negative, the optimal solution would be to finance the firm with 100% equity.

These two extreme solutions really have no practical significance, the actual problem facing the financial manager is to choose a financial strategy (capital structure) in a realistic setting in which future sales prices, costs, and hence net operating income, are uncertain. That is to say, he does *not* know in advance if the *NOI* will always lie to the right of the break-even point. Consequently, the firm cannot be certain that the financial leverage will be positive.

Essentially, the impact of financial leverage, given the realistic assumption that uncertainty prevails, can be reduced to three alternative scenarios:

(a) Situations in which leverage increases risk, but at the same time decreases expected *EPS*;

(b) neutral situations in which the increase of risk following the introduction of leverage leaves expected *EPS* unchanged;

(c) and finally, situations in which the introduction of leverage increases expected *EPS* and risk simultaneously.

These alternative situations are described schematically in Fig. 14.3. The three solid curves in the diagram describe the *EPS* probability distributions of a firm financed by 100% equity; thus, these curves present a pictorial description of the firm's expected profit and business risk. Future *EPS* is not known with certainty, and the solid curves set out the probabilities of occurrence for various alternatives of *EPS*.

The dashed curves in the same diagram represent the probability distribution of *EPS* when leverage is introduced. In all three cases leverage increases the variability of earnings, i.e., leverage increases shareholders' risk. Diagrammatically, the dashed curves are flatter which reflects the fact that leverage *increases* variability (risk). However, the three curves which are drawn in Fig. 14.3 differ with respect to the degree of impact that leverage has on expected (mean) earnings.

Figure 14.3(a) depicts a situation in which leverage increases risk but decreases expected *EPS*. This can occur if the mean post-tax unlevered *EPS* is less than the post-tax interest cost. In such an instance one would expect the firm to adopt an unlevered financial strategy. The second alternative is illustrated in Fig. 14.3(b). In this case, introducing leverage increases the variability of the *EPS* but the mean *EPS* is unaffected. This can occur should the mean unlevered *EPS* be just equal to the after-tax interest cost. Again, the optimal strategy is to eschew the use of leverage, since introducing debt does *not* raise profitability, but does increase risk.

Although the first two cases conceivably could occur in real life they are relatively uninteresting; in both instances the firm would simply forgo debt financing completely. The only relevant, and by far the most challenging situation confronting financial management is the third alternative in which the use of leverage increases both *EPS* and risk. This type of scenario is depicted in Fig. 14.3(c). Here, the introduction of leverage increases expected *EPS* and risk simultaneously. In this instance, the expected *EPS* of the unlevered firm exceeds the after-tax interest cost; hence any increase in the degree of leverage increases expected profitability. In terms of Fig. 14.3(c), the mean of the levered alternative (dashed curve) lies to the right of the mean of the unlevered distribution.

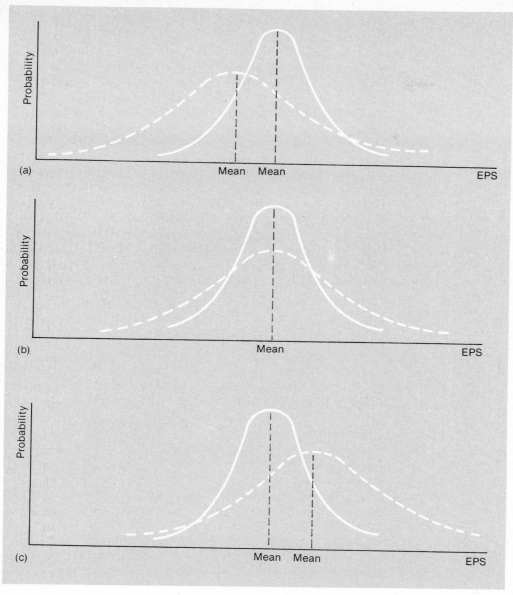

(a)   Mean Mean   EPS

(b)   Mean   EPS

(c)   Mean Mean   EPS

Fig. 14.3

Again the increase in variance is reflected by the relative flatness of the dashed curve. Unfortunately the solution to the financing problem in this case, which incidentally characterizes almost all firms, is neither straightforward nor simple. The analysis of the tradeoff between the increased profitability and greater risk engendered by the use of leverage will occupy us for the remainder of this, and for the next, chapter. Here we shall briefly discuss some of the basic factors which can affect a firm's financing policy; a more rigorous analysis of capital structure, which requires considerations of stock valuation, is postponed to the next chapter.

In reality the firm's long-term financing decision can be influenced by a variety of considerations. Among these we find the following.

Location of Earnings Distribution

The willingness of a firm to accept the increased risk which is engendered by the use of financial leverage depends on the characteristics of the distribution of earnings. Other things being equal, the lower the probability of negative leverage, the greater will be the recourse to the use of financial leverage. Thus firms with relatively high rates of operating profit can better afford to undertake the risk of greater leverage which in turn further magnifies their net earnings. Financial leverage, on the other hand, can become a dangerous strategy when employed by the firm with an inadequate operating profit base. Once again, management is confronted by the fact that in the world of finance the old adage "to him that has, is given" tends to hold with almost frustrating frequency.

Stability of Sales and Earnings

Another key factor which determines the range of earnings, and hence the amount of debt that the firm borrows, is the stability of sales, which in turn influences the stability of operating earnings. The more stable the earnings, the better the chances that the firm can meet its fixed charges and obligations. Thus we expect firms having relatively stable earnings to finance a larger proportion of their investments with debt.

Figure 14.4 describes two firms whose average earnings before interest and taxes are identical, but which differ in the stability of their earnings streams. Three alternative financing strategies (pure equity, 25% debt and 50% debt) are assumed for each of the two firms. The shaded areas of Fig. 14.4 denote the anticipated *range* of possible operating results. The reader should note that the range of outcomes is considerably greater in the case of firm B which reflects the assumption that that firm has less stable operating earnings.

Now let's suppose that both firms adopt the same financial strategy of financing their operations with 50% debt. (Such a policy is represented in Fig. 14.4 by the two lines marked "50% debt".) A comparison of the two cases shows that the probability of the first firm's *EPS* being negative is very small; hence there is also a good chance that its fixed interest charges will be covered out of normal operating income. Clearly this conclusion does not hold for firm B. Should that firm adopt a 50% leverage ratio there would exist a relatively large probability that the *NOI* will fall in the range of operating events for which *EPS* is negative, which implies that the firm would be unable to pay its fixed interest charges out of current operating earnings. In order to achieve a comparable degree of certainty regarding the coverage of its fixed interest

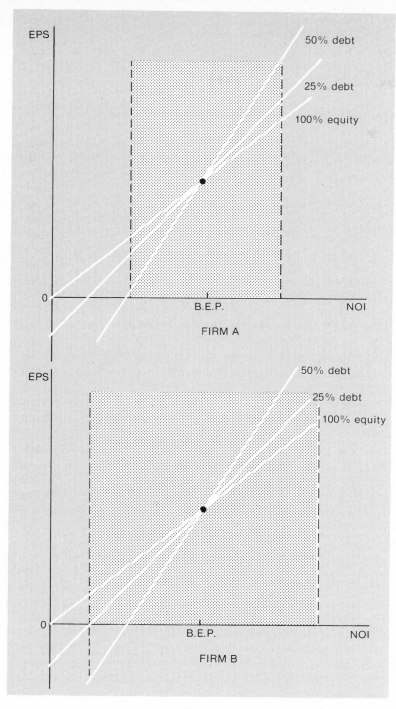

Fig. 14.4

payments firm B would have to reduce the proportion of debt in its capital structure to 25% (see Fig. 14.4).

Risk of Bankruptcy[4]

This factor is also strongly associated with the stability of sales and earnings. A firm with highly unstable earnings will be reluctant to adopt a high degree of leverage, since conceivably it might be unable to meet its fixed obligations at all! Negative earnings in any one year do not usually induce bankruptcy, but a firm which experiences a loss over a series of consecutive years may find itself in very serious financial straits. Clearly, for a given pattern of sales and earnings, the higher the financial leverage, the higher the probability that the firm will face such a series of losses, and hence the higher is the risk of bankruptcy.

The chances of bankruptcy do not depend solely on the statistical distribution of earnings, but also on the firm's assets and borrowing power. For example, some firms can more readily sell off some of their assets in order to meet debt charges which also enhances the collateral value of such assets, thereby increasing the firm's borrowing power as well; while others hold relatively large cash reserves. In general the greater the firm's liquidity, either from holding cash assets or from the convertibility of its other assets to cash, the smaller will be its vulnerability to bankruptcy and the greater will be its willingness to undertake the risks of leverage.

Dividend Policy

Although the analysis of a firm's dividend policy is deferred to Chapter 19 below, it is noteworthy that almost all firms attach great importance to achieving an "unbroken" dividend record, i.e. one in which the dividend payment is never skipped or even temporarily reduced. The implications of such an objective for financial policy are straightforward — for any given dividend rate, the higher the leverage ratio, other things being equal, the greater is the chance that the firm will be unable to meet its dividend payments out of current operating income.

The relationship between leverage and dividend policy is illustrated in Fig. 14.5 which sets out the break-even chart for a hypothetical firm, assuming three alternative financing strategies — pure equity, 25% debt and 50% debt; and two alternative dividend policies — cash dividends of 45 cents or one dollar per share. Figure 14.5 clearly shows that the greater the leverage ratio the higher is the chance of not meeting the cash dividend out of operating earnings. For example, under the pure equity option, the 45 cent dividend will not be covered if *NOI* falls in the range labeled OA; however, as debt financing is successively increased to 25% and 50%, larger operating incomes are required to ensure

---

4 Bankruptcy risk is analyzed in greater detail in Chapter 16.

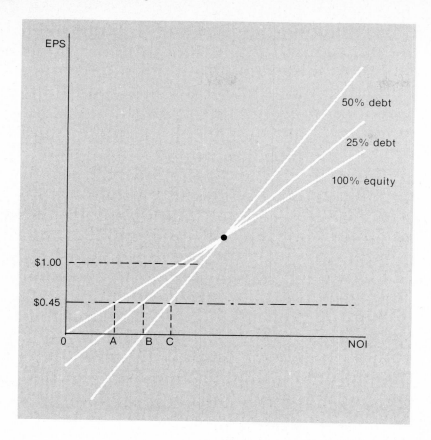

EPS

50% debt

25% debt

100% equity

$1.00

$0.45

0   A   B   C

NOI

Fig. 14.5

dividend coverage. In the case of 25% leverage, *NOI* must exceed OB; should a 50% leverage ratio be adopted the *NOI* must lie to the right of point C. Similarly, a higher dividend payout, say one dollar per share, also shifts the "dividend coverage point" to the right.

Control

In some cases, firms may resort to the use of intensive leverage in order to retain effective control over the corporation. A loss of control might occur, for example, should the company issue additional shares to the public. In such an instance the firm might well prefer to use additional debt rather than issue equity even though the debt increases the risk beyond what otherwise might be considered as a critical maximum.

OPERATING LEVERAGE vs FINANCIAL LEVERAGE

A major disadvantage of financial leverage is that it increases the variability of earnings. Hence, in establishing its financial strategy each firm is confronted with a difficult decision regarding the amount of risk which it is willing to undertake. In this context it is worthwhile noting that any given risk level can be achieved in principle either by changing the firm's financial structure or by changing its asset structure. The larger the proportion of its fixed assets, the greater is its *operating leverage*, and such a firm might be expected to adopt a relatively conservative financial leverage ratio.[5]

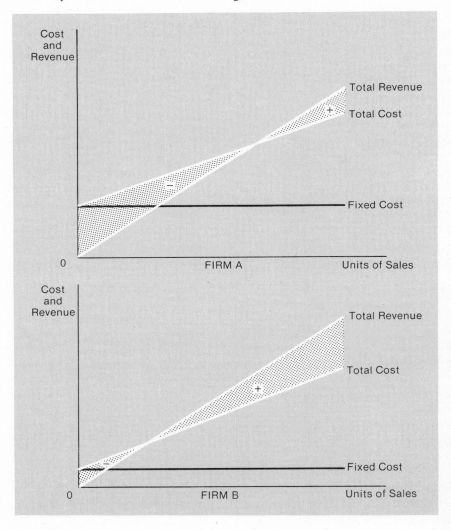

Fig. 14.6

5 For evidence of the relationship between operating leverage and risk, see Baruch Lev, "On the Association Between Operating Leverage and Risk", *Journal of Financial and Quantitative Analysis*, September 1974.

Figure 14.6 sets out operating leverage charts for two firms which differ only in the composition of their assets. Both firms sell the same product at the same price and hence have the same total revenue. However, firm A has a higher operating leverage; its variable cost is lower and its fixed investment is higher than those of firm B. The fact that firm A has a *lower* variable cost is reflected in the smaller slope of its "total cost" function, which for diagramatic simplicity is assumed to be linear.

Clearly, the operating break-even points of the two firms are *not* identical. Moreover, a per unit shift of sales induces a relatively greater change in the profit (or loss) of firm A. This follows from our assumption that the difference in the slopes of the "total cost" and the "total revenue" lines of firm A is greater than the difference between the slopes of the relevant cost and revenue lines of firm B. Firms with relatively high fixed costs and operating leverage, and which as a result, are also characterized by relatively high variability of operating earnings, might reach their desired risk levels by adopting a relatively conservative debt policy. Conversely, firms with lower operating leverage might conceivably reach the same target risk level with a far larger debt-equity ratio; the willingness to undertake the additional financial risk, reflecting, in this instance, the greater stability of the underlying operating earnings stream.

The "tradeoff" between operating and financial leverage is illustrated in Table 14.4 by means of a simple numerical example. In actual practice, of course, these two strategies are not perfect substitutes, as the over-simplified example might seem to imply, however both do affect the variability of earnings per share in the same direction. In the example we have assumed that there is an equal probability of sales being 100,000 or 500,000 units. Each unit is sold for $1 and hence the total revenue is either $100,000 or $500,000. Firm A has a larger operating leverage, since its fixed cost is $50,000, as compared with only $35,000 for firm B. However, firm A is a pure equity company; the firm issued

Table 14.4

	Firm A		Firm B	
	"Bad" Year	"Good" Year	"Bad" Year	"Good" Year
	$	$	$	$
Sales	100,000	500,000	100,000	500,000
Fixed cost not including interest	50,000	50,000	35,000	35,000
Interest	—	—	5,000	5,000
Total fixed cost	50,000	50,000	40,000	40,000
Variable cost	50,000	250,000	60,000	300,000
Total cost	100,000	300,000	100,000	340,000
Net earning before tax	0	200,000	0	160,000
Corporate Tax	0	100,000	0	80,000
Net earning after corporate tax	0	100,000	0	80,000
Number of shares	100,000	100,000	80,000	80,000
Earnings per share	**0**	**$1.00**	**0**	**$100**

100,000 shares at $5 each, i.e. its total equity equals $500,000. Firm B, on the other hand issued only 80,000 shares of $5 each, and an additional $100,000 worth of bonds bearing interest at the rate of 5%. The variable cost of firm A is assumed to be 50 cents per unit, while the variable cost of firm B (with the low fixed cost) is higher — 60 cents per unit. Taking all this data into account, the earnings per share of both firms will either be zero or $1.00, depending on the actual sales realized.

Thus, the two firms offer the same variability of earnings to their stock-holders. This goal is achieved in the case of firm B through the use of more intensive financial leverage; and in firm A, by a combination of a higher operating leverage with a lower level of debt financing. But choosing between financial and operating leverage is not as simple as it might seem. In many cases the firm has only limited discretion regarding its plant and equipment, and in other instances the variable costs are not linear, a fact which greatly complicates the firm's calculations. The modest objective of the above example is merely to point out that the firm must consider the impact of *both* kinds of leverage when setting its financial strategy, and that a good rule to remember is the higher the operating leverage, the more risky is the recourse to financial leverage.

SUMMARY

This chapter has been devoted to the analysis of financial leverage. As we have seen financial leverage is a two-edged sword: if the leverage is *positive* the use of debt raises *EPS*; however should it be *negative EPS* can fall. Although, in general, we may assume that on balance leverage is positive, the use of debt also increases the fluctuations of *EPS*, thereby increasing financial risk. Hence financial management is confronted with the difficult task of weighing the advantages and disadvantages of levering the firm's financial structure. To this end it is convenient to differentiate a firm's business risk from its financial risk. The former is related to the industry to which a company belongs and to the general conditions prevailing in the economy. The variability of the firm's net operating income or *NOI* per share (i.e., earnings before interest and taxes) is an appropriate measure of its business risk. Financial risk, as we have already noted, is associated with the firm's use of leverage. An appropriate measure of this element of risk is the *additional* variance in per share earnings (*EPS*) induced by leverage.

A rather simple device, the financial break-even chart, provides an efficient and useful tool for visualizing the alternative choice situations confronting the firm. Combined with some basic probability concepts, this type of analysis can be used to identify and evaluate some of the factors which may affect a firm's financing strategy.

Location of earnings distribution. Other things being equal, the use of leverage is inversely related to the probability that the leverage will be negative.

Stability of sales and earnings. The more stable a firm's sales and earnings, the greater is the probability that it will be able to meet its fixed charges out of operating income. Hence we expect such a firm to finance a relatively larger proportion of its assets out of debt.

Risk of bankruptcy. Risk of bankruptcy is perhaps the greatest single deterrent to the use of leverage. The degree of such risk again depends on the stability of the earnings distribution as well as on the liquidity of its assets.

Dividend policy. Another deterrent to the use of leverage is the strong desire of many firms never to skip or reduce a regular dividend payment. Since leverage increases the variability of *EPS*, higher leverage ratios increase the probability that the firm will be unable to cover its dividend payments out of current operating revenues.

Control. The desire to retain effective control of a company, on the other hand, could conceivably lead management into adopting a higher debt ratio than would otherwise be desirable in order to avoid issuing additional voting stock.

We conclude this chapter with a brief analysis of the tradeoff between financial and operating leverage. Although the two strategies are not substitutes — many firms find it difficult if not impossible to alter significantly their operating leverage — both affect the variability of *EPS*, and therefore risk, in the same direction. Hence, we may presume that a high degree of instability of earnings due to operating leverage will have a mitigating effect on the firm's willingness to undertake the additional financial risk inherent in a high debt-equity ratio.

We have now carried the analysis of leverage as far as we can without introducing considerations of valuation. In the following two chapters we shall explicitly examine the impact of financial leverage on the value of the firm's securities in order to isolate the factors which determine its optimal financing strategy, i.e. that financial structure which maximizes the market value of the firm to its shareholders.

QUESTIONS AND PROBLEMS

14.1 A new firm is faced with three mutually exclusive alternatives for financing its investments:

(i) Issuing 10,000 shares at $20 each.

(ii) Issuing 7,500 shares at $20 each and an additional $50,000 worth of bonds bearing interest at the rate of 5%.

(iii) Issuing 5,000 shares at $20 each and an additional $100,000 worth of 5% bonds.

Assume that the net operating income is $25,000 and answer the following questions:

(a) Calculate the *EPS* for each alternative, assuming no corporate tax.

(b)   How do you explain the fact that the larger the proportion of the bonds, the higher is the *EPS*?

(c)   Calculate the *EPS* for each alternative, assuming a corporate tax of 48%.

14.2 With respect to question 14.1, assume now that the firm issues preferred stock instead of the bonds.

(a)   Calculate the post-tax *EPS* for each alternative, assuming the substitution of a 5% preferred stock for the bonds.

(b)   How can you explain the difference in your results when preferred stock is used?

(c)   Calculate the post-tax *EPS*, for each alternative, assuming that the firm issues preferred stock which pays dividends at the rate of 6.5%. Explain your results.

14.3 Assume a firm, whose expectation regarding future net operating income can be characterized by the following distribution: $24,000 with a probability of 1/4, $14,000 with a probability of 1/2 and $4,000 with a probability of 1/4.

Assume, also, that the firm has only two mutually exclusive financing alternatives: (a) 100% equity, i.e. 10,000 shares at $10 each and (b) equal amounts of stock and bonds, i.e. 5,000 shares at $10 each and $50,000 bonds bearing interest at the rate of 8%.

(a)   Define "economic risk" and "financial risk".

(b)   Calculate the expected value and variance of *EPS* for each alternative, ignoring corporate taxes.

(c)   Measure the economic risk and the financial risk.

14.4 Does a bakery or a cosmetics manufacturer normally have greater economic risk? Explain.

14.5 How might you explain the fact that mining companies are characterized by a debt component of almost 30%; industrial companies by a debt component of about 50%, and utility companies by a debt component of almost 80%?

14.6 Distinguish between "location of earnings distribution" and "stability of sales and earnings" and try to give a numerical or diagrammatic example to illustrate each factor.

14.7 "Firms with relatively stable sales and earnings tend to use relatively high proportions of debt." Appraise this quotation.

14.8 "Firms who forego financial leverage are in a better position to protect their dividend." Appraise.

14.9 (a)   Define *operating leverage*. What impact does operating leverage have on the riskiness of the firm?

(b)   In what way are operating leverage and financial leverage substitutes?

(c)   What is the connection between a firm's business risk and its operating leverage?

14.10 "A firm which desires to increase its financial leverage only slightly should consider issuing preferred stock rather than bonds." Critically appraise this quotation.

14.11 A firm examines two mutually exclusive alternatives: (1) financing the firm with 100% equity, i.e. 10,000 shares of $10 per share; and (2) financing the firm with 5,000 shares of $10 per share and 50,000 bonds bearing interest at the rate of 8%.

(a)   Ignoring corporate tax, calculate the *EPS* for the two alternatives as a function of *NOI*, for the following values of *NOI*: $24,000; $20,000; $16,000; $12,000; $8,000; $4,000; $0; — $4,000.

(b)   Graph *EPS* as a function of *NOI* for each alternatives.

(c)   Find the break-even point.

(d)   How can you explain the statement: "Financial leverage is a two-edged sword" in view of the results you obtained above?

14.12 Three firms face two mutually exclusive alternatives:

(1)   Financing the firm with 100% equity (10,000 shares, of $10 each); or

(2)   Financing the firm with equal amounts of stock and bonds (5,000 shares of $10 each, $50,000 bonds bearing interest at the rate of 8%). The probabilities of the net operating income of the three firms are given in the following table:

NOI	0	4,000	8,000	12,000	16,000	
Firm			Total Probability			
A	2/8	1/8	2/8	1/8	2/8	1
B	2/8	3/8	1/8	1/8	1/8	1
C	1/8	1/8	1/8	3/8	2/8	1

Which financing alternative should firm A adopt? Which alternative should firm B and firm C adopt? (Assume that the firms use the $E - V$ criterion and ignore corporate tax.)

14.13 A firm is faced with three mutually exclusive financing alternatives:

(1)   10,000 shares at $10 per share

(2)   7,500 shares at $10 per share and $25,000 in bonds (8%)

(3)   5,000 shares at $10 per share and $50,000 in bonds (8%)

Assume that the firm expects the following values of *NOI*: $16,000; $14,000; $12,000; $10,000; $8,000; $6,000; $2,000; $0 and — $2,000, with equal probability. (There is no corporate tax.)

(a)   Calculate the *EPS* for each alternative as a function of *NOI*.

(b)   Graph *EPS* as a function of *NOI* for each alternative.

(c)   Assume that the firm pays a dividend of 20 cents per share, and that it seeks a probability of *at least* 70% to meet this dividend payment out of current income. Which alternatives are capable of fulfilling this goal?

(d)   Suppose, now, that the firm wants to increase its dividend payment to 60 cents per share and it desires a chance of *at least* 60% of achieving this goal. Which alternatives are relevant in this case? Graph your answers to (c) and (d) on the diagram of part (b) above.

14.14 Two firms, "Alpha" and "Beta" sell the same product at the same price — $5 per unit.

Alpha has fixed costs (not including interest) of $150,000 compared with only $80,000 for Beta. The variable cost of Alpha is assumed to be $2 per unit while the variable cost of Beta is $3 per unit.

Alpha is a pure equity company — the firm issued 75,000 shares at $10 each. Beta, on the other hand, issued only 50,000 shares of $10 each and additional $250,000 worth of bonds bearing interest at the rate of 8%.

(a)   Draw the operating leverage charts for the two firms, ignoring interest expenses, and find the operating break-even point for each firm.

(b)   Draw (on the same diagram) the operating leverage charts taking interest into account.

(c)   Assume that there is equal probability of sales being 50,000 units ("Bad" year) or 200,000 units ("Good" year) and a corporate tax of 50%, and calculate the *EPS* for each firm in a "good" year and in a "bad" year.

(d)   Explain the results you got in (c).

APPENDIX 14A BREAK-EVEN CHARTS AND FINANCIAL ANALYSIS

In the text we defined the financial break-even point using a numerical example. In this appendix we derive the general relationship between the *EPS* generated by levered and unlevered capital structures. Consider a firm that requires C dollars for investment, the outlay on which can be financed either by equity or by a mixed financial strategy — the proportion p of bonds, bearing r percent interest, and the remaining proportion $(1 - p)$ in the form of common stock. For simplicity, we shall further assume that the issue price of the stock equals $1, so that C shares are required in the unlevered pure equity financing option, while $(1 - p)C$ shares are required for the levered financing option.

Denoting the *pre-tax* net operating income (net earnings before interest and taxes) by *NOI*, we can write the *post-tax* earnings per share (*EPS*) of the unlevered strategy as follows:

$$EPS = \frac{(1 - T)\, NOI}{C}$$

where: T denotes the corporate tax tate.

The relevant formula for the levered option is,

$$EPS = \frac{(1 - T)(NOI - rpC)}{(1 - p)C}$$

where rpC denotes the total interest expense, and $(1 - p)C$ denotes the levered firm's equity, as well as the number of its shares. Since NOI appears in both equations, the break-even point, i.e. the value of NOI for which the EPS of both the levered and unlevered alternatives are equal can be derived by equating the two equations:

$$\frac{(1 - T)NOI}{C} \overset{!}{=} \frac{(1 - T)(NOI - rpC)}{(1 - p)C}$$

Multiplying both sides of this equation by $C/(1 - T)$ yields:

$$NOI = \frac{NOI - rpC}{1 - p}$$

which can be written as

$$(1 - p)NOI = NOI - rpC$$

Rearranging terms we have,

$$p \cdot NOI = rpC$$

If we cancel out p, which appears on both sides of the equation, we find that the break-even value of the pre-tax operating income is given by $NOI = rC$ or alternatively,

$$r = \frac{NOI}{C}$$

Thus, if the firm's pre-tax operating rate of return on total investment (assets) is just equal to the interest rate, the use of leverage will not affect the return to shareholders, i.e. its EPS.

Similarly, we can derive the break-even point in terms of *post-tax EPS*, rather than pre-tax *NOI*. Recall that for the unlevered firm we have the following relationship:

$$EPS = \frac{(1 - T)NOI}{C}$$

Dividing each side of this equation by $(1 - T)$, and substituting this result in the preceding equation, we obtain,

$$r = \frac{EPS}{1 - T}$$

or

$$EPS = (1 - T)\, r$$

Thus, financial leverage wil be neutral and therefore will have no impact on *EPS*, provided the *post-tax EPS* of the unlevered firm equals the *post-tax* interest rate. The lower after-tax break-even point reflects the tax deductibility of the interest charges. Hence, for an interest rate of 5% and corporate tax rate of 50%, the post-tax break-even return on total assets is $2\frac{1}{2}\%$. The firm "pays" only $2\frac{1}{2}\%$ out of its net after-tax earnings; the remaining $2\frac{1}{2}\%$ being deducted from taxes, and therefore being "paid", so to speak, by the government.

The break-even point is *not* a function of the degree of financial leverage, i.e., of the proportion of debt (p) in the capital structure. But despite the fact that the proportion of debt has no impact on *EPS* at the break-even point, it remains one of the most important determining factors of *EPS*. A little manipulation of the formal relationship between *EPS* and the degree of leverage suffices to show that the variability of *EPS* increases as the leverage ratio p is increased:

$$EPS = \frac{(1 - T)\,(NOI - rpC)}{(1 - p)C}$$

Separating terms and cancelling out *C,* yields

$$EPS = -\frac{1 - T}{1 - p} \cdot rp + \frac{1 - T}{(1 - p)C} \cdot NOI$$

Since the *EPS* is a linear function of the *NOI*, this equation can be rewritten in the familiar linear form:[1]

$$EPS = a + bNOI$$

where: $\quad a = -\dfrac{1 - T}{1 - p}\, rp \;$ and $\; b = \dfrac{1 - T}{(1 - p)C}$

For a given corporate tax rate, *T*, interest rate *r* and investment outlay *C,* a higher debt ratio *p* implies a lower value of the intercept *a.* (The reader should

---

1 This equation can be used to draw the break-even chart. For each value of *p*, the two parameters *a* and *b* can be calculated, and then used to draw the appropriate linear *EPS-NOI* relationship; each individual line illustrating the potential impact of a given financing strategy on shareholders' earnings.

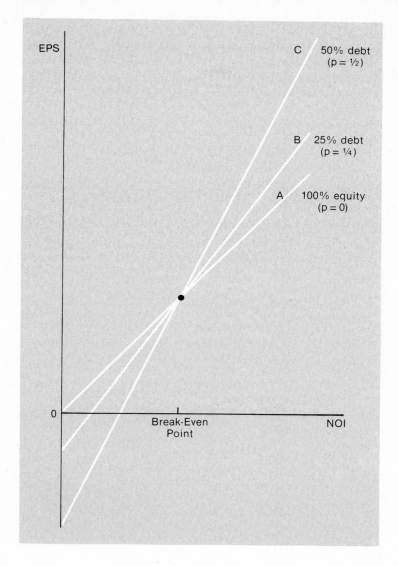

Fig. 14.A1

note the minus sign in the definition of the intercept *a*.) On the other hand, the higher the debt-equity ratio, the greater will be the slope of the leverage line; an increase in *p* implying a rise in *b*. These results are illustrated in Fig. 14A.1 which sets out the by now familiar break-even chart for three levels of leverage: zero leverage, i.e. 100% equity financing, 25% debt and 50% debt. Figure 14A.1 confirms the mathematical relationships: the higher the debt ratio, the steeper is the *EPS* line, and all lines intersect at the same break-even point, i.e. the latter is independent of the degree of leverage.

QUESTIONS AND PROBLEMS

14A.1. Assume that the interest rate on bonds has risen.
- (a) What happens to the post-tax *EPS* when the rate of interest (r) increases?
- (b) How much is the post-tax *EPS* changed when r increases by 1%?
- (c) What is the change in the break-even-point caused by a 1% increase of r, in terms of pre-tax *NOI*?

14A.2
- (a) Draw the break-even-point in terms of post-tax *EPS* as a function of the rate of interest, for the following values of T:0%, 25%, 50%, 75%.
- (b) Find on the diagram the appropriate *EPS* for a rate of interest of 8% for each value of T.
- (c) Find on the diagram the appropriate rate of interest for an *EPS* of 3%, for each value of T.

14A.3 A few years ago, the corporate tax rate decreased from 52% to 48%.
- (a) What is the change in the break-even point, in terms of pre-tax *NOI*, caused by the decline in the corporate tax rate?
- (b) What is the change in the *BEP* in terms of post-tax *EPS*?

14A.4 What is the impact of the proportion of debt in the capital structure on the break-even point in terms of post-tax *EPS*? Prove your answer, mathematically and diagramatically.

14A.5
- (a) Express the *expected value* of a levered strategy's post-tax *EPS* as a function of an unlevered strategy's post-tax *EPS*.
- (b) Express the *variability* of a levered firm's post-tax *EPS* as a function of an unlevered firm's post-tax *EPS*.

SELECTED REFERENCES

Adar, Z., Barnea, A. and Lev, B., "A Comprehensive Cost-Volume-Profit Analysis under Uncertainty", *Accounting Review,* January 1977.

Aivazian, V. A. and Callen, J. L., "Corporate Leverage and Growth: The Game-Theoretic Issues", *Journal of Financial Economics,* December, 1980.

Ang, J. S., "The Intertemporal Behavior of Corporate Debt Policy", *Journal of Financial and Quantitative Analysis,* November 1976.

Ang, J. S., "A Note on the Leverage Effect on Portfolio Performance Measures", *Journal of Financial and Quantitative Analysis,* September 1978.

Arditti, Fred D. and Peles, Yoram C., "The Regulatory Process and the Firm's Capital Structure", *The Financial Review,* Winter 1980.

Barges, Alexander, *The Effect of Capital Structure on the Cost of Capital,* Englewood Cliffs, N.J.: Prentice-Hall, 1963.

Bierman, H. Jr. and Oldfield, G. S., Jr., "Corporate Debt and Corporate Taxes", *Journal of Finance,* September 1979.

Boot, John C. G. and Frankfurter, George M., "The Dynamics of Corporate Debt Management, Decision Rules, and Some Empirical Estimates", *Journal of Financial and Quantitative Analysis,* September 1972.

Bowman, Robert G., "The Importance of a Market-Value Measurement of Debt in Assessing Leverage", *Journal of Accounting Research,* Spring 1980.

Briscoe, G. and Hawke, G., "Long-term Debt and Realisable Gains in Shareholder Wealth: An Empirical Study", *Journal of Business Finance & Accounting,* Spring 1976.

Davenport, Michael, "Leverage and the Cost of Capital: Some Tests Using British Data", *Economic,* May 1971.

Donaldson, Gordon, "Corporate Debt Capacity", *Division of Research, Harvard Business School,* 1961.

Ghandhi, J. K. S., "On the Measurement of Leverage", *Journal of Finance,* December 1966.

Haley, Charles W. and Schall, Lawrence D., *The Theory of Financial Decisions,* New York: McGraw-Hill, 1973.

Haslem, John A., "Leverage Effects on Corporate Earnings", *Arizona Review,* March 1970.

Jones, W. H. and Ferri, M. G., "Short-Term Leverage and Attributes of the Firm", *Review of Business and Economic Research,* Fall 1979.

Krainer, R. E., "Interest Rates, Leverage, and Investor Rationality", *Journal of Financial and Quantitative Analysis,* March 1977.

Lev, Baruch and Pekelman, Dov, "A Multiperiod Adjustment Model for the Firm's Capital Structure", *The Journal of Finance*, March 1975.

Litzenberger, Robert H. and Sosin, Howard B., "A Comparison of Capital Structure Decisions of Regulated and Non-Regulated Firms", *Financial Management*, Autumn 1979.

Malkiel, Burton G., *The Debt-Equity Combination of the Firm and the Cost of Capital: An Introductory Analysis,* New York: General Learning Press, 1971.

Martin, John D. and Scott, David F., Jr., "Debt Capacity and the Capital Budgeting Decision", *Financial Management,* Summer 1976.

Martin, Linda J. and Henderson, Glen V., Jr., "The Effect of ERISA on Capital Structure Measures", *The Financial Review,* Spring 1980.

Percival, John R., "Operating Leverage and Risk", *Journal of Business Research,* April 1974.

Pfahl, John K., Crary, David T. and Howard, R. Hayden, "The Limits of Leverage", *Financial Executive,* May 1970.

Remmers, Lee, Stonehill, Arthur, Wright, Richard and Beekhuisen, Theo, "Industry and Size as Debt Ratio Determinants in Manufacturing Internationally", *Financial Management,* Summer 1974.

Schwartz, Eli and Aronson, Richard J., "Some Surrogate Evidence in Support of the Concept of Optimal Capital Structure", *Journal of Finance,* March 1967.

Scott, David, F., Jr., "Evidence on the Importance of Financial Structure", *Financial Management*, Spring 1972.

Scott, David F., Jr. and Martin, John D., "Industry Influence on Financial Structure", *Financial Management,* Spring 1975.

Shalit, Sol S., "On the Mathematics of Financial Leverage", *Financial Management*, Spring 1975.

Tinsley, P. A., "Capital Structure, Precautionary Balances, and Valuation of the Firm: The Problem of Financial Risk", *Journal of Financial and Quantitative Analysis,* July, 1979.

Turnbull, S. M., "Debt Capacity", *Journal of Finance*, September 1979.

Vickers, Douglas, "Disequilibrium Structures and Financing Decisions in the Firm", *Journal of Business Finance & Accounting*, Autumn, 1974.

Walker, Ernest W. and Petty, J. William, II, "Financial Differences Between Large and Small Firms", *Financial Management,* Winter 1978.

White, William L, "Debt Management and the Form of Business Financing", *Journal of Finance*, May 1974.

Whittington, Ray and Wittenburg, Gerald, "Judicial Classification of Debt Versus Equity — An Empirical Study", *The Accounting Review*, July 1980.

Williams, Edward E., "Cost of Capital Functions and the Firm's Optimal Level of Gearing", *Journal of Business Finance*, September 1972.

15

Capital Structure and Valuation

In the preceding chapter we saw that financial leverage can be either positive or negative depending on the relationship between the rate of return on invested capital and the rate of interest payable to the firm's debtors. Where the former exceeds the latter the leverage effect was defined as positive since *EPS* is enhanced; where the rate of return is less than the rate of interest paid on the debt, we defined the leverage as negative because *EPS* is thereby decreased. Since a firm that does not succeed in earning a return in excess of the interest rate presumably will not survive for long, financial leverage appears, on balance, to be positive in almost all instances. However, as we have already noted, the increase in expected *EPS* has its "price" i.e., the increase in the variability of the income stream to the common stockholders. Or in other words, financial leverage increases the total risk associated with the investment in the company's shares.

Since leverage increases expected return and risk simultaneously, this raises the question of the *net* impact of leverage on shareholders' economic welfare. Off hand, it is not clear which of these two factors outweighs the other. Since we have taken the goal of the firm to be the maximization of stockholders' wealth, i.e., the maximization of the market value of its common stock, the only unambiguous way to measure the relative strength of these two factors is to examine the behavior of the market price of the shares themselves. Should the market price of the stock *fall* as a result of the introduction of financial leverage, this would indicate that the increase in shareholders' risk outweighs the increase in expected earnings per share. The opposite conclusion holds if the market value of the stock should rise. The firm's optimal financing strategy (capital structure) is that which maximizes the market value of its outstanding common stock. By definition, any deviation in either direction from the optimal financing mix will induce a decline in value of the common stock, and hence in the market value of the firm.

LEVERAGE AND VALUATION

A necessary preliminary step in analyzing alternative financial policies is to determine the extent (if any) to which a shareholder can actually benefit from the firm's use of leverage. And as we have already noted, the answer to this question depends on the *security market's* evaluation of the tradeoff between risk and return which characterizes the firm's use of debt.

This is an exceedingly complicated question, and for simplicity we shall initially assume a world without taxes. It will also help to simplify matters and help to sharpen distinctions, if at this stage we examine two diametrically opposed approaches to the valuation problem: the capitalization of net operating income, or *NOI* approach as it is usually called; and the *NI* approach, which in contrast capitalizes a firm's net income.[1] The differences between the two methods can be illustrated by considering a firm which is financed partly by 4% bonds and partly by common stock. The net operating income of the firm is assumed to be $2,000,000. Table 15.1 sets out the two alternative approaches to the valuation of the firm's common stock.

Table 15.1

NOI Method

	A	B	C
Net Operating Income	$2,000,000	$2,000,000	$2,000,000
Capitalization Rate (10%)	× 10	× 10	× 10
Total Market Value of Company	20,000,000	20,000,000	20,000,000
Total Market Value of Bonds	—	5,000,000	10,000,000
Total Market Value of Stock	20,000,000	15,000,000	10,000,000
Number of Shares	2,000,000	1,500,000	1,000,000
Value per Share	$10	$10	$10

NI Method

	A	B	C
Net Operating Income	$2,000,000	$2,000,000	$2,000,000
Interest (4% on bonds)	—	200,000	400,000
Net Income	2,000,000	1,800,000	1,600,000
Capitalization Rate (10%)	× 10	× 10	× 10
Total Market Value of Stock	20,000,000	18,000,000	16,000,000
Total Market Value of Bonds	—	5,000,000	10,000,000
Total Market Value of Company	20,000,000	23,000,000	26,000,000
Number of Shares	2,000,000	1,500,000	1,000,000
Value per Share	$10	$12	$16

---

1 The terms *NI* and *NOI*, as well as the examples given in the text, are taken from the pioneering article by David Durand, "Cost of Debt and Equity Funds for Business: Trends and Problems of Measurement", in *Conference on Research in Business Finance*, New York: National Bureau of Economic Research, 1952.

In the *NOI* method the total value of the firm's securities is derived by capitalizing the net operating income at the market rate of discount, which we shall assume is 10%.

$$V \equiv S + B = \frac{X}{k}$$

where: V = total market value of the firm's securities
S = market value of its common stock
B = market value of its bonds (debt)
X = net operating income (*NOI*)
k = 10%, the market capitalization rate

The market value of the equity, in turn, is derived by subtracting the market value of the debt from the total value of the firm's securities.

$$S = \frac{X}{k} - B$$

The essence of the *NOI* approach is that the total value of the firm remains constant at $20,000,000 *independent* of its capital structure (see Table 15.1). For example, if the firm is financed by 2,000,000 shares of stock and no bonds (Alternative A), the total value of the firm is $20,000,000 and the value per share (price) of its common stock is $10. If it is financed with $10,000,000 in bonds and one million shares (Alternative C), the total value of all securities (stocks and bonds) remains $20,000,000 and the value of the common stock ($20,000,000 less the value of the bonds) equals $10,000,000, or again $10 per share. This approach implies that any increase in expected return induced by the leverage is *exactly offset* by the increase in risk to the common shareholder, so that the total value of the firm and the value (price) of an individual share of common stock remain invariant.

In the alternative *NI* method, the net income, rather than the net operating income, is capitalized to derive the total market value of the stock:

$$S = \frac{X - rB}{k}$$

Where *r* denotes the rate of interest paid on the bonds. To this sum, the market value of the bonds is added to derive the total market value of the firm's securities:

$$V \equiv S + B = \frac{X - rB}{k} + B$$

Table 15.1 also shows that using the *NI* method successive increases in the proportion of bonds in the capital structure *increase* the total value of the firm's common stock; the price of a share of common stock rises from $10 in the unlevered case to $16 when $10,000,000 worth of bonds are used. In terms of our previous discussion, the *NI* approach assumes no penalty whatsoever to compensate the shareholder for the additional financial risk incurred. All increases in *EPS* are automatically translated into increases in the price of the common stock. The *NOI* approach represents the other extreme and allows for no influence whatsoever of leverage-induced increases in *EPS* on the price of the shares, that is, it is assumed that the increase in financial risk *exactly offsets* the increase in expected profitability.

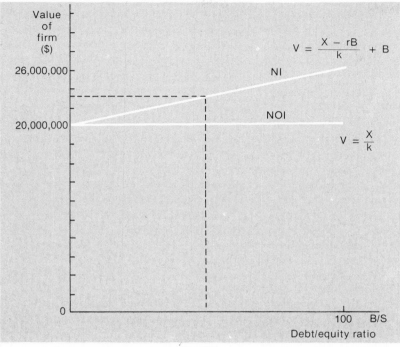

Fig. 15.1

These relationships (in a world without taxes) are summarized in Fig. 15.1, which provides a convenient diagrammatic representation of the two alternative methods of valuation. Note that both approaches give the same valuation for the 100% equity case. As debt is introduced into the capital structure, the degree to which leverage increases the value of the firm under the *NI* method depends on the proportion of debt in the capital structure and the differential between the rate of return earned on total assets (*k*) and the rate of interest paid on the bonds (*r*). Other things being equal, the higher the proportion of debt and/or the greater the differential, the greater the leverage effect, that is, the steeper will be the *NI* line of Fig. 15.1. Clearly, many intermediate positions can be defined, but the essence of the problem still hinges on our assumption regarding the market's appraisal of the financial risk created by leverage in relation to the increase in potential net earnings to shareholders.

THE MODIGLIANI AND MILLER ANALYSIS

Although Durand expressed a personal preference for the *NOI* approach, it was Franco Modigliani and Merton H. Miller (hereafter referred to as M & M) who in a series of justly famous articles provided a rigorous justification for the *NOI* method.[2] We shall present their analysis by means of simple (we trust not simple-minded) numerical examples followed by their general "arbitrage" proof — initially assuming a world without taxes and then for the more realistic situation in which firms are subject to corporate taxation.

Before examining the M & M position in detail, a prefatory remark is called for. In their original 1958 article a set of very restrictive assumptions was required to establish the relationship between leverage and the value of a firm's shares. Subsequently, owing to further work, much of it by M & M themselves, it has been shown that the original propositions hold under far less severe assumptions than were originally thought necessary. Consequently we no longer need many of the implicit and explicit restrictions of the original paper, and shall replace them with the following three assumptions:

(a)   Individuals can borrow or lend at the same market rate of interest as firms.
(b)   There is no bankruptcy.
(c)   There are no transaction costs, or other barriers to the free flow of information in security markets.

These three assumptions are sufficient to derive M & M's basic and most important first proposition.[3]

The No Tax Case: Proposition I

M & M argue that in such a world, without taxes, firms cannot gain from leverage (which is equivalent to the claim that the *NOI* method is the only correct method of valuation). Their Proposition I states that in the absence of corporate taxes the value of the firm is *independent* of its capital structure, i.e., of the debt-equity mix:[4]

$$V_L = V_U$$

where
$$V_U \equiv S_U = \text{the market value of an unlevered firm's securities}$$
$$S_U = \text{the market value of an unlevered firm's shares}$$
$$V_L \equiv S_L + B_L = \text{the market value of a levered firm's securities}$$
$$S_L = \text{the market value of a levered firm's shares}$$
$$B_L = \text{the market value of a levered firm's bonds (debt)}$$

The proposition can be illustrated by a numerical example. Suppose that there are two firms (which we denote by A and B) which are *identical* in all respects except for their capital structures. Let us further assume that both firms have

---

2 The original article, "The Cost of Capital, Corporation Finance, and the Theory of Investment", appeared in the *American Economic Review*, June 1958.
3 See J. E. Stiglitz, "A Re-examination of the Modigliani-Miller Theorem", *American Economic Review*, December 1969.
4 A formal proof of Proposition I is given in Appendix 15B at the end of the chapter.

just started their operations and require an investment of $1,000 which will return $50 (annually) with probability of 1/2 or $150 with probability of 1/2. Firm A raises the required money by issuing 100 shares of common stock at a price of $10 per share; firm B raises the required $1,000 by issuing 50 shares at $10 per share and later issues $500 of 6% bonds. The essence of the M & M position is that if one ignores corporate taxes, the market price of the stocks of the two firms must be the same, despite the fact that they differ in their capital structures. They argue that economic forces exist which ensure the equality of the share prices of the two firms and hence of their market values as well, even though the difference in capital structures confronts investors with different distributions of return. Table 15.2 summarizes the distribution of earnings per share for the two firms.

Table 15.2

	Firm A (100% Equity)		Firm B (50% Equity, 50% Debt)	
	Return per Share	Probability	Return per Share	Probability
	0.50	·1/2	0.40	1/2
	1.50	1/2	2.40	1/2
Expected (average) return*	$1.00		$1.40	

*The expected return of firm A is given by 1/2 × 0.50 + 1/2 × 1.50 = $1.00.
The expected return of firm B is given by 1/2 × 0.40 + 1/2 × 2.40 = $1.40.

Since firm A's cash flow is comprised of $50 with probability 1/2 and $150 with probability 1/2, and it issued 100 shares, the return per share is 50 cents with probability 1/2 and $1.50 with probability 1/2. Similarly, the second firm's cash flow is characterized by an equal probability of earning either $50 or $150. However, in the case of firm B, should $50 be realized from operations, the return per share *after* the payment of interest (6% of $500 = $30) will be only 40 cents ($20 ÷ 50 shares = 40 cents), i.e. in such an event the effect of the leverage is negative and *EPS* falls from 50 to 40 cents. If, on the other hand, $150 is realized from operations, the net return per share equals $2.40 ($150 − $30 = $120 and $120 ÷ 50 shares = $2.40).

In *contradistinction* to the M & M analysis, let us assume for the moment that investors are *unable* to borrow or lend money, and that they are offered, free of charge, the choice of either distribution A or distribution B. Which alternative will be chosen? Clearly, this depends on an investor's preferences, or in terms of Chapter 9, on his utility function. Figures 15.2 and 15.3 set out the utility functions of two different investors. The expected utility from the results of firms A and B are identified in each diagram by the letters *a* and *b* respectively. Note that the investor whose utility function is given in Fig. 15.2 prefers firm B to A (point *b* lies above point *a*), while the opposite holds for the investor whose preferences are drawn in Fig. 15.3. The latter prefers the cash flow of firm A (point *a* lies above point *b* in Fig. 15.3). Clearly, the market value of firm A

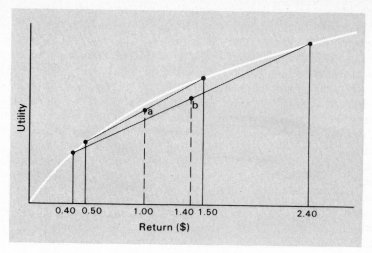

Fig. 15.2

might differ from the market value of firm B; the exact relationship between the prices of their common stock depends on the weighted average of the preferences of investors (in terms of the dollar amount of investment rather than the number of individuals). Thus equilibrium in such a market depends on individuals' preferences for particular income streams, i.e. for particular capital structures.

Now let us drop the restriction against borrowing and lending, and explicitly incorporate M & M's assumption that individuals can borrow and lend at the same interest rate as do the firms. In terms of our numerical example this means that individuals can borrow or lend at 6%. Given this assumption, M & M argue that the market values of the two firms must be identical independent

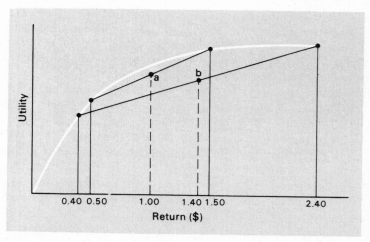

Fig. 15.3

of investors' preferences. This also implies, of course, that capital structure does not matter, since all financing mixes will result in the same market value for the two firms.

This can be proved, using the same numerical example as before. Consider the case of an investor with the preferences depicted in Fig. 15.2 above. Recall that his personal preference is for the income stream generated by the levered firm B. Let us further assume that the market price of firm B's shares is greater than the share price of firm A, i.e. $P_B > P_A$, where P_A and P_B denote the market price of one share of the stock of A and B respectively. On the surface this situation seems to make sense since, by assumption, the investor prefers the income stream of B to that of A and hence one would expect that be should be willing to pay more for a share of firm B's stock. However, despite its apparent plausibility this is not the case. The price differential in favor of firm B (i.e. $P_B > P_A$) cannot persist even in the extreme situation in which *every* investor in the market is assumed to prefer the income stream of firm B to that of A.

Let us assume for convenience that $P_A = \$10.00$; hence the total market value of firm A equals $1,000 (100 shares $\times$ $10 = $1,000). If $P_B > P_A$, an investor who owns one share of the stock of firm B can sell it for more than $10, say $11. (Recall P_B is greater than P_A by assumption.) He then can borrow $10 at 6%, and use the proceeds of the sale *and* the loan to buy two shares of stock in the unlevered firm A (at a price of $10 per share), putting aside the $1 premium which he earned by selling his share in firm B. The investor's return before and after these transactions is given in Table 15.3. Clearly the suggested switch of shares provides the investor with the *identical* income stream as before, but with a saving of the $1 which he put aside, i.e. his net investment is $1 smaller. The difference $P_B - P_A$ is the measure of his profit on this transaction, and therefore he will continue to sell shares in firm B and buy those of A (thereby lowering the price of B and raising the price of A), so long as the price of B exceeds that of A (i.e. as long as $P_B > P_A$). And this process will continue until the prices of the shares are equalized.

The reader should recall that when we imposed the constraint that investors are not permitted to borrow or lend, the market values of the otherwise identical levered and unlevered firms were not necessarily the same. But when the assumption that investors can freely lend or borrow on the same terms as firms is introduced, this conclusion changes drastically. In particular, given this

Table 15.3

Investment	Income Stream	
	Probability	Return
1. Initial Position		
One share of B	1/2	$0.40
	1/2	$2.40
2. New Position		
Two shares of A	1/2	(2 × 0.50) − 0.60 = $0.40
plus $10 loan	1/2	(2 × 1.50) − 0.60 = $2.40

assumption, firms cannot increase their market values by employing financial leverage. Since the opportunity to lever themselves (i.e. borrow) is open also to individuals, investors will not be willing to pay a "premium" in the form of an enhanced market price for the shares of a levered firm, because they can achieve the same income stream by borrowing themselves and by "levering" the income stream of the unlevered firm. Given the *NOI* valuation framework and the assumption of no taxes, this "*homemade leverage*" is a perfect substitute for corporate leverage, and therefore the latter will have no impact on the value of the firm.

As we have just seen, the levered firm's shares cannot command a premium in the market, if investors can freely substitute personal borrowing for corporate borrowing. However, the question arises as to whether the opposite possibility, i.e. $P_A > P_B$, can exist. Once again let us take an extreme case in which every investor in the market is assumed to prefer the return of A to that of B. (That is to say, they are characterized by the preferences illustrated in Fig. 15.3 above.) Using the same switching technique as before we can easily show that in equilibrium, the price of the unlevered shares P_A *cannot* exceed the price of the shares of the levered firm P_B.

To demonstrate this, let us initially assume that the price per share of A is $11 and that of firm B is only $10, i.e. a premium for "safety" exists in the market which reflects investors' assumed preferences for more stable returns. Now assume for numerical convenience that an individual who owns two shares of the unlevered stock of A sells his shares, using the proceeds from the sale (2 × $11 = $22) to purchase one share of B at $10 and $10 worth of bonds of firm B. His total investment outlay is only $20 so he can put $2 aside. The investor's returns both before and after these transactions are given in Table 15.4. Once again the suggested switch permits the investor to achieve the identical income stream as before, but with a saving of the $2 which he puts aside. Once again this "profit" can be earned as long as P_A exceeds P_B. Thus, the price differential $P_A > P_B$ will generate market forces which will raise the price of B and lower that of A; and this process will continue until equality between the share prices is restored. In equilibrium, the share prices of levered and unlevered firms must be equal; or in other words, in the M & M world of no taxes, no bankruptcy and perfectly efficient securities markets, leverage cannot affect the value of the firm. Hence no optimal financing strategy can be identified and the firm is indifferent to the use of debt.

Table 15.4

Investment	Income Stream	
	Probability	*Return*
1. Initial Position	1/2	$1.00
One share of A	1/2	$3.00
2. New Position		
Two shares of B	1/2	0.40 + 0.60 = $1.00
plus $10 of bonds	1/2	2.40 + 0.60 = $3.00

The No Tax Case: Proposition II

From their first proposition which relates the value of the firm to its capital structure, M & M derive a second proposition which deals with the relationship of the required rate of return on equity to leverage. In the preceding discussion we suggested by means of a numerical example that the required rate of return (yield) on equity rises with leverage. Utilizing the M & M apparatus, it is possible to spell out the exact functional relationship between the return on equity and leverage.

Denoting a firm's net operating income by X, the rate of return on equity of an unlevered firm (Y_U) is given by

$$Y_U = \frac{X}{V_U}$$

and the rate of return on the equity of a levered firm (Y_L) is given by

$$Y_L = \frac{X - rB_L}{V_L - B_L} = \frac{X - rB_L}{S_L} = \frac{X}{S_L} - \frac{rB_L}{S_L}$$

where r = the interest rate on the firm's bonds, assumed to be riskless. Multiplying and dividing the first term on the right-hand side by V_U, we get

$$Y_L = \frac{X}{V_U} \cdot \frac{V_U}{S_L} - \frac{rB_L}{S_L}$$

and by adding and subtracting $(X/V_U)(B_L/S_L)$ we obtain

$$Y_L = \frac{X}{V_U}\left(\frac{V_U}{S_L} - \frac{B_L}{S_L}\right) + \left(\frac{X}{V_U} - r\right)\frac{B_L}{S_L} = \frac{X}{V_U} + \left(\frac{X}{V_U} - r\right)\frac{B_L}{S_L}$$

Since by definition $X/V_U = Y_U$, the rate of return on the equity of a levered firm (Y_L) is equal to the rate of return on an unlevered firm's shares Y_U, plus a risk premium ($Y_U - r$) (B_L/S_L), which depends on the degree of leverage. The higher the proportion of debt in the capital mixture, B_L/S_L, the greater is an investor's risk, and hence the higher is the required return on equity.

One can interpret M & M's two propositions in the no tax case as follows: by increasing the proportion of debt in its capital structure, a firm cannot affect its total value, and therefore no change occurs in the value of its equity (Proposition I). On the other hand, by Proposition II, increasing the proportion of debt in the capital structure increases the rate of return on the firm's equity (Y_L). When these two propositions are examined simultaneously, we can see that any increase in the proportion of low cost debt also increases investors' risk, therefore raising their required rates of return, i.e. the cost of equity (see Chapters 17 and 18 below). Since these two influences exactly cancel one another in an M & M world without taxes and bankruptcy, the value (price) of a firm's shares is invariant to leverage.

THE IMPACT OF CORPORATE TAXES

The invariance of the value of the firm to leverage was established on the explicit assumption that taxes are not imposed on earnings. In this section we shall deal with the much more realistic, and hence much more important, case which assumes the existence of a corporate income tax. Table 15.5 calculates the net operating income, *after taxes*, for three financing alternatives assuming a 4% interest rate and 50% corporate income tax. Although, as we have just seen, a firm cannot benefit from the use of debt in a tax free world, no question arises regarding the advantages of debt once the effects of tax are recognized. As can be seen from Table 15.5, the after-tax net operating income, and not just *EPS, increases* as the proportion of bonds in the capital structure rises. This also implies an increase in the value of the firm's common stock as the proportion of

Table 15.5

	A 100% Equity	B 75% Equity 25% Bonds	C 50% Equity 50% Bonds
	$	$	$
1. Operating Income	2,000,000	2,000,000	2,000,000
2. Interest (4% on bonds)	—	200,000	400,000
3. Taxable Net Income	2,000,000	1,800,000	1,600,000
4. Income Tax at 50%	1,000,000	900,000	800,000
5. Net Income after Taxes	1,000,000	900,000	800,000
6. Net Operating Income (line 5 + line 2)	1,000,000	1,100,000	1,200,000
Number of shares	2,000,000	1,500,000	1,000,000

debt is increased.[5] The reader should note that the *NOI* rises from $1 million in the case of pure equity financing to $1,200,000 when we assume a capital structure equally divided between debt and equity.

The post-tax relationship between the value of the firm and its capital structure is shown graphically in Fig. 15.4. Note that in sharp contrast to the pre-tax case, the total value of the firm depends on the proportion of debt in the capital structure. To be more explicit, the use of debt can potentially increase the value of the firm so long as the deduction of interest for tax purposes is permitted.

M & M also provide a rigorous analysis of the impact of corporate taxation. Retaining the three previous assumptions regarding the borrowing and lending opportunities open to individual investors, the absence of bankruptcy and the absence of all transactions (and information) costs in the capital market, they

---

5 For a detailed discussion of the relationship between maximizing the total value of the firm's and maximizing the market price of the firm's common stock, see Appendix 15 A at the end of the chapter.

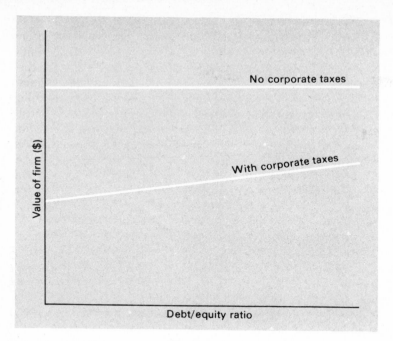

Fig. 15.4

provide a formal arbitrage proof of the contention that shareholders can gain when the firm introduces leverage as long as corporate earnings are taxed.[6]

The introduction of taxes destroys the necessary equivalence between the total market values of otherwise identical levered and unlevered firms. And in fact M & M show that the equilibrium relation with corporate taxation is given by:

$$V_L = V_U + TB_L$$

where T = the corporate income tax rate.

It is clear from this relationship that a market premium, TB_L (which depends on the tax rate and the proportion of debt), is created on the shares of the levered firm, and therefore the levered firm's market value is higher than the market value of its unlevered counterpart.[7] Moreover, the greater is the proportion of debt in the capital structure, the higher is the value of the firm. Thus

---

6 The formal arbitrage proof is given in Appendix 15B at the end of this Chapter.

7 In a world with corporate taxation M & M's. Second Proposition can also be derived. The after-tax rate of return on equity (Y_L^*) becomes:

$$Y_L^* = Y_U^* + (1 - T)(Y_U^* - r)\frac{B_L}{S_L}$$

where the asterisks denote after-tax values. The formal derivation of this proposition is given in Appendix 15B at the end of this Chapter.

a firm which takes advantage of the tax deductibility of interest payments can increase its value by levering its capital structure.

Although the rigorous incorporation of risk in the leverage model greatly enhances our understanding of basic financial relationships, it leaves many important questions unresolved. In particular, the M & M analysis leads to an extreme *corner solution* in the more important post-tax case, that is a firm's optimum capital structure is comprised mainly of debt. Clearly, such an unrealistic result is unsatisfactory and we shall return to the perplexing question of the firm's financing mix in the next chapter.

CAPM AND CAPITAL STRUCTURE

The M & M analysis assumes that investors hold a portfolio comprised of the shares of the firm in question plus bonds (or borrowing). Let's now turn to the question of the impact of leverage on the value of the firm in a world in which investors hold *fully diversified* portfolios of shares plus bonds (or borrowing).

Invoking the Capital Asset Pricing Model (*CAPM*) the following equilibrium relationship between expected return and systematic risk holds[8] (see Chapter 13 above):

$$E(X_i) = r + (EX_m - r)\beta_i$$

where $E(X_i)$ = expected return on stock i
$\quad\quad E(X_m)$ = expected return on the market portfolio
$\quad\quad r$ $\quad\quad$ = risk-free rate of interest
$\quad\quad \beta_i$ $\quad\quad$ = systematic risk of the ith stock

Let us assume that we have two firms which are identical in every respect except for their capital structure. The above relationship between (systematic) risk and return has important implications for the relationship between the value of the firm and its capital structure. We begin the analysis under the assumption of no corporate taxation and then go on to the analysis of capital structure with corporate taxation.

The Analysis without Taxes

Consider two firms, one levered and the other unlevered, who differ only in their capital structures. Since the two firms are otherwise identical, they both have the same earnings before interest payments, i.e., the same net operating income. However, the rate of return on investment to shareholders is calculated differently for each firm.

---

8 For convenience, and to avoid unnecessary confusion, we shall use the *CAPM* notation as set out in Chapter 13 above. Hence the return on shares will be denoted by X rather than Y.

(1) $\quad X_L = \dfrac{NOI - rB_L}{S_L}$ for the levered firm, and

(2) $\quad X_U = \dfrac{NOI}{V_U}$ for the unlevered firm

where: $\quad X_U$ = return on equity of the unlevered firm
$\qquad X_L$ = return on equity of the levered firm
$\qquad S_L$ = value of the levered firm's stock
$\qquad V_U$ = value of the unlevered firm (= value of its stock)
$\qquad B_L$ = amount of debt

From the first equation we obtain,

$$X_L = \frac{NOI}{V_U} \cdot \frac{V_U}{S_L} - \frac{rB_L}{S_L} = \frac{X_U V_U}{S_L} - r \frac{B_L}{S_L}$$

Taking the expected value of this expression yields,

$$E(X_L) = E(X_U) \frac{V_U}{S_L} - r \frac{B_L}{S_L}$$

The systematic risk, β_U, of the unlevered firm is given by

$$\beta_U = \frac{Cov(X_U, X_m)}{\sigma_m^2} = \frac{Cov(NOI/V_U, X_m)}{\sigma_m^2}$$

where X_m is the rate of return on the "market portfolio", and σ_m^2 is its variance. The systematic risk of the levered firm, β_L, is:[9]

$$\beta_L = \frac{Cov(X_L, X_m)}{\sigma_m^2} = \frac{Cov[(NOI - rB_L/S_L, X_m)]}{\sigma_m^2}$$

$$= \frac{1}{\sigma_m^2} Cov\left(\frac{NOI}{S_L}, X_m\right) - \frac{1}{\sigma_m^2} Cov\left(\frac{rB_L}{S_L}, X_m\right)$$

since r is *not* a random variable the last term is zero, which leaves the following expression:

$$\beta_L = Cov\left(\frac{NOI}{V_U} \cdot \frac{V_U'}{S_L}, X_m\right) = \frac{V_U}{S_L} Cov\left(\frac{NOI}{V_U}, X_m\right) \bigg/ \sigma_m^2$$

Hence, it is clear, by the definition of beta that,

$$\beta_L = \frac{V_U}{S_L} \beta_U$$

Clearly, the systematic risk of the levered firm differs from that of the otherwise

---

9 Recall that (a) $Cov(X + Y, m) = Cov(X, m) + Cov(Y, m)$. Since r, B_L and S_L are given at that point of time they are constants and therefore have zero covariance with X_m. (b) For any constant c, $Cov(cX, m) = c \cdot Cov(X, m)$.

identical firm which is unlevered by a constant which reflects the degree of financial leverage.

Now let's examine the implication of the *CAPM* for the analysis of the relationship between leverage and the value of the firm.

For any security, *i* we have,

$$\frac{E(X_i) - r}{\beta_i} = E(X_m) - r$$

Thus, we expect that $[E(X_i) - r]/\beta_i$ will be a constant for *all* securities. This holds true for our two hypothetical firms as well, hence:

$$\frac{E(X_U) - r}{\beta_U} = \frac{E(X_L) - r}{\beta_L}$$

Substituting for $E(X_L)$ and B_L we get,

$$\frac{E(X_U) - r}{\beta_U} = \left[\frac{V_U}{S_L} E(X_U - r \frac{B_L}{S_L}) - r \right] \Big/ \frac{V_U}{S_L} \beta_U$$

We can multiply both the numerator and the denominator of the right-hand side by S_L/V_U without affecting its value:

$$\frac{E(X_U) - r}{\beta_U} = \left[EX_U - r \frac{B_L}{V_U} - r \frac{S_L}{V_U} \right] \Big/ \beta_U$$

This equality, which is implied by the *CAPM*, holds only if

$$-r = -r \frac{B_L}{V_U} - r \frac{S_L}{V_U}$$

or

$$r\left(\frac{B_L}{V_U} + \frac{S_L}{V_U} \right) = r$$

But this, in turn, implies

$$V_U = S_L + B_L$$

This is merely a restatement of M & M Proposition I of no taxation which asserts that in the absence of corporate taxes, the value of unlevered and levered firms will be the same. In other words, the value of the firm is invariant to changes in its financial structure. However, the reader should note that the *systematic risk* of the levered firm:[10]

$$\beta_L = \beta_U \frac{V_U}{S_L}$$

The relationship between beta and leverage can be clarified by considering

---

10 The equality $V_U = V_L = S_L + B_L$ implies $V_U > S_L$. A simple formula for deriving the relationship between unlevered and levered betas is given on page 371 below.

a numerical example. Let's assume that the distribution of the rates of return on the shares of an unlevered firm (X_U) and on the market portfolio (X_m) are as follows:

X_U	X_m
0.10	0.10
0.10	0.15
0.21	0.30
0.23	0.38
0.27	0.40

Let's further assume that each *pair* of returns has an equal probability of occurrence. The beta coefficient of the unlevered shares is given by the following formula:

$$\beta_U = \frac{Cov(X_U X_m)}{Var(X_m)} = \frac{\Sigma X_U X_m - [(\Sigma X_U)(\Sigma X_m)]/N}{\Sigma X_m^2 - N\bar{X}_m^2}$$

$$= \frac{0.293 - 0.242}{0.4265 - 0.3537} = 0.5638$$

Now suppose that the firm had been financed by 50% debt (i.e., $B_L/V_L = 0.5$). What would be its Beta coefficient? Since we know that:

$$\beta_L = \frac{V_U}{S_L} \beta_U$$

and, as we have already proven $V_L = V_U$. It follows that $\beta_L = (V_L/S_L) \beta_U$. Hence, with 50% debt, $V_L/S_L = 2$ and $\beta_L = 2\beta_U = 1.127$. For any amount of debt, one may use the following simple formula to find the value of V_L/S_L that one should multiply by β_U in order to get β_L.

$$\frac{V_L}{S_L} = \frac{V_L}{V_L - B_L} = \frac{V_L/V_L}{(V_L/V_L) - (B_L/V_L)} = \frac{1}{1 - (B_L/V_L)}$$

Table 15.6 (below) sets out the precise numerical relationship between leverage and beta on the specific assumption that $\beta_U = 0.5$:

Analysis with Corporate Taxes

The post-tax rate of return per dollar of investment in the unlevered firm is given by

$$X_U^* = \frac{(1 - T)NOI}{V_U}$$

Table 15.6

(1)	(2)	(3)
Leverage Ratio (B_L/V_L)	$\dfrac{V_L}{S_L} = \dfrac{1}{1 - (B_L/V_L)}$	$\beta_L = \beta_U \cdot (V_L/S_L)$
No leverage	1.00	0.50
0.1	1.11	0.56
0.2	1.25	0.63
0.3	1.43	0.71
0.4	1.67	0.83
0.5	2.00	1.00
0.6	2.50	1.25
0.7	2.33	1.66
0.8	5.00	2.50
0.9	10.00	5.00

For the levered firm we have:

$$X_L^* = \frac{(1 - T)(NOI - rB_L)}{S_L} = \frac{(1 - T)NOI}{V_U}\ \frac{V_U}{S_L} - (1 - T)\,r\,\frac{B_L}{S_L}$$

where the asterisk denotes a *post-tax* variable.

Thus, $X_L^* = \dfrac{V_U}{S_L}\,X_U^* - (1 - T)\,r\,\dfrac{B_L}{S_L}$

Taking expected values of both sides of the last equation we get,

$$E(X_L^*) = \frac{V_U}{S_L}\,E(X_U^*) - (1 - T)\,r\,\frac{B_L}{S_L}$$

Similarly, for the systematic risk of the unlevered firm:

$$\beta_U^* = \frac{Cov(X_U^*, X_m)}{\sigma_m^2}$$

Using the same technique as in the pre-tax analysis we find the following relationship for the levered firm:

$$\beta_L^* = \frac{Cov(X_L^*, X_m)}{\sigma_m^2} = \frac{V_U}{S_L}\ \frac{Cov(X_U^*, X_m)}{\sigma_m^2}$$

Thus, as before we find:

$$\beta_L^* = \frac{V_U}{S_L}\,\beta_U^*$$

Note that we again use the functional relationship between X_U^* and X_L^* and the fact that the covariance between $r(B_L/S_L)$ and X_m is zero to obtain this result.

In equilibrium the following must hold:

$$\frac{E(X_U^*) - r}{\beta_U^*} = \frac{E(X_L^*) - r}{\beta_L^*}$$

Substituting, as before, for EX_L^* and β_L^*,

$$\frac{EX_U^* - r}{\beta_U^*} = \left[\frac{V_U}{S_L} E(X_U^*) - \frac{(1 - T)rB_L}{S_L} - r \right] \bigg/ \frac{V_U}{S_L} \beta_U^*$$

Multiplying all the terms on the right hand side by S_L/V_U we obtain:

$$\frac{EX_U^* - r}{\beta_U^*} = \left[EX_U^* - (1 - T) r \frac{B_L}{V_U} - r \frac{S_L}{V_U} \right] \bigg/ \beta_U^*$$

This equation holds only if:

$$- r = -(1 - T) r \frac{B_L}{V_U} - r \frac{S_L}{V_U}$$

which reduces to

$$V_U = (1 - T)B_L + S_L$$

or

$$V_U + TB_L = B_L + S_L$$

But as by definition $B_L + S_L \equiv V_L$ we can rewrite this as

$$V_L = V_U + TB_L$$

which is the M & M proposition for the case of corporate taxation. Hence the *CAPM* result leads to the same disturbing conclusion, i.e. that the firm should maximize its value by taking on as much debt as possible.

Even casual empiricism shows that this is an unsatisfactory picture of actual corporate behavior. The next chapter will be devoted to the resolution of this seemingly paradoxical result.

SUMMARY

This chapter has been devoted to measuring the impact of financial leverage on shareholders' earnings and risk. As we have seen financial leverage is a two-edged sword: if the leverage is *positive* the use of debt raises *EPS*; however, should it be negative *EPS* can fall. Although in general we may assume that on balance leverage is positive, the use of debt also increases the fluctuations of *EPS*, thereby increasing financial risk. Hence financial management is confronted with the difficult task of weighing the advantages and disadvantages of levering the firm's financial structure.

Since leverage affects both expected return and risk a way must be found to evaluate the tradeoff between risk and return. The only unambiguous way to measure the relative strength of the two factors is to measure their combined impact on the price of the firm's shares. To this end two methods (*NI* and *NOI*) of valuation are distinguished.

A rigorous analysis of the impact of leverage on the market value of a firm's equity has been provided by Modigliani and Miller (M & M) both for a taxless world and one with corporate taxes. In a world without corporate taxes, no bankruptcy or liquidation costs and perfectly efficient capital markets, M & M demonstrate that leverage *cannot* affect the value of the firm, and, therefore, an *optimal* capital structure cannot be identified. Under these assumptions the firm is indifferent between the use of debt or equity to finance its investments. In the more important case of corporate taxation the M & M analysis leads to an extreme "corner solution", that is the firm's *optimal* financial structure is made up mainly of debt.

Application of the *CAPM* to the analyis reinforces the basic M & M proposition. In the pre-tax case the value of the firm is invariant to changes in the debt-equity mix; and in the post-tax case the *CAPM* framework again implies a maximum use of debt. In terms of the *CAPM* this also implies that a firm's systematic risk (beta coefficient) rises with the degree of leverage.

QUESTIONS AND PROBLEMS

15.1 Define the term "homemade leverage".

15.2 Modigliani and Miller claim that in a world without taxes, firms cannot benefit from leverage. Prove that statement by using a numerical example. Explain carefully the arbitrage transaction.

15.3 Assume that there are two firms, Alpha and Beta, which have just commenced operations and both of which require an initial investment of $4 million. Futhermore assume that these firms are *identical* in all respects except for their capital structures.

Alpha raises the required money by issuing 200,000 shares of common stock at a price of $20 per share, while Beta raises the required $4 million by issuing 120,000 shares at $20 per share and by using $7\frac{1}{2}\%$ bonds for the remainder.

Assume that both firms expect a return of $240,000 on their investment with a probability of 1/3 and $960,000 with a probability of 2/3. Answer the following questions, ignoring corporate taxes:

(a)   Assuming that investors are unable to borrow and lend, is it possible that the market price of Beta's shares will be greater than the share price of Alpha?

(b)   Is it possible that the price of Alpha's shares will be higher than the price of Beta's shares? Prove your answers to (a) and (b).

(c)   Can Beta's share price be greater than Alpha's under M & M's assumption that individuals can borrow or lend at the same market rate of interest as firms? (In your answer, show the details of the arbitrage (selling and buying) process.)

15.4 With respect to question 15.3, can Alpha's share price be greater than Beta's given M & M's borrowing and lending assumption? (In your answer again show the details of the arbitrage process.)

15.5 A new firm which expects $800,000 in operating income before taxes is confronted with four mutually exclusive alternatives for financing its required investment:
(i) By 100% equity ($5 million in shares of stock).
(ii) By $4 million in shares of stock and $1 million of 7.5% bonds.
(iii) By $3 million in shares and $2 million of bonds.
(iv) By $2 million in shares and $3 million of bonds.
Assume a corporate tax rate of 48% and answer the following questions:
(a) Calculate the net income and the net operating income after taxes for each of the above alternatives.
(b) Calculate for each one of the four alternatives the value of the firm according to M & M's post-tax equilibrium relationship. (Assume that the capitalization rate for unlevered firms is 10%.)
(c) Graph the value of the firm as a function of the debt/equity ratio.

15.6 Distinguish between the *NOI* and *NI* approach to valuation. Which of the two methods is the more optimistic?

15.7 The Aladin Lamp Company has this year an operating income of $6,000,000. The firm has 1,600,000 shares of stock and no bonds.
(a) Calculate the total value of the firm and the value per share, using the *NOI* method and capitalization rate of 15%.
(b) What would your answer be to part (a) if the firm has $15,000,000 of debt (bonds) with an 8% interest charge and 1,000,000 shares of stock?
(c) What would your answer to part (a) be if the firm has $30,000,000 of debt (bonds) and 400,000 shares of stock?
(d) Answer parts (a), (b) and (c), using the *NI* method to valuation.

15.8 "The *NI* method automatically translates any increase in *EPS* to an increase in the price of the common stock". Prove the above quotation by a numerical example.

15.9 Modigliani and Miller claim that in a world of no corporate tax, firms cannot benefit from leverage. Prove that statement by using a numerical example. Explain carefully the arbitrage transaction.

15.10 Consider two corporations A and B identical in all respects, except for their financial structures. While firm A has debt in its capital structure, firm B finances all its operations only with equity. The earnings before interest and tax of each firm (*EBIT*) is a random variable denoted by *X*. The following data describe the two firms and the random variable *X*.

	Firm A	Firm B
Number of shares of Common Stock (N)	1,000,000	2,000,000
Long term debt (B_L)	$10,000,000	—

Distribution of *EBIT* for the two firms:

X	$Pr(X)$
$2,000,000	0.50
$1,200,000	0.25
$ – 500,000	0.25

The market value of the stock of firm B is $20,000,000, and the interest rate that firm A pays on its debt is 7%.

(a) In the absence of corporate taxes can the share price of firm A be higher than the share price of firm B, or vice versa? Prove your answer by means of a numerical example using two-way arbitrage.

(b) Now assume a corporate tax of $T = 0.50$. What should be the price of corporation A stock, given that the price of stock of corporation B is $10? Prove your answer by carrying out the two-way arbitrage and show that the price that you suggest is indeed an equilibrium price.

15.11 Assume two identical firms which differ only in their capital structure. Prove by numerical example that if the corporate tax is $T\%$, the following equilibrium holds,

$$V_L = V_U + TB_L$$

where

V_L = the market value of the levered firm.

V_U = the market value of the unlevered firm.

B_L = the market value of bonds issued by the levered firm.

T = the corporate tax rate.

In your answer, use detailed tables to show the way the arbitrage mechanism ensures that deviations from the above equality cannot be permanent. (See Appendix 15B.)

15.12 What is the optimal capital structure that will be chosen by a firm's manager, who adopts the M & M model? Do firms in practice behave according to the M & M model?

15.13 Define and prove M & M's Proposition II in the absence of income taxes. What is the relationship of the pre-tax Proposition II to its post-tax counterpart? (See Appendix 15B.)

15.14 Assume an unlevered firm whose net operating income is equal to $700,000 and its total market value is $5,000,000.

(a) What will be the required rate of return on the equity of a levered firm in equilibrium in the absence of taxes, if the interest rate on the firm's bonds is 8%, and the proportion of the debt in the capital structure $B/(B+S)$ is 20%? 40%? 60%? 80%?

(b) Illustrate graphically the rate of return on the levered firm's equity as a function of the debt/equity ratio (B/S).

(c) Answer the above in post-tax terms assuming a 50% corporate tax rate. (See Appendix 15B.)

15.15 John McKinney, Jr. is planning to establish an electronic company which will require an initial capital investment of $12,500,000. His financial manager offers five mutually exclusive alternatives for financing this investment:

(i)   1 million shares, and no debt.
(ii) 800,000 shares and $2,500,000 worth of 7.5% bonds.
(iii) 600,000 shares and $5 million worth of bonds.
(iv) 400,000 shares and $7,500,000 worth of bonds.
(v)   200,000 shares and $10 million worth of bonds.

Assume a corporate income tax of 48% and answer the following questions:

(a) Calculate the market value of the firm for each financing alternative, using the M & M post-tax equilibrium formula.

(b) Calculate the maximum possible price per share, for which the firm can sell its shares, in each alternative.

(c) What is the meaning of a "corner solution" in the above case? Why is such a solution unsatisfactory?

15.16 Consider the following data concerning the income and investment of a given firm and some market parameters (assume no-tax framework):

Current income $X_0 = \$5,000$; current investment $I_0 = \$3,000$; expected rate of return on the market portfolio $\bar{r}_m = 0.14$; standard deviation of the market rate of return $\sigma_m = 0.12$; risk-free interest rate $r = 0.06$; expected end-of-period income $\bar{X}_1 = \$6,000$; $Cov(\tilde{X}_1, \tilde{r}_m) = 100$.

(a) Determine the value of the firm at t_0.

(b) Suppose the firm issues (at time t_0) debt which yields return $\tilde{y}^b$ with the following characteristics:

$$\tilde{y}^b = \$2,000$$
$$Cov(\tilde{y}^b, r_m) = 10$$

In other words, the firm does not change its investment but finances it partly by debt and partly by stock. Determine the value of the debt, and the value of the firm at t_0. Does the value of the firm change as a result of the debt issue?

15.17 (a) Given that $\beta_U = 1$ (unlevered), calculate β_L for a levered firm with 50% debt in its capital mix. Assume a corporate tax rate equal to zero.

(b) Now answer the same question assuming a 50% corporate tax.

15.18   Suppose there are no taxes. Calculate the Beta of a levered firm with a *25% debt to equity* ratio given the following data.

Year	Rate of Return on the Unlevered Firm X_U	Rate of Return on the Market Portfolio X_m
1978	0.1	0.08
1979	0.12	0.06
1980	0.05	0.10
1981	0.02	0.12

15.19   Given the following data, calculate β_U and β_L assuming a *debt to equity* ratio of 0.5. Explain your results.

Year	Rate of Return on the Unlevered Firm X_U	Rate of Return on the Market Portfolio X_m
1978	0.1	0.05
1979	0.05	0.075
1980	0.025	0.15
1981	0.0415	0.05

APPENDIX 15A ALTERNATIVE FORMULATIONS OF THE GOAL OF THE FIRM [1]

In this book we have assumed throughout that the firm takes as its goal the maximization of the wealth of its existing stockholders. Several variants of this objective have been referred to in the course of our discussion of leverage. Depending on the particular context, the objective of the firm has also been defined in terms of the maximization of the value of the firm, the price per share of its common stock, or the value of the owners' equity. The purpose of this Appendix is to show that the three alternatives come to the same thing and that all three imply the maximization of stockholders' wealth.

Let's start by demonstrating the equivalence between maximizing the total market value of the firm and the maximization of share price. [2] Consider an unlevered firm whose total capitalization consists of n_0 shares of common stock with a market price per share of P_0. The total value of this firm is given by

$$V_0 = n_0 P_0$$

---

1 The appendix follows the proof set out in Haim Levy and Marshall Sarnat, "A Pedagogic Note on Alternative Formulation of the Goal of the Firm", *Journal of Business,* October 1977.

2 Obviously the number of shares, and hence their price, can be changed arbitrarily by stock splits or stock dividends. In such an event, the "price" per share would have to be adjusted to reflect these alterations.

Now, suppose the firm considers an alternative capital structure, which includes B_0 dollars of bonds, the remainder to be financed by equity. As a result, the firm can maintain the same level of economic activity by issuing a smaller number of shares. Denoting the required number of shares by n_1 we can determine the number of shares needed when B_0 dollars of bonds are issued as follows:

$$n_1 = \frac{V_0 - B_0}{V_0} \cdot n_0$$

Denoting the price of the shares of the levered alternative by P_1, the total market value of the levered firm, V_1, can be written as follows:

$$V_1 = n_1 P_1 + B_0 = \frac{V_0 - B_0}{V_0} \cdot n_0 \cdot P_1 + B_0$$

Since by definition $n_0 = V_0 / P_0$ we can rewrite this expression as

$$V_1 = (V_0 - B_0) \frac{P_1}{P_0} + B_0$$

Now if leverage increases the value of the firm, so that $V_1 > V_0$, we have

$$V_1 \equiv (V_0 - B_0) \frac{P_1}{P_0} + B_0 > V_0$$

But this relationship can hold *if and only if* $P_1 > P_0$, i.e. if the price of the shares of the levered alternative is higher than the share price of the unlevered strategy. Hence the financial policy which maximizes the value of the firm also maximizes the price of the firm's common stock. Thus, we use interchangeably the objective functions "maximizing of the value of the firm" and "maximizing the value per share".

A numerical example might prove helpful. Suppose that the firm wants to raise $100,000 by selling 1,000 shares of common stock at a price of $100 per share. Now let us assume that the firm decides on an alternative financial policy, say issuing $50,000 of bonds. In order to make the relevant comparison, the firm should issue only 500 shares $\left(\frac{V_0 - B_0}{V_0} \cdot n_0 = 500 \right)$ since it needs to raise only half of the equity that it previously required. If the "levered" firm succeeds in selling its stock for more than $100 per share, the leverage is *positive* and the total market value of the firm (bonds plus stock), as well as the price per share of stock increase.[3]

---

3 The reader should note that if the firm raises $50,000 by means of a bond issue and also issues 500 shares at a price P_1, $P_1 > P_0$, the total capital raised will exceed $100,000. In order to hold the level of investment unchanged, we assume that the firm immediately distributes any excess as a dividend to its shareholders. The need to preserve a given level of overall economic activity is a sine qua non for the rigorous analysis of problems involving leverage, as has been emphasized by Franco Modigliani and Merton H. Miller in their pioneering 1958 article, and in their subsequent work (see Modigliani and Miller, "The Cost of Capital, Corporation Finance and the Theory of Investment", *American Economic Review*, June 1958.

Note that the maximization of the price per share is not identical in the above example to the maximization of the total market value of the equity, since for a given investment (i.e. a given size of the firm), the higher the proportion of debt employed the lower is the total required equity. Thus it is not intuitively obvious that the maximization of the market value of the firm (share price) implies the maximization of the value of owners' wealth (or equity).

In order to clarify this question, let's consider the case of an unlevered firm which repurchases 50% of its outstanding shares at the going market price P_0, using for this purpose the proceeds of a new debt issue. Let's further assume that the debt issue is announced one day *after* the repurchase agreement, which is tantamount to assuming that the change in financial policy (increase in leverage) is not anticipated by the market on the day the shares are repurchased. To show in this case that the maximization of the value of the firm is consistent with the maximization of equity (or wealth) of its *existing* stockholders, we shall employ a simple device. Consider the previous example: A firm which issues n_0 shares at a market price of P_0; hence its total market value is again given by $V_0 = n_0 P_0$. Now assume that the firm considers repurchasing $n_0/2$ of its shares, at the going price of P_0. Since the firm wishes to maintain the same level of operations, it raises an additional amount of debt, $B = V_0/2$, to finance the partial repurchase of its shares. Recalling that $n_0 = V_0/P_0$, the total value of the firm after these transactions can be written as $V_1 = n_0/2 \cdot P_1 + B = n_0/2 \cdot P_1 + V_0/2 = V_0/2 \cdot P_1/P_0 + V_0/2 = V_0(P_1/P_0 + 1)/2$, where P_1 denotes the new price of shares after the introduction of debt into the capital structure. Clearly, if $V_1 > V_0$ this again implies that $P_1 > P_0$. Hence, each *existing* stockholder who held two shares before the bonds were issued received P_0 for one share (through the firm's repurchase of 50% of the outstanding shares); in addition his second share is now worth P_1, $P_1 > P_0$, and as a result the shareholder's total wealth is also enhanced because $(P_0 + P_1) > 2P_0$.

Now let's consider a somewhat more plausible scenario in which the firm first incurs the debt and only later uses the proceeds to repurchase "some" of its outstanding shares. In this instance we cannot stipulate with certainty the exact number of shares, B/P_1, which will be repurchased; the market can be expected to react to the "new information" regarding the firm's new financial policy, and as a result, the repurchase will be effected at a new market price P_1, $P_1 \gtreqless P_0$. In this case the value of the firm after the transactions (debt issue and share repurchase) becomes:

$$V_1 = \left(n_0 - \frac{B}{P_1} \right) P_1 + B = n_0 P_1 - B + B = n_0 P_1.$$

Recalling that $V_0 = n_0 P_0$, we once again find that $V_1 > V_0$ if and only if $P_1 > P_0$. Moreover, since stockholders total wealth prior to the debt issue was $V_0 = n_0 P_0$ and following the share repurchase their total wealth is given by $n_0 P_1 - B = V_1 - B$ *plus* B which was received in payment for the repurchased shares, total wealth increases if and only if $V_1 > V_0$, or equivalent if $P_1 > P_0$.

As we have just seen, the total value of equity (held by the firm *and* the stockholders) rises when the market price per share and the total value of the firm increase. Thus, when our problem is correctly stated, the three alternative goals of the firm: maximum total market value; maximum share price and maximum value of owners' equity are identical after all, and all three imply the maximization of the wealth of the firm's existing stockholders.

APPENDIX 15B   A FORMAL PROOF OF THE MODIGLIANI AND MILLER PROPOSITIONS

In the text we have illustrated the M & M Analysis, in the absence of taxation, by means of specific numerical examples. However, by employing the arbitrage mechanism which characterizes a perfectly efficient capital market, the general proof of their argument is straightforward.

PROPOSITION I: NO TAXES

M & M's first proposition states that the value of the firm is independent of its capital structure. In other words, *other things being equal*, the value of a levered firm will be exactly equal to its unlevered counterpart. To prove this statement,[1] let us first define the following notations:

$$V_U \equiv S_U = \text{the market value of an unlevered firm's securities}$$
$$S_U = \text{the market value of an unlevered firm's shares}$$
$$V_L \equiv S_L + B_L = \text{the market value of a levered firm's securities}$$
$$S_L = \text{the market value of a levered firm's shares}$$
$$B_L = \text{the market value of a levered firm's bonds (debt)}$$
$$r = \text{the interest rate}$$
$$X = \text{net operating income, which is identical for both the levered}$$

and unlevered firms. This income stream is gross of interest payments (if any), but net of all other operating expenses.

Proposition I can be proved by showing that if V_U does not equal V_L, then it would be possible for holders of the shares of the "overvalued" firm to achieve a better investment combination by selling their shares and buying the shares of the undervalued firm, and that this shift will continue until the following equilibrium relationship is restored:

$$V_L = V_U$$

Consider an investor who holds any fraction α of the shares of the unlevered firm. His investment is $\alpha S_U \equiv \alpha V_U$ and his return is αX. If $V_U > V_L$, the investor can build a new portfolio which increases his return, without increasing his investment. Table 15B.1 describes the suggested transaction.

1 The proof is taken from F. Modigliani and M. H. Miller, "Reply to Heins and Sprenkle", *American Economic Review*, September 1969.

Table 15B.1

	Investment Required	Return Produced
Initial Position	αV_U	αX
Transaction		
(a) Buy the fraction α of the shares in the levered firm	$S_L \equiv \alpha(V_L - B_L)$	$\alpha(X - rB_L)$
(b) Buy the fraction α of the bonds of the levered firm	αB_L	$\alpha r B_L$
TOTAL INVESTMENT (a + b)	αV_L	αX

Before the change in the investment portfolio the investor received a return αX for an investment $\alpha S_U = \alpha V_U$. Following the change in the portfolio he still receives a return of αX, but his investment outlay is αV_L. Now, if we assume that $V_U > V_L$, it will be worthwhile to sell the shares of the unlevered firm and to use the proceeds from the sale to buy the stocks and bonds of the levered firm. But this process will tend to raise the market price of the levered firm's shares, while at the same time the price of the unlevered firm's shares will tend to fall. This can be expected to continue until $V_L = V_U$, at which time equilibrium will have been restored. For when $V_U = V_L$ investors have no further incentive to change their portfolios.

Let us now examine the reverse case, in which we assume that $V_L > V_U$. In order to show that this inequality cannot hold in equilibrium, we shall assume initially that an investor holds a fraction α of the levered firm's stock. Hence his investment is $\alpha S_L \, \alpha(V_L - B_L)$, and his return equals $\alpha(X - rB_L)$. Table 15B.2 shows that if $V_L > V_U$, as assumed, the investor can gain by switching his investment from the levered firm to the unlevered firm. In this manner the investor still receives the same return $\alpha(X - rB_L)$ that he had before, but his investment is now $\alpha(V_U - B_L)$ rather than $\alpha(V_L - B_L)$. As long as $V_U < V_L$ it is worthwhile to shift to the shares of the unlevered firm, thereby obtaining the *same* stream

Table 15B.2

	Investment Required	Return Produced
Initial Position	$\alpha S_L = \alpha(V_L - B_L)$	$\alpha(X - rB_L)$
Transaction		
(a) Buy the fraction α of the shares of the unlevered firm	$\alpha S_U = \alpha V_U$	αX
(b) Borrow αB_L on personal account	$-\alpha B_L$	$-\alpha r B_L$
TOTAL INVESTMENT (a + b)	$\alpha(V_U - B_L)$	$\alpha(X - rB_L)$

of returns for *less* cost. By switching from the overvalued firm to the under-valued firm, market forces are again created which, in equilibrium, restore the equality $V_L = V_U$.

To summarize, the arbitrage mechanism of a perfect capital market ensures that in equilibrium neither $V_L > V_U$ nor $V_L < V_U$ can persist, and therefore, V_L must equal V_U. This means that the value of the firm is independent of its capital structure, which is the proposition that we set out to prove. This formal proof confirms the numerical examples given in the text.

It should be noted that we have assumed here, as before, that the two firms are characterized by the same level of profitability (X) and by the same economic risk, and that they differ only in their capital structures. However, there is really no need to think about two firms at all; we seek to determine the impact of a change in the capital structure of a given firm on the value of its securities. Thus the relevant example would be to consider the same firm in two different hypothetical situations rather than two different firms in a given time period. The use of two firms serves only as convenient expository device, and is not necessary for the argument.[2]

PROPOSITION I: WITH CORPORATE TAXES

Taking corporate taxes into account, M & M argue that the equilibrium value of the levered firm will be higher than its unlevered counterpart. The precise equilibrium relationship is given by their post-tax Proposition I:

$$S_L + B_L \equiv V_L = V_U + TB_L$$

This can be proved as follows:

Denoting the corporate tax rate by T, the net income of the shareholders of the unlevered firm is $(1 - T)X$, while the net income to the shareholders of the levered firm is $(X - rB_L)(1 - T)$. Consider first a case in which we assume that $S_L + B_L \equiv V_U + TB_L$, which implies that $S_L > V_U - (1 - T)B_L$. An investor who owns αS_L of the levered firm's shares can gain by making the portfolio switch that is spelled out in Table 15B.3. The return to the investor, both before and after the transaction, is the same, and is given by $\alpha(X - rB_L)(1 - T)$. But by switching to the unlevered firm, and borrowing on his personal account, his outlay is $\alpha[V_U - (1 - T)B_L]$, which by assumption is smaller than his previous outlay αS_L. Thus he can gain by selling the levered firm's shares and buying the unlevered firm's shares, so long as $V_L > S_U + TB_L$. Thus in equilibrium the last inequality can not hold, and V_L must equal $V_U + TB_L$.

To complete the post-tax presentation, we must prove that $V_L < V_U + TB_L$ also cannot hold. Let us assume that an investor owns a fraction α of the unlevered firm's shares; that is, his investment outlay is $\alpha S_U \equiv \alpha V_U$ which

---

2 As Stiglitz, *op. cit.*, has shown, this enables us to dispense with the awkward device of postulating the so-called "equal risk classes" which plagued earlier proofs of the M & M pro-positions.

Table 15B.3

	Investment Required	Return Produced
Initial Position	αS_L	$\alpha(X - rB_L)(1 - T)$
Transaction		
(a) Buy the fraction α of the shares of the unlevered firm	$\alpha S_U \equiv \alpha V_U$	$\alpha X(1 - T)$
(b) Borrow $\alpha(1 - T)B_L$ on personal account	$-\alpha(1 - T)B_L$	$-\alpha(1 - T)rB_L$
TOTAL INVESTMENT (a + b)	$\alpha[V_U - (1 - T)B_L]$	$\alpha[X - rB_L(1 - T)]$

affords him a return of $\alpha X(1 - T)$. But if the investor carries out the switch indicated in Table 15B.4 that is, selling the shares of the over-valued unlevered firm and purchasing the shares and bonds of the levered firm, he can achieve the same level of return at a reduced investment outlay. And since this shift will be worthwhile so long as $V_L < V_U + TB_L$ market forces are again created which will restore the equilibrium equality between V_L and $V_U + TB_L$.

Table 15B.4

	Investment Required	Return Produced
Initial Position	$\alpha S_U \equiv \alpha V_U$	$\alpha X(1 - T)$
Transaction		
(a) Buy the fraction α of the shares of the levered firm	$\alpha S_L = \alpha(V_L - B_L)$	$\alpha(X - rB_L)(1 - T)$
(b) Buy a fraction $\alpha(1 - T)B_L$ of the bonds of the levered firm	$\alpha B_L(1 - T)$	$\alpha rB_L(1 - T)$
TOTAL INVESTMENT (a + b)	$\alpha(V_L - TB_L)$	$\alpha X(1 - T)$

PROPOSITION II

In a world of taxes M & M's second proposition can also be derived. Denoting the *after-tax* rate of return as Y_U^* for the case of levered shares we can write the following post-tax relationships:

$$Y_U^* = \frac{(1 - T)X}{V_U}$$

$$Y_L = \frac{(1 - T)(X - rB_L)}{V_L^* - B_L} = \frac{(1 - T)(X - rB_L)}{S_L}$$

$$= \frac{(1 - T)X}{S_L} - \frac{(1 - T)(rB_L)}{S_L}$$

Multiplying and dividing the first term on the right-hand side of the latter by V_U, we have

$$Y_L^* \quad \frac{(1 - T)X}{V_U} \cdot \frac{V_U}{S_L} - \frac{(1 - T)rB_L}{S_L} = Y_U^* \frac{V_U}{S_L} - \frac{(1 - T)rB_L}{S_L}$$

Now if we add and subtract

$$\frac{Y_U^*(1 - T)B_L}{S_L}$$

we obtain

$$Y_L^* = Y_U^* \left[\frac{V_U}{S_L} - \frac{(1 - T)B_L}{S_L} \right] + Y_U^* \frac{(1 - T)B_L}{S_L} - \frac{(1 - T)rB_L}{S_L}$$

Since by Proposition I, $V_U - B_L + TB_L = S_L$, we have

$$Y_L^* = Y_U^* + (1 - T)(Y_U^* - r) \frac{B_L}{S_L}$$

Thus the post-tax yield on the equity of the levered firm is equal to the post-tax yield of the unlevered firm plus a risk premium which is a function of leverage, the interest rate, and the corporate tax rate.

Proposition II, for both the no-tax and post-tax cases, is represented graphically in Fig. 15B.1. The line $Y_U a$ shows the required rate of return on equity as a function of the degree of leverage. The higher B_L/S_L, the higher is the required rate of return. The slope of this line ($Y_U - r$) represents the required risk premium when B_L/S_L is changed by one unit.

The line $Y_U^* b$ sets out this relationship for the corporate tax case. Since by

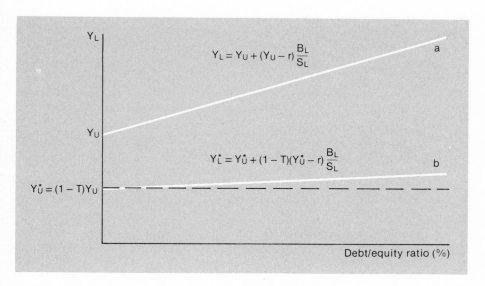

Fig. 15.B1

definition $(1 - T) < 1$ and $(Y_U^* - r) < (Y_U - r)$, the slope of line $Y_U^* b$ is smaller than previously. Thus because of the tax advantage of debt, the required risk premium is much lower than in the no-tax case. For example, assuming $Y_U = 10\%$, $r = 4\%$, and $T = 50\%$, the slope of line $Y_U a$ is 6% as compared with a slope of only $\frac{1}{2}\%$ for line $Y_U^* b$.

SELECTED REFERENCES

Arditti, F., Levy, H., and Sarnat M., "Taxes, Uncertainty and Optimal Dividend Policy", *Financial Management*, Vol. 5, No. 1, 1977.

Bailey, F.A. and Fung, W.K.F., "A Note on Extreme Leverage, MM and Ezra Solomon", *Journal of Business Finance & Accounting*, Summer 1978.

Baumol, William and Malkiel, Burton G., "The Firm's Optimal Debt-Equity Combination and the Cost of Capital", *Quarterly Journal of Economics*, November 1967.

Becker, J., "General Proof of Modigliani-Miller Propositions I and II Using Parameter-Preference Theory", *Journal of Financial and Quantitative Analysis*, March 1978.

Boness, A., Chen, Andrew H. and Jatusipitak, Som, "On Relations Among Stock Price Behavior and Chances in the Capital Structure of the Firm", *Journal of Financial and Quantitative Analysis*, September, 1972.

Boness, A.J. and Frankfurter, G.M., "Evidence of Non-Homogeneity of Capital Costs within "Risk-Classes", *Journal of Finance*, June 1977.

Booth, Laurence, D., "Capital Structure, Taxes, and the Cost of Capital", *The Quarterly Review of Economics and Business*, Autumn 1980.

Bradford, William D., "Valuation, Leverage and the Cost of Capital in the Case of Depreciable Assets: Comment", *The Journal of Finance*, March 1975.

Brennan, M.L. and Schwartz, E.S., "Corporate Income Taxes, Valuation, and the Problem of Optimal Capital Structure", *Journal of Business*, January 1978.

Brewer, D.E. and Michaelson, J., "The Cost of Capital, Corporation Finance, and the Theory of Investment: Comment", *American Economic Review*, January 1965.

Brigham, Eugene F. and Schome, Dilip K., "International Harvester Lecture: Effects of Inflation on Capital Structure and the Cost of Capital in the 1980s", *Journal of the Midwest Finance Association*, Vol. 9, 1980.

Conine, Thomas E. Jr., "Corporate Debt and Corporate Taxes: An Extension", *The Journal of Finance*, September 1980.

Durand, David, "Costs of Debt and Equity Funds for Business: Trends and Problems of Measurement", *The Management of Corporate Capital*, New York: The Free Press, 1959.

Fama, Eugene and Miller, Merton H., *The Theory of Finance*, New York: Holt, Rinehart and Winston, 1972.

Hamada, Robert S., "The Effect of the Firm's Capital Structure on the Systematic Risk of Common Stocks", *Journal of Finance*, May 1972.

Haugen, Robert A. and Wichern, Dean W., "The Intricate Relationship Between Financial Leverage and the Stability of Stock Prices", *Journal of Finance*, December 1975.

Heins, James A. and Sprenkle, Case M., "A Comment on the Modigliani-Miller Cost of Capital Thesis", *American Economic Review*, September 1969.

Hite, G.L., "Leverage, Output Effects and the M-M Theorems", *Journal of Financial Economics*, March 1977.

Hong, Hai and Rappaport, Alfred, "Debt Capacity, Optimal Capital Structure, and Capital Budgeting Analysis", *Financial Management*, Autumn 1978.

Husale, Gloria J., "Leverage, Risk, Market Structure and Profitability", *The Review of Economics and Statistics*, November 1974.

Inselbag, I., "Optimal Financing and Capital Structure Programs for the Firm: Comment", *Journal of Finance*, June 1976.

Keenen, Michael, "Models of Equity Valuations: The Great Serm Bubble", *Journal of Finance*, May 1970.

Kim, E.H., "A Mean-Variance Theory of Optimal Capital Structure and Corporate Debt Capacity", *Journal of Finance*, March 1978.

Kim, E.H., McConnell, J.J. and Greenwood, P.R., "Capital Structure Rearrangements and Me-First Rules in an Efficient Capital Market", *Journal of Finance*, June 1977.

Kraus, Alan and Litzenberger, Robert H., "A State-Preference Model of Optimal Financial Leverage", *Journal of Finance*, September 1973.

Krouse, Clement G., "Optimal Financing and Capital Structure Programs for the Firm", *Journal of Finance*, December 1972.

Litzenberger, Robert H. and Joy, O. M., "Target Rates of Return and Corporate Asset and Liability Structure under Uncertainty", *Journal of Financial and Quantitative Analysis*, March 1971.

Lloyd-Davis, P. R., "Optimal Financial Policy in Imperfect Markets", *Journal of Financial and Quantitative Analysis*, September 1975.

Melnyk, Lew Z., "Cost of Capital as a Function of Financial Leverage", *Decision Sciences*, July – October 1970.

Merton, R. C., "On the Pricing of Contingent Claims and the Modigliani-Miller Theorem", *Journal of Financial Economics*, November 1977.

Miller, M. H., "Debt and Taxes", *Journal of Finance*, May 1977.

Modigliani, Franco and Miller, M. H., "The Cost of Capital, Corporation Finance, and the Theory of Investment", *American Economic Review* (June 1958).

Modigliani, Franco and Miller, M. H., "The Cost of Capital, Corporation Finance and the Theory of Investment: Reply", *American Economic Review*, September 1958; "Taxes and the Cost of Capital: A Correction", *Ibid*, June 1963; "Reply", *Ibid*, June 1965; "Reply to Heins and Sprenkle", *Ibid*, September 1969.

Myers, Stewart C., "Interactions of Corporate Financing and Investment Decisions — Implications for Capital Budgeting", *Journal of Finance*, March 1974.

Myers, S. C., "Determinants of Corporate Borrowing", *Journal of Financial Economics*, November 1977.

Peles, Yoram C. and Sarnat, Marshall, "Corporation Taxes and Capital Structure: Some Evidence Drawn from the British Experience", *The Review of Economics and Statistics*, February 1979.

Resek, Robert W., "Multidimensional Risk and the Modigliani-Miller Hypothesis", *Journal of Finance*, March 1970.

Robichek, Alexander A., Higgins, Robert C. and Kinsman, Michael D., "The Effect of Leverage on the Cost of Equity Capital of Electric Utility Firms", *Journal of Finance*, May 1973.

Ross, S. A. "The Determination of Financial Structure: The Incentive-Signalling Approach", *Bell Journal of Economics*, Spring 1977.

Schall, Lawrence, D., "Firm Financial Structure and Investment", *Journal of Financial and Quantitative Analysis*, June 1971.

Schneller, M. I., "Taxes and the Optimal Capital Structure of the Firm", *Journal of Finance*, March 1980.

Senchack, A. J. Jr., "The Firm's Optimal Financial Policies: Solution, Equilibrium and Stability", *Journal of Financial and Quantitative Analysis*, November 1975.

Solomon, Ezra, "Leverage and the Cost of Capital", *Journal of Finance*, May 1963.

Stapleton, Richard C. and Burke, Christopher M., "European Tax Systems and the Neutrality of Corporate Financing Policy", *Journal of Banking and Finance*, June 1977.

Stiglitz, Joseph E., "On the Irrelevance of Corporate Financial Policy", *The American Economic Review*, December 1974.

Sullivan, Timothy G., "Market Power, Profitability and Financial Leverage", *Journal of Finance*, December 1974.

Taggart, Robert A. Jr., "Taxes and Corporate Capital Structure in an Incomplete Market", *The Journal of Finance*, June 1980.

Tuttle, Donald L. and Litzenberger, Robert H., "Leverage, Diversification and Capital Market Effects on a Risk-Adjusted Capital Budgeting Framework", *Journal of Finance*, June 1968.

Weston, J. Fred, "A Test of Cost of Capital Propositions", *Southern Economic Journal*, October 1963.

Wippern, Ronald F., "Financial Structure and the Value of the Firm", *Journal of Finance*, December 1966.

Wrightsman, D., "Tax Shield Valuation and the Capital Structure Decision", *Journal of Finance*, May 1978.

16

Bankruptcy Risk and the Choice of Financial Structure

Numerous factors can affect financing decisions, and some of them clearly operate against the use of debt to finance a firm's operations. This chapter will be devoted to the role played by bankruptcy risk which appears to be the crucial factor precluding the excessive use of debt in corporate capital structures.

THE PROBLEM OF EXTREME CORNER SOLUTIONS

As we noted at the end of the preceding chapter, the Modigliani and Miller analysis of a firm's capital structure, in the relevant case in which the firm is assumed to pay corporate taxes, leads to an extreme "corner solution" in the sense that a firm's capital structure is comprised of nearly 100% debt. The fact that the M & M analysis implies such a solution can easily be verified from the equilibrium relationship which states that $V_L = V_U + TB_L$. In the numerical example given in Table 16.1 and graphed in Fig. 16.1, we have used their equilibrium equation to calculate the maximum price for which the firm can sell its common stock in the market. Suppose that a new firm decides to sell 20,000 shares and to use the proceeds to finance some specific business activities. The firm issues no debt and, of course, tries to sell its shares at the highest possible price. Let us assume that it succeeds in selling its stock at a net price of $1 per share; hence the total amount of money available for investment is $20,000. Now suppose that the same firm considers the possibility of financing the same operations by borrowing $5,000 and issuing only 15,000 shares. Assuming a 50% corporate tax rate and applying the M & M *post-tax* equilibrium condition ($V_L = V_U + TB_L$), we find that

$$V_L = \$20,000 + 1/2 \times \$5,000 = 22,500$$

Table 16.1

| | Zero Debt | Alternative Financing Policies* | | |
		$5,000 Debt	$10,000 Debt	$15,000 Debt
	$	$	$	$
Value of the firm	20,000	22,500	25,000	27,500
Total value of debt	—	5,000	10,000	15,000
Total value of stock	20,000	17,500	15,000	12,500
Number of shares	20,000	15,000	10,000	5,000
Price per share	$1	$1.16	$1.50	$2.50

*Assuming a corporate tax rate equal to 50%.

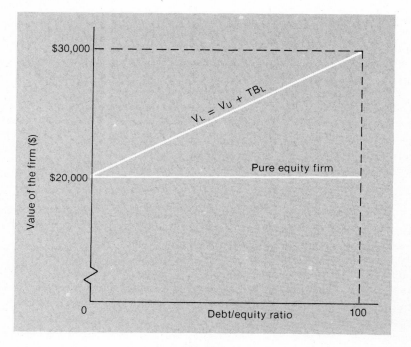

Fig. 16.1

Since the value of the debt is $5,000, it follows that the value of stock is $17,500, i.e. the firm can sell 15,000 shares at a price of $1.16 per share ($17,500/15,000 = 1.16) as compared with a price of $1 in the unlevered case. Similarly, should the firm decide to borrow $10,000 and issue only 10,000 shares it can succeed in selling the shares for $1.50 per share. The firm will maximize its market value, and hence the market price of a share of its stock, if management adopts an extreme policy of issuing nearly 100% debt. Such a "corner solution" is, of course, an unsatisfactory result in the positive sense, because in reality firms do not, and in fact cannot, achieve anywhere near that degree of leverage. Clearly, the analysis of the previous chapter did not capture all of the relevant factors influencing the financing decision.

RISK OF BANKRUPTCY

In practice, a firm is confronted with steeply rising interest rates beyond fairly low levels of the debt-equity ratio, since lenders and borrowers are sensitive to the possibility of "gamblers ruin", i.e. bankruptcy, which as we have already noted is ruled out in the M & M analysis. Similarly the M & M analysis assumes that investors and firms can borrow at the same interest rate. In effect this means that the investor will be indifferent between the leverage achieved by the firm and the so-called "homemade" leverage which he achieves by borrowing on his own account. Once again this reflects the absence of possible bankruptcy in the model, for unless this assumption holds, considerations of limited liability will logically lead the investor to prefer corporate to homemade leverage. Thus to the degree that substantial differences in borrowing rates exist, which is tantamount to the introduction of differential bankruptcy risk into the model, one can expect a firm's optimal capital structure to fall far short of the extreme corner solution. The actual degree of leverage used will reflect the particular firm's ability to absorb the financial risk inherent in the use of debt without incurring a penalty from the financial community in the form of increased interest rates and/or a fall in the price of its stock.

THE NATURE OF FINANCIAL FAILURE[1]

Broadly speaking, we shall denote by the term *economic failure* a firm whose net rate of return, adjusted for risk, is significantly lower than the prevailing rate of interest. A corporation is a *legal failure* if the corporation's assets are not sufficient to meet the legally enforceable claims of creditors. These two concepts of business failure are not identical: the former measures success or failure in terms of earnings on invested capital; the latter uses a corporation's ability to meet its legally enforceable liabilities as the benchmark of performance.[2]

Two other terms are commonly used with respect to financial failure:

(a) *Technical Insolvency.* This refers to a state in which a firm finds itself unable to meet its current obligations even though its total assets exceed its total liabilities.

(b) *Bankruptcy (or equivalently insolvency in an equity sense).* A firm is bankrupt or insolvent in an equity sense when its total liabilities exceed a fair valuation of its total assets.

For convenience we shall use the term "failure" to include both of these aspects of the problem.

---

1 This section relies on the classic analysis of Arthur Stone Dewing, *The Financial Policy of Corporations*, 5th edn., New York, Ronald Press, 1953 (1st edn. 1919).

2 The reader should note that the term "legal failure" is somewhat misleading since this condition can exist even in the absence of any formal legal proceedings.

Underlying Causes of Failure

The usual "causes" given for financial failure, e.g. lack of capital, faulty accounting, poor planning, etc., are more often not causes but rather rationalizations or excuses for the poor performance. The underlying cause of most failures can best be summarized by the term *management incompetence*. It is the lack of managerial skills which appears to be the fundamental cause of business failure, independent of the size or nature of the business undertaking. Ultimately business success or failure depends on the quality of human management.[3]

Scope of Financial Failure[4]

As we have already mentioned, the extreme corner solution implied by the M & M analysis must be rejected because it does not reflect the essential properties of the capital structure decision, and therefore fails to "explain" (i.e. account for) the behavior patterns of actual firms. The source of much of this distortion of economic reality can be traced to the failure of the M & M model to reflect the risks and costs associated with the possibility of financial failure. The significance of this omission can be gauged by examining the data of Table 16.2. From 1925 to 1978 the failure rate of corporations ranged from a low of 4 per 10,000 during World War II to a high of 154 per 10,000 during the Great Depression of the 1930s. If, for illustrative purposes only, we take the average failure rate during the decade of the 1960s, i.e. slightly more than 50 per 10,000, this means that if one chooses a firm at random from the corporations constituting that population of Table 16.2, there exists a probability of $\frac{1}{2}\%$ that the firm so chosen will go bankrupt during the year. If we apply the average failure rate for the period as a whole, this probability rises to 1%. Clearly, even a relatively small probability of such a disaster as financial failure will be a cause of great concern to management and, therefore, will affect the financial decision-making process.

BANKRUPTCY RISK AND OPTIMAL CAPITAL STRUCTURE

Now let us turn our attention to the question of how the probability of bankruptcy can be expected to affect the firm's financial structure decision. Clearly, the probability of going bankrupt depends on many economic factors; however, the two most important factors for our purposes are the firm's

---

3 Dun and Bradstreet lists management incompetence as the cause in almost 90% of all business failures. See *The Failure Record Through* 1969.

4 For a comprehensive analysis of the trends in corporate bankruptcy in the United States, see Edward I. Altman, *Corporate Bankruptcy in America*, Lexington, Mass., Heath Lexington Books, 1971. Altman also sets out a multivariate statistical model designed to explain the aggregate failure rate and liability experience.

Table 16.2

Year	Number of Failures	Failure Rate per 10,000 Listed Concerns	Average Liability per Failure ($)
1925	21,214	100	20,918
1926	21,773	101	18,795
1927	23,146	106	22,471
1928	23,842	109	20,534
1929	22,909	104	21,094
1930	26,355	122	25,357
1931	28,285	133	26,032
1932	31,822	154	29,172
1933	19,859	100	23,038
1934	12,091	61	27,621
1935	12,244	62	25,366
1936	9,607	48	21,148
1937	9,490	46	19,310
1938	12,836	61	19,204
1939	14,768	70	12,359
1940	13,619	63	12,239
1941	11,848	55	11,488
1942	9,405	45	10,713
1943	3,221	16	14,076
1944	1,222	7	25,908
1945	809	4	37,361
1946	1,129	5	59,654
1947	3,474	14	58,898
1948	5,250	20	44,690
1949	9,246	34	33,323
1950	9,162	34	27,099
1951	8,058	31	32,210
1952	7,611	29	37,224
1953	8,862	33	44,477
1954	11,086	42	41,731
1955	10,969	42	40,968
1956	12,686	48	44,356
1957	13,739	52	44,784
1958	14,964	56	48,667
1959	14,053	52	49,300
1960	15,445	57	60,772
1961	17,075	64	68,843
1962	15,782	61	76,898
1963	14,374	56	94,100
1964	13,501	53	98,454
1965	13,514	53	97,800
1966	13,061	52	106,091
1967	12,364	49	102,332
1968	9,636	39	97,654
1969	9,154	37	125,000
1970	10,748	40	176,000
1971	10,326	42	186,000
1972	9,566	38	209,000
1973	9,345	36	246,000
1974	9,915	38	308,000
1975	11,432	43	383,000
1976	9,628	35	313,000
1977	7,919	28	391,000
1978	6,619	24	356,000

Source: U.S. Statistical Abstract 1979, p. 575.

economic and financial risks. Economic risk is associated mainly with the industry to which the firm belongs and with the general conditions of the economy. Hence even competent management can do very little to reduce economic risk, once the underlying decision regarding the type of economic activity to be pursued is taken. Financial risk, on the other hand, is subject almost completely to the discretionary control of management. By reducing the use of leverage the firm can decrease the variability of earnings, thereby decreasing the probability of not being able to meet fixed charges (interest and redemptions) during a series of consecutive years. Conversely, by increasing its use of leverage the firm also increases its financial risk and thereby the probability of financial failure.

Fortunately, the probability of bankruptcy and its impact on financial decision making can be incorporated in the basic capital structure model developed in Chapter 15 by utilizing a convenient hypothetical device. Suppose that each year the firm pays a premium to an insurance company (or to the government) in order to insure itself against the possibility of bankruptcy. Such an arrangement implies that the insurance company will pay the interest (and other fixed charges) to the firm's creditors in years in which losses are sustained. This assumption allows us to retain the M & M assumption of no bankruptcy, while also reflecting the costs of avoiding this risk. This, in turn, implies a significant change in the valuation equation, because the payments involved in the insurance transaction also affect the value of the firm.

The essential feature of the insurance arrangement lies in the fact that the insurance company pays the firm in years of negative cash flow but also receives an annual premium from the firm. In the unlikely event that the expected value of the cash receipts from the insurance company is equal to the stream of insurance premiums paid by the firm, no change will occur in the valuation equation for the firm, and therefore the corner solution will persist. However, under the more realistic assumption that the insurance company sets its premium sufficiently high to cover administrative costs and to provide a return on its investment, the net expected value of the insurance transaction is negative from the firm's viewpoint. Due to risk aversion, the firm is prepared to pay the "extra" premium required to cover the expenses and provide the insurance company's required profit. But this premium in excess of the expected value of the insurance coverage constitutes a net outlay from the firm to the insurance company and therefore must be deducted from the firm's cash flow, thereby changing its market value.

Since the insurance company's required return reflects its perception of the firm's risk, we expect that for a *given* level of business risk, the size of the excess premium will depend on the firm's financial risk, i.e. on the degree to which it uses leverage. The higher the financial leverage ratio the higher the risk of bankruptcy, and therefore the higher will be the extra required premium. Figure 16.2 illustrates a typical situation in which this payment is assumed to be quite moderate for low debt/equity ratios but increases at an accelerated rate as the firm resorts to more and more financial leverage.

Figure 16.3 illustrates the impact of deducting the present value of the extra

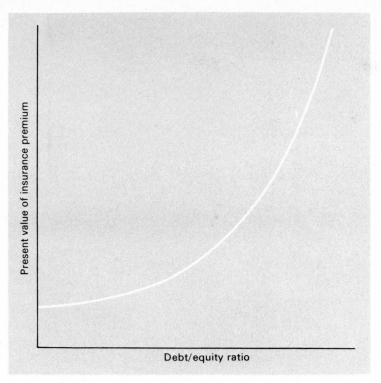

Fig. 16.2

insurance premium on the M & M valuation model. If one deducts from the basic after-tax valuation formula ($V_L = V_U + TB_L$) the present value of the costs (i.e. the excess premium) of avoiding bankruptcy, the corner solution is precluded. The line V_L of Fig. 16.3 sets out the relationship between the value of the firm and its financial leverage as postulated in the non bankruptcy case. As we have previously shown, this model implies an extreme capital structure comprised largely of debt. The U-shaped curve denoted by V_B in Fig. 16.3 is derived by deducting the present value of the excess premium paid to avoid bankruptcy from the line V_L. The particular shape of the V_B curve reflects our assumption that the risk of bankruptcy (and, therefore, the size of this premium) rises at an *increasing* rate as additional leverage is employed.

The striking feature of explicitly incorporating bankruptcy risk in the M & M valuation model is that it permits us to avoid the extreme corner solution. Up to point L^* of Fig 16.3 the value of the firm rises as debt is introduced into the capital structure; however, beyond this point, increasing the use of leverage lowers the value of the firm. It follows that such a firm will not (and should not) strive to maximize the use of debt in its capital structure. Increasing leverage raises expected profits and owing to the tax effect it increases the value of the firm as well (line V_L); but the introduction of debt also increases the risk

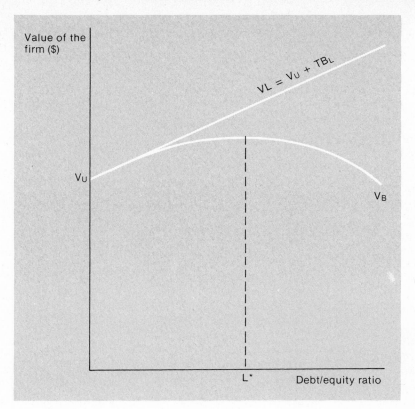

Fig. 16.3

of financial failure. For moderate degrees of debt the overall impact of leverage is positive (i.e. the value of the firm rises), but beyond some point the risk of bankruptcy becomes dominant and the impact of further increases in debt is negative. Such a critical turning point, denoted by L^* in Fig. 16.3, defines the firm's *optimal* capital structure. And in general it can safely be expected to fall far short of a 99% debt level.

The incorporation of bankruptcy risk can also serve to resolve another paradoxical result of the M & M model. The original valuation model (ignoring bankruptcy) implies not only an extreme corner solution, but also that this extreme debt/equity ratio is optimal for all firms, independent of their economic activity. Once again, this implication stands in sharp contrast to reality. Table 16.3 sets out a rough measure of the actual debt/equity ratios in eight industries. The data confirm the well-known fact that public utilities tend to employ relatively more debt than do manufacturing and mining concerns.[5] The ratio of long-term debt to equity is 0.9 for the former and 0.3 for the latter.

The reason for the variation in debt/equity ratios is not difficult to find.

5 The data of Table 16.3 reflect only long-term debt; however, the inclusion of short-term debt does not change the basic conclusion that the degree of leverage used by utilities is significantly greater than that in manufacturing and mining.

Table 16.3
Capital Structure in Selected Industries

	(1) Long-term Debt (*in million $*)	(2) Net Worth	(3) Debt/Equity Ratio (*in %*)
Agriculture, Forestry and Fishery	2,730	3,990	0.7
Mining	3,920	12,379	0.3
Contract Construction	4,815	10,936	0.4
Manufacturing	95,725	299,548	0.3
Transportation, Communication, Electric, Gas and Sanitary services	101,598	113,468	0.9
Wholesale and Retail Trade	22,115	74,987	0.3
Finance, Insurance and Real Estate	78,835	194,362	0.4
Services	16,286	17,854	0.9

Source: Department of the Treasury, Internal Revenue Service, *Statistics of Income 1969, Corporation Income Tax Returns.*

Utilities are less vulnerable to the risk of economic failure; the demand for their services is relatively stable, i.e. their economic risk is relatively low, although one should alway bear in mind that some risk alway exists. On the other hand, the economic risk in mining and manufacturing is much greater; due to changes in fashion or to the introduction of new products, the demand for industrial products, for example, is far less stable. This difference by itself can help to explain the variety of financial policies followed by various industry groups. Figure 16.4 illustrates two firms that would command the same market value if they did not use debt at all (V_U). Now, assume that the curve labeled A represents a mining or manufacturing firm and the curve denoted by B is a public utility. Ignoring bankruptcy risk, the two firms would adopt a policy of maximum debt financing and both would have the same market value as described by line V_L. However, once the risk of bankruptcy is recognized, the manufacturing firm can be expected to use far less debt than does the public utility, i.e. the optimal debt/equity ratio of the former L_A lies to the left of the optimal debt/equity mix of the latter, L_B. This result follows from the assumption that the *economic risks* in manufacturing are greater than those of a public utility. Thus even though both firms are confronted by the risk of financial failure, the degree of risk is greater for the manufacturing concern. In terms of our convenient insurance device, both firms can insure themselves against failure, but the excess premium charged to the manufacturing firm will be significantly higher than that required of the utility. Thus, the explicit incorporation of bankruptcy risk into the model bridges the gap between the theoretical results and empirical observation; the revised valuation model, which incorporates the penalty for financial failure, can serve as a useful guide and benchmark for corporate financial strategy.[6]

---

6 The reader should note that the device of insurance is employed as a means of formally incorporating bankruptcy risk into the model. The risk exists even though a firm does not actually insure itself, the hypothetical premium serving as a convenient proxy for the economic costs of bearing a given level of bankruptcy risk.

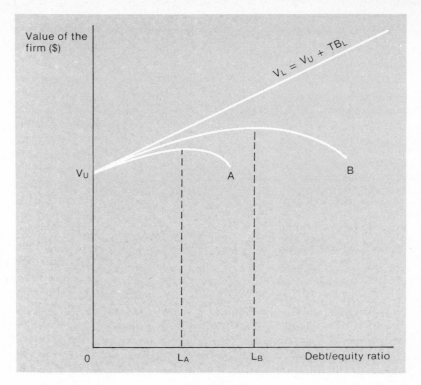

Fig. 16.4

A NUMERICAL EXAMPLE

In order to make the crucial role of default risk even more transparent, let us consider a specific numerical example. Table 16.4 reproduces the four financing alternatives originally set out in Table 16.1 above. In this particular example, the value of the unlevered firm, V_U, equals \$20,000. The unadjusted valuation formula, $V_L = V_U + TB_L$ (assuming $T = 50\%$), was then used to calculate the value of the firm for three alternative degrees of leverage. These values are given in line 1 of Table 16.4. In order to simplify the exposition we further assume that the firm can insure itself against bankruptcy, and that the size of the annual extra premium is \$4,000 (\$2,000 on an after-tax basis) multiplied by the probability of bankruptcy. Clearly, the higher the latter, the higher will be the required extra premium which reflects the insurance company's higher required return on the riskier undertaking.

This annual excess premium for Firm A is given in line 5 of Table 16.4. To calculate the net present value of the firm, with bankruptcy risk eliminated, one must deduct the present value of the extra premiums from line 1 (the value of the firm using the unadjusted M & M model). This present value has been

Table 16.4

	Alternative Financing Policies			
	Zero Debt	$5,000 Debt	$10,000 Debt	$15,000 Debt
1. Value of the firm	20,000	22,500	25,000	27,500
2. Total value of debt	—	5,000	10,000	15,000
3. Total value of shares	20,000	17,500	15,000	12,500
		Firm A		
4. Probability of failure (in %)	1	5	7½	15
5. After-tax excess premium paid ($2,000) × (4)	20	100	150	300
6. Present value of the excess premium (at 5% discount rate)	400	2,000	3,000	6,000
7. Net value of firm (1) − (6)	19,600	20,500	**22,000**	21,500
		Firm B		
8. Probability of failure (in %)	5	10	20	30
9. After-tax excess premium paid ($2,000) × (8)	100	200	400	600
10. Present value of the excess premium (at 5% discount rate)	2,000	4,000	8,000	12,000
11. Net value of firm (1) − (10)	18,000	**18,500**	17,000	15,500

calculated using a 5% discount rate. The net present value of the firm when the possibility of financial failure is taken into account is given in line 7.

The reader should note that while the original M & M hypothesis leads to an extreme debt policy, successive increments of debt to the capital structure increase the value of the firm (line 1); once the economic costs of bankruptcy are taken into account this "corner solution" disappears. An examination of line 7 reveals that the value of the firm increases with leverage up to the $10,000 debt alternative but declines when $15,000 of debt is employed. Hence $10,000 of debt, i.e. a 50% debt-equity ratio, represents the *optimal* financial policy for firm A. This result was obtained by explicitly incorporating the cost of bankruptcy risk into the M & M valuation model, using the very realistic assumption that the probability of financial failure *increases* as the financial leverage ratio increases (see lines 4 and 8 of Table 16.4).

Table 16.4 also presents a parallel set of calculations for a second firm denoted as B. This firm is similar in all respects to the first firm with the exception that its economic risk is assumed to be much higher. The probability of failure in the unlevered alternative is 5% for firm B as compared with only 1% for firm A (compare lines 4 and 8). As a result, the total risk of bankruptcy in firm B becomes quite large as leverage is introduced.

The relationship between firms A and B is illustrated graphically in Fig. 16.5. In the original M & M model (ignoring bankruptcy risk) the continuously rising line, V_L, sets out the value of *both* firms for various financing alternatives. When bankruptcy costs are explicitly included in the valuation model, the value of firm A reaches a maximum at a $10,000 debt level, while that of B

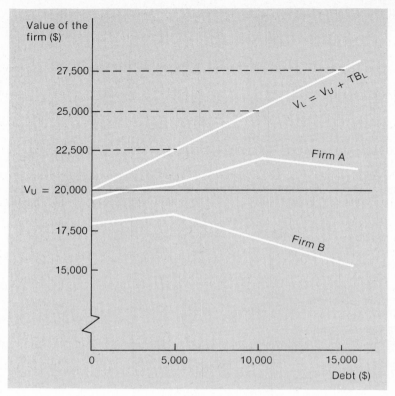

Fig. 16.5

reaches a maximum at a lower level of debt, i.e. $5,000. Once again this illustrates the fact that, other things being equal, firms with higher economic risks (e.g. mining companies) will tend to use proportionately less debt than do firms with lower levels of economic risk (e.g. public utilities).

LIQUIDATION COSTS

Even with the possibility that the firm may go bankrupt, it can be shown that given certain restrictive assumptions the relationship between the value of the firm and its leverage as proposed by M & M still holds. The most restrictive and unrealistic assumption necessary for this result is that bankruptcy be costless.

In order to better understand the assumption, recall that bankruptcy is the financial state that bondholders may choose to precipitate when the firm fails to meet the interest and principal payments on its debt as those payments come due. If the firm's failure to meet its cash obligations results in bondholders suing for the interest and principal owed them, a state of bankruptcy is entered. The firm's assets are liquidated, the fees of lawyers representing both sides are paid,

Table 16.5
Administrative Expenses of Bankruptcy Cases in U.S. District Courts Fiscal Years 1968 and 1976*

	1969	Per-centage 1969	1976	Per-centage 1976
Total Realization	$113,137,000	100	$229,535,533	100
Total Administrative Expenses	26,446,000	23.4	52,534,678	22.9
Receivers' Commissions	777,000	0.7	835,466	0.4
Receivers' Expenses	234,000	0.2	414,900	0.2
Trustees' Commissions	4,009,000	3.5	7,133,560	3.1
Referees' Salary and Expense Fund	2,808,000	2.5	7,630,861	3.3
Reporting and Transcribing Testimony	339,000	0.3	626,657	0.3
Accountants' Fees	576,000	0.5	1,234,297	0.5
Auctioneers' Fees	1,611,000	1.4	3,174,835	1.4
Appraisers' Fees	462,000	0.4	711,973	0.3
Attorneys for Creditors	460,000	0.4	359,104	0.2
Attorneys for Trustees	7,268,000	6.4	15,497,324	6.8
Attorneys for Receivers	781,000	0.7	840,231	0.4
Attorneys for Bankrupts	1,314,000	1.2	1,762,663	0.8
Attorneys for Others	560,000	0.5	1,566,256	0.7
Rental Expenses	1,241,000	1.1	2,239,956	1.0
Trustees for All Other Expenses	4,014,000	3.5	8,506,595	3.7

Source: Table of Bankruptcy Statistics, Washington D.C., Administrative Office of the United States Courts, June 30, 1969 and June 30, 1976.
* The figures relate to liquidation from July 1 – June 30 of the following year.

and the residual funds obtained from liquidation are distributed among security holders with bondholders having prior claim. Thus, bankruptcy involves costs; liquidation costs are estimated to comprise anywhere from 30% to 70% of the assets' going-concern value. Table 16.5 shows that the administrative expenses associated with bankruptcy alone can consume almost a quarter (about 23%) of the asset's realized value. Note also that administrative expenses contributed a constant percentage of liquidated assets in 1969 and 1976 even though the value of the liquidated assets themselves increased from about 113 million in 1969 to 239 million in 1976.

Clearly cost considerations of such a magnitude vitiate the M & M proposition about the relationship between leverage and the value of the firm. In the real world firms do not adopt extremely leveraged positions which increase the possibility of bankruptcy beyond acceptable levels. Moreover, even if bankruptcy were costless, the managers would still tend to lose their jobs once bankruptcy occurs, which again implies that firms normally will not willingly take on the extreme amount of debt that is implied by the M & M theorem with corporate taxation.

SUMMARY

The last two chapters have surveyed the factors affecting the firm's financing mix, including: location of the earnings distribution; stability of sales and earnings; dividend policy; control and the risk of bankruptcy. The latter consideration appears to be most crucial in precluding the excess use of debt.

The inclusion of bankruptcy risk in the M & M valuation model permits us to explain and account for two features of the observed financial policies of corporations:

(1)   Despite the tax advantages attached to the use of debt, firms in practice do not adopt extremely levered capital structures.

(2)   The degree to which leverage is employed depends inversely on the firm's underlying economic risk: the greater the economic risk the smaller will be the financial leverage ratio.

QUESTIONS AND PROBLEMS

16.1 Explain how the removal of the "no bankruptcy" assumption affects the M & M conclusion regarding leverage and valuation.

16.2 Distinguish between "economic failure" and "legal failure".

16.3 Give a numerical example of a firm which is bankrupt or insolvent in an equity sense.

16.4 "If firms were able to insure themselves against bankruptcy by paying a premium in excess of the expected value of the contract M & M's post-tax result would hold, and the optimal capital structure would be comprised of nearly 100% debt." Critically appraise this quotation.

16.5 In November 1976, the New Electronic Laboratories Coporation (NELCO) asked the L & S Insurance Company, which specializes in bankruptcy insurance, to underwrite its risk of failure. The insurance company undertook an obligation to pay a required constant sum to the firm's creditors in years in which losses are sustained, for an annual premium on this sum. The "excess" insurance premium required to induce the insurance company to underwrite the risk varied as a function of the rate of the debt in the capital structure as set out in the table on p. 403. NELCO had five alternatives for financing its initial required investment of $10 million:

(i)   100% shares;
(ii)   80% shares and 20% debt;
(iii)   60% shares and 40% debt;
(iv)   40% shares and 60% debt;
(v)   20% shares and 80% debt.

Assume that the required sum of money to be paid by the insurance

Percentage of Debt in the Capital Structure $B/(B+S)$	Annual "Extra" Premium (in %)
0.0	0.5
0.1	2
0.2	2.5
0.3	3.5
0.4	5
0.5	7
0.6	10
0.7	14.5
0.8	20
0.9	27

company in years of losses, in order to avoid NELCO's bankruptcy, is $1 million. Assume also that the corporate tax rate is 50% and that the discount rate (for present value calculations) is $6\frac{2}{3}\%$.

(a) Plot the present value of the insurance premium offered to NELCO as a function of the debt/equity ratio $[B/(B+S)]$.

(b) Calculate for each alternative the net value of the firm, with bankruptcy risk eliminated.

(c) Find the optimal financial policy for NELCO, from the above five alternatives.

(d) Plot the value and the net value of NELCO as a function of its financial leverage ratio.

16.6 Another compay — COMP — was offered a similar arrangement by L & S, with the same conditions as NELCO, except for the premium rates, which were higher:

Percentage of Debt in the Capital Structure $B/(B+S)$	Annual "Extra" Premium (in %)
0.0	1
0.1	2.5
0.2	3.5
0.3	5
0.4	7.5
0.5	11.5
0.6	17
0.7	24
0.8	32
0.9	42

Except for its economic risk, COMP is similar in all respects to NELCO (i.e. in its initial investment, the sum of money needed to avoid bankruptcy, the tax rate and the discount rate). Answer the following question assuming that COMP has the same financial alternatives as NELCO:

(a)   Plot the present value of the insurance premium offered to COMP as a function of the debt/equity ratio.

(b)   Calculate, for each alternative, the net value of the firm with bankruptcy risk eliminated.

(c)   Find the optimal financial policy for COMP.

(d)   Plot the value and the net value of COMP as a function of its financial leverage ratio.

(e)   Compare your results in 16.6 with those of 16.5. How do you account for the differences in optimal financial strategies?

SELECTED REFERENCES

Aharony, Joseph, Jones, Charles P. and Swary, Itzhak, "An Analysis of Risk and Return Characteristics of Corporate Bankruptcy Using Capital Market Data", *The Journal of Finance*, September 1980.

Altman, E. I., Haldeman, Robert G. and Narayanan, P., "ZETA Analysis: A New Model to Identify Bankruptcy Risk of Corporations", *Journal of Banking and Finance*, June 1977.

Altman, E. I., *Corporation Bankruptcy in America*, Lexington, Mass.: Heath Lexington Books, 1971.

Altman, E. I., Baidya, T. K. N. and Ribeiro Dias, L. M., "Assessing Potential Financial Problems for Firms in Brazil", *Journal of International Business Studies*, Fall 1979.

Arbel, A., Kolodny, R. and Lakonishok, J., "The Relationship between Risk of Default and Return on Equity: An Empirical Investigation", *Journal of Financial and Quantitative Analysis*, November 1977.

Baron, D. P., "Firm Valuation, Corporate Taxes and Default Risk", *The Journal of Finance*, December 1975.

Baron, D. P., "Default Risk and the Modigliani-Miller Theorem: A Synthesis", *American Economic Review*, March 1976.

Baxter, Nevins D., "Leverage, Risk of Ruin, and the Cost of Capital", *The Journal of Finance*, September 1967.

Beaver, William H., "Market Prices, Financial Ratios, and the Prediction of Failure", *Journal of Accounting Research*, Autumn 1968.

Cheng, P. L. "Default Risk, Scale, and the Homemade Leverage Theorem: Note", *American Economic Review*, September 1975.

Feder, Gershon, "Note on Debt, Assets and Lending under Default Risk", *Journal of Financial and Quantitative Analysis*, March 1980.

Flath, D. and Knoeber, C. R., "Taxes, Failure Costs and Optimal Industry Capital Structure: An Empirical Test", *The Journal of Finance*, March 1980.

Hagen, K. P., "Default Risk, Homemade Leverage and the Modigliani-Miler Theorem: Note", *American Economic Review*, March 1976.

Haugen, R. A. and Senbet, L. W., "The Insignificance of Bankruptcy Costs to the Theory of Optimal Capital Structure", *The Journal of Finance*, May 1978.

Lawler, Thomas A., "Yield Spreads, Relative Yield Spreads and Default Risk", *The Financial Review*, Winter 1980.

Machol, Robert F. and Lerner, Eugene, M., "Risk, Ruin and Investment Analysis", *Journal of Financial and Quantitative Analysis*, December 1969.

Milne, F., "Choice over Asset Economies: Default Risk and Corporate Leverage", *Journal of Financial Economics*, June 1975.

Ohlson, James A., "Financial Ratios and the Probabilistic Prediction of Bankruptcy", *Journal of Accounting Research*, April 1980.

Scott, J. H., Jr., "Bankruptcy, Secured Debt, and Optimal Capital Structure", *The Journal of Finance*, March 1977.

Smith, Vernon, L., "Default Risk, Scale, and the Homemade Leverage Theorem", *American Economic Review*, March 1972.

Smith, C. W., Jr. and Warner, J. B., "Bankruptcy, Secured Debt, and Optimal Capital Structure: Comment", *The Journal of Finance*, March 1979.

Stapleton, R. C., "A Note on Default Risk, Leverage and the MM Theorem", *Journal of Financial Economics*, December 1975.

Stiglitz, Joseph E., "Some Aspects of the Pure Theory of Corporate Finance: Bankruptcies and Takeovers", *Bell Journal of Economics and Finance*, Autumn 1972.

Warner, J. B., "Bankruptcy, Absolute Priority, and the Pricing of Risky Debt Claims", *Journal of Financial Economics*, May 1977.

17

Defining the Cost of Capital

In the preceding chapter we concluded that, up to a limit, the use of financial leverage can potentially increase the value of the firm. If we denote the proportions of debt and equity which correspond to this limit by the letter L^*, the latter represents the firm's *optimal* capital structure. And as we have assumed that the goal of the firm is to maximize its market value (thereby maximizing the market value of the stockholders' equity as well), it follows that the firm should strive to achieve that financing mix which it believes to be optimal in the long run.

In this chapter we turn our attention to the problem of defining the cost of capital, that is a firm's minimum required rate of return on new investment. Initially we shall set out the theoretical arguments supporting the use of a *weighted average* of the various sources of financing as the measure of the cost of capital, the weights being determined by the proportion of each source in the optimal capital structure, L^*. In the following chapter we shall discuss the ways in which each individual type of financing (debt, preferred stock, common stock, retained earnings, etc.), can be measured, and conclude the discussion by setting out a practical method for calculating the cost of capital using General Motors Corporation and IBM as examples.

THE WEIGHTED AVERAGE COST OF CAPITAL

For simplicity, let us first assume that all new investments are financed in the exact proportions of debt and equity given by the optimal financial structure, L^*. What is the cost of capital (discount rate) that the firm should use when evaluating a new project? Table 17.1 illustrates the case of a firm which has adopted a policy of financing investments with 40% debt and 60% equity, presumably on the assumption that this capital structure is optimal, given the firm's risk-return profile. Thus its initial capital structure (column 1 of Table

Table 17.1

	Before the New Investment	New Investment	After the New Investment
	$	$	$
Capital Structure:			
Bonds (5%)	4,000,000	400,000	4,400,000
Stock	6,000,000	600,000	6,600,000
Total	10,000,000	1,000,000	11,000,000
Cash Flows:			
Net Operating Income	1,100,000	110,000	1,210,000
Interest	200,000	20,000	220,000
Dividends	900,000	90,000	990,000

17.1) is comprised of $6 million of common stock yielding 15% in dividends, and $4 million of bonds on which it pays 5% interest. To simplify the discussion we assume that the firm distributes *all* of its net earnings as dividends; hence the required rate of return by the stockholder (for the given capital structure) is equal to the dividend yield.

Ignoring corporate taxes for the moment, we assume in Table 17.1 that the firm earns $1,100,000 on its $10 million of capital, paying out $200,000 (5% × $4 million) as interest to its bondholders and the remaining $900,000 as dividends to its common stockholders. Hence, the yield on the existing equity is 15% ($900,000/$6 million = 15%).

Column 2 of Table 17.1 sets out the expected results of a proposed new investment. An additional $1 million is required to finance the investment, and the firm decides to raise 40% of this sum by issuing 5% bonds and the remaining 60% by issuing additional common stock, i.e. the firm desires to preserve its existing debt/equity ratio. What is the minimum required rate of return on the new investment, i.e. the rate of return which will leave the value of the existing shareholder equity unchanged? In order to answer this question let us analyze the cost component of each element of the financing mix. Clearly one component of the required return consists of the $20,000 (5% × $400,000 = $20,000) which the firm must pay the new bondholders. But in addition Table 17.1 shows that the firm must earn an additional $90,000 if it does not want to reduce the earnings (dividends) on the existing equity. The $90,000 represents a 15% return on the new equity ($90,000/$600,000 = 15%) which will enable the firm to pay a 15% dividend to the new shareholders without affecting the dividends of the old shareholders. In other words, the new investment must earn $20,000 + $90,000 = $110,000 if the value of the existing equity is to remain unchanged by the new investment. If the operating returns are *less* than $110,000 the investment should be rejected out of hand; if it yields more than $110,000 it should be accepted since the position of the existing shareholders will be improved.

This contention can be illustrated using the data in column 3 of Table 17.1 which gives the firm's capital structure and cash flows *after* the new investment is accepted, on the explicit assumption that the critical amount, i.e. $110,000, is earned on the new project. As can be seen, the $110,000 is just sufficient to leave the position of the old stockholders unchanged; the earnings available for dividends for all classes of shareholders is $990,000 which represents an unchanged dividend (earnings) yield of 15% ($990,000/$6,600,000 = 15%). Should the firm earn less than this amount on the new investment, say only $44,000 rather than $110,000, the earnings available for dividends, after interest is paid, will be only $924,000 ($900,000 + 24,000); hence the dividend yield will decline from 15% to 14% ($924,000/$6,600,000 = 14%). Similarly, should the return on the new investment be more than $110,000, say $176,000, the existing stockholders will be better off. In this case, the firm again pays $20,000 to the new bondholders leaving $156,000 as the contribution of the new investment of the firm's shareholders. Thus, the total earnings available for distribution to the stockholders is $1,056,000 ($900,000 + $156,000) and the new dividend yield rises to 16% ($1,056,000/$6,600,000 = 16%).

Now let us turn to the analogous question of the discount rate which this firm should apply when evaluating an investment proposal's net present value (*NPV*). For the sake of convenience we assume that the project in our example involves an initial outlay of $1 million and generates a perpetual cash flow of $110,000 per year. Denoting the discount rate by k, the *NPV* calculation reduces to:

$$NPV = \frac{110,000}{k} - 1,000,000$$

To be consistent with our previous analysis, we must make the further stipulation that for the case in which $110,000 is earned, the *NPV* must be zero: otherwise the existing shareholders will not be indifferent to the project. Imposing this condition we have:

$$NPV = \frac{110,000}{k} - 1,000,000 = 0$$

The discount rate which equates the *NPV* to zero is given by

$$k = \frac{110,000}{1,000,000} = 11\%$$

Thus in this example, the cost of capital is 11%. If the annual cash flow of the new project is greater than $110,000, the *NPV* (at 11%) will be positive and the firm should accept the project. If the annual cash flow is less than $110,000, the *NPV* calculated at the 11% cost of the capital will be negative, and the project should be rejected. These results are consistent with the previous analysis and confirm our conclusion that for earnings exceeding $110,000 the existing stockholders are better off; for earnings below $110,000 they are worse off; and for earnings exactly equal to $110,000 the stockholders are indifferent to the proposal. This relationship between the interests of existing shareholders and the *NPV* calculation of project acceptability can be ensured, in our example, *if and only if* the discount rate is set at 11%.

How should the 11% discount rate be interpreted? An examination of Table 17.2 shows that the 11% rate represents a *weighted average* of the required

Table 17.2

	Amount Raised (in dollars)	Proportion of Total Money Raised	Cost of the Specific Components	Contribution to the Cost of Capital
	(1)	*(2)*	*(3)*	*(4)* = *(2)* × *(3)*
Debt	400,000	0.40	5%	0.40 × 5% = 2%
Stocks	600,000	0.60	15%	0.60 × 15% = 9%
				Weighted average cost of capital **11%**

rate of return of the individual sources of financing, with each type of financing being given its proportionate weight in the firm's long-run target capital structure. Alternatively, the 11% can be viewed as the weighted average of the cost components. Since debt accounts for 40% of the firm's total financing mix, the contribution of the debt component to the cost of capital is 2% (0.40 × 0.05 = 0.02 = 2%). Similarly, the contribution of the equity component is 9% (0.60 × 0.15 = 0.09 = 9%). Combining the two components gives an overall cost of capital equal to 11%. The justification for using a discount rate (cost of capital) which reflects the costs of the individual sources of financing, weighted by their share in the firm's optimal (target) capital structure, reflects the fact that such a calculation insures that the value of the existing owners' equity will be maximized. Setting a lower rate, as our numerical example showed, would induce the firm to accept projects which are not in the existing shareholders' best interest; setting the rate above the weighted average, on the other hand, would lead the firm to forgo projects whose acceptance would increase the value of the existing shareholders' equity.

FINANCING A NEW PROJECT IN PRACTICE

We have assumed in the preceding analysis that the firm finances each new project by 40% debt and 60% equity, i.e. it was assumed that the firm finances *each* project in the same proportions as its optimal (target) capital structure. However, it is well known that firms in practice do not issue stocks and bonds simultaneously every time a need for additional long-term financial resources arises. This is especially true when the firm raises relatively small amounts of money, since often it is not economical to split such sums, by raising part of it by a bond issue and the rest by a stock issue. Thus, even a firm which has set a target financial structure will tend to deviate from this optimal mix from time to time. Figure 17.1 illustrates the financing policy of a hypothetical firm with a target capital structure of 40% debt and 60% equity. As can be seen from the graph, the proportion of debt decreases in both 1974 and 1975. This does not necessarily mean that the firm issued common stock in these years; the decline in the share of debt in the total financing mix might reflect an increase in retained earnings during these same years, or the retirement of part of the firm's

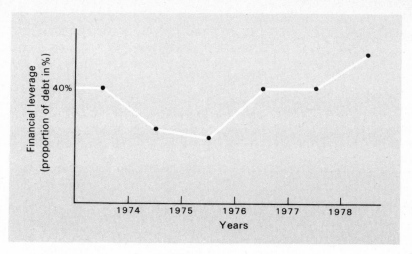

Fig. 17.1

outstanding debt. In 1976 the firm "corrects" for these deviations from its target capital structure by issuing bonds, thereby restoring the proportion of debt in the capital structure to 40%. This financing mix is retained in 1977; however, due perhaps to unusually favorable market conditions the firm raises additional debt in 1978, and the proportion of debt rises above the 40% target. In the future the firm presumably will meet its financial requirements by raising additional equity, once again restoring the long-run target capital structure. Thus even though the firm has set a specific debt policy, it will probably deviate in the short run from its target debt/equity ratio, because practical considerations (flotation costs, market considerations, etc.) make the alternative of raising capital each year by issuing a financing "package", in fixed proportions of debt and equity, undesirable.

Should the fact that firms tend to deviate from their long-run optimal financial structure change our conclusion that the weighted average cost of capital be used as the discount rate for evaluating new investments? In order to answer this question let us once again turn to the numerical example given in Table 17.1, in which the cost component of debt is assumed to be 5%, the cost component of equity is 15% and the firm's target financial structure has been set at 40% debt and 60% equity. As noted in Fig. 17.1, the firm does *not* issue bonds and stock each year, and as a result it tends to deviate temporarily from the optimal financial structure. Now suppose that the firm considers a project whose internal rate of return is 7% and which will be financed by a bond issue. Should the project be accepted? If we compare the project's internal rate of return (7%) with the cost of the debt component (5%) the project is clearly acceptable. However, if the internal rate of return is compared with the *weighted average* cost of capital of 11% (see Table 17.2), the project will be rejected. The question remains: which is the appropriate discount rate?

It is the accepted view that the firm should ignore temporary deviations from its long-run policy and use the weighted average cost of capital as a discount rate (i.e. 11% in our example). Thus the above project, whose internal rate of return is 7%, should be rejected, even though it is financed with the proceeds of a 5% bond issue. To clarify this line of reasoning, the reader should recall that the raising of low cost debt capital to finance this particular project will tend to raise the proportion of debt in the firm's capital structure above the target level of 40%. This, in turn, implies an increase in risk so that the firm will have to finance its projects in future years with relatively expensive equity capital, if the optimal debt level is to be restored. Should the firm use the specific interest rate, rather than the weighted average, it might conceivably accept a project with an internal rate of return of 7% in the years in which bonds are issued, while a project with a 14% rate of return might be rejected in a year in which equity capital was being raised.

To avoid such a dilemma, firms should ignore transitory deviations from their target debt/equity ratios. Since increasing the proportion of debt this year *implies* that the firm must issue additional equity in the future, both of these sources must be taken into account when evaluating a new project. By using the weighted average cost of capital, the firm can avoid situations in which relatively low-return projects are accepted, while high-return projects are rejected, solely because of timing. In our example, using the 11% weighted average cost of capital, the project with a 7% rate of return will be rejected even though it is financed by debt, and the project with a 14% internal rate of return will be accepted even though the firm finances it with high cost equity.

To sum up, the individual types of financing constitute a "joint product" which must be evaluated together if the firm is to optimize its investment decisions.[1]

LEVERAGE AND THE SPECIFIC COSTS OF FINANCING

So far we have tried to show that the firm should employ a cutoff rate for new investment which reflects the weighted average of the costs of its specific sources of financing — debt, equity etc. However, it is crucial to recognise that *these individual costs are neither constant over time nor independent of the firm's overall financial strategy.* In general, all of the specific costs tend to rise as leverage is increased. Bondholders settle for a fixed annual income. However, for intensive degrees of leverage, the risk of bankruptcy rises; hence the bondholders may lose all or part of their interest income and/or principal. The larger the risk of bankruptcy the higher will be the interest rate required to compensate the bondholders for incurring the greater risk. Thus, even relatively small firms who do not ordinarily influence money market rates will be confronted by an upward sloping supply curve for loans. The higher the proportion

---

1 A theoretical justification for using the weighted average cost of capital is given in Appendix 17A.

of debt, the higher the risk from the bondholders' point of view, and hence the higher will be the required interest rate. By an analogous argument we also expect the cost of preferred stock to rise with leverage. The higher the risk of bankruptcy, the higher will be the required return and hence the higher will be the specific cost of preferred stock. Similarly, as we pointed out in Chapter 15, the variability of per-share earnings increases with leverage. Since most, if not all, stockholders are risk-averse, *the greater the variability of the earnings stream, the higher will be the average required return on equity.* And needless to add the common stockholders are the most vulnerable to bankruptcy as well. Thus we also expect the cost of equity to rise with leverage.

In general, the larger the risk, the larger will be the required return, and therefore the higher will be the financing cost. However, one should remember that financial leverage is only one of the risk factors which affect the cost of capital. A second factor is the firm's economic or business risk. Each specific cost component is composed of the riskless interest rate (representing the time value of money) plus risk premium. This risk premium, in turn, is determined by the firm's economic risk (which exists even when financial leverage is zero) plus its financial risk. Thus each specific source can be decomposed into two parts:

$$k_i = r + BRP + FRP$$

where

k_i = the ith cost component
r = the riskless interest rate
BRP = the premium for business risk
FRP = the premium for financial risk

Does the above analysis necessarily imply that the firm's weighted average cost of capital must also rise with leverage? As can be seen from Table 17.3, the firm's cost of capital can have U-shaped properties even when the cost of each individual component increases with leverage. This reflects the fact that the firm's cost of capital is a *weighted average* of the individual sources. Up to a point, the inclusion of relatively low-cost debt in the capital structure reduces the average cost; however, for highly levered financing structures, both the cost of debt and of equity rise sharply, and these factors combine to reverse the impact of the inclusion of additional debt in the capital structure.

The numerical example of Table 17.3 is illustrated in Fig. 17.2 which graphs the relationship between the cost of capital and financial leverage. Although both the cost of debt and equity are assumed to rise with leverage, the firm's weighted average cost of capital is U-shaped: initially decreasing to a leverage ratio of 40% and then rising. Since the goal of the firm is to minimize its cost of capital, thereby maximizing the value of the firm, 40% debt represents the *optimal* financial leverage in our specific exmple.[2]

---

2 For detailed discussion of the relationship of the minimization of the cost of capital to the maximization of the value of the firm, see F.D. Arditti, "The Weighted Average Cost of Capital: Some Questions on its Definition, Interpretation and Use", *Journal of Finance,* September 1973.

Table 17.3

| Capital Structure | | Cost of Debt Component | Cost of Equity Component | Weighted Average Cost of Capital |
Debt (1)	Equity (2)	(3)	(4) (in %)	(5) = (1) × (3) + (2) × (4)
0.1	0.9	5.0	15.0	14.00
0.2	0.8	5.0	16.0	13.80
0.3	0.7	6.0	17.0	13.70
0.4	0.6	7.0	18.0	**13.60**
0.5	0.5	7.5	20.0	13.75
0.6	0.4	8.0	24.0	14.40
0.7	0.3	9.0	28.0	14.70
0.8	0.2	12.0	30.0	15.60
0.9	0.1	15.0	35.0	17.00

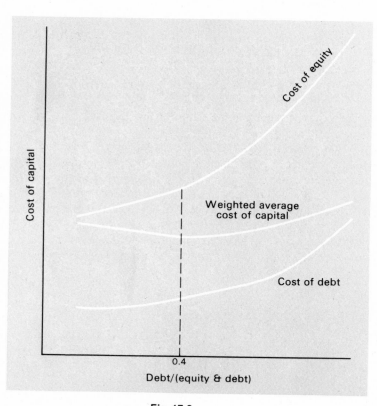

Fig. 17.2

COST OF EQUITY: THE *CAPM* APPROACH

As we have just noted the firm's cost of equity can be decomposed into two components: the risk-free interest rate and a risk premium. This premium depends on the firm's risk level; the higher the risk the greater is the required rate of return on equity. Clearly a firm's business risk as well as the intensity of its financial leverage have a direct impact on the risk premium. Following this approach we found that the variability of a firm's earnings per share constitutes the appropriate measure of its riskiness.

An alternative approach, based on the capital asset pricing model (*CAPM*) takes into account not only a firm's own earnings variability but also the covariability of its earnings with those of other firms. Using this approach we assume that investors in the stock market hold a portfolio of stocks of many firms. Hence even though the variability of a firm's own earnings may be relatively high, its stock might still not be considered very risky due to the negative covariance with other securities in the portfolio.

Recalling the result of Chapter 13, the firm's risk, using the *CAPM* approach, is measured by its systematic risk, i.e. beta, and not by its variance alone. Thus, the required rate of return on equity is given by k_i:

$$k_i = r + (Ex_m - r)\beta_i$$

where:
r = the risk-free interest rate
Ex_m = the expected rate of return on the market portfolio
β_i = the firm's systematic risk
k_i = the required rate of return on the firm's equity

Finally note that the *CAPM* approach does not ignore the variability of earnings, since the latter is included in beta. However, in the *CAPM* approach the variance is only one component of the systematic risk; beta reflects many covariances which may have a much stronger impact on the size of beta than does the firm's own variance. However, it is noteworthy that empirical studies have shown that a strong positive correlation often exists between the firm's beta coefficients and its variability. This implies that even if one accepts the underlying logic of the *CAPM* approach, variance can still be used as a useful proxy of the firm's systematic risk.

CHANGES IN LONG-TERM FINANCIAL POLICY

At the beginning of this chapter, we distinguished between a firm's long-run optimal financial strategy and temporary deviations around this target ratio (see Fig. 17.1). Although purely transitory deviations can properly be ignored, this does *not* mean that the firm should not re-examine from time to time its long-term financial policy. Capital market conditions, government policy, the tax structure and a myriad of other influences can, and do, change over time,

Table 17.4

| Capital Structure | | Cost of Debt Component | Cost of Equity Component | Weighted Average Cost of Capital |
| Debt (1) | Equity (2) | (3) | (4) | (5) = (1) × (3) + (2) × (4) |
		(in %)		
0.1	0.9	3.0	15.0	13.80
0.2	0.8	3.0	16.0	13.40
0.3	0.7	4.0	17.0	13.10
0.4	0.6	5.0	18.0	12.80
0.5	0.5	5.5	20.0	**12.75**
0.6	0.4	6.0	24.0	13.20
0.7	0.3	7.0	28.0	13.30
0.8	0.2	10.0	30.0	14.00
0.9	0.1	13.0	35.0	15.20

often generating significant changes in the relative cost of alternative sources of finance. The need for such a revaluation of financial policy is illustrated in Table 17.4 which reproduces the data of Table 17.3 with one difference — we now assume that the interest rate has fallen by two percentage points. As a direct result, the weighted average cost of capital given in Table 17.4 is lower than that in the previous illustration. Moreover, as we can see from Fig. 17.3, the proportion of debt in the optimal capital structure also changes. Prior to the

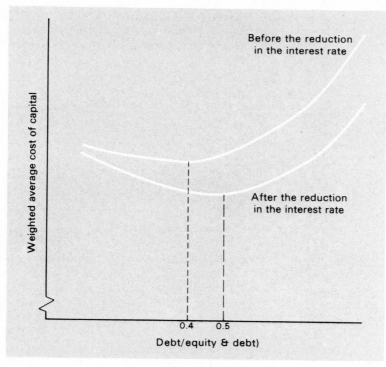

Before the reduction in the interest rate

After the reduction in the interest rate

Weighted average cost of capital

0.4   0.5

Debt/equity & debt)

Fig. 17.3

fall in interest rates, the optimal proportion of debt was 40%; following the drop in interest rates, this proportion rises to 50%. Thus significant changes in the required returns on debt and equity not only change the absolute magnitude of the cost of capital, but the proportions of the optimal capital structure as well. Similarly, economic and social changes which affect the character of the firm's operations, particularly those which significantly change its business risk, can have a parallel effect on its long-term financial strategy. All of these dynamic considerations suggest the dangers of getting "locked-in" to a particular financial strategy, and the need for a periodic reassessment of the firm's long-term financial policies.

MARKET VALUE vs BOOK VALUE

A firm's weighted-average cost of capital can be calculated either on the basis of book (i.e. accounting) values or on the basis of market values. However, considerable confusion can be avoided if we emphasize from the very outset that market value provides the only acceptable method for estimating the cost of capital. Market values should be used when calculating each specific cost component; market weights should be used for calculating the weighted average. Perhaps the easiest way to justify the reliance on market, rather than accounting, values is to consider a highly simplified yet not unrealistic example. Consider the case of a firm which issued a $100 bond bearing 5% interest a number of years ago. For the sake of simplicity we shall assume zero corporate taxes and flotation costs, and that the bond (like the famous consols issued by Britain at the time of Napoleon) is a perpetuity having no maturity. The interest yield of the debt, therefore, is 5%:

$$100 = \frac{5}{1 + k_d} + \frac{5}{(1 + k_d)^2} + \ldots = \frac{5}{k_d} \text{ and}$$

$$k_d = \frac{5}{100} = 5\%$$

where: k_d denotes the interest yield.

Now let us assume that after a number of years, world-wide inflation induces a sharp rise in domestic interest rates. To be specific let us assume that the interest rate on bonds of similar risk and duration doubles to 10%. Now given these circumstances, what do you expect the *market* price of the old bond to be? Clearly, they must now afford investors a return of 10% rather than 5% or no one will hold them; but since the firm's interest payment is fixed (forever), at $5 per bond, the only way that this can be achieved is by fall in the market price to $50. Hence in a free and competitive securities market, bondholders will try to sell the bonds as long as the price is over $50 (and the yield below 10%) but no investor will buy them until the price falls to $50 (and the yield equals the going market rate of 10%).

What impact does the above price change have on the interest cost of debt?

If we use historical accounting book values, the issue price remains $100 and, therefore, the yield remains 5% as before. However, if we use the new market price of $50, the interest cost rises to 10%:

$$50 = \frac{5}{1 + k_d} + \frac{5}{1 + k_d} + \dots = \frac{5}{k_d}, \text{ and}$$

$$k_d = \frac{5}{50} = 10\%$$

Which of these two calculations is appropriate for our purposes? Recall that we have defined the cost of capital as the minimum required rate of return on investment, i.e. the discount rate to be used when evaluating new capital investment projects. Assuming for a moment a *hypothetical world in which all investment is financed by debt*, the use of accounting values suggests that investments should be accepted if they earn a return of more than 5%. The market value approach would stipulate 10% as the correct cutoff rate. However, only the latter is correct, because the firm can always earn more than 5% simply by repurchasing two of its own bonds in the market for $100 (recall that their market price is now $50) thereby saving $10 in interest payments and earning a rate of return of 10%. Thus the cost of the debt component cannot be less than its opportunity cost to the firm which in this case is 10%. Historical accounting costs and prices are simply irrelevant.

An analogous argument can readily be found to support the use of market prices when evaluating preferred and common stocks. Since market values are used in calculating each cost component, market weights should be used in calculating the weighted average cost of capital. Note that market values rather than accounting values should be used *even if the firm does not plan a new issue*. Retirement of existing debt or the repurchase of its own securities always represent alternative investment options to the firm. Although market values are the only conceptually correct figures to be used, it would be uneconomic and impractical to revise the calculation of the cost of capital daily, i.e. every time the market price of its securities changes. A compromise with reality is required in which the *average* market price or trend is identified; temporary deviations around the trend line can, and should, be ignored.[3]

QUESTIONS AND PROBLEMS

17.1 Assume a firm with an intitial capital structure comprised of $15 million of common stock, yielding 18% in dividends and $5 million of bonds on which it pays 6% interest. Assume also that the firm distributes all of its net earnings as dividends, and answer the following questions, ignoring

3 In practice the book and market values of equity often differ markedly so that the use of book values would impart a serious bias to the estimate of the cost of capital. This is not usually true for debt, and in many instances substituting the book value of debt for its market value does not materially change the analysis.

corporate taxes:

(a)   How much is the net operating income of the firm?

(b)   Suppose that the firm needs $4 million to finance new investments but desires to preserve its existing debt/equity ratio. What is the minimum required *NOI* on new investment?

17.2 A firm which pays 40% corporate tax desires to raise $2 million by issuing bonds at an interest rate of 7.5%.

(a)   How much must the firm earn on the additional capital in order to preserve the return on equity?

(b)   What is the specific after-tax cost of bonds?

17.3 The Extraplast Colours Inc. was established at the end of 1966. The initial required investment was $5,400,000 and the firm issued 120,000 shares of common stock at a price of $30 per share and $1,800,000 of bonds. The retained earnings at the end of 1967 were $600,000 and the firm was considering a new common stock issue in 1976. The financial policy of the firm during the years from 1967 till 1975 is summarized in the following table:

Year	Retained Earnings After Tax ($)	Common Stock Issues Number of Shares	Common Stock Issues Price per Share ($)	Debt Issues Amount of Money Raised by Bonds ($)
1967	600,000	—	35	—
1968	400,000	30,000	38	—
1969	700,000	—	40	2,200,000
1970	1,200,000	—	48	600,000
1971	500,000	50,000	50	—
1972	600,000	—	56	1,700,000
1973	1,400,000	40,000	60	—
1974	1,000,000	—	65	2,100,000
1975	1,500,000	—	70	—

(a)   Calculate for each year (from 1966 to 1975) the capital structure of the firm in dollars and in %.

(b)   Illustrate graphically the financial policy of the firm.

(c)   Did the firm follow a consistent policy? Explain.

17.4 "A firm which pays 7.5% as interest on debt should always accept a project whose internal rate of return is 13% as long as it can be financed by a bond issue." Critically evaluate this statement.

17.5 Consider the following balance sheet and profit and loss statement of Gamma Corporation.

Balance Sheet
(in thousand $)

Assets		Liabilities	
Cash	20,000	Bonds ($1,000 par value)	60,000
Inventories	180,000	Short term loan	10,000
Plant and Equipment	50,000	Common Stock ($ par value)	180,000
	250,000		250,000

Income Statement
(in thousand $)

Earnings before interest and tax	100,000
Operating expenses	60,850
Operating income	39,150
Interest payments	3,150
Net income	36,000
Less 50% tax	18,000
Net income after tax	18,000
Net earnings per share	$0.10

The market price of a share of stock is $1.25
The market price of a bond is $750

Suppose that Gamma distributes all of its net earnings as dividends and that the specific cost of debt is equal to $\dfrac{\text{interest after tax}}{\text{market price of a bond}}$:

(a) Should the firm accept a project whose after-tax internal rate of return is 7%?

(b) Should the project be accepted if the firm's long-term target capital structure is 30% debt and 70% equity?

APPENDIX 17A THE WEIGHTED AVERAGE COST OF CAPITAL

In the text we have presented the argument on behalf of the use of the weighted average cost of capital by means of numerical examples. In this appendix we present the Modigliani-Miller analysis of the appropriate cutoff rate for new investments — their Proposition III.

Ignoring corporate taxes, the value of the unlevered firm is given by $V_U = X/k$, where X is the average net operating income and k is the discount rate of the unlevered firm (which is equal to the yield Y_U on the stock of a pure equity firm). M & M's Proposition III asserts *that k should also be used as the cost of capital for a levered firm.* To illustrate this proposition it is sufficient to consider the extreme case in which a levered firm finances a new investment of I dollars solely out of debt.

Since by Proposition I (see Appendix 15B)

$$V_L = S_L + B_L = V_U$$

the value of the equity before the new investment was

$$S_b = V_U - B_L$$

Assume that the rate of return on the new investment is R, hence the new net operating income is $X + RI$ and the value of the firm becomes

$$V = \frac{X + RG}{k} - I = V_U + \frac{RI}{k} - I$$

and the value of equity after the investment (S_a) is given by

$$S_a = V_U + \frac{RI}{k} - B_L - I = S_b + I\left(\frac{R}{k} - 1\right)$$

Thus the value of the equity rises only if $R > k$, i.e., if the internal rate of return on the new project exceeds k, hence k should be used as the cost of capital of levered, as well as unlevered, firms. The same conclusion holds when the firm finances the new investment I by equity or by any combination of debt and equity.

Now let us turn to the question of whether the proposed discount rate, k, is indeed the weighted average cost of equity and debt.

A levered firm has a capital structure with the proportion B/V of debt and S/V of equity. Since the cost of debt is $r\%$, and the cost of equity is $Y_L = Y_U + (Y_U - r) B/S$ (by Proposition II), the weighted average cost of capital is given by

$$\frac{B}{V} r + \frac{S}{V} Y_L = \frac{B}{V} r + \frac{S}{V}\left[Y_U + (Y_U - r)\frac{B}{S}\right]$$

$$= \frac{B}{V} r + \frac{S}{V} Y_U + \frac{S}{V}\frac{B}{S} Y_U - \frac{S}{V}\frac{B}{S} r$$

$$= Y_U\left(\frac{S}{V} + \frac{B}{V}\right)$$

but since $V = S + B$, the weighted average cost of capital is simply equal to Y_U. If we recall that $Y_U = X/V_U$ or $V_U = X/Y_U$, this can be rewritten as $V_U = X/k$, when $k = Y_U$. Thus, the weighted average cost of capital Y_U is the proper cut-off rate, k, that should be used in project evaluation.

SELECTED REFERENCES

Agmon, T., Ofer, A. P. and Tamir, A., "Variable Rate Debt Instruments and Corporate Debt Policy", *Journal of Finance*, December 1980.

Alberts, W.W. and Archer, S.H., "Some Evidence on the Effect of Company Size on the Cost of Equity Capital", *Journal of Financial and Quantitative Analysis*, March 1973.

Archer, Stephen H. and Faerber, LeRoy G., "Firm Size and the Cost of Equity Capital", *Journal of Finance*, March 1966.

Barnea Amir, Haugen, Robert A. and Senbet, Lemma W., "A Rationale for Debt Maturity Structure and Call Provisions in the Agency Theoretic Framework", *Journal of Finance*, December 1980.

Baron, David P. and Holmström Bengt, "The Investment Banking Contract for New Issues Under Asymmetric Information: Delegation and the Incentive Problem", *Journal of Finance*, December 1980.

Bear, Robert M. and Curley, Anthony J., "Unseasoned Equity Financing", *Journal of Financial and Quantitative Analysis*, June 1978.

Beranek, William, "The Cost of Capital, Capital Budgeting, and the Maximation of Shareholder Wealth", *Journal of Financial and Quantitative Analysis*, March 1975.

Black, F. and Cox, J.C., "Valuing Corporate Securities: Some Effects of Bond Indenture Provisions", *Journal of Finance*, May 1976.

Block, Stanley and Block, Marjorie, "The Financial Characteristics and Price Movement Patterns of Companies Approaching the Unseasoned Securities Market in the Late 1970s", *Financial Management*, Winter 1980.

Bodie, Z. and Friedman, B.M., "Interest Rate Uncertainty and the Value of Bond Call Protection", *Journal of Political Economy*, February 1978.

Boquist, J.A., Racetta, G.A. and Schlarbaum, G.G., "Duration and Risk Assessment for Bonds and Common Stocks", *Journal of Finance*, December 1975.

Craine, R.N. and Pierce, J.L., "Interest Rate Risk", *Journal of Financial and Quantitative Analysis*, November 1978.

Dobrovolsky, S.P., "Economics of Corporation Internal and External Financing", *Journal of Finance*, March 1958.

Ederington, L.H., "Uncertainty, Competition, and Costs in Corporate Bond Underwriting", *Journal of Financial Economics*, March 1975.

Edmister, R.O., "Commission Cost Structure Shifts and Scale Economies", *Journal of Finance*, May 1978.

Elton, Edwin J. and Gruber, Martin J., "The Effect of Share Repurchases on the Value of the Firm", *Journal of Finance*, March 1968.

Fabozzi, F. J. Hershkoff, R.A., "The Effect of the Decision to List on a Stock's Systematic Risk", *Review of Business and Economic Research*, Spring 1979.

Fox, A.F., The Cost of Retained Earnings — A Comment'', *Journal of Business Finance & Accounting*, 4/4 1977.

Gentry, James A. and Pyhrr, Stephen A., "Stimulating an EPS Growth Model", *Financial Management*, Summer 1973.

Gordon, M.J. and Gould L.I., "The Cost of Equity Capital: A Reconsideration", *Journal of Finance*, June 1978.

Gordon, Myron J. and Shapiro, Eli, "Capital Equipment Analysis: The Required Rate of Profit", *Management Science*, October 1956.

Grier, P. and Katz, S., "The Differential Effects of Bond Rating Changes among Industrial and Public Utility Bonds by Maturity", *Journal of Business*, April 1976.

Hakansson, Nils H., "On the Dividend Captialization Model under Uncertainty", *Journal of Financial and Quantitative Analysis*, March 1969.

Haley, Charles W., "Taxes, The Cost of Capital, and the Firm's Investment Decisions", *Journal of Finance*, September 1971.

Harris, Robert S., "The Refunding of Discounted Debt: An Adjusted Present Value Analysis", *Financial Management*, Winter 1980.

Henderson, Glenn V., Jr., "Shareholder Taxation and the Required Rate of Return on Internally Generated Funds", *Financial Management*, Summer 1976.

Ibbotson, R.G., "Price Performance of Common Stock New Issues", *Journal of Financial Economics*, September 1975.

Johnson, K.B., Morton, T.G. and Findlay, M.C., III, "An Empirical Analysis of the Flotation Cost of Corporate Securities, 1971 – 1972", *Journal of Finance*, September 1975.

Keenan, Michael and Maldonado, Rita M., "The Redundancy of Earnings Leverage in a Cost of Capital Decision Framework", *Journal of Business Financing & Accounting*, Summer 1976.

Kolodny, R., Seely, P. and Polakoff, M.E., "The Effect of Compensating Balance Requirements on the Profitability of Borrowers and Lenders", *Journal of Financial and Quantitative Analysis*, December 1977.

Kummer, D.R. and Hoffmeister, J.R., "Valuation Consequences of Cash Tender Offers", *Journal of Finance*, May 1978.

Lakonishok, Joseph and Ofer, Aharon R., "The Value of General Price Level Adjusted Data to Bond Rating", *Journal of Business Finance & Accounting*, Spring 1980.

Lee, Sang M. and Lerro, A.J., "An Appraisal of Price Earnings, Dividends and Retained Earnings", *The Southern Journal of Business*, February 1978.

Livingston, M., "Taxation and Bond Market Equilibrium in a World of Uncertain Future Interest Rates", *Journal of Financial and Quantitative Analysis*, March 1979.

Livingston, M., "The Pricing of Premium Bonds", *Journal of Financial and Quantitative Analysis*, September 1979.

Mandelker, G. and Raviv, A., "Investment Banking: An Economic Analysis of Optimal Underwriting Contracts", *Journal of Finance*, June 1977.

McDonald, John G. and Osborne, Alfred E., Jr., "Forecasting the Market Return on Common Stocks", *Journal of Business Finance & Accounting*, Summer 1974.

McDonald, John G., "Market Measures of Capital Cost", *Journal of Business Finance*, Autumn 1970.

Merten, Robert C., "On the Pricing of Corporate Debt: The Risk Structure of Interest Rates", *Journal of Finance*, May 1974.

Ofer, A.R. and Taggart, R.A., Jr., "Bond Refunding: A Clarifying Analysis", *Journal of Finance*, March 1977.

Petry, Glenn H., "An Unidentified Corporate Risk — Using the Wrong Cost of Funds", *MSU Business Topics*, Autumn 1975.

Pinches, G.E., and Singleton, J.C., "The Adjustment of Stock Prices to Bond Rating Changes", *Journal of Finance*, March 1978.

Reilly, F.K. and Joehnk, M.D., "The Association between Market-Determined Risk and Measures for Bonds and Bond Ratings", *Journal of Finance*, December 1976.

Shiller, R.J. and Modigliani, F., "Coupon and Tax Effects on New and Seasoned Bond Yields and the Measurement of the Cost of Debt Captial", *Journal of Financial Economics*, June 1979.

Smith, C.W., Jr., "Alternative Methods for Raising Capital: Rights versus Underwritten Offerings", *Journal of Financial Economics*, December 1977.

Soldofsky, Robert M. and Miller, Roger, L., "Risk-Premium Curves for Different Classes of Long-Term Securities, 1950 – 66", *Journal of Finance*, June 1969.

Stoll, H.R., "The Pricing of Security Dealer Services: An Empirical Study of NASDAQ Stocks", *Journal of Finance*, September 1978.

Tallman, Gary D., Rush, David F. and Melicher, Ronald W., "Competitive Versus Negotiated Underwriting Costs for Regulated Industries", *Financial Management*, Summer 1974.

Vickers, Douglas, "Profitability and Reinvestment Rates: A Note on the Gordon Paradox", *Journal of Business*, July 1966.

Weinstein, M.I., "The Effect of a Rating Change Announcement on Bond Price", *Journal of Financial Economics*, December 1977.

White R.W. and Lusztig, P.A., "The Price Effects of Rights Offerings", *Journal of Financial and Quantitative Analysis*, March 1980.

Whitington, G., "The Profitability of Retained Earnings", *Review of Economics and Statistics*, May 1972.

Wrightsman, Duayne and Harrigon, James O., "Retention, Risk of Success, and the Price of Stock", *Journal of Finance*, December 1975.

Yawitz, J.B., "Risk Premia on Municipal Bonds", *Journal of Financial and Quantitative Analysis*, Setpember 1978.

Zanker, F.W.A., "The Cost of Capital for Debt-Financed Investments", *Journal of Business Finance and Accounting*, 4, 3 (1977).

Zwick, B., "Yields on Privately Placed Corporate Bonds", *Journal of Finance*, March 1980.

18

Measuring the Cost of Capital

Having surveyed the theoretical arguments supporting the use of a weighted average cost of capital as the cutoff rate for evaluating new investments, we turn in this chapter to the prosaic, but no less important, question of its measurement. We shall first discuss the ways in which the cost of each individual type of financing (debt, preferred stock, common stock and retained earnings) can be estimated, *given the firm's target capital structure.* We then set out a practical method for calculating the firm's weighted average cost of capital using General Motors Corporation and IBM as examples.

COST OF INDIVIDUAL COMPONENTS

The specific cost of each component is the minimum rate of return required by the suppliers of the capital. For example, the specific cost of the bond component of the financing mix is the yield required by the bondholders. Clearly the payment of interest *without* dilution of earnings per share implies that the firm must earn at least this rate on its investment. It is this minimum rate of return, which ensures no dilution of shareholders' earnings, which constitutes the "specific cost" of debt or the "cost of debt component". A similar definition will be used for the equity component.

To avoid any confusion the reader should note that these specific costs should *not* be used as the cutoff rate in project evaluation. The former are estimated solely for the purpose of calculating the weighted average cost of capital; and it is the weighted average which constitutes the appropriate cutoff point (i.e. discount rate) when evaluating the feasibility of investments. Thus the specific costs of debt and equity presented in this chapter are the appropriate costs to be used when calculating the weighted average cost of capital. They are not the appropriate concepts to be used when analyzing proposed changes in the financing mix.

424

SPECIFIC COST OF DEBT

Given the firm's target debt-equity ratio L^*, let us first turn our attention to the calculation of the specific cost which is to be assigned to the debt component of the weighted average cost of capital. Suppose that a firm raises $1 million by issuing 1,000 bonds at a unit price of $1,000 and at an interest rate of 8%, i.e. the firm pays the holder of each bond $80 interest at the end of each year. Also assume that these bonds will be redeemed after ten years. Hence, at the end of the tenth year the firm pays the bondholder $80 interest plus an additional $1,000 to retire the bond's principal. Ignoring corporate taxes for a moment, Table 18.1 shows that the firm must earn *at least* $80,000, i.e. 8% on the $1 million raised by the bond issue in order to meet the interest payments without any dilution of earnings. If the firm invests the proceeds of the bond issue at exactly 8%, net operating income will be increased by $80,000, i.e. by an amount just sufficient to pay the bond interest. As a result net income is again $1 million and therefore the rate of return on the initial investment is also not affected by the new investment and financing and remains 10%. Hence the minimum rate of return on the new investment which preserves the return on existing investment is 8%. In terms of this chapter 8% is the "specific cost" of the debt component which should be used when calculating the weighted average cost of capital.

Table 18.1

	Before the Bond Issue	After the Bond Issue
	$	$
Initial Investment	10,000,000	10,000,000
Additional Investment	—	1,000,000
Total	10,000,000	11,000,000
Net Operating Income	1,000,000	1,080,000
Interest	—	80,000
Net Income	1,000,000	1,000,000
Rate of Return on Equity	10%	10%

Table 18.1 sets out the cash flow for only one year. The entire financing picture can be seen more clearly when we consider the firm's aggregate cash outflows to the bondholders. Over the entire life of the bonds, the firm must pay the bondholders the following stream of cash payments:

First year	*Second year*	. . .	*Tenth year*
$80,000	$80,000	. . .	$1,080,000

The bondholders receive $80,000 interest per year over a period of ten years, plus an additional $1 million at the end of the tenth year which represents the redemption of principal. Since we assume that each bond is sold for $1,000, we can now analyze the cash flow of a single bond in order to determine the specific cost of the bonds. Clearly, the new investment must yield sufficient funds to meet the cash outflows to the bondholders. Denoting the specific cost of the debt component by k_d, we have:

$$1000 = \frac{80}{1 + k_d} + \frac{80}{(1 + k_d)^2} + \ldots + \frac{1080}{(1 + k_d)^{10}}$$

The discount rate, k_d, which solves this equation is exactly 8%. If the firm earns 8% on the new investment it will just be able to pay the interest and principal of the bonds out of the proceeds of the investment. Any project whose internal rate of return is lower than 8% will not generate sufficient cash flows to pay the interest and principal to the bondholders, and therefore will reduce earnings per share. In this sense 8% represents the specific cost to be assigned to the debt component of the weighted average cost of capital.

Adjustment for Corporate Taxes

To this point we have ignored corporate taxes. In reality, the specific cost of debt is significantly lower, because corporate interest payments are deductible for tax purposes. Table 18.2 illustrates the calculation of the after-tax of debt, assuming a 50% corporate tax rate. (We again employ the basic data of Table 18.1.) Column 1 of Table 18.2 sets out the firm's financial condition *before* the new bond issue, but *after* the payment of corporate taxes. Due to the impact of the corporate tax, the rate of return on invested capital is only 5% compared

Table 18.2

	Before the Bond Issue	After the Bond Issue but Before the Investment	After the Bond Issue and Investment
	(1)	(2)	(3)
	$	$	$
Total Investment	10,000,000	10,000,000	11,000,000
Operating Income	1,000,000	1,000,000	1,080,000
Interest	—	80,000	80,000
Earnings after Interest	1,000,000	920,000	1,000,000
Corporate Tax (50%)	500,000	460,000	500,000
Net After-tax Earnings	500,000	460,000	500,000
Existing Investment	10,000,000	10,000,000	10,000,000
New Debt	—	1,000,000	1,000,000
After-tax Rate of Return on Equity	5%	4.6%	5%

with the pre-tax return of 10%. Column 2 of Table 18.2 isolates the *changes* in the financial figures generated by the new $1 million bond issue on the assumption that, for the moment at least, the firm does not invest the proceeds of the bond issue. As a result, operating income remains unchanged at $1 million. However, as the firm must pay interest on the debt, earnings after interest are reduced by $80,000 to $920,000. Since interest payments are tax-deductible, the firm's tax bill is only $460,000, and the after-tax rate of return on existing equity falls from 5% to 4.6%.

How can we account for the fact that although the firm pays $80,000 interest to the bondholders, its post-tax flow is reduced by only $40,000? Do the bondholders get only $40,000? Although the bondholders do receive $80,000 each year as interest, only $40,000 is payable out of net profits, the remaining $40,000 coming from the reduction in corporate tax. The firm pays the bondholders $40,000 and the Internal Revenue Service, so to speak, pays the other $40,000, because of its willingness to recognize corporate interest payments as a tax-deductible expense.

If we denote the annual pre-tax interest payment by the letter C and the corporate tax rate by the letter T, the annual *after-tax* interest cost to the firm is only $(1 - T)C$. The specific after-tax cost of the debt component is given by that rate of discount, $k_d{}^*$ which equates the after-tax cash flow generated by the bond with its initial purchase price:

$$1000 = \frac{(1 - T)80}{1 + k_d{}^*} + \frac{(1 - T)80}{(1 + k_d{}^*)^2} + \ldots + \frac{(1 - T)80}{(1 + k_d{}^*)^{10}} + \frac{1000}{(1 + k_d{}^*)^{10}}$$

Assuming $T = 50\%$, the discount rate which solves the equation is 4%. If the proceeds of the bond issue are invested to yield either 8% on a pre-tax basis, *or equivalently* 4% on an after-tax basis, the firm's return on equity will remain unchanged. This is illustrated in column 3 of Table 18.2. Hence the after-tax specific cost of debt is 4%, or more generally,

$$k_d{}^* = (1 - T)k_d$$

where: k_d denotes the pre-tax specific cost of debt, $k_d{}^*$ denotes the after-tax cost and T denotes the corporate tax rate. Other things being equal, the higher the corporate tax rate, the lower will be the effective cost of using debt, since the Internal Revenue Service will cover a large share of the total interest cost. Moreover, it should be emphasized that it is the after-tax cost of debt financing which is relevant to the firm and its shareholders. On occasion, we employ "pre-tax", or "no tax", examples for simplicity or for illustrative purposes only. In actual practice, however, no firm can afford to ignore the tax implications of its investment and financing policies.[1]

---

1 See for example, F. D. Arditti and H. Levy, "Pre-tax and Post-tax Discount Rates", *Journal of Business Finance*, 1971.

Flotation Costs

In general, a new issue of any type of security will incur flotation costs which reflect the administrative expenses, registration and legal fees, and risks associated with the raising of the funds, as well as the need to underprice the issue relative to outstanding securities in order to induce investors to acquire the new securities. The effect of these costs is to reduce the proceeds to the firm, thereby raising the specific cost of the capital raised. Using our previous example of the 8% bond issue, whose specific after-tax cost is 4%, let us now assume that the "spread" between the price the public pays for the bonds (i.e. $1 million) and the net proceeds to the firm is 4% or $40,000, that is $40 per bond. The latter sum reflects all of the costs (including any underpricing) necessary to float the bond issue. How does this affect the cost of the bonds? The after-tax specific cost is now given by the solution of the following formula:

$$960 = \frac{(1 - T)80}{(1 + k_d{}^*)} + \frac{(1 - T)80}{(1 + k_d{}^*)^2} + \ldots + \frac{(1 - T)80 + 1000}{(1 + k_d{}^*)^{10}}$$

and $k_d{}^*$ rises to 4.5%. Thus the effective after-tax cost of the bond component is increased by the necessity to cover the expenses incurred by the bond issue, and in general the higher the flotation costs, the higher will be the specific cost of the capital raised.

The impact of a given flotation cost on the specific cost of the bonds also depends on the maturity of the debt. Figure 18.1 illustrates the relationship for 2% and 10% flotation costs. For simplicity, we continue to assume a bond with a face value of $1,000 which pays 8% interest after taxes, i.e. annual after-tax interest of $80. The curve marked 2% describes the case in which the net proceeds to the firm are $980 for each bond sold; the graph marked 10% sets out the case in which the net proceeds to the firm are only $900. For short-term bonds, the specific cost of debt rises sharply. For example, for a one-year bond, the cost rises from 8% to 10.2% when flotation costs are 2% and to 20% when flotation costs are assumed to be 10%. However, in the relevant range for long-term debt, say twenty years, the specific cost rises only moderately to 8.21% when flotation costs are 2% and to 9.1% when flotation costs are assumed to be 10%. In general, the greater the number of years to maturity, the smaller is the impact of a given spread on the cost of the debt component.

SPECIFIC COST OF PREFERRED STOCK

A preferred stock is a hybrid security in the sense that it has some properties of bonds and others which are similar to equities. Like bondholders, preferred shareholders typically receive a *fixed* annual income, in this instance the preferred dividend; but as is true of common stock, failure to pay the preferred dividend will not cause bankruptcy. On the other hand, in the event that the firm fails, preferred shareholders are in an inferior position to the firm's debtors; the latter are compensated *before* the preference shareholders, although as the name

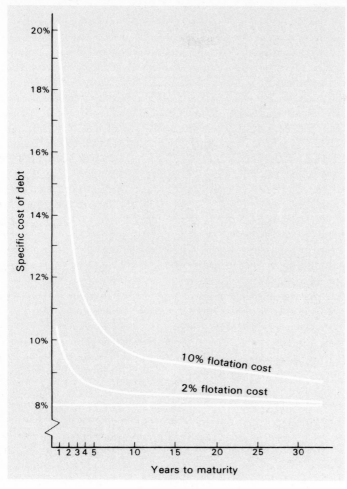

Fig. 18.1

itself suggests, preferred stockholders have a prior claim to the firm's income and assets *vis à vis* the holders of common stock.

For the purposes of calculating the weighted average cost of capital, the specific cost of a preferred stock will be defined as follows:

$$k_p^* = \frac{D}{P}$$

where D denotes the fixed annual dividend and P is the *net* issuing price (after deducting flotation costs). Assuming a net price of $95 and a dividend of $5, the specific cost of the preferred stock would be:

$$k_p{}^* = \frac{5}{95} = 5.26\%$$

Because a preferred stock represents a greater risk to the investor than a perpetual bond, the dividend yield of preferred stocks will usually be greater than the interest yield on long-term bonds. This gap is even greater from the viewpoint of the firm because dividends, unlike interest, are *not* tax deductible. The tax consideration is illustrated in Table 18.3 which reproduces our previous numerical example of a firm confronted with a $1 million investment with an 8% internal rate of return. In column 2 of Table 18.3 we assume that the project is financed by a bond issue yielding 8% interest. As we have already noted, the specific after-tax cost of debt is 4%. Since the project also earns 4% *after taxes*, earnings per share are not diluted by this investment-financing combination. Column 3 analyzes the cash flows when the same project is financed by 8% preferred stock. In this case the pre-tax internal rate of return on the project does not suffice to cover the 8% preferred dividend and, as a result, the rate of return to the firm's existing shareholders falls to 4.6%. Column 4 repeats the experiment assuming a project return of 16%. In this instance, the annual *pre-tax* return of $1,160,000 is just sufficient to cover the *post-tax* 8% preferred dividend, leaving the existing investor's return unchanged at 5%. Unlike the case of the 8% bond, whose *after-tax* specific cost is only 4%, the *after-tax*

Table 18.3

	Before the New Investment	After the New Investment Pre-tax Rate of Return = 8%		Pre-tax Rate of Return = 16%
		Financed by Bonds	Financed by Preferred Stock	Financed by Preferred Stock
	(1)	(2)	(3)	(4)
	$	$	$	$
Total Investment	10,000,000	11,000,000	11,000,000	11,000,000
Operating Income	1,000,000	1,080,000	1,080,000	1,160,000
Interest (8%)	—	80,000	—	—
Earnings after Interest	1,000,000	1,000,000	1,080,000	1,160,000
Corporate Tax (50%)	500,000	500,000	540,000	580,000
Net Earnings after Interest and Taxes	500,000	500,000	540,000	580,000
Dividend on Preferred Stock (8%)	—	—	80,000	80,000
Net Earnings Available for Common Stock	500,000	500,000	460,000	500,000
Equity	10,000,000	10,000,000	10,000,000	10,000,000
Bonds	—	1,000,000	—	—
Preferred Stock	—	—	1,000,000	1,000,000
Rate of Return on Equity	5%	5%	4.6%	5%

specific cost of an 8% preferred share remains 8%, because the firm must earn 8% *after-tax* to meet its obligation to the preferred shareholders. Dividends, unlike interest, must be paid out of net after-tax profits. Analogously we might say if k_p^* denotes the *after-tax* specific cost of a preferred stock, its pre-tax specific cost is given by:

$$\frac{k_p^*}{1 - T}$$

In our numerical example in which $k_p^* = 8\%$ and $T = 50\%$, we find that the pre-tax specific cost k_p is 16%:

$$k_p = \frac{k_p^*}{1 - T} = \frac{0.08}{0.5} = 16\%$$

These relationships are summarized in Table 18.4. A 50% corporate tax rate greatly enhances the desirability of using debt. In the case of preferred stock the firm must earn $2 (before taxes) for every $ of dividends just to break even. In the case of a bond, $1 of (pre-tax) earnings is sufficient to pay $1 of interest. The explanation is straightforward; the Internal Revenue Service simply refuses to share in the cost of equity financing, thereby creating a strong bias in favor of debt financing. In terms of our analysis, the specific cost of preferred stock will usually be substantially greater than that of debt.

Table 18.4

	Bonds	Preferred Stock
Pre-tax Specific Cost	K_d	$k_p^*/(1 - T)$
Post-tax Specific Cost	$(1 - T)k_d$	k_p^*
Numerical example assuming same 8% interest and dividend payments		
Pre-tax Specific Cost	8%	16%
Post-tax Specific Cost	4%	8%

COST OF EQUITY

A firm's equity includes both common stock and retained earnings.[2] Hence a firm can increase its equity either by selling additional stock or by retaining part of its current profits. These two modes of finance essentially are two components of the same financing source, i.e. owners' equity. However, due to flotation costs, the specific cost of raising new equity capital in the market will be somewhat greater than that of retained earnings, but the principle remains the same in both cases.

Let us initially assume that investors in the common stock of the Omega

---

2 We define "equity" to *exclude* preferred stock. The reader should note that the term "retained earnings" refers to that part of current earnings which is reinvested in the business rather than being paid out as dividends, and *not* to the "accumulated surplus" of the balance sheet.

Company expect to receive an annual dividend of $10, and that they also expect the market price of the stock will rise to $110 by the end of the year. Given these hypothetical expectations, investors are willing to pay $100 for this stock in today's market. Ignoring flotation costs for the moment, what is the required rate of return on Omega's common stock? The answer is given by the discount rate, k_e, which solves the following equation:[3]

$$\$100 = \frac{\$10}{1 + k_e} + \frac{110}{1 + k_e} = \frac{120}{1 + k_e}$$

In this case $k_e = 0.2$ or 20%. Thus if the firm issues additional common stock at the going market price of $100 per share, it must realize at least 20% on new investment just in order to provide the minimum rate of return required by stockholders. Hence 20% is the specific cost of equity which should be used when calculating the weighted average cost of capital. Suppose now that investors do not change their expectations but attribute greater uncertainty to the firm's ability to earn this expected profit. Since the firm's shares are now perceived to be more risky, investors will be willing to buy the stock only at a lower price, say $95. What is the specific cost of equity in this instance? The cost of equity in this case is given by that rate of discount which equates the present value of the expectation with the current price, i.e. with $95:

$$\$95 = \frac{\$120}{1 + k_e}; \ k_e = 26\%$$

Because the firm can sell new shares for only $95, a higher rate of return (26%) must be earned on the investment in order to cover the stockholders' required rate of return. Just the opposite result holds should the stockholders attribute a greater degree of certainty to their future expectations. In such a case shareholders will be ready to pay a higher price for the stock, say $110; and the specific cost becomes:

$$\$110 = \frac{\$120}{1 + k_e}; \ k_e = 9.1\%$$

So far, we have assumed that the stock is held for one year and then sold. In the more general case, stockholders can hold their shares for an unrestricted number of years, thereby obtaining a stream of future dividends. If the firm sells new stock for a net price P, the specific cost of common stock is given by:

$$P = \frac{D_1}{1 + k_e} + \frac{D_2}{(1 + k_e)^2} + \ldots = \sum_{t=1}^{\infty} \frac{D_t}{(1 + k_e)^t}$$

---

3 Since we capitalize dividends, which by definition represent a cash flow *after* the payment of corporate tax k_e denotes the *post-tax* discount rate. However, to simplify the notation we have dropped the asterisk from the specific costs of equity and debt for the remainder of the chapter.

and if we further assume that the dividend stream is expected to remain constant, i.e. $D_1 = D_2 = \ldots = D$, this equation reduces to:[4]

$$P = \frac{D}{k_e}$$

and the specific cost of common stock is given by the dividend yield:

$$k_e = \frac{D}{P}$$

However, as we shall see below, a constant annual dividend implies that the firm pays out all of its earnings every year, and that the earnings themselves are constant over time. Hence in this case the cost of equity is given by

$$k_e = \frac{D}{P} = \frac{E}{P}$$

where E denotes earnings per share.

Let us leave aside this special case in which the firm distributes all its earnings as dividends and examine the more realistic case in which firms retain some proportion of their annual earnings, distributing the rest as dividends. If we denote net earnings per share (after deduction of depreciation, interest and taxes) by E, and cash dividends by D, the first year dividend is given by

$$D_1 = (1 - b)E$$

where b denotes the fraction of earnings which the firm desires to reinvest ($0 \leqslant b \leqslant 1$). It is clear from this definition that if the firm follows a policy of reinvesting a *fixed* proportion of its annual earnings, dividends in the following years will not remain constant. This can readily be seen from the following calculation of the earnings available for distribution in the second year, assuming that the firm earns an average rate of return R on the reinvested portion of the previous year's earnings:

$$E_2 = E + RbE = E(1 + bR)$$

If the firm follows the assumed policy of paying out a fixed proportion $(1 - b)$ of its annual earnings as dividends, the second-year dividend, D_2, becomes:

$$D_2 = (1 - b)E_2 = (1 - b)E(1 + bR)$$

In the third year the earnings available for allocation equal the earnings of year 2 plus the additional earnings on the investments financed out of the retention of part of the previous year's earnings. Thus the level of earnings per share in

---

4 This follows from the summation of an infinite geometric progression:

$$P = \frac{D}{1 + k_e} + \frac{D}{(1 + k_e)^2} + \ldots + \frac{D}{(1 + k_e)^n} + \ldots$$

$$= \frac{D}{1 + k_e} \cdot \frac{1}{1 - \dfrac{1}{1 + k_e}} = \frac{D}{k_e}$$

the third year will be

$$E_3 = E_2 + bE_2 R = E(1 + bR) + bE(1 + bR) \cdot R$$

which can also be written as

$$E(1 + bR)(1 + bR) = E(1 + bR)^2$$

and the dividend in the third year becomes

$$D_3 = (1 - b)E(1 + bR)^2$$

Given the investment policy, the dividend will go on increasing from year to year at the rate bR. If we assume that the firm retains 50% of its earnings ($b = 0.5$) and earns 10% on the average on new investments, the dividends will grow at a 5% rate each year ($bR = 0.5 \times 0.10 = 0.05$).

Having identified the components of the dividend flow, we can compute the present value of the future dividend stream, using the post-corporate tax required rate of return k_e as the discount rate:

$$P = \frac{(1 - b)E}{1 + k_e} + \frac{(1 - b)E(1 + bR)}{(1 + k_e)^2} + \frac{(1 - b)E(1 + bR)^2}{(1 + k_e)^3} + \dots$$

Denoting bR by g, for growth rate, and the first year dividend $(1 - b)E$ by D, we derive the Gordon dividend growth model,[5]

$$P = \frac{(1 - b)E}{k_e - bR} = \frac{D}{k_e - g}$$

Recalling that P is the observed market price of the stock, i.e., *the maximum price per share for which the firm can sell additional shares*, k_e is the specific cost of common stock. Rewriting the above formula we get

$$k_e = \frac{D}{P} + g$$

Thus in the more general case, the cost of equity is equal to the dividend yield D/P plus the growth rate of future earnings, which for a given retention policy,

---

5 The equation is an infinite geometric progression with the common factor $(1 + bR)/(1 + k_e)$ Summing the progression yields

$$P = (1 - b)E \frac{1}{1 + k_e} \left[1 + \frac{1 + bR}{1 + k_e} + \frac{(1 + bR)^2}{(1 + k_e)^2} + \dots + \right]$$

$$= (1 - b)E \frac{1}{1 + k_e} \cdot 1/1 - \frac{1 + bR}{1 + k_e} = \frac{(1 - b)E}{k_e - bR}$$

Note that $bR < k_e$ constitutes a necessary condition for the convergence of the geometric progression. Since, in general, $b < 1$ (that is dividends are paid) R can be greater or smaller than k_e. The specific model presented in the text was developed by Myron J. Gordon, *The Investment, Financing and Valuation of the Corporation*, Homewood, Ill., Irwin, 1962.

b, also constitutes the growth rate of dividends. Although it is quite clear that the discount rate k_e which equates the present value of future dividends with the market price of the stock is the specific cost of common stock, a numerical example may be helpful.

Suppose that a firm which is financed only by equity earns $10 per share each year and pays all of this amount to the shareholders as a dividend. If the market price of the stock is, say $100, k_e is given by

$$\$100 = \frac{10}{1 + k_e} + \frac{10}{(1 + k_e)^2} + \ldots = \frac{10}{k_e}$$

and

$$k_e = \frac{10}{100} = 10\%$$

Assume now that at the end of the first year the firm needs $10 per share to finance a new investment. Should the firm undertake this project? The answer of course depends on whether the market price of the stock will rise or fall as a result of the new investment. In other words, it depends on whether the net present value calculated at the appropriate discount rate is positive or negative. In order to show that the appropriate discount rate for the new investment is k_e (and, therefore, k_e is indeed the specific cost of common stock), let us assume that the firm omits its dividend payment at the end of the first year, and uses the money to finance the new investment, which yields $R\%$ every year thereafter. Let us further assume that commencing in the second year, the firm returns to its previous policy of paying out all earnings as dividends. The new dividend equals $10 + 10R$, i.e. $10 plus the additional earnings from the new investment, and the share's market price is given by[6]

$$P = \frac{0}{1 + k_e} + \frac{10 + 10R}{(1 + k_e)^2} + \frac{10 + 10R}{(1 + k_e)^3} + \ldots = \frac{10}{k_e} \cdot \frac{1 + R}{1 + k_e}$$

But as $k_e = 10\%$ we get

$$P = \frac{10}{0.1} \cdot \frac{1 + R}{1.1} = \$100 \cdot \frac{1 + R}{1.1}$$

Since the market price of the stock before undertaking the new investment was $100, we can verify that the market price of the stock will rise only if $R > 10\%$, i.e. only if the internal rate of return on the new investment is greater than the specific cost of common stock. If we use k_e as the discount rate for evaluating the new project, it will have a positive *NPV* only if $R > k_e$ and therefore any project with a positive *NPV*, calculated at k_e, also induces a rise in the market price of the stock. Hence, by definition, k_e is the rate of return required by

---

6 Again summing the infinite progression we derive:

$$P = \frac{10 + 10R}{(1 + k_e)^2} \cdot 1/1 - \frac{1}{1 + k_e} = \frac{10 + 10R}{k_e(1 + k_e)} = \frac{10}{k_e} \cdot \frac{(1 + R)}{(1 + k_e)}$$

shareholders and should be used as the cost of the equity component when calculating the weighted average cost of capital.

SUPER GROWTH COMPANIES

It is common practice, especially among financial analysts, to capitalize future earnings rather than dividends when evaluating common stocks. Despite the popularity of such calculations, it must be emphasized that replacing dividends with earnings in the valuation formula is conceptually incorrect and may lead to serious error: the relevant cash flow to the investor is the dividend stream. Moreover, discounting current earnings (part of which are reinvested) would constitute *double counting* of the retained earnings, the return on which, R, already is reflected in the growth rate of future earnings, bR. One explanation for the widespread use of earnings in valuation is that a very simple version of the present value of earnings provides a good rule of thumb approximation of the cost of capital for companies with only moderate growth prospects.

In order to examine the relationship between earnings and dividend valuation models, let us rewrite the dividend growth model on the explicit assumption that the average rate of return on reinvested earnings, R, is exactly equal to the specific cost of equity, k_e:

$$P = \frac{(1 - b)E}{k_e - bR} = \frac{(1 - b)E}{k_e - bk_e} = \frac{(1 - b)E}{(1 - b)k_e} = \frac{E}{k_e}$$

Given this assumption, the price of the stock, as derived from the dividend model, is equivalent to the price that would be derived from the calculation of the present value of a fixed stream of future earnings. And the firm's cost of capital is equal to the current earnings yield, E/P:

$$k_e = \frac{E}{P}$$

where E denotes earnings per share in the current year. However, since we derived our results from the dividend growth model, we can equivalently set out the cost of capital as follows:

$$k_e = \frac{E}{P} = \frac{D}{P} + g$$

Thus for the class of firms under consideration, i.e. those for whom the average rate of return on reinvested earnings equals the specific cost of equity capital ($R = k_e$), the easily calculated and very popular earnings yield provides a good estimate of the cost of common stock.

Do these results necessarily imply that the per share earnings of such a company are constant, i.e. that the growth rate is zero? The answer is no! We have defined this class of companies in terms of the relationship between R and k_e, but earnings per share (and dividends) can increase over time even if extraordinary profit opportunities ($R > k_e$) do not exist. For example, a high retention policy in itself can cause an expansion of earnings even though the rate of return on reinvestment is only moderate. In such a case we would still refer to such a company as a "moderate-growth" firm despite the significant rate of increase in its earnings over time.

To clarify this argument, assume that a firm which earns $1 per share in the current year adopts a policy of retaining 50% of its earnings ($b = 50\%$). In order to emphasize the role played by the retention policy, let us further assume that the reinvested profits earn only 5%. Given this relatively low rate of return, will future earnings grow? Clearly, the answer is in the affirmative. Next year's per-share earnings will increase to $1.025 ($1 as before plus 5% of $0.50 = 2½ cents). Similarly next year's dividend, given the fixed retention policy, will also grow at the same rate, i.e. from 50 cents to 51¼ cents per share. Thus, both earnings and dividends will grow at the rate $g = bR$, which is 2½% per year in our example. Moreover, this growth rate can be increased to 4% per year merely by increasing the retention rate to 0.80%, even though we assume that the additional funds are reinvested at a very low rate of return. It follows that even relatively unprofitable firms might display relatively high growth rates if they retain high proportions of their earnings.

A more meaningful distinction between firms can be made on the basis of the gap between the average reinvestment rate R, and the required return of stockholders, k_e. Firms characterized by a relatively small difference between R and k_e should be considered as "moderate-growth" companies. On the other hand, firms like IBM whose average rate of return R is considerably greater than the cost of equity capital will be defined as "super-growth" stocks. Alternatively, we can distinguish between stocks by comparing the "rule of thumb" and "dividend growth model" estimates of the cost of capital:

$$k_e = \frac{E}{P} \quad \text{and} \quad k_e = \frac{D}{P} + g \text{ respectively}$$

If the difference between the two estimates is negligible we are dealing with a *moderate-growth* stock, no matter how high the actual growth rate; if the E/P rule of thumb provides a poor estimate of $D/P + g$ then we are dealing with a *super-growth* stock.

SUPER GROWTH FOR A LIMITED PERIOD

Using the formula $k_e = D/P + g$ to estimate the firm's cost of equity may lead to a paradoxical result, i.e., to an unreasonably high cost of equity. Let us illustrate the point using the case of Xerox Corporation. Suppose that one wants to estimate the firm's cost of equity at the end of 1969, using the adjusted *EPS* for the years 1960–69 to estimate the growth rate $\hat{g}$. Moody's Industrial Manual reveals the following figures:

Year	1960	1961	1962	1963	1964	1965	1966	1967	1968	1969
Adjusted *EPS* ($)	0.045	0.093	0.33	0.38	0.63	0.93	1.24	1.49	1.73	2.08

For simplicity we use the geometric mean and not the logarithmic regression (see Appendix 18A) to obtain the estimated growth rate, $\hat{g}$:

$$\hat{g} = \left(\frac{EPS_{1969}}{EPS_{1960}} \right)^{1/9} - 1 = \left(\frac{2.08}{0.045} \right)^{1/9} - 1 = 53.1\% \cong 53\%$$

Since D/P for Xerox at the end of 1969 was about 1%, the cost of equity for Xerox, applying the dividend growth model can be estimated as follows:

$$k_e = \frac{D}{P} + \hat{g} = 1\% + 53\% = \textbf{54\%}$$

Does it make sense that the cost of equity even of this supergrowth firm was 54% in 1969?

Recalling that by definition the cost of equity consists of the riskless interest rate plus a risk premium, such a high cost of equity is reasonable only if the probability of default is very high, and in such a case the stock price should be very low. Obviously this is not the case of most supergrowth firms and certainly not of Xerox.

The apparent paradox can be resolved if we note that a firm cannot earn extraordinarily high profits forever. As new firms enter the highly profitable industry the extraordinary profits will tend to disappear after a few years. Even in the case of a firm which earns extraordinary profits due to an invention protected by patent, the reader should note that patents have only finite lives. Hence, one should consider the possibility of a reduction in future growth and not rely solely on past data when applying the dividend growth formula. This is crucial in the case of supergrowth firms.

Let us now develop a formula to estimate the cost of equity for the case of limited growth periods. Suppose that profits and dividends are expected to grow at an extraordinary rate g_1 for $n-1$ years and then will continue to grow at a normal rate g_2, where $g_2 < g_1$. Applying the dividend growth approach, the stock price is given by

$$P_0 = \frac{D}{1 + k_e} + \frac{D(1 + g_1)}{(1 + k_e)^2} + \ldots + \frac{D(1 + g_1)^{n-1}}{(1 + k_e)^n} +$$

$$+ \frac{D(1 + g_1)^{n-1}(1 + g_2)}{(1 + k_e)^n(1 + k_e)} + \frac{D(1 + g_1)^{n-1}(1 + g_2)^2}{(1 + k_e)^n(1 + k_e)^2} + \ldots$$

This can be rewritten as,

$$P = \sum_{t=1}^{n} \frac{D(1 + g_1)^{t-1}}{(1 + k_e)^t} + \frac{D(1 + g_1)^{n-1}}{(1 + k_e)^n} \sum_{i=1}^{\infty} \frac{(1 + g_2)^t}{(1 + k_e)^t}$$

Using the summation formula for an infinite geometric progression, this equation can be rewritten as,

$$P = \sum_{t=1}^{n} \frac{D(1 + g_1)^{t-1}}{(1 + k_e)^t} + \frac{D(1 + g_1)^{n-1}}{(1 + k_e)^n} \cdot \frac{1 + g_2}{1 + k_e} \cdot 1 \Big/ 1 - \frac{1 + g_2}{1 + k_e}$$

which after multiplying through becomes

$$P = \sum_{t=1}^{n} \frac{D(1 + g_1)^{t-1}}{(1 + k_e)^t} + \frac{D(1 + g_1)^{n-1}}{(1 + k_e)^n} \cdot \frac{1 + g_2}{k_e - g_2}$$

Since P (the stock's current price) and d_0 (its current dividend) are given, the cost of equity, k_e, is a function of the supergrowth rate g_1, the normal growth rate g_2, and the duration of the supergrowth period, $n - 1$ years.

A Numerical Example

Let $P = \$100$, $d_0 = \$1$ and $g_1 = 50\%$ for 9 years (i.e., $n - 1 = 9$). After the 10th year the firm's patent will expire, so that the earnings and dividends will grow at $g_2 = 5\%$ per year. If the growth rate is 50% *forever*, the cost of equity would be

$$k_e = \frac{d}{p} + g = \frac{1}{100} + 50\% = 51\%,$$

which does not make sense. However, applying the above formula which takes into account that the extraordinary growth rate will be reduced in the future to 5%, we obtain

$$\$100 = \sum_{t=1}^{10} \$1 \cdot \frac{(1.5)^{t-1}}{(1 + k_e)^t} + \$1 \cdot \frac{(1.5)^9}{(1 + k_e)^{10}} \cdot \frac{1.05}{k_e - 0.05}$$

By trial and error one can plug in values for k_e until the present value of future dividends is just equal to $100. In this special case, $k_e \cong 17.2\%$, which is a much more reasonable estimate of the cost of equity.

So far we have assumed that the supergrowth phase will last for nine years at the rate $g_1 = 50\%$ per annum. How sensitive is the cost of equity k_e to errors in the length of the supergrowth period or in the growth rate estimate? Table 18.5 gives the values of k_e obtained by the same trial-and-error method for alternative values of n and g_1 (assuming that g_2, the normal growth rate remains 5%).

In general, as the length of the supergrowth period increases, the discount rate increases, approaching in the limit the theoretical infinite growth value $k_e = (D/P) + g_1$. As the supergrowth period becomes shorter, the discount rate decreases steeply, but always remains higher than the permanent growth rate, which in this case is assumed to be 5%.

Table 18.5

The Value of k_e for Various Values of g_1 and n(*in percent*)

g_1	1	3	5	10	15	20	50	100
5	6.0	6.0	6.0	6.0	6.0	6.0	6.0	6.0
10	6.0	6.1	6.2	6.5	6.8	7.2	8.9	9.9
25	6.0	6.4	6.9	9.3	12.0	14.0	22.0	24.5
50	6.0	7.0	8.8	17.2	26.0	32.0	45.0	49.0

Let us return to the case of Xerox Corporation. Suppose that the high growth rate of about 50% was expected to continue for the next 9 years and that a normal growth of 5% was expected thereafter. Since the price of the firm's stock at the end of 1969 was about $100, Table 18.5 indicates that the cost of equity is 17.2% and not 51% as noted previously. In reality growth rates tend to decrease gradually over time; the per share earnings of Xerox after 1969 were as follows:

Year	1970	1971	1972	1973	1974	1975	1976	1977	1978
Adjusted *EPS* ($)	2.40	2.71	3.16	3.81	4.16	3.07	4.53	5.03	5.92

which constitutes an average growth rate of about 12% per annum over the eight year period.

$$\hat{g}_2 = \left(\frac{EPS_{78}}{EPS_{70}}\right)^{1/8} - 1 = \left(\frac{5.92}{2.40}\right)^{1/8} - 1 \approx 12.3\%$$

The supergrowth which prevailed in the sixties did not persist, and the firm enjoyed only a reasonable growth rate in the seventies. Thus, when future growth opportunities, rather than ex-post growth, are taken into account in estimating the cost of equity the cost of equity *paradox* is resolved.

To sum up, the dividend model must be based on a realistic estimate of *future growth rates*. However, for many mature firms which have reached a stable development, the past growth rate serves as a good estimate of the future growth in profits and dividends. But for supergrowth firms, e.g. firms with temporary monopoly power or patents, basing our analysis solely on past growth can lead to a gross overestimate of the true cost of equity.

ADJUSTING EARNINGS PER SHARE (*EPS*)

Since we are primarily concerned with the past record of a firm's earnings in order to help us estimate the crucial growth rate, some adjustment of the *EPS* figures may be necessary. The need to adjust the *EPS* figures in order to ensure comparability between the years can be illustrated by the hypothetical example

Table 18.6

Earnings per Share for a Hypothetical Company

Year	Net Earnings	Number of Shares	Earnings per Share
1979	100,000	50,000	2
1980	100,000	100,000	1

given in Table 18.6. Although net after-tax profits remained the same between 1979 and 1980, the number of shares doubled in 1980, thereby reducing *EPS* by 50%, that is, from $2 per share in 1979 to $1 per share in 1980. How should we interpret this drop in *EPS*?

To the degree that the company issued new shares to the public, and that sufficient time has elapsed for the new investments financed by the issue to reach fruition, the conclusion that profitability dropped drastically seems justified. If the company issued new shares and the funds were not properly used, this is tantamount, from the investor's point of view, to acquiring a new partner who adds nothing to the company's overall profitability but shares in the earnings. However, if the drop in *EPS* is due to a 2 for 1 stock split, no additional capital was raised, but neither have the former shareholders acquired new partners. For every share owned in 1979 a shareholder now has two shares, so *EPS* did not really drop but remained stable at $2 per *adjusted* share in 1980. Hence, if paradoxical results are to be avoided, *EPS* figures must be adjusted.

Adjusting *EPS* for Stock Splits and Stock Dividends

In a stock dividend or split a company's stockholders are given additional shares to represent their ownership interest. No additional investment on the part of the shareholders is required, and of course, no additional capital is raised by the corporation. The difference between the stock dividend and the split is technical and need not concern us here: in a split, as the name suggests, the par or stated value of the stock is reduced, while in a stock dividend the par or stated value remains unchanged, and a transfer is effected from earned surplus to the capital account. In both instances no transaction takes place, and the split or stock dividend represents a bookkeeping entry.[7]

To clarify the procedure for adjusting *EPS* for splits or stock dividends, let us consider the example given in Table 18.7 of a company which declared a 10% stock dividend in 1977 and a 2 for 1 split (equivalent for our purposes to a 100% stock dividend) in 1979. As a first step, a base year is chosen; in our example it is

---

7 Large stock dividends and splits may broaden the market for a firm's stock by lowering the per unit price, thereby lowering the minimum investment required to secure the preferential commission on 100 share round lots. The case for a small stock dividend or split is far less clear, although where the cash dividend rate remains unchanged it affords management the opportunity to "announcing" a dividend rise in advance.

Table 18.7

Unadjusted Earnings per Share and Stock Dividends (Splits) of a Hypothetical Company

Year	Net Earnings after Tax (1)	Number of Shares (2)	Unadjusted Earnings per Share (3)	Splits and Stock Dividends (4)
1975	1,000	1,000	1.00	—
1976	1,100	1,000	1.10	—
1977	1,200	1,100	1.09	10%
1978	1,500	1,100	1.36	—
1979	1,500	2,200	0.68	2:1
1980	1,600	2,200	0.73	—

Table 18.8

Year	Number of Shares at Beginning of Each Year	Splits and Stock Dividends	Number of Shares at End of Each Year
1975	100	—	100
1976	100	—	100
1977	100	10%	110
1978	110	—	110
1979	110	2:1	220
1980	220	—	220

1975. An "index" of the *number* of shares a 1975 shareholder owns in each of the following years, *without additional investment*, is constructed. Such an index is given in Table 18.8. For simplicity, consider a shareholder with 100 shares in 1975. In 1977, following the 10% stock dividend, the *number* of shares which he owned increases to 110, without any additional investment, and the index is set at 110 from 1977 on. In 1977 following the 2 for 1 split the number of shares which he owned increased to 220 (not 200, since he held 110 shares when the split occurred). From that date the index becomes 220. When calculating the adjusted *EPS*, Table 18.9, the observed *EPS* (Column 1) is multiplied by the index (Column 2), and the resulting product (Column 3) represents the *EPS*, adjusted for stock splits and stock dividends.[8]

The need for the adjustment becomes clear when we compare the record of

8 Alternatively 1980 could be chosen as the base year and the index constructed backwards by *dividing* the annual unadjusted earnings-per-share data by 1 plus the relevant percentage change in the number of shares. This is the procedure commonly employed by Moody's and other reporting services when adjusting for splits or stock dividends.

Table 18.9

Year	Unadjusted Earnings per Share (1)	Index (2)	Adjusted Earnings per share (1) · (2) /100 = (3)
1975	1.00	100	1.00
1976	1.10	100	1.10
1977	1.09	110	1.20
1978	1.36	110	1.50
1979	0.68	220	1.50
1980	0.73	220	1.61

unadjusted earnings per share for the company (Column 1 of Table 18.9) with its adjusted *EPS* (Column 3 of Table 18.9). These fluctuations in *unadjusted EPS* which were induced by the accounting manipulations clearly are of no significance to the investor and must be offset when the *rate of growth* in earnings is being calculated. The company did not experience a 27% drop in profitability between 1975 and 1980, as the unadjusted *EPS* figures suggest. On the contrary, a glance at Table 18.9 suffices to show that the company's profits (for a given investment) *increased* by 61% (adjusted *EPS* were $1.61 in 1980 compared with $1.00 in 1971) during those years. Similarly the increase in profitability between 1977 and 1975 was 20% (adjusted) and not 9% as the unadjusted figures suggest. Since we are examining the past record of *EPS* in order to discern *trends* in the rate of growth, only the *adjusted* record is relevant for this purpose.[9]

Adjusting *EPS* in Practice: Georgia-Pacific Corporation

To illustrate the *EPS* adjustments in practice, let's consider an actual case of a corporation which declared stock dividends and split its stock. The Georgia-Pacific Corporation is an integrated manufacturer and distributor of forest products and chemicals. It employs over 40,000 people in 205 plants over the USA. Table 18.10 lists the basic financial data taken from the firm's annual statements which shows a very slight growth rate of about 3% per year during the period 1972 – 78.

$$\left(\frac{EPS_{78}}{EPS_{72}}\right)^{1/6} - 1 = \left(\frac{2.95}{2.44}\right)^{1/6} - 1 = 3.2\%$$

But 3.2% is *not* the true growth rate in earnings per share. In order to calculate the true rate of growth the *EPS* figures must be adjusted for stock dividends

9 A similar adjustment should be made for the stock dividend component of a rights offering as well. See Haim Levy and Marshall Sarnat, *Investment and Portfolio Analysis*, New York, Wiley, 1972, Chapter 2.

Table 18.10
Georgia – Pacific Corporation — Earnings per Share

Year	Net Income (Thousand $) (1)	Number of Common Shares (Thousand Shares) (2)	EPS (3) = (1)/(2)	Annual Growth Rate in EPS, (%)
1972	$128,500	52,675	$2.44	—
1973	162,810	53,825	3.02	23.8
1974	164,350	56,250	2.92	− 3.3
1975	148,020	60,325	2.45	− 16.1
1976	215,300	98,750	2.18	− 11.0
1977	262,000	102,500	2.56	17.4
1978	302,000	102,500	2.95	15.2

and splits. Table 18.11 provides the basic information on stock dividends and splits and the standard share index. Georgia – Pacific distributed stock dividends of 2% − 4% a year, and in 1976 it split its stock 3 for 2 which is equivalent to a 50% stock dividend. Starting with 100 shares and denoting the adjustment factor by α, the index at the end of 1973 is

$$100(1 + \alpha) = 100 \cdot 1.02 = 102$$

At the end of 1974 it is $102 \cdot 1.02 \cdot 1.02 = 106.12$ since it reflects two additional 2% stock dividends in that year and the stock issued in March was entitled to receive the stock dividend declared in September. In the same way, the appropriate standard share index is calculated each year. The index at the end of 1978 was 172.3. Thus an investor who held 100 shares of stock in 1972 had accumulated 172.3 shares by the end of 1978 without additional investment.

Table 18.11
Calculation of the Standard Share Index for Georgia – Pacific Corporation

Year	Standard Share Index, Beginning of Period	Stock Dividends or Stock Splits	Adjustment Factor	Standard Share Index, End of Period
1972	—	—	—	100.00
1973	100	2% stock dividend	1.02	102.00
1974	102	2% stock dividend March 1974	1.02	104.04
	104.04	2% stock dividend Sept. 1974	1.02	106.12
1975	106.12	2% stock dividend March 1975	1.02	108.24
	108.24	2% stock dividend Sept. 1975	1.02	110.40
1976	110.40	2% stock dividend March 1976	1.02	112.61
	112.61	3-for-2 stock split August 1976	1.5	168.92
1977	168.92	2% stock dividend Aug. 1977	1.02	172.30
1978	172.30	—	—	172.30

Table 18.12
Adjusted Earnings per Share for Georgia — Pacific Corporation

Year	Earnings per Share, as Reported (1) ($)	Standard Share Index (2)	Adjusted EPS $(3) = \dfrac{(1) \cdot (2)}{100}$ ($)	"Backward" Standard Share Index $(4) = [(2)/172.30] \cdot 100$	"Retroactively" Adjusted EPS ($) $(5) = \dfrac{(3) \cdot}{(4)}$ 100
1972	2.44	100.00	2.44	58.04	1.42
1973	3.02	102.00	3.08	59.20	1.79
1974	2.92	106.12	3.10	61.27	1.79
1975	2.45	110.40	2.70	64.07	1.57
1976	2.18	168.92	3.68	98.04	2.14
1977	2.56	172.30	4.41	100.00	2.56
1978	2.95	172.30	5.08	100.00	2.95

Table 18.12 sets out the "reported" and "adjusted" *EPS* of Georgia – Pacific; Fig. 18.2 plots the two *EPS* series. Clearly the impact of the adjustment is very significant, and therefore, it is the common practice to always refer to the *adjusted* earnings per share whenever the results of several years are compared. The true (adjusted) growth rate for the period is

$$\left(\frac{5.08}{2.44}\right)^{1/6} - 1 = 13\% \text{ and not } 3\%$$

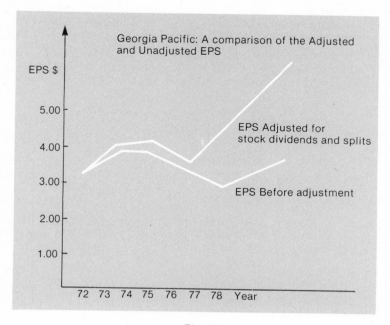

Fig. 18.2

We have performed a *forward* adjustment from the base year (1972) to the current year (1978). This is the most convenient procedure; for each additional year we only have to determine the additional adjustment factor. Most investment analysts do a "retroactive" or "backward" adjustment: the last year's index is set at 100 and the standard share index is adjusted backward by *dividing* the current index by the adjustment factor. The advantage of this method is that the last year's earnings per share are simply computed from the reported results. Its major shortcoming stems from the fact that the entire adjusted *EPS* series has to be recalculated each year, as the base year (index equal to 100) always advances to coincide with the last year. The last two columns in Table 18.12 give the "backward" standard share index and the "retroactively" adjusted earnings per share. Note that although the numbers are different, the percentage changes and growth rates are the *same* with both methods.

SPECIFIC COST OF RETAINED EARNINGS

The typical business firm finances a large share of its long-term capital investments internally out of retained earnings. Although such funds might appear to be "free" in the sense that the firm does not incur an actual outlay cost, there is no conceptual difference between the use of retained earnings or the proceeds of a stock issue to finance new investments. Both of these sources have a well-defined opportunity cost, i.e. the rate of return which stockholders expect from the stock. Retained earnings should be treated like a common stock issue with one notable exception. No flotation costs are incurred when internal, rather than external, funds are employed. Hence there is no need to deduct such costs from the current market price, P, when calculating the specific cost of equity. As a result, the cost of retained earnings will always be somewhat less than the cost of common stock, the exact differential depending on the magnitude of the flotation costs.

CALCULATING THE COST OF CAPITAL IN PRACTICE

Having got the theoretical underpinnings of the analysis of the cost of capital under our belts, let us now turn to the thorny question of its practical application. More specifically let us see if the procedures outlined in the previous sections can be applied to actual business firms. The question of application is absolutely crucial; for as we have tried to emphasize throughout the book, a theory or analytical apparatus which is "good in theory but bad in practice" is simply a bad theory. The ultimate test of the theory of corporate finance is not its formal elegance but lies rather in our ability to apply the theoretical concepts to actual business problems. To this end we shall now illustrate the calculation of the weighted average cost of capital in 1972 for two well-known firms — General Motors Corporation (GM) and International Business Machines (IBM). We use 1972 as a benchmark in order to analyze the impact of the oil crisis on the cost of capital. In later sections the cost of capital will be estimated for 1979 as well.

General Motors Corporation

As a first step in the analysis we shall estimated the specific cost of equity capital for GM at the end of 1972. As we have already noted, this requires the estimation of the future growth of earnings (dividends). For the purpose of this analysis, let us estimate the growth rate by means of regression analysis, using historical data on earnings per share over the period 1953 – 72 (see Table 18.13).

Table 18.13
General Motors Corporation: Net Earnings Per Share of Common Stock*

Year	Earnings per Share	Year	Earnings per Share
	($)		($)
1953	2.24	1963	5.56
1954	3.03	1964	6.05
1955	4.30	1965	7.41
1956	3.02	1966	6.24
1957	2.99	1967	5.66
1958	2.22	1968	6.02
1959	3.06	1969	5.95
1960	3.35	1970	2.09
1961	3.11	1971	6.72
1962	5.10	1972	7.51

*Adjusted for stock dividends and splits.
Source: General Motors Corporation, Annual Report 1972.

Using this approach the annual growth rate of per share earnings (and dividends) was estimated to be 4.7%.[10] Given GM's 1972 dividend of $4.45, a market price at the end of 1972 of $81.125, the specific cost of equity (retained earnings) is 10.19%. (For simplicity, we shall ignore flotation costs throughout the analysis.)

$$k_e = \frac{D}{P} + g = \frac{4.45}{81.125} + 0.047 = 10.19\%$$

Clearly 10.19% represents the estimate of GM's *after-tax* specific cost of equity, because the per-share earnings of Table 18.13 have been calculated *net* of corporate taxes.

Now let us deviate from our main task for a moment in order to examine one of the basic characteristics of GM stock. Does the 4.7% growth rate indicate that GM should properly be considered a so-called "super-growth stock"? As we have already noted, the fact that observed earnings increase over time is not in itself sufficient evidence to support an affirmative answer to this question. And in fact, in the case of GM we can readily demonstrate that despite an observed growth rate of almost 5%, it does not represent a true growth situation. This contention can be verified by calculating the *E/P* rule of

10 The estimation procedure is set out in Appendix 18A. Alternatively, the growth rate could be calculated from estimates of *b* and *R*.

thumb estimate of GM's specific cost of equity:

$$k_e = \frac{7.51}{81.125} = 9.2\%$$

where \$7.51 denotes GM's earnings per share in 1972. Since 9.2% is a fairly good approximation of GM's cost of equity capital as calculated from the $D/P + g$ formula (10.2%), we can conclude that *extraordinarily* profitable investment opportunities have not been the major factor accounting for the growth of GM's earnings.

Now, let us return to our calculation of the cost of capital. Again, ignoring flotation costs, we have calculated the specific cost of GM's preferred stock at about 6.5%:[11]

GM 3.75% Preferred Stock

$$k_p = \frac{D}{P} = \frac{\$3.75}{57.125} = 6.56\%$$

GM 5% Preferred Stock

$$k_p = \frac{D}{P} = \frac{\$5.00}{77.50} = 6.45\%$$

where 57.125 and 77.50 are the market prices of the two preferred stocks on 31 December 1972. Similarly the after-tax specific cost of debt $(1 - T)k_d$ was estimated to be 3.07% at the end of 1972. Although market prices were employed in the calculation of the specific costs of equity and preference shares, book values were used to estimate the cost of debt. In the case of GM, the use of book values for that purpose does not materially affect the calculation of the weighted average.

Table 18.14 sets out the specific costs of debt, preferred stock and common equity and the market value of each source of financing (number of shares outstanding times their market price).[12] Assuming that the observed capital structure constitutes GM's target financing mix, its after-tax weighted average cost of capital is approximately 10%, and *the latter should be used as the cutoff rate for evaluating investment projects.*

A word of caution is in order. Our calculation of GM's cost of capital is only illustrative. In particular, the all-important growth rate was estimated solely on the basis of historical earnings data. Presumably the company's finan-

11 The relatively low yields on preferred stock reflect the fact that under US tax regulations the preferred dividends are tax-free to other corporations.

12 The reader should note that with regard to equity, the market value of the common stock (number of shares times market price) reflects the full market value of the firm's equity so that there is no need to make any additional calculation of the value of any other balance sheet equity items such as surplus, retained earnings or various reserve accounts.

In the case of GM, substituting book for market value changes the calculation only slightly. The cost of capital using the former is 9.6% as compared with the 9.9% estimate using market weights. However this close relationship does not necessarily hold true for other companies.

Table 18.14
General Motors Corporation: Weighted Average Cost of Capital, 1972

	Capital Structure in Million $	in %	After-tax Specific Costs (in %)	Contribution to the Weighted Average Cost of Capital (in %)
	(1)	(2)	(3)	(4) = (2) × (3)
Debt*	790.9	3.25	3.07	0.100
3.75% Preferred Stock†	57.1	0.23	6.56	0.015
5% Preferred Stock†	145.3	0.60	6.45	0.039
Common Equity†	23,332.9	95.92	10.19	9.774
	24,326.2	100.00	Weighted average cost of capital	**9.928%**

*Based on book value.
†Based on market value.

cial analysts and economists could use additional sources of information, drawn from general economic, industry and company forecasts, when estimating the future growth pattern of GM's earnings.

International Business Machines

Having estimated the cost of capital in the moderate growth situation represented by General Motors, let us now turn to the firm whose very name has become a synonym for rapid growth — IBM. The source of IBM's reputation can readily be found by examining the historical record of its per-share earnings

Table 18.15

Year	Earnings Per Share ($)	Year	Earnings Per Share ($)
1963	3.39	1968	7.71
1964	4.00	1969	8.21
1965	4.40	1970	8.92
1966	4.71	1971	9.38
1967	5.81	1972	11.03

*Adjusted for stock dividends and splits.
Source: International Business Machines, Annual Report 1972.

for the decade 1963–72 which is set out in Table 18.15. Earnings per share (adjusted for splits and stock dividends) grew threefold during the period — from $3.39 per share to $11.03 per share. Applying the same regression technique as before (see Appendix 18A), the estimated annual growth rate of IBM's earnings (dividends) is 14.3%. Given its 1972 dividend of $5.40 and end-of-year market price of $402, the specific cost of equity for IBM (ignoring flotation costs) at the end of 1972 is 15.64%:

$$k_e = \frac{D}{P} + g = \frac{5.4}{402} + 0.143 = 15.64\%$$

In the case of IBM we can readily verify that the E/P rule of thumb cannot be used to estimate its cost of equity:

$$\frac{E}{P} = \frac{11.03}{402} = 2.7\%$$

Clearly 2.7% is a nonsensical result which only serves to emphasize the dangers inherent in the use of the popular E/P measure.

Table 18.16 sets out all of the relevant data on specific costs and capital structure required to estimate IBM's weighted average cost of capital at the end of 1972. The after-tax specific cost of debt was 3.31%. Combining this with the cost of equity results in a weighted average of 15.4%. Thus the cutoff rate was significantly higher for IBM (about 15%) than for GM (about 10%). This implies a pre-tax required rate of return of about 30% in the case of IBM.

Table 18.16
IBM: Weighted Average Cost of Capital, 1972

	Capital Structure in Million $	in %	After-tax Specific Costs (in %)	Contribution to the Weighted Average Cost of Capital (in %)
	(1)	(2)	(3)	(4) = (2) × (3)
Debt*	772.9	1.62	3.31	0.054
Common Equity†	46,792.4	98.38	15.64	15.387
			Weighted average cost of capital	**15.441%**

*Based on book value.
†Based on market value.

THE IMPACT OF THE ENERGY CRISIS

Having estimated the cost of capital for GM and IBM at the end of 1972, let us turn our attention to the events of the following year. The year 1973 was a watershed year for the world economy; in that year the energy crisis became apparent to all as the petroleum exporting nations sharply increased the price of oil. All over the globe it was a year of boycotts, excess demands, short-supplies, balance of payments problems and shifting relative prices.

What was the impact of these events on the cost of capital of IBM and GM? Let us start with IBM. For all practical purposes our estimate of the all-important growth rate remains constant when estimated from the time series

1964 – 73 rather than 1963 – 72; the compounded average annual growth rate rising from 14.3% to 14.4%. However, due to falling stock prices and rising interest rates (falling bond prices) the specific costs of equity and debt rose at the end of 1973 to 16.22% and 4.45% respectively, compared with 15.64% and 3.31% at the end of 1972. As a result, IBM's weighted average cost of capital rose from 15.44% in 1972 to 16.01% at the end of 1973.

This result makes good sense. The rise in the cost of capital is only moderate, reflecting the changes in capital market conditions which were engendered by the increase in the rate of inflation, part, but certainly not all of which, reflects the energy crisis. The relative stability of the estimated cost of equity capital reflects the fact that any change in expected earnings (and dividends) is offset by changes in the share's current market price; any differences between the specific costs of equity capital of various firms largely reflect differences in their risk class. And since the oil crisis did not *directly* change the riskiness of IBM's various lines of activity, the change in the cost of capital is only moderate.

At first glance, a very different picture emerges when General Motors' cost of capital is re-estimated at the end of 1973. As was true of IBM, the specific costs of GM's debt and near debt (i.e. preferred stock) rose along with the general change in capital market conditions. The cost of bonds rose from 3.07% in 1972 to 4.54% in 1973; the relevant figures for preferred stock are from about 6.5% at the end of 1972 to almost 7.3% at the end of 1973. Again as was true of IBM, the expected growth rate at the end of 1973 remained the same as in 1972 — 4.7% in both years. GM's specific cost of equity capital and, as a result, its weighted average cost of capital, rose dramatically in 1973. The cost of equity and weighted average cost of capital were 10.19% and 9.93% respectively in 1972; the relevant figures for 1973 are 16.08% and 15.35%!

Do the events of 1973 justify such a jump in the cost of capital? Hardly. While it is true that the oil crisis could be expected to affect (and did affect) the sales of automobiles adversely, it could still be argued that the underlying riskiness of GM did not change that dramatically. The explanation for the sharp rise in the estimated cost of equity actually reflects a shortcoming of our statistical procedure. This will become apparent if we write out the equations for GM's specific cost of equity at the end of 1972 and 1973:

1972

$$k_e = \frac{D}{P} + g = \frac{4.45}{81.125} + 0.047 = 10.18\%$$

1973

$$k_e = \frac{D}{P} + g = \frac{5.25}{46.125} = 0.047 = 16.08\%$$

It is clear from the calculations that the sharp rise in GM's cost of equity reflects the sharp drop in the price of GM stock combined with a *rise* in its current dividend and *unchanged* growth rate. Clearly the fall in price was engendered by the market's apprehension of the negative impact of the oil crisis on GM's future profits and dividends. Our estimation procedure, based solely on ex-post historical data, does not reflect this change in expectations, and as a result our estimate of GM's future earnings and dividends is biased upwards. If we were to plug in GM's own revised forecasts of sales and earnings, following the sharp rise in gasoline prices, we would obtain a lower growth rate, perhaps a cut in the dividend rate and again a much more moderate rise in GM's cost of capital, reflecting the changes in capital market rates, which in turn reflect inflation and the underlying riskiness of the firm.

MEASURING THE COST OF CAPITAL USING THE CAPITAL ASSET PRICING MODEL (*CAPM*)

As noted in the theoretical discussion of Part II, the evaluation of a project's desirability must reflect both its contribution to profitability and its contribution to the firm's risk level. In the CAPM approach, the contribution of a new project's risk should be measured by taking its covariance not only with the firm's own earnings, but also the covariances with other firms' earnings as well. The reasoning underlying this approach is based on the assumption that the investor in the stock market holds many securities in his portfolio. Hence from his point of view, risk should be measured by the covariance of the returns on the new project with the market portfolio rather than with the returns on the firm's existing investments. Thus, if the firm evaluates a new project i, with systematic risk β_i, the required rate of return on the new project is k_i:

$$k_i = r + (Ex_m - r)\beta_i$$

where:
r = the risk free interest rate
Ex_m = the expected return on the market portfolio

Using the *CAPM* approach there is no unique cutoff rate that the firm should employ in project evaluation. Each project has its own cutoff point, i.e. its required rate of return, which depends directly on the project's risk as measured by beta. Unfortunately, the implementation of this approach in practice is quite complicated. By its very nature, the investment in physical assets requires a multiperiod analysis; the capital asset pricing model, as we have seen, is a one-period model. Theoretically, a way out of this impasse can be found by evaluating the market value of the assets at the end of each interim period and then breaking down the total return into period (e.g. annual) rates of return. However, this type of analysis is rarely operational in actual practice.

An alternative approach is to use the *CAPM* to estimate the specific cost of each individual source of financing. For simplicity, we shall confine our illustration to the case of the specific cost of equity. However, the same technique can be used to estimate the specific costs of preferred stock and debt.

In calculating the weighted average cost of capital, the specific cost of equity was estimated by the present value of future cash flows as measured by the dividend growth model:

$$k_e = \frac{d}{p} + g$$

where k_e denotes the required rate of return on equity, d is the annual cash dividend and g is the annual growth rate of earnings (and hence the dividend growth rate as well).

Table 18.17 presents estimates of the cost of equity, based on the *CAPM*, for the five "aggressive" and five "defensive" stocks whose betas were estimated in Chapter 13 above. The analysis refers to the years 1948 – 68. During this period the average rate of return on the market portfolio (Fisher Index) was 17.43% and the average risk-free interest rate (on treasury bills) was 3.31%. Applying the formula for the specific cost of equity:

$$k_e = r + (Ex_m - r)\beta_i$$

and substituting the observed values for Ex_m and r, we derive the following equation:

$$k_e = 0.0331 + (0.1743 - 0.0331)\beta_i$$

This formula is applied to each of the ten companies in Table 18.17. Column 2 sets out the risk premium for each firm; the specific cost of equity is given in column 3. The cost of equity for "defensive" stocks ranged from a low of 9.24% for Abbot Laboratory to 16.3% for Union Carbide. (The reader should note that the required return on Union Carbide stock was very close to the return on the market as a whole since its beta was close to one). The minimum

Table 18.17

	(1) Systematic Risk β_i	(2) Risk Premium $(14.12) \times (1)$	(3) Specific Cost of Equity $k_i = 3.31 + (2)$
Abbot Laboratory	0.42	5.93	9.24
General Telephone	0.60	8.47	11.78
Greyhound Corporation	0.62	8.75	12.06
R.H. Macy Corporation	0.65	9.18	12.43
Union Carbide Corporation	0.92	12.99	16.30
Bethlehem Steel	1.37	19.43	22.65
Hooper Chemical	1.43	20.19	23.50
Cerro Corporation	1.67	23.58	26.89
Medusa Portland	1.86	26.26	29.57
Conalco inc.	3.44	48.57	51.88

required rates of return (specific cost of equity) for aggressive stocks were all greater than 20%.

Calculating the Cost of Capital in Practice: The *CAPM* Approach

In this subsection we use the *CAPM* to calculate the cost of capital for two firms in the same industry, General Motors (GM) and American Motors (AMC).

   Table 18.18 presents the annual rates of return on the stock of GM and AMC as well as of the market portfolio for the years 1956 – 78. (We can use Standard & Poor's 500 as a proxy for the market portfolio).

   In calculating the cost of capital by the *CAPM* approach we first estimate each firm's systematic risk, β.

$$\beta_{GM} = \frac{Cov(X_{GM}, X_m)}{\sigma_m^2} = 1.555$$

$$\beta_{AMC} = \frac{Cov(X_{AMC}, X_m)}{\sigma_m^2} = 3.174$$

where X_m denotes the rate of return on the market portfolio.

Table 18.18
Annual Rates of Return on GM, AMC and the Market Portfolio (S & P 500 Index)
for the Years 1956 – 1968 (%)

Year	GM	AMC	Market Portfolio
1956	− .5	− 40.1	2.2
1957	− 19.9	52.5	− 10.7
1958	55.2	415.3	43.5
1959	14.4	121.2	11.9
1960	− 22.2	− 33.9	.4
1961	47.5	3.7	26.9
1962	7.7	3.1	− 8.6
1963	42.8	17.2	22.8
1964	30.7	− 16.9	16.5
1965	11.4	− 32.8	12.5
1966	− 32.5	− 30.4	− 10.06
1967	30.5	114.0	23.9
1968	1.8	− 3.7	11.1
1969	− 6.2	− 33.0	− 8.5
1970	22.3	− 33.2	3.9
1971	4.3	21.6	14.3
1972	6.5	17.8	19.1
1973	− 37.8	7.5	− 14.7
1974	− 27.6	− 62.3	− 26.5
1975	97.1	65.4	37.3
1976	45.85	− 28.02	23.8
1977	− 11.25	− 6.33	− 7.15
1978	− 4.7	26.67	12.16

Now, using these βs we can estimate the cost of equity of the above two firms as follows:

$$k_e = r + (\bar{X}_m - r)\beta_i$$

where k_e is the estimate of the cost of equity, r the risk-free interest rate and X_m is the average return on the market portfolio.

If we assume that in the period in question (1956 – 68) the risk-free interest rate, r, was about 4.5%, the costs of equity for the two firms are as follows:

> For GM, $k_e = 4.5 + (8.52 - 4.50)\ 1.555 = 10.75\%$.
> For AMC, $k_e = 4.5 + (8.52 - 4.50)\ 3.174 = 17.26\%$.

where 8.52% is the average rate of return on S & P 500 index.

Using book values [13] of equity, debt and preferred stock as weights we can calculate the weighted average cost of capital of these two firms as follows:

General Motors

Capital Structure (1978):	Amount (in Million $)	%	Specific Cost	Contribution to the Weighted Average Cost of Capital
Common Equity	17,286.3	0.9319	10.75	10.0179
Preferred Stock	283.6	0.0153	4.54	0.069
Debt	978.9	0.0528	4.96	0.262
	18,548.8	1.0000	Cost of Capital	10.3489%

The specific cost of debt k_d was calculated as follows:

$$k_d = \frac{\text{interest payment}}{\text{debt}}\ (1 - \text{tax rate}) = \frac{90.0}{978.9}\ (1 - 0.46) = 4.96\%$$

The specific cost of preferred stock was calculated as follows:

$$k_p = \frac{\text{preferred dividend}}{\text{preferred stock}} = \frac{12.9}{283.6} = 4.54\%$$

Using the *CAPM* approach we estimate General Motors cost of capital at about 10.3%, which is the after-tax discount rate which the firm should use for project evaluation.

Looking at the capital structure of AMC we find that this firm had a much higher proportion of debt in its capital structure than did GM. In 1978 it paid interest of $22,318,000 on a debt of $148,334,108, which yields an after-tax specific cost of debt of 9.02%:

$$k_d = \frac{22,318,000}{148,334,108} \cdot (1 - 0.40) = 0.0902 = 9.02\%$$

13 We use the book values for simplicity only. However, in these two cases market values yield almost identical results.

Note that the firm's effective tax rate is lower than that of GM, but its weighted average cost of capital is higher: 14.8%:

American Motors

Capital Structure (1978):	Amount (in Thousands)	%	Specific Cost	Contribution to the Weighted Average Cost of Capital
Common Equity	351,880	0.707	17.26	12.2028
Debt	148,341	0.293	9.02	2.6429
	500,221	1.000	Cost of Capital	14.8457%

The higher cost of equity for AMC is induced at least in part by the high proportion of debt (30%) in its capital structure. By comparison GM had only about 5% debt. Thus, even if the two firms had the same business risk one would expect to find a higher β for AMC and therefore a higher cost of equity. AMC's weighted average cost of capital is also higher than that of GM. This may reflect differences in the size of the firms: GM is much larger and hence more diversified (across products) which in turn reduces its business risk in comparison to AMC.

Finally, a word of caution is called for. Estimating the cost of capital for GM by applying the dividend approach or the *CAPM* approach yields almost the same result (9.928% by the dividend approach and 10.3335% by the *CAPM* approach). The student may be tempted to believe that one can employ either method and obtain almost the same result. While this was the case for GM, in general it is not true. The *CAPM*'s estimate cost of capital and the dividend model's estimate can, and often do, differ significantly. In such an event the dividend growth model, which is a pragmatic approach, is the more reliable. As we noted in Chapter 13 the explanatory power of the *CAPM* leaves much to be desired given the current state of the art.

SUMMARY

This chapter has presented an operational method for measuring the weighted average cost of capital in actual practice. The principles underlying the measurement of the specific cost of the individual components are discussed and the necessary adjustments to reflect corporate taxation and flotation costs are spelled out. After analyzing the impact of growth on the calculations, estimates of the cost of capital are presented for General Motors Corporation and for IBM. We conclude the chapter with an illustration of how the capital asset pricing model can be used to estimate the cost of equity capital, using for this purpose data on the returns of five "aggressive" and five defensive stocks over a 20-year period.

QUESTIONS AND PROBLEMS

18.1　What is the specific cost of a $500 *perpetual* bond paying $45 in interest each year?

18.2　How much must a firm which pays 48% coporation tax earn on a new investment of $2 million which is financed by 7.5% bonds if the common stockholder's rate of return is to remain unchanged? What is the specific after-tax cost of the debt component?

18.3　What is the effective specific after-tax cost of a five-year bond with a face value of $500 which pays $72.50 interest *before tax* if the flotation costs are 4% and the corporate tax rate is 48%?

18.4　What is the effective specific after-tax cost of a ten-year bond with a face value of $500 which pays 7% interest, if the flotation costs are:
(a)　2%;
(b)　4%;
(c)　6%;
(d)　8%?
Assume a 50% corporation tax rate.

18.5　Answer question 18.4, assuming that the bond is issued for fifteen years.

18.6　How much must a firm which pays 55% corporate tax earn on a new investment of $5 million which is financed by preferred stock yielding a dividend of 9%, if the common stockholder's return is to remain unchanged? How much must it earn if the same investment is financed by 9% bonds? Explain your results.

18.7　Investors in the common stock of Amgal Corporation expect to receive an annual dividend of $12.50 and also expect that the market price of the stock will rise to $105 by the end of the year.
Answer the following questions, ignoring flotation costs:
(a)　What is the required rate of return on Amgal's common stock if the investors are willing to pay $100 for this stock in today's market?
(b)　What is the specific cost of equity if investors are only willing to buy the stock for $94?

18.8　Derive the dividend valuation model on the assumption that earnings are expected to increase at a given rate over time.

18.9　The Gamma Company earns 25% on new investments and pays 40% of its earnings as dividends.
(a)　Calculate the growth rate of its future earnings according to the dividend growth model.
(b)　Find Gamma's current earnings yield (E/P), assuming that the specific cost of its equity is equal to 20%.

(c)   Is Gamma a "moderate-growth" or "super-growth" company? Explain.

18.10   What is the maximum price you will be willing to pay for a share of common stock that is paying $1.80 annual dividend, if you expect the dividend to grow at a rate of 7% in perpetuity and your required rate of return is 10%?

18.11   A high-technology electronics firm and a national food manufacturer both pay an annual dividend of $4 per share. Both firms have no debt and a stable earnings record and pay all their earnings as cash dividend. Neither firm anticipates changing the expected dividend in the future, but such changes cannot be completely ruled out. Yet the market price of the electronics stock is $32 per share whereas the food manufacturer's stock sells at $40. What is the required rate of return of the two stocks implied by these figures? How can we account for the difference?

18.12   Two chemical corporations, both equity financed with no debt, are essentially in the same business and therefore have the same risk and the same required rate of return. However, whereas one of the corporations has a stable earnings and dividend record, paying out all its earnings in dividends, the other is a growth stock increasing its earnings and dividends annually through a different management strategy. The current dividend is $5 per share for both corporations. The stable corporation's stock trades for $40 per share, whereas the price of the growth stock is $50.

Estimate the investors' required rate of return on these stocks and the steady future growth rate of the growing corporation as perceived by the market.

18.13   The following table lists some selected financial data of IBM for the years 1973−78. The last column gives the consumer price index (CPI) for the corresponding period.

Year	Cash Dividend ('000 $)	Net Income ('000 $)	Number of Shares	CPI
1973	654,554	1,575,467	146,712,688	116.3
1974	824,320	1,837,939	148,259,260	130.5
1975	973,986	1,989,877	149,844,582	139.6
1976	1,205,552	2,398,093	150,694,548	146.3
1977	1,474,709	2,719,414	147,470,876	156.3
1978	1,679,731	3,110,568	145,810,364	170.4

(a)   Calculate the *EPS* and the dividend per share and estimate the geometric mean growth rate over the period in nominal and in real (inflation-adjusted) terms.

(b) Assuming that the reported earnings indeed represent the true economic income, which of the two growth rates would you use to estimate IBM's cost of capital? (Hint: look at the payout ratio.)

(c) Suppose that due to inflation the reported earnings overestimate the true economic income. What can you say about the payout ratio trend? Which growth rate is the most relevant in this case?

18.14 The following two excerpts from the IBM annual reports for 1978 and 1979 show an apparently puzzling contradiction: The 1978 *annual* cash dividend is stated as $11.52 in the 1978 annual report and as $2.88 in the 1979 annual report. A closer look reveals that the 1978 cash dividends in the 1979 report were "adjusted for 1979 stock split".

FROM 1979 REPORT

Quarter	1979	1978
First	$0.86	$0.72
Second	0.86	0.72
Third	0.86	0.72
Fourth	0.86	0.72
	$3.44	$2.88

FROM 1978 REPORT

Quarter	1978	1977
First	$2.88	$2.50
Second	2.88	2.50
Third	2.88	2.50
Fourth	2.88	2.50
	$11.52	$10.00

(a) Using the dividend figures before and after adjustment, determine the ratio in which the stock was split.

(b) Use the result of (a) to adjust the 1977 cash dividend and calculate the average growth rate of cash dividends over the three years 1977−79.

18.15 The following table shows the net income and the number of common stock shares of Phillips Petroleum Company for the 10 years 1970−79:

Year	1979	1978	1977	1976	1975	1974	1973	1972	1971	1970
Net income ($ millions)	891	718	531	412	335	388	212	148	132	111
No. of shares of common stock (million shares)	154.4	154.4	76.8	76.4	76.4	76.4	76.0	76.0	76.0	76.0

Source: Moody's Industrial Manual, 1979.

In 1977 the stock was split two-to-one.

(a) Calculate the stated earnings per share (*EPS*) and adjust the *EPS* for the 1977 stock split.

(b) Use the adjusted *EPS* series to calculate the average annual growth rate for 1970−79 as the geometric mean over the period.

18.16 How would you formulate the dividend valuation model for a case in which earnings are expected to increase for the next five years and to remain stable from the sixth year on and that the firm pays a percentage of its earnings as dividends?

18.17 Consider the following balance sheet and the income statement of Delta Inc.

Balance Sheet (in thousand $)

Assets		*Liabilities*	
Cash	11,000	Current Liabilities	20,000
Receivables	20,000	Long term Debt* Bonds	80,000
Inventories	139,000	Equity Common Stock**	160,000
Plant and Equipment	90,000		
Total Assets	260,000	Total Liabilities	260,000

* $1000 par value
**$10 par value

Income Statement (in thousand $)

Operating Revenue	140,000
Operating Expense	76,000
Net Operating Income	64,000
Interest Payments	6,400
Net Income	57,600
Taxes (50%)	28,800
Net Income after Taxes	28,800

Assume that the market price of Delta's stock is $12, the market price of its bonds is $800 and that the bonds have fifty years to maturity.

(a) Suppose that Delta is a "non-growth" company. Should it accept a project with an after-tax internal rate of return of 12%?

(b) How will your answer to (a) be affected if you know that the financing mix (in book values) is the firm's optimal (target) capital structure?

18.18 Use the accounting data of IBM to carry out the following calculations:

(a) Calculate the growth rate in the earnings per share for the period 1970–1979.

(b) Estimate post-tax cost of equity for 31 December 1979, using the growth rate of *EPS* as an estimate to the growth rate of dividends.

(c) Estimate the post-tax cost of debt for 31 December 1979.

(d) Calculate weighted average cost of capital for 31 December 1979.

IBM Selected Accounting Data 1975–1979

	1979	1978	1977	1976	1975
	(Dollars in thousands except per share amounts)				
Gross income from sales, rentals and services:					
Sales	$ 9,472,649	$ 8,754,794	$ 7,090,157	$ 5,959,475	$ 4,545,359
Rentals and services	13,390,127	12,321,295	11,043,027	10,344,858	9,891,182
	22,862,776	21,076,089	18,133,184	16,304,333	14,436,541
Cost of sales	3,266,605	2,838,225	2,256,135	1,959,631	1,630,978
Cost of rentals and services	5,146,353	4,645,800	4,042,448	3,865,813	3,717,709
Selling, development and engineering, and general and administrative expenses	9,205,367	8,151,129	7,177,080	6,409,315	5,664,897
Interest on debt	140,487	55,175	40,350	44,950	62,607
Other income, principally interest	449,295	411,808	475,243	494,469	360,527
Earnings before income taxes	5,553,259	5,797,568	5,092,414	4,519,093	3,720,877
US Federal and non-US income taxes	2,542,000	2,687,000	2,373,000	2,121,000	1,731,000
Net earnings	$ 3,011,259	$ 3,110,568	$ 2,719,414	$ 2,398,093	$ 1,989,877
Per share †	$5.16	$5.32	$4.58	$3.99	$3.34
Average number of shares outstanding† . .	583,373,269	584,428,584	594,298,448	601,701,768	596,177,708
Cash dividends paid	$ 2,007,572	$ 1,684,612	$ 1,487,627	$ 1,203,791	$ 968,989
Per share†	$3.44	$2.88	$2.50	$2.00	$1.63
Number of shares outstanding†	583,594,543	583,241,454	589,883,503	602,778,192	599,378,326
Net investment in plant, rental machines and other property	$ 12,193,019	$ 9,302,228	$ 7,889,326	$ 6,962,908	$ 6,695,043
Long-term debt	$ 1,589,358	$ 285,534	$ 255,776	$ 275,127	$ 295,115
Working capital	$ 4,405,877	$ 4,510,789	$ 4,864,073	$ 5,838,125	$ 4,751,829
Number of stockholders	696,918	580,572	581,513	577,156	586,470

†Adjusted for 1979 stock split.
Source: *IBM Annual Report, 1979*

In your answer to (d) use book value of debt and market value of equity as weights.

Additional information:

— Stock price at 31 December 1979 is $64.25.
— Earnings per share adjusted for stock splits (which do not appear in the five years data)

	$
1974	3.12
1973	2.70
1972	2.76
1971	2.35
1970	2.23

— Dividend in 1979 = $3.44
— Long-term debt including current portion = $1,628,198,000.

18.19 In April 1979, the Xerox Corporation asked you to estimate its cost of capital and you decide to rely upon Xerox's 1978 annual report, excerpts from which are given on pp. 462 and 463. In addition, you will find that the number of outstanding shares on 31 December 1978 was

XEROX CORPORATION: TEN YEARS IN REVIEW	1978	1977	1976[3]
Yardsticks of Progress			
Income (Loss) per Common Share			
Continuing Operations	$ 5.77	$ 503	$ 4.49
Discontinued Operations	–	–	–
Extraordinary Income	.15	–	–
Net Income per Common Share	5.92	5.03	4.49
Dividends Declared per Common Share	2.00	1.50	1.10
Operations (Dollars in millions)			
Total Operating Revenues	$ 5,902	$ 5,082	$ 4,418
Rentals and Services	4,015	3,714	3,495
Sales	1,887	1,368	923
Cost of Rentals, Services and Sales	2,400	2,057	1,805
Depreciation of Rental Equipment	509	484	502
Depreciation and Amortization of Buildings and Equipment	155	149	144
Research and Development Expenses	311	269	226
Operating Income	1,142	995	878
Interest Expense	123	111	134
Income before Income Taxes	1,067	913	805
Income Taxes	515	441	376
Outside Shareholders' Interests	87	68	69
Income from Continuing Operations	465	404	360
Income (Loss) from Discontinued Operations[1]	–	–	–
Extraordinary Income (Net of Income Taxes)	12	–	–
Net Income	477	404	360
Financial Position (Dollars in millions)			
Current Assets	$ 2,567	$ 2,269	$ 2,059
Rental Equipment and Related Inventories at Cost	4,071	3,909	3,800
Accumulated Depreciation of Rental Equipment	2,595	2,512	2,386
Land, Buildings and Equipment at Cost	1,763	1,662	1,596
Accumulated Depreciation and Amortization of Buildings and Equipment	738	633	548
Total Assets	5,578	5,047	4,803
Current Liabilities	1,339	1,146	1,081
Long-Term Debt	908	1,020	1,176
Outside Shareholders' Interests	349	315	301
Shareholders' Equity	2,786	2,460	2,173
Additions to Rental Equipment and Related Inventories	696	552	456
Additions to Land, Buildings and Equipment	190	168	198
General and Ratios			
Average Common Shares Outstanding	80,517,659	80,343,003	80,342,521
Shareholders at Year End	117,924	125,549	129,077
Employees at Year End — Continuing Operations	104,736	103,977	97,558
Income before Income Taxes to Total Operating Revenues	18.1%	18.0%	18.2%
Net Income to Average Shareholders' Equity	18.2%	17.4%	17.7%
Long-Term Debt to Total Capitalization[2]	22.5%	26.9%	32.2%

1 The revenues, costs and expenses of discontinued operations for 1975 and prior years have been excluded from the respective captions and the income (loss) from discounted operations is reported separately. Income (loss) from discontinued operations is net of income tax and outside shareholders' interests.

2 Total capitalization is defined as the sum of long-term debt, outside shareholders' interests in equity of subsidiaries, and shareholders' equity.

3 Certain data have been restated for the years 1973 through 1977 to give effect to the retro-

	1975[3]	1974[3]	1973[3]	1972	1971	1970	1969
	$ 4.29	$ 4.37	$ 3.76[4]	$ 3.50	$ 2.95	$ 2.64	$ 1.89
	(1.22)	(.23)	(.19)	(.26)	(.28)	(.22)	.15
	–	–	–	–	–	–	–
	3.07	4.14	3.57[4]	3.24	2.67	2.42	2.04
	1.00	1.00	.90	.84	.80	.65	.58⅓
	$ 4,054	$ 3,505	$ 2,915	$ 2,338	$ 1,896	$ 1,636	$ 1,357
	3,316	2,866	2,430	1,904	1,541	1,324	1,073
	738	639	485	434	355	312	284
	1,648	1,309	1,024	558	459	398	417
	460	391	325	291	231	192	174
	122	98	73	46	35	32	27
	198	179	154	117	96	87	101
	844	865	766	645	537	496	381
	149	111	66	37	35	32	22
	757	788	692	621	516	474	361
	341	363	328	291	244	233	192
	74	77	61	53	39	33	22
	342	348	298[4]	277	233	208	147
	(98)	(19)	(15)	(21)	(22)	(18)	11
	–	–	–	–	–	–	–
	244	329	283[4]	256	211	190	158
	$ 1,687	$ 1,632	$ 1,276	$ 1,053	$ 918	$ 825	$ 649
	3,574	3,221	2,452	1,928	1,626	1,322	1,068
	2,058	1,706	1,354	1,063	869	696	549
	1,443	1,253	999	668	542	432	353
	447	376	299	215	172	144	116
	4,614	4,207	3,209	2,484	2,145	1,844	1,516
	1,127	1,050	852	659	556	492	419
	1,279	1,167	703	445	426	359	263
	259	221	155	114	108	89	71
	1,898	1,733	1,475	1,249	1,041	883	726
	582	862	595	438	382	312	267
	269	281	226	125	121	89	76
	79,550,021	79,548,124	79,388,281	79,228,281	78,821,232	78,591,401	77,712,417
	135,578	137,471	138,314	143,666	143,640	146,605	129,981
	93,532	97,399	90,200	72,237	62,638	55,367	49,335
	18.7%	22.5%	23.7%	26.6%	27.2%	29.0%	26.6%
	13.4%	20.5%	20.8%	22.4%	21.9%	23.6%	24.0%
	37.2%	37.4%	30.1%	24.6%	27.0%	27.0%	24.8%

active change in the method of accounting for capital leases and to reflect changes in the classification of components of operating revenues and related costs and the change in the classification of service expense to cost of rentals and services from the selling, administrative and general expense category.

4 Income from continuing operations, net income, and related per share amounts reflect a decrease of $5 million ($.06 per share) for the cumulative effect at January 1, 1973 of retroactively applying the new method of accounting for capital leases.

80,521,180 and, that the amount of interest Xerox paid on its long term debt (including $49,400,000 current portion) was $123,000,000. The price of Xerox common stock on 31 December 1978 was $153.25.

(a) Estimate the growth rate of Xerox using historical data on earnings per share over the period 1969–78.

(b) Ignoring flotation costs, calculate the after-tax weighted average cost of capital. (Assume that the existing proportions of debt and equity are optimal. Also assume that the firm plans to raise more money in the same proportion of debt/equity which currently exists.)

(c) Calculate the after-tax average cost of capital, assuming that half of the equity comes from new issues with a flotation cost of 5% (and half from retained earnings) and that the flotation cost of bonds is 3%.

(d) Suppose now that as a result of inflation, the future rate of interest is expected to rise to 10%, and that the target capital structure changes to 28.45% debt and 71.55% equity. Ignoring flotation costs, calculate the after-tax weighted average cost of capital.

18.20 Define the specific cost of equity using the *CAPM* approach. Using this same approach, how would you define the specific cost of preferred stock?

18.21 Assume that the riskless interest rate (r) is 6%; the expected return on the market portfolio (Ex_m) is 14%; and the coefficients of the systematic risk (β_i) for five firms are as follows:

$$\beta_A = 0.25; \ \beta_B = 0.75; \ \beta_C = 1; \ \beta_D = 1.45; \ \beta_E = 2.25$$

(a) Calculate the specific cost of equity for each firm.

(b) What is the relationship between beta and the specific cost of equity? Explain.

18.22 (a) Calculate the systematic risk (beta) for the following three firms, *A, B* and *C*, whose specific costs of equity are: $k_A = 10\%$; $k_B = 12\%$; and $k_C = 16\%$, assuming that $r = 7\%$ and $Ex_m = 12\%$.

(b) Which firm's stocks are "aggressive"? Which are defensive? Explain.

18.23 A firm is considering two investment projects, each with several alternative levels of activity corresponding to different amounts of investment and different return distributions (the firm may choose only one activity level in each project). The projects are specified by the schedules on p. 465 (x_m is the return on the market portfolio):

The following market parameters are given: the expected return of the market portfolio $Ex_m = 0.15$; standard deviation of the market return $\sigma_m = 0.10$; risk-free interest rate $r = 0.05$.

(a) How much should the firm invest in each project?

(b) Suppose you want to apply the risk-adjusted discount rate (k) to projects 1 and 2. What rate should be applied to each project at each level of investment? (You have to derive 10 different rates.)

(c) Estimate the cost of capital by the formula

$$k_i = r + (Ex_m - r)\beta_i = r + \lambda Cov(x_i, x_m)$$

where x_i is the return per \$1 of investment so that k_i is in percent. Carry out this calculation only for the first investment of project 1. Compare your result to (b) above. Explain the differences!

Hint: Recall that the *SML* holds only for assets in equilibrium; in equilibrium the *NPV* must be equal to zero.

Project 1			Project 2		
Investment ($)	Expected Return ($)	Covariance with x_m	Investment ($)	Expected Return ($)	Covariance with x_m
100	300	8	100	150	4
200	500	16	200	360	8
300	650	24	300	560	12
400	730	32	400	730	16
500	800	40	500	800	20

18.24 Details of Argo Industries Inc. are given in the following pages. After studying them, answer the following questions.

1. What is the investment strategy of Argo?
2. What are the most pressing problems that Mr. Simon Taylor faces in Argo?
3. What do you think of Mr. Taylor's claim that the Argo stock is underpriced?

   In your answer, estimate the growth rate of Argo and try to estimate the value of the stock. Is Argo's stock indeed underpriced?

ARGO INDUSTRIES INC.

Argo Industries Inc. (formerly Argo Textile Dye Works Inc.) holds a leading position in textile dyeing and finishing in the Mid-West, serving many of the small- and medium-sized textile manufacturers (except the large integrated concerns, which have their own dyeing and finishing operations). Argo has the capability to handle a large variety of textile products, including natural and man-made yarn, woven fabrics and knits.

Argo was established in 1934 as a family business in one of Chicago suburbs, where it operated for over 30 years. In 1967 the Argo management began relocating the production facilities in one of the developing areas in Iowa. The Iowa plant was designed with a much larger production capacity than the old Chicago plant, but the relocation plans caused considerable labor difficulties; the skilled Argo workers, who lived in the Chicago metropolitan area, refused to move to Iowa, despite the management's offer of assistance with housing, moving expenses, etc. Argo had to recruit and train a virtually new labor force in Iowa, and in 1977 the new plant employed about 700 workers, in modern industrial buildings sprawling over 25 acres.

In June 1972, Mr. Simon Taylor was appointed Argo's Managing Director. Simon, the founder's son, held an engineering degree from MIT and had previously headed the task force in charge of the Iowa project.

"Operation Iowa" was conducted in several stages. The cotton dyeing plant was the first to move to the new premises in 1967, and the relocation of the entire concern was completed in 1970. The Iowa plant was financed from a variety of sources: a rights offering to Argo shareholders, a private stock placement with Midwestern Investment Company — one of Argo's major shareholders, capital gains accruing from the sale of the Chicago property and a long-term loan through the Iowa Industrial Development Bank. The running-in of the manufacturing divisions had been completed by 1971 and Argo began operating at full capacity.

Argo has since established several subsidiaries specializing in different textile-related businesses. The expansion reflects some new investment opportunities, but to a certain extent it was dictated by the operating potential of the Iowa plant.

ARGO SUBSIDIARIES

(1)   *Ardaf Inc.*

A wholly-owned subsidiary established in 1969, Ardaf specializes in textile printing and merchandises printed fabrics. It sells printing services to textile manufacturers and markets original Ardaf prints. Ardaf prints are finished in the Argo textile-finishing plant. Argo further provides Ardaf with complete administrative, laboratory and technical backup.

(2)   *Ariel Control Systems Inc.*

Established in 1971, Ariel specializes in the development, manufacturing and marketing of advanced control systems for textile dyeing machines. Ariel is targeted on large automated dyeing plants, and its control systems have been successfully installed by Argo and a number of other textile manufacturers.

(3)   *Argo-line Inc.*

Argo-line was established in 1971 to design, manufacture and market textile dyeing and finishing equipment. Originally a joint venture with a West German investor who had considerable experience in the European textile-equipment market, Argo-line became a wholly owned subsidiary in 1977 when Argo exercised its option to purchase the West German investor's share. To fully utilize its skilled work force, Argo-line has also ventured into producing equipment for the chemical, food and paper industries.

The recent slump in the world textile markets has of necessity led to a reduction in capital investments and equipment orders for the textile industry. Argo management is of the opinion, however, that cyclic recovery in the textile markets, combined with intro-duction of advanced equipment by Argo-line, will enable the subsidiary to increase its production and exports.

Argo-line initially had a knowhow agreement with the West German investor which precluded it from direct marketing efforts in Europe. This agreement expired on 31 March, 1975 and Argo-line now has research and development capability of its own. Argo-line equipment is sold in Europe and export sales accounted for about 50% of Argo-line's output in 1976–77.

(4)   *Umar Textiles Inc.*

Umar was incorporated in 1964 with the object of setting up a cotton weaving plant. It is a joint venture with United Merchants and Manufacturers, Inc., one of the largest diversified textile concerns in the US, with textile sales of around US $1 billion in 1974 and foreign subsidiaries in South America, Canada, France and England (UMM's diversified activities include commercial factoring and finance operations, with a gross volume of about $1.4 billion in 1974). Argo owns 65% of Umar stock, the remaining 35% held by UMM.

A marketing agreement ensures that UMM will purchase half the Umar output during the first five years of operation on a "cost plus" basis. Umar plans to export independently most of the remaining capacity.

Umar's requirements for investment funds are as follows:

Plant and infrastructure	$ 6,986,000
Equipment	$30,615,000
Working capital	$ 2,500,000
	$40,101,000

The investment will be financed from the following sources:

Long-term debt	$28,021,000
Equity (65% Argo, 35% UMM)	$12,080,000
	$40,101,000

Umar became fully operational in 1976−77. The projected annual output initially will be 5 million tons of cotton fabrics. The plant eventually could be expanded to double its capacity.

Umar-woven fabrics will be dyed and printed by Argo and Ardaf, and Umar will merchandise the finished product. Mr. Taylor, Managing Director of Argo Industries, indicated that this arrangement would increase the output of both Argo and Ardaf and thus contribute indirectly to the profitability of the entire group. Umar also will be used as a convenient source of supply for other subsidiaries (Ardaf will purchase Umar fabrics for its printing operation), as no other textile manufacturer will be able to match Umar's delivery times.

(5)   *Argotex Vertriebs GmbH*

Argotex was incorporated in West Germany to market Ariel's and Argo-line's equipment. Argo owns 51% of Argotex and the remaining 49% are owned by a West German investor. Argotex began its operations in 1976 and sold during the first year several systems and machines in West Germany, Switzerland and Austria.

(6)   *Arcom Inc.*

Incorporated in 1977, Arcom will market domestically surplus lines from Umar's and Ardaf's export collections. These domestic sales are expected to account for some 20%−25% of Umar's and Ardaf's capacity.

(7)   *Worsted Weaving Plant*

In June 1976 Argo acquired a worsted weaving plant that had gone into receivership. The plant had been over the years the largest customer of Argo's wool dyeing operation.

The reorganization of the worsted weaving plant as a manufacturing division of Argo was completed in 1977. Efforts are being made to find export markets for the plant's output.

ORGANIZATION

The parent company and its various subsidiaries are organized in three operating divisions in Argo Industries:

1.   A division incorporating the four Argo dyeing and finishing plants (cotton, wool and synthetic fabrics, knits, and yarn dyeing plant) and the manufacturing operations of the Ardaf printing plant.
2.   A division incorporating the equipment manufacturing subsidiaries, Argo-line and Ariel Control Systems.
3.   A marketing division, incorporating Umar Textiles and the marketing operations of Ardaf.

The three divisions receive backup services from a central pool. These include secretarial services, centralized finance and control, management information services and R & D.

The joint R & D operations concentrate on the development of dyeing and finishing processes, design of dyeing and finishing equipment, and development of control systems for the textile industry.

The Argo Industries management is of the opinion that a central R & D body serves the needs of the group more effectively than separate R & D facilities in the individual plants.

THE EFFECT OF INFLATION ON ARGO'S OPERATIONS

The actual investment in Iowa exceeded the original projections, as domestic inflation caused severe cost overruns.

Argo's traditional policy was to extend 90-days credit to its customers, whereas its payables were always kept to a minimum.

The Argo management has introduced several measures in order to cope with the inflationary pressures:

(1)   *Reducing the Receivables*

Argo usually extended 90- and even 120-days credit to its domestic customers. As of 15 February, 1976, however, the net credit terms were reduced to 60 days. Yet it was clear from the start that many of Argo's customers simply would not be able to meet the new terms of payment: no additional lines of bank credit were available to the smaller customers, whereas Argo could easily get additional short-term bank financing against its ample collateral. Argo therefore agreed to continue its policy of 90 days to pay whenever necessary, but all accounts remaining unpaid after 60 days were charged at the market rate of interest.

The administration's anti-inflationary measures, however, led to a further credit squeeze and resulted in a significant increase in the market rate of interest. Argo was forced to further restrict its credit terms to the customers and the new arrangement went into effect in December 1976. Details of the revised credit policy will be found in Exhibits A1 and A2.

(2)   *Leasing Equipment*

Argo decided to lease new equipment, instead of purchasing it. A financial lease contract was regarded as a convenient method of avoiding the need for new financing.

EXHIBIT A1   CHANGE IN CREDIT TERMS AS OF 15 FEBRUARY 1976

16 January 1976

Dear Sir,

RE: Terms of payment for dyeing, finishing and printing

You are no doubt aware of the severe credit restrictions imposed by the banks during the last year. Despite accelerating inflation, our credit lines have been frozen at previous year's level and the banks have raised the interest rate on overdrafts in excess of the approved lines of credit.

Cognizant of our special position as a service industry to all textile manufacturers in the Mid-West, we are nevertheless unable to bear this financial load, especially as most of our obligations are either prepaid (such as dyes and chemicals) or are payable in cash (fuel, water, electricity, rent, taxes, etc.) We were thus forced to notify our clients in our circular letter dated 24 November 1974 that it would no longer be possible for us to grant credit in excess of 60 days.

However, as most of our customers seem to have run into difficulties in meeting the new terms of payment and were unable to arrange the necessary lines of credit with their banks, we have decided as a special sign of goodwill to help them with financing during the interim period and for as long as sufficient credit lines are available to us.

Our customers may therefore continue paying their accounts within 90 days of the biweekly statement. Every customer may choose at his discretion to pay cash or to schedule his payment for any period up to 90 days and will be entitled to appropriate discounts in accordance with the attached table. The customers are kindly reminded to send in their drafts or postdated checks within 3 weeks of the date of each statement. We would like to stress that on no account will we be able to stretch credit terms beyond 90 days.

TABLE OF DISCOUNTS

For Payment Within	Discount
3 weeks	4.5%
4 weeks	4.0%
5 weeks	3.5%
6 weeks	3.0%
7 weeks	2.5%
8 weeks	2.0%
9 weeks	1.5%
10 weeks	1.0%
11 weeks	0.5%
12 weeks	NIL

Sincerely yours,

ARGO Textile Dye Works Inc.

EXHIBIT A2   CHANGE IN CREDIT TERMS AS OF 15 DECEMBER 1976

27 September 1976

Dear Sir,

RE: *Adjustment of credit terms to prevailing market conditions*

Because of continued inflation, deterioration of credit terms allowed by our suppliers and restriction of bank credit, we are regretfully obliged to reduce by two weeks the terms of credit extended to our customers.

The customers are kindly requested to date their drafts and checks for periods not exceeding 6 weeks from date of statement and the table of discounts has been revised accordingly:

For payment within	Discount
3 weeks	4.2%
4 weeks	3.6%
5 weeks	3.0%
6 weeks	2.4%
7 weeks	1.8%
8 weeks	1.2%
9 weeks	0.6%
10 weeks	NIL

The new terms come into effect as of 15 December 1976, so that our customers should have ample time to make the necessary arrangements.

We trust that our customers will accept the new terms with friendly understanding. We would like to assure you of our continued goodwill and high-quality service.

Sincerely,

ARGO Textile Dye Works Inc.

DEVELOPMENT OF THE SHARE CAPITAL AND PUBLIC OFFERINGS

Argo made its first public offering over the counter in 1961. The original issue was 3,750,000 shares of common stock and the share capital remained unchanged through the end of 1963. In 1964 Argo made a rights offering of 1,250,000 shares at $1.50. The total proceeds of this issue ($1,771,000) were earmarked for the Iowa project. In 1966 the share capital was increased to 6,250,000 shares by a stock dividend of 250,000 shares and a private placement of 1,000,000 shares with Midwestern Investment Company, one of Argo's major shareholders, at $1.50. Midwestern's stock was paid up in two instalments: 10% of the placement in 1965–66 and the remaining 90% in 1966–67.

In 1973 the share capital was increased to 10,015,620 shares by a 25% stock dividend (1,562,446 shares), a rights offering at $1.80 (1,953,124 shares) and an offering to Argo employees (250,000 shares).

The share capital was increased to 13,221,000 shares in 1975 by another stock dividend. In November 1975 the share capital was further increased to 18,509,000 shares by a stock dividend of 2,664,000 shares and another rights offering of 2,664,000 shares made at $1.25. In the same year Argo placed a $7.5 million 6% convertible bonds issue. In 1976 Argo authorized another 20% stock dividend and the share capital increased to 22,211,000 shares by the end of the 1976–77 fiscal year.

Most of the funds raised through the various stock issues were invested in the Iowa project, and the bulk of the recent investment funds were intended for Umar.

Despite the repeated infusion of new equity, Argo's financing expenses have steadily increased, mainly due to inflation and the inevitable lag between price increases announced by the company and the inflationary increase in the cost of its production inputs. Mr. Taylor, Argo's Managing Director, rejected the possibility of another public issue in 1976.

"The market value of our stock is about $50 million, while the value of our plant and equipment, including the surrounding property, is over $300 million at 1976 prices. Thus our stock is grossly underpriced, and it is not reasonable to raise new equity under these conditions."

Argo's share capital in 1976 consisted of 18.5 million shares of common stock and its stock traded at $3.45 in October 1976.

Exhibits B, C, and D present some selected financial data from Argo's consolidated reports.

EXHIBIT C
ARGO INDUSTRIES INC.
CAPITAL STRUCTURE FOR THE PERIOD
1964 – 77 ('000 $)

Fiscal Year (end March 31)	Equity	Debt		
		Long-term debt*	Short-term loans	Total debt
1965	7,495	21	1,090	1,111
1966	8,833	2,000	1,088	3,088
1967	9,256	4,000	1,498	5,498
1968	8,989	5,504	990	6,494
1969	9,684	6,392	1,669	8,061
1970	10,487	7,828	2,173	10,001
1971	11,169	8,729	3,406	12,135
1972	12,965	10,329	6,067	16,396
1973	19,896	11,033	6,837	17,870
1974	23,640	11,104	9,547	20,651
1975	28,441	20,205	14,041	34,246
1976	38,664	42,450	21,190	63,640
1977	45,478	58,377	47,133	105,510

* Including currently maturing portion of long-term debt, including $7.5 million convertible bonds issued in 1976.

EXHIBIT B
ARGO INDUSTRIES INC.
SELECTED FINANCIAL DATA FOR THE PERIOD
1964–77

Fiscal Year	1964–5	1965–6	1966–7	1967–8	1968–9	1969–70	1970–1	1971–2	1972–3	1973–4	1974–5	1975–6	1976–7
Common stock, beg. year (thou. shares)	5,000	5,000	5,350	6,250	6,250	6,250	6,250	6,250	6,250	10,016	11,017	13,221	18,509
Stock dividend (%)	—	5%	—	—	—	—	—	—	25%	10%	20%	20%	20%
Stock dividend (thou. shares)	—	250	—	—	—	—	—	—	1,563	1,001	2,203	2,664	3,702
Rights (thou. shares)	—	—	—	—	—	—	—	—	1,953³	—	—	2,664⁵	—
Other issues (thou. shares)	—	100¹	900²	—	—	—	—	—	250⁴	—	—	—	—
Common stock, end year	5,000	5,350	6,250	6,250	6,250	6,250	6,250	6,250	10,016	11,017	13,221	18,509	22,211
Earning per share EPS^8 (cents)	92.90	48.28	36.85	32.16	45.40	64.49	68.56	154.67	109.36	101.37	66.08	44.06	36.95
Average return of Argo stock⁷ (%)	—	–14.1	–17.7	–6.7	60.0	–34.5	21.1	273.3	41.4	8.5	–33.4	66.4	65.6
Cash dividend (cents per share)	10	10	8	8	8	8	10	10	10	10	10	10	10

Notes: (1) A private placement of 1 million shares with Midwestern Investment Company in 1965–66, paid up in two instalments: 10% of the total was paid up in 1965–66, adding 100,000 shares to Argo's share capital account.

(2) The remaining 90% of the Midwestern placement paid up in fiscal year 1966–67 (see note (1) above).

(3) A 1-to-4 rights offering according to a prospectus dated November 30, 1972 (with stock dividend distributed during the current fiscal year participating). Subscription price $P_s = \$1.80$, ex-rights date December 7, 1972, price of Argo stock with rights on $P_c = \$3.44$ (November 29, 1972), price ex-rights $P_{xr} = \$3.38$.

The stock dividend components of a rights issue is defined as

$$\alpha = \frac{P_c - P_s}{NP_c + P_s}$$

where N is the number of previously held shares entitled to a single right (see H. Levy and M. Sarnat, *Investment and Portfolio Analysis*, Wiley, New York 1972).

(4) Shares issued and distributed to Argo employees according to a prospectus dated November 30, 1972.

(5) A 1-to-6 rights offering according to a prospectus dated November 12, 1975 (with stock dividend distributed during the current fiscal year participating). Subscription price $P_s = \$1.25$, ex-rights date November 13, 1975, price of Argo stock with rights on $P_c = \$2.65$ (November 4, 1975), price ex-rights $P_{xr} = \$2.41$.

(6) EPS is net earnings per share after extraordinary items in consolidated financial statements.

(7) Average annual return on Argo stock calculated from quarterly data, adjusted for all distributions (stock dividend, rights and cash dividends).

EXHIBIT D
ARGO INDUSTRIES INC. — CONSOLIDATED BALANCE SHEET
FOR YEAR ENDING 31 March 1977 (in '000 $)

ASSETS:

Current assets:

Cash		151
Receivables		48,917
Inventories		39,505
Prepaid expenses		5,166
Marketable securities		12,955
	Total current assets	106,694
Fixed assets, at cost		114,682
Less accumulated depreciation		27,612
	Net fixed assets	87,070
		193,764

LIABILITIES AND STOCKHOLDER'S EQUITY:

Current liabilities:

Loans payable		58,539
Accounts payable		11,611
Accrued liabilities		12,373
Dividends payable		2,112
	Total current liabilities	84,635

Long-term Debt:

Convertible bonds		7,500
Other		39,471
	Total long-term debt	46,971
Retirement compensation reserve		1,302
Tax-equalization reserve		11,910
	Total liabilities	144,818
Minority Interest		3,468

Stockholder's Equity:

Common stock, par value $1.00 per share		22,211
Stock dividend reserve		4,442
Additional paid-in capital		5,390
Reinvested earnings		13,435
	Total stockholder's equity	45,478
		193,764

APPENDIX 18A ESTIMATING THE GROWTH RATE FROM HISTORICAL DATA

As noted in the text, the growth rate of earnings per share constitutes one of the most important components in the analysis of the cost of equity capital. This appendix spells out a simple regression procedure for estimating the growth rate from *ex-post* data using the standard statistical technique of least-squares regression.

Since the growth rate has a cumulative effect on earnings, the relationship between the earnings per share in any year t (E_t), and the earnings per share in the base year (E_0) can be formulated as follows:

$$E_t = E_0(1 + g)^t$$

where *g* denotes the compounded average annual growth rate. In order to estimate the growth rate statistically, we first take the logarithms of both sides of the above equation, which gives

$$\log E_t = \log E_0 + t \log (1 + g)$$

This equation is linear in logarithms, and has a slope equal to $\log (1 + g)$.

Using the least-squares regression technique we can now estimate $\log (1 + g)$. Denoting the *i*th observation of the log of earnings per share by x_i, the estimate of the slope of the regression line [i.e. $\log(1 + g)$] is given by

$$\log (1 + g) = \frac{\sum_{i=1}^{n}(x_i - \bar{x})(t_i - \bar{t})}{\sum_{i=1}^{n} t_i^2 - n\bar{t}^2}$$

where t_i denotes the *i*th year, bars denote averages and *n* is the total number of years included in the study. Subtracting the average year $\bar{t}$ from all the variables t_i, the average of the derived series, i.e. the average of $(t_i - \bar{t})$, becomes zero and we obtain the expression:

$$\log (1 + g) = \frac{\sum_{i=1}^{n} x_i t_i^*}{\sum_{i=1}^{n} t_i^{*2}}$$

where $t_i^* = t_i - \bar{t}$, i.e. in deviation notation.

Plugging in the data on the per-share earnings of General Motors for the period 1953 – 72, we have

$$\log (1 + g) = \frac{13.3938}{665} = 0.0201$$

Hence $(1 + g) =$ antilog $(0.0201) = 1.047$, i.e. the estimated annual growth rate for GM is 4.7%.

The relevant figures for IBM for the period 1963 – 72 are as follows:

$$\log (1 + g) = \frac{\sum_{i=1}^{n} x_i t_i^*}{\sum_{i=1}^{n} t_i^{*2}} = \frac{4.7914}{82.5} = 0.0581$$

Hence $(1 + g)$ = antilog (0.0581) = 1.143, and the estimated compounded average annual growth rate of IBM's earnings per share is 14.3%.

PROBLEM

18A.1 Use your results for problem 18.15 to recalculate the average annual growth rate of the Phillips Petroleum earnings per share in 1970 – 79 by the logarithmic regression method. Compare the result to the geometric mean growth in problem 18.15. How do you account for the difference in the two figures?

SELECTED REFERENCES

Aivazian, V. A. and Callen, J. L., "Investment, Market Structure, and the Cost of Capital", *Journal of Finance*, March 1979.

Ang, J. S., "Weighted Average is True Cost of Capital", *Financial Management*, Spring 1974.

Arditti, Fred D., "The Weighted Average Cost of Capital: Some Questions on its Definition, Interpretation and Use", *Journal of Finance*, September 1973.

Arditti, F. D., Levy, H. and Sarnat, M., "Taxes, Capital Structure, and the Cost of Capital: Some Extensions", *Quarterly Review of Economics and Business*, Summer 1977.

Arditti, F. D. and Pinkerton, J. M., "The Valuation and Cost of Capital of the Levered Firm with Growth Opportunities", *Journal of Finance*, March 1978.

Auerbach, Alan, "Wealth Maximization and the Cost of Capital", *Quarterly Journal of Economics*, August 1979.

Ben-Horim, Moshe, "Comment on 'The Weighted Average Cost of Capital as a Cutoff Rate'", *Financial Management*, Summer 1979.

Beranek, W., "The Weighted Average Cost of Capital and Shareholder Wealth Maximization", *Journal of Financial and Quantitative Analysis*, March 1977.

Bones, James A., "A Pedagogic Note on the Cost of Capital", *Journal of Finance*, March 1964.

Boudreaux, Kenneth J. and Long, Hugh W., "The Weighted Average Cost of Capital as a Cutoff Rate: A Further Analysis", *Financial Management*, Summer 1979.

Brennan, Michael J., "A New Look at the Weighted Average Cost of Capital", *Journal of Business Finance*, Spring 1973.

Brigham, Eugene F., and Smith, Keith V., "The Cost of Capital to the Small Firm", *The Engineering Economist* Fall 1967.

Budd, A. F. and Litzenberger, R. H., "Changes in the Supply of Money, the Firm's Market Value and Cost of Capital", *Journal of Finance*, March 1973.

Elliott, Walter J., "The Cost of Capital and U.S. Capital Investment: A Test of Alternative Concepts", *The Journal of Finance*, September 1980.

Ezzamel, Mahmoud A., "Estimating the Cost of Capital for a Division of a Firm, and the Allocation Problem in Accounting: A Comment", *Journal of Business Finance & Accounting*, Spring 1980.

Ezzell, J. R. and Porter, R. B., "Flotation Costs and the Weighted Average Cost of Capital." *Journal of Financial and Quantitative Analysis*, September 1976.,

Ezzell, J. R. and Porter, R. B., "Correct Specification of the Cost of Capital and Net Present Value", *Financial Management*, Summer 1979.

Findlay, M. Chapman, III, "The Weighted Average Cost of Capital and Finite Flows", *Journal of Business Finance & Accounting*, 1977.

Gordon, Myron J. and Halper, Paul J., "Cost of Capital for a Division of a Firm", *Journal of Finance*, September 1974.

Haley, C. W. and Schall, L. D., "Problems with the Concept of the Cost of Capital", *Journal of Financial and Quantitative Analysis*, December 1978.

Jarrett, Jeffrey E., "Estimating the Cost of Capital for a Division of a Firm, and the Allocation Problem in Accounting", *Journal of Business Finance & Accounting*, Spring 1978.

Keane, Simon M., "The Cost of Capital as a Financial Decision Tool", *Journal of Business Finance & Accounting*, Autumn 1978.

Kim, Moon H., "Weighted Average vs. True Cost of Capital", *Financial Management*, Spring 1974.

Lewellen, Wilbor G., "A Conceptual Reappraisal of Cost of Capital", *Financial Management*, Winter 1974.

Linke, Charles M., "Weighted Average vs. True Cost of Capital", *Financial Management*, Spring 1974.

Litzenberger, Robert H. and Rao, C. U., "Portfolio Theory and Industry Cost-of-Capital Estimates", *Journal of Financial and Quantitative Analysis*, March 1972.

Long, Michael S. and Rasette, George A., "Stochastic Demand, Output and the Cost of Capital", *Journal of Finance*, May 1974.

Miles, James A. and Ezzell, John R., "The Weighted Average Cost of Capital, Perfect Capital Markets, and Project Life: A Clarification", *Journal of Financial and Quantitative Analysis*, September 1980.

Nantell, Timothy J. and Carlson, Robert C., "The Cost of Capital as a Weighted Average", *Journal of Finance*, December 1975.

Reilly, Raymond R. and Wecker, William E., "On the Cost of Capital as a Weighted Average Cost of Capital", *Journal of Financial and Quantitative Analysis*, January 1973.

Shapiro, Alan C., "In Defense of the Traditional Weighted Average Cost of Capital as a Cutoff Rate", *Financial Management*, Summer 1979.

Tepper, Irwin, "Revealed Preference Methods and the Pure Theory of the Cost of Capital", *Journal of Finance*, March 1973.

Vickers, Douglas, "The Cost of Capital and the Structure of the Firm", *Journal of Finance*, March 1970.

Weston, J. E. and Lee, W. Y., "Cost of Capital for a Division of a Firm: Comment", *Journal of Finance*, December 1977.

19

Dividend Policy

As we have already seen, the firm is continually faced with two crucial and inter-related problems: the capital investment and long-term financing decisions. Along with its investment and financing policies, the firm must also decide on its dividend policy, that is the proportion of earnings which should be distributed to its shareholders in the form of cash dividends. In this chapter we focus attention on a question which has occupied the attention of leading financial experts for more than two decades: why do firms almost universally pay out a substantial portion of their earnings as cash dividends?

The key to this problem can be found in the answers to two additional, albeit related, questions:

(a)   What impact (if any) does dividend policy have on the market price of a firm's common stock? Essentially this question asks whether dividend policy is a significant factor in determining the market value of the shareholders' investment.

(b)   If dividend policy *does* affect shareholders' wealth (the market value of common stock), what constitutes the firm's *optimal* dividend policy?

Dividend policy has been (and remains today) a subject of considerable controversy. Much ink and invective have been spilled, yet operational solutions to the problem of dividend policy are far from perfect, and qualitative judgmental factors, the so-called intangibles of financial decisions, remain of considerable importance in determining dividend policy. The purpose of this chapter is not to resolve the irresolvable; our more modest goal is to clarify some of the more important issues so that an intelligent choice can be made between alternative theories. The goal is to improve, not to replace, judgment! To this end we shall analyze dividend policies under various assumptions regarding the degree of competition and uncertainty prevailing in the securities markets; however, it should be emphasized, *not* in the hopeless quest for the Grail of the optimum but rather in order to help achieve a better foundation on which to base corporate dividend decisions.

DIVIDENDS AND VALUATION: NO EXTERNAL FINANCING

To help clarify the underlying theoretical foundation of the dividend decision, let us initially imagine a pleasant world in which no taxes are levied on current income or capital gains. For simplicity, we shall also assume the absence of a new issue market for securities, so that firms must finance their investment programs solely from internally generated sources.

The analysis of the impact of dividend policy on the value of a firm's common stock requires a prior stipulation of a formal valuation model. Numerous variants exist, but perhaps the best known of these models defines the price of a firm's common stock as the present value of all future dividend payments:

$$P = \frac{d_1}{1 + k_e} + \frac{d_2}{(1 + k_e)^2} + \cdots = \sum_{t=1}^{\infty} \frac{d_t}{(1 + k_e)^t}$$

where:
P = the initial price of a share of common stock
d_t = the cash dividend per share distributed in year t
k_e = the cost of equity capital

According to this view the underlying earnings are only a means to an end: if the retained portion of earnings are reinvested for the benefit of the shareholders they too will produce future dividends and therefore will be reflected in the cash flow. If they do *not* produce future dividends, such reinvested earnings are correctly excluded from the discounted value of future benefits. Or as John B. Williams unforgettably expressed it in the form of some sage advice of an old farmer to his son:

> A cow for her milk.
> A hen for her eggs,
> And a stock by heck,
> For her dividends.
>
> An orchard for fruit,
> Bees for their honey,
> And stocks, besides,
> For their dividends.[1]

Now let us follow the farmer's advice, and use the dividend valuation formula to analyze the impact of a change in dividend policy on stock prices. For example, let us assume that the firm decides to forgo its cash dividend in the first year in order to reinvest the additional sum d_1, *for one year,* distributing in the second year $d_2 + d_1(1 + R)$; that is the company increases its second-year dividend by d_1 plus the one-year return on this additional investment, Rd_1.

Obviously, shifting the dividend from the first year to the second year constitutes a change in dividend policy. But what is the impact of this change on the

---

1 See John B. Williams, *The Theory of Investment Value*, Cambridge, Mass., Harvard University Press, 1938, p. 58. Williams continues: "The old man knew where milk and honey came from, but he made no such mistake as to tell his son to buy a cow for her cud or bees for their buzz". *Ibid.*

value of the company's stock? To answer this question we re-write the valuation equation in a form which explicitly reflects the above change in dividend policy. The new valuation formula, following the dividend change, is given by:

$$P' = \frac{0}{1 + k_e} + \frac{d_2 + d_1(1 + R)}{(1 + k_e)^2} + \sum_{t=3}^{\infty} \frac{d_t}{(1 + k_e)^t}$$

where:

P' = the new stock price

R = the rate of return on reinvestment in year 1.

Subtracting the previous equation from this formula we derive the change in the value of the stock (ΔP) which results from the assumed change in dividend policy:

$$\Delta P = P' - P = \frac{d_1(1 + R)}{(1 + k_e)^2} - \frac{d_1}{1 + k_e} = \frac{d_1}{1 + k_e} \left[\frac{1 + R}{1 + k_e} - 1 \right] =$$

$$\frac{d_1}{(1 + k_e)^2} (R - k_e)$$

If $R = k_e$ (that is if the reinvestment rate R is equal to the market required rate of return k_e), then the change in dividend policy has no impact on the value of the stock, that is, $P' - P = 0$. On the other hand, if $R > k_e$, the reinvestment of the first year "dividend", d_1, increases the market value of the shares; conversely, should R be less than k_e, the price of the stock will fall.

The reader should recall the assumption underlying this highly simplified model, i.e., that no external sources of financing are available to the firm. In such a case a decision by the firm to increase its investment induces a parallel change in its dividend policy, and vice versa. Thus dividend policy is tied to investment policy, and apart from the special case in which $R = k_e$, changes in dividend policy can be expected to have a substantial and direct impact on the value of the firm.

These results can easily be generalized to cover the case of constant growth. Recall that in this case we assume that the firm retains a constant fraction b out of its earnings per share, earns a rate of return, R, on its investments, and employs no external sources of financing. Given these assumptions, per share earnings and dividends will grow at a compounded average annual rate equal to bR and the price of a share, that is the present value of future dividends, is given by:

$$P = \frac{(1 - b) E}{1 + k_e} + \frac{(1 - b) E (1 + bR)}{(1 + k_e)^2} + \frac{(1 - b) E (1 + bR)^2}{(1 + k_e)^3} + \dots$$

where:

E	= current earnings per share
b	= the fraction of retained earnings
$(1 - b) E \equiv d$	= current dividend per share
R	= the rate of return on reinvested earnings
k_e	= the cost of equity

As we have shown in Chapter 18, the summation of all the terms on the right hand side of the equation yields the solution:

$$P = \frac{(1 - b)\,E}{k_e - bR}$$

Since b, the fraction of earnings per share which is reinvested, represents the firm's dividend policy it is clear that in the growth model dividend policy "counts", that is share price depends on a firm's dividend policy. The relationship of share price to alternative dividend policies (alternative values of b) can be seen in Table 19.1 which sets out the solutions of the valuation equation on the assumption that earnings per share in the first year (E) are \$10, and k_e, the discount rate, is 20%: solutions for two alternative values of the reinvestment rate of return, R (25% and 10%), are given.

An examination of Table 19.1 shows that a share's market price rises as the percentage retained, b, increases when the rate of return on reinvestment is greater $(R = 25\%)$ than the cost of equity. The opposite relationship holds when $R = 10\%$, that is when R is less than the discount rate. In the simple dividend growth model, valuation depends on dividend policy, and on the relationship between k_e and R. If the company expects to earn a rate of return on reinvested profits which is higher than the alternative cost of the distributed profits (dividends) to the stockholders, the increase in the proportion of retained earnings is desirable. However, if the investment opportunities confronting the firm are relatively poor $(R < k_e)$, a decrease in retained earnings (increase in the dividend payout ratio) increases the value of the firm.

Finally, in cases where $R = k_e$, the valuation equation can be rewritten as follows:

$$P = \frac{(1 - b)E}{k_e - bR} = \frac{(1 - b)E}{k_e - bk_e} = \frac{(1 - b)E}{(1 - b)k_e} = \frac{E}{k_e}$$

Table 19.1
Theoretical Share Prices for Alternative Retention Ratios (b) and Rates of Return (R)*

Retention Ratio as % of Earnings (b)	Share Price in $ (P)
R = 25%	
0	50.00
0.1	51.40
0.2	53.30
0.5	66.70
R = 10%	
0	50.00
0.1	47.40
0.2	44.40
0.5	33.30

* Calculated from the formula: $P = \frac{(1 - b)E}{k - bR}$ on the assumption that $k = 20\%$ and $E = \$10$.

The dividend term itself as well as the dividend policy variable b are eliminated from the valuation formula, which indicates that when $R = k_e$, dividend policy is irrelevant for valuation purposes since it has no effect on shareholders' wealth. The intuitive explanation for this phenomenon is straightforward: the shareholders' opportunity cost is k_e, but since the firm can earn exactly the same rate of return ($R = k_e$) on its retained earnings, the shareholders are indifferent as to whether the firm reinvests the earnings for them, or whether they receive cash dividends and reinvest them elsewhere themselves — assuming, of course, the absence of transaction costs and taxes.

DIVIDENDS AND VALUATION: WITH EXTERNAL FINANCING

To this point we have assumed retained earnings are the only source which the firm can draw upon to finance new investment projects. This of course forges a link, as we have seen, between a firm's investment and dividend policies — the only way to finance investment projects is through retention of earnings, and given the level of earnings, the only way to increase retention is by raising the proportion retained, thereby decreasing dividends. In practice such situations might, and undoubtedly do, exist. In the short run, access to outside financing may become difficult or impossible, and for a variety of reasons (for example, family control) a firm may find itself constrained to retained earnings even in the long run.

The typical corporation, however, usually has recourse to alternative means of financing its investment projects, and is not necessarily restricted to the use of retained earnings. The availability of external sources of financing breaks the link between dividend and investment policies. Given the ability to raise outside capital, the firm can simultaneously increase investment and dividends.[2] In such a situation the previously analyzed *tradeoff* between investment and dividends no longer obtains since the firm can always raise additional funds to finance its investment program and the payment of dividends simultaneously.

The Miller and Modigliani Model[3]

Perhaps the best known advocates of the incorporation of external financing in valuation models are Merton Miller and Franco Modigliani (hereafter referred to as M & M) who have used this approach to show that the price of a firm's common stock is *independent* of its dividend policy in a perfect riskless capital market in which no individual trader or firm can influence the price of securities; information is freely and immediately available to all; there are no

---

2 However, the reader should note that many major corporations, such as IBM and Xerox, have issued common stock only once in the post-World War II period.

3 See Merton H. Miller and Franco Modigliani, "Dividend Policy, Growth, and the Valuation of Shares", *Journal of Business*, October 1961.

482 Chapter 19 — Dividend Policy

transactions costs or other legal and institutional impediments to investment; and there is no differential taxation of personal income (i.e. dividends) and capital gains.

In order to focus attention on the crucial role played by the existence of external sources of financing let's initially assume a world of perfect certainty.

To prove the M & M invariance theorem, we define the following notation: let

$d_{j(t)}$ = the dividend per share paid by firm j on the *last* day of period t, and

$P_{j(t)}$ = the price (ex-any-dividend in t-1) of a share of firm j at the *start* of period t.

As we assume *certainty* and a perfect capital market, the price of each share must be such that the rate of return to investors $r_{(t)}$ on every share will be the same over any given interval of time; and equal to the riskless interest rate[4] that is,

$$r_{(t)} = \frac{d_{j(t)} + P_{j(t+1)} - P_{j(t)}}{P_{j(t)}}$$

and, therefore:

$$P_{j(t)} = \frac{1}{1 + r_{(t)}} [d_{j(t)} + P_{j(t+1)}]$$

for every firm's shares.[5]

Market forces assure that the last two equations will hold. If the rate of return on one firm's shares is lower than that of another firm's shares, investors will sell the low return shares and buy the shares which offer the higher return, and this process will continue until the rate of return on all shares is equal to r. To analyze the impact of dividend policy on stock valuation let us reformulate the valuation equation in terms of the total value of the firm rather than in terms of an individual share. Without loss of generality we drop the subscript j and introduce the following additional notations:

$n_{(t)}$ = number of shares on record at the start of period t;

$m_{(t+1)}$ = number of new shares sold during t at the ex-dividend closing price $P_{(t+1)}$.

It is clear from these definitions that $n_{(t+1)} = n_{(t)} + m_{(t+1)}$.

$V_{(t)} = n_{(t)}P_{(t)}$ = total value of the enterprise at the start of period t, and

$D_{(t)} = n_{(t)}d_{(t)}$ = total dividends paid at the end of t to shareholders on record at the start of period t.

Using these symbols and the relationship: $n_{(t)} P_{(t+1)} = V_{(t+1)} - m_{(t+1)}P_{(t+1)}$, the valuation equation can be rewritten as

4 Hence we denote the rate of return by r rather than by the Greek letter ρ which was used in M & M's original article.

5 Since M & M assume a perfect market and complete certainty, there is no need to distinguish between bonds and stocks. In effect, ρ equals the riskless rate of interest in such a market.

$$V_{(t)} = \frac{1}{1 + r_{(t)}} [D_{(t)} + n_{(t)}P_{(t+1)}] = \frac{1}{1 + r_{(t)}} [D_{(t)} + V_{(t+1)} - m_{(t+1)}P_{(t+1)}]$$

Hence the end-of-year dividend $D_{(t)}$, the terminal value $V_{(t+1)}$, and the term $m_{(t+1)}P_{(t+1)}$ would appear to be the factors which determine $V_{(t)}$. It would appear, therefore, that dividend policy really affects share values since the value of the firm ($V_{(t)}$) depends, *inter alia* on $D_{(t)}$. Nevertheless, M & M have succeeded to prove the irrelevance of dividend policy. Suppose now that the company decides to invest $I_{(t)}$ dollars in year t. The company may finance this investment by reducing $D_{(t)}$ or by raising external capital, thereby increasing $m_{(t)}P_{(t+1)}$. As we can see from the valuation equation the dividend policy decision affects the value of firm $V_{(t)}$ in two ways: (a) directly through the dividend payment, $D_{(t)}$, and (b) indirectly through the amount of outside capital required to finance the investment program, $- m_{(t+1)}P_{(t+1)}$. The latter is determined by the relationship:

$$m_{(t+1)}P_{(t+1)} = I_{(t)} - [X_{(t)} - D_{(t)}]$$

where $X_{(t)}$ is the firm's total net profit for the period t. This relationship reflects the fact that the portion of investment not covered by retained earnings must be financed by raising external capital. Substituting this expression for $m_{(t+1)}P_{(t+1)}$ in the valuation formula yields:

$$V_{(t)} = n_{(t)}P_{(t)} = \frac{1}{1 + r_{(t)}} [X_{(t)} - I_{(t)} + V_{(t+1)}]$$

Thus the value of the firm depends on earnings $X_{(t)}$, investment $I_{(t)}$, and $V_{(t+1)}$, but does *not* depend on the current dividend $D_{(t)}$. However, if we assume that future dividends are independent of the first-year dividend $D_{(t)}$, and that they are known with certainty, it follows that $V_{(t+1)}$ is also independent of the current dividend $D_{(t)}$, but still might be dependent on future dividends. However, we can repeat the same line of reasoning for $V_{(t+1)}$ and show that this value is also independent of $D_{(t+1)}$, and similarly that $V_{(t+2)}$ is independent of $D_{(t+2)}$, and so on. Therefore, the current value of the firm, $V_{(t)}$ is also independent of all future dividends. In sum, the level of future earnings $X_{(t)}$ is the key variable which determines the value of the firm. In the absence of a link between dividend and investment decisions dividend policy in a riskless perfect capital market is irrelevant.[6]

---

6 It is clear from the M & M analysis that $D_{(t)} = X_{(t)} - I_{(t)} + EF_{(t)}$, where $EF_{(t)}$ denotes the firm's external financing during the period. Thus the firm should first find its *optimal* level of investment and then adjust its dividend policy and external financing to the desired level. It follows that the irrelevancy of dividend policy under conditions of certainty can be derived directly from the investment-consumption analysis of Chapter 4. Simply replace the consumption in the two periods, C_0 and C_1 (see Table 4.14 above), by the dividends in each period, D_0 and D_1. The separation property between investment and financial decisions remains. As a result, any dividend policy is optimal so long as the firm follows the *NPV* rule when evaluating its investments. If some shareholders have a preference for a different dividend policy (combination of D_1 and D_2) they can borrow or lend thereby adjusting the cash flow to their preferences. The particular dividend policy chosen by the firm is, under these circumstances, irrelevant. *(footnote continued overleaf)*

INTERNAL AND EXTERNAL FINANCING: A RECONCILIATION

The dividend growth model and the M & M results can be reconciled by noting that dividend changes do not affect share prices in both cases when the investment effect is neutralized. In order to isolate the impact of dividend policy on valuation, M & M hold firms' net investment constant, that is they compare situations with identical investment programs but which differ in their dividend policies. In the growth model, on the other hand, investment varies with changes in dividend policy. In order to neutralize the effects of investment in the dividend growth model, we must set the net present value of any new investment equal to zero.[7] Thus investment can be permitted to differ but only as long as $R = k_e$.

Consider the following example of a firm which pays out all of its earnings as dividends. In such a case the value of the company's shares is given by:

$$P = \frac{Y}{(1 + k_e)} + \frac{Y}{(1 + k_e)^2} \cdots + \frac{Y}{(1 + k_e)^t} + \cdots$$

where Y denotes the company's expected earnings all of which it expects to pay out as cash dividends and k_e is the cost of equity capital. Now assume that the firm suspends its first-year dividend and reinvests that same amount in an annuity yielding an annual rate of return of R which is exactly equal to k_e. In this case no dividend is paid in the first year and the firm earns an additional RY per annum in perpetuity all of which is paid out as future dividends:

$$P' = \frac{0}{1 + k_e} + \frac{Y + RY}{(1 + k_e)^2} + \cdots \frac{Y + RY}{(1 + k_e)^t} +$$

Recall that investment is neutralized, as we have already shown, so long as $R = k_e$. Hence P' is exactly equal to P and dividend policy has no effect on share prices.

The same result can be reached using the growth model formula:

$$P = \frac{(1 - b)Y}{k_e - Rb}$$

(*Footnote 6 continued*)
Note that in this type of analysis we assume liquidation of the firm at the end of the period. The value of the firm today (V_0) is

$$V_0 = (X_0 - I_0) + \frac{X_1^*}{1 + r}$$

where: X_0 = the return today
X_1^* = tomorrow's return *after* the investment
I_0 = today's investment

Given the assumption of liquidation this is also equal to

$$V_0 = D_0 + \frac{D_1}{1 + r}$$

7 See Myron J. Gordon, "Optimal Investment and Financing Policy", *Journal of Finance*, May 1961.

Given the assumption $R = k_e$, this can be rewritten as

$$\frac{(1 - b)Y}{k_e - k_e b} = \frac{(1 - b)Y}{(1 - b)k_e} = \frac{Y}{k_e}$$

Since b can be eliminated from the valuation formula, dividend policy is again irrelevant for valuation.

Thus, given the assumptions of certainty and of perfect capital markets, *both* the dividend growth and the M & M models assert that once investment policy is neutralized dividend policy can have no effect on share prices.[8] However, this should not be interpreted to mean that dividend policy is not important.

FACTORS AFFECTING DIVIDEND DECISIONS

The assumption that securities are traded in frictionless capital markets under conditions of perfect certainty clearly is intended only as an approximation of reality. Real-life capital markets are neither perfect nor riskless. In this section we shall examine some of the implications of relaxing these assumptions before tackling the formidable task of introducing taxation into the theoretical models.

Flotation and Transaction Costs

The irrelevance of dividend policy in a perfect market assumes of course zero flotation costs. Thus a firm is indifferent between the financing of its new projects either out of the retained earnings or by issuing new securities. However, in practice these two sources of finance are not perfect substitutes; external financing is the more expensive alternative due to the existence of flotation costs which reflect the need to cover the costs of underwriting. Other things being equal, the smaller the firm, or the smaller the new issue, the larger will be the proportion of such costs. Again this is a factor which favors the use of retained earnings, that is a low-dividend payment ratio.

Another factor which may favor retained earnings is the existence of transaction costs. Thus a shareholder who desires to increase his investment in the firm would prefer not to receive cash dividends, thereby increasing his investment in the firm without paying commissions which are proportionately high, particularly when the amount of investment is relatively small. However, this sword cuts two ways. Investors who desire to decrease their investment in the firm, say in order to increase current consumption, will by an analogous argu-

---

8 They do disagree with respect to the impact of uncertainty. However, it has been shown that the two approaches can also be reconciled in the case of uncertainty, see M.J. Brennan, "A Note on Dividend Irrelevance and the Gordon Valuation Model", *Journal of Finance*, December 1971.

ment prefer to receive dividends thereby avoiding the commission which applies to the alternative of selling off part of their shares.

Control

Many firms, particularly small family-owned firms, operate under a self-imposed constraint which limits the amount of external financing which can be raised; the reason being that management is afraid to lose control of the firm. New issues of common stock dilute control, while after a point further increases in debt become undesirable or even impossible. Thus, after a point at least dividend and investment decisions are tied to one another. In such a situation the dividend growth model is appropriate and offers useful insight with respect to the optimal payout ratio (dividend policy).

Informational Content of Dividends

Many researchers place special emphasis on the so-called informational content of dividends.[9] In the real world the relevant information regarding a firm's future prospects is neither readily available nor costless. In such a situation dividends can be (and probably are) important purveyors of information to investors. Thus shifts in dividend policy may affect an investor's expectations regarding the future prospects of the firm, thereby affecting its current share price as well. According to this approach, rises in a firm's dividend rate will be interpreted as an optimistic signal from management regarding the expected level of future profits. Conversely, decreases in the dividend rate will be treated as harbingers of ill tidings. And these two effects need not be offsetting. Cuts in dividends are likely to have a greater negative impact on share prices than a corresponding increase in dividends, which reflects the fact that the current price of most shares already includes a significant premium for some future growth.

Stability of Earnings

A firm's cash position is another important factor that must be taken into account when determining long-run dividend policy. A rapidly expanding and very profitable firm is often faced with a chronic shortage of cash. Such a firm usually prefers to set a relatively low payout ratio, and to plow back most of its earnings in order to finance further growth. Although it is true that the firm

---

9 See M & M, *op. cit.*; R. Watts, "The Information Content of Dividends", *Journal of Business*, April 1973; Stephen Ross, "The Determination of Financial Structures: The Incentive Signalling Approach", *Bell Journal of Economics*, Spring 1977; and Sudipto Bhattacharya, "Imperfect Information, Dividend Policy, and 'The Bird in the Hand' Fallacy", *Bell Journal of Economics*, Spring, 1979.

could turn to the capital market for funds, the uncertainty engendered by rapid expansion often leads such a firm to set a "safe" payout ratio, that is one which it can maintain should the rate of earnings growth decline in the future.

In general the greater the risk of larger fluctuations in future earnings, the greater is the probability that the firm will adopt a policy of setting a relatively low payout ratio. The line of reasoning which underlies such a policy is as follows:

(a)   Most firms are anxious to avoid the negative "information content" of a decline in the cash dividend rate. One way to minimize the risk that large fluctuations in earnings will force a cut in dividends is to set a low payout ratio which can be maintined even in the face of a relatively serious or prolonged decline in earnings.

(b)   The existence of large fluctuations in earnings materially increases the risk of default and as a result the firm will try to avoid a high proportion of debt in its capital structure, thereby limiting its access to this source of external sources of financing. A parallel policy of paying out a low proportion of earnings as dividends is especially appropriate for such a firm since it helps provide the relatively large proportion of equity capital required to finance its investment program.

TAXES AND DIVIDENDS

To this point we have ignored taxes — a strategy which cannot be recommended (for long) either in theory or practice. The introduction of taxes raises a fundamental question. In view of the differential taxation of dividend income and capital gains, why should firms pay dividends at all?[10] Current dividends are taxed at marginal personal income tax rates while retained earnings incur no immediate personal tax liability. Any increase in the value of a firm's shares which stems from the reinvestment of income is taxed as a capital gain only when the shares are sold, i.e. at a rate lower than the marginal personal tax rate. Since many investors are in relatively high personal tax brackets this could be expected to create a strong preference for capital gains. Despite this, US corporations distribute a substantial part of their real earnings as dividends. Hence the expression "dividend puzzle".

Clearly no problem arises in a world without taxes. As we have just seen, the M & M analysis suggests that investors would be indifferent to dividends, i.e., no systematic preference for retained earnings would exist.[11] But once

---

10 The question of *why corporations pay dividends* has been raised explicitly by Fischer Black and Myron Scholes, "The Effects of Dividend Yield and Dividend Policy on Common Stock Prices and Returns", *Journal of Financial Economics*, 1974; Fischer Black, "The Dividend Puzzle", *Journal of Portfolio Managment*, Winter, 1975; Merton Miller and Myron Scholes, "Dividends and Taxes", *Journal of Financial Economics*, December, 1978; and Martin Feldstein and Jerry Green, "Why Do Companies Pay Dividends?" *Working Paper 413*, National Bureau of Economic Research, December 1979.

11 But even here the M & M analysis does not account for the observed stability of corporate dividend policy, see p. 495 below.

taxes are recognized, the nagging question of why firms do not eliminate (or at least sharply reduce) their cash dividends crops up. Several, not necessarily mutually-exclusive, ways to resolve the dividend dilemma have been suggested.

Transaction Costs

As we have already noted, investors who desire to receive a steady income stream from their equity holdings might prefer the receipt of periodic dividends to the alternative of selling off a portion of their shares from time to time, thereby reducing the costs of such transactions. This argument could be significant with respect to small investors in low tax brackets. Similarly some types of institutional investors are sensitive to the formal difference between spending "capital" or "income".

The Clientele Effect

The idea that different classes of investors might have differing "tastes" regarding dividend policy is not new. In their 1961 article M & M suggested that the differential taxation of capital gains and dividends might conceivably lead to a tendency for each corporation to attract a particular "clientele" comprised of those investors who have a preference for its dividend policy (payout ratio). Given such a distribution of shareholders among corporations, a firm would be indifferent between alternative payout ratios. However, once a particular dividend policy has been established, the firm would be reluctant to change its payout ratio since this would lead to clientele shifts, and the latter generate undesirable transactions costs for investors.

Table 19.2
Mean Dividend Payouts and Implied Tax Brackets of Investors

Decile	Dividend Payout Mean	Implied Tax Bracket
1	0.204	0.4883
2	0.316	0.4945
3	0.371	0.3889
4	0.409	0.4245
5	0.447	0.4108
6	0.486	0.4848
7	0.533	(unavailable)
8	0.594	0.1889
9	0.674	0.0806
10	1.040	0.2245

Source: E. J. Elton and M. J. Gruber, "Marginal Stockholder Tax Rates and the Clientele Effect", *Review of Economics and Statistics*, February 1970.

Perhaps the best known attempt to measure the clientele effect was made in 1970 by Elton and Gruber[12] who used the average decline of share prices as a stock goes *ex-dividend* to estimate the marginal tax bracket of investors. Using data from April 1966 to March 1967, they found that this tax bracket was 36.4%. Elton and Gruber also presented empirical evidence supporting the existence of a clientele effect, which indicates that, in general, the higher a firm's dividend payout ratio, the lower the tax bracket of its stockholders. However, their general conclusion must be qualified, for although they found a negative correlation between investors' tax brackets and firms' dividend payouts, there are departures from this general rule. Thus, Table 19.2 shows that as one systematically moves from low to high dividend-payout firms, investors in some of the higher tax brackets *prefer* dividends to retentions. For example, a move from the fifth dividend-payout decile to the sixth is accompanied by an *increase* in the implied personal tax rate.

The Miller—Scholes Thesis

Recently Merton Miller and Myron Scholes[13] have used an often overlooked features of US tax law to restore the equivalence between dividend income and capital gains. Since 1969 individuals' deductions for interest on investments (i.e., excluding interest paid on mortgages and business loans) have been limited to their investment income plus $25,000. Thus each extra dollar of dividend income increases the allowable interest tax deduction by one dollar. Clearly, for the relevant investor the additional dollar of income is exactly offset by the additional dollar of deduction which leaves his taxable income unchanged! Thus such an individual will be indifferent between the receipt of dividends or a capital gain via the firm's repurchase of its shares, if he can offset the tax effect by borrowing.[14] Unfortunately two empirical findings limit the usefulness of this ingenious, albeit somewhat convoluted argument.

(a)   Since the limit on interest deductions was only introduced in 1969, the Miller – Scholes approach does not provide an explanation for observed dividend policy before that year.

(b)   Very few investors with dividend income make sufficiently large interest payments on debt to make the constraint binding.[15]

---

12 E.J. Elton and M.J. Gruber, "Marginal Stockholder Tax Rates and the Clientele Effect", *Review of Economics and Statistics*, February 1970.

13 Miller and Scholes, *op. cit.*, 1978.

14 Miller and Scholes show how this can be accomplished through borrowing and simultaneously investing in risk-free assets. Clearly this implies some level of transactions costs, but the basic point remains — much if not all of the marginal personal tax on dividends can be avoided.

15 See Feldstein and Green, *op. cit.*

The Portfolio Approach

Another alternative explanation for observed dividend behavior can be found by applying the portfolio principle. In a recent paper,[16] Feldstein and Green use the idea that shareholders' risk-aversion provides a limit to corporate growth. They consider an economy with shareholders in diverse tax situations, i.e. two groups of taxable individuals and untaxed institutions, but the same line of reasoning holds for investors in "low" and "high" tax brackets. Firms can either distribute their profits as dividends or reinvest them and grow larger, eventually distributing these funds to shareholders as capital gains. Under certainty, this would lead to a segmented market in which taxable individuals invest only in firms which forgo dividend payments, while untaxed institutions would prefer the firms which pay dividends. However, if we assume that investors regard each firm's return as uncertain, they will desire to diversify their holdings. Feldstein and Green demonstrate that in such a market share price maximization implies that each firm must attract both types of investors, and this in turn implies that some fraction of earnings must be distributed as dividends. Market equilibrium of the segmented form can take place only in the case of little or no uncertainty or if we assume a constraint on investors' ability to diversify risk.

The Information Signalling Approach

Finally, an intuitively appealing explanation for observed dividend payments, in the face of differential taxation, can be found by considering one of the many implications of the separation of ownership and management. According to this approach management employs dividends to convey information regarding the *sustainable* level of its real income.[17]

In the highly uncertain world confronting investors, the use of dividend changes as a proxy for the trend in earnings is readily understandable and makes good sense. Reported earnings per share can be manipulated by means of "imaginative" accounting (or worse!) even by a firm in dire financial straits. The same cannot be said for cash dividends which represent a drain on the firm's real resources. And while a firm might conceivably raise dividends in the face of declining earnings or even losses, this process cannot continue indefinitely. Investors are likely to treat a raise in reported earnings, which is *confirmed* by a corresponding change in the dividend rate, with far greater confidence, presumably on the grounds that such a dual rise represents a higher level of *substainable* earnings and not just a transitory fluctuation of profits.

---

16 *Ibid.*

17 See Fred Arditti, Haim Levy and Marshall Sarnat, "Taxes, Uncertainty and Optimal Dividend Policy", *Financial Management*, Spring 1976; Stephen Ross, "The Determination of Financial Structures: The Incentive Signalling Approach", *The Bell Journal of Economics*, Spring 1977; and Sudipto Bhattacharya, "Imperfect Information, Dividend Policy and 'The Bird in the Hand' Fallacy", *The Bell Journal of Economics*, Spring 1979.

UNCERTAINTY AND DIVIDEND POLICY

In reality there is probably some truth in all of the above explanations. Dividend policy, like financial management in general, is a multi-faceted activity. In this section, however, we shall focus attention on the information-signalling effect and demonstrate, in a formal manner, how the explicit introduction of uncertainty of information[18] can account for the observed policy of paying dividends even when personal tax rates exceed the rate of tax on capital gains.

In a Perfect Capital Market

Let us initially turn to the question of the impact of dividends on the market value of the firm in a perfect capital market, using the following notation:

S = market value of a firm's common stock

B = market value of a firm's debt

X = random variable representing a firm's earnings before interest and taxes but after the deduction of depreciation expense.

T = the corporate tax rate.

T_p = the personal tax rate, assumed to be the same for all individuals.

T_g = the capital gains tax rate, assumed to be the same for all individuals and applicable to any gains from the price appreciation of common stock. Obviously $T_g < T_p$.

q = the dividend-payout (or dividend-earnings) ratio; while $(1-q)$ represents that fraction of after-tax earnings not paid out as dividends, which we assume results in an equivalent increase in the market value of the firm's equity value.

r = the riskless rate of interest; all interest income is taxed at T_p and interest payments are tax deductible against personal income.

Given our assumptions and the above notation, it follows that $q(1 - T_p)$ denotes that part of each dollar of the firm's *after-tax* income paid as dividends, which accrues to the shareholder after the payment of his personal income tax. The fraction of each dollar of the firm's after-tax income that is retained $(1 - q)$, generates a capital gains tax payment by the shareholder equal to $(1 - q)T_g$, so that the residual amount accruing to the stockholder is $(1 - T_g)(1 - q)$. Hence, out of each *post-tax* corporate dollar earned by the firm, the amount received by the shareholders, after the payment of all taxes (corporate, personal and capital gains), denoted by w, is given by the expression:

$$w = q(1 - T_p) + (1 - T_g)(1 - q)$$

or equivalently

$$w = (1 - T_g) - q(T_p - T_g)$$

18 This follows the approach of Arditti, Levy and Sarnat, *op. cit.*

Clearly, w decreases as the dividend payout ratio increases, when the personal tax rate exceeds the rate of tax on capital gains. For example if $T_p = 0.50$ and $T_g = 0.20$, then a payout ratio of 40% ($q = 0.40$) results in an after-tax income of 68 cents ($w = 0.68$); but if the dividend payment, q, is increased to 60%, then investors' after-tax income is reduced to 62 cents ($w = 0.62$). Hence a firm's best policy, under the above assumptions, is to pay zero dividends. The reasoning behind this result is as follows: an investor who receives one dollar in a *perfect capital market* attaches the same degree of risk to the dollar of future income independent of the way it is received. Hence, a dollar of capital gains or a dollar of dividends are of equal value. But the existence of differential taxation destroys this equality; because of taxation, greater value will be attached to low dividend payouts which leads to the conclusion that the lowest dividend payout, namely zero, will be optimal.[19]

In an Imperfect Capital Market

As we have just seen the taking into account of personal and capital gains taxes, in addition to corporate taxes, implies an optimal dividend payout of zero. Clearly, it is the fact that the tax rate on capital gains is lower than the tax rate on income which induces this corner solution. However, even the most cursory empirical examination suffices to show the inadequacy of such a result; in reality the typical corporation retains only a part of its earnings, the remainder being paid out to its shareholders as dividends. Thus the explanatory property of such a model is seriously impaired.

A solution to the dilemma created by the discrepancy between observed corporate behavior in the real world and the prescription for such behavior spelled out by the formal theoretical model presented above can be found by relaxing the assumption of a perfect capital market. More specifically, we shall introduce an assumption which reflects the differential risk which a corporate shareholder may impute to the two components of corporate profits — dividends and retained earnings.

We shall assume that due to management's ability to influence or even manipulate reported earnings the typical shareholder will view that portion of reported earnings which is not "confirmed" by a dividend payment as a less reliable indicator of a firm's true earning power. Numerous examples can be given of management's ability to influence the relationship of a firm's reported accounting profits to its underlying economic earnings. For example, the allowance for bad debts and the reserve for outstanding claims which are important components of the earnings statement of banks and insurance companies are highly subjective estimates made by management. Similarly, the degree of management discretion in determining the reported earnings of a

19 See D.E. Farrar and L.L. Selwyn, "Taxes, Corporate Financial Policy and Return to Investors", *National Tax Journal*, December 1967; and S.C. Myers, "Taxes, Corporate Financial Policy and Return to Investors: Comment", *National Tax Journal*, December 1967. For a formal proof see Arditti, Levy and Sarnat, *op. cit.*

highly diversified conglomerate firm has been a cause of much concern to the Securities and Exchange Commission.

In essence, we propose to relax a key part of the perfect capital market assumption, namely that all market participants have equal and costless access to all information. Here it is suggested, that since shareholders are in an inferior "information position" *vis à vis* management because of management's ability to influence accounting magnitudes they will view reported earnings with suspicion. Cash dividends, on the other hand, require an actual expenditure of a firm's resources, and, in the long run, should reflect underlying profitability. Thus by paying a dividend the firm provides investors with some additional information regarding the estimated permanence of earnings. *This reduces the conditional variability of deviations of reported accounting earnings from underlying economic profits,* since such uncertainty relates only to the retained portion of earnings. Hence, the variance of earnings narrows as the payout ratio increases.

Simultaneously considering the personal-capital gains tax differential and the uncertainty attached to undistributed earnings, the investor's expected return-risk opportunity is given by[20]

$$\bar{Y} = E(1 - T_p) + E\ \frac{(T_p - T_g)\ \sigma Y}{(1 - T_g)\ \sigma E''}$$

where $\bar{Y}$ denotes the expected value of shareholders after-tax income; E = reported *EPS*; σ_Y = standard deviation of Y; and $\sigma_{E''}$ = maximum standard deviation of earnings per share when all earnings are retained.

A simple graphical device can now be employed to illustrate the dividend policy problem. The above equation describes a straight line in the $\bar{Y}$ and σ_Y plane; each point on this line corresponds to a given value of q, i.e., to a particular dividend policy. For the value of $q = 1$, $\bar{Y} = (1 - T_p)E$ and $\sigma_Y = 0$. On the other hand, for $q = 0$, i.e. when all earnings are retained, $\sigma_Y = (1 - T_g)\sigma_{E''}$ and $\bar{Y} = (1 - T_g)E$, which are the *maximum* expected earnings and *maximum* risk points. Figure 19.1 illustrates such a transformation line (*aa'*) superimposed on a set of indifference curves for a typical risk averter. The tangency point P^* represents that dividend policy which this individual considers optimal — the value q that corresponds to $\bar{Y}^*$ and σ_{Y^*}. In general the optimal point will *not* lie at a corner of the transformation line.

It is also instructive to look at the transformation lines as a function of the tax rates T_p and T_g. In a world in which there are no personal or capital gains taxes, the transformation curve simply becomes a horizontal line (for example the line *Eb* of Fig. 19.2) and the optimal dividend payout is $q^* = 1$, shown as point E in Fig. 19.2. If we consider the other extreme case in which personal taxes exist but $\sigma_{E''} = 0$, i.e. there is no uncertainty, then the vertical line *mm'* which lies on the vertical axis of Fig. 19.2 portrays the transformation curve, and its locus of points is defined by

$$\bar{Y} = E(1 - T_g) + qE(T_g - T_p)$$

---

20 The derivation of this equation is given in the Appendix to this chapter.

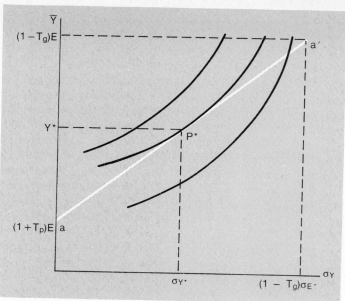

Fig. 19.1

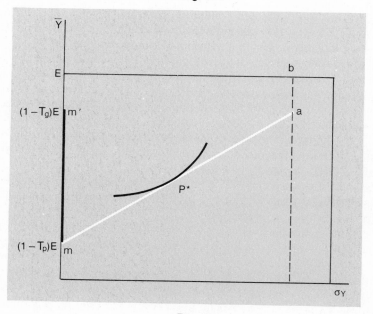

Fig. 19.2

In this instance, the optimal point is given by *m'* which means that the optimal payout ratio, *q**, is zero. However, when both taxes and uncertainty are considered, the transformation curve is again a rising line such as *ma* in Fig. 19.2, and the optimal dividend payout typically lies *between* zero and one.

The introduction of an information imperfection which stipulates that stockholders do not know a firm's true economic profits with certainty results in an optimal dividend policy which calls for the distribution of part of a firm's earnings to shareholders. To obtain this result there is no need to assume that management knows precisely the firm's true profits. Due to measurement problems, arbitrary cost allocations, etc., this is rarely the case. However, for our purposes, it is sufficient to assume that the firm's management is in a better position than its shareholders to estimate economic profits. While such an assumption complicates the presentation of the argument, it does not alter any of the conclusions.

DIVIDEND POLICY IN PRACTICE

Now let's take a look at the time series of actual dividend payments taken in the aggregate. Figure 19.3 graphs the dividends and earnings per share of Moody's Industrial Stocks for the period 1929 to 1978. Even a cursory glance suffices to show that the fluctuations in earnings have been much more pronounced than the fluctuations in dividends during these years. Especially noteworthy is the relatively small magnitude of downturns in dividends per share compared with those of per share earnings. Moreover, in several of the years, earnings per share actually fell below dividends per share which means that even in years of losses firms attempt to avoid a parallel drastic cut in cash dividends. This is illustrated in Table 19.3 which presents data on total dividends and earnings of private US corporations for selected years during the period 1929 – 74. In the years of the Great Depression earnings were very low or even negative; however corporations in the aggregate declared dividends in excess of earnings. For example, in 1932 although the firms lost 2.7 billion dollars, cash dividends amounting to 2.5 billion dollars were paid to shareholders. But no matter how strong the desire to maintain dividends, firms cannot continue to distribute earnings at the same pace in the face of losses during a number of consecutive years. And as Table 19.3 shows, US firms, taken in the aggregate, cut their dividends drastically, albeit not by the same amount as the decline in earnings, during the first half of the 1930s. It was only in the latter half of the 1940s that total corporate dividends again reached their 1929 level, even in nominal terms.

The Partial Adjustment Hypothesis

This historical pattern of dividends and earnings has fascinated economists and specialists in business finance for many years. The seminal work in this area is John Lintner's pioneering 1956 empirical study,[21] in which he proposed a lagged model to explain individual firms' dividend policies, as well as dividends in the aggregate. On the basis of field interviews, Lintner hypothesized the

21 J. Lintner, "Distribution of Incomes of Corporations Among Dividends Retained Earnings and Taxes", *American Economic Review*, May 1956.

496

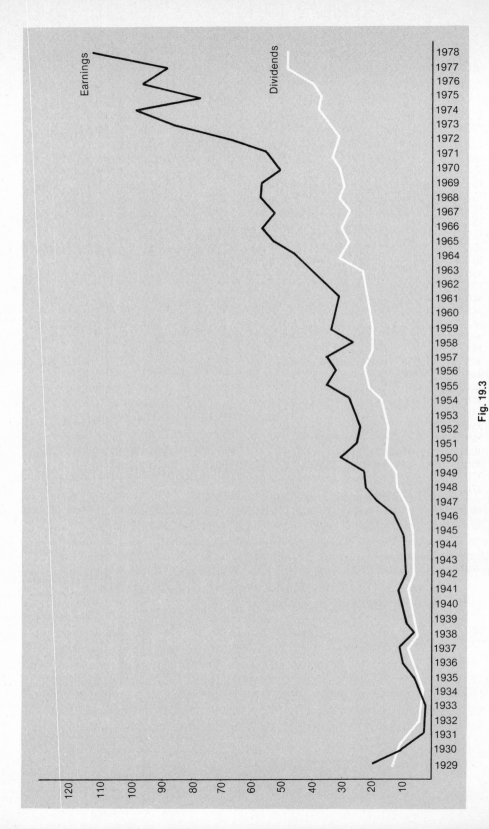

Fig. 19.3

Dow – Jones Industrials 1929 – 1978 Dividends – Earnings per share

Source Moody's Industrial Manual, 1979, p. 50a

Table 19.3
Profits after Taxes and Dividends, all Private US Corporations, Selected Years
1929 – 1974
(Billions of dollars)

Year	Corporate Profits After Taxes	Dividends
1929	8.6	5.8
1930	2.9	5.5
1931	− 0.9	4.1
1932	− 2.7	2.5
1933	.4	2.0
1934	1.6	2.6
1935	2.6	2.8
1936	4.9	4.5
1937	5.3	4.7
1938	2.9	3.2
1939	5.6	3.8
1940	7.2	4.0
1941	10.1	4.4
1942	10.1	4.3
1943	11.1	4.4
1944	11.2	4.6
1945	9.0	4.6
1946	15.5	5.6
1947	20.2	6.3
1948	22.7	7.0
1949	18.9	7.2
1950	24.9	8.8
1955	27.0	10.5
1960	26.7	13.4
1965	46.5	19.8
1970	39.3	24.7
1974	85.2	32.7

Source: *Economic Report of the President*, 1971 Table C-73, p. 282 and *Economic Report of the President*, 1975 Table C-74, p. 335.

following relationship to explain dividend decisions:

$$\Delta D_{it} = a_i + c_i\,(D^*_{it} - D_{i(t-1)}) + u_{it}$$

where D^*_{it} is the target payout ratio; ΔD_i is the change in dividend payments; and D_t and D_{t-1} are the amounts of dividends paid in the years identified by the dating subscripts t. The subscript i identifies the individual company and D^*_{it} represents the dividends which the company would have paid in the current year if its dividends were based simply on its fixed target payout ratio applied to current profits. The parameter c_i indicates the fraction of the difference between this "target" dividend D^*_{it}, and the actual payment made in the preceding year $D_{i(t-1)}$. The lagged Lintner model views current dividends as a function not only of current earnings but of past dividends as well. This reflects the firms' desire to avoid raising current dividends to levels which cannot be maintained, a policy which might force the firm to cut dividends in the future. According to Lintner, corporations follow a policy of setting a *target* dividend payout ratio which they apply to earnings. However due to the strong bias against dividend cuts, increases in earnings are translated into increases in dividends only gradually so as to avoid the necessity of future downward revisions. The lag in the adjustment of current dividends to increases in earnings is a sort of safety device designed to make dividends a function of *permanent* rather than transitory earnings which cannot be sustained.[22]

Consider a case in which a firm earns an unusual profit in a given year, but management knows that there is only a slight probability that the high level of profit will be maintained in the future. Let us further assume that the company in question pays cash dividends of two dollars per share. In such cases a firm desiring to increase dividends in the profitable year, will often prefer to declare an "extra" dividend, say, of one dollar per share rather than to raise its "regular" dividend rate. The motive underlying such a policy is not to disappoint the shareholder should earnings and dividends return to their previous levels in the following year. Such behavior, and Lintner's lagged adjustment hypothesis in general, are clearly consistent with the theoretical view which emphasizes the importance of the *informational content* of dividends in a capital market which is less than perfect.

Another argument in favor of regularity of dividend payments is that such a policy not only enhances the investment position of the company's stock, but also its credit standing, when raising debt capital in the open market. A strong dividend record is often an important consideration for institutional investors when the firm's bonds are being examined.

DIVIDENDS AND VALUATION: THE EMPIRICAL EVIDENCE

It is clear enough that in a perfect capital market in which external financing is *freely* available, rational investors would be indifferent between the components of their return: dividends and capital gains. However, it is equally clear that in an imperfect market the firm should consider the possible effects of the differential tax brackets of its stockholders, dilution of control, flotation and transaction costs, the stability of earnings, etc., when reaching its dividend

---

22 John A. Brittain has modified the basic Lintner model by treating dividends as a function of the cash flow (earnings and depreciation). The rationale for such a procedure is that changes in the liberality of depreciation allowances for tax purposes during wartime and economic recessions makes net profits a poor measure of firms' "ability" to pay dividends. See J. A. Brittain, *Corporate Dividend Policy*, Washington, D.C.: The Brookings Institution, 1966. Another variation on this same theme has been presented by Keith V. Smith who hypothesizes that a company faced with a serious and prolonged secular decline in earnings will prefer a once-and-for-all large cut in its payout ratio rather than a gradual series of cuts in its payout ratio over a period of years. According to this so-called *increasing stream of dividends hypothesis*, dividend increases will lag behind the rise in earnings, but should a cut in dividends become unavoidable, the firm will prefer large rather than a small downward revision of its dividend policy. See Keith V. Smith, "Increasing Stream Hypothesis of Corporate Dividends Policy", *California Management Review*, Fall 1971, pp. 56 – 64.

decisions. Under these circumstances, it is not clear if dividends would be preferred to capital gains or vice versa.

In order to examine the impact of dividends on share prices, the following type of regression equation has been applied, empirically, to cross-sections of common stock:

$$P_i = a + b_1 D_i + b_2(E_i - D_i) + u_i$$

where:

P_i = the price of the ith company's shares
D_i = the dividend per share of the ith company
$E_i - D_i$ = the retained earnings of the ith company's shares
u_i = an error term

Most empirical studies using the above type of regression equation have found that $b_1 > b_2$, and have concluded, therefore that cash dividends are systematically preferred to retained earnings, that is in real-life situations dividend policy seems to count. However, Irwin Friend and Marshall Puckett[23] have raised serious doubts regarding the interpretation of such empirical results. For example, they argue that where $b_1 > b_2$, firms could clearly increase their market values by gradually increasing their dividend payout ratios until $b_1 = b_2$. The latter equality is a necessary condition for a firm to reach its optimal dividend policy. Hence empirical studies which find b_1 significantly higher than b_2 indicate either that a permanent state of disequilibrium exists in the market or that the above type model is inadequate to capture the essentials of the valuation process.

In their critical analysis, Friend and Puckett stress the statistical limitations of the regression model which imparts serious bias to the results. Although we cannot go into all their arguments in any detail, one particular source of bias appears to be of crucial importance. A simple regression model is obviously incomplete in the sense that it does not include all of the relevant variables which may affect valuation.

The most important of these omitted variables is a firm's risk. As we have already mentioned, firms which are characterized by high degrees of uncertainty regarding future earnings (that is by large fluctuations in their earnings) tend to adopt low dividend payout ratios, since such a policy reduces the probability that the firm will be forced to cut its dividends at some future time due to a drop in earnings. Thus, high-risk firms tend to have low payout ratios. This negative correlation between the omitted variable (risk) and the payout ratio creates a bias in favor of cash dividends. We know that, other things being equal, high risk lowers a share's market price. But as high-risk firms also adopt low payout ratios, the regression analysis findings that firms with low payout ratios are characterized by low market prices may well reflect, as Friend and Puckett have suggested, the negative correlation between payout ratios and risk, rather than investors' preference for dividends.

23 Irwin Friend and Marshall Puckett, "Dividends and Stock Prices", *American Economic Review*, September 1964.

This analysis suggests that the inclusion of a risk variable in the regression equations should eliminate the bias, and hence the preference for dividends induced by the bias should also disappear.[24] However, after making a number of corrections in the regression model and adding risk and other variables, Friend and Puckett found the evidence on the effects of dividend policy tenuous and inconclusive. While little support can be found for the hypothesis that a strong market preference exists for cash dividends rather than retained earnings, a moderate preference was found in non-growth industries. The opposite preference (that is favoring retained earnings) seemed to hold for growth companies. Friend and Puckett conclude their work with a warning that the empirical validation of the existence or absence of an optimal dividend payout ratio will require more sophisticated statistical techniques than have been applied hitherto to such empirical studies.

THE CON EDISON EXPERIENCE

The combination of complex alternative theoretical models with, at best, controversial empirical evidence would seem to provide little solace for a worried financial executive in a world of inflation and extreme uncertainty. And clearly dividend policy remains one of the more difficult decisions confronting the business firm. Although magic answers to management's dilemmas are not likely to jump out of a computer printout, the preceding analysis, by pointing out the significance of the information content of unanticipated dividend changes in an uncertain world can provide a framework for analyzing actual decisions.

A case in point is provided by Con Edison which in the wake of the oil crisis stunned Wall Street[25] with an announcement that it would *not* pay any dividend in the second quarter of 1974. The decision marked the first time since the concern was formed in 1881 (i.e., 89 years) that the Company had failed to make a regular dividend payment, and served to disprove a favorite Wall Street axiom that utilities *always* pays their dividends.

The suspension of cash dividend payments reinforced the parallel announcement that operating profits had fallen by 21% in the same quarter. The market's reaction was not long to follow. After a delayed opening, the price of Con Edison's shares fell by 32% on a turnover which placed it at the top of the New York Stock Exchange's most active list for the day.

---

24 It is noteworthy that Fred Arditti has obtained some results which support the analysis of Friend and Puckett. In a regresbion analysis which omits risk variables a preference for cash dividends is observed. However, when he adds the risk factor, thereby correcting for the statistical bias, the regression coefficient of the payout variable becomes insignificant. See Fred D. Arditti, "Risk and the Required Return on Equity", *Journal of Finance*, March 1967.

25 See *Wall Street Journal*, April 24, 1974.

INTEGRATING DIVIDEND POLICY AND CAPITAL STRUCTURE

The desire to avoid such shocks helps account for much of actual dividend behavior. Risk aversion is a powerful force in the corporate boardroom, and we are now in a position to integrate the previous analysis of the effect of leverage on risk with the dividend decision. Figure 19.4 reproduces the, by now, familiar breakeven chart for a firm under two alternative assumptions regarding its financial mix — all equity or 50% debt. We have also superimposed on the graph the probability distribution for the firm's operating earnings. This firm is in the particularly enviable position that there is practically no probability of its losing money. Perhaps it is a regulated industry. But there does exist a positive probability (the area "a" under the curve) that operating earnings will be too low to meet its dividend payments, which we have assumed to be one dollar per share, even when it follows a policy of pure equity financing. Should the firm lever its capital structure, say by introducing 50% debt, the probability that the *NOI* will not be sufficient to pay the one dollar per share dividend rises, and is

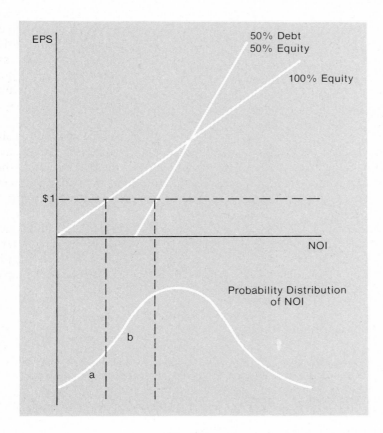

Fig. 19.4

measured by the area "a" + "b". This reflects the fact that interest payments take precedence over dividends.

Although such a graph is rarely (if ever) drawn on the wall of a board chairman's office, it does illustrate the type of thinking which underlies what often appear on the surface to be purely judgmental decisions.

SUMMARY

This chapter has examined a number of problems relating to both the theoretical and practical aspects of dividend policy. Attention was initially directed to the impact of dividend policy on the market valuation of the firm's shares in an effort to determine the theoretically optimal policy to be followed by a firm desiring to maximize owners' wealth.

Perfect Capital Market: No External Financing

When external sources of financing are *not* available the firm's decisions to invest are tied to its dividend policy: in such a case a decision by the firm to increase its investment induces a parallel change in its dividend policy. As a result changes in dividend policy can be expected to have a direct impact on the valuation of common stock, except in the limiting case in which the net present value of the additional investment is zero. This conclusion holds both for *growth* and *non-growth* situations. Hence, dividend policy is of special significance to a firm which for one reason or another is constrained to financing its further expansion solely out of retained earnings. In such situations a proposed increase in dividends must be carefully weighed against the incremental return of any forgone investment.

Perfect Capital Market: With External Financing

The availability of external sources of financing breaks the link between dividend and investment policies, since given the ability to raise outside capital, the firm can simultaneously increase investment and dividends.

Imperfect Capital Markets

Real-life capital markets are not perfect. The firm is confronted, in practice, by numerous factors which are often neglected in the theoretical models. Differential taxation of capital gains and dividends, flotation and transaction costs, control, the psychological impact of dividend changes on investors, the stability of earnings and the possibiilty of bankruptcy and the information conveyed by dividend payments in an uncertain world are all factors which must be given consideration when setting a firm's dividend policy. When all of the dimensions of the dividend decision are recognized, it is clear that dividend policy remains one of the most difficult financial decisions facing the firm.

Empirical Studies: Dividends vs Retained Earnings

Due to the complexity of the factors affecting actual dividend decisions, it is not clear from the theoretical analysis whether investors systematically prefer dividends to capital gains, or vice versa. Numerous empirical studies have been made; however, the results of these regression analyses are not conclusive because of the statistical limitations of the underlying models. Attempts to correct for the statistical bias of the earlier studies have been made, but given the present state of the art in statistics, empirical analysis has only succeeded in narrowing, but not in closing, the gap which exists between the alternative hypotheses regarding the impact of dividend policy on valuation. In practice, the picture is somewhat brighter. Despite the considerable controversy regarding the theoretical aspects of dividends and the interpretation of the empirical record, important practical insights can be derived from the academic models. In particular, the need to avoid "negative information" signals provides a useful guideline for practical decision-making at the level of the firm.

QUESTIONS AND PROBLEMS

19.1   What will be the impact (the change in the value of the firm's stock) of shifting a cash dividend of $6.05 from the first year to the second, if the rate of return on reinvestment in year 1 is 14% and the relevant discount rate is 10%? (In your answer, assume that no external sources of financing are available to the firm.)

19.2   Answer question 19.1, assuming that the rate of return on reinvestment in year 1 is equal to 8%.

19.3   Calculate the theoretical prices for the following alternative retention ratios (b) and rates of return (R) using the Gordon valuation model. (Assume that earnings per share in the first year (E) are $6 and the discount rate (k) is 15%.)

(a) $R = 20\%$; $b = 0, 15\%, 25\%, 50\%, 60\%$
(b) $R = 10\%$; $b = 0, 15\%, 25\%, 50\%, 60\%$

19.4   In what sense does the dividend valuation model lead to a "corner solution"? How can this shortcoming be overcome?

19.5   What is meant by the "information content" of dividends?

19.6   Several studies have been carried out to test investors' preferences for dividends as opposed to capital gains. A regression model of the following type has been used in most of these studies:

$$P_i = a + b_1 D_i + b_2(E_i - D_i) + u_i$$

Discuss the statistical limitations of this model.

19.7   The equity of Hagayon Ltd. consists of $N = 50,000$ shares of common stock. The price of the stock on January 1, 1980 is $130 and the expected net income in 1980 is $500,000. The discount rate used by the shareholders of this firm is $k = 10\%$. Ignore personal taxes on cash dividends.

(a)   Suppose that the firm will not pay cash dividend in 1980. What is the expected price of its stock on December 31, 1980. What is the expected price at the end of the year if the firm pays 10% stock dividend but no cash dividend?

(b)   Make now the alternative assumption that the firm pays on December 31, 1980 a cash dividend of $4 per share. What is the ex-dividend expected price of the stock? What is the impact of the distribution of the cash dividend on the shareholders' wealth?

(c)   Assume that at the end of the year the firm distributes a cash dividend of $4 per share and a few hours later also a 10% stock dividend. What is the impact of this distribution on the investors' wealth?

(d)   Suppose that the firm decides to invest at the end of the year in a new project which requires an initial outlay of $500,000, but still to pay cash dividend of $4 per share. The project is highly profitable. Would you recommend the firm to skip the payment of the cash dividend and to use the retained earnings to finance the new project? Prove your answer.

(e)   Suppose that a financial consultant advises the firm to pay a cash dividend of $4 per share. How many shares should the firm issue in order to finance the new project?

19.8   A given share is sold for $30 just before time t_0. If the firm pays a $3 dividend per share, the price will immediately drop to $27. Suppose you own 100 shares. If the firm decides not to distribute the dividends, you would need to sell 10 shares (at $30 a share) since you need to have a $300 cash income. Assume that the shares were originally bought for $20 each.

(a)   If both ordinary personal tax rate and capital gains tax are 25%, what is your after-tax wealth under the two alternative situations?

(b)   Answer part (a) again, this time assuming that the ordinary income tax is 40%, while the capital gains tax is 25%.

19.9   The firm is capitalized by 100,000 shares of common stock which trade at the beginning of the period at $10 per share. The expected net income in period one is $X_1 = $200,000 and the firm has declared a cash dividend of $1 per share, to be paid at the end of the period. The firm's cost of equity is 10%.

Ignoring personal taxes, answer the follow questions:

(a) What is the ex-dividend share price? What would have been the end-of-period stock price if the firm skipped the dividend?
(b) How many shares of common stock will the firm have to sell at the ex-dividend price in order to undertake an investment project which requires an investment $I_1 = \$200,000$?
(c) What is the value of the firm just after the new issue? What would have been the value of the firm if it skipped the dividend and used the retained earnings to finance the investment?

19.10 Assume a situation in which the firm will be liquidated one period from now (thus, now is time t_0 and one period from now is time t_1). Also assume perfect certaity, perfect capital markets and no taxes. Suppose earnings at time t_0 are $X_0 = \$100,000$, investment is $I_0 = \$40,000$ and earnings plus liquidation value at time t_1 are $X_1 = \$200,000$. The interest rate for borrowing and lending is $r_0 = 8\%$. Determine the cash dividends D_0 and D_1 for the following alternative amounts of external financing (*EF*) that the firm decides to borrow at time t_0: $EF = \$10,000$; $\$50,000$; and $\$80,000$. Also determine the value of the firm V_0 at time t_0. Is it a function of the dividend policy?

19.11 The XYZ Corporation traditionally pays out around 40% of its annual earnings in cash dividends. Up to last year it had had 100,000 shares of common stock outstanding and a steady earnings record at an annual level of $X_0 = \$500,000$. Last year the XYZ Corporation went to the market and sold another 50,000 shares of common stock for $\$1,000,000$ in order to finance new promising investments.

(a) What was the cash dividend per share prior to the new stock issue?
(b) The XYZ Corporation will want to maintain the same cash dividend per share after the new stock issue. Assuming that the investment has not yet affected this year's earnings and they remain at the previous level, what will be the new payout ratio?
(c) What should be the future earnings in order to enable the XYZ Corporation to maintain the same cash dividend per share without exceeding the traditional payout ratio of 40%?
(d) Assume that the investment will indeed raise the earnings to the new level you calculated in (c) and maintain it indefinitely. What is the after-tax internal rate of return on the investment? Compare it to the last year's *dividend yield* and to the earnings per $1 of equity.
(e) Now assume that because of transaction costs (underwriters' premium, broker fees, etc.) the net proceeds to the firm are only 90% of the gross stock issue. What should be the internal rate of return on investment in this case in order to maintain the same earnings and dividends per share?

19.12   A shareholder owns 1,000 shares of ABC Corporation's common stock, trading on January 1, 1981 at $10 per share (cum dividends). A cash dividend of $2 per share is declared, which will be distributed to the stockholders on February 1, 1981.

(a) What is the value of the shareholder's ABC stock valued at the ex-dividend price? How can the shareholder maintain the previous value of his holdings (before the dividend was declared)? Ignore personal tax and transaction costs.

(b) Instead of distributing a cash dividend, the firm considers declaring an "equivalent" stock dividend. What stock dividend will produce the same ex-dividend share price as in (a)? What is the number of ABC shares that the shareholder owns after the stock dividend? What is the value of his holding?

(c) Now assume that there is a transaction cost of 2% of the price of each share purchased (although there are no personal taxes). What is the difference between the cash dividend and the stock dividend option in this case?

19.13   The long-term investment plan of a firm calls for an investment of $I_0 = \$100,000$ in the current period. The annual income of the firm is $X_0 = \$100,000$. The firm traditionally pays out 40% of its net income as cash dividend to its shareholders.

Can the firm keep up with its dividend payments and undertake the entire investment as planned?

Show the firm's sources and uses of funds on the assumption that it maintains the same dividend and undertakes the planned investment.

19.14   Assume a one-period situation with full certainty and perfect capital markets. Also let:

$$X_0 \quad = 400$$
$$X_1 \quad = 600$$
$$r_0 \quad = 20\%$$
$$\Delta X_1 \quad = 100 + 100 \ \ln I_0 \ (I_0 \geqslant 0)$$

Here, time $t = 0$ is now and $t = 1$ is one year from now. Also X_0 and X_1 stand for the firm's current income and the income one year from now, respectively. I_0 is the investment and ΔX_1 is the additional income one year from now resulting from the new investment. Thus, if investment I_0 is undertaken now, the total income one period from now will be $X_1^* = X_1 + \Delta X_1$. After reaching the optimal investment, the firm distributes as dividends all cash available now (D_0) and one period from now (D_1).

(a) Find the optimal investment and the cash dividends D_0, D_1. What is the value of the firm V_0?

(b) If $D_0 = \$500$, determine the external financing EF_0 and the dividend D_1 and calculate the value of the firm. Compare to your result in (a) above.

19.15 Consider a one-period case with full certainty and perfect capital markets. Firms and individuals can borrow and lend at 5%. Assume X_0 = 0, and X_1 is a function of the investment I_0 as follows:

$$X_1 = 1000 - 1000 \, e^{-0.002I_0}$$

Here X_0 and X_1 is the firm's income now and one year from now respectively.

(a) What is the optimal amount to be invested at time t_0?
(b) What is the value of the firm?
(c) What must be the cash dividends D_0 and D_1 if they are to be of equal amounts (ie. if $D_0 = D_1$)?
(d) Determine the external financing EF_0 required to sustain the dividend policy of (c).

19.16 Consider a two-period case with full certainty and perfect capital markets (note that now there are *three* relevant points in time: t_0, t_1, and t_2). Investment at time t_0 will yield *net* return at time t_1 *only*, in accordance with the following schedule:

Marginal Investment at t_0	Marginal Net Return at t_1
$	$
100	80
100	50
100	20
100	6
100	1

Investment at time t_1 will yield *net* return at time t_2 *only*, in accordance with the following schedule:

Marginal Investment at t_1	Marginal Net Return at t_2
$	$
100	50
100	40
100	30
100	20
100	10
100	10

If the firm does not invest, its income in all three periods is zero, namely $X_0 = X_1 = X_2 = 0$.

The firm decides to undertake some of the above investments. Furthermore it adopts a dividend policy such that dividends increase each year by 20%. At the end of period t_2 the firm is liquidated and its liquidation value is distributed to shareholders.

Determine the optimal investment, the dividends and the external financing for times t_0, t_1, and t_2 assuming a borrowing and lending rate of 12% in both periods.

19.17   One important consequence of equal borrowing and lending rates facing the individual, as we have seen in Chapter 4, is that the wealth of an individual depends on his or her investment decision, not consumption decision. This problem deals with the implication of the above conclusion to the firm by illustrating that one can apply the investment-consumption analysis of Chapter 4 to the question of the impact of dividend policy in perfect and imperfect markets. Assume a framework of one period under *full certainty* where transactions take place at the beginning of the period and the firm is liquidated at the end of the period. Past investments will give the firm income at the beginning of the period (time t_0) in an amount equal to $X_0 = \$10,000$. If no additional investment takes place at time t_0, then the income at the end of the period (time t_1) will be $X_1 = \$5,000$. However, if new investment is made at time t_0, the income at t_1 will be $X_1^* = X_1 + \Delta X_1$, where ΔX_1 is the return (at t_1) on the investment that was made at t_0. The firm faces the following investment projects — all independent of one another:

Project	Investment Required at t_0	Return at t_1
	$	$
A	800	1,200
B	1,500	1,600
C	700	800
D	2,300	3,200
E	400	600
F	350	500
G	1,000	1,400

Assume that the lending and borrowing rate is 20%. The firm is fully equity financed and it has no liabilities.

(a) If the firm makes no investment at the current time (time t_0), what is the total value of the firm?

(b) Which investment projects should the firm undertake and which should it reject? What is the total investment amount at the current time, and what will be the total return on this investment at time t_1? What is the total value of the firm after making the investments?

(c) Suppose the firm distributes all its income except amounts allocated to new investment to stockholders as dividends. If no investment is made at the current time, what will be the current dividend (D_0) and the end-of-period dividend (D_1)? Using the PV of dividends what is the present value of this dividend stream and how does it compare with the value of the firm?

(d) Now suppose the firm undertakes and invests in all the profitable investment projects out of A through G. If the firm does not engage in any borrowing, what is the current dividend (D_0) and the future dividend (D_1)? Using the PV of dividends what is the value of the firm in this case?

(e) It is known that stockholders prefer high dividend at t_0. In order to satisfy the stockholders the firm decides to borrow $5,000 at time t_0. The money will be used to finance the investment and any left-over will be distributed as dividends. What are D_0 and D_1 in this case? What is the value of the firm? Compare your answers to parts (c) and (d).

(f) Suppose now that the market is imperfect and the firm and stockholders cannot borrow at all, but they can lend at 20%. The firm decides to pay out $D_0 = \$8,250$. What investments does it make? What is D_1? Does the dividend policy affect the value of the firm in this case? Why? Can you indicate the optimum dividend policy?

(g) Suppose now that the firm can borrow and lend money. However, for each $100 (or a fraction of $100) that it borrows it pays apart from the 20% interest also transaction costs (banker's fee or commission) of $10. The stockholders do not face such transaction cost. What projects would you suggest the firm to undertake? What is the *NPV* of the firm if it pays out $D_0 = \$5,150$? What is the *NPV* of the firm if it pays out $D_0 = \$8,250$? Is dividend policy relevant in this case? If yes, what is the optimal dividend policy? Illustrate your answer graphically.

APPENDIX 19A DERIVATION OF INVESTORS OPPORTUNITY SET

In order to formalize this discussion, we assume a one period model in which the firm knows its true economic earnings of the past period with certainty, but the stockholder does not. E' denotes the true earnings per share figure known by the firm, and E symbolizes the earnings figure reported to shareholders. Now let us assume that the firm declares a dividend of M dollars per share, such that

$$M = q'E', \qquad (A1)$$

where q' is some number that represents the proportion of true earnings paid out as dividends. Symbolizing the stockholder per share after-tax income by Y, we obtain

$$Y = (1 - T_p)q'E' + (1 - T_g)(1 - q')E' = (1 - T_g)E' + (T_g - T_p)q'E' \quad (A2)$$

Note that in spite of the fact that q' and E' are unknown to the stockholders, the product $q'E'$ is known with certainty since it is the cash dividend, M, paid by the firm. However, since E' remains unknown, stockholders view Y as a random variable.

The expected value of Y is then given by

$$\bar{Y} = (1 - T_g)\bar{E}' + (T_g - T_p)M \tag{A3}$$

where the bar indicates the expected value. Assuming for simplicity, and without loss of generality, that $\bar{E}' = E$, and considering that M is by definition also equal to reported earnings per share, E, multiplied by the reported dividend payment, q, equation (A3) can be rewritten as follows:

$$\bar{Y} = (1 - T_g)E + (T_g - T_p)qE \tag{A4}$$

A glance at equation (A2) above indicates that the variability of E' determines the variability of Y. Thus, from equation (A2) we have,

$$\sigma_Y = (1 - T_g)\sigma_{E'} \tag{A5}$$

where σ_Y denotes the standard deviation of Y. (Recall that $q'E' = M$ is known to the investor with certainty.) Following our argument in the text that one can view the variability of E' as a *conditional* variability that decreases as the reported dividend payout, q, increases, we write

$$\sigma_{E'} = (1 - q)\sigma_{E''}, \tag{A6}$$

where $\sigma_{E''}$ denotes the maximum value attained by the standard deviation of E' when the firm retains all earnings. Substituting equation (A6) into equation (A5) yields,

$$\sigma_Y = (1 - T_g)(1 - q)\sigma_{E''}. \tag{A7}$$

Employing (A4) and (A7) to eliminate q, we obtain,

$$\bar{Y} = E(1 - T_p) + E \frac{(T_p - T_g)}{(1 - T_g)} \frac{\sigma_Y}{\sigma_{E''}} \tag{A8}$$

SELECTED REFERENCES

Aharony, J. and Swary, Itzhak, "Quarterly Dividend and Earnings Announcements and Stockholders' Returns: An Empirical Analysis", *The Journal of Finance*, March 1980.

Ang, James S., "Dividend Policy: Informational Content or Partial Adjustment?" *The Review of Economics and Statistics*, February 1975.

Bar-Yosef, Sasson and Kolodny, Richard, "Dividend Policy and Capital Market Theory", *Review of Economics and Statistics*, May 1976.

Ben-Zion, U. and Shalit, S. S., "Size, Leverage and Dividend Record as Determinants of Equity Risk", *Journal of Finance*, September 1975.

Bhattacharya, Sudipto, "Imperfect Information, Dividend Policy and 'The Bird in the Hand' Fallacy", *The Bell Journal of Economics*, Spring, 1979.

Black, Fischer, "The Dividend Puzzle", *Journal of Portfolio Management*, Winter 1976.

Black, Fisher and Schjoles, Myron, "The Effects of Dividend Yield and Dividend Policy on Common Stock Prices and Returns", *Journal of Financial Economics*, 1974.

Blume, Marshall E., "Stock Returns and Dividend Yields: Some More Evidence", *The Review of Economics and Statistics,* November 1980.

Bradford, David, "The Incidence and Allocation Effect of a Tax on Corporate Distributions", NBER Working Paper No. 349, May 1979.

Brennan, Michael J., "A Note on Dividend Irrelevance and the Gordon Valuation Model", *Journal of Finance*, December 1971.

Brigham, Eugene F. and Gordon, Myron J., "Leverage, Dividend Policy and the Cost of Capital", *Journal of Finance*, March 1968.

Brittain, John A., *Corporate Dividend Policy*, Washington, D.C.: The Brookings Institution, 1966.

Charest, G., "Dividend Information, Stock Returns and Market Efficiency — II", *Journal of Financial Economics*, June/September 1978.

Chen, Carl R., "The Dividend and Investment Decisions of Firms: A Varying Parameter Approach", *Journal of the Midwest Finance Association*, Vol. 9, 1980.

Darling, Paul G., "The Influence of Expectations and Liquidity on Dividend Policy", *Journal of Political Economy*, June 1957.

DeAngelo, Harry and Masulis, Ronald W., "Leverage and Dividend Irrelevancy Under Corporate and Personal Taxation", *Journal of Finance*, May 1980.

Dhrymes, Phoebus J., and Kurz, Mordicai, "On the Dividend Policy of Electric Utilities", *Review of Economics and Statistics*, February 1964.

Edwards, Charles E. and Hilton, James G., "Stockholders' Returns: Dividend or Earnings? Words of Caution", *Mississippi Valley Journal of Business and Economics*, Fall 1970.

Elton, Edwin J. and Gruber, Martin, J., "Marginal Stockholder Tax Rates and the Clientele Effect", *Review of Economics and Statistics*, February 1970.

Fama, Eugene F. and Babiak, Harvey, "Dividend Policy: An Empirical Analysis", *Journal of the American Statistical Association*, December 1968.

Feldstein, Martin, "Corporate Taxation and Dividend Behavior", *Review of Economic Studies*, 1970.

Foster, T. W. III and Vickrey, D., "The Information Content of Stock Dividend Announcements", *Accounting Review*, April 1978.

Friend, Irwin and Puckett, Marshall, "Dividends and Stock Prices", *American Economic Review*, September 1964.

Gordon, Myron J., "Optimal Investment and Financing Policy", *Journal of Finance*, May 1963.

Gordon, Myron J., *The Investment, Financing and Valuation of the Corporation*, Homewood, Ill.: Richard D. Irwin, Inc., 1964.

Gupta, M. C. and Walker, D.A., "Dividend Disbursal Practices in Commercial Banking", *Journal of Financial and Quantitative Analysis*, September 1975.

Higgens, Robert C., "The Corporate Dividend-Saving Decision", *Journal of Financial and Quantitative Analysis*, March 1972.

Keane, Simon, "Dividends and the Resolution of Uncertainty", *Journal of Business Finance & Accounting*, Autumn, 1974.

Krainer, Robert E., "A Pedagogic Note on Dividend Policy", *Journal of Financial and Quantitative Analysis*, September 1971.

Laub, P. M., "On the Informational Content of Dividends", *Journal of Business*, January 1976.

Lee, C. F., "Functional Form and the Dividend Effect in the Electric Utility Industry", *Journal of Finance,* December 1976.

Lerner, Eugene, M. and Carleton, Willard T., *A Theory of Financial Analysis*, New York: Harcourt Brace Jovanovich, 1966.

Litzenberger, R. H. and Ramaswamy, K., "The Effect of Personal Taxes and Dividends on Capital Asset Prices: Theory and Empirical Evidence", *Journal of Financial Economics*, June 1979.

Litzenberger, R. H. and Van Horne, J. C., "Elimination of the Double Taxation of Dividends and Corporate Financial Policy", *Journal of Finance*, June 1978.

Lintner, John, "Distribution of Incomes of Corporations Among Dividends, Retained Earnings and Taxes", *American Economic Review*, May 1956.

Long, J. B., Jr., "The Market Valuation of Cash Dividends: A Case to Consider", *Journal of Financial Economics*, June/September 1978.

Mayne, Lucille S., "Bank Dividend Policy and Holding Company Affiliation. Preliminary Programme of the 15th Annual Conference of the Western Finance Association", *Journal of Financial and Quantitative Analysis*, June 1980.

McDonald, J. G., Jacquillat, B. and Nussbaum, M., "Dividend, Investment and Financing Decisions: Empirical Evidence on French Firms", *Journal of Financial and Quantitative Analysis*, December 1975.

McEnally, Richard W., "An Evaluation of Some Costs and Consequences of Dividend-Oriented Investment Strategies", *Journal of Business Research*, January 1974.

Mehta, D. R., "The Impact of Outstanding Convertible Bonds on Corporate Dividend Policy", *Journal of Finance*, May 1976.

Michel, Allen, "Industry Influence on Dividend Policy", *Financial Management*, Autumn 1979.

Miller, Merton H. and Modigliani, Franco, "Dividend Policy, Growth and the Valuation of Shares", *Journal of Business*, October 1961.

Miller, Merton and Scholes, Myron, "Dividends and Taxes", *Journal of Financial Economics*, December 1978.

Moore, Basil, "Equity Values and Inflation: The Importance of Dividends", *Lloyds Bank Review*, July 1980.

Petit, R. R., "The Impact of Dividend and Earnings Announcements: A Reconcilliation", *Journal of Business*, January 1976.

Petit, R. R., "Taxes, Transactions Costs and the Clientele Effect of Dividends", *Journal of Financial Economics*, December 1977.

Pogue, Thomas F., "A Cross-Section Study of the Relationship between Dividends and Investments", Yale Economic Essays, Fall, 1971.

Porteus, Evan L., "On Optimal Dividend, Reinvestment, and Liquidation Policies for the Firm", *Operations Research*, September-October 1977.

Pye, Gordon, "Preferential Tax Treatment of Capital Gains, Optimal Dividend Policy, and Capital Budgeting", *Quarterly Journal of Economics*, May 1972.

Ryan, Terence M., "Dividend Policy and Market Valuation in British Industry", *Journal of Business Finance & Accounting*, Autumn 1974.

Stapleton, R. C. and Burke, C. M., "Taxes, the Cost of Capital and the Theory of Investment. A Generalisation to the Imputation System of Dividend Taxation", *Economic Journal*, December 1975.

Van Horne, James C. and McDonald, John G., "Dividend Policy and New Equity Financing", *Journal of Finance*, May 1971.

West, Richard R. and Bierman, Harold, Jr., "Corporate Dividend Policy and Pre-emptive Security Issues", *Journal of Business*, January 1968.

Watts, Ross, "The Information Content of Dividends", *Journal of Business*, April 1973.

Wilkes, F. M., "Dividend Policy and Investment Appraisal in Imperfect Capital Markets", *Journal of Business Finance and Accounting*, Vol. 4, No. 2, 1977.

Williams, John B., *The Theory of Investment Value*, Cambridge, Mass: Harvard University Press, 1938.

20

Capital Investment Decisions under Capital Rationing

Throughout the book we have made the implicit assumption that the capital necessary to finance a given investment project is always available to the firm, at some cost of course. And it is this cost of capital which constitutes the appropriate discount rate for evaluating cash flows. In this chapter we change our viewpoint somewhat in order to focus attention on an analogous problem which often confronts many firms in practice. For such firms the amount of capital which can be invested in any time period is more or less fixed, independent of the capital market. Hence their capital budgeting problem involves the allocation of scarce capital resources among competing economically desirable projects, not all of which can be carried out due to a capital (or other) constraint. This problem is often referred to as "capital rationing".

THE NATURE OF CAPITAL RATIONING

Despite its name, a capital rationing situation can arise for a variety of reasons, not all of which are concerned with the capital market *per se*. Of course some far-reaching imperfection in the capital markets may preclude the raising of additional debt and/or equity beyond some stipulated amount, but more often than not the restriction on the supply of capital reflects *non-capital* constraints or bottlenecks within the firm. For example, the supply of key personnel necessary to carry out the projects may be severely limited, thereby restricting the dollar amount of feasible investment. Similarly, considerations of management time may preclude the adoption of programs beyond some level. For example, the board of directors may insist on reviewing and approving all major projects, thereby limiting the overall scope of investment. A classic example of such constraints on capital investment is provided by a co-operative or collective enterprise which does *not* employ hired labor. (Israel's Kibbutzim, i.e. collective

513

settlements, provide one such example.) No matter how ample the supply of capital or how attractive the projects may be, once the fixed supply of labor has been allocated no more investment projects can be executed.

Of course it might well be argued that such constaints on a firm's freedom to invest should more properly be called "labor" or "management" constraints rather than capital constraints. But whatever their origin all of these restrictions operate so as to limit or fix the maximum amount of investment which can be undertaken by the firm. Hence, for simplicity, it is very convenient to discuss the analytical problems which arise from such complex situations *as if* a capital constraint on the total amount of investment funds had been imposed, thereby avoiding the necessity to discuss the difficult problems of labor or management relations or of technology which in reality are often the underlying causes of the necessity to ration capital.

Finally, the reader should be cautioned that to the professional economist the capital rationing problem, as we have defined it, represents a "short-run" problem. In the long run additional personnel can be trained, top management can be recruited or authority can be delegated thereby removing the investment bottlenecks. But in this context, it is well to recall the dictum of Lord Keynes (the most famous economist of his time) that "in the long run we are all dead". Investment decisions have to be taken *now* and it is of little solace to be told that somewhere over the rainbow lies a better world in which all of the required human and capital resources are always available. For the remainder of this chapter we shall be concerned, therefore, with the practical question of how to function within the constraints as they exist. Admittedly all such solutions are sub-optimal in the sense that the firm can always improve its situation by removing the constraint. But that takes time, and as you know by now, time is also a very scarce resource.

ANALYZING CAPITAL RATIONING PROBLEMS: A FIRST APPROXIMATION

To facilitate the analysis we shall follow Henry Kissinger and adopt a step by step approach to the question of capital rationing; first considering relatively simple questions and then going on to more complex, and therefore more realistic, problems.

Consider the example of a firm faced with a variety of investment proposals and a fixed budget, on the assumption that:

(1)   The timing and magnitude of the cash flows of all projects are known at the outset with complete certainty.

(2)   The cost of capital is known (*independent* of the investment decisions under consideration) so that the present values of all of the projects are also given.

(3)   All projects are strictly independent, i.e. the execution of one project does not affect the costs and benefits of some other project.

Under these simplifying assumptions our problem becomes one of how to select among those projects which have *positive* net present values.

Single Period Case

In a classic article Lorie and Savage[1] proposed a solution to the rationing problem when all outlays are assumed to take place in a single period. Their solution was to rank all projects by the ratio of present value to investment outlay, and then select from the top of the list until the budget is exhausted. The procedure is simple and easily understood; however, it depends on a set of very limiting and unrealistic assumptions: namely that cash flows are known; the cost of capital is independent of the investment decision; mutually exclusive projects are ruled out; and all outlays occur in a single period of time so that the budget constraint applies to a single period.

Multiperiod Case

Lorie and Savage drop the latter restriction by also considering the selection process in which the budget limitation occurs in more than one period. Like so many seminal articles in finance and economics it is the question they asked, and not the particular solution which they proposed, which is of lasting interest. By formulating the capital rationing problem in a multiperiod context they paved the way for the application of mathematical programming techniques to the analysis of capital budgeting decisions.[2]

A PRIMER ON LINEAR PROGRAMMING

Before turning to the linear programming (LP) solution of the capital rationing problem, let us digress very briefly on the LP technique itself. Those readers who already *know* that LP is too complicated for them to understand can skip on to the next section; those who remain are in for a very pleasant surprise. For our purposes, as *consumers* of results, the LP technique can be made sufficiently clear by means of a numerical example. Of course, if there are any "do it yourselfers" in the audience they had better sign up for a course in LP.[3]

1 See J. H. Lorie and L. J. Savage, "Three Problems in the Rationing of Capital", *Journal of Business*, October 1955.

2 Lorie and Savage proposed a rather cumbersome procedure based on Lagrangian multipliers: subsequently, H. M. Weingartner extended this approach by applying linear programming techniques; see his *Mathematical Programming and the Analysis of Capital Budgeting Problems*, Englewood Cliffs N. J., Prentice-Hall, 1963.

3 Those readers who wish to pursue the application of LP to financial decision-making somewhat further should read Weingartner, *op. cit.* A painless introduction to the field is provided by Gerald Salkin and Jonathan Kornbluth, *Linear Programming in Financial Planning*, London, Haymarket Publishing, 1973.

Financial managers are almost continuously confronted by the necessity to allocate scarce resources over a very wide range of alternative courses of action. Before computers became available for corporate data processing, only a small number of alternative strategies could be considered explicitly. Now with the aid of high-speed digital computers and powerful mathematical techniques such as LP, the firm can examine very large-scale choice problems in which the number of alternatives is virtually unlimited in the relevant range. Since the process of choosing an optimal strategy invariably involves the comparison of the "value" to the firm of various alternative uses of its resources, the LP technique has the further advantage, as we shall see below, of both allocating and evaluating scarce resources. Thus the LP technique can also provide decision-makers with some very insightful information regarding the marginal value of resources. All LP problems have certain common features:

(a)   The problem can be defined in terms of a series of possible courses of action or activities.
(b)   The decision-makers must choose the best level for each activity.
(c)   This choice is limited by the availability of scarce inputs.
(d)   Alternative strategies are capable of being compared in terms of a well-defined quantity such as money, profits, net present value, etc.

In order to illustrate the LP technique let us consider a simple example of a firm confronted by two possible courses of action:

(1)   operating swimming pools in Florida.
(2)   operating sauna baths in Michigan.

Table 20.1 summarizes the necessary data for each activity. In our hypothetical (and incidentally very cheap) world, building a swimming pool entails investment outlays of $3 and $4 in periods 1 and 2 respectively; while a sauna bath requires an outlay of $4 in the first period and $2 in the second. The *NPVs* of both types of project are positive: $6 for each swimming pool and $7 for each bath.

The two investment opportunities — swimming pools or saunas — are *not* mutually exclusive. Moreover, the firm can invest in more than one pool or bath. The only constraint on the firm's freedom of action is an assumed restriction on the total money resources available for investment in each of the two

Table 20.1

	Swimming Pool	Sauna Bath
Outlays:		
Period 1	3	4
Period 2	4	2
Net Present Value	6	7

outlay periods. For our purposes we shall assume that only $10 are available in each of the periods. Thus the firm is faced with a capital rationing situation.

The problem confronting the firm is to choose among its investment opportunities (pools and/or saunas) so as to maximize net present value. If we denote by the letters X_p and X_s the number (or fractions) of pools and saunas which are constructed,[4] this choice can be set out as a linear programming problem:

Maximize $NPV = 6X_p + 7X_s$

Subject to:
$$3X_p + 4X_s \leqslant 10$$
$$4X_p + 2X_s \leqslant 10$$
$$X_p, X_s \geqslant 0$$

The first equation sets out the so-called *objective function*, in our case the *NPV* to be earned from operating saunas and swimming pools, which is to be maximized. The next two inequalities set out the budget constraints in each of the two periods. The last line restricts us to positive (or zero) investment; we cannot build negative pools or saunas, or in the jargon of Wall Street we cannot sell them short.

The simplicity of our problem permits us to visualize the solution by utilizing a simple graphical device. (In practice, complex LP problems are usually solved by the simplex method which involves a procedure of successive iterations.) Figure 20.1 plots the two linear constraints of periods 1 and 2.[5] The first period constraint restricts the firm to combinations of pools and saunas below the line extending from $3\frac{1}{3}$ on the vertical axis, to $2\frac{1}{2}$ on the horizontal axis. The interpretation of this constraint is straightforward. If all the available resources in period 1 are devoted to the investment in swimming pools $3\frac{1}{3}$ can be built. Conversely, if all of the first period resources are devoted to saunas, $2\frac{1}{2}$ can be built. The area under the first period constraint gives the combinations of pools and saunas which *satisfy* that constraint. Similarly, the area under the second period constraint contains those combinations of pools and saunas which satisfy the second period constraint. Since we also have the constraints, $X_p \geqslant 0$, and $X_s \geqslant 0$, it follows that all *feasible* investment combinations, i.e. those which satisfy all constraints, lie in the cross-hatched area of Fig. 20.1. The optimal solution, i.e. that combination which maximizes *NPV*, is given by the

---

4 A decision to build a fraction (say one half) of a pool or sauna could be interpreted as a partnership arrangement.

5 The intercepts on the two axes are found by replacing the two inequalities with equalities and solving them first on the assumption that $X_s = 0$, and then on the assumption that $X_p = 0$. For example, taking the constraint in the first period, the intercepts on the vertical and horizontal axes are $3\frac{1}{3}$ and $2\frac{1}{2}$ respectively:

$$3X_p + 4X_s = 10$$

Setting $X_s = 0$, we have
$$3X_p = 10$$
$$X_p = 3\tfrac{1}{3}$$

Setting $X_p = 0$, we have
$$4X_s = 10$$
$$X_s = 2\tfrac{1}{2}$$

The intercepts of the second period constraint, $2\frac{1}{2}$ and 5, can be derived in a similar manner.

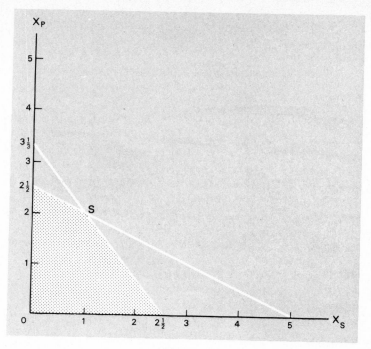

Fig. 20.1

inflection point denoted by the letter S in the diagram. This point corresponds to an investment in two swimming pools and one sauna, and results in a total *NPV* of 19. No other *feasible* combination lies above point S (in a north-easterly direction) and therefore no other combination can have a greater *NPV*.

In order to show graphically that S is the optimal solution Fig. 20.2 superimposes a set of "equal-present value" lines on the set of feasible solutions. The slopes of these lines are given by the objective function $NPV = 6X_p + 7X_s$. Clearly point S permits us to maximize *NPV*, i.e. reach the highest equal-present value line, without violating any of the constraints.

The fact that the budget is exhausted in both periods suggests that the company could increase its *NPV* if additional resources were available for investment in either of the two periods. This is true, and can readily be shown, by adding $1 to the $10 already available in period 1 and solving the original problem subject to the constraints that

$$3X_p + 4X_s \leqslant 11$$
$$4X_p + 2X_s \leqslant 10$$

This results in a *NPV* of 20.6, an increase of 1.6 over the previous result. Similarly, we can relax the second period constraint by solving the original problem subject to the constraints:

$$3X_p + 4X_s \leqslant 10$$
$$4X_p + 2X_s \leqslant 11$$

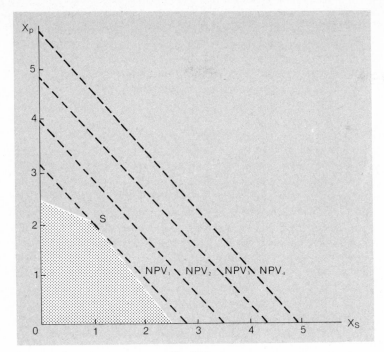

Fig. 20.2

The addition of $1 of resources in period 2 results in a total *NPV* of 19.3, i.e. an increase in *NPV* of 0.3 compared with the original solution. This procedure provides us with an estimate of the value of an extra dollar of resources in each of the two periods, 1.6 and 0.3 respectively. These two values represent the "marginal value" to the firm of the budget constraints and are obtained by comparing the total *NPV with* and *without* the extra dollar of resources. In LP such values are usually referred to as *dual variables* or *shadow prices*; from the viewpoint of economics they represent (whatever the name) the opportunity costs of using a unit of the firm's resources.

The LP technique has the advantage of providing the decision-maker with both the optimal allocation *and* the optimal valuation, i.e. shadow prices, of the resources being used. This follows from the fact that any LP maximization problem can always be rewritten as a corresponding minimization problem, and vice versa. Thus from our original two-period investment problem we can construct its "dual":

Minimize $V = 10Y_1 + 10Y_2$

Subject to: $3Y_1 + 4Y_2 \geqslant 6$
$4Y_1 + 2Y_2 \geqslant 7$
$Y_1,\ Y_2 \geqslant 0$

where Y_1 and Y_2 denote the dual variables. If, as before, we plot and solve this cost minimization version of the problem, we find that $Y_1 = 1\frac{3}{5}$ and $Y_2 = \frac{3}{10}$.

Thus the dual variables of the LP technique are economically meaningful measures of the value of the marginal resources (in our case the marginal dollar of each period's budget) used in the optimal investment program. These variables measure the alternative cost to the firm (in terms of foregone income) of the budget constraints. Thus the LP model automatically generates the opportunity costs of funds in each of the planning periods.

THE LP FORMULATION OF THE CAPITAL RATIONING PROBLEM

Having briefly reviewed some of the underlying principles of the LP model, let us apply this type of model to the two-period capital rationing problem which was suggested by Lorie and Savage (see Table 20.2). In this case the selection process is subject to restrictions on the total amount of dollar investment in each of the periods: $50 in period 1 and $20 in the second period. Unlike our previous example, however, a particular project can only be executed once or fractionally. If we restrict the solution set to whole projects, integer programming methods must be utilized. Once again, we assume that the *NPVs* of the projects are given; hence the problem confronting the firm is to allocate the fixed investment budget so as to maximize its *NPV*.

Table 20.2

Projects	NPV	Present Value of Outlays	
		Period 1	Period 2
1	14	12	3
2	17	54	7
3	17	6	6
4	15	6	2
5	40	30	35
6	12	6	6
7	14	48	4
8	10	36	3
9	12	18	3

This problem can readily be formulated in LP form. Let X_j ($j = 1, 2, \ldots,$ 9) denote the proportion of the *j*th project which is executed. By restricting $0 \leqslant X_j \leqslant 1$ we ensure that a project can only be executed once while also allowing for the acceptance of partial (i.e. fractional) projects. The LP model can be written as:

Maximize $NPV = 14X_1 + 17X_2 + \ldots + 10X_8 + 12X_9$

Subject to the two budget constraints:

$$12X_1 + 54X_2 + \ldots + 36X_8 + 18X_9 \leqslant 50$$
$$3X_1 + 7X_2 + \ldots + 3X_8 + 3X_9 \leqslant 20$$
$$0 \leqslant X_j \leqslant 1 \; (j = 1, 2, \ldots 9)$$

This problem can be solved by adding so-called *slack variables* (S_1 and S_2) to convert the inequalities to equalities:

$$12X_1 + 54X_2 + \ldots + 36X_8 + 18X_9 + S_1 = 50$$
$$3X_1 + 7X_2 + \ldots + 3X_8 + 3X_9 + S_2 = 20$$
$$X_1 + q_1 = 1 \quad X_4 + q_4 = 1 \quad X_7 + q_7 = 1$$
$$X_2 + q_2 = 1 \quad X_5 + q_5 = 1 \quad X_8 + q_8 = 1$$
$$X_3 + q_3 = 1 \quad X_6 + q_6 = 1 \quad X_9 + q_9 = 1$$

The solution to the problem is similar in principle to the one presented in the preceding section, but now requires more calculations. The model examines all feasible sets of projects and chooses the portfolio of projects with a maximum *NPV*.

The solution is:

$$NPV^* = \$70.27$$

$$S^*_1 = 0 \qquad\qquad S^*_2 = 0$$
$$X_1^* = 1.0 \quad X_4^* = 1.0 \quad X_7^* = 0.045$$
$$X_2^* = 0.0 \quad X_5^* = 0.0 \quad X_8^* = 0.0$$
$$X_3^* = 1.0 \quad X_6^* = 0.97 \quad X_9^* = 1.0$$

where stars denote the *optimal* values of the variables. The two slack variables, S_1 and S_2, are zero which indicates that the available budget is exhausted in both periods. The optimal portfolio consists of projects 1, 3, 4 and 9 *in toto* (i.e. those for whom $X^* = 1.0$). The solution $X_6^* = 0.97$ and $X_7^* = 0.045$ indicates that only a fraction of projects 6 and 7 (97% and 4½%, respectively) should be undertaken. If the partial solution is meaningful (e.g. building different size parking lots) the LP solution can be implemented at once. However, if the execution of partial projects is not feasible a more detailed study using the information on alternative costs provided by the dual can help to determine which of the projects should be executed.[6]

In the optimal solution the values of the two dual variables associated with the budget constraints are $p_1^* = 0.136$ and $p_2^* = 1.864$, where p_1^* and p_2^* denote the shadow prices of the budget constraints in the first and second periods. The interpretation of these variables is straightforward: for example, $p_1^* = 0.136$ implies that if the total capital available for investment in period one were increased by 1 dollar, total *NPV* would rise by $0.136. Similarly an addition of 1 dollar to the second period's budget would increase total *NPV* by $1.864. These figures, therefore, represent the opportunity cost of funds to the firm, and indicate that the budget restriction in period 2 is the more serious of the two.

The model has nine more dual variables; one associated with each of the nine projects. The values of those associated with projects which are accepted *in toto* are positive and indicate the *net* values of the investment after deducting

---

6 Fractional problems are less of a problem than might appear at first glance. The number of fractional projects cannot exceed the number of time periods for which budget constraints exist.

use of the rationed capital resources, valued at the shadow price. For example the value for project 1, μ_1*, is **6.776**:

$$\mu_1{}^* = 14 - (12 \times 0.136 + 3 \times 1.864) = \mathbf{6.776}$$

Since the project has a positive net present value, after allowing for the opportunity cost of the funds used in periods 1 and 2, it is accepted. On the other hand, projects which are completely rejected or only partially accepted have a zero shadow price, i.e. $\mu_j^* = 0$. The *net* values of such projects are either zero or negative, for example the net value of project 6 which is partially accepted is *zero*:

$$\mu_6^* = 12 - (6 \times 0.136 + 6 \times 1.864) = 0$$

A RULE OF THUMB APPROXIMATION

The simple LP model of the Lorie and Savage two-period capital rationing problem has much to recommend it. The problem is easy to formulate, the data inputs are available and the LP can be given an intuitively appealing economic interpretation in terms of the opportunity costs or the shadow prices of the constraints. Upon reflection, however, the model has one particularly glaring defect. Although the opportunity cost of funds is measured by the value of the dual variables, the objective function is set out in terms of the net present values of the projects, calculated at some predetermined arbitrary discount rate. Clearly the opportunity cost of scarce funds should be used to calculate the *NPV*; but this leads to an apparent dilemma, because the opportunity costs were determined "after" the *NPVs* were already stipulated.

These difficulties can be overcome by applying the insights drawn from the LP model in an informal manner without resorting to the mathematical apparatus. Clearly, the key to such an application is the estimation of the relevant future discount rates using forecasts of the demand and supply for funds. These rates should always reflect the shadow price or opportunity cost of the funds, although in some cases the internal opportunity cost may be equal to some external borrowing or lending rate.[7]

This argument can be clarified by considering the two highly simplified cases drawn in Figs. 20.3(a) and 20.3(b). Figure 20.3(a) graphs the familiar diagram from economic theory of the firm's demand for investment funds in a perfect capital market under certainty. For simplicity, the projects facing the firm are assumed to be independent and infinitely divisible and therefore the opportunity set can be drawn as a continuous curve in descending order of the projects' internal rates of return.

Given the assumption of a perfect capital market with complete certainty

---

[7] This point is emphasized by Tsvi Ophir, "Optimum Capital Budgeting: Lessons of a Linear Programming Formulation", Research Report No. 6, School of Business Administration, The Hebrew University, Jerusalem.

A way to overcome this difficulty can be found in Fred D. Arditti, Richard C. Grinold, and Haim Levy, "The Investment Consumption Decision under Capital Rationing: An Efficient Analysis", *Review of Economic Studies*, July 1973.

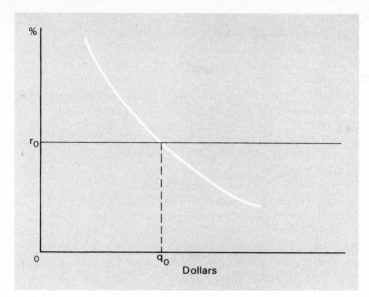

Fig. 20.3a

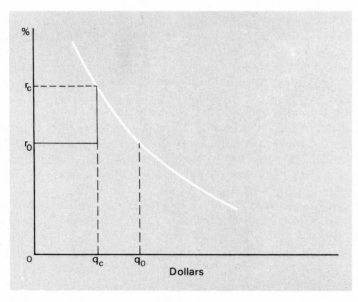

Fig. 20.3b

the supply of funds can be portrayed by the horizontal line drawn at the level of the riskless interest rate r_0, which is the cost of capital. The firm executes all projects with a positive *NPV* (i.e. those with an *IRR* greater than r_0), and the optimum initial outlay is denoted by $0q_0$. Figure 20.3b assumes that for some reason or other the firm is constrained to a total outlay of $0q_c$ dollars. Although the capital funds up to that amount are still made available at a cost of r_0, it is apparent that the opportunity cost or shadow price of the budget constraint is given by r_c which is considerably higher than r_0. If we add one dollar to the budget the firm will earn r_c, and not r_0, on the additional investment. Hence the opportunity cost of funds is given by the internal rate of return of the marginal project which in LP terms corresponds to the value of the dual evaluator of the budget constraint. Thus r_c is the appropriate discount rate to be used in the *NPV* calculation.[8]

A Numerical Example

The use of *NPV* rather than *IRR* for the capital rationing case is imperative once we relax the assumption of independence and permit mutually exclusive projects. This can be clarified by considering a specific example. Consider the hypothetical case of the Gavka Company which is a subsidiary of the Brosh Investment Holding Company. Let us assume that each year the parent company allocates a *fixed sum* of $100,000 to Gavka which serves as the latter's *maximum* capital budget. Gavka is charged 8% interest per year on any funds which it utilizes, but $100,000 constitutes the effective ceiling on Gavka's annual capital expenditure budget.

In 1981 Gavka is faced with four *independent* investment opportunities: Projects 1, 2, 3 and 4, but in each instance there are several alternative ways to execute the projects. These alternatives are designated by the letters of the alphabet a, b or c. Since each project can be executed only once, the alternative ways of carrying out a particular project constitute *mutually exclusive* alternatives.

To simplify our calculations let's further assume that the entire investment outlay is made immediately, that the equal annual net receipts are received at the end of each year, and that the project's terminal (scrap) values are zero. Table 20.3 summarizes the data available to Gavka on the four projects.

Given Gavka's budget constraint of $100,000, which projects should be executed and in which way, i.e., which of the alternative methods should be used to execute the accepted projects? Table 20.3 sets out three possible answers using three well-known decision rules[9]: the *IRR*, *NPV* and profitability index (*PV/I*). As a first step, the *best* alternative is chosen out of the mutually exclusive sets of alternative ways to execute each project. The projects chosen by each evaluation method are set out in Table 20.4. Two striking features of the capital budgets can be readily discerned. First, all four projects are desirable in a world in which the cost of investment funds is 8%. However, the acceptance of the

---

8 In the more general multiperiod case, the firm would make a rough estimate of a diagram such as 20.3b for every relevant future period in which the constraint is expected to be binding, thereby deriving a series of discount rates which reflect the estimated value of the marginal dollar in each period. These rates would then be used to calculate the *NPVs* of the projects currently confronting the firm. And as we have already shown, the *NPV* calculation using differing discount rates over time presents no difficulty (see Chapter 4 above).

9 For details see Chapter 4 above.

Table 20.3

The GAVKA Company

	Initial Investment Outlay ($)	Annual Net Receipts ($)	Project's Duration (in years)	IRR	NPV (k = 8%)	Profitability Index (k = 8%)
Project 1a	15,000	6,000	5	28.7	**8958**	**1.6**
1b	7,000	4,000	3	**32.7**	3308	1.5
Project 2a	50,000	17,000	5	20.8	**17881**	1.4
2b	32,000	12,000	5	25.4	15916	**2.1**
2c	45,000	15,000	5	19.9	14895	1.3
Project 3a	70,000	20,000	8	23.2	**44940**	**1.6**
3b	53,000	20,000	5	**25.7**	26860	1.5
Project 4a	30,000	10,000	5	19,9	9930	1.3
4b	33,000	9,000	8	**21.6**	**18723**	**1.6**
4c	25,000	8,500	5.	20.8	8941	1.4

*Present value ÷ initial investment outlay ($PV ÷ I$)

four projects by each method violates the budget constraint. More importantly, the actual projects chosen differ remarkably in each method. One explanation immediately suggests itself. As we noted in Chapter 4 above, neither the *IRR* nor profitability index are appropriate measures of investment feasibility in mutually exclusive choice situations. Since Gavka is confronted by mutually exclusive choices, our attention will be focused on the *NPV* solution.

Since the budget constraint is violated, one project must be eliminated — in this instance project 3a. The final choice, therefore, is to execute projects 1a, 2a and 4b which entail a total initial outlay of $98,000 which satisfies the $100,000 budget constraint. But is this solution correct? Applying the insights of the LP analysis and Fig. 20.3(b) above, it is clear that in a situation of capital rationing 8% is not the true cost of the funds used. Given additional financing Gavka would also execute project 3a which has an *IRR* of over 23%! Furthermore, the choice between alternatives in the first three projects was made on the implicit assumption that Gavka's opportunity cost was only 8%, which clearly is not the case.

Table 20.4

Projects Chosen and Total Required Outlay by Method of Evaluation

IRR	NPV k = 8%	Profitability Index
1b	1a	1a
2b	2a	2b
3b	3a	3a
4b	4b	4b

	Total Required Outlay	
$125,000	$168,000 (98,000)	$150,000

Table 20.5

Projects Chosen and Total Required Outlay by the *NPV* Method Using Alternative Discount Rates

$k = 8\%$	$k = 16\%$	$k = 22\%$
1a	1a	1a
2a	2b	2b
3a	3a	3b
4b	4b	—
Total Required Outlay		
$168,000	$150,000	$100,000

A way out of our dilemma can be found by applying the *NPV* method using the higher opportunity cost of financing and without violating the budget constraint. This can be done by a process of trial and error (see Table 20.5). The discount rate is raised, in the example to 16%, but the total required investment outlay ($150,000) still exceeds the $100,000 budget constraint. The discount rate is raised again, this time to 22%. At this rate, projects 1a, 2b and 3b are chosen, and the required investment outlay satisfies the constraint.

The striking feature of the solution using the 22% opportunity cost of funds, rather than the arbitrary 8% interest rate, is the significant difference in the composition of the projects chosen. Using the opportunity cost, projects 2b and 3b are chosen; using the irrelevant 8% discount rate, the firm would prefer projects 2a and 3a. Finally, when the 8% method is used the firm satisfies the budget constraint by dropping the third project and executing projects 1a, 2a and 4b.

But which solution is correct? The answer is straightforward. In the best of all possible worlds the budget constraint would be relaxed, Gavka would receive an additional $68,000 in investment funds, and would execute the *NPV* solution using an 8% discount rate (projects 1a, 2a, 3a and 4b would be chosen). The marginal opportunity cost (shadow price) of an additional dollar is 8% and that is the appropriate discount rate. But in the assumed situation in which the $100,00 budget constraint is binding, the opportunity cost of the marginal dollar to Gavka is much higher. Given additional funds, the company would execute a project with a rate of return in excess of 22%. Hence 22%, and not 8%, is the relevant opportunity cost (shadow price) to be applied in this case.

SUMMARY

This chapter has been devoted to the discussion of capital rationing — a situation in which the firm finds the amount of capital which can be invested in particular time periods fixed more or less independently of the capital market. More often than not, the restriction on the supply of capital reflects *non-capital* constraints or bottlenecks within the firm, for example a shortage of some key labor input.

The capital rationing problem can be analyzed using the formal framework provided by the linear programming model. The LP model is appropriate for relatively large-scale resource allocation problems while also providing valuable information regarding the marginal value of scarce resources through its *dual variables* or *shadow prices*. An analysis of the LP model emphasizes the crucial importance of using the appropriate discount rate(s) when evaluating the *NPV* of projects. The appropriate rate is *always* the *opportunity cost* of capital, that is the internal rate of return of the marginal project, since this rate measures the income forgone, or cost, of the budget constraint. In a free unconstrained capital market the external financial cost of capital always equals the opportunity cost; in the typical rationing situation in which the constraint is binding the internal opportunity cost exceeds the external financial cost, and the higher of the two rates is the relevant measure to be used when reaching capital budgeting decisions.

QUESTIONS AND PROBLEMS

20.1 Give two examples of *non-capital* constraints on capital investment.

20.2 Amigus Sport Club Enterprises (ASCE) is confronted by the following two *non-mutually exclusive* opportunities:

(a) Operating tennis clubs in San Francisco.
(b) Operating golf clubs in Los Angeles.

Building a tennis club entails an investment outlay of $50,000 in the first year and $70,000 in the second, while a golf club requires outlays of $75,000 and $35,000 in each of the two years. Assume that the net present value of the tennis clubs project is $40,000 for each, while the *NPV* for the golf clubs is $25,000 each. Finally assume that the total money resources available for investment are $300,000 in the first year, and $280,000 in the second. The ASCE can invest in more than one tennis or golf club.

(a) Set out the firm's choice situation as a linear programming problem. (Denote by the letters X_t and X_g the number of tennis and golf clubs which are constructed and express the amounts of money in thousands of dollars.)

(b) Describe graphically the above problem, and identify the set of *feasible* investment combinations.

(c) Find the optimal solution, i.e. that combination of tennis and golf clubs which maximizes the total *NPV*.

(d) Calculate the maximum total *NPV* of the above combination.

20.3 (a) Answer question 20.2 under the assumption that an additional $100,000 is available to ASCE in the first year.

(b) Calculate the "marginal value" to the firm of the budget constraints, in absolute terms (dollars) and in %.

20.4   (a) Answer question 20.2 under the assumption that an additional $140,000 is available to ASCE in the second year.

       (b) Calculate the "marginal value" to the firm of the budget constraints, in absolute terms (dollars) and in %.

20.5   Rewrite the two-period investment problem of ASCE (in question 20.2) as a corresponding minimization problem (i.e. construct its "dual"). Calculate (in %) the *dual variables* of the budget constraints.

20.6   The Hercules Rubber & Tire Corporation is examining the feasibility of the following seven projects:

Project	NPV	Present Value of Outlays Period 1 (in thousand $)	Period 2
1	3,000	2,500	1,000
2	4,500	3,200	1,800
3	3,900	5,400	600
4	2,500	1,600	1,200
5	3,600	1,100	4,200
6	1,300	300	400
7	1,700	3,700	2,600

Assume that there are restrictions on the total amount of dollar investment in each of the periods: $10 million in period 1 and $6 million in period 2. Assume also that a particular project can only be executed once or fractionally.

       (a) Formulate the LP model for maximizing *NPV*.

       (b) Convert the inequalities (in part (a)) to equalities by adding *slack variables*.

SELECTED REFERENCES

Bernhard, Richard H., "Mathematical Programming Models for Capital Budgeting — A Survey, Generalization, and Critique", *Journal of Financial and Quantitative Analysis*, June 1969.

Bey, R. P. and Porter, R. B., "An Evaluation of Capital Budgeting Portfolio Models Using Simulated Debts", *Engineering Economics*, Fall 1977.

Bhaskar, Krish, "Linear Programming and Capital Budgeting: The Financing Problem", *Journal of Business Finance and Accounting*, Summer 1978.

Bradley, S. P. and Frey, S. C. Jr., "Equivalent Mathematical Programming Models of Pure Capital Rationing", *Journal of Financial and Quantitative Analysis*, June 1978.

Burton, R. M. and Damon, W. W., "On the Existence of a Cost of Capital Under Pure Capital Rationing", *Journal of Finance*, September 1974.

Charnes, A., Cooper, W. W. and Miller, M. H., "Application of Linear Programming to Financial Budgeting and the Costing of Funds", *Journal of Business*, January 1959.

Cheng, Pal L. and Shelton, John P., "A Contribution to the Theory of Capital Budgeting — The Multi-Investment Case", *Journal of Finance*, December 1963.

Cohen, Kalman J. and Elton, Edwin J., "Inter-Temporal Portfolio Analysis Based upon Simulation of Joint Returns", *Management Science*, September 1967.

Cord, Joel, "A Method for Allocating Funds to Investment Projects When Returns are Subject to Uncertainty", *Management Science*, January 1964.

Ederington, L. H. and Henry, W. R., "On Costs of Capital in Programming Approaches to Capital Budgeting", *Journal of Financial and Quantitative Analysis*, December 1979.

Elton, Edwin J., "Capital Rationing and External Discount Rates", *Journal of Finance*, June 1970.

Fogler, H. Russell, "Ranking Techniques and Capital Rationing", *Accounting Review*, January 1972.

Freeland, J. R. and Rosenblatt, M. J., "An Analysis of Linear Programming Formulations for the Capital Rationing Problem", *Engineering Economist*, Fall 1978.

Goldberger, Juval and Paroush, Jacob, "Capital Budgeting of Interdependent Projects", *Management Science*, July 1977.

Hughes, John S. and Lewellen, Wilbur G., "Programming Solutions to Capital Rationing Problems", *Journal of Business Finance & Accounting*, Winter 1974.

Krainer, Robert E., "A Neglected Issue in Capital Rationing — The Asset Demand for Money", *Journal of Finance*, December 1966.

Kryzanowski, Lawrence, Lustig, Peter and Schwab, Bernhard, "Monte Carlo Simulation and Capital Expenditure Decisions — a Case Study", *The Engineering Economist*, Fall 1972.

Lorie, J. H. and Savage, L. J., "Three Problems in Rationing Capital", *Journal of Business*, October 1955.

Myers, Stewart C., "A Note on Linear Programming and Capital Budgeting", *Journal of Finance*, March 1972.

Myers, Stewart C. and Pogue, Gerald A., "A Programming Approach to Corporate Financial Management", *Journal of Finance*, May 1974.

Ophir, T., "Optimum Capital Budgeting Lessons of a Linear Programming Formulation", Research No. 6, The Hebrew University, Israel.

Salkin, G. and Kornbluth, J., *Linear Programming in Financial Planning*, London: Haymarket Publishing Limited, 1973.

Sealey, C. W. Jr., "Utility Maximization and Programming Models for Capital Budgeting", *Journal of Business Finance and Accounting*, Autumn 1978.

Spies, Richard R., "The Dynamics of Corporate Capital Budgeting", *Journal of Finance*, June 1974.

Thompson, H. E., "Mathematical Programming the Capital Asset Pricing Model and Capital Budgeting of Interrelated Projects", *Journal of Finance*, March 1976.

Weingartner, H. M., *Mathematical Programming and the Analysis of Capital Budgeting Problems*, Englewood Cliffs, N.J.: Prentice-Hall, 1963.

Weingartner, H. M., "Capital Rationing: Authors in Search of a Plot", *Journal of Finance*, December 1977.

21

The Lease or Buy Decision

Capital budgeting techniques were developed for the analysis of capital investment decisions. In this chapter we apply the risk-adjusted net present value rule
to the analysis of an alternative means of acquiring the services of productive
assets through leasing.

IMPORTANCE OF LEASING

In general a *lease* can be defined as a contractual relationship in which the
owner of the asset or property (*lessor*) grants to a firm or person (*the lessee*) the
use of the property's services for a specified period of time. Thus in a lease contract, the firm is able to use the leased assets without assuming their ownership.
The idea that leasing can provide an alternative to the use of long-term debt has
been around for many years, but it was not until the early 1950s that the leasing
of capital equipment became a generally accepted method. At present, industrial leasing companies are prepared to offer almost any type of asset. The
use of land, warehouses, manufacturing facilities, retail stores, jet engines,
computers, trucks or even beer kegs all can be acquired by lease. A popular
variant is the so-called "sale and lease-back" — an arrangement in which an institutional investor such as an insurance company or university endowment
fund buys an asset from a firm (or builds a new one to the firm's specifications)
and then leases it back to the firm on a long-term basis (twenty years or more).

Some idea of the magnitude of the leasing industry today can be had from
an examination of the rental revenues of two giants — IBM and Xerox Corporation. The bulk of Xerox's operating revenue is derived from leasing:

Operating Revenue Xerox Corp.
(in millions of dollars)

	1970	1975	1978
(1) Total Operating Revenues	1,636	4,054	5,902
(2) Rentals and Services	1,324	3,316	4,015
(3) Line (2) as % of Line (1)	81%	82%	68%

Throughout the first half of the 1970s income from rentals and services accounted for over 80% of Xerox Corporation's total operating revenues. And although this percentage was somewhat lower in 1978 — 68% — the absolute magnitude of its leasing revenue that year was over 4 billion dollars.

Much the same picture emerges from an examination of IBM:

Operating Revenue of IBM
(in millions of dollars)

	1975	1976	1977	1978	1979
(1) Total Operating Revenues	14,436	16,304	18,133	21,076	22,863
(2) Rentals and Services	9,891	10,345	11,043	12,321	13,390
(3) Line (2) as % of Line (1)	69%	63%	61%	59%	59%

In the case of IBM over 60% of its total operating revenues in the second half of the 1970s was generated by leasing arrangements. Over the five-year period from 1975 – 79 income from rentals and services amounted to 57 billion dollars.

Types of Lease

In general, the types of leases offered in the market today can be classified into two categories: the *operating* lease and the *financial* lease.

The operating lease is not financial in nature and is written for a short period of time; usually for a period substantially shorter than the equipment's useful life. Durations of this type of lease run typically from a few months to a few years; some, however, run for as short as a few hours.

Under an operating lease, the lessor assumes most or all the responsibilities of ownership including maintenance, service, insurance, liability, property taxes, etc. The lessee can cancel an operating lease on short notice and does not involve the long-term fixed future commitment of the financial lease.[1] Thus, the operating lease is similar to renting; a good example of this type of lease is an office copying machine lease.

The *financial lease*, on the other hand, is a contract that is primarily financial in nature; the lessee agrees to pay the lessor a series of payments, the sum of

---

1 See V.J. McGugan, *Competition and Adjustment in the Equipment Leasing Industry,* Boston, Mass.; Federal Reserve Bank of Boston, 1972.

which equals or exceeds the purchase price of the asset. Typically, the total cash flows over the term from the lease payments, the tax savings and the equipment's residual value will be sufficient to pay back the lessor's investment and provide a profit.

Most financial leases are "net" leases, i.e., the fundamental ownership responsibilities such as maintenance, insurance, property and sales taxes are placed upon the *lessee*. And, since the agreement entered into by the lessors are long-term, financial leases are not cancellable by either party. Some contracts, however, provide that in case of unforseen events, the contract can be cancelled but the lessor imposes a substantial pre-payment penalty which will assure the return of his investment and a profit, at least up to the date of termination.[2] Upon termination of the financial lease, the equipment is returned to the lessor, or, as in some cases, the lessee is given the option to purchase the asset.

In the remainder of this chapter we shall devote our attention to the analysis of the long-term financial lease. Given the character of such contracts, the emphasis will be on the analysis of leasing as a "financial decision", i.e. as a substitute for debt-financing.

POSSIBLE ADVANTAGES OF LEASING

Many reasons are given for leasing rather than purchasing assets. Let us critically examine some of the chief claims which are often made on behalf of leasing.

Release of Cash

A lease arrangement provides "complete financing" in the sense that the lessee avoids the cash downpayment required to purchase the asset. Moreover, the firm may benefit if the rental payments are "slower" than the relevant instalment payments. In addition, the sale and lease-back contract, as we have already noted, permits the extension of such arrangements to existing equipment already owned by the firm.

Shift of Ownership Risk

At first glance, the lease appears to allow the firm to avoid completely the substantial risk of owning obsolete equipment. However, the lessor obviously includes an estimate of the cost of obsolescence when calculating the rental payment. The cost of "insuring" the lessor against the risk of obsolescence may be significantly lower than the comparable cost to the lessee, especially in cases where the leased equipment has alternative uses in other firms or industries. Moreover, like an insurance company, the lessor can spread the risk of osbolescence over many contracts.

2 See Richard Contino, *Legal and Financial Aspects of Equipment Leasing Transactions*, Englewood Cliffs, N.J., Prentice-Hall, 1979.

Flexibility

Relatively short-term leases permit the firm to acquire the use of equipment as needed. Thus the cost of idle equipment can be avoided by not renewing the lease. This advantage does not hold for long-term leases in which case the firm is obligated to continue its rental payments until the lease is terminated.

Tax Advantage

A tax advantage may be gained in cases in which the term of the lease is shorter than the depreciation period which the tax authorities would allow if the assets were owned.

Enhanced Leverage

Some financial executives contend that through the judicious use of lease contracts the firm can increase its total amount of credit. The proponents of this argument emphasize that a lease represents "off the balance sheet" financing. However skilled analysts are quick to recognize the fixed charges implicit in a long-term lease. Despite this, some relief may be afforded from the restrictions on further borrowing or on the use of assets which are often imposed when the assets are financed by a regular debt issue or term loan.

Bankruptcy Risk

The lease is conceptually similar to borrowing since it represents an obligation of the firm to make a series of *fixed* rental payments. The impact of these payments on the firm's per share earnings is similar to that of the payment schedule of interest and principal on borrowed money. But there is one further advantage to the lease arrangement. In the case of financial difficulty the leasing company simply takes back the equipment, legal title to which remains with the lessor. In the case of a loan, inability to meet the fixed charges may cause bankruptcy, especially in cases where the equipment has only limited marketability.

Clearly these "advantages" have a price, and the degree to which the firm can benefit from them depends on the terms of the lease contract. Hence we now turn to the problem of evaluating the desirability of leasing from the standpoint of the lessee, i.e. the firm which is considering the financing of equipment or property by a lease contract.

DEFINING THE CASH FLOW

Let us first turn to the problem of determining the cash flows which are relevant for the analysis of the lease or buy decision. Although the valuation of the desirability of a leasing arrangement appears, on the surface at least, to be straightforward and perhaps even simple, nothing could be further from the truth.

Some of the difficulty in evaluating a lease proposal reflects an underlying ambiguity regarding the relevant alternative that should be used as the benchmark for comparison with the lease. Should the lease be compared with buying or borrowing? Obviously, a "lease or borrow" comparison also implies a "lease or buy" comparison, so to avoid possible confusion we shall denote by "lease or buy" the comparison with a purchase that is financed by the firm's standard debt-equity mix.

On the surface, it would appear that the choice between the two alternatives — lease or buy — is relatively simple. Assuming that both options have *positive* net present values, it might be argued that the firm should follow the alternative with the higher *NPV*. If the present value of the lease, *NPV(L)*, is greater than the net present value of the purchase option, *NPV(B)*, the machine should be leased, and conversely in the case in which *NPV(B)* exceeds *NPV(L)*. But despite the apparent plausibility of this approach such a solution is incorrect.

Comparing the net present values of the buy or lease alternatives involves us in a comparison of apples and oranges, because the two cash flows differ in a fundamental sense. The lease arrangement is like borrowing in that it commits the firm to a series of fixed rental payments. Thus, even if the lease alternative has a greater *NPV*, it may also use more of the firm's borrowing capacity, thereby exposing the firm's shareholders to greater financial risk. The differential financial risk can be identified by carefully specifying the cashflows of the two alternatives.

Lease Cash Flow

Let us first turn to the problem of determining the cash flow engendered by the lease. For convenience we shall assume that the lease is for the life of the asset and there is no residual value. Consider a firm which leases a machine for n years and pays a rent of L_t in year t, and that the firm earns revenue from the sale of the machine's output equal to S_t in year t. The production cost associated with this output is C_t (labor, raw materials, electricity, etc.). The firm has no depreciation cost since it does not actually own the machine. Hence the *net* cash flow engendered by the lease can be written as follows:

$$(1 - T)(S_t - C_t - L_t) = (1 - T)(S_t - C_t) - (1 - T)L_t$$

where T denotes the appropriate corporate tax rate.

Now if we assume that the riskiness of the net receipts from this investment, $(S_t - C_t)$, does not deviate significantly from the firm's standard risk, and that the after-tax cost of capital is equal to k, the latter constitutes the appropriate discount rate which should be applied to the $(S_t - C_t)$ component of the cash flow. On the other hand, the "after-tax" lease payment $(1 - T)L_t$, like the payments on a bond or bank loan, constitutes a fixed charge and therefore should be discounted using the interest rate, r. Thus the *net present value* of the lease, $NPV(L)$ is given by,

$$NPV(L) = \sum_{t=1}^{n} \frac{(1 - T)(S_t - C_t)}{(1 + k)^t} - \sum_{t=1}^{n} \frac{(1 - T)L_t}{(1 + r)^t}$$

Purchase Cash Flow

Suppose now that the firm decides to buy rather than lease the machine. Assuming a purchase price of I dollars, and an annual depreciation allowance of D_t, the relevant cash flow of the purchase option in year t is given by

$$(1 - T)(S_t - C_t - M_t - D_t) + D_t$$

Again, the reader should note that we first subtract the depreciation expense, D_t, in order to calculate the corporate tax liability, but then add it back because depreciation is not a cash outflow. We also deduct M_t, which denotes any additional maintenance, insurance, or other costs engendered by the decision to buy rather than lease the machine. For simplicity, we shall assume that the sum of all these costs (i.e. M_t) is zero. Hence the net cash flow in year t of the purchase option reduces to

$$(1 - T)(S_t - C_t) + TD_t$$

Again ignoring any salvage values the net present value of the purchase option, $NPV(B)$, is given by the formula,

$$NPV(B) = \sum_{t=1}^{n} \frac{(1 - T)(S_t - C_t)}{(1 + k)^t} + \sum_{t=1}^{n} \frac{TD_t}{(1 + r)^t} - I$$

The reader should note that the tax shelter, TD_t, is discounted using the interest rate, r. As we pointed out in Chapter 6 above, the tax shelter is for all practical purposes almost completely certain since it can be realized against the income of other projects should the project in question fail to generate any taxable income. However, even in the case in which the firm suffers an overall loss, the tax claim can still be carried forward (or backward) and applied against the firm's future (or past) years' taxable income. Because the tax shield is considered to be virtually certain this component of the cash flow is discounted using the interest rate, r, rather than the cost of capital, k, as the latter reflects the firm's overall risk level.

COMPARING ALTERNATIVES

The differential annual cash flow for any year which is engendered by the decision to buy can now be derived by subtracting the *annual* lease cash flow from the *annual* buy cash flow:

$$(1 - T)L_t + TD_t$$

The lease commits the firm to a series of annual fixed after-tax rentals, $(1 - T)L_t$, the purchase option of course involves an initial investment outlay of I but adds with certainty the annual tax shield from depreciation, TD_t. Before we can make a meaningful comparison of the two alternatives, we must first neutralize any additional financial risk inherent in the lease i.e., we must hold the risk constant when comparing the two alternatives. Only if the risk incurred in both of these alternatives is identical can the difference in net present values be used as a guide to action.

Since the discount rate k is a weighted cost of capital which implies some standard (target) level of borrowing against the cash flows generated by the firm's assets, a simple comparison of the NPV's of the leasing and borrowing alternatives depends on the implicit assumption that obligating the firm under the lease, and giving up the depreciation shelter, induces no change in the firm's overall risk level (borrowing power). Clearly this is not the case. The lease option, as we have already noted, commits the firm to a stream of rental payments, fixed in advance, which implies the using up of some of the firm's borrowing capacity. Hence, in order to neutralize the financial risk differential, the analysis of the purchase option must be made on the explicit assumption that the purchase is partially financed by a loan which commits the firm to a stream of fixed payments (or principal and interest) equal to that implied by the lease alternative.

Since interest payments constitute a tax deductible expense, the *interest tax shield* engendered by the additional debt must also be taken into account. Thus, the annual payments stream on the loan (principal repayment plus *pre-tax* interest actually paid) which is required to neutralize the differential risk between the lease and the purchase options is given by,[3]

$$(TD_t + (1 - T)L_t + TZ_t)$$

where TZ_t denotes the interest tax shield in year t.

A fully equivalent and a more readily applicable formulation sets out the critical risk-equating payment stream on the loan in terms of principal repayment and the *after-tax* interest payment:

$$(TD_t + (1 - T)L_t).$$

Using the *pre-tax* formulation, a correct, and incidentally practical, way to choose between the two alternatives is to find the critical level of lease payment that leaves the firm indifferent between the lease and buy alternatives. This

---

3 The proof that this procedure actually neutralizes the differential riskiness of the two alternatives is given in Appendix 21A at the end of the chapter.

critical value is the maximum lease payment, L_t^* that the firm can pay before the purchase option becomes preferable, and is given by

$$\sum_{t=1}^{n} \frac{TD_t + (1 - T)L_t^* + TZ_t}{(1 + r)^t} = I$$

This formula has an obvious disadvantage; the tax shield on the borrowed funds is difficult to calculate since it diminishes over time. Fortunately the tax shield can be eliminated from the numerator by discounting the *post-tax* formulation of the risk-equating payments stream using the *after-tax* interest rate $(1 - T)r$. This transformation yields the more operational formula:[4]

$$\sum_{t=1}^{n} \frac{TD_t + (1 - T)L_t^*}{[1 + (1 - T)r]^t} = I$$

If we assume, for simplicity, constant annual lease payments the critical level of lease payments can be found by solving this expresssion[5] explicitly for L^*:

$$L^* = \frac{I - \sum_{t=1}^{n} TD_t / [1 + (1 - T)r]^t}{\sum_{t=1}^{n} (1 - T) / [1 + (1 - T)r]^t}$$

Should the firm choose the buy or lease alternative? If the proposed lease payments are less than L^*, the equipment in question should be leased; for lease payments greater than L^*, the purchase option is preferable. This is illustrated in Fig. 21.1. For lease payments greater than L^* the gain from purchasing is positive, but for lease payments below L^*, purchasing involves a loss of *NPV* and the lease alternative should be chosen.

A Numerical Example

Now let's apply the lease evaluation formula to a concrete numerical example. Assume that the firm has already decided to acquire a given machine, but is considering whether it should be purchased or leased. The price of the machine (I) is $10,000 and its estimated economic (and accounting) life span (n) is 10 years. The interest rate (r) is 10%; the corporate tax rate (T) is 50%; the annual straight-line depreciation charge ($D = I/n$) is equal to $1,000; and, if leased, the annual rental payment (L) would be $2,000.

Should the firm buy or lease the machine? Plugging in the data of this specific example we solve the lease evaluation formula for the critical "break-

4 A formal proof of the equivalence of these two formulae is given in Appendix 21A.
5 This formula can also be derived from the valuation formula set out in S. C. Myers, D. A. Dill, and A.J. Bautista, "Valuation of Finanical Lease Contracts", *Journal of Finance*, June 1976, pp. 799 – 819.

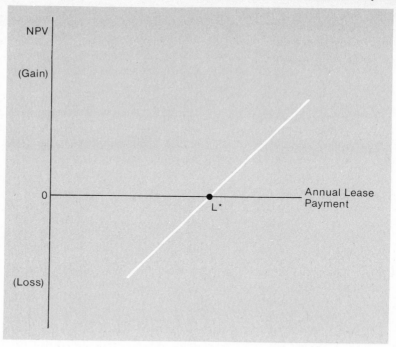

Fig. 21.1
NPV Gain (or loss) from purchasing rather than leasing equipment

even" rental payment L^*, that is for the maximum annual rental payment which the firm can offer:

$$L^* = \frac{I - PV \text{ of the depreciation tax shelter at 5\% discount}}{PV \text{ of } (1 - T) \text{ at 5\% discount}}$$

From Appendix Table B we find that the coefficient of present value of a 10 year annuity, using the 5% *after-tax* interest rate, equals 7.722. Hence the critical lease payment, in this instance, is $1,590.

$$L^* = \frac{10,000 - 3861}{0.5 \times 7.722} = \frac{6139}{3.861} = \textbf{\$1,590}$$

Since the terms of the lease call for an annual rental of $2,000, which exceeds the critical break-even point, the machine should be purchased rather than leased in this case.

SALE AND LEASE BACK IN AN INFLATIONARY ECONOMY[6]

Suppose that a firm which uses straight-line depreciation purchased a machine five years ago for one million dollars. Thus, half the investment has already been depreciated and the machine's book value is half a million dollars. Due to double-digit inflation the market value of the machine after five years of operation is much higher than the net book value, for example $900,000 if the firm continues to operate the machine, it will get (in addition to the cashflow from sales) the following present value of the depreciation tax shelter, TD:

$$\sum_{t=1}^{5} \frac{TD_t}{(1 + r)^t} = \sum_{t=1}^{5} T \frac{100,000}{(1 + r)^t}$$

Suppose that the corporate tax rate is 50% and the riskless nominal interest rate adjusted for inflation is 15%. Furthermore assume that the capital gain tax is $T_g = 0.25$. Thus, if the firm does not change its policy the PV of the depreciation tax shelter remaining from this machine is

$$50,000 \times 3.352 = \$167,600$$

However, since the depreciation tax shelter is based on historical cost, the firm can exploit the fact that the market price of the machine is now higher, i.e., $900,000. The firm can sell the machine for $900,000 and pay capital gains tax at a rate of 25% on the difference between the sale price and the book value of the machine $(900,000 - 500,000)$ and buy a new machine which will induce a higher depreciation tax shelter in the future. An alternative way to achieve the same goal would be to *sell and lease back* the same machine. This implies no change in operating costs and no change in the physical assets which the firm holds. Suppose that the firm sells the machine for $900,000 and leases it back for five years (which is the technological life of the machine). If the annual lease payment is $400,000 which is all tax-deductible, the firm's cash flow from this transaction would be

$$NPV = 900,000 - (900,000 - 500,000)T_g - \sum_{t=1}^{5} \frac{(1 - T)360,000}{(1 + r)^t}$$

Plugging in $T = 0.5$, $T_g = 0.25$ and $r = 0.15$ we get $NPV = 900,000 - 100,000 - 180,000 \times 3.352 = 800,000 - 603,360 = \$196,640$. Recall that if the firm continues its regular operation without this transaction the PV of the tax shelter is only $167,600. Thus, the lessee benefits from this transaction. However, is it possible that the lessee benefits because the lease payments taken in the above calculation are too low? This is not the case since the NPV from the lessor's point of view is also positive. He pays $900,000 and gets annual lease payments of $360,000. Since he is the owner of the new asset he is allowed to depreciate it

---

6 For discussion of the impact of inflation on the lease-buy decision see H. Wyman, "Financial Lease Evaluation Under Conditions of Uncertainty", *Accounting Review*, July 1973, pp. 489 – 93; M. Ungar, "The Impact of Inlation on Leasing", *Review of Business and Economic Research*, Winter 1977, pp. 46 – 55; R. C. Waters and R. L. Bullock, "Inflation and Replacement Decisions", *The Engineering Economist*, Vol. 21, no. 4, pp. 249 – 57; R. P. Marcus, "The Cost of Leasing: Inflation and Residual Value", *Financial Analysts Journal*, March – April 1978, pp. 58 – 60.

over five years so that his annual depreciation is $900,000/5 = $180,000$. His after-tax annual cash flow is

$$(1 - T)(360,000 - 180,000) + 180,000 = 0.5 \times 180,000 + 180,000 = 270,000$$

And the *NPV* of the transaction from his point of view is,

$$NPV = -900,000 + \sum_{t=1}^{5} \frac{270,000}{(1.15)^t} = -900,000 + 270,000 \times 3.352$$
$$= -900,000 + 905,040 = \$5,040$$

Thus both parties benefit from the transaction. This mutual benefit can be explained only when we recognize that there is a third party, the IRS, who loses from the above transaction. Since the capital gains tax is lower than the corporate tax rate, the firm pays only the lower rate on the captial gain created by selling the machine but all the lease payments are tax deductible at the higher corporate tax rate. The lessor on the other hand starts depreciating the machine according to its market value ($900,000) and not according to its historical value. Thus, this transaction is similar to a revaluation of the machine, for tax purposes.

Obviously, the higher the inflation rate, the greater is the gap between the book value and the market value of assets. This provides an incentive for early replacement of equipment or for a sale and lease back transaction. Not every transaction like the one described above is recognized for tax purposes and the IRS has some restrictions on such transactions, but despite these restrictions there is ample room for both sides to benefit, which helps to explain the increasing popularity of sale and lease back transactions during inflationary years.

SUMMARY

This chapter has attempted to analyze a problem that has been growing in importance as more and more types of assets become available for long-term rental. Although at first glance the lease or buy question appears relatively simple, a correct decision requires an appraisal of almost all aspects of financial decision-making. The lease or buy decision is a type of capital budgeting problem requiring the application of present value techniques. It also has tax implications, and the relevant after-tax cash flows of the two alternatives must be set out with great care. The choice of discount rates requires a decomposition of the cash flows into their risky and riskless components. And finally, the correct solution requires a neutralization of the differential financial risk implicit in the lease vs. purchase comparison.

21.1 In what sense can leasing be considered as a hedge against obsolescence?

21.2 The Sisra Textile Corporation leases a machine for ten years, and must pay a rental of $35,000 every year.

    The annual revenue from the sale of the machine's output is expected to be $90,000, while the production costs are $40,000 a year.

    Assume corporate tax of 48%, an after-tax cost of capital of 12% and an interest rate of 8%. Also assume that the risk involved in both options is identical.

    (a)   Calculate the net present value of the lease.

    (b)   What is the maximal rental payment the firm can make before the net present value of the lease becomes negative?

21.3 Suppose now that the Sisra Textile Co. decides to buy rather than lease the machine. Assume a purchase price of $190,00 and straight-line depreciation for ten years. Also assume that the sum of the maintenance, insurance or other costs engendered by the decision to buy rather than lease is zero:

    (a)   Calculate the net present value of the purchase option.

    (b)   Compare the result you got to the result you got in part (a) of question 21.2; did the firm choose the optimal alternative?

21.4 Suppose that a firm is confronted with two mutually exclusive alternatives: to buy a machine which costs $25,000 and has an economic life of ten years; or to lease it for $4,500 a year. Assume straight-line depreciation, 50% corporate tax, and interest rate of 6%.

    (a)   Should the firm "buy or lease" the machine?

    (b)   How much will the firm gain (or lose) if it decides to buy the machine rather than lease it?

    (c)   Answer parts (a) and (b) assuming now that the required rental payments are $4,000 a year.

    (d)   Illustrate graphically the relationship between the gain (or loss) from the decision to buy rather than lease and the level of lease payments.

21.5 Assume now that the interest rate is 8% and answer the following questions: (Also assume that the riskiness of both options is the same.)

    (a)   Should the firm "buy or lease" the machine (assume in your answer annual rental payments of $4,500)?

    (b)   Calculate the gains (or losses) incurred if the firm should decide to buy the machine rather than lease it, for the following alternative levels of lease payments: $4,500, $5,000, and $5,500.

    (c)   Illustrate graphically the relationship between the gain (or loss) from the decision to buy rather than lease and the level of lease payments. Compare this relationship to that of the 6% interest case.

21.6 The United Carton Corporation has decided to acquire a cutting machine which is required for its current production. The company is considering whether to purchase the machine or to lease it.

The price of the machine is $40,000 and its economic (and account-ing) life is 8 years. If the machine is leased, the annual rental payments would be $9,000.

Assume that the company uses straight-line depreciation, the interest rate is 12%, and the corporate tax rate is 50%.

Should the company "buy" or "lease" the machine?

To solve this problem, answer the following questions:

(a) What are the annual payments of interest and principal required to equalize the annual cash flows of *both* alternatives?

(b) Find the size of the loan which the company should take in order to *neutralize* the leverage implicit in the annual lease payments. (Hint: Calculate the present value of the annual payments of principal and interest required to neutralize the leverage, at the *post-tax* riskless discount rate).

(c) Prove, using a table of principal and interest payments, that the loan you found in part (b) requires *equal annual* payments of principal and after-tax interest which are equal to the amounts you found in part (a).

21.7 Answer question 21.6, assuming that the annual lease payment is $7,000.

21.8 With reference to question 21.6, find the *critical value* of the lease pay-ment (L^*).

APPENDIX 21A PROOF OF THE EQUIVALENCE OF THE POST-TAX AND PRE-TAX LEASE OR BUY ANALYSIS

In this appendix we derive the pre-tax and post-tax equations of the text, and show that they are equivalent, and therefore, that they can be used interchange-ably to evaluate a lease or buy decision.

Let us denote by B_t the balance of a loan outstanding at the end of period t. Hence, for any n period project, $B_n = 0$, and B_0 is the total amount borrowed. In the text it is argued that in order to equate the riskiness of the lease and buy options, the firm should borrow a sum that requires a total payments stream (repayment of principal and after-tax interest) which is just equal to

$$(1 - T)L_t + TD_t \tag{A1}$$

Thus the neutralization of the differential risk in year t implies that the following relationship should hold:

$$B_{t-1} - B_t + (1 - T)rB_{t-1} = (1 - T)L_t + TD_t \tag{A2}$$

That is, the debt repayment $(B_{t-1} - B_t)$ plus after-tax interest payment $(1 - T)rB_{t-1}$ should equal the after-tax lease payment plus depreciation shelter. From Equation (A2) we derive:

$$B_{t-1} = \frac{(1 - T)L_t + TD_t + rTB_{t-1} + B_t}{1 + r} \tag{A3}$$

Since, by definition, $B_n = 0$, we obtain for $t = n - 1$:

$$B_{n-1} = \frac{(1-T)L_n + TD_n + rTB_{n-1}}{1 + r} \tag{A4}$$

Using (A3) and (A4) we have

$$B_{n-2} = \frac{(1-T)L_{n-1} + TD_{n-1} + rTB_{n-2} + B_{n-1}}{1 + r}$$

$$= \frac{(1-T)L_{n-1} + TD_{n-1} + rTB_{n-2}}{1 + r} + \frac{B_{n-1}}{1 + r}$$

Substituting the right hand side of Equation (A4) for B_{n-1} yields,

$$B_{n-2} = \frac{L_{n-1}(1-T) + TD_{n-1} + TB_{n-2}\,r}{1 + r} + \frac{L_n(1-T) + TD_n + TB_{n-1}\,r}{(1 + r)^2}$$

which simplifies to

$$B_{n-2} = \sum_{t=n-1}^{n} \frac{L_t(1-T) + TD_t + TB_{t-1}\,r}{(1 + r)^{t-(n-2)}} \tag{A5}$$

Continuing this substitution procedure we finally obtain

$$B_0 = \sum_{t=1}^{n} \frac{L_t(1-T) + TD_t + TB_{t-1}\,r}{(1 + r)^t} \tag{A6}$$

To find the critical lease payment, L_t^*, which leaves the firm indifferent between the buy and lease options, we simply substitute $B_0 = I$ and solve for L_t^*,

$$I = \sum_{t=1}^{n} \frac{L_t^*(1-T) + TD_t + TB_{t-1}\,r}{(1 + r)^t} \tag{A7}$$

Recalling that $TB_{t-1}r$ is identical to TZ_t, where Z_t is defined as the interest paid on the loan at the end of period t, Equation (A7) is clearly the same as the pre-tax equation of the text.

In order to show the equivalence to the post-tax equation let us write (A2) as follows:

$$B_{t-1}(1 + r) - TB_{t-1}r = L_t(1 - T) + TD_t + B_t \tag{A8}$$

Hence:

$$B_{t-1} = \frac{L_t(1-T) + TD_t + B_t}{1 + (1-T)\,r} \tag{A9}$$

Using the same substitution procedure as above, and recalling that $B_n = 0$, the critical lease payment L_t^* can be found from the following equation:

$$B_0 = I = \sum_{t=1}^{n} \frac{(1-T)L_t^* + TD_t}{[1 + (1-T)r]^t} \tag{A10}$$

which is equivalent to the post-tax equation of the text. Since both the pre-tax and post-tax formulations yield the *same* estimate of the critical lease payment, L^*, they lead to the *same* decision regarding the relative desirability of the lease and buy alternatives.

SELECTED REFERENCES

Allen, C.L., Martin, J.D. and Anderson, P.F., "Debt Capacity and the Lease-Purchase Problem: A Sensitivity Analysis", *Engineering Economist*, Winter 1978.

Ashton, D.J., "The Reasons for Leasing — A Mathematical Programming Framework", *Journal of Business Finance & Accounting*, Summer 1978.

Beechy, T.H., "Quasi-Debt Analysis of Financial Leases", *Accounting Review*, April 1969.

Bloomfield, E.C. and Ronald, M.A., "The Lease Evaluation Solution", *Accounting and Business Research*, Autumn 1979.

Bower, Richard S., "Issues in Lease Financing", *Financial Management*, Winter 1973.

Bower, Richard S. and Bower, Dorothy H., "Risk and the Valuation of Common Stock", *Journal of Political Economy*, May – June 1969.

Bowles, G.N., "Some Thoughts on the Lease Evaluation Solution", *Accounting and Business Research*, Spring 1977.

Bowman, R.G., "The Debt Equivalence of Leases: An Empirical Investigation", *Accounting Review*, April 1980.

Brealey, R.A. and Young, C.M. "Debt, Taxes and Leasing — A Note", *Journal of Finance*, December 1980.

Cooper, Kerry and Strawser, Robert H., "Evaluation of Capital Investment Projects Involving Asset Leases", *Financial Management*, Spring 1975.

Doenges, R. Conrad, "The Cost of Leasing", *Engineering Economist*, Fall 1971.

Fawthrop, R.A. and Terry, Brian, "Debt Management and the Use of Leasing Finance in UK Corporate Financing Strategies", *Journal of Business Finance and Accounting*, Autumn 1975.

Findlay, M. Chapman, III, "A Sensitivity Analysis of IRR Leasing Models", *Engineering Economist*, Summer 1975.

Finnerty, Joseph E., Fitzsimmons, Rick N. and Oliver, Thomas W., "Lease Capitalization and Systematic Risk", *Accounting Review*, October 1980.

Franks, J.R. and Hodges, S.D., "Valuation of Financial Lease Contracts: A Note", *Journal of Finance*, May 1978.

Gaumnitz, Jack E., and Ford, Allen, "The Lease or Sell Decision", *Financial Management*, Winter 1978.

Gordon, Myron J., "A General Solution to the Buy or Lease Decision: A Pedagogical Note", *Journal of Finance*, March 1974.

Gritta, Richard D., "The Impact of Lease Capitalization", *Financial Analysts Journal*, March/April 1974.

Henderson, G.V., Jr., "A Decision Format for Lease or Buy Analsyis", *Review of Business & Economic Research*, Fall 1976.

Honic, Lawrence E. and Colley, Stephen C., "An After-tax" equivalent Payment Approach to Conventional Lease Analysis", *Financial Management*, Winter 1975.

Johnson, Keith B. and Hazuka, Thomas B., "The NPV-IRR Debate in Lease Analysis", *Mississippi Valley Journal*.

Johnson, Robert W. and Lewellen, Wilbur G., "Analysis of the Lease or Buy Decision", *Journal of Finance*, September 1972.

Keller, Thomas, F. and Peterson, Russell J., "Optimal Financial Structure, Cost of Capital, and the Lease-or-Buy Decision", *Journal of Business Finance and Accounting*, Autumn 1974.

Kim, E.H., Lewellen, W.G. and McConnell, J.J., "Sale-and-Leaseback Agreements and Enterprise Valuation", *Journal of Financial and Quantitative Analysis*, December 1978.

Levy, Haim and Sarnat, Marshall, "On Leasing, Borrowing and Financial Risk", *Financial Management*, Winter 1979.

Lewellen, W.G., Long, M.S. and McConnell, J.J., "Asset Leasing in Competitive Capital Markets", *Journal of Finance*, June 1976.

Long, M.S., "Leasing and the Cost of Capital", *Journal of Financial and Quantitative Analysis*, November 1977.

Middleton, K.A., "Lease Evaluation: Back to Square One", *Accounting and Business Research*, Spring 1977.

Miller, M.H. and Upton, C.W., "Leasing, Buying, and the Cost of Capital Services", *Journal of Finance*, June 1976.

Mitchell, G.B., "After-Tax Cost of Leasing", *Accounting Review*, April 1970.

Morgan, Eleanor, Lowe, Julian and Tomkins, Cyril, "The UK Financial Leasing Industry — A Structural Anaysis", *The Journal of Industrial Economics*, June 1980.

Moyer, R. Charles, "Lease Evaluation and the Investment Tax Credit: A Framework for Analysis," *Financial Management*, Summer 1975.

Myers, S.C., Dill, D.A. and Bautista, A.J., "Valuation of Financial Lease Contracts", *Journal of Finance*, June 1976.

Nantell, Timothy J., "Equivalence of Lease vs. Buy Analyses", *Financial Management*, Autumn 1973.

Ofer, Aharon R., "The Evaluation of the Lease Versus Purchase Alternatives", *Financial Management*, Summer 1976.

Perg, Wayne, F., "Leveraged Leasing: The Problem of Changing Leverage", *Financial Management*, Autumn 1978.

Roenfeldt, Rodney L. and Osteryoung, Jerome S., "Analysis of Financial Leases", *Financial Management*, Spring 1973.

Sartoris, William L. and Paul, Ronda S., "Lease Evaluation — Another Capital Budgeting Decision", *Financial Management*, Summer 1973.

Schall, L.D., "The Lease-or-Buy Asset Acquisition Decision", *Journal of Finance*, September 1974.

Sorenson, Ivar W. and Johnson, Ramon E., "Equipment Financial Leasing Practices and Costs: An Empiricial Study", *Financial Management*, Spring 1977.

Van Horne, J.C., "The Cost of Leasing with Capital Market Imperfections", *Engineering Economist*, Fall 1977.

Wiar, Robert C., "Economic Implications of Multiple Rates of Return in the Leveraged Lease Context", *Journal of Finance*, December 1973.

22

Inflation and Financial Decision Making

The double-digit inflation which has characterized much of the world economy in the 1970s has refocused attention on the financial and economic implications of monetary instability. In this chapter we briefly review some of the key features of the inflationary process[1] and then go on to the analysis of the impact of the decline in the purchasing power of the dollar on the underlying logic of financial decision making.

DEFINING INFLATION

The Oxford English Dictionary defines *inflation* as the increase of prices beyond proper limits. More recently, Robert Solow has provided a variant of this definition which most of us would accept: "A substantial sustained increase in the general level of prices." Both definitions have the advantage of eliminating minor or transitory price fluctuations although it is admittedly difficult to agree on a precise interpretation of *proper limits, substantial* or *sustained*. Solow's version has the further advantage of emphasizing the idea that inflation has to do with the *general* price level, that is the terms so to speak on which some representative bundle of goods and services exchanges for money. Alternatively we could define inflation using the reciprocal of the general price level, i.e. in terms of the purchasing power of money. Thus if the general level of prices doubles, we can equivalently speak of a decline by one half of the purchasing power of the dollar, or as your wife (or husband) might put if after returning from the grocer, "a dollar is worth only 50 cents".

Table 22.1 summarizes the changes in the general price level and the purchasing power of the dollar over the period 1939 – 79. During these years the

1 The review draws on Robert Solow's essay, "The Intelligent Citizen's Guide to Inflation", *The Public Interest*, Winter 1975.

Table 22.1

U.S. Consumer Price Index*

(Annual Averages)

Year	Price Index	Purchasing Power of One Dollar
1939	100.0	1.00
1945	129.6	0.77
1950	173.3	0.58
1955	192.8	0.52
1960	213.2	0.47
1965	227.2	0.44
1970	279.6	0.36
1973	320.0	0.31
1974	355.0	0.28
1975	387.4	0.26
1976	409.8	0.24
1977	436.3	0.22
1978	468.1	0.21
1979	530.4	0.18

*1939 = 100

Source: Economic Report of The President, Washington, D.C., 1979.

general price level (as measured by the Consumer Price Index) rose more than fourfold, and as a result a dollar in 1979 was worth only 18 cents in terms of its 1939 purchasing power.

Like most important concepts, the notion of a general price level (or generalized purchasing power) is not as simple as it might appear. In reality there are hundreds of thousands of goods and services and during any given period of time their prices fluctuate, some rising, some falling and some remaining the same. For example, it is not unlikely that a sharp rise in gasoline prices may be accompanied by a fall in the prices of used cars.

The problem of measuring inflation is to build up out of these often con-flicting price changes a single index number which will show at a glance the change in the general level of prices. But before we can decide on the type of index required, we must first determine the purpose which it is to serve. For example, if we desire a very general measure of the change in prices, we should include all of the goods and services which are subject to exchange. On the other hand, if we desire to measure changes in the cost of living of, say, blue-collar workers we should try to build an index based on the "basket" of goods and services which they consume. Clearly, the relevant basket for white-collar workers or farmers may differ considerably.

Perhaps the best known price index is the *Consumer Price Index* (CPI) often referred to as the cost of living index. This index, which is calculated and published monthly by the Bureau of Labor Statistics, is based on a budget that reflects the spending habits of a cross-section of families of varying size, income and other characteristics. (The CPI is based on retail prices; a second index based on wholesale prices is also published monthly.)

Another, but perhaps less well known index, is the so-called *GNP Deflator*. This index differs from the CPI in that it covers only currently produced goods and services. Used cars, mortgage payments, sales taxes and so on, which are all part of the consumer's actual expenditure, and therefore are properly included in the CPI, are excluded from the GNP Deflator. Thus the latter is a very good indicator of the price experience of currently produced goods and services, but of course, for that very reason, may not be a good indicator of the current price experience of consumers.[2]

THE HISTORICAL RECORD

To this generation of Americans it often appears that inflation, like death and taxes, is inevitable. Curiously enough, the price history of the United States does not confirm this popular impression. Fig. 22.1 charts the general price level (as measured by the GNP Deflator) from 1867 (the close of the Civil War) to 1973. The index has been drawn on a logarithmic scale in order to focus atten-

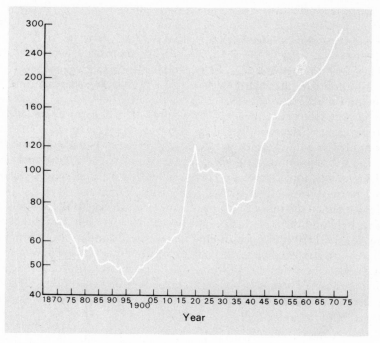

Fig. 22.1: The Price Index, 1867 – 1973* (1929 = 100)

Source Robert M. Solow, 'The Intelligent Citizen's Guide to Inflation', *The Public Interest,* Winter 1975, p. 37. Reprinted with permission of *The Public Interest,* No. 28 (Winter 1975) copyright © 1975 by National Affairs, Inc.

2 Numerous technical difficulties are encountered in the building of any index number; not the least of which are the problems engendered by the changing quality over time of the goods and services. Clearly a 1982 Ford Mustang is not the same animal as a 1920 model T.

Table 22.2

World Consumer Prices

(average annual percentage increases)

	1950-54	1955-59	1960-64	1965-69	1970-74	1975-79
World	3.4	3.2	3.5	4.8	8.5	11.5
Industrial countries	3.0	2.2	2.2	3.6	7.3	8.8
Oil exporting countries	...	3.1	2.0	2.5	8.5	14.2
Non-oil developing countries	5.2	9.4	11.9	12.0	15.9	26.4

Source: International Monetary Fund *IFS Yearbook for 1980*

tion on *proportional*, rather than absolute changes. Although prices almost quadrupled from 1867 to 1973, the overall trend from the end of the Civil War to the close of the nineteenth century was actually deflationary — prices fell by more than 40% between 1867 and 1896. And again in this century, the trend following the First World War was also deflationary. A glance at the chart suffices to show that what we have learned to call the economy's "inflationary bias" has largely been the product of the country's involvement in war. The big bursts of inflation (i.e. the steep portions of the chart) coincide with the two world wars and the Korean and Vietnamese conflicts.

Table 22.2 emphasizes the world-wide character of the recent inflationary experience. In the two decades preceding 1970, world consumer prices rose at a relatively moderate annual rate averaging 3.7% in the twenty years from 1950 to 1969. The average annual rate of increase for industrial countries in that period (2.75%) was lower than the world average while that for the non-oil developing nations was significantly higher (9.26%). The pace of inflation gathered momentum during the 1970s especially following the quadrupling of oil prices in 1973 and the sharp rise in the prices of other commodities. By the second half of the 1970s the average annual rate of world inflation had reached double digits. Especially noteworthy is the rise in consumer prices in the non-oil developing countries which exceeded 26% per annum in the second half of the decade. The peak inflation year during the period was 1974 in which year consumer prices rose by over 15% in industrial countries and 29% in the non-oil developing countries.

TYPES OF INFLATION

Let us pause for a moment and examine the concept of inflation. As we have just noted, the US economy has been characterized by rising prices since 1939, but a glance back at Fig. 22.1 shows that the pace of inflation (the slope of the curve) has varied from time to time. Many economists would also distinguish between at least two types of inflation. The first or classic type of inflation is related to an excess demand for goods and services — or to put it more simply, is a case of too much money chasing too few goods, thereby creating market pressures which increase prices. The second type, popularly known as *cost-push*, associates the rise in prices with a prior rise in wages and other costs. Too fine a distinction should not be drawn between the two types of inflation. Clearly, a cost-push inflation cannot continue indefinitely unless a corresponding expansion in the money supply takes place. Historically inflation (of both types) has been associated, more often than not, with prosperity; stable or slowly rising prices, on the other hand, have been more often associated with periods of recession. However, in the 1970s, the world was confronted by a new phenomenon. In the United States and Western Europe relatively rapid inflation was accompanied by stagnation or even decline in economic growth — hence the popular barbarism *stagflation*. And this situation has been aggravated further by the activities of the cartel formed in the 1970s by the Organization of Petroleum Exporting Countries (OPEC).

Some other distinctions between types of inflation are useful. To properly understand the inflationary process, it is often helpful to consider an abstraction from reality which we shall call *pure*, or equivalently *neutral*, inflation, i.e. one in which all prices (including wages) rise in the same proportion, so that relative prices remain unchanged. In such a situation everyone seems to retain the same purchasing power, but upon reflection it is apparent that the holders of monetary claims will suffer a reduction of their *real* wealth even in a neutral inflation. Thus creditors and the holders of cash assets suffer a loss in welfare. And if we relax the assumption that *all* prices and incomes rise in the same proportion we can add to the list of those who suffer from inflation, pensioners and others living on fixed or relatively fixed incomes — a group by the way which is considerably larger than the lip service which is usually paid to "widows and orphans" might suggest.

Similarly it is helpful to distinguish between perfectly and imperfectly anticipated rises in the price level. In the latter case, which is also the realistic one, inflation can generate massive, and often socially undesirable, shifts in the allocation of wealth between the buyers and sellers of some goods and services and between debtors and creditors. And although these "gains" and "losses" cancel in the aggregate, this provides little solace to the individual who finds himself an unwilling victim of an imperfectly anticipated inflation.[3]

In the spirit of Part II of this book we should also add the conjecture, at least, that the uncertainty regarding inflation increases the general level of uncertainty of business decisions in general. And since we have assumed the firm and its shareholders to be "risk-averse" this enhanced level of uncertainty will translate itself into a utility loss for the economy as a whole.

---

3 See, for example, Stanley Fischer and Franco Modigliani, "Towards an Understanding of the Real Effects and Costs of Inflation", *Weltwirtschaftliches Archiv*, 4: 1978.

PURCHASING POWER RISK AND THE INTEREST RATE

In addition to a premium to cover the financial risk of default, the yields on fixed-income securities also reflect the risk of a general rise in consumer prices during the lifetime of the contract. Such a premium becomes necessary since as we have already mentioned creditors (bondholders) suffer a real economic loss when consumer prices rise. Inflation reduces the purchasing power of the fixed nominal amounts (interest and return of principal) which the bondholder is entitled to receive; hence the need for an additional premium to induce him to give up present money in return for a promise to receive a fixed amount of future money.

The role of purchasing power risk can be clarified by using the well-known distinction between the "money" (nominal) and "real" rates of interest. The former, as its name implies, measures the rate of interest in terms of money, while the latter measures the rate of interest in terms of the command over commodities, that is in terms of the purchasing power of money.[4] Unless the general price level remains stable over the duration of the loan, the two rates are not identical.

The formula relating the *real* and nominal rates of interest is given by:

$$1 + m = \frac{1 + r}{1 + h}$$

where:

m = the *real* rate of interest
r = the nominal rate of interest
h = the rate of change of consumer prices

By cross-multiplying this equation we obtain:

$$m = r - h - mh$$

which reduces to the following rule of thumb when m and h are small:

$$m = r - h$$

The real rate of interest can be approximated by deducting the increase in the general price level from the nominal rate of interest.[5] Thus if the rate of interest on a one-year bond is 8% but inflation raises prices by 6%, the *real* rate of interest in terms of purchasing power is only about 2%. The investor gave up $100 at the beginning of the year and receives $108 at the end of the year. However the $108 can only purchase $102 ($101.89 to be exact) worth of goods in terms of beginning year prices. If we consider a more extreme case in which prices are expected to rise by 8% the real rate becomes zero; and if the rate of

---

4 We owe this distinction to Irving Fisher, *The Rate of Interest*, New York, Macmillan, 1907. The algebraic formulation is taken from Don Patinkin, "Secular Price Movements and Economic Development: Some Theoretical Aspects", in *The Challenge of Development*, A Bonne, Jerusalem, The Hebrew University, 1958, p. 28.

5 Where the real rate and inflation rate are significantly large the rule of thumb approximation should not be used, see Chapter 7, above.

price increase exceeds the money rate of interest, the real rate is negative; that is the bondholder gives up more current purchasing power than he receives at the end of the year. Thus if the general level of consumer prices is increasing, the real rate is less than the money rate; conversely, when prices are decreasing the real rate exceeds the money rate.

Since individuals invest their savings in order to enhance their eventual command over consumer goods, strong expectations of inflation undermine the willingness to loan money (buy bonds) at a *given* nominal interest rate. As a result, bond prices will tend to fall and yields to rise until the investing public is offered a nominal interest return sufficiently high to ensure the desired real rate of interest. Thus the specific cost (yields) of fixed-income bearing securities will tend to rise, other things being equal, during inflation.

COST OF CAPITAL AND INFLATION

Now let us turn our attention to the impact of pure or neutral inflation, that is a proportional increase in all prices, on the cost of capital. Recall that in such an event revenues, expenses, profits, wages, etc. increase at the same rate. Hence, no change occurs in relative prices, and a fully anticipated price rise will have no impact on the *present* market price of shares. Thus, even if we assume that the general level of prices will increase by 5%, 10% or even 20% per year, no immediate change in the prices of common stocks need occur. However, the cost of capital will tend to rise along with inflation.

To illustrate this contention, consider the simple case of a pure equity firm, which distributes all its earnings as dividends. (This assumption will be relaxed later on.) In the absence of inflation the cost of capital, k_R, of such a firm is given by

$$P_0 = \sum_{t=1}^{\infty} \frac{D_t}{(1 + k_R)^t} = D \sum_{t=1}^{\infty} \frac{1}{(1 + k_R)^t} = \frac{D}{k_R}$$

and

$$k_R = \frac{D}{P_0} = \frac{E}{P_0}$$

Where P_0 denotes the present market price of the stock, D_t is the dividend in year t which by assumption is also equal to E_t, the earnings in year t, and k_R is the real cost of capital in the absence of inflation. Note also that for simplicity we assume that earnings and hence dividends are constant over time. Now, suppose that consumer prices are expected to rise at a rate of $h\%$ a year, and that the firm's revenues and expenses and therefore its earnings, are also expected to grow at the same rate. Since the firm distributes all its earnings as dividends, its *nominal* cost of capital, k_h, is determined as follows:

$$P_0 = \sum_{t=1}^{\infty} \frac{D_t}{(1 + k_h)^t} = \frac{D(1 + h)}{(1 + k_h)} + \frac{D(1 + h)^2}{(1 + k_h)^2} + \frac{D(1 + h)^3}{(1 + k_h)^3} + \ldots$$

$$= \frac{D(1 + h)}{1 + k_h} \left[1 + \frac{1 + h}{1 + k_h} + \frac{(1 + h)^2}{(1 + k_h)^2} \cdots \right]$$

or

$$P_0 = \frac{D(1 + h)}{1 + k_h} \cdot 1 \left| 1 - \frac{1 + h}{1 + k_h} = \frac{D(1 + h)}{k_h - h} \right.$$

and hence the nominal cost of capital is given by:

$$k_h = \frac{D}{P_0} (1 + h) + h$$

Comparing this result with the zero inflation case in which $k_R = \dfrac{D}{P_0}$ it is clear that

$$k_h = k_R(1 + h) + h = k_R + h + k_R \cdot h$$

which reduces to a simple rule of thumb when k_R and h are small:

$$k_h = k_R + h$$

Thus the new nominal cost of capital, k_h, can be approximated by adding the expected increase in the general level of prices to the appropriate cost of capital which would exist in the absence of inflation. The latter is often called the *real* cost of capital and should be distinguished from its nominal counterpart.

This approach can be clarified by considering the following simplified numerical example: Suppose that in the absence of inflation the minimum required *real* rate of return on investment is 10%, i.e. the firm requires a minimum return of $110 on a $100 investment with a duration of one year. Now what will be the impact of an expected rate of inflation of say 10% on the *nominal* cost of capital, k_h? Using the formula derived above we have:

$$k_h = 0.10 \cdot (1.10) + 0.10 = 21\%$$

which can also be approximated fairly closely by simply adding the 10% rate of inflation to the 10% *real* required rate of return.

The explanation for the rise in the cost of capital from 10% to 21% is straightforward. Given the expected 10% rise in prices a rate of return of 11% is equivalent to a 10% rate of return in the absence of inflation. The additional 10% return is required to preserve the purchasing power (i.e. real value) of the initial $100 investment; given the 10% inflation rate, an end of year sum of $110 is needed to acquire the same goods and services which cost only $100 at the beginning of the year. Putting the two together, we require $121 at the end of the year in order to earn 10% in terms of *constant* prices.

So far we have assumed a pure equity firm, but as we have already noted the required yield on debt also rises with inflation; a firm which can issue bonds at an interest rate of $r\%$ in the absence of inflation, will be required to pay $r(1 + h) + h$ in a case of an expected annual inflation rate of $h\%$. Otherwise the *real* interest rate (taking into account the principal as well as the interest) will decline. In actual practice, however, the adjustment of the interest rate often lags behind the rise in prices, because the rate of inflation is *not* fully anticipated. But for our purposes, the adjusted interest rate should be calculated using the *long-run* anticipated inflation rate (appropriate to the maturity of the debt) and not the rate of inflation at a given point of time. Thus, both the cost of equity as well as the cost of debt rise approximately by the rate of anticipated inflation, h, and therefore the weighted average cost of capital also rises at the same rate.

The implications of this analysis for capital budgeting are straightforward. In evaluating its investment opportunities the firm makes forecasts of future revenues and costs, both of which reflect a forecast of the rate of inflation as well. Hence the appropriate discount rate to be used in discounting such a cash flow is the nominal cost of capital. Alternatively, the firm can project into the future *current* prices and costs, i.e. base its cash flow forecast on the relationship between current prices and costs *without* an upward adjustment for secular inflation. In such a case, the appropriate discount rate would be the *real* cost of capital.[6]

In Chapter 7, we saw that in a fully anticipated neutral inflation of h percent per year, the *NPV* of a project is given by:

$$NPV = \sum_{t=1}^{N} \frac{(1 - T)S_t (1 + h)^t}{[(1 + k_R)(1 + h)]^t} + \sum_{t=1}^{N} \frac{TD_t}{[(1 + r)(1 + h)]^t} - I$$

$$= \sum_{t=1}^{N} \frac{(1 - T)S_t}{(1 + k_R)^t} + \frac{TD_t}{[(1 + r)(1 + h)]^t} - I$$

where:

r = the risk free interest rate
k_R = cost of capital in the absence of inflation
S_t = net receipt in year t
T = corporate tax rate
D_t = depreciation allowance in year t
I = initial investment outlay.

But in reality, inflation is rarely neutral. The price of oil, for example, has risen in recent years much faster than has the price of large cars. Price changes of food products have been very different from those of durable goods, and so on. Assuming that stockholders consume a mixed basket of goods and services, it is only reasonable to assume that their required rate of return on investment will change proportionally to the average price change rather than the price change of any specific product or service. Hence, the cost of capital increases with inflation from $(1 + k_R)$ to $(1 + k_R)(1 + h)$. But a firm which produces only a limited number of products is usually confronted by an increase in its prices at a rate h^* which generally differs from h. Hence, the *NPV* of a project with non-neutral inflation becomes

---

6 The reader should be cautioned that the underlying assumption of the *real* analysis is that relative prices and costs will remain unchanged over the life of the project. Clearly this may be an inappropriate assumption for many firms..

$$NPV = \sum_{t=1}^{N} \frac{(1 - T)S_t (1 + h^*)^t}{[(1 + k_R)(1 + h)]^t} + \sum_{t=1}^{N} \frac{TD_t}{[(1 + r)(1 + h)]^t} - I$$

Clearly, this sum is different from the *NPV* with neutral inflation. As long as h^* differs from h, the inflation rate cannot be ignored in the numerator of the first term.

A non-neutral inflation in which h^* is different from h introduces a new dimension of risk to the firm. These differential inflation rates increase the business risk of all firms, and as a result, may also increase the real cost of capital k_R. To be more specific, in a neutral inflation, the first year cashflow is given in *real* terms by $[S_1 (1 + h)]/1 + h$. In a non-neutral inflation the first year cashflow, in real terms, becomes $[S_1 (1 + h^*)]/(1 + h)$. Since in practice h^* as well as h are not fully anticipated, inflation may increase the dispersion of the real cashflow which implies that the mean $\bar{S}$ must be discounted at a real discount rate greater than k_R. Thus a non-neutral inflation increases risks thereby raising the cost of capital. This in turn decreases projects' net present values which reduces a firm's capital expenditures.

From the above discussion one might be tempted to infer that so long as inflation is neutral, no additional risk is produced by inflation. But this is not the case since the inflation rate itself is not known with certainty. As we have just seen, the cashflow in year t, in real terms, is $[S_t (1 + h)^t]/(1 + h)^t$ which is unaffected by inflation; and as the distribution of the cashflow in real terms is not affected by inflation, there is no need to change the real cost of capital k_R. The depreciation tax-shelter TD_t, however, which is discounted at $(1 + r)$ because we assume it to be certain, now becomes a random variable given by $TD_t/[(1 + r)(1 + h)]^t$. This is a random variable since h (even in a neutral inflation) is a random variable. Hence, a risky discount rate r^*, which is greater than the risk-free rate, r, should be used when discounting the depreciation tax shelter. (The nominal discount rate applied to TD_t therefore is $(1 + r^*)(1 + h)$.)

To sum up, non-neutral inflation increases risk, thereby increasing the cost of capital. It also causes the depreciation tax shelter to become risky. A neutral inflation, on the other hand, has no impact on the firm's real cost of capital but it still introduces an element of risk into the depreciation tax shelter, which reduces the present value of this term. In both cases, a project's *NPV* is reduced either by an increase in k_R, or an increase in r, or by an increase in both. All these factors discourage investment, in particular for unlevered firms who do not enjoy the "capital gain" on their debts (see Chapter 7 above). Since the latter seems to be the only real benefit accruing to firms from inflation, we expect the corporate sector to increase their debt in an inflationary environment. And indeed in late 1979 IBM floated the largest industrial debt issue in the history of the US; Du Pont tripled its outstanding debt, and many other companies began to follow suit.

STOCK PRICES AND INFLATION

In the preceding section we noted that in a fully anticipated neutral inflation the cost of capital will tend to rise in direct proportion to the rise in the price level.

In this section we turn our attention to the relationship between stock prices and inflation, a subject which has been the source of some confusion.

As we noted above, a fully anticipated price rise one year hence will have no impact on the *present* market price of shares. However, their future prices will reflect the rate of inflation; the relevant end of period price of the shares will rise in proportion to the rate of inflation. Let us consider a simple case of *no growth*, that is a firm with constant earnings, E, and which distributes all of these earnings as dividends, so that $E = D$. The price of the stock in period t is given by:

$$P_t = \frac{D}{1 + k_R} + \frac{D}{(1 + k_R)^2} + \ldots = \frac{D}{k_R}$$

The price of the stock one year later, in period $t + 1$, remains the same:

$$P_{t+1} = \frac{D}{1 + k_R} + \frac{D}{(1 + k_R)^2} + \ldots = \frac{D}{k_R} = P_t$$

Now let us assume a fully anticipated neutral inflation of $h\%$ per year. What will be the impact of this rate of price increase on the present and future share prices of our hypothetical firm? Today's price is given by the capitalization of the new dividends (= earnings) stream which by the definition of neutral inflation will rise at the same rate as the inflation:

$$P_t = \frac{D(1 + h)}{1 + k_h} + \frac{D(1 + h)^2}{(1 + k_h)^2} + \ldots$$

where k_h denotes the new *nominal* cost of capital. Recalling the dividend growth model, the present price of the share in this instance is given by:[7]

$$P_t = \frac{D(1 + h)}{k_h - h} = \frac{D(1 + h)}{k_R + h + kh - h} = \frac{D(1 + h)}{k_R(1 + h)} = \frac{D}{k_R}$$

i.e. there is no immediate impact on the stock price. However, one year later the price of the share is given by the capitalization of the following dividend stream:

$$P_{t+1} = \frac{D(1 + h)^2}{1 + k_h} + \frac{D(1 + h)^3}{(1 + k_h)^2} + \ldots \text{ and}$$

$$P_{t+1} = \frac{D(1 + h)^2}{k_h - h}$$

Thus $P_{t+1} = (1 + h)P_t$, i.e. the end of period share price rises at the same rate as inflation. This is not too surprising. After all it is precisely this phenomenon

---

7 Summing the geometric progression yields:

$$\frac{D(1 + h)}{1 + k_h} \left[1 + \frac{1 + h}{1 + k_h} + \frac{(1 + h)^2}{(1 + k_h)^2} + \ldots \right]$$

$$= \frac{D(1 + h)}{1 + k_h} \cdot \frac{1}{1 - \dfrac{1 + h}{1 + k_h}} = \frac{D(1 + h)}{k_h - h}$$

Also note that by definition $k_h = k_R + h + k_R h$.

which underlies the popular view that common stock can provide a hedge against inflation.

STOCK PRICES AND STAGFLATION

In the early 1970s the economy was confronted by a new situation which has been popularly dubbed as stagflation. In recent years, the rise in the cost of living index has been acompanied by recession and an increase in unemployment. In such a case, common stock no longer provides a hedge against inflation since the prices of stocks fall in real, and even in nominal, terms during stagflation. To be more specific, let us consider a firm which distributes all its earnings as dividends. The stock price in the absence of inflation, as we have already seen, is

$$P = \frac{D}{1 + k_R} + \frac{D}{(1 + k_R)^2} + \ldots = \frac{D}{k_R}$$

where k_R is the discount rate in the absence of inflation. Now, suppose that there is inflation of $h\%$ a year and hence the new discount rate is approximately $k_h = k_R + h$. If the nominal earnings (dividends) remain unaffected by inflation we obtain

$$P_h = \frac{D}{1 + k_h} + \frac{D}{(1 + k_h)^2} + \ldots = \frac{D}{k_h}$$

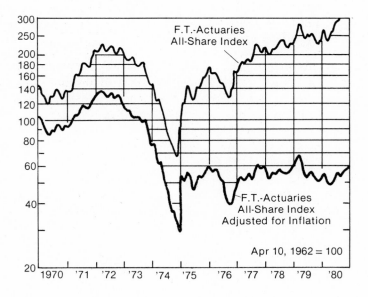

Fig. 22.2
Share Price Movements in Real Terms
Source: *Financial Times*

where P_h denotes the price of the stock assuming inflation. Since k_h by construction must be higher than k_R then $P_h < P$, that is the price of the stock *falls* with inflation in this instance. The explanation is straightforward. In stagflation a firm's profits lag behind the rise in the general price level (or even fall) and due to this imperfect adjustment *real* profits decline. The decline in profits reflects the "cost-push" nature of recent inflation in which firms' input prices have risen at a faster rate than the prices paid for final output. As a result, stock prices which reflect the anticipated real earnings stream also fall, and common stocks lose some of their appeal as an inflation hedge.

This is illustrated, for the case of England, in Fig. 22.2 which plots the London common stock index in nominal and real terms. The impact of stagflation on share prices can easily be discerned from the graph. Following the 1973 oil crisis, common stock prices fell dramatically in nominal, and even more in real, terms. And although share prices recovered towards the end of the decade of the 1970s in nominal terms, their real values remained below their 1970 level.

STOCK PRICES AND INFLATION: THE EMPIRICAL EVIDENCE[8]

The classical view of inflation asserts that common stock returns and inflation are positively related, a view which gives rise to the investment maxim that ordinary shares provide a good hedge against the attrition of price instability.[9] Recently, researchers have questioned this viewpoint and have attempted to estimate empirically the historical relationship between inflation and the return on equities. Although their results depend on the time period chosen, data from many countries suggest that the positive long run correlation beween inflation and stock prices has been impaired, and even reversed, in the post-World War II period. The empirical evidence shows that, with the single exception of Japan, common stocks have not provided a good inflation hedge during the past decade in all countries having a major stock exchange.[10]

The discrepancy between traditional theory and reality has led to a number of empirical studies with the purpose of explaining the relationship between equity values and inflation. In a series of articles John Lintner[11] has examined

8 See M. Ben Horim and H. Levy, "Financial Management in an Inflationary Economy", in E. Altman (editor), *Financial Handbook*, New York: Wiley, forthcoming.

9 This is an extension of Irving Fisher's hypothesis that in a perfect capital market under certainty the nominal rate of interest will be equal to the real rate plus the new rate of inflation. See Irving Fisher, *The Theory of Interest*, New York: Macmillan, 1930. The implications of this hypothesis with respect to interest rates have been studied empirically by E. F. Fama, *Foundations of Finance*, New York: Basic Books, 1975; P. J. Hess and J. L. Bicksler, "Capital Asset Prices versus Time Series Models as Predictors of Inflation: the Expected Real Rate of Interest and Market Efficiency", *Journal of Financial Economics*, December 1975; and C. R. Nelson and G. W. Schwert, "Short-Term Interest Rates as Predictors of Inflation: On Testing the Hypothesis that the Real Rate of Interest is Constant", *American Economic Review*, June 1977.

10 See B. Moore, "Equity Values and Inflation: The Importance of Dividends", *Lloyds Bank Review*, July 1980.

11 See J. Lintner, "Inflation and Security Returns", *The Journal of Finance*, May 1975; and "Inflation and Common Stock Prices in a Cyclical Context", in National Bureau of Economic Research, *53rd Annual Report*, September 1973.

the relationship between annual stock price changes and annual changes in the general price level. His main findings are as follows:

(a) A simple regression between the annual percentage change in stock prices and the annual percentage change in the wholesale price index over a 70-year period shows *no correlation* between these two variables. This result is obtained largely because both high inflation rates and serious deflation tend to reduce stock returns. Lintner found that a 10% deflation reduces stock prices by 15%; however, a 10% inflation also reduces equity returns by 4.1%.

(b) When percentage changes in earnings and interest rates are added to the regression equation, as explanatory variables, the explained variance of stock price changes (i.e., the dependent variable) rises to about 33%. Deflation is the most powerful explanatory variable in the equation; a 10% price fall was estimated to *reduce* prices by 33%. A 10% inflation, on the other hand, was estimated to *reduce* stock prices by only about 6.7%. Since these are estimates in a multiple regression analysis in which percentage changes in earnings and interest rates are included as explanatory variables, these effects on stock prices are *net* of the effect of earnings and interest rates.

Lintner concludes that the classical theory of the relationship between changes in the price level and stock prices is not valid. He notes that the theory will hold if the *real* returns to ownership of capital goods and the real interest rate are invariant to inflation, but adds that there are good reasons to believe that neither premise holds.

Additional evidence contradicting the traditional view has been provided by Zvi Bodie[12] who applies a portfolio approach to the question of common

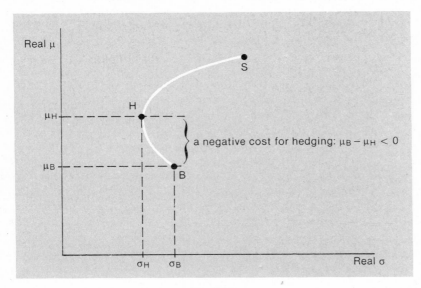

Fig. 22.3
The Efficient Frontier between S and B.
The Stock Portfolio S is Held Long at the Minimum Variance Portfolio H

12 See Z. Bodie, "Common Stocks as a Hedge Against Inflation", *Journal of Finance*, May 1976.

stock returns and inflation. He focuses on the variance of a bond free of default, the risk of which originates solely from the *inflation uncertainty*. Bodie seeks to determine the extent to which an investor can reduce the uncertainty of the real return on such a nominal bond by combining it with a well diversified portfolio of common stocks.

Consider Fig. 22.3 in which the expected return and standard deviation of a default-free bond (B) and a well diversified portfolio of common stock (S) are shown. Portfolio theory teaches that B and S can be combined into a portfolio whose expected return and standard deviation lie along the curve BS (see Chapter 12 above). The precise location of the portfolio depends on the proportion of investment allocated to B and S, and Bodie was concerned with the proportions that bring the portfolio's variance (or standard deviation) to a minimum. If a combination of B and S can result in a portfolio such as H in the figure, where the standard deviation of H (σ_H) is smaller than the standard deviation of $B(\sigma_B)$, then, equities do provide (at least some) hedge against inflation. Clearly, common stocks provide a perfect hedge against inflation when $\sigma_H = 0$ and a partial hedge when $\sigma_H > 0$. The *cost of hedging* is defined as the difference between the mean real return on the nominal bond (μ_B) and the mean real return on the minimum variance portfolio (μ_H). In Fig. 22.3, ($\mu_B - \mu_H$) < 0; hence the cost is negative since combining a well diversified portfolio of common stocks with B not only decreases the risk from σ_B to σ_H, it also increases the return from μ_B to μ_H.

But the situation described by Fig. 22.3 is not the only possible one. Consider Fig. 22.4 in which the minimum variance portfolio, H, is not located between the points B and S, but on the extension of the curve SB beyond B. Portfolio theory advises that to attain portfolio H, B must be *held* long and S *short*. If empirical findings indicate that the minimum variance portfolio includes the well-diversified stock portfolio S with a negative proportion, i.e., S is held short, the situation corresponds to Fig. 22.4, and the conclusion is that stocks do not provide a hedge against inflation (when held in long position). The cost of hedging in Fig. 22.4 is positive ($\mu_B - \mu_H$) > 0, so that one can reduce the variance below σ_B, but only at the cost of reducing the expected value below μ_B.

Using data for 1953 – 72, Bodie found that the minimum variance portfolio could be attained only when the common stock portfolio were held short, not long. To attain the minimum variance portfolio, the investor must sell short about $0.03 worth of equity for every $1.03 invested in nominal bonds. By doing that, the hedge can eliminate roughly 18% of the variance of the real return on the bonds. The cost of such a hedge would have been a reduction in expected return of 0.34%. Moreover, Bodie found that not only is the real return on equity negatively correlated with unanticipated inflation, but it is also inversely related to anticipated inflation. The estimate he obtained was that an increase of 1 percentage point in the expected rate of inflation is associated with a decline of 4 percentage points in the real return on equity.

Fama and Schwert[13] have examined the empirical relationship between

13 E. F. Fama and G. W. Schwert, "Asset Returns and Inflation", *Journal of Financial Economics*, November 1977.

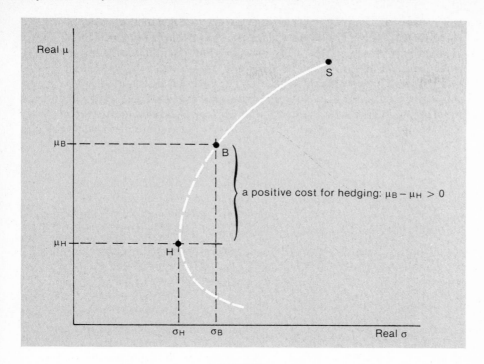

Fig. 22.4

realized rates of return on various assets and the rate of inflation. Their study was concerned with both expected and unexpected inflation and used the returns to stock portfolios, US Treasury bills, longer-term US government bonds, the returns on privately held residential real estate and nominal income from human capital. The period covered by the study is 1953 through 1971.

The main tests in the study involve separate time series regression analyses for each asset. The dependent variable in such a regression is the asset's nominal rate of return and the two explanatory variables are measures of expected and unexpected inflation. The variable that was used as a proxy for the expected inflation was the Treasury Bill nominal interest rate. The rationale for such a procedure is that if the expected real return on the bill is constant through time, and if the bill market is efficient, the nominal rate on the bill is equal to a constant expected real return plus the expected inflation rate. Unexpected inflation was estimated as the difference between the ex-post realized inflation rate. Denoting expected inflation by x_1, unexpected inflation by x_2, and the nominal rate of return on an asset by R, the regression used for each asset is given by,

$$R_t = \beta_0 + \beta_1 x_{1t} + \beta_2 x_{2t}$$

where the subscript t denotes a value for period t.

A coefficient $\beta_1 = 1.0$ in the regression indicates that when anticipated inflation rises by one percentage point ("on the average") so does the nominal rate of return on the asset, which means that the asset is a good hedge against anticipated inflation. Similarly, a coefficient $\beta_2 = 1.0$ means that when unantici-pated inflation rises by one percentage point ("on the average") so does the nominal rate of return on the asset. Such an asset is a good hedge against unanticipated inflation.

Running the returns of the aforementioned assets against the anticipated and unanticipated rates of inflation using monthly, quarterly and semi-annual data, Fama and Schwert reached the following conclusions:[14]

(a)   Of all assets, only private residential real estate was a complete hedge against both expected and unexpected inflation during the 1953 – 71 period.
(b)   Government debt instruments (i.e., bonds and bills) are a complete hedge against *expected* inflation, but not against unanticipated inflation.
(c)   Common stock returns are negatively related to expected and unexpected inflation. They are also negatively related to changes in expected inflation.

Similarly, Irwin Friend and Joel Hasbrouck[15] have also found a negative correlation between rates of return on equity and the rate of inflation. They attribute this finding to two principal factors:

(a)   a decline in real dividends and earnings of the firms
(b)   an increase in the real required rates of return on stocks.

The Friend – Hasbrouck findings, i.e., that inflation reduces profits while at the same time increasing risk (hence the rise in required rates of return on stocks), is especially appropriate for what we have called "stagflation". They found that a one percentage point increase in steady-state inflation is accom-panied by a 5% decline in dividends and about 10% decline in real economic earnings per share. Thus, inflation tends to decrease economic earnings per share more sharply than cash dividends implying that the payout ratio increases under inflation. The decrease in dividends and the increase in risk (due to the fact that typically inflation is *non-neutral*), depresses stock prices and produces the negative relationship between rates of return on equity and the rate of inflation.[16]

The interaction between the returns on common stock and the rate of infla-tion has also been investigated by other researchers. Oudet found, using quarterly data over the period 1953 – 70, that expected returns on common stock are negatively correlated with ex-post rates as well as anticipated rates of

14 More recently, Fama has conjectured that stock returns are determined by forecasts of real economic variables. Hence the observed negative stock return — inflation relationship reflects the underlying negative relationships between inflation and many aspects of real income activity.
15 See I. Friend and J. Hasbrouck, "Effect of Inflation on the Profitability and Valuation of U.S. Corporations", in M. Sarnat and G. Szego (editors), *Saving, Investment and Capital Markets in an Inflationary Economy*, Ballinger, forthcoming.
16 In a fully indexed economy with a neutral inflation one would expect stock prices to increase along with inflation. However, since corporate earnings are not indexed, the effective tax burden increases with inflation. As a result, the economy is better described by a scenario of stagflation which has induced stock prices to fall even in nominal terms during the recent bout of double-digit inflation.

inflation.[17] Jaffe and Mandelker using monthly data provide similar evidence that ex-post rates of return on common stock are negatively correlated with expected as well as unexpected inflation rates.[18] Similar results have been reported by Bodie, Jaffe and Mandelker, and Nelson[19]; while Brenner and Galai[20] found that even in the inflation-intensive environment of Israel quarterly changes in the rate of return on common stocks cannot be explained by quarterly changes in the inflation rate.

INDEXATION OF FINANCIAL ASSETS

When uncertainty regarding the purchasing power of money becomes very great, investors may become unwilling to acquire fixed-income bearing securities unless an explicit purchasing power guarantee is added to the contract. Thus the worldwide inflation during and after the Second World War led a number of countries to introduce investments whose interest and/or principal were linked to various price indexes. Such experiments with indexation have been tried in Finland, Israel, Brazil and recently for small saving deposits in the UK. In addition, purchasing power guarantees, or escalator clauses as they are often called, have been included in wage contracts and pension contracts in the United States and many European countries.

Although the overwhelming weight of theoretical authority has favored indexation, in principle, for the past century,[21] it is remarkable that so few experiments with indexation have actually taken place. Much of the practical opposition to indexation reflects the reluctance of the financial community to introduce a new and untried investment medium whose impact on the capital market and existing financial institutions is uncertain. Thus it is somewhat paradoxical that a device designed to help the capital market function in times of financial stress should engender the most opposition among the practitioners in that market.

Part of this opposition reflects technical difficulties. Since inflation is typically non-neutral, which particular price index should be used for financial

---

17 See B. A. Oudet, "The Variation of the Return on Stocks in Periods of Inflation", *Journal of Financial and Quantitative Analysis*, March 1973.

18 See J. F. Jaffe and G. Mandelker, "The Fisher Effect for Risky Assets: An Empirical Test", Working Paper, Carnegie-Mellon University, Pittsburgh Pa., September 1974.

   More recently the same authors have reported a slight positive correlation, between the holding period returns on fixed-interest bearing securities and anticipated inflation, see Jaffe and Mandelker, "Inflation and the Holding Period Returns on Bonds", *Journal of Financial and Quantitative Analysis*, December 1979.

19 See Z. Bodie, "Common Stocks as a Hedge Against Inflation", *Journal of Finance*, May 1976; J. Jaffe and G. Mandelker, "The 'Fisher Effect' for Risky Assets: An Empirical Investigation", *Journal of Finance*, May 1976; and C. R. Nelson, "Inflation and Rates of Return on Common Stocks", *Journal of Finance*, May 1976.

20 See M. Brenner and D. Galai, "The Empirical Relationship between Inflation and Financial Assets' Returns in an Inflation-Intensive Capital Market", in M. Sarnat (editor), *Inflation and Capital Markets*, Cambridge, Mass. Ballinger Publishing Company, 1978.

21 For a summary of the arguments on behalf of indexation, see M. Sarnat "Purchasing Power Risk, Portfolio Analysis and the Case for Index-Linked Bonds", *Journal of Money, Credit and Banking*, August 1973.

contracts? Clearly, firms whose product prices lag behind the general average may be very reluctant to enter into debt contracts which tie their liability to future rises in the general index. How should the gains from indexation be treated for tax purposes? And how should the indexed contracts be reflected in the corporation's accounts?

All of these questions, and others, represent serious obstacles to the introduction of indexation. However, should the reduced effectiveness of common stock as an inflation hedge which became apparent during the stagflation of the 1970s continue, the case for indexation will be greatly strengthened. Although stable purchasing power debt instruments are not a panacea for all of the economy's ills, and most certainly are not a desirable substitute for price stability itself, they potentially can make an important contribution to the orderly functioning of the capital market especially in a highly uncertain inflationary environment.

SUMMARY

This chapter has briefly surveyed the impact of inflation on financial decision-making. To this end it is convenient to draw several distinctions:

(a)   An inflation characterized by *excess* demand vs. *cost push* inflation in which the rise in prices is associated with a prior rise in wages and other costs.

(b)   A *pure* or neutral inflation in which all prices (and wages) rise in the same proportion so that relative prices do not change.

(c)   *Real* vs. nominal interest rates. The former can be approximated by deducting the increase in the general price level from the nominal interest rate.

(d)   *Real* vs. nominal cost of capital. In a typical excess demand type of inflation in which both revenues and costs rise, the required return on both debt and equity will tend to rise at the rate of inflation, and therefore, the weighted average cost of capital will also rise at that rate.

The chapter concludes with an analysis of the relationship between stock prices and inflation. In a fully anticipated neutral inflation the prices of common stocks will rise at the same rate as the inflation. However, in the case of the stagflation which has affected much of the world in recent years, the prices of common stock have fallen in real terms. As a result, the bulk of the empirical evidence shows that common stock is no longer a very effective hedge against inflation.

QUESTIONS AND PROBLEMS

22.1   What are the major problems associated with the measurement of inflation?

22.2 Define the following terms:

(a) Consumer Price Index (CPI);
(b) GNP Deflator;
(c) Cost-push inflation;
(d) Stagflation;
(e) Pure inflation.

22.3 Explain the term "purchasing power risk" and give examples of cases in which it exists.

22.4 Assume that the rate of interest on a one-year bond is 9%.
Calculate the real rate of interest on this bond, assuming that the general level of consumer prices rises by:

(a) 4%;
(b) 6%;
(c) 8%;
(d) 10%.

22.5 Assume that the general level of consumer prices is expected to increase by 7% in the coming year.
What nominal interest rate do you require in order to earn a:

(a) real rate of 3%;
(b) real rate of 4%;
(c) real rate of 5%?

22.6 What nominal interest rate is required on a one-year bond in order to earn a real rate of 3.5% if prices are expected to rise in the coming year, by:

(a) 5%;
(b) 7%;
(c) 9%?

22.7 Assume a firm which distributes all its earnings as dividends. What will be the market price of its stock if the dividend is $4.80 per share (and will remain in future years at this level), the cost of capital (in the absence of inflation) is 12%, and inflation is expected to raise all prices at a rate of 4% a year?

22.8 Assume a firm which distributes $2.70 per share as dividends every year. What will be the impact of an increase in the expected rate of inflation from 5% to 8% on the minimum required return (cost of capital)? Assume that the market price of the firm's stock was initially $30.

22.9 What are the alternative ways to evaluate investment opportunities under conditions of inflation?

22.10   Show, using a numerical example, that stock prices tend to rise at the same rate as inflation, in the no growth case.

22.11   Assume a firm which distributes all its earnings as dividends. The annual dividend of the firm is $3.60 per share and the cost of capital (in the absence of inflation) is 10%. Assume a case of *stagflation*, in which the general price level rises at a rate of 8% a year, and the nominal earnings of the firm at a rate of only 3%. What will be the impact of the stagflation on the value of the firm's stock?

SELECTED REFERENCES

Amihud, Y. and Barnea, A., "A Note on Fisher Hypothesis and Price Level Uncertainty", *Journal of Financial and Quantitative Analysis*, September 1977.

Baesel, Jerome B. and Biger, Nahum, "The Allocation of Risk: Some Implications of Fixed versus Index-linked Mortgages", *Journal of Financial and Quantitative Analysis*, June 1980.

Baran, Arie, Lakonishik, Josef and Ofer, Aharon R., "The Value of General Price Level Adjusted Data to Bond Rating", *Journal of Business Finance & Accounting*, Spring 1980.

Bhattacharya, Sudipto, "Welfare and Savings Effects of Indexation", *Journal of Money, Credit and Banking*, May 1979.

Bicksler, J. L. and Hess, P. J., "More on Purchasing Power Risk, Portfolio Analysis and the Case for Index-Linked Bonds: Comment", *Journal of Money, Credit and Banking*, May 1976.

Biger, N., "Portfolio Selection and Purchasing Power Risk: Recent Canadian Experience", *Journal of Financial and Quantitative Analysis*, June 1976.

Biger, N. and Kahane, Yehuda, "Purchasing Power Risk and the Performance of Non-Life Insurance Companies", *The Journal of Risk and Insurance*, March 1976.

Blejer, Mario I. and Eden, Benjamin, "A Note on the Specification of the Fisher Equation Under Inflation Uncertainty", *Economics Letters*, Vol. 3 1979.

Bodie, Z., "Common Stocks as a Hedge against Inflation", *Journal of Finance*, May 1976.

Bomberger, W. A. and Makinen, G. E., "The Fisher Effect: Graphical Treatment and Some Econometric Implications", *Journal of Finance*, June 1977.

Bradford, William D., "Monetary Position, Unanticipated Inflation, and Changes in the Value of the Firm", *The Quarterly Review of Economics and Business*, Winter 1976.

Branch, Ben, "Common Stock Performance and Inflation: An International Comparison", *The Journal of Business*, January 1974.

Brealey, R. and Schaefer, S. "Term Structure with Uncertain Inflation", *Journal of Finance*, May 1977.

Cargill, T. F. and Meyer, R. A. "Intertemporal Stability of the Relationship beween Interest Rates and Price Chances", *Journal of Finance*, September 1977.

Chen, A. H., "Effects of Purchasing Power Risk on Portfolio Demand for Money", *Journal of Financial and Quantitative Analysis*, June 1979.

Choate, G. M. and Archer, S. H., "Irving Fisher, Inflation, and the Nominal Rate of Interest", *Journal of Financial and Quantitative Analysis*, November 1975.

Cohn, R. A. and Lessard, D. R., "Recent Research on Indexation and the Housing Market", *Journal of Finance*, May 1976.

Cornell, W. B., "Which Inflation Rate Affects Interest Rates?" *Business Economics*, May 1977.

Cukierman, Alex, "The Effects of Wage Indexation on Macroeconomic Fluctuations: A Generalization", *Journal of Monetary Economics*, April 1980.

De Alessi, Louis, "Do Business Firms Gain from Inflation? Reprise", *Journal of Business*, April 1975.

Fama, E. F., "Inflation Uncertainty and Expected Returns on Treasury Bills", *Journal of Political Economy*, June 1976.

Fama, E. F. and Schwert, G. W., "Asset Returns and Inflation", *Journal of Financial Economics*, November 1977.

Fama, E. F., "Interest Rates and Inflation: The Message in the Entrails", *American Economic Review*, June 1977.

Feldstein, Martin, "Inflation and the Stock Market", *The American Economic Review*, December 1980.

Fischer, Stanley, "The Demand for Index Bonds", *Journal of Political Economy*, June 1975.

Friend, I., Landskroner, Y. and Losq, E., "The Demand for Risky Assets under Uncertain Inflation", *Journal of Finance*, December 1976.

Hagerman, R. L. and Kim, E. H., "Capital Asset Pricing with Price Level Changes", *Journal of Financial and Quantitative Analysis*, September 1976.

Hess, P. J. and Bicksler, J. L., "Capital Asset Prices versus Time Series Models as Predictors of Inflation: The Expected Real Rate of Interest and Market Efficiency", *Journal of Financial Economics*, December 1975.

Hong, H., "Inflation and the Market Value of the Firm: Theory and Tests", *Journal of Finance*, September 1977.

Ibbotson, R. G. and Sinquefield, R. A., "Stocks, Bonds, Bills and Inflation: Simulations of the Future", *Journal of Business*, July 1976.

Ibbotson, R. G. and Sinquefield, R. A., *Stocks, Bonds, Bills and Inflation: The Past (1926 – 1976) and the Future (1977 – 2000)*, Charlottesville , Va.: The Financial Analysis Research Foundation, 1977.

Jaffe, J. F. and Mandelker, G., "The 'Fisher Effect' for Risky Assets: An Empirical Investigation", *Journal of Finance*, May 1976.

Jaffe, J. F. and Mandelker, G., "Inflation and the Holding Period Returns on Bonds", *Journal of Financial and Quantitative Analysis*, December 1979.

Laidler, D. E. and Parkin, J. M., "Inflation: A Survey", *Economic Journal*, December 1975.

Lee, C. F., Lee, J. C. and Zumwalt, J. K., "An Analytical Examination of Real versus Nominal Rates of Return Matrices in Portfolio Management", *Journal of Economics and Business*, Fall, 1979.

Levi, M. D. and Makin, J. H., "Fisher, Phillips, Friedman and the Measured Impact of Inflation on Interest", *Journal of Finance*, March 1979.

Logue, Dennis E. and Willett, Thomas D., "A Note on the Relation between the Rate and Variability of Inflation", *Economica*, May 1976.

McCulloch, J. Huston, "The Ban on Indexed Bonds, 1933 – 77", *American Economic Review*, December 1980.

Manaster, S., "Real and Nominal Efficient Sets", *Journal of Finance*, March 1979.

Nelson, C. R., "Inflation and Rates of Return on Common Stocks", *Journal of Finance*, May 1976.

Nelson, C. R. and Schwert, G. W., "Short-Term Interest Rates as Predictors of Inflation: On Testing the Hypothesis that the Real Rate of Interest is Constant", *American Economic Review*, June 1977.

Pyun, C. S., "A Note on Capital Asset Pricing Model under Uncertain Inflation", *Journal of Financial and Quantitative Analysis*, June 1980.

Reilly, F. K., Smith, R. E. and Johnson, G. L., "A Correction and Update Regarding Individual Common Stocks as Inflation Hedges", *Journal of Financial and Quantitative Analysis*, December 1975.

Reilly, F. K., Johnson, G. L. and Smith, R. E., "A Note on Common Stocks as Inflation Hedges — The After-Tax Case", *The Southern Journal of Business*, November 1972.

Sarnat, Marshall, "Purchasing Power Risk, Portfolio Analysis and the Case for Index-Linked Bonds", *Journal of Money, Credit and Banking*, August 1973.

Siegel, J. J. and Warner, J. B., "Indexation, the Risk-Free Asset, and Capital Market Equilibrium", *Journal of Finance*, September 1977.

Soldofsky, Robert M. and Max, Dale F., "Securities as a Hedge against Inflation: 1910 – 1969", *Journal of Business Research*, April 1975.

Solnik, B. H., "Inflation and Optimal Portfolio Choices", *Journal of Financial and Quantitative Analysis*, December 1978.

Spahr, R. W., "The Impact of Inflation on the Measure of Security Risk", *Review of Business and Economic Research*, Winter 1978 – 79.

Von Furstenberg, G. M. and Malkiel, B. G., "Financial Analysis in an Inflationary Environment", *Journal of Finance*, May 1977.

Yaari, Uzi, Palmon, Dan and Marcus, Matityahu, "Stock Prices Under Inflation with Taxation of Nominal Gains", *The Financial Review*, Winter 1980.

PART III: SUGGESTIONS FOR FURTHER READING

The reader who wishes to examine the impact of capital structure on the value of the firm at greater length can well start with the classic article by Franco Modigliani and Merton Miller and then go on to the extensive literature which has emerged in recent years:

F. Modigliani and M. H. Miller, "The Cost of Capital, Corporation Finance and the Theory of Investment", *American Economic Review*, June 1958.

F. Modigliani and M. H. Miller, "Reply to Heins and Sprenkle," *American Economic Review*, September 1969.

E. F. Fama and M. H. Miller, *The Theory of Finance*, New York, Holt Rinehart & Winston, 1972.

The significance of bankruptcy risk for financial decision-making is analyzed in the following:

E. I. Altman, *Corporate Bankruptcy in America*, Lexington Mass., Heath Lexington Books, 1971.

N. D. Baxter, "Leverage, Risk of Ruin, and the Cost of Capital", *Journal of Finance*, September 1967.

J. E. Stiglitz, "On the Irrelevance of Corporate Financial Policy", *American Economic Review*, December 1974.

D. P. Baron, "Firm Valuation, Corporate Taxes and Default Risk", *Journal of Finance*, December 1975.

J. H. Scott Jr., "A Theory of Optimal Capital Structure", *Bell Journal of Economics*, Spring 1976.

The Weighted Average Cost of Capital has been re-examined:

F. D. Arditti, "The Weighted Average Cost of Capital: Some Questions on its Definition, Interpretation and Use", *Journal of Finance*, September 1973.

E. J. Elton and M. J. Gruber, "Valuation and the Cost of Capital for Regulated Industries", *Journal of Finance*, June 1971.

M. J. Gordon and P. J. Halpern, "Cost of Capital for a Division of a Firm", *Journal of Finance*, September 1974.

Dividend policy has also been the subject of numerous articles and books but the flavor of the debate can be sampled in:

M. H. Miller and F. Modigliani, "Dividend Policy, Growth and the Valuation of Shares", *Journal of Business*, October 1961.

M. J. Gordon, "Optimal Investment and Financing Policy", *Journal of Finance*, May 1963.

M. J. Brennan, "A Note on Dividend Irrelevance and the Gordon Valuation Model", *Journal of Finance*, December 1971.

A critical review of empirical studies of dividend effects is given by:

I. Friend and M. Puckett, "Dividends and Stock Prices", *American Economic Review*, September 1964.

T. E. Copeland and J. Fred Weston, *Financial Theory and Corporate Policy*, Reading, Mass., Addison-Wesley, 1979.

The Linear Programming Approach to capital rationing is developed by:

H. M. Weingartner, *Mathematical Programming and the Analysis of Capital Budgeting Problems*, Englewood Cliffs, N. J., Prentice Hall, 1963.

W. J. Baumol and R. E. Quandt, "Investment and Discount Rates Under Capital Rationing — a Programming Approach", *Economic Journal*, June 1965.

F. D. Arditti, R. C. Grinold and H. Levy, "The Investment-Consumption Decision Under Capital Rationing: An Efficiency Analysis", *Review of Economic Studies*, July 1973.

Appendix
Tables A – E

TABLE A   Present Value of 1

Periods	1%	2%	3%	4%	5%	6%	7%	8%	9%	10%
1	0.990	0.980	0.971	0.962	0.952	0.943	0.935	0.926	0.917	0.909
2	0.980	0.961	0.943	0.925	0.907	0.890	0.873	0.857	0.842	0.826
3	0.971	0.942	0.915	0.889	0.864	0.840	0.816	0.794	0.772	0.751
4	0.961	0.924	0.888	0.855	0.823	0.792	0.763	0.735	0.708	0.683
5	0.951	0.906	0.863	0.822	0.784	0.747	0.713	0.681	0.650	0.621
6	0.942	0.888	0.837	0.790	0.746	0.705	0.666	0.630	0.596	0.564
7	0.933	0.871	0.813	0.760	0.711	0.665	0.623	0.583	0.547	0.513
8	0.923	0.853	0.789	0.731	0.677	0.627	0.582	0.540	0.502	0.467
9	0.914	0.837	0.766	0.703	0.645	0.592	0.544	0.500	0.460	0.424
10	0.905	0.820	0.744	0.676	0.614	0.558	0.508	0.463	0.422	0.386
11	0.896	0.804	0.722	0.650	0.585	0.527	0.475	0.429	0.388	0.350
12	0.887	0.788	0.701	0.625	0.557	0.497	0.444	0.397	0.356	0.319
13	0.879	0.773	0.681	0.601	0.530	0.469	0.415	0.368	0.326	0.290
14	0.870	0.758	0.661	0.577	0.505	0.442	0.388	0.340	0.299	0.263
15	0.861	0.743	0.642	0.555	0.481	0.417	0.362	0.315	0.275	0.239
16	0.853	0.728	0.623	0.534	0.458	0.394	0.339	0.292	0.252	0.218
17	0.844	0.714	0.605	0.513	0.436	0.371	0.317	0.270	0.231	0.198
18	0.836	0.700	0.587	0.494	0.416	0.350	0.296	0.250	0.212	0.180
19	0.828	0.686	0.570	0.475	0.396	0.331	0.277	0.232	0.194	0.164
20	0.820	0.673	0.554	0.456	0.377	0.312	0.258	0.215	0.178	0.149
21	0.811	0.660	0.538	0.439	0.359	0.294	0.242	0.199	0.164	0.135
22	0.803	0.647	0.522	0.422	0.342	0.278	0.226	0.184	0.150	0.123
23	0.795	0.634	0.507	0.406	0.326	0.262	0.211	0.170	0.138	0.112
24	0.788	0.622	0.492	0.390	0.310	0.247	0.197	0.158	0.126	0.102
25	0.780	0.610	0.478	0.375	0.295	0.233	0.184	0.146	0.116	0.092
26	0.772	0.598	0.464	0.361	0.281	0.220	0.172	0.135	0.106	0.084
27	0.764	0.586	0.450	0.347	0.268	0.207	0.161	0.125	0.098	0.076
28	0.757	0.574	0.437	0.333	0.255	0.196	0.150	0.116	0.090	0.069
29	0.749	0.563	0.424	0.321	0.243	0.185	0.141	0.107	0.082	0.063
30	0.742	0.552	0.412	0.308	0.231	0.174	0.131	0.099	0.075	0.057
40	0.672	0.453	0.307	0.208	0.142	0.097	0.067	0.046	0.032	0.022
50	0.608	0.372	0.228	0.141	0.087	0.054	0.034	0.021	0.013	0.009

Table A (contd.) – Present Value of 1

Periods	11%	12%	13%	14%	15%	16%	17%	18%	19%	20%
1	0.901	0.893	0.885	0.877	0.870	0.862	0.855	0.847	0.840	0.833
2	0.812	0.797	0.783	0.769	0.756	0.743	0.731	0.718	0.706	0.694
3	0.731	0.712	0.693	0.675	0.658	0.641	0.624	0.609	0.593	0.579
4	0.659	0.636	0.613	0.592	0.572	0.552	0.534	0.516	0.499	0.482
5	0.593	0.567	0.543	0.519	0.497	0.476	0.456	0.437	0.419	0.402
6	0.535	0.507	0.480	0.456	0.432	0.410	0.390	0.370	0.352	0.335
7	0.482	0.452	0.425	0.400	0.376	0.354	0.333	0.314	0.296	0.279
8	0.434	0.404	0.376	0.351	0.327	0.305	0.285	0.266	0.249	0.233
9	0.391	0.361	0.333	0.308	0.284	0.263	0.243	0.225	0.209	0.194
10	0.352	0.322	0.295	0.270	0.247	0.227	0.208	0.191	0.176	0.162
11	0.317	0.287	0.261	0.237	0.215	0.195	0.178	0.162	0.148	0.135
12	0.286	0.257	0.231	0.208	0.187	0.168	0.152	0.137	0.124	0.112
13	0.258	0.229	0.204	0.182	0.163	0.145	0.130	0.116	0.104	0.093
14	0.232	0.205	0.181	0.160	0.141	0.125	0.111	0.099	0.088	0.078
15	0.209	0.183	0.160	0.140	0.123	0.108	0.095	0.084	0.074	0.065
16	0.188	0.163	0.141	0.123	0.107	0.093	0.081	0.071	0.062	0.054
17	0.170	0.146	0.125	0.108	0.093	0.080	0.069	0.060	0.052	0.045
18	0.153	0.130	0.111	0.095	0.081	0.069	0.059	0.051	0.044	0.038
19	0.138	0.116	0.098	0.083	0.070	0.060	0.051	0.043	0.037	0.031
20	0.124	0.104	0.087	0.073	0.061	0.051	0.043	0.037	0.031	0.026
21	0.112	0.093	0.077	0.064	0.053	0.044	0.037	0.031	0.026	0.022
22	0.101	0.083	0.068	0.056	0.046	0.038	0.032	0.026	0.022	0.018
23	0.091	0.074	0.060	0.049	0.040	0.033	0.027	0.022	0.018	0.015
24	0.082	0.066	0.053	0.043	0.035	0.028	0.023	0.019	0.015	0.013
25	0.074	0.059	0.047	0.038	0.030	0.024	0.020	0.016	0.013	0.010
26	0.066	0.053	0.042	0.033	0.026	0.021	0.017	0.014	0.011	0.009
27	0.060	0.047	0.037	0.029	0.023	0.018	0.014	0.011	0.009	0.007
28	0.054	0.042	0.033	0.026	0.020	0.016	0.012	0.010	0.008	0.006
29	0.048	0.037	0.029	0.022	0.017	0.014	0.011	0.008	0.006	0.005
30	0.044	0.033	0.026	0.020	0.015	0.012	0.009	0.007	0.005	0.004
40	0.015	0.011	0.008	0.005	0.004	0.003	0.002	0.001	0.001	0.001
50	0.005	0.003	0.002	0.001	0.001	0.001	0.000	0.000	0.000	0.000

Table A (contd.) – Present Value of 1

Periods	21%	22%	23%	24%	25%	26%	27%	28%	29%	30%
1	0.826	0.820	0.813	0.806	0.800	0.794	0.787	0.781	0.775	0.769
2	0.683	0.672	0.661	0.650	0.640	0.630	0.620	0.610	0.601	0.592
3	0.564	0.551	0.537	0.524	0.512	0.500	0.488	0.477	0.466	0.455
4	0.467	0.451	0.437	0.423	0.410	0.397	0.384	0.373	0.361	0.350
5	0.386	0.370	0.355	0.341	0.328	0.315	0.303	0.291	0.280	0.269
6	0.319	0.303	0.289	0.275	0.262	0.250	0.238	0.227	0.217	0.207
7	0.263	0.249	0.235	0.222	0.210	0.198	0.188	0.178	0.168	0.159
8	0.218	0.204	0.191	0.179	0.168	0.157	0.148	0.139	0.130	0.123
9	0.180	0.167	0.155	0.144	0.134	0.125	0.116	0.108	0.101	0.094
10	0.149	0.137	0.126	0.116	0.107	0.099	0.092	0.085	0.078	0.073
11	0.123	0.112	0.103	0.094	0.086	0.079	0.072	0.066	0.061	0.056
12	0.102	0.092	0.083	0.076	0.069	0.062	0.057	0.052	0.047	0.043
13	0.084	0.075	0.068	0.061	0.055	0.050	0.045	0.040	0.037	0.033
14	0.069	0.062	0.055	0.049	0.044	0.039	0.035	0.032	0.028	0.025
15	0.057	0.051	0.045	0.040	0.035	0.031	0.028	0.025	0.022	0.020
16	0.047	0.042	0.036	0.032	0.028	0.025	0.022	0.019	0.017	0.015
17	0.039	0.034	0.030	0.026	0.023	0.020	0.017	0.015	0.013	0.012
18	0.032	0.028	0.024	0.021	0.018	0.016	0.014	0.012	0.010	0.009
19	0.027	0.023	0.020	0.017	0.014	0.012	0.011	0.009	0.008	0.007
20	0.022	0.019	0.016	0.014	0.012	0.010	0.008	0.007	0.006	0.005
21	0.018	0.015	0.013	0.011	0.009	0.008	0.007	0.006	0.005	0.004
22	0.015	0.013	0.011	0.009	0.007	0.006	0.005	0.004	0.004	0.003
23	0.012	0.010	0.009	0.007	0.006	0.005	0.004	0.003	0.003	0.002
24	0.010	0.008	0.007	0.006	0.005	0.004	0.003	0.003	0.002	0.002
25	0.009	0.007	0.006	0.005	0.004	0.003	0.003	0.002	0.002	0.001
26	0.007	0.006	0.005	0.004	0.003	0.002	0.002	0.002	0.001	0.001
27	0.006	0.005	0.004	0.003	0.002	0.002	0.002	0.001	0.001	0.001
28	0.005	0.004	0.003	0.002	0.002	0.002	0.001	0.001	0.001	0.001
29	0.004	0.003	0.002	0.002	0.002	0.001	0.001	0.001	0.001	0.000
30	0.003	0.003	0.002	0.002	0.001	0.001	0.001	0.001	0.000	0.000
40	0.000	0.000	0.000	0.000	0.000	0.000	0.000	0.000	0.000	0.000
50	0.000	0.000	0.000	0.000	0.000	0.000	0.000	0.000	0.000	0.000

Table A (contd.) – Present Value of 1

Periods	31%	32%	33%	34%	35%	36%	37%	38%	39%	40%
1	0.763	0.758	0.752	0.746	0.741	0.735	0.730	0.725	0.719	0.714
2	0.583	0.574	0.565	0.557	0.549	0.541	0.533	0.525	0.518	0.510
3	0.445	0.435	0.425	0.416	0.406	0.398	0.389	0.381	0.372	0.364
4	0.340	0.329	0.320	0.310	0.301	0.292	0.284	0.276	0.268	0.260
5	0.259	0.250	0.240	0.231	0.223	0.215	0.207	0.200	0.193	0.186
6	0.198	0.189	0.181	0.173	0.165	0.158	0.151	0.145	0.139	0.133
7	0.151	0.143	0.136	0.129	0.122	0.116	0.110	0.105	0.100	0.095
8	0.115	0.108	0.102	0.096	0.091	0.085	0.081	0.076	0.072	0.068
9	0.088	0.082	0.077	0.072	0.067	0.063	0.059	0.055	0.052	0.048
10	0.067	0.062	0.058	0.054	0.050	0.046	0.043	0.040	0.037	0.035
11	0.051	0.047	0.043	0.040	0.037	0.034	0.031	0.029	0.027	0.025
12	0.039	0.036	0.033	0.030	0.027	0.025	0.023	0.021	0.019	0.018
13	0.030	0.027	0.025	0.022	0.020	0.018	0.017	0.011	0.014	0.013
14	0.023	0.021	0.018	0.017	0.015	0.014	0.012	0.011	0.010	0.009
15	0.017	0.016	0.014	0.012	0.011	0.010	0.009	0.008	0.007	0.006
16	0.013	0.012	0.010	0.009	0.008	0.007	0.006	0.006	0.005	0.005
17	0.010	0.009	0.008	0.007	0.006	0.005	0.005	0.004	0.004	0.003
18	0.008	0.007	0.006	0.005	0.005	0.004	0.003	0.003	0.003	0.002
19	0.006	0.005	0.004	0.004	0.003	0.003	0.003	0.002	0.002	0.002
20	0.005	0.004	0.003	0.003	0.002	0.002	0.002	0.002	0.001	0.001
21	0.003	0.003	0.003	0.002	0.002	0.002	0.001	0.001	0.001	0.001
22	0.003	0.002	0.002	0.002	0.001	0.001	0.001	0.001	0.001	0.001
23	0.002	0.002	0.001	0.001	0.001	0.001	0.001	0.001	0.001	0.000
24	0.002	0.001	0.001	0.001	0.001	0.001	0.001	0.000	0.000	0.000
25	0.001	0.001	0.001	0.001	0.001	0.000	0.000	0.000	0.000	0.000
26	0.001	0.001	0.001	0.000	0.000	0.000	0.000	0.000	0.000	0.000
27	0.001	0.001	0.000	0.000	0.000	0.000	0.000	0.000	0.000	0.000
28	0.001	0.000	0.000	0.000	0.000	0.000	0.000	0.000	0.000	0.000
29	0.000	0.000	0.000	0.000	0.000	0.000	0.000	0.000	0.000	0.000
30	0.000	0.000	0.000	0.000	0.000	0.000	0.000	0.000	0.000	3.000
40	0.000	0.000	0.000	0.000	0.000	0.000	0.000	0.000	0.000	0.000
50	0.000	0.000	0.000	0.000	0.000	0.000	0.000	0.000	0.000	0.000

Table A (contd.) – Present Value of 1

Periods	41%	42%	43%	44%	45%	46%	47%	48%	49%	50%
1	0.709	0.704	0.699	0.694	0.690	0.685	0.680	0.676	0.671	0.667
2	0.503	0.496	0.489	0.482	0.476	0.469	0.463	0.457	0.450	0.444
3	0.357	0.349	0.342	0.335	0.328	0.321	0.315	0.308	0.302	0.296
4	0.253	0.246	0.239	0.233	0.226	0.220	0.214	0.208	0.203	0.198
5	0.179	0.173	0.167	0.162	0.156	0.151	0.146	0.141	0.136	0.132
6	0.127	0.122	0.117	0.112	0.108	0.103	0.099	0.095	0.091	0.088
7	0.090	0.086	0.082	0.078	0.074	0.071	0.067	0.064	0.061	0.059
8	0.064	0.060	0.057	0.054	0.051	0.048	0.046	0.043	0.041	0.039
9	0.045	0.043	0.040	0.038	0.035	0.033	0.031	0.029	0.028	0.026
10	0.032	0.030	0.028	0.026	0.024	0.023	0.021	0.020	0.019	0.017
11	0.023	0.021	0.020	0.018	0.017	0.016	0.014	0.013	0.012	0.012
12	0.016	0.015	0.014	0.013	0.012	0.011	0.010	0.009	0.008	0.008
13	0.011	0.010	0.010	0.009	0.008	0.007	0.007	0.006	0.006	0.005
14	0.008	0.007	0.007	0.006	0.006	0.005	0.005	0.004	0.004	0.003
15	0.006	0.005	0.005	0.004	0.004	0.003	0.003	0.003	0.003	0.002
16	0.004	0.004	0.003	0.003	0.003	0.002	0.002	0.002	0.002	0.002
17	0.003	0.003	0.002	0.002	0.002	0.002	0.001	0.001	0.001	0.001
18	0.002	0.002	0.002	0.001	0.001	0.001	0.001	0.001	0.001	0.001
19	0.001	0.001	0.001	0.001	0.001	0.001	0.001	0.001	0.001	0.000
20	0.001	0.001	0.001	0.001	0.001	0.001	0.000	0.000	0.000	0.000
21	0.001	0.001	0.001	0.000	0.000	0.000	0.000	0.000	0.000	0.000
22	0.001	0.000	0.000	0.000	0.000	0.000	0.000	0.000	0.000	0.000
23	0.000	0.000	0.000	0.000	0.000	0.000	0.000	0.000	0.000	0.000
24	0.000	0.000	0.000	0.000	0.000	0.000	0.000	0.000	0.000	0.000
25	0.000	0.000	0.000	0.000	0.000	0.000	0.000	0.000	0.000	0.000
26	0.000	0.000	0.000	0.000	0.000	0.000	0.000	0.000	0.000	0.000
27	0.000	0.000	0.000	0.000	0.000	0.000	0.000	0.000	0.000	0.000
28	0.000	0.000	0.000	0.000	0.000	0.000	0.000	0.000	0.000	0.000
29	0.000	0.000	0.000	0.000	0.000	0.000	0.000	0.000	0.000	0.000
30	0.000	0.000	0.000	0.000	0.000	0.000	0.000	0.000	0.000	0.000
40	0.000	0.000	0.000	0.000	0.000	0.000	0.000	0.000	0.000	0.000
50	0.000	0.000	0.000	0.000	0.000	0.000	0.000	0.000	0.000	0.000

TABLE B Present Value of Annuity of 1

Periods	1%	2%	3%	4%	5%	6%	7%	8%	9%	10%
1	0.990	0.980	0.971	0.962	0.952	0.943	0.935	0.926	0.917	0.909
2	1.970	1.942	1.913	1.886	1.859	1.833	1.808	1.783	1.759	1.736
3	2.941	2.884	2.829	2.775	2.723	2.673	2.624	2.577	2.531	2.487
4	3.902	3.808	3.717	3.630	3.546	3.465	3.387	3.312	3.240	3.170
5	4.853	4.713	4.580	4.452	4.329	4.212	4.100	3.993	3.890	3.791
6	5.795	5.601	5.417	5.242	5.076	4.917	4.767	4.623	4.486	4.355
7	6.728	6.472	6.230	6.002	5.786	5.582	5.389	5.206	5.033	4.868
8	7.652	7.325	7.020	6.733	6.463	6.210	5.971	5.747	5.535	5.335
9	8.566	8.162	7.786	7.435	7.108	6.802	6.515	6.247	5.995	5.759
10	9.471	8.983	8.530	8.111	7.722	7.360	7.024	6.710	6.418	6.145
11	10.368	9.787	9.253	8.760	8.306	7.887	7.499	7.139	6.805	6.495
12	11.255	10.575	9.954	9.385	8.863	8.384	7.943	7.536	7.161	6.814
13	12.134	11.348	10.635	9.986	9.394	8.853	8.358	7.904	7.487	7.103
14	13.004	12.106	11.296	10.563	9.899	9.295	8.745	8.244	7.786	7.367
15	13.865	12.849	11.938	11.118	10.380	9.712	9.108	8.559	8.061	7.606
16	14.718	13.578	12.561	11.652	10.838	10.106	9.447	8.851	8.313	7.825
17	15.562	14.292	13.166	12.166	11.274	10.477	9.763	9.122	8.544	8.024
18	16.398	14.992	13.754	12.659	11.690	10.828	10.059	9.372	8.756	8.204
19	17.226	15.678	14.324	13.134	12.085	11.158	10.336	9.604	8.950	8.362
20	18.046	16.351	14.877	13.590	12.462	11.470	10.594	9.818	9.129	8.511
21	18.857	17.011	15.415	14.029	12.821	11.764	10.836	10.017	9.292	8.649
22	19.660	17.658	15.837	14.451	13.163	12.042	11.061	10.201	9.442	8.772
23	20.456	18.292	16.444	14.857	13.489	12.303	11.272	10.371	9.580	8.883
24	21.243	18.914	16.936	15.247	13.799	12.550	11.469	10.529	9.707	8.985
25	22.023	19.523	17.413	15.622	14.094	12.783	11.654	10.675	9.823	9.077
26	22.795	20.121	17.877	15.983	14.375	13.003	11.826	10.810	9.929	9.161
27	23.560	20.707	18.327	16.330	14.643	13.211	11.987	10.935	10.027	9.237
28	24.316	21.281	18.764	16.663	14.898	13.406	12.137	11.051	10.116	9.307
29	25.066	21.844	19.188	16.984	15.141	13.591	12.278	11.158	10.198	9.370
30	25.808	22.396	19.600	17.292	15.372	13.765	12.409	11.258	10.274	9.427
40	32.835	27.355	23.115	19.793	17.159	15.046	13.332	11.925	10.757	9.779
50	39.196	31.424	25.730	21.482	18.256	15.762	13.801	12.233	10.962	9.915

Table B (contd.) – Present Value of Annuity of 1

Periods	11%	12%	13%	14%	15%	16%	17%	18%	19%	20%
1	0.901	0.893	0.885	0.877	0.870	0.862	0.855	0.847	0.840	0.833
2	1.713	1.690	1.668	1.647	1.626	1.605	1.585	1.566	1.547	1.528
3	2.444	2.402	2.361	2.322	2.283	2.246	2.210	2.174	2.140	2.106
4	3.102	3.037	2.974	2.914	2.855	2.798	2.743	2.690	2.639	2.589
5	3.696	3.605	3.517	3.433	3.352	3.274	3.199	3.127	3.058	2.991
6	4.231	4.111	3.998	3.889	3.784	3.685	3.589	3.498	3.410	3.326
7	4.712	4.564	4.423	4.288	4.160	4.039	3.922	3.812	3.706	3.605
8	5.146	4.968	4.799	4.639	4.487	4.344	4.207	4.078	3.954	3.837
9	5.537	5.328	5.132	4.946	4.772	4.607	4.451	4.303	4.163	4.031
10	5.889	5.650	5.426	5.216	5.019	4.833	4.659	4.494	4.339	4.192
11	6.207	5.938	5.687	5.453	5.234	5.029	4.836	4.656	4.486	4.327
12	6.492	6.194	5.918	5.660	5.421	5.197	4.988	4.793	4.611	4.439
13	6.750	6.424	6.122	5.842	5.583	5.342	5.118	4.910	4.715	4.533
14	6.982	6.628	6.302	6.002	5.724	5.468	5.229	5.008	4.802	4.611
15	7.191	6.811	6.462	6.142	5.847	5.575	5.324	5.092	4.876	4.675
16	7.379	6.974	6.604	6.265	5.954	5.668	5.405	5.162	4.938	4.730
17	7.549	7.120	6.729	6.373	6.047	5.749	5.475	5.222	4.990	4.775
18	7.702	7.250	6.840	6.467	6.128	5.818	5.534	5.273	5.033	4.812
19	7.839	7.366	6.938	6.550	6.198	5.877	5.584	5.316	5.070	4.843
20	7.963	7.469	7.025	6.623	6.259	5.929	5.628	5.353	5.101	4.870
21	8.075	7.562	7.102	6.687	6.312	5.973	5.665	5.384	5.127	4.891
22	8.176	7.645	7.170	6.743	6.359	6.011	5.696	5.410	5.149	4.909
23	8.266	7.718	7.230	6.792	6.399	6.044	5.723	5.432	5.167	4.925
24	8.348	7.784	7.283	6.835	6.434	6.073	5.746	5.451	5.182	4.937
25	8.422	7.843	7.330	6.873	6.464	6.097	5.766	5.467	5.195	4.948
26	8.488	7.896	7.372	6.906	6.491	6.118	5.783	5.480	5.206	4.956
27	8.548	7.943	7.409	6.935	6.514	6.136	5.798	5.492	5.215	4.964
28	8.602	7.984	7.441	6.961	6.534	6.152	5.810	5.502	5.223	4.970
29	8.650	8.022	7.470	6.983	6.551	6.166	5.820	5.510	5.229	4.975
30	8.694	8.055	7.496	7.003	6.566	6.177	5.829	5.517	5.235	4.979
40	8.951	8.244	7.634	7.105	6.642	6.233	5.871	5.548	5.258	4.997
50	9.042	8.304	7.675	7.133	6.661	6.246	5.880	5.554	5.262	4.999

Table B (contd.) – Present Value of Annuity of 1

Periods	21%	22%	23%	24%	25%	26%	27%	28%	29%	30%
1	0.826	0.820	0.813	0.806	0.800	0.794	0.787	0.781	0.775	0.769
2	1.509	1.492	1.474	1.457	1.440	1.424	1.407	1.392	1.376	1.361
3	2.074	2.042	2.011	1.981	1.952	1.923	1.896	1.868	1.842	1.816
4	2.540	2.494	2.448	2.404	2.362	2.320	2.280	2.241	2.203	2.166
5	2.926	2.864	2.803	2.745	2.689	2.635	2.583	2.532	2.483	2.436
6	3.245	3.167	3.092	3.020	2.951	2.885	2.821	2.759	2.700	2.643
7	3.508	3.416	3.327	3.242	3.161	3.083	3.009	2.937	2.868	2.802
8	3.726	3.619	3.518	3.421	3.329	3.241	3.156	3.076	2.999	2.925
9	3.905	3.786	3.673	3.566	3.463	3.366	3.273	3.184	3.100	3.019
10	4.054	3.923	3.799	3.682	3.571	3.465	3.364	3.269	3.178	3.092
11	4.177	4.035	3.902	3.776	3.656	3.543	3.437	3.335	3.239	3.147
12	4.278	4.127	3.985	3.851	3.725	3.606	3.493	3.387	3.286	3.190
13	4.362	4.203	4.053	3.912	3.780	3.656	3.538	3.427	3.322	3.223
14	4.432	4.265	4.108	3.962	3.824	3.695	3.573	3.459	3.351	3.249
15	4.489	4.315	4.153	4.001	3.859	3.726	3.601	3.483	3.373	3.268
16	4.536	4.357	4.189	4.033	3.887	3.751	3.623	3.503	3.390	3.283
17	4.576	4.391	4.219	4.059	3.910	3.771	3.640	3.518	3.403	3.295
18	4.608	4.419	4.243	4.080	3.928	3.786	3.654	3.529	3.413	3.304
19	4.635	4.442	4.263	4.097	3.942	3.799	3.664	3.539	3.421	3.311
20	4.657	4.460	4.279	4.110	3.954	3.808	3.673	3.546	3.427	3.316
21	4.675	4.476	4.292	4.121	3.963	3.816	3.679	3.551	3.432	3.320
22	4.690	4.488	4.302	4.130	3.970	3.822	3.684	3.556	3.436	3.323
23	4.703	4.499	4.311	4.137	3.976	3.827	3.689	3.559	3.438	3.325
24	4.713	4.507	4.318	4.143	3.981	3.831	3.692	3.562	3.441	3.327
25	4.721	4.514	4.323	4.147	3.985	3.834	3.694	3.564	3.442	3.329
26	4.728	4.520	4.328	4.151	3.988	3.837	3.696	3.566	3.444	3.330
27	4.734	4.524	4.332	4.154	3.990	3.839	3.698	3.567	3.445	3.330
28	4.739	4.528	4.335	4.157	3.992	3.840	3.699	3.568	3.446	3.331
29	4.743	4.531	4.337	4.158	3.994	3.841	3.700	3.569	3.446	3.332
30	4.746	4.534	4.339	4.160	3.995	3.842	3.701	3.570	3.447	3.332
40	4.760	4.544	4.347	4.166	3.910	3.846	3.703	3.571	3.448	3.333
50	4.762	4.545	4.348	4.167	3.910	3.846	3.703	3.571	3.448	3.333

Table B (contd.) – Present Value of Annuity of 1

Periods	31%	32%	33%	34%	35%	36%	37%	38%	39%	40%
1	0.763	0.758	0.752	0.746	0.741	0.735	0.730	0.725	0.719	0.714
2	1.346	1.331	1.317	1.303	1.289	1.276	1.263	1.250	1.237	1.224
3	1.791	1.766	1.742	1.719	1.696	1.673	1.652	1.630	1.609	1.589
4	2.130	2.096	2.062	2.029	1.997	1.966	1.935	1.906	1.877	1.849
5	2.390	2.345	2.302	2.260	2.220	2.181	2.143	2.106	2.070	2.035
6	2.588	2.534	2.483	2.433	2.385	2.339	2.294	2.251	2.209	2.168
7	2.739	2.677	2.619	2.562	2.508	2.455	2.404	2.355	2.308	2.263
8	2.854	2.786	2.721	2.658	2.598	2.540	2.485	2.432	2.380	2.331
9	2.942	2.868	2.798	2.730	2.665	2.603	2.544	2.487	2.432	2.379
10	3.009	2.930	2.855	2.784	2.715	2.649	2.587	2.527	2.469	2.414
11	3.060	2.978	2.899	2.824	2.752	2.683	2.618	2.555	2.496	2.438
12	3.100	3.013	2.931	2.853	2.779	2.708	2.641	2.576	2.515	2.456
13	3.129	3.040	2.956	2.876	2.799	2.727	2.658	2.592	2.529	2.469
14	3.152	3.061	2.974	2.892	2.814	2.740	2.670	2.603	2.539	2.478
15	3.170	3.076	2.988	2.905	2.825	2.750	2.679	2.611	2.546	2.484
16	3.183	3.088	2.999	2.914	2.834	2.757	2.685	2.616	2.551	2.489
17	3.193	3.097	3.007	2.921	2.840	2.763	2.690	2.621	2.555	2.492
18	3.201	3.104	3.012	2.926	2.844	2.767	2.693	2.624	2.557	2.494
19	3.207	3.109	3.017	2.930	2.848	2.770	2.696	2.626	2.559	2.496
20	3.211	3.113	3.020	2.933	2.850	2.772	2.698	2.627	2.561	2.497
21	3.215	3.116	3.023	2.935	2.852	2.773	2.699	2.629	2.562	2.498
22	3.217	3.118	3.025	2.936	2.853	2.775	2.700	2.629	2.562	2.498
23	3.219	3.120	3.026	2.938	2.854	2.775	2.701	2.630	2.563	2.499
24	3.221	3.121	3.027	2.939	2.855	2.776	2.701	2.630	2.563	2.499
25	3.222	3.122	3.028	2.939	2.856	2.777	2.702	2.631	2.563	2.499
26	3.223	3.123	3.028	2.940	2.856	2.777	2.702	2.631	2.564	2.500
27	3.224	3.123	3.029	2.940	2.856	2.777	2.702	2.631	2.564	2.500
28	3.224	3.124	3.029	2.940	2.857	2.777	2.702	2.631	2.564	2.500
29	3.225	3.124	3.030	2.941	2.857	2.777	2.702	2.631	2.564	2.500
30	3.225	3.124	3.030	2.941	2.857	2.778	2.702	2.631	2.564	2.500
40	3.226	3.125	3.030	2.941	2.857	2.778	2.703	2.632	2.564	2.500
50	3.226	3.125	3.030	2.941	2.857	2.778	2.703	2.632	2.564	2.500

Table B (contd.) – Present Value of Annuity of 1

Periods	41%	42%	43%	44%	45%	46%	47%	48%	49%	50%
1	0.709	0.704	0.699	0.694	0.690	0.685	0.680	0.676	0.671	0.667
2	1.212	1.200	1.188	1.177	1.165	1.154	1.143	1.132	1.122	1.111
3	1.569	1.549	1.530	1.512	1.493	1.475	1.458	1.441	1.424	1.407
4	1.822	1.795	1.769	1.744	1.720	1.695	1.672	1.649	1.627	1.605
5	2.001	1.969	1.937	1.906	1.876	1.846	1.818	1.790	1.763	1.737
6	2.129	2.091	2.054	2.018	1.983	1.949	1.917	1.885	1.854	1.824
7	2.219	2.176	2.135	2.096	2.057	2.020	1.984	1.949	1.916	1.883
8	2.283	2.237	2.193	2.150	2.109	2.069	2.030	1.993	1.957	1.922
9	2.328	2.280	2.233	2.187	2.144	2.102	2.061	2.022	1.984	1.948
10	2.360	2.310	2.261	2.213	2.168	2.125	2.083	2.042	2.003	1.965
11	2.383	2.331	2.280	2.232	2.185	2.140	2.097	2.055	2.015	1.977
12	2.400	2.346	2.294	2.244	2.196	2.151	2.107	2.064	2.024	1.985
13	2.411	2.356	2.303	2.253	2.204	2.158	2.113	2.071	2.029	1.990
14	2.419	2.363	2.310	2.259	2.210	2.163	2.118	2.075	2.033	1.993
15	2.425	2.369	2.315	2.263	2.214	2.166	2.121	2.078	2.036	1.995
16	2.429	2.372	2.318	2.266	2.216	2.169	2.123	2.079	2.037	1.997
17	2.432	2.375	2.320	2.268	2.218	2.170	2.125	2.081	2.038	1.998
18	2.434	2.377	2.322	2.270	2.219	2.172	2.126	2.082	2.039	1.999
19	2.435	2.378	2.323	2.271	2.220	2.172	2.126	2.082	2.040	1.999
20	2.436	2.379	2.324	2.271	2.221	2.173	2.127	2.083	2.040	1.999
21	2.437	2.379	2.324	2.272	2.221	2.173	2.127	2.083	2.040	2.000
22	2.438	2.380	2.325	2.272	2.222	2.173	2.127	2.083	2.041	2.000
23	2.438	2.380	2.325	2.272	2.222	2.174	2.127	2.083	2.041	2.000
24	2.438	2.380	2.325	2.272	2.222	2.174	2.127	2.083	2.041	2.000
25	2.439	2.381	2.325	2.272	2.222	2.174	2.128	2.083	2.041	2.000
26	2.439	2.381	2.325	2.273	2.222	2.174	2.128	2.083	2.041	2.000
27	2.439	2.381	2.325	2.273	2.222	2.174	2.128	2.083	2.041	2.000
28	2.439	2.381	2.325	2.273	2.222	2.174	2.128	2.083	2.041	2.000
29	2.439	2.381	2.326	2.273	2.222	2.174	2.128	2.083	2.041	2.000
30	2.439	2.381	2.326	2.273	2.222	2.174	2.128	2.083	2.041	2.000
40	2.439	2.381	2.326	2.273	2.222	2.174	2.128	2.083	2.041	2.000
50	2.439	2.381	2.326	2.273	2.222	2.174	2.128	2.083	2.041	2.000

TABLE C

Future Value of 1

Periods	1%	2%	3%	4%	5%	6%	7%	8%	9%	10%
1	1.010	1.020	1.030	1.040	1.050	1.060	1.070	1.080	1.090	1.100
2	1.020	1.040	1.061	1.082	1.102	1.124	1.145	1.166	1.188	1.200
3	1.030	1.061	1.093	1.125	1.158	1.191	1.225	1.260	1.295	1.331
4	1.041	1.082	1.126	1.170	1.216	1.262	1.311	1.360	1.412	1.464
5	1.051	1.104	1.159	1.217	1.276	1.338	1.403	1.469	1.539	1.611
6	1.062	1.126	1.194	1.265	1.340	1.419	1.501	1.587	1.677	1.772
7	1.072	1.149	1.230	1.316	1.407	1.504	1.606	1.714	1.828	1.949
8	1.083	1.172	1.267	1.369	1.477	1.594	1.718	1.851	1.993	2.144
9	1.094	1.195	1.305	1.423	1.551	1.689	1.838	1.999	2.172	2.358
10	1.105	1.219	1.344	1.480	1.629	1.791	1.967	2.159	2.367	2.594
11	1.116	1.243	1.384	1.539	1.710	1.898	2.105	2.332	2.580	2.853
12	1.127	1.268	1.426	1.601	1.796	2.012	2.252	2.518	2.813	3.138
13	1.138	1.294	1.469	1.665	1.886	2.133	2.410	2.720	3.066	3.452
14	1.149	1.319	1.513	1.732	1.980	2.261	2.579	2.937	3.342	3.797
15	1.161	1.346	1.558	1.801	2.079	2.397	2.759	3.172	3.642	4.177
16	1.173	1.373	1.605	1.873	2.183	2.540	2.952	3.426	3.970	4.595
17	1.184	1.400	1.653	1.948	2.292	2.693	3.159	3.700	4.328	5.054
18	1.196	1.428	1.702	2.026	2.407	2.854	3.380	3.996	4.717	5.560
19	1.208	1.457	1.754	2.107	2.527	3.026	3.617	4.316	5.142	6.116
20	1.220	1.486	1.806	2.191	2.653	3.207	3.870	4.661	5.604	6.727
21	1.232	1.516	1.860	2.279	2.786	3.400	4.141	5.034	6.109	7.400
22	1.245	1.546	1.916	2.370	2.925	3.604	4.430	5.437	6.659	8.140
23	1.257	1.577	1.974	2.465	3.072	3.820	4.741	5.871	7.258	8.954
24	1.270	1.608	2.033	2.563	3.225	4.049	5.072	6.341	7.911	9.850
25	1.282	1.641	2.094	2.666	3.386	4.292	5.427	6.848	8.623	10.835

Table C (contd.) – Future Value of 1

Periods	11%	12%	13%	14%	15%	16%	17%	18%	19%	20%
1	1.110	1.120	1.130	1.140	1.150	1.160	1.170	1.180	1.190	1.200
2	1.232	1.254	1.277	1.300	1.322	1.346	1.369	1.392	1.416	1.490
3	1.368	1.405	1.443	1.482	1.521	1.561	1.602	1.643	1.685	1.728
4	1.518	1.574	1.630	1.689	1.749	1.811	1.874	1.939	2.005	2.074
5	1.685	1.762	1.842	1.925	2.011	2.100	2.192	2.228	2.386	2.488
6	1.870	1.974	2.082	2.195	2.313	2.436	2.565	2.700	2.840	2.986
7	2.076	2.211	2.353	2.502	2.660	2.826	3.001	3.185	3.379	3.583
8	2.305	2.476	2.658	2.853	3.059	3.278	3.511	3.759	4.021	4.300
9	2.558	2.773	3.004	3.252	3.518	3.803	4.108	4.435	4.785	5.160
10	2.839	3.106	3.395	3.707	4.046	4.411	4.807	5.234	5.695	6.192
11	3.152	3.479	3.836	4.226	4.652	5.117	5.624	6.176	6.777	7.430
12	3.498	3.896	4.335	4.818	5.350	5.936	6.580	7.288	8.064	8.916
13	3.883	4.363	4.898	5.492	6.153	6.886	7.699	8.599	9.596	10.699
14	4.310	4.887	5.535	6.261	7.076	7.988	9.007	10.147	11.420	12.839
15	4.785	5.474	6.254	7.138	8.137	9.266	10.539	11.974	13.590	15.407
16	5.311	6.130	7.067	8.137	9.358	10.748	12.330	14.129	16.172	18.488
17	5.895	6.866	7.986	9.276	10.761	12.468	14.426	16.672	19.244	22.186
18	6.544	7.690	9.024	10.575	12.375	14.463	16.879	19.673	22.901	26.623
19	7.263	8.613	10.197	12.056	14.232	16.777	19.748	23.214	27.252	31.948
20	8.062	9.646	11.523	13.743	16.367	19.461	23.106	27.393	32.429	38.338
21	8.949	10.804	13.021	15.668	18.822	22.574	27.034	32.324	38.591	46.005
22	9.934	12.100	14.714	17.861	21.645	26.186	31.629	38.142	45.923	55.206
23	11.026	13.552	16.627	20.362	24.891	30.376	37.006	45.008	54.649	66.247
24	12.239	15.179	18.788	23.212	28.625	35.236	43.297	53.109	65.032	79.497
25	13.585	17.000	21.231	26.462	32.919	40.874	50.658	62.669	77.388	95.396

Table C (contd.) – Future Value of 1

Periods	21%	22%	23%	24%	25%	26%	27%	28%	29%	30%
1	1.210	1.220	1.230	1.240	1.250	1.260	1.270	1.280	1.290	1.300
2	1.464	1.488	1.513	1.538	1.563	1.588	1.613	1.638	1.664	1.690
3	1.772	1.816	1.861	1.907	1.953	2.000	2.048	2.097	2.147	2.197
4	2.144	2.215	2.289	2.364	2.441	2.520	2.601	2.684	2.769	2.856
5	2.594	2.703	2.815	2.932	3.052	3.176	3.304	3.436	3.572	3.713
6	3.138	3.297	3.463	3.635	3.815	4.002	4.196	4.398	4.608	4.827
7	3.797	4.023	4.259	4.508	4.768	5.042	5.329	5.629	5.945	6.275
8	4.595	4.908	5.239	5.590	5.960	6.353	6.768	7.206	7.669	8.157
9	5.560	5.987	6.444	6.931	7.451	8.005	8.595	9.223	9.893	10.604
10	6.727	7.305	7.926	8.594	9.313	10.086	10.915	11.806	12.761	13.786
11	8.140	8.912	9.749	10.657	11.642	12.708	13.862	15.112	16.462	17.922
12	9.850	10.872	11.991	13.215	14.552	16.012	17.605	19.343	21.236	23.298
13	11.918	13.264	14.749	16.386	18.190	20.175	22.359	24.759	27.395	30.288
14	14.421	16.182	18.141	20.319	22.737	25.421	28.396	31.691	35.339	39.374
15	17.449	19.742	22.314	25.196	28.422	32.030	36.062	40.565	45.587	51.186
16	21.114	24.086	27.446	31.243	35.527	40.358	45.799	51.923	58.808	66.542
17	25.548	29.384	33.759	38.741	44.409	50.851	58.165	66.461	75.862	86.504
18	30.913	35.849	41.523	48.039	55.511	64.072	73.870	85.071	97.862	112.455
19	37.404	43.736	51.074	59.568	69.389	80.731	93.815	108.890	126.242	146.192
20	45.259	53.358	62.821	73.864	86.736	101.721	119.145	139.380	162.852	190.050
21	54.764	65.096	77.269	91.592	108.420	128.169	151.314	178.406	210.080	247.065
22	66.264	79.418	95.041	113.574	135.525	161.492	192.168	228.360	271.003	321.184
23	80.180	96.889	116.901	140.831	169.407	203.480	244.054	292.300	349.593	417.539
24	97.017	118.205	143.788	174.631	211.758	256.385	309.948	374.144	450.976	542.801
25	117.391	144.210	176.859	216.542	264.698	323.045	393.634	478.905	581.759	705.641

Table C (contd.) – Future Value of 1

Periods	31%	32%	33%	34%	35%	36%	37%	38%	39%	40%
1	1.310	1.320	1.330	1.340	1.350	1.360	1.370	1.380	1.390	1.400
2	1.716	1.742	1.769	1.796	1.822	1.850	1.877	1.904	1.932	1.960
3	2.248	2.300	2.353	2.406	2.460	2.515	2.571	2.628	2.686	2.744
4	2.945	3.036	3.129	3.224	3.322	3.421	3.523	3.627	3.733	3.842
5	3.858	4.007	4.162	4.320	4.484	4.653	4.826	5.005	5.189	5.378
6	5.054	5.290	5.535	5.789	6.053	6.328	6.612	6.907	7.213	7.530
7	6.621	6.983	7.361	7.758	8.172	8.605	9.058	9.531	10.025	10.541
8	8.673	9.217	9.791	10.395	11.032	11.703	12.410	13.153	13.935	14.758
9	11.362	12.166	13.022	13.930	14.894	15.917	17.001	18.151	19.370	20.661
10	14.884	16.060	17.319	18.666	20.107	21.647	23.292	25.049	26.925	28.925
11	19.498	21.199	23.034	25.012	27.144	29.439	31.910	34.568	37.425	40.496
12	25.542	27.983	30.635	33.516	36.644	40.037	43.717	47.703	52.021	56.694
13	33.460	36.937	40.745	44.912	49.470	54.451	59.892	65.831	72.309	79.371
14	43.833	48.757	54.190	60.182	66.784	74.053	82.052	90.846	100.510	111.120
15	57.421	64.359	72.073	80.644	90.158	100.713	112.411	125.368	139.708	155.568
16	75.221	84.954	95.858	108.063	121.714	136.969	154.003	173.008	194.194	217.795
17	98.540	112.139	127.491	144.804	164.314	186.278	210.984	238.751	269.930	304.913
18	129.087	148.024	169.562	194.038	221.824	253.338	289.048	329.476	375.203	426.879
19	169.104	195.391	225.518	260.011	299.462	344.540	395.996	454.677	521.532	597.630
20	221.527	257.916	299.939	348.414	404.274	468.574	542.514	627.454	724.930	836.683
21	290.200	340.449	398.919	466.875	545.769	637.261	743.245	865.886	1007.653	1171.356
22	380.162	449.393	530.562	625.613	736.789	866.674	1018.245	1194.923	1400.637	1639.898
23	498.012	593.199	705.647	838.321	994.665	1178.677	1394.996	1648.994	1946.885	2295.857
24	652.396	783.023	938.511	1123.350	1342.797	1603.001	1911.145	2275.611	2706.171	3214.200
25	854.638	1033.590	1248.220	1505.289	1812.776	2180.081	2618.268	3140.344	3761.577	4499.880

Table C (contd.) – Future Value of 1

Periods	41%	42%	43%	44%	45%	46%	47%	48%	49%	50%
1	1.410	1.420	1.430	1.440	1.450	1.460	1.470	1.480	1.490	1.500
2	1.988	2.016	2.045	2.074	2.102	2.132	2.161	2.190	2.220	2.250
3	2.803	2.863	2.924	2.986	3.049	3.112	3.177	3.242	3.308	3.375
4	3.953	4.066	4.182	4.300	4.421	4.544	4.669	4.798	4.929	5.063
5	5.573	5.774	5.980	6.192	6.410	6.634	6.864	7.101	7.344	7.594
6	7.858	8.198	8.551	8.916	9.294	9.685	10.090	10.509	10.943	11.391
7	11.080	11.642	12.228	12.839	13.476	14.141	14.833	15.554	16.304	17.086
8	15.623	16.531	17.486	18.488	19.541	20.645	21.804	23.019	24.294	25.629
9	22.028	23.474	25.005	26.623	28.334	30.142	32.052	34.069	36.197	38.443
10	31.059	33.334	35.757	38.338	41.085	44.008	47.117	50.422	53.934	57.665
11	43.794	47.334	51.132	55.206	59.573	64.251	69.261	74.624	80.362	86.498
12	61.749	67.214	73.119	79.497	86.381	93.807	101.814	110.444	119.739	129.746
13	87.066	95.444	104.561	114.475	125.252	136.958	149.667	163.457	178.411	194.620
14	122.763	135.530	149.522	164.845	181.615	199.959	220.010	241.916	265.832	291.929
15	173.096	192.453	213.816	237.376	263.342	291.939	323.415	358.035	396.090	437.894
16	244.065	273.284	305.757	341.822	381.846	426.232	475.420	529.892	590.174	656.841
17	344.132	388.063	437.233	492.224	553.676	622.298	698.867	784.240	879.360	985.261
18	485.226	551.049	625.243	708.802	802.831	908.555	1027.335	1160.676	1310.246	1477.892
19	684.169	782.490	894.097	1020.675	1164.105	1326.491	1510.182	1717.800	1952.266	2216.833
20	964.678	1111.135	1278.559	1469.772	1687.952	1936.677	2219.968	2542.344	2908.877	3325.257
21	1360.196	1577.812	1828.339	2116.471	2447.530	2827.548	3263.353	3762.669	4334.227	4987.885
22	1917.876	2240.493	2614.525	3047.718	3548.919	4128.220	4797.129	5568.750	6457.998	7481.828
23	2704.205	3181.500	3738.771	4388.714	5145.932	6027.201	7051.779	8241.750	9622.417	11222.741
24	3812.929	4517.730	5346.442	6319.749	7461.602	8799.714	10366.115	12197.790	14337.401	16834.112
25	5376.230	6415.177	7645.413	9100.438	10819.322	12847.582	15238.189	18052.730	21362.728	25251.168

TABLE D Present Value of Depreciation Charges Using the Sum-of-the-Years'-Digits Method*

n	1%	2%	3%	4%	5%	6%	7%	8%	9%	10%
3	0.98358	0.96764	0.95216	0.93712	0.92251	0.90830	0.89449	0.88105	0.86797	0.85525
4	0.98034	0.96136	0.94300	0.92526	0.90810	0.89149	0.87541	0.85984	0.84476	0.83014
5	0.97712	0.95514	0.93398	0.91363	0.89403	0.87515	0.85696	0.83941	0.82248	0.80614
6	0.97392	0.94897	0.92509	0.90222	0.88029	0.85927	0.83909	0.81972	0.80110	0.78321
7	0.97073	0.94287	0.91633	0.89102	0.86688	0.84382	0.82179	0.80073	0.78057	0.76128
8	0.96756	0.93683	0.90769	0.88004	0.85377	0.82880	0.80504	0.78242	0.76086	0.74030
9	0.96440	0.93085	0.89918	0.86926	0.84097	0.81419	0.78882	0.76475	0.74191	0.72022
10	0.96126	0.92492	0.89079	0.85868	0.82846	0.79997	0.77310	0.74771	0.72371	0.70099
11	0.95814	0.91905	0.88251	0.84830	0.81624	0.78614	0.75786	0.73126	0.70620	0.68257
12	0.95503	0.91324	0.87436	0.83812	0.80429	0.77268	0.74310	0.71537	0.68934	0.66491
13	0.95193	0.90749	0.86632	0.82812	0.79262	0.75958	0.72878	0.70003	0.67315	0.64798
14	0.94885	0.90177	0.85839	0.81830	0.78121	0.74683	0.71490	0.68521	0.65755	0.63174
15	0.94579	0.89614	0.85057	0.80867	0.77006	0.73441	0.70144	0.67089	0.64253	0.61616
16	0.94274	0.89055	0.84287	0.79921	0.75915	0.72232	0.68838	0.65704	0.62806	0.60120
17	0.93970	0.88501	0.83527	0.78992	0.74849	0.71054	0.67570	0.64366	0.61412	0.58683
18	0.93668	0.87952	0.82778	0.78080	0.73806	0.69906	0.66340	0.63071	0.60067	0.57302
19	0.93368	0.87409	0.82039	0.77185	0.72786	0.68788	0.65146	0.61818	0.58771	0.55974
20	0.93069	0.86871	0.81310	0.76306	0.71788	0.67680	0.63986	0.60606	0.57521	0.54697
21	0.92771	0.86338	0.80591	0.75442	0.70812	0.66637	0.62860	0.59433	0.56314	0.53469
22	0.92475	0.85809	0.79882	0.74594	0.69858	0.65602	0.61766	0.58297	0.55150	0.52286
23	0.92180	0.85286	0.79184	0.73760	0.68923	0.64593	0.60703	0.57196	0.54025	0.51148
24	0.91887	0.84768	0.78494	0.72942	0.68009	0.63609	0.59670	0.56130	0.52938	0.50051
25	0.91595	0.84254	0.77814	0.72138	0.67114	0.62650	0.58666	0.55097	0.51889	0.48994
26	0.91305	0.83746	0.77143	0.71348	0.66238	0.61713	0.57689	0.54096	0.50874	0.47974
27	0.91016	0.83242	0.76481	0.70572	0.65381	0.60800	0.56740	0.53124	0.49892	0.46992
28	0.90728	0.82743	0.75828	0.69809	0.64541	0.59909	0.55816	0.52183	0.48943	0.46043
29	0.90442	0.82248	0.75184	0.69059	0.63719	0.59039	0.54917	0.51269	0.48025	0.45127
30	0.90157	0.81759	0.74549	0.68322	0.62914	0.58191	0.54043	0.50382	0.47136	0.44243

* per $1.00 of assets depreciated over n years. The calculation assumes zero salvage values.

Table D (contd.) – Sum-of-the-Years'-Digits

n	11%	12%	13%	14%	15%	16%	17%	18%	19%	20%
3	0.84286	0.83079	0.81904	0.80758	0.79642	0.78553	0.77492	0.76456	0.75446	0.74460
4	0.81596	0.80221	0.78887	0.77592	0.76335	0.75114	0.73927	0.72774	0.71653	0.70563
5	0.79036	0.77512	0.76039	0.74615	0.73238	0.71904	0.70614	0.69364	0.68153	0.66980
6	0.76600	0.74944	0.73350	0.71814	0.70334	0.68907	0.67530	0.66201	0.64918	0.63678
7	0.74279	0.72507	0.70807	0.69176	0.67609	0.66104	0.64656	0.63263	0.61923	0.60632
8	0.72068	0.70194	0.68402	0.66689	0.65050	0.63479	0.61974	0.60531	0.59147	0.57817
9	0.69959	0.67995	0.66126	0.64343	0.62643	0.61020	0.59470	0.57987	0.56569	0.55212
10	0.67947	0.65906	0.63969	0.62128	0.60379	0.58713	0.57127	0.55615	0.54173	0.52796
11	0.66026	0.63918	0.61924	0.60035	0.58245	0.56547	0.54934	0.53401	0.51942	0.50553
12	0.64192	0.62026	0.59984	0.58056	0.56234	0.54510	0.52878	0.51330	0.49862	0.48467
13	0.62439	0.60224	0.58142	0.56182	0.54336	0.52594	0.50948	0.49392	0.47920	0.46524
14	0.60763	0.58507	0.56392	0.54408	0.52543	0.50788	0.49136	0.47576	0.46104	0.44712
15	0.59160	0.56869	0.54728	0.52725	0.50848	0.49086	0.47430	0.45872	0.44404	0.43019
16	0.57626	0.55306	0.53146	0.51129	0.49244	0.47479	0.45825	0.44271	0.42811	0.41435
17	0.56157	0.53815	0.51638	0.49613	0.47725	0.45961	0.44311	0.42766	0.41315	0.39952
18	0.54750	0.52390	0.50203	0.48173	0.46285	0.44525	0.42883	0.41348	0.39910	0.38561
19	0.53400	0.51027	0.48834	0.46803	0.44918	0.43166	0.41534	0.40011	0.38587	0.37254
20	0.52107	0.49724	0.47528	0.45500	0.43621	0.41878	0.40258	0.38749	0.37341	0.36025
21	0.50866	0.48477	0.46282	0.44258	0.42388	0.40657	0.39051	0.37557	0.36166	0.34867
22	0.49674	0.47284	0.45091	0.43075	0.41216	0.39498	0.37907	0.36430	0.35056	0.33776
23	0.48530	0.46140	0.43953	0.41946	0.40099	0.38396	0.36821	0.35362	0.34007	0.32745
24	0.47430	0.45044	0.42864	0.40869	0.39036	0.37349	0.35791	0.34350	0.33014	0.31772
25	0.46373	0.43992	0.41822	0.39840	0.38022	0.36352	0.34812	0.33390	0.32073	0.30850
26	0.45356	0.42983	0.40825	0.38856	0.37055	0.35402	0.33881	0.32478	0.31180	0.29979
27	0.44378	0.42014	0.39869	0.37915	0.36131	0.34497	0.32995	0.31611	0.30333	0.29149
28	0.43436	0.41083	0.38952	0.37015	0.35249	0.33633	0.32150	0.30786	0.29527	0.28362
29	0.42528	0.40188	0.38072	0.36153	0.34404	0.32808	0.31345	0.30000	0.28761	0.27615
30	0.41654	0.39328	0.37228	0.35326	0.33597	0.32020	0.30576	0.29251	0.28031	0.26904

TABLE E

Present Value of Depreciation Charges Using the Twice Straight-Line Declining Balance Depreciation Method*

n	1%	2%	3%	4%	5%	6%	7%	8%	9%	10%
3	0.98575	0.97189	0.95840	0.94526	0.93246	0.92000	0.90785	0.89601	0.88446	0.87320
4	0.98157	0.96376	0.94654	0.92988	0.91376	0.89816	0.88305	0.86840	0.85421	0.84045
5	0.97762	0.95613	0.93547	0.91561	0.89650	0.87811	0.86010	0.84333	0.82687	0.81100
6	0.97359	0.94839	0.92433	0.90133	0.87934	0.85829	0.83814	0.81882	0.80030	0.78252
7	0.96972	0.94100	0.91374	0.88784	0.86320	0.83976	0.81742	0.79613	0.77582	0.75642
8	0.96578	0.93353	0.90310	0.87435	0.84717	0.82144	0.79707	0.77396	0.75202	0.73118
9	0.96196	0.92632	0.89290	0.86150	0.83197	0.80418	0.77798	0.75326	0.72991	0.70782
10	0.95809	0.91906	0.88267	0.84869	0.81692	0.78716	0.75927	0.73308	0.70846	0.68528
11	0.95432	0.91203	0.87283	0.83643	0.80258	0.77104	0.74162	0.71412	0.68840	0.66430
12	0.95050	0.90496	0.86100	0.82425	0.78840	0.75519	0.72435	0.69568	0.66898	0.64407
13	0.94677	0.89810	0.85350	0.81254	0.77485	0.74010	0.70801	0.67830	0.65075	0.62516
14	0.94301	0.89121	0.84402	0.80093	0.76149	0.72531	0.69205	0.66140	0.63311	0.60694
15	0.93933	0.88451	0.83485	0.78974	0.74868	0.71119	0.67688	0.64542	0.61649	0.58985
16	0.93562	0.87779	0.82571	0.77867	0.73606	0.69735	0.66210	0.62991	0.60044	0.57340
17	0.93197	0.87124	0.81685	0.76798	0.72394	0.68412	0.64802	0.61520	0.58527	0.55791
18	0.92831	0.86469	0.80804	0.75741	0.71201	0.67117	0.63430	0.60093	0.57062	0.54300
19	0.92471	0.85830	0.79948	0.74719	0.70053	0.65876	0.62121	0.58736	0.55673	0.52893
20	0.92110	0.85190	0.79097	0.73709	0.68925	0.64661	0.60846	0.57420	0.54332	0.51539
21	0.91754	0.84565	0.78270	0.72731	0.67838	0.63496	0.59628	0.56167	0.53059	0.50257
22	0.91397	0.83942	0.77448	0.71766	0.66770	0.62356	0.58441	0.54952	0.51829	0.49023
23	0.91046	0.83331	0.76648	0.70830	0.65739	0.61261	0.57305	0.53792	0.50659	0.47852
24	0.90694	0.82722	0.75855	0.69907	0.64727	0.60191	0.56198	0.52667	0.49528	0.46725
25	0.90346	0.82125	0.75082	0.69011	0.63749	0.59160	0.55138	0.51592	0.48450	0.45653
26	0.89998	0.81531	0.74316	0.68128	0.62789	0.58154	0.54105	0.50550	0.47409	0.44620
27	0.89655	0.80948	0.73568	0.67270	0.61861	0.57184	0.53114	0.49552	0.46415	0.43637
28	0.89311	0.80367	0.72827	0.66425	0.60950	0.56236	0.52149	0.48583	0.45453	0.42689
29	0.88972	0.79797	0.72104	0.65603	0.60068	0.55321	0.51221	0.47655	0.44534	0.41784
30	0.88633	0.79230	0.71387	0.64793	0.59203	0.54428	0.50318	0.46755	0.43644	0.40911

* per $1.00 of assets over *n* years. The calculation assumes zero salvage values.

Table E (contd.) – Twice Straight-Line Declining Balance

n	11%	12%	13%	14%	15%	16%	17%	18%	19%	20%
3	0.86220	0.85148	0.84101	0.83078	0.82080	0.81104	0.80151	0.79219	0.78308	0.77418
4	0.82710	0.81414	0.80156	0.78934	0.77748	0.76594	0.75473	0.74383	0.73322	0.72290
5	0.79568	0.78088	0.76659	0.75278	0.73943	0.72651	0.71401	0.70190	0.69018	0.67882
6	0.76546	0.74907	0.73331	0.71816	0.70357	0.68952	0.67599	0.66295	0.65037	0.63823
7	0.73789	0.72017	0.70321	0.68698	0.67142	0.65650	0.64218	0.62844	0.61523	0.60254
8	0.71136	0.69250	0.67453	0.65740	0.64105	0.62545	0.61053	0.59627	0.58261	0.56954
9	0.68692	0.66711	0.64833	0.63049	0.61353	0.59741	0.58205	0.56742	0.55346	0.54014
10	0.66344	0.64284	0.62338	0.60498	0.58756	0.57105	0.55539	0.54051	0.52637	0.51292
11	0.64168	0.62043	0.60043	0.58160	0.56383	0.54705	0.53119	0.51617	0.50194	0.48844
12	0.62080	0.59901	0.57860	0.55944	0.54144	0.52449	0.50852	0.49344	0.47920	0.46513
13	0.60134	0.57914	0.55841	0.53902	0.52086	0.50381	0.48780	0.47273	0.45854	0.44514
14	0.58269	0.56016	0.53920	0.51966	0.50142	0.48436	0.46837	0.45336	0.43926	0.42599
15	0.56524	0.54247	0.52135	0.50173	0.48346	0.46643	0.45051	0.43561	0.42163	0.40851
16	0.54852	0.52557	0.50437	0.48473	0.46649	0.44953	0.43373	0.41896	0.40515	0.39221
17	0.53282	0.50977	0.48853	0.46891	0.45074	0.43389	0.41822	0.40362	0.38999	0.37724
18	0.51778	0.49467	0.47344	0.45389	0.43584	0.41913	0.40363	0.38921	0.37578	0.36324
19	0.50362	0.48050	0.45932	0.43986	0.42195	0.40540	0.39008	0.37586	0.36263	0.35030
20	0.49003	0.46695	0.44586	0.42654	0.40878	0.39242	0.37730	0.36329	0.35028	0.33817
21	0.47722	0.45419	0.43322	0.41405	0.39646	0.38030	0.36538	0.35159	0.33880	0.32691
22	0.46492	0.44199	0.42116	0.40216	0.38477	0.36881	0.35412	0.34055	0.32798	0.31632
23	0.45328	0.43047	0.40980	0.39098	0.37380	0.35805	0.34358	0.33022	0.31788	0.30643
24	0.44210	0.41945	0.39895	0.38034	0.36336	0.34784	0.33359	0.32046	0.30834	0.29711
25	0.43150	0.40901	0.38870	0.37029	0.35354	0.33823	0.32420	0.31130	0.29940	0.28838
26	0.42132	0.39900	0.37890	0.36071	0.34418	0.32910	0.31530	0.30262	0.29093	0.28012
27	0.41164	0.38951	0.36962	0.35164	0.33534	0.32048	0.30690	0.29443	0.28296	0.27235
28	0.40233	0.38041	0.36073	0.34298	0.32690	0.31228	0.29891	0.28666	0.27539	0.26498
29	0.39347	0.37175	0.35229	0.33477	0.31891	0.30451	0.29136	0.27932	0.26824	0.25803
30	0.38494	0.36343	0.34420	0.32691	0.31128	0.29709	0.28416	0.27232	0.26145	0.25142

Index

NAMES

SUBJECTS